Fundamentals of ... ing

This work was funded in part by the National Institute of Justice (NIJ) through interagency agreement 2008-DN-R-121 with the NIST Office of Law Enforcement Standards. Points of view in this document are those of the author and do not necessarily represent the official position or policies of the U.S. Department of Justice. Certain commercial equipment, instruments, and materials are identified in order to specify experimental procedures as completely as possible. In no case does such identification imply a recommendation or endorsement by the National Institute of Standards and Technology nor does it imply that any of the materials, instruments, or equipment identified are necessarily the best available for the purpose.

Completed January 2009

Fundamentals of Forensic DNA Typing

John M. Butler

National Institute of Standards and Technology
Gaithersburg, Maryland, USA

AMSTERDAM • BOSTON • HEIDELBERG • LONDON • NEW YORK • OXFORD
PARIS • SAN DIEGO • SAN FRANCISCO • SINGAPORE • SYDNEY • TOKYO
Academic Press is an imprint of Elsevier

Contribution of the National Institute of Standards and Technology, 2010.

Academic Press is an imprint of Elsevier
30 Corporate Drive, Suite 400, Burlington, MA 01803, USA
525 B Street, Suite 1900, San Diego, California 92101-4495, USA
84 Theobald's Road, London WC1X 8RR, UK

Library of Congress Cataloging-in-Publication Data
Butler, John M. (John Marshall), 1969-
   Fundamentals of forensic DNA typing / John M. Butler.
      p. ; cm.
   Includes bibliographical references and index.
   ISBN 978-0-12-374999-4 (pbk. : alk. paper) 1. DNA fingerprinting.
      2. Forensic genetics. I. Title.
   [DNLM: 1. DNA Fingerprinting—methods. 2. DNA—physiology.
      3. Forensic Medicine—methods. W 786 B985f 2010]
   RA1057.55.B883 2010
   614'.1—dc22

                                                    2009009659

British Library Cataloguing-in-Publication Data
A catalogue record for this book is available from the British Library.

ISBN: 978-0-12-374999-4

For information on all Academic Press publications
visit our Web site at www.elsevierdirect.com

Working together to grow
libraries in developing countries

www.elsevier.com | www.bookaid.org | www.sabre.org

ELSEVIER   BOOK AID International   Sabre Foundation

Transferred to Digital Printing 2009

To my parents
who fostered my love for learning,
and to my wife, Terilynne, and six children
who tolerate it.

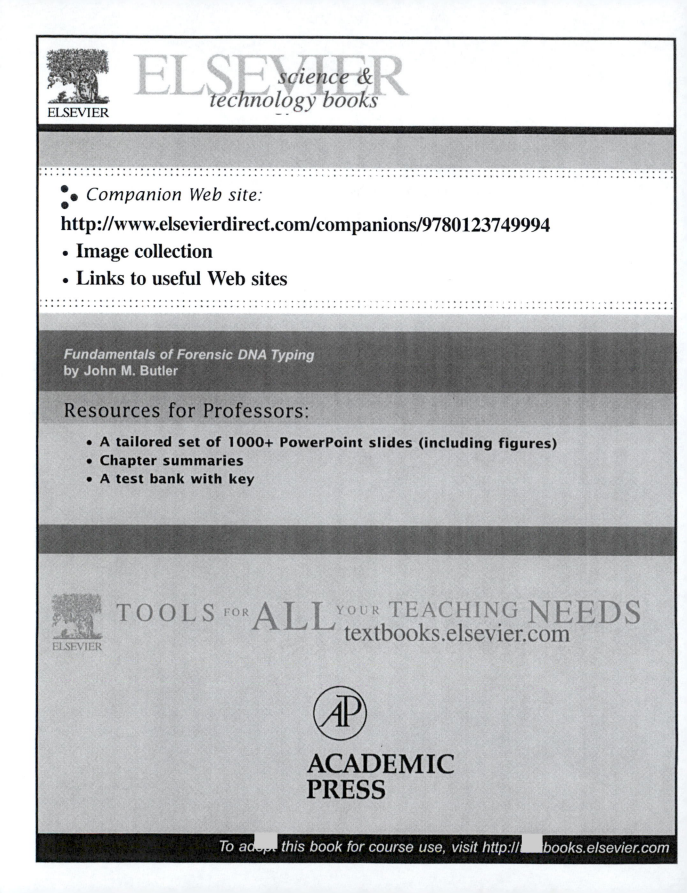

Contents

References are provided at the end of each chapter by subtopic (but without direct citation within the text).

High-profile cases and other interesting information are included as D.N.A. (Data, Notes, and Applications) boxes scattered throughout the book in the chapter pertaining to a particular subject.

Foreword

In the fast-moving field of forensic DNA, there is always the danger that a textbook will become quickly out of date. It is a tribute to John's remarkable tenacity and attention to detail that his work has never been endangered in this way.

In his latest book, John explains how and why the organization of his texts has evolved into this latest iteration. Not wishing to write an encyclopedia, he explains that his solution has necessitated splitting the original format of *Forensic DNA Typing* into two volumes. The first volume is entitled *Fundamentals of Forensic DNA Typing*. There is a forthcoming companion volume entitled *Advanced Topics in Forensic DNA Typing*.

Forensic science attracts a very broad audience from a wide diversity of backgrounds. Devising a framework that is able to appeal to such an audience is perhaps the biggest challenge. The scientist, the lawyer, the law enforcement officer, and the student will all expect a different emphasis from a book that deals with all aspects of DNA profiling.

Dividing *Forensic DNA Typing* into two volumes is a masterful stroke. The first volume, *Fundamentals of Forensic DNA Typing*, is written from a more general perspective. It is subdivided into 18 chapters ordered into a logical sequence. Thus we begin with an extensive overview and history in Chapter 1 and end with Chapter 18 on future trends. In between, chapters progress through sample collection, DNA extraction, PCR, and interpretation. There is a brand new section on DNA databases that describes the growth of this 'industry' since the first U.K. use in 1995. Ethical concerns are discussed in relation to the retention of DNA profiles, and the proposed expansion of databases to allow for close relatives to be searched for (so-called familial searching). Chapter 13 provides an expanded section on quality assurance. What is meant by validation? What procedures are in place that maintain public confidence? How can we learn from mistakes that have been made in the past?

Although slightly shorter than *Forensic DNA Typing*, skillful arrangement of chapters and extensive use of cross-referencing enhance the reading experience. It can easily be read from cover to cover. The specialist reader requiring more information is directed to the companion volume, *Advanced Topics in Forensic DNA Typing*. In addition, there are extensive references to material that is freely available on the Internet (the NIST Web site is itself a tremendous resource). *Fundamentals of Forensic DNA Typing* admirably succeeds in its goal of reaching a diverse audience. It does this by acting as a portal—if a specific piece of information isn't explicitly written down, it will tell you where to find it. Consequently, it fulfills the same function as an encyclopedia but in a very user-friendly way.

Peter Gill, PhD FIBiol

Strathclyde, UK

Introduction

An expert is one who knows more and more about less and less until they know absolutely everything about nothing…

—Nicholas Butler, *Bartlett's*, 585:10

Being directly involved in the forensic DNA typing community over the past 15 years has been rewarding yet challenging as the field continues to grow rapidly. The popularity of television shows like *CSI: Crime Scene Investigation* and *Law & Order* have sparked interest by the general public. Since the first edition of *Forensic DNA Typing* was published in January 2001 and expanded on in the second edition in February 2005, I have had the opportunity to directly teach thousands of scientists, students, and lawyers regarding the fundamentals of forensic DNA analysis. Questions raised during my lectures and discussions held as part of training workshops conducted have aided in refinement of the information provided herein.

A number of forensic science programs have arisen on college campuses around the world to meet the needs and interests of students. The purpose of this book is to aid students, beginning scientists, and members of the legal community in gaining an introductory understanding of and a fundamental foundation to forensic DNA testing. A companion volume for practitioners (*Advanced Topics in Forensic DNA Typing, 3rd Edition*) touches on more advanced topics and provides further details to the basic information in this volume. Rather than creating an encyclopedic single text to be all things to all people, we have decided with the third edition of *Forensic DNA Typing* to divide the material into fundamental information and advanced topics.

Several significant things have happened since the first edition of *Forensic DNA Typing* was published in January 2001. The Human Genome Project published a draft sequence of the human genome in February 2001 and completed the reference sequence in April 2003. In addition, human mitochondrial DNA population genomics is under way and thousands of full mitochondrial genomes have been published. Soon hundreds if not thousands of full human genomes will be available due to next-generation sequencing capabilities. Technology for DNA sequencing and typing continues to advance as does our understanding of genetic variation in various population groups around the world. These milestones are a tribute to the progress of science and will benefit the field of forensic DNA typing.

The literature on the short tandem repeat (STR) markers used in forensic DNA testing has more than tripled in the 8 years since the first edition of this book became available. More than 3500 publications now detail the technology and report the allele frequencies for forensically informative STR loci. Hundreds of different population groups have been studied. New technologies for rapidly typing DNA samples have been developed. Standard protocols have been validated in laboratories worldwide. Yet DNA results are still sometimes challenged in court—not usually because of the technology, which is sound—but rather to question the ability of practitioners to perform the tests carefully and correctly. A major purpose of this book is to help in the training of professionals in the field of forensic DNA testing. The knowledge of forensic scientists, lawyers, and students coming into the field will be enhanced by careful review of the materials found herein.

In the past few years, the general public has become more familiar with the power of DNA typing as the media has covered efforts to identify remains from victims of the World Trade Center Twin Towers collapse following the terrorist attacks of 11 September 2001, the O.J. Simpson murder trial in 1994 and 1995, the parentage testing of Anna-Nicole Smith's daughter in 2007, and the ongoing Innocence Project that has led to the exoneration of over 200 wrongfully convicted individuals. News stories featuring the value of forensic DNA analysis in solving crime seem commonplace today. In another popular application, DNA testing with Y-chromosome markers is now used routinely to aid genealogical investigations. In addition, the medical community is poised to benefit from the tremendous amount of genomic DNA sequence information being generated. DNA testing has an important role in our society that is likely to grow in significance and scope in the future.

Though high-profile cases have certainly attracted widespread media attention in recent years, they are only a small fraction of the thousands of forensic DNA and paternity cases that are conducted each year by public and private laboratories around the world. The technology for performing these tests has evolved rapidly over the past two decades to the point where it is now possible to obtain results in a few hours on samples with only the smallest amount of biological material.

This book will examine the science of current forensic DNA typing methods by focusing on the biology, technology, and genetic interpretation of short tandem repeat (STR) markers, which encompass the most common forensic DNA analysis methods used today. The materials in this book are intended primarily for two audiences: (1) students learning about forensic DNA analysis in an academic environment and (2) forensic science professionals and members of the law enforcement and legal communities who want to gain a better understanding of the fundamentals behind STR typing. Further information on each of the subjects presented here is available in the second volume, *Advanced Topics in Forensic DNA Typing, 3rd Edition.*

NEW MATERIAL IN THIS EDITION

In many ways, this is a completely new book. Those familiar with the previous two editions of my book will come to find that *Fundamentals of Forensic DNA Typing* is substantially enhanced with additional information. A chapter has been added reviewing historical methods used in the first two decades of forensic DNA testing (Chapter 3). Topics have been reordered to reflect the DNA testing process, which progresses from sample collection (Chapter 4) to statistical interpretation of a DNA match (Chapter 11). A number of new figures have been added, including Figure 1.3, which provides an overview of the entire DNA testing process. A chapter discussing my perspectives on future trends in the field has also been added (Chapter 18). A number of additional Data, Notes, and Applications (D.N.A.) boxes have been added as well as an extensive glossary to aid newcomers to the field (Appendix 1). Major updates have been made to all of the content, bringing the information contained herein current as of the time of publication.

At the end of each chapter are points for discussion to foster thought on the topics covered. To avoid interrupting the flow of ideas, the references and Web sites listed at the end of each chapter are not cited within the text but are provided to indicate sources of material as well as to enable readers to be aware of additional resources on each topic. These reference lists are subdivided by topic to enable easy access to further information desired on a specific subject. The citation format has also changed. Author lists have been shortened to only the first author, and titles for each article have been added to make it more meaningful. Links are provided to Web sites including the online training available from http://www.dna.gov (Appendix 2).

In this edition, we again utilize D.N.A. boxes to cover specific topics of general interest. These D.N.A. boxes include high-profile cases—such as the O.J. Simpson trial (D.N.A. Box 4.2)—along with other topics of interest relevant to a specific section of the book. These are scattered throughout the book near the sections dealing with the science or issues behind these cases. It is hoped that these D.N.A. boxes will help readers see the practical value of forensic DNA typing.

Acknowledgments

I express a special thanks to colleagues and fellow researchers who kindly provided important information and supplied some of the figures for this book or previous editions of *Forensic DNA Typing*. These individuals include Michael Baird, Susan Ballou, Martin Bill, George Carmody, Mike Coble, David Duewer, Dan Ehrlich, Nicky Fildes, Lisa Forman, Ron Fourney, Lee Fraser, Chip Harding, Doug Hares, Debbie Hobson, Bill Hudlow, Margaret Kline, Carll Ladd, Steve Lee, Bruce McCord, Ruth Montgomery, Steve Niezgoda, Richard Schoske, Jim Schumm, Bob Shaler, Melissa Smrz, Amanda Sozer, Mark Stolorow, Kevin Sullivan, and Lois Tully. I am indebted to the dedicated project team members, past and present, who work with me at the U.S. National Institute of Standards and Technology: Pete Vallone, Mike Coble, Margaret Kline, Jan Redman, David Duewer, Jill Appleby, Amy Decker, Becky Hill, Dennis Reeder, Christian Ruitberg, and Richard Schoske. It is a pleasure to work with such supportive and hard-working scientists.

Several other people deserve specific recognition for their support of this endeavor. The information reported in this book was in large measure made possible by a comprehensive collection of references on the STR markers used in forensic DNA typing. For this collection now numbering more than 3000 references, I am indebted to the initial work of Christian Ruitberg for tirelessly collecting and cataloging these papers and the steady efforts of Jan Redman to update this STR reference database monthly. A complete listing of these references may be found at http://www.cstl.nist.gov/biotech/strbase.

My wife, Terilynne, who carefully reviewed the manuscript and made helpful suggestions, was always a constant support in the many hours that this project took away from our family. As the initial editor of all my written materials, Terilynne helped make the book more coherent and readable. In addition, David Duewer and Katherine Sharpless provided a fine technical review. The support of NIST management, especially Laurie Locascio and Willie May, made completion of this book possible.

I was first exposed to forensic DNA typing in 1990 when a friend gave me a copy of Joseph Wambaugh's *The Blooding* to read, and since then I have watched with wonder as the forensic DNA community has rapidly evolved. DNA testing that once took weeks can now be performed in a matter of hours. I enjoy being a part of the developments in this field and hope that this book will help many others come to better understand the fundamental principles behind the biology, technology, and genetics of STR markers.

About the Author

John Marshall Butler grew up in the U.S. Midwest and, enjoying science and law, decided to pursue a career in forensic science at an early age. After completing an undergraduate education in chemistry at Brigham Young University, he moved east to pursue his graduate studies at the University of Virginia. While a graduate student, he enjoyed the unique opportunity of serving as an FBI Honors Intern and guest researcher for more than 2 years in the FBI Laboratory's Forensic Science Research Unit. His Ph.D. dissertation research, which was conducted at the FBI Academy in Quantico, Virginia, involved pioneering work in applying capillary electrophoresis to STR typing. After receiving his Ph.D. in 1995, Dr. Butler obtained a prestigious National Research Council postdoctoral fellowship to the National Institute of Standards and Technology (NIST). While a postdoc at NIST, he designed and built STRBase, the widely used Short Tandem Repeat Internet Database (http://www.cstl.nist.gov/biotech/strbase) that contains a wealth of standardized information on STRs used in human identity applications. Dr. Butler then went to California for several years to work as a staff scientist and project leader at a startup company named GeneTrace System to develop rapid DNA analysis technologies involving time-of-flight mass spectrometry. In the fall of 1999, he returned to NIST to lead their efforts in human identity testing with funding from the National Institute of Justice.

Dr. Butler is currently a NIST Fellow and Group Leader of Applied Genetics in the Biochemical Science Division at NIST. He is a regular invited guest of the FBI's Scientific Working Group on DNA Analysis Methods (SWGDAM) and a member of the Department of Defense Quality Assurance Oversight Committee for DNA Analysis. Following the terrorist attacks of 11 September 2001, Dr. Butler's expertise was sought to aid the DNA identification efforts, and he served as part of the distinguished World Trade Center Kinship and Data Analysis Panel (WTC KADAP). He is a member of the International Society of Forensic Genetics and serves as an associate editor for *Forensic Science International: Genetics*.

He has received numerous awards during his career for his work in advancing forensic DNA typing, including the Presidential Early Career Award for Scientists and Engineers (2002), the Department of Commerce Silver Medal (2002) and Gold Medal (2008), the Arthur S. Flemming Award (2007), Brigham Young University's College of Physical and Mathematical Sciences Honored Alumnus (2005), and the Scientific Prize of the International Society of Forensic Genetics (2003).

Dr. Butler has more than 100 publications describing aspects of forensic DNA testing, making him one of the most prolific active authors in the field with articles appearing regularly in every major forensic science journal. He has been an invited speaker to numerous national and international forensic DNA meetings and in the past few years has spoken in Germany, France, England, Canada, Mexico, Denmark, Belgium, Poland, Portugal, Cyprus, and Australia. He is well qualified to present the information found in this book, much of which has come from his own research efforts over the past 15 years. In addition to his busy scientific career, Dr. Butler and his wife serve in their community and church and are the parents of six children, all of whom have been proven to be theirs through the power of DNA typing.

CHAPTER 1

Overview and History of DNA Typing

DNA testing is to justice what the telescope is for the stars; not a lesson in biochemistry, not a display of the wonders of a magnifying glass, but a way to see things as they really are.

—Barry Scheck and Peter Neufeld, *Actual Innocence*

In the darkness of the early morning hours of 26 August 1999, a young University of Virginia student awoke to find a gun pointed at her head. The assailant forced her and a male friend spending the night to roll over on their stomachs. Terrorized, they obeyed their attacker. After robbing the man of some cash, the intruder put a pillow over the man's head and raped the woman. She was then blindfolded with her own shirt and led around the house while the intruder searched for other items to steal.

During the sexual assault, the intruder kept his gun to the back of the male student's head, daring him to look at him and telling him if he tried he would blow his head off. The assailant forced the young woman to take a shower in the hope that any evidence of the crime would be washed away. After helping himself to a can of beer, the attacker left before dawn, taking with him the cash, the confidence, and the sense of safety of his victims. However, even though the assailant had tried to be careful and clean up after the sexual assault, he had left behind enough of his personal body fluids to link him to this violent crime.

The police investigating the crime collected some saliva from the beer can. In addition, evidence technicians found some small traces of semen on the bed sheets that could not be seen with the naked eye. These samples were submitted to the Virginia Department of Forensic Sciences in Richmond along with control samples from other occupants of the residence where the crime occurred. The DNA profiles from the beer can and the bed sheets matched

Contribution of the National Institute of Standards and Technology, 2010.

each other, but no suspect had been developed yet. Because of intense darkness and then the blindfold, the only description police had from the victims was that the suspect was black, medium height, and felt heavy set.

A suspect list was developed by the Charlottesville Police Department that contained the names of more than 40 individuals, some from the sex offender registry and some with extensive criminal histories who were stopped late at night in the area of the home invasion. Unfortunately, no further leads were available, leaving the victims as well as other University of Virginia students and their parents suspicious and fearful. The police were at the end of their rope and considered asking many of the people on the suspect list to voluntarily donate blood samples for purposes of a DNA comparison. The top suspects were systematically eliminated by DNA evidence, leaving the police frustrated.

Then on 5 October, six long weeks after the crime had been committed, the lead detective on the case, Lieutenant J.E. 'Chip' Harding of the Charlottesville Police Department, received a call that he describes as being 'one of the most exciting phone calls in my 22 years of law enforcement.' A match had been obtained from the crime scene samples to a convicted offender sample submitted to the Virginia DNA Database several years before. The DNA sample for Montaret D. Davis of Norfolk, Virginia, was among 8000 samples added to the Virginia DNA Database at the beginning of October 1999. (Since 1989, a Virginia state law has required all felons and juveniles ages 14 and older convicted of serious crimes to provide blood samples for DNA testing.)

A quick check for the whereabouts of Mr. Davis found him in the Albemarle-Charlottesville Regional Jail. Ironically, because of a parole violation, he had been court ordered weeks before to report to jail on what turned out to be the same day as the rape. Amazingly enough he had turned himself in at 6 p.m., 14 hours after committing the sexual assault! Unless he would have bragged about his crime, it is doubtful that Mr. Davis would ever have made it onto the suspect list without the power of DNA testing and an expanding DNA database. At his jury trial in April 2000, Mr. Davis was found guilty of rape, forcible sodomy, and abduction, among other charges, and sentenced to a 90-year prison term.

DNA typing, since it was introduced in the mid-1980s, has revolutionized forensic science and the ability of law enforcement to match perpetrators with crime scenes. Thousands of cases have been closed with guilty suspects punished and innocent ones freed because of the power of a silent biological witness at the crime scene. This book explores the science behind DNA typing and the biology, technology, and genetics that make DNA typing the most useful investigative tool to law enforcement since the development of fingerprinting more than 100 years ago.

OVERVIEW OF THE CRIMINAL JUSTICE SYSTEM

As illustrated in Figure 1.1, the criminal justice system consists of three broad areas: (1) law enforcement, (2) scientific analysis, and (3) legal proceedings. Detectives or investigators serving in police agencies submit evidence collected from crime scenes to forensic laboratories. This evidence is then compared to suspect reference samples (when available) or—in the case of DNA or fingerprints—searched against a database of previous offenders as performed in the Virginia case just described. A scientific report of the analysis of the evidence and comparison to the reference samples is then produced. This report is used by law enforcement and the legal community (prosecutors or defense attorneys) to make further decisions that may result in the evidence being presented in a court of law.

Provided that the defendant does not plead guilty, legal proceedings are typically pursued in a court of law with the scientific report and testimony from the forensic expert conducting the analysis being admitted to strengthen one side or the other in the court proceedings against the defendant. Following review of the evidence against a defendant, a verdict of guilt or innocence, in the form of conviction (and fine or imprisonment or both) or acquittal, will result.

Thanks to popular television programs like *CSI: Crime Scene Investigation* and *Law & Order*, the public has become more aware of forensic science. Unfortunately, this increased awareness has also come with an inaccurate

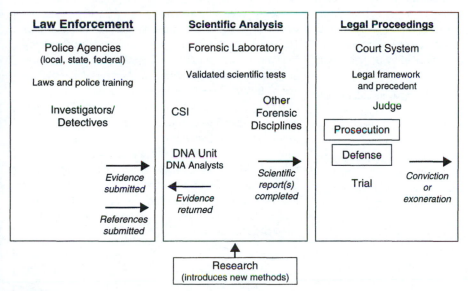

FIGURE 1.1

Illustration of the interactions between the three components of the criminal justice system.

understanding of the time and effort required to obtain a result—and equally unrealistic, the feeling that every case is solved in a simple and straightforward manner. Nevertheless, forensic science does play a center stage role in solving many crimes. The guilty are convicted and the innocent freed thanks in large measure to the power of DNA testing (D.N.A. Box 1.1).

A BRIEF HISTORY AND OVERVIEW OF FORENSIC DNA ANALYSIS

'DNA fingerprinting,' or DNA typing (profiling) as it is now known, was first described in 1985 by an English geneticist named Alec Jeffreys. Dr. Jeffreys found that certain regions of DNA contained DNA sequences that were repeated over and over again next to each other. He also discovered that the number of repeated sections present in a sample could differ from individual to individual. By developing a technique to examine the length variation of

D.N.A. Box 1.1 The Innocence Project: Using DNA Evidence to Exonerate Wrongfully Convicted Individuals

Forensic DNA testing can play a role in protecting the innocent as well as implicating the guilty. In recent years, the use of DNA evidence to free people from prison has been highly publicized and has altered some perceptions of the criminal justice system. For example, capital punishment in Illinois was put on hold in 2000 by the governor after learning of several inmates being exonerated by postconviction DNA testing.

As of December 2008, a total of 225 people, including some 'death row' inmates previously incarcerated for crimes they did not commit, have been released from prison thanks to the power of modern forensic DNA typing technologies. Many of these wrongfully convicted individuals were found guilty prior to the development of DNA typing methods in the mid-1980s based on faulty eyewitness accounts or circumstantial evidence. Fortunately for the more than 200 individuals exonerated so far by postconviction DNA testing, some items from the crime scenes were preserved in police evidence lockers that after many years could still be used for DNA testing. Results from testing these old crime scene materials successfully excluded them as the perpetrator of the crimes for which they were falsely convicted and imprisoned.

Defense attorneys Barry Scheck and Peter Neufeld launched the Innocence Project in 1992 at the Benjamin N. Cardozo School of Law in New York City. This nonprofit legal clinic promotes cases where evidence is available for postconviction DNA testing and can help demonstrate innocence. The Innocence Project has grown to include an Innocence Network of more than 40 law schools and other organizations around the United States and Australia. Law students and staff carefully evaluate thousands of requests for DNA testing to prove prisoners' innocence. In spite of careful screening, when postconviction testing is conducted, DNA test results more often than not further implicate the defendant. However, the fact that truly innocent people have been behind bars for a decade or more has prompted legislation in a number of states and also at the federal level to fund postconviction DNA testing. The increased use of DNA analysis for this purpose will surely impact the future of the criminal justice system.

Source:
http://www.innocenceproject.org; see also Grisham, J. (2006). *The innocent man: Murder and injustice in a small town.* New York: Doubleday.

these DNA repeat sequences, Dr. Jeffreys created the ability to perform human identity tests.

These DNA repeat regions became known as VNTRs, which stands for *variable number of tandem repeats*. The technique used by Dr. Jeffreys to examine the VNTRs was called restriction fragment length polymorphism (RFLP) because it involved the use of a restriction enzyme to cut the regions of DNA surrounding the VNTRs. This RFLP method was first used to help in an English immigration case and shortly thereafter to solve a double homicide case (D.N.A. Box 1.2). Since that time, human identity testing using DNA typing methods has been widespread. Chapter 3 provides a historical review of methods involved in forensic DNA analysis leading up to the short tandem repeat (STR) markers used today.

The past two-and-a-half decades have seen tremendous growth in the use of DNA evidence in crime scene investigations as well as paternity and genetic

D.N.A. Box 1.2 First Use of Forensic DNA Testing: Catching Colin Pitchfork

The first use of DNA testing in a forensic setting came in 1986. Two young girls, Lynda Mann and Dawn Ashworth, were sexually assaulted and then brutally murdered in 1983 and 1986. Both murders occurred near the village of Narborough in Leicestershire, England, with similar features, leading the police to suspect that the same man had committed both crimes. Under public pressure, police obtained a confession from a local man to killing one of the girls. His blood was compared to semen recovered from the crime scenes. The man's DNA did not match DNA evidence from either crime! Thus, the first forensic application of DNA technology was to demonstrate the innocence of someone who might otherwise have been convicted.

A mass screening to collect blood for DNA testing from all adult men in three local villages was conducted in a thorough search for the killer. More than 4000 men were tested without a match. About a year later a woman at a bar overheard someone bragging about how he had given a blood sample for a friend named Colin Pitchfork. The police interviewed Mr. Pitchfork, collected a blood sample from him, and found that his DNA profile matched semen from both murder scenes. He was subsequently convicted and sentenced to life in prison.

The story behind the first application of forensic DNA typing or genetic fingerprinting, as it was then called, has been well told in Joseph Wambaugh's *The Blooding*. The DNA typing methods used were Alec Jeffreys's multi-locus RFLP probes, which he first described in 1985. Since it was first used more than 20 years ago, DNA testing has progressed to become a sensitive and effective tool to aid in bringing the guilty to justice and in exonerating the innocent.

Important lessons from this first forensic application of DNA include (1) the connection of two separate crimes through development and comparison of DNA profiles from the biological evidence in the individual cases, (2) development and use of a DNA database to search for the perpetrator of both crimes, (3) exoneration of an innocent suspect who had apparently confessed to the police, and (4) realization that DNA is merely an investigative tool, because it did not solve the case by itself but rather relied on the confession of an accomplice and further detective work to bring Colin Pitchfork to justice.

Source:
Wambaugh, J. (1989). *The blooding.* New York: Bantam Books; http://www.forensic.gov.uk

genealogy testing. Today around 200 public and private forensic laboratories and several dozen private paternity testing laboratories conduct hundreds of thousands of DNA tests annually in North America. In addition, most countries in Europe, South America, and Asia as well as Australia, New Zealand, and some countries in Africa have forensic DNA programs. The number of laboratories around the world conducting DNA testing will continue to grow as the technique gains in popularity within the law enforcement community.

Since the mid-1990s, computer databases containing DNA profiles from crime scene samples, convicted offenders, and in some cases persons simply arrested for a crime, have provided law enforcement with the ability to link offenders to their crimes. Application of this technology has enabled tens of thousands of crimes—particularly horrible serial crimes by repeat offenders— to be solved around the world.

Due to the growth and effectiveness of national DNA databases of convicted offenders, which now contain in some cases millions of DNA profiles with a specific set of core STR loci, it is unlikely that other classes of genetic markers will have a major impact in the forensic community for the foreseeable future. Rather, as noted in Chapter 15, single nucleotide polymorphisms (SNPs) and other possible forensic DNA typing systems will probably see use in a supplemental rather than a supplanting role over the core STR loci that provide the common currency of data exchange in today's national DNA databases.

Some basic principles

As we begin reviewing the fundamentals of forensic DNA typing, it is worth noting a few basic principles of DNA analysis. First, with the exception of identical twins, the genome (i.e., the complete genetic composition) of each individual is unique and is inherited from an individual's parents with one-half coming from the mother and one-half from the father. However, to limit the expense and time of testing, forensic DNA analysis only examines a small subset of genetic variation within the human genome in order to differentiate among individuals. Current DNA tests based on STR markers do not look at genes. With the STR markers in use today, little to no information can be gleaned regarding ethnicity, predisposition to disease, or other phenotypic characteristics such as eye color, height, or hair color. Out of the more than 6 billion nucleotides present in the diploid human genome, fewer than 4000 nucleotides, or 0.0006% of the material, are examined from highly variable and nondescript regions. By way of comparison, if each nucleotide were 1 inch (2.5 cm) in length, the nuclear DNA in a single cell would be more than 100,000 miles (160,000 km) long—yet forensic DNA tests only examine about 300 feet (90 m) of this information. Because only a fraction of the available DNA information is examined, statistical calculations are performed to estimate the occurrence of a random match based on measured frequencies of particular genetic attributes among unrelated individuals.

As noted in Chapter 17, there are a number of applications for human identity testing involving DNA analysis using STR markers including (1) parentage analysis to help identify a child's father, (2) disaster victim identification to literally help put the pieces back together after a major natural or man-made disaster, (3) genetic genealogy and ancestry tests to attempt to gain a better understanding of one's heritage, and (4) historical and missing persons investigations to help link recovered bones from unknown individuals back to their family members. Since the early 1990s, the U.S. military has collected direct reference blood stains from service members; these blood stains are stored for future analysis in the event the soldier is killed in action and his or her remains need to be identified. In this manner, the military's goal of no more unknown soldiers can be met.

It is important to keep in mind that forensic DNA tests must be performed carefully in order to obtain reliable results. Stringent standards and precise protocols are faithfully followed by forensic DNA laboratories to help maintain a high level of quality in the data obtained. The information produced as part of a forensic examination must be reliable and able to hold up in court under rigorous scrutiny. The steps involved in processing a forensic DNA sample are reviewed in the next section.

STEPS IN DNA SAMPLE PROCESSING

Chapters 4 through 11 of this book describe the steps involved in processing forensic DNA samples with STR markers. STRs are a smaller version of the VNTR sequences first described by Dr. Jeffreys. Samples obtained from crime scene investigations or used in other forms of human identity testing are subjected to defined processes involving biology, technology, and genetics (Figure 1.2). Each of these steps will be described in more detail in subsequent chapters of this book and its companion volume, *Advanced Topics in Forensic DNA Typing*, 3rd edition.

Biology

Following collection of biological material from a crime scene or paternity investigation (Chapter 4), the DNA is first extracted from its biological source material (Chapter 5) and then measured to evaluate the quantity of DNA recovered (Chapter 6). After isolating the DNA from its cells, specific regions are copied with a technique known as the polymerase chain reaction, or PCR (Chapter 7). PCR produces millions of copies of each DNA segment of interest and thus permits very minute amounts of DNA to be examined. Multiple

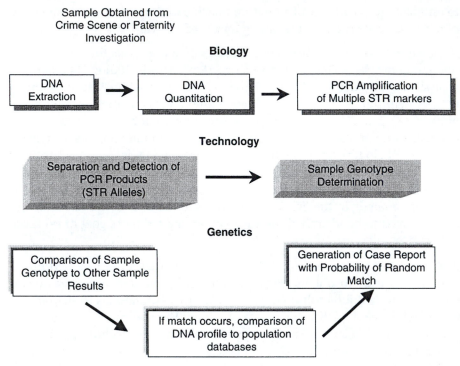

FIGURE 1.2

Overview of biology, technology, and genetic components of DNA typing using short tandem repeat (STR) markers.

STR regions can be examined simultaneously to increase the amount of information obtained from each DNA test as well as to minimize the amount of DNA consumed (Chapter 8).

Technology

The resulting PCR products are then separated based on their size and detected in order to characterize the STR region being examined (Chapter 9). The separation methods used today primarily involve capillary electrophoresis (CE). Fluorescence detection methods have greatly aided the sensitivity and ease of measuring PCR-amplified STR alleles compared to earlier methods (Chapter 3). Today, the primary instrument platforms used in the United States and around the world for fluorescence detection of STR alleles are the ABI Prism 310 and 3130xl Genetic Analyzers. After detecting the STR alleles, the number of repeats in a DNA sequence is determined, a process known as sample genotyping (Chapters 8 and 10).

The specific methods used for DNA typing are validated (Chapter 13) by individual laboratories to ensure that reliable results are obtained before new technologies (Chapter 18) are implemented. DNA databases (Chapter 12), such as the one described earlier in this chapter to match Montaret Davis to his crime scene, are extremely valuable tools and play an increasingly important role in law enforcement efforts.

Genetics

The resulting DNA profile for a sample, which is a combination of individual STR genotypes, is compared to other samples. In the case of a forensic investigation, these other samples would include known reference samples such as those taken from the victim or suspects, which are compared to the crime scene evidence. With paternity investigations, a child's genotype would be compared to his or her mother's and the alleged father(s) under investigation (Chapter 17). If there is no match between the questioned forensic sample and the known sample, then the samples may be considered to have originated from different sources. If there is no biological relationship demonstrated between the DNA profile of a child and that of the alleged father, then the alleged father is eliminated as the biological father. The term used for failure to match between two DNA profiles is 'exclusion.'

If a match or 'inclusion' results, then an estimate is made of the rarity of the obtained DNA profile by comparing it to a population database, which is a collection of DNA profiles obtained from unrelated individuals of a particular ethnic group (Chapter 11). For example, due to minor genetic differences between the groups, African Americans and Caucasians have different population databases for comparison purposes (see Table 11.1). Finally a case report or paternity test result is generated. This report typically includes the random match probability (i.e., an estimate of the rarity of the observed DNA profile) for the match in question. This random match probability is the chance that a randomly selected individual from a population will have an identical STR profile or combination of genotypes at the DNA markers tested.

DNA ANALYSIS INVOLVES COMPARISONS

It is important to keep in mind that a DNA profile by itself is fairly useless because it has no context. DNA analysis always requires that a comparison be made between two samples: (1) a questioned sample, commonly referred to as a 'Q,' and (2) a known sample, referred to as a 'K' (Figure 1.3). In forensic cases, crime scene evidence (Q) is always compared to a single suspect (K) or multiple suspects (K_1, K_2, K_3, etc.). In a case without a suspect, the evidence DNA profile may be compared to a computer database containing DNA profiles from previous offenders ($K_1, \ldots, K_n$).

Note that in Figure 1.3 under the reference sample steps, no characterization of the sample is performed nor is there a statistical interpretation given of the

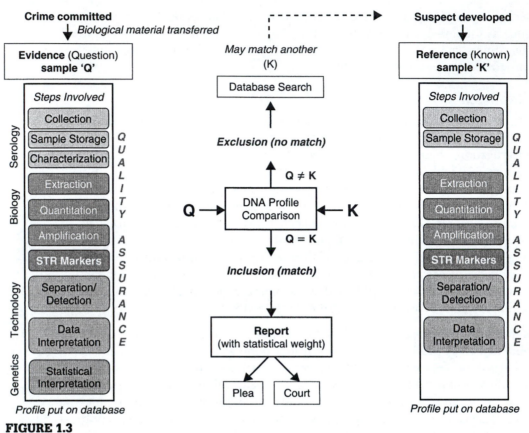

FIGURE 1.3

Steps involved in a Q-K comparison.

rarity of the DNA profile. Because sample K is from a known source, there is no need to determine its origin (e.g., bloodstain vs. saliva stain) or to calculate a random match probability because through accurate chain-of-custody records the DNA analyst should truly know the source of the sample.

Other applications of DNA testing also involve direct or biological kinship comparisons. With paternity testing, an alleged father or fathers (Q) are compared to a child (K). The victim's remains (Q) in missing persons or mass disaster cases are identified through use of biological relatives (K). Likewise, a soldier's remains (Q) may be identified through comparison to the direct reference bloodstain (K) that was collected for each soldier prior to combat and is maintained by a country's military. In each situation, the known sample K is used to assess or determine the identity of the unknown or questioned sample Q. A simple way to think about this comparison is that a K sample has the name of an individual associated with it, whereas a Q sample does not.

The results of this Q-K comparison are either (1) an inclusion, (2) an exclusion, or (3) an inconclusive result. Sometimes different language is used to describe these results. An inclusion may also be referred to as a 'match' or as 'failure to exclude' or 'is consistent with.' Another way that lab reports often state this information is 'the DNA profile from sample Q is consistent with the DNA profile of sample K—therefore sample K cannot be eliminated as a possible contributor of the genetic material isolated from sample Q.' An exclusion may be denoted as 'no match' or 'is not consistent with.'

As will be described further in later chapters and in the companion *Advanced Topics* volume, there may be many reasons why an inconclusive result is reported for the Q-K comparison. As illustrated in Figure 1.3, if a comparison finds the Q and K samples equivalent or indistinguishable, then a statistical evaluation is performed and a report issued stating an assessment of the rarity of the match. This number is commonly referred to as the random match probability (RMP). Methods for calculating the RMP will be described in more detail in Chapter 11.

THE LABORATORY REPORT

The end result of a forensic examination is a laboratory report, which represents a brief summary of work conducted by a forensic examiner (i.e., DNA analyst). The work represented in a laboratory report is based on standard operating procedures that must be followed. Prior to release of a lab report, data and conclusions are vetted through an internal review process culminating with a second reviewer and/or the DNA technical leader approving the work. This type of lab report is typically submitted to police investigators to describe DNA typing results obtained from evidence and reference samples submitted. Depending on the results, this report may also be used by a prosecuting attorney during court proceedings to illustrate that a defendant's DNA matches (or cannot be eliminated as a possible contributor to) DNA evidence from a crime scene.

An example generic laboratory report is shown in D.N.A. Box 1.3. Information such as the laboratory name and location, report date, examiner performing the work, and case file number are usually provided at the top of a lab report. A report is often addressed to the submitting agency ('customer') along with date(s) on which the evidence was received by the laboratory.

The next section of a report typically lists items tested and their sources, such as a blood sample from a suspect or a swab taken from a bloodstain on a broken pane of glass. Each item may have multiple identifiers, such as item #2 and Q1. The item number was probably assigned originally by the submitting agency, whereas the laboratory assigns unique identifiers as part of their analysis process in order to track the sample by case and sample number.

D.N.A. Box 1.3 Example Laboratory Report from a DNA Examination

ABC Laboratory

Hometown, U.S.A.

Report of Examination

Date: December 8, 2008

Examiner Name: Sherlock Holmes

Unit: Forensic Biology

Case File Number: 08-3101-042

The specimens listed below were received in the Forensic Biology unit under cover of communication dated April 1, 2008 (080412001) and April 15, 2008 (080412312):

Q1 Swab from broken, bloodstained glass in window frame (Item #2)

Q2 Swab from keyboard of laptop computer (Item #7)

K1 Blood sample from SUSPECT 1

K2 Buccal swab from SUSPECT 2

This report contains the results of the serological and nuclear DNA analyses.

Results of Examinations:

Blood was identified on specimen Q1. Specimen Q2 was examined for the presence of blood; however, no evidence of blood was found.

Deoxyribonucleic acid (DNA) was isolated from specimens Q1, Q2, K1 (SUSPECT 1), and K2 (SUSPECT 2) and subjected to DNA typing by the polymerase chain reaction (PCR) at the amelogenin sex typing locus and fifteen (15) short tandem repeat (STR) loci of the AmpF*l*STR Identifiler PCR Amplification Kit. The DNA typing results are detailed below:

Specimen	D8	D21	D7	CSF	D3	TH01	D13	D16	D2	D19	VWA	TPOX	D18	AMEL	D5	FGA
Q1	12,14	28,30	9,9	10,10	16,17	6,6	11,14	9,11	22,23	12,14	17,18	8,8	14,16	X,Y	12,13	21,22
Q2	12,14	28,30	9,9	10,10	16,17	6,6	11,14	9,11	22,23	12,14	17,18	8,8	14,16	X,Y	12,13	21,22
K1	12,14	28,30	9,9	10,10	16,17	6,6	11,14	9,11	22,23	12,14	17,18	8,8	14,16	X,Y	12,13	21,22
K2	13,14	30.2,32	8,12	10,12	17,17	6,9	8,12	7,8	23,25	14,14	17,20	8,10	14,17	X,X	11,13	21,25

Based on the typing results from the amelogenin locus (for sex determination), male DNA is present in the DNA obtained from specimens Q1, Q2, and K1 (SUSPECT 1). Based on the STR typing results and to a reasonable degree of scientific certainty, the contributor of specimen K1 (SUSPECT 1) is the source of the DNA obtained from specimens Q1 and Q2. The probability of selecting an unrelated individual at random having an STR profile matching the DNA obtained from the questioned specimens is approximately 1 in 840 trillion from the Caucasian population, 1 in 16 quadrillion from the African American population, and 1 in 18 quadrillion from the Hispanic population.

The STR typing results for specimen Q1 will be entered into the Combined DNA Index System (CODIS) and maintained by the ABC Laboratory for future comparisons.

No further serological or nuclear DNA examinations were conducted.

Known samples may be submitted sometime after submission of the initial crime scene evidence. These K samples can be from victim(s), suspect(s), or elimination samples from consensual sex partners, family members, and roommates who may have had access to the crime scene. In addition, DNA profiles from crime scene technicians, detectives, laboratory personnel, and others who may have had legitimate contact with the biological evidence in the course of the investigation may also be compared to the Q sample(s) to eliminate concerns over potential contamination of the evidence.

Serology results are often the first information provided under the 'Results of Examinations' portion of the report. These results may state something like 'blood was identified on specimen Q1' and indicate that the submitted sample has been characterized through a chemical or serological test prior to proceeding with DNA analysis.

The next section of the lab report typically lists what DNA tests were performed (e.g., PCR with the Identifiler kit that examines 15 STRs and permits gender determination) followed in some cases by a listing of the DNA typing results. Note that some laboratories prefer to keep the DNA typing results in the case file notes (which are available to the defense through discovery requests) and not provide them in the report in order to protect the privacy of the known individuals tested.

A lab report will typically summarize the gender of the donor (based on a sex-typing test called amelogenin) and a statistical statement regarding the weight of the evidence in terms of a random match probability or a source attribution statement. Finally, if the STR results were entered into a DNA database for potential future comparisons, this may also be mentioned in the report.

COMPARISONS TO COMPUTER TECHNOLOGY

To get a better feel for how rapidly forensic DNA analysis methods have progressed in the first two decades of development, a comparison to computer technology may be helpful. The use of computers at home and in the workplace has increased dramatically since personal computers became available in the mid-1980s. These computers become faster and more powerful every year. It is almost inconceivable that the Internet, which has such a large impact on our daily lives, was just an idea only a few years ago. DNA testing has had a similar impact on forensic science.

Table 1.1 lists some of the major historical events in forensic DNA typing. The implementation of new methods by the FBI Laboratory has been listed in this historical timeline because the DNA casework protocols used by the FBI create an important trend within the United States and around the world.

Table 1.1 Major historical events in forensic DNA typing shown by year (1985–2003). The events relating to forensic DNA (first column) are described in context with parallel developments in biotechnology (second column) and key events relating to Microsoft Corporation, which have impacted the computer age (final column).

Year	Forensic DNA Science & Application	Parallel Developments in Biotechnology	Microsoft Corporation Chronology
1985	Alec Jeffreys develops multi-locus RFLP probes	PCR process first described	First version of Windows shipped
1986	DNA testing goes public with Cellmark and Lifecodes in United States	Automated DNA sequencing with four colors first described	Microsoft goes public
1988	FBI begins DNA casework with single-locus RFLP probes		
1989	TWGDAM established; NY v. Castro case raises issues over quality assurance of laboratories	DNA detection by gel silver-staining, slot blot, and reverse dot blots first described	
1990	Population statistics used with RFLP methods are questioned; PCR methods start with DQA1	Human Genome Project begins with goal to map all human genes	Windows 3.0 released (quality problems); exceeds $1 billion in sales
1991	Fluorescent STR markers first described; Chelex extraction		Windows 3.1 released
1992	NRC I Report; FBI starts casework with PCR-DQA1	Capillary arrays first described	
1993	First STR kit available; sex typing (amelogenin) developed	First STR results with CE	
1994	Congress authorizes money for upgrading state forensic labs; 'DNA wars' declared over; FBI starts casework with PCR-PM	Hitachi FMBIO and Molecular Dynamics gel scanners; first DNA results on microchip CE	
1995	O.J. Simpson saga makes public more aware of DNA; DNA Advisory Board setup; UK DNA Database established; FBI starts using D1S80/amelogenin	ABI 310 Genetic Analyzer and TaqGold DNA polymerase introduced	Windows 95 released
1996	NRC II Report; FBI starts mtDNA testing; first multiplex STR kits become available	STR results with MALDI-TOF and GeneChip mtDNA results demonstrated	
1997	Thirteen core STR loci defined; Y-chromosome STRs described		Internet Explorer begins overtaking Netscape
1998	FBI launches national Combined DNA Index System; Thomas Jefferson and Bill Clinton implicated with DNA	2000 SNP hybridization chip described	Windows 98 released; antitrust trial with U.S. Justice Department begins

(Continued)

Table 1.1 Continued

Year	Forensic DNA Science & Application	Parallel Developments in Biotechnology	Microsoft Corporation Chronology
1999	Multiplex STR kits are validated in numerous labs; FBI stops testing DQA1/PM/D1S80	ABI 3700 96-capillary array for high-throughput DNA analysis; chromosome 22 fully sequenced	
2000	FBI and other labs stop running RFLP cases and convert to multiplex STRs; PowerPlex 16 kit enables first single amplification of CODIS STRs	First copy of human genome completed	Bill Gates steps down as Microsoft CEO; Windows 2000 released
2001	Identifiler STR kit released with 5-dye chemistry; first Y-STR kit becomes available	ABI 3100 Genetic Analyzer introduced	Windows XP released
2002	FBI mtDNA population database released; Y-STR 20plex published		Windows XP Tablet PC Edition released
2003	U.S. DNA database (NDIS) exceeds 1 million convicted offender profiles; the U.K. National DNA Database passes the 2 million sample mark	Human Genome Project completed with the 'final' sequence coinciding with 50th anniversary of Watson–Crick DNA discovery	Windows Server 2003 released; 64-bit operating systems expand capabilities of software

When multi-locus RFLP probes were first reported in 1985, the average computer operating speed was less than 25 MHz. Now, more than 20 years later, computing speeds of 3000 MHz (3 GHz) are common. Just as computer processing speeds and capabilities have increased rapidly, the ability of laboratories to perform DNA typing methods has improved along a similar timeline due to rapid progress in the areas of biology, technology, and application of genetic theories. In addition, the power of discrimination for DNA tests steadily increased in the late 1990s and into the new century (see Chapter 3).

Some interesting parallels can be drawn between the Microsoft Corporation, the company that has led the computer technology revolution, and the timing for advancements in the field of forensic DNA typing (Table 1.1). In 1985, the year that Alec Jeffreys first published his work with multi-locus RFLP probes, Microsoft shipped its first version of Windows software to serve as a computer operating system. In 1986, as DNA testing began to 'go public' in the United States with Cellmark and Lifecodes performing RFLP, Microsoft launched a successful initial public offering.

In the late 1980s, single-locus RFLP probes began to be used by the FBI Laboratory in DNA casework. Due to issues over the use of statistics for population genetics and the quality of results obtained in forensic laboratories,

RFLP methods were questioned by the legal community in 1989 and the early 1990s. At this same time, Microsoft had quality problems of their own with the Windows 3.0 operating system. However, they 'turned the corner' with their product release of Windows 3.1 in 1991. In the same year, improved methods for DNA typing were introduced, namely, fluorescent STR markers and Chelex extraction.

The popularity of Microsoft products improved in 1995 with the release of Windows 95. During this same year, forensic DNA methods gained public exposure and popularity due to the O.J. Simpson trial. The United Kingdom also launched a National DNA Database that revolutionized the use of DNA as an investigative tool. The United States launched its National DNA Index System (NDIS) utilizing the Combined DNA Index System (CODIS) software in 1998, concurrent with the release of Windows 98.

To aid sample throughput and processing speed, the FBI Laboratory and many other forensic labs stopped running RFLP cases as of the year 2000. On 13 January 2000, Bill Gates stepped down as the CEO of Microsoft in order to help his company move in new directions.

The development and release of Windows 2000 and Windows XP at the beginning of the 21st century continue to improve the capabilities of multi-tasking computer software. In like manner, the development and release of new DNA testing kits capable of single amplification reactions for examining 16 regions of the human genome simultaneously further the capability of multiplexing DNA information. Improved instrumentation and chemistry will continue to fuel the forensic DNA field just as computer technologies grow with both hardware and software development.

We recognize that due to the rapid advances in the field of forensic DNA typing, some aspects of this book may be out of date by the time it is published, much like a computer is no longer the latest model by the time it is purchased. However, a reader should be able to gain a fundamental understanding of forensic DNA typing from the following pages. Although we cannot predict the future with complete certainty, short tandem repeat DNA markers have had and will continue to have an important role to play in forensic DNA typing due to their use in DNA databases and their extraordinary effectiveness in answering legal questions surrounding human identification.

The match on Mr. Davis described at the beginning of this chapter was made with eight STR markers. These eight STRs are a subset of a larger set of core STR markers described in detail throughout this book that will most likely be used in DNA databases around the world for many years to come. DNA technology is enabling forensic scientists to aid the criminal justice system and to help catch violent criminals like Mr. Davis.

Points for Discussion

- What role does a forensic laboratory play in the criminal justice system?
- What are some ways in which DNA testing has impacted forensic science and the criminal justice system?
- Discuss some communication skills that might be beneficial for a forensic DNA scientist to have in interacting with law enforcement and the legal community.
- Why is a DNA profile considered 'useless' without another sample for comparison purposes?
- What are the important elements of a DNA lab report?

READING LIST AND INTERNET RESOURCES

Overview of Criminal Justice System

Bond, J. W. (2007). Value of DNA evidence in detecting crime. *Journal of Forensic Sciences, 52*, 128–136.

Crime Scene and DNA Basics for Forensic Analysts. http://dna.gov/training/evidence

Grisham, J. (2006). *The innocent man: Murder and injustice in a small town*. New York: Doubleday.

The Innocence Project. http://www.innocenceproject.org

Lazer, D. (Ed.), (2004). *DNA and the criminal justice system: The technology of justice*. Cambridge, MA: The MIT Press.

History of Forensic DNA Analysis

Alec Jeffreys Web site at University of Leicester. http://www.le.ac.uk/ge/ajj

Jeffreys, A. J. (2005). Genetic fingerprinting. *Nature Medicine, 11*, 1035–1039.

Jobling, M. A., & Gill, P. (2004). Encoded evidence: DNA in forensic analysis. *Nature Reviews Genetics, 5*, 739–751.

National Commission on the Future of DNA Evidence. (2000). *The future of forensic DNA testing: Predictions of the research and development working group*. Washington, DC: National Institute of Justice.

U.K. Forensic Science Service Casefiles. http://www.forensic.gov.uk/forensic_t/inside/news/casefiles.php

Wambaugh, J. (1989). *The blooding*. New York: Bantam.

Steps in DNA Sample Processing

Budowle, B., et al. (2000). *DNA typing protocols: Molecular biology and forensic analysis*. Natick, MA: Eaton Publishing.

Butler, J. M. (2004). Short tandem repeat analysis for human identity testing. *Current Protocols in Human Genetics*, Chapter 14, Unit 14.8.

Doak, S., & Assimakopoulos, D. (2007). How do forensic scientists learn to become competent in casework reporting in practice: A theoretical and empirical approach. *Forensic Science International, 167*, 201–206.

Watson, J. D., et al. (2007). DNA fingerprinting and forensics. In: *Recombinant DNA: Genes and genomes—A short course* (3rd ed.) (pp. 431–457). Cold Spring Harbor, NY: Cold Spring Harbor Press.

Comparisons to Computer Technology

Computer History Museum. http://www.computerhistory.org

Microsoft Corporation. http://www.microsoft.com

Resources

Denver District Attorney's Office (court case summaries involving DNA testing). http://www.denverda.org

DNA: A Prosecutor's Practice Notebook. http://dna.gov/training/prosecutors-notebook

DNA Resource.com. http://www.dnaresource.com

DNA.gov. http://www.dna.gov

FBI Combined DNA Index System (CODIS). http://www.fbi.gov/hq/lab/codis/index1.htm

FBI Laboratory. http://www.fbi.gov/hq/lab/labhome.htm

National Institute of Justice. http://www.ojp.usdoj.gov/nij

Principles of Forensic DNA for Officers of the Court. http://www.dna.gov/training/otc

STRBase. http://www.cstl.nist.gov/biotech/strbase

Other Books on Forensic DNA

Balding, D. J. (2005). *Weight-of-evidence for forensic DNA profiles.* Hoboken, NJ: Wiley.

Buckleton, J., Triggs, C. M., & Walsh, S. J. (Eds.), (2005). *Forensic DNA evidence interpretation.* Boca Raton, FL: CRC Press.

Carracedo, A. (Ed.), (2005). *Forensic DNA typing protocols (Methods in molecular biology): Vol. 297.* Totowa, NJ: Humana Press.

Evett, I. W., & Weir, B. S. (1998). *Interpreting DNA evidence: Statistical genetics for forensic scientists.* Sunderland, MA: Sinauer.

Goodwin, W., Linacre, A., & Hadi, S. (2007). *An introduction to forensic genetics.* Hoboken, NJ: Wiley.

Kobilinsky, L., Liotti, T. F., & Oeser-Sweat, J. (2005). *DNA: Forensic and legal applications.* Hoboken, NJ: Wiley.

Li, R. (2008). *Forensic biology.* Boca Raton, FL: CRC Press.

Lincoln, P. J., & Thomson, J. (Eds.), (1998). *Forensic DNA profiling protocols (Methods in molecular biology): Vol. 98.* Totowa, NJ: Humana Press.

Michaelis, R. C., Flanders, R. G., & Wulff, P. H. (2008). *A litigator's guide to DNA: From the laboratory to the courtroom.* San Diego: Elsevier Academic Press.

Rapley, R., & Whitehouse, D. (Eds.), (2007). *Molecular forensics.* Hoboken, NJ: Wiley.

Rudin, N., & Inman, K. (2002). *An introduction to forensic DNA analysis* (2nd ed.). Boca Raton, FL: CRC Press.

CHAPTER 2

Basics of DNA Biology and Genetics

Today, we are learning the language in which God created life.
—President Bill Clinton, 26 June 2000, announcing
the first draft sequence of the human genome

BASIC DNA PRINCIPLES

The basic unit of life is the *cell*, which is a miniature factory producing the raw materials, energy, and waste removal capabilities necessary to sustain life. Thousands of different proteins are required to keep these cellular factories operational. An average human being is composed of approximately 100 trillion cells, all of which originated from a single cell (the *zygote*) formed through the union of a father's sperm and a mother's egg. Each cell contains the same genetic programming. Within the nucleus of our cells is a chemical substance known as DNA that contains the informational code for replicating the cell and constructing the needed proteins. Because the DNA resides in the nucleus of the cell, it is often referred to as *nuclear DNA*. As will be discussed in Chapter 16, some minor extranuclear DNA, known as *mitochondrial DNA*, exists in human mitochondria, which are the cellular powerhouses.

Deoxyribonucleic acid, or DNA, is sometimes referred to as our genetic blueprint because it stores the information necessary for passing down genetic attributes to future generations. Residing in every nucleated cell of our bodies (note that red blood cells lack nuclei), DNA provides a 'computer program' that determines our physical features and many other attributes. The complete set of instructions for making an organism, that is, the entire DNA in a cell, is referred to collectively as its *genome*.

Contribution of the National Institute of Standards and Technology, 2010.

Table 2.1 Comparison of printed and genetic information.

Printed Information	Genetic Information
Library	Body
Book	Cell
Chapter	Nucleus
Page	Chromosome
Paragraph	Locus or gene
Word	Short DNA sequence
Letter	DNA nucleotide

DNA molecules store information in much the same way that text on a page conveys information through the order of letters, words, and paragraphs. Information in DNA is stored based on the order of nucleotides, genes, and chromosomes. Table 2.1 provides a simple comparison of how information is stored in both printed text and genetic formats.

DNA has two primary purposes: (1) to make copies of itself so cells can divide and carry the same information; and (2) to carry instructions on how to make proteins so cells can build and maintain the machinery of life. Information encoded within the DNA structure itself is passed on from generation to generation with one-half of a person's DNA information coming from his or her mother and one-half coming from his or her father.

DNA structure and definitions

Nucleic acids including DNA are composed of nucleotide units that are made up of three parts: a nucleobase, a sugar, and a phosphate (Figure 2.1). The nucleobase or 'base' imparts the variation in each nucleotide unit, while the phosphate and sugar portions form the backbone structure of the DNA molecule.

The DNA alphabet is composed of only four characters representing the four nucleobases: A (adenine), T (thymine), C (cytosine), and G (guanine). The various combinations of these four letters, known as nucleotides or bases, yield the diverse biological differences among human beings and all living creatures. Humans have approximately 3 billion nucleotide positions in their genomic DNA. Thus, with four possibilities (A, T, C, or G) at each position, literally zillions of combinations are possible. The informational content of DNA is encoded in the order (sequence) of the bases just as computers store binary information in a string of ones and zeros.

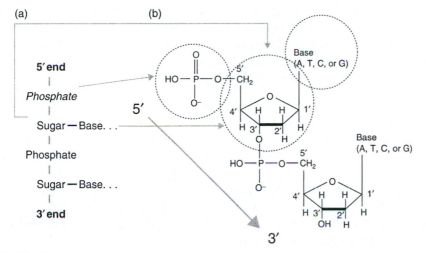

FIGURE 2.1

Basic components of nucleic acids: (a) phosphate sugar backbone with bases coming off the sugar molecules; (b) chemical structure of phosphates and sugar molecules illustrating numbering scheme on the sugar carbon atoms. DNA sequences are conventionally written from 5′ to 3′.

Directionality is provided when listing a DNA sequence by designating the 'five-prime' (5′) end and the 'three-prime' (3′) end. This numbering scheme comes from the chemical structure of DNA and refers to the position of carbon atoms in the sugar ring of the DNA backbone structure (Figure 2.1). A sequence is normally written (and read) from 5′ to 3′ unless otherwise stated. DNA polymerases, the enzymes that copy DNA, only 'write' DNA sequence information from 5′ to 3′, much like the words and sentences in this book are read from left to right.

Base pairing and hybridization of DNA strands

In its natural state in the cell, DNA is actually composed of two strands that are linked together through a process known as *hybridization*. Individual nucleotides pair up with their 'complementary base' through hydrogen bonds that form between the bases. The base-pairing rules are such that adenine can only hybridize to thymine and cytosine can only hybridize to guanine (Figure 2.2). There are two hydrogen bonds between the adenine–thymine base pair and three hydrogen bonds between the guanine–cytosine base pair. Thus, GC base pairs are stuck together a little stronger than AT base pairs. The two DNA strands form a twisted ladder shape or double helix due to this 'base-pairing' phenomenon (Figure 2.2).

The two strands of DNA are 'anti-parallel'; that is, one strand is in the 5′ to 3′ orientation and the other strand lines up in the 3′ to 5′ direction relative to the first strand. By knowing the sequence of one DNA strand, its complementary sequence can easily be determined based on the base-pairing rules of A with T and G with C. These combinations are sometimes referred to as Watson–Crick base pairs for James Watson and Francis Crick who discovered this structural relationship in 1953.

Hybridization of the two strands is a fundamental property of DNA. However, the hydrogen bonds holding the two strands of DNA together through base pairing may be broken by elevated temperature or by chemical treatment, a process known as *denaturation*. A common method for denaturing double-stranded DNA is to heat it to near boiling temperatures. The DNA double helix can also be denatured by placing it in a salt solution of low ionic strength or by exposing it to chemical denaturants such as urea or formamide, which destabilize DNA by forming hydrogen bonds with the nucleotides and preventing their association with a complementary DNA strand.

Denaturation is a reversible process. If a double-stranded piece of DNA is heated up, it will separate into its two single strands. As the DNA sample cools, the single DNA strands will find their complementary sequence and rehybridize or *anneal* to each other. The process of the two complementary DNA strands coming back together is referred to as *renaturation* or *reannealing*.

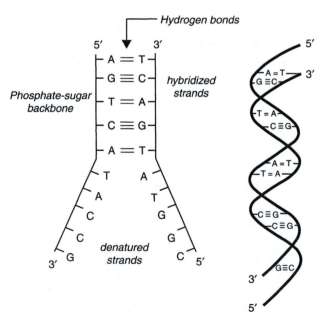

FIGURE 2.2
Base pairing of DNA strands to form double-helix structure.

Chromosomes, genes, and DNA markers

Obtaining a complete catalog of our genes was the focus of the Human Genome Project, which announced a final reference sequence for the human genome in April 2003 (D.N.A. Box 2.1). In 2007, DNA pioneers James Watson and Craig Venter released their fully sequenced genomes to the public. The information from the Human Genome Project will benefit medical science as well as forensic human identity testing and help us better understand our genetic makeup.

Within human cells, DNA found in the nucleus of the cell (nuclear DNA) is divided into chromosomes, which are dense packets of DNA and protection proteins called histones. The human genome consists of 22 matched pairs of autosomal chromosomes and two sex-determining chromosomes (Figure 2.3). Thus, normal human cells contain 46 different chromosomes or 23 pairs of chromosomes. Males are designated XY because they contain a single copy of the X chromosome and a single copy of the Y chromosome, while females contain two copies of the X chromosome and are designated XX. Most human

---

D.N.A. Box 2.1 The Human Genome Project and Beyond

Molecular biology's equivalent to NASA's *Apollo* space program began in 1990 when a multibillion-dollar, 15-year project was launched to decipher the DNA sequence contained inside a human cell. The Human Genome Project began under the leadership of James Watson, the scientist who, with Francis Crick, first determined the double-helix structure of DNA in 1953. With joint funding from the U.S. National Institutes of Health and the Department of Energy, efforts in the United States began with examining genetic and physical maps of human DNA and other model organisms such as yeast, *Drosophila* (fruit fly), and the mouse. In 1992, Francis Collins took the helm of the Human Genome Project. Amazingly over the years the project met or exceeded its milestones and stayed under budget. In 1999, a private sector enterprise named Celera under the leadership of Craig Venter challenged the public effort to a sequencing duel. The competition in large measure drove the Human Genome Project forward, leading to the announcement of a draft sequence in June 2000, its publication in February 2001, and a 'final' sequence in April 2003.

The medical community will likely be the largest beneficiaries of the Human Genome Project as scientists come to better understand the genetic basis for various diseases. This information raises legal and ethical issues as scientists and policymakers struggle with genetic privacy concerns and intellectual property rights. Undertaking such an enormous project has accelerated technology development and will continue to aid in the understanding of our species. With a human genome reference sequence in place, the International Haplotype Mapping ('HapMap') Project worked from 2002 to 2007 to help better understand normal genetic variation that occurs among different individuals by examining millions of single nucleotide polymorphisms (SNPs) in 270 individuals representing four population groups. In 2007, James Watson's and Craig Venter's genome sequences were completed and publicly released. The U.S. National Human Genome Research Institute announced in January 2008 plans to sequence 1000 human genomes. Next-generation sequencing has significantly cut the costs for genome scale analysis. The future looks promising for this field.

Sources:
http://www.genome.gov
http://hapmap.org

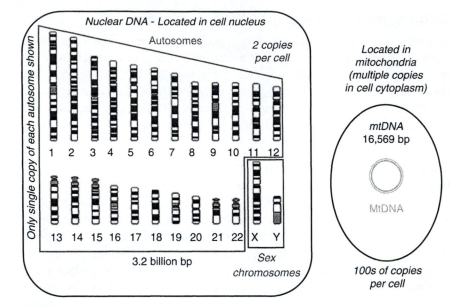

FIGURE 2.3

The human genome contained in every cell consists of 23 pairs of chromosomes and a small circular genome known as mitochondrial DNA. Chromosomes 1 through 22 are numbered according to their relative size and occur in single copy pairs within a cell's nucleus with one copy being inherited from an individual's mother and the other copy coming from the father. Sex chromosomes are either X,Y for males or X,X for females. Mitochondrial DNA is inherited only from one's mother and is located in the mitochondria with hundreds of copies per cell. Together the nuclear DNA material amounts to over 3 billion base pairs (bp), while mitochondrial DNA is only about 16,569 bp in length.

identity testing is performed using markers on the autosomal chromosomes, and gender determination is done with markers on the sex chromosomes. As will be discussed in Chapter 16, the Y chromosome and mitochondrial DNA, a small, multi-copy genome located in cell's mitochondria, can also be used in human identification applications.

Chromosomes in all body (somatic) cells are in a *diploid* state; they contain two sets of each chromosome. On the other hand, gametes (sperm or egg) are in a *haploid* state; they have only a single set of chromosomes. When an egg cell and a sperm cell combine during conception, the resulting zygote becomes diploid. Thus, one chromosome in each chromosomal pair is derived from each parent at the time of conception.

Mitosis is the process of nuclear division in somatic cells that produces daughter cells, which are genetically identical to each other and to the parent cell. *Meiosis* is the process of cell division in sex cells or gametes. In meiosis, two consecutive cell divisions result in four rather than two daughter cells, each with a haploid set of chromosomes.

The DNA material in chromosomes is composed of 'coding' and 'noncoding' regions. The coding regions are known as *genes* and contain the information necessary for a cell to make proteins. A gene usually ranges from a few thousand to tens of thousands of base pairs in size. One of the big surprises to come out of the Human Genome Project is that humans have fewer than 30,000 protein-coding genes rather than the 50,000 to 100,000 previously thought.

Genes consist of *exons* (protein-coding portions) and *introns* (the intervening sequences). Genes only make up ~5% of human genomic DNA. Non-protein-coding regions of DNA make up the rest of our chromosomal material. Because these regions are not related directly to making proteins, they have been referred to as 'junk' DNA although recent research suggests that they may have other essential functions. Markers used for human identity testing are found in the noncoding regions either between genes or within genes (i.e., introns) and thus do not code for genetic variation.

Polymorphic (variable) markers that differ among individuals can be found throughout the noncoding regions of the human genome. The chromosomal position or location of a gene or a DNA marker in a noncoding region is commonly referred to as a *locus* (plural: *loci*). Thousands of loci have been characterized and mapped to particular regions of human chromosomes through the worldwide efforts of the Human Genome Project.

Pairs of chromosomes are described as *homologous* because they are the same size and contain the same genetic structure. A copy of each gene resides at the same position (locus) on each chromosome of the homologous pair. One chromosome in each pair is inherited from an individual's mother and the other from his or her father. The DNA sequence for each chromosome in the homologous pair may or may not be identical since mutations may have occurred over time.

The alternative possibilities for a gene or genetic locus are termed *alleles*. If the two alleles at a genetic locus on homologous chromosomes are different they are termed *heterozygous*; if the alleles are identical at a particular locus, they are termed *homozygous*. Detectable differences in alleles at corresponding loci are essential to human identity testing.

A *genotype* is a characterization of the alleles present at a genetic locus. If there are two alleles at a locus, A and a, then there are three possible genotypes: AA, Aa, and aa. The AA and aa genotypes are homozygous, whereas the Aa genotype is heterozygous. A DNA *profile* is the combination of genotypes obtained for multiple loci. DNA typing or DNA profiling is the process of determining the genotype present at specific locations along the DNA molecule. Multiple loci are typically examined in human identity testing to reduce the possibility of a random match between unrelated individuals.

To help understand these concepts better, consider a simple analogy. Suppose you are in a room with a group of people and are conducting a study of twins. You instruct each member of the group to line up matched with his or her twin (homologue). You notice that there are 22 sets of identical twins (autosomes) and one fraternal set consisting of one boy and one girl (sex chromosomes). You have the twin pairs rearrange their line by average height from tallest pair of twins to the shortest with the fraternal twins at the end and number the pairs 1 through 23 beginning with the tallest. Now choose a location on one twin, say the right forearm (locus). Compare that to the right forearm of the other twin. What is different (allele)? Perhaps one has a mole, freckles, more hair. There are several possibilities that could make them different (heterozygous) or perhaps they both look exactly the same (homozygous).

Nomenclature for DNA markers

The nomenclature for DNA markers is fairly straightforward. If a marker is part of a gene or falls within a gene, the gene name is used in the designation. For example, the short tandem repeat (STR) marker TH01 is from the human *tyrosine hydroxylase* gene located on chromosome 11. The '01' portion of TH01 comes from the fact that the repeat region in question is located within intron 1 of the tyrosine hydroxylase gene. Sometimes the prefix HUM- is included at the beginning of a locus name to indicate that it is from the human genome. Thus, the STR locus TH01 would be correctly listed as HUMTH01.

DNA markers that fall outside of gene regions may be designated by their chromosomal position. The STR loci D5S818 and DYS19 are examples of markers that are not found within gene regions. In these cases, the 'D' stands for DNA. The next character refers to the chromosome number, 5 for chromosome 5 and Y for the Y chromosome. The 'S' refers to the fact that the DNA marker is a single copy sequence. The final number indicates the order in which the marker was discovered and categorized for a particular chromosome. Sequential numbers are used to give uniqueness to each identified DNA marker. Thus, for the DNA marker D16S539:

D16S539

D: DNA

16:    chromosome 16

S: single copy sequence

539: 539th locus described on chromosome 16

Designating physical chromosome locations

The basic regions of a chromosome are illustrated in Figure 2.4. The center region of a chromosome, known as the *centromere*, controls the movement of the chromosome during cell division. On either side of the centromere are 'arms' that terminate with *telomeres*. The shorter arm is referred to as 'p' (for petite) while the longer arm is designated 'q' (because it comes after p in the alphabet).

Human chromosomes are numbered based on their overall size with chromosome 1 being the largest and chromosome 22 the smallest. The complete sequence of chromosome 22 was reported in December 1999 to be over 33 million nucleotides in length. Since the Human Genome Project completed its monumental effort, we now know the sequence and relative length of all 23 pairs of human chromosomes.

During most of a cell's life cycle, the chromosomes exist in an unraveled linear form. In this form, they can be transcribed to code for proteins. Regions of chromosomes that are transcriptionally active are known as *euchromatin*.

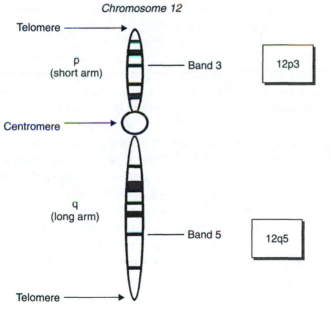

FIGURE 2.4

Basic haploid chromosome structure and nomenclature. The centromere is a distinctive feature of chromosomes and plays an important role during mitosis. On either side of the centromere are 'arms' that extend to terminal regions, known as telomeres. The short arm of a chromosome is designated 'p' while the long arm is referred to as 'q.' The band nomenclature refers to physical staining with a Giemsa dye (G-banded). Band localization is determined by G-banding the image of a metaphase spread during cell division. Bands are numbered outward from the centromere with the largest values near the telomeres.

The transcriptionally inactive portions of chromosomes, such as centromeres, are *heterochromatin* regions and are generally not sequenced due to complex repeat patterns found therein. Prior to cell division, during the metaphase step of mitosis, the chromosomes condense into a more compact form that can be observed under a microscope following chromosomal staining. Chromosomes are visualized under a light microscope as consisting of a continuous series of light and dark bands when stained with different dyes. The pattern of light and dark bands results because of different amounts of A and T versus G and C bases in regions of the chromosomes.

A common method for staining chromosomes to obtain a banding pattern is the use of a Giemsa dye mixture that results in so-called 'G-bands' via the 'G-staining' method. These G-bands serve as signposts on the chromosome highway to help determine where a particular DNA sequence or gene is located compared to other DNA markers. The differences in chromosome size and banding patterns allow the 24 chromosomes (22 autosomes and X and Y) to be distinguished from one another, an analysis called a *karyotype*.

A DNA or genetic marker is physically mapped to a chromosome location using banding patterns on the metaphase chromosomes. Bands are classified according to their relative positions on the short arm (p) or the long arm (q) of specific chromosomes (Figure 2.4). Thus, the chromosomal location 12p1 means band 1 on the short arm (p) of chromosome 12. The band numbers increase outward from the centromere to the telomere portion of the chromosome. Thus, band 3 is closer to the telomere than band 2. When a particular band is resolved further into multiple bands with additional staining, its components are named p11, p12, etc. If additional sub-bands are seen as techniques are developed to improve resolution, then these are renamed p11.1, p11.11, etc. For DNA markers close to the terminal ends of the chromosome, the nomenclature 'ter' is often used as a suffix to the chromosome arm designation. The location of a DNA marker might therefore be listed as 15qter, meaning the terminus of the long arm of chromosome 15. Sometimes a DNA marker is not yet mapped with a high degree of accuracy, in which case the chromosomal location would be listed as being in a particular range, that is, 2p23-pter or somewhere between band 23 and the terminus of the short arm on chromosome 2.

POPULATION VARIATION

It is estimated that a vast majority of our DNA bp sequence (over 99.7%) is the same between people. Only a small fraction of our DNA (around 0.3% or ~10 million nucleotides) differs between people and makes us unique individuals. New genomic information will provide a better understanding of human variation as more and more human genome sequences are completed and compared to one another. Variable regions of the human genome provide the capability to use DNA information for human identity purposes. Methods have been developed to locate and characterize this genetic variation at specific sites in the human genome.

Types of DNA polymorphisms

DNA variation is exhibited in the form of different alleles, or various possibilities at a particular locus. Two primary forms of variation are possible at the DNA level: sequence polymorphisms and length polymorphisms (Figure 2.5). It is worth noting that since the completion of the Human Genome Project (and now comparison of multiple completed human genomes) it has been discovered that another layer of genetic variation is possible, known as copy number variants (CNVs), where large segments of chromosomes can be inverted, duplicated, deleted, or even moved to different regions of the genome. Thus, we are discovering that our genomes are more complex than they were originally thought to be.

As discussed earlier, a genotype is an indication of a genetic type or allele state. A sample containing two alleles, one with 13 and the other with 18 repeat units, would be said to have a genotype of '13,18.' This shorthand method of designating the alleles present in a sample makes it easier to compare results from multiple samples.

In DNA typing, multiple markers or loci are examined. The more DNA markers examined and compared, the greater the chance that two unrelated individuals will have different genotypes. Alternatively, each piece of matching information adds to the confidence in connecting two matching DNA profiles from the same individual. If each locus is inherited independent of the other loci, then a calculation of a DNA profile frequency can be made by multiplying each individual genotype frequency together. This is known as the *product rule*.

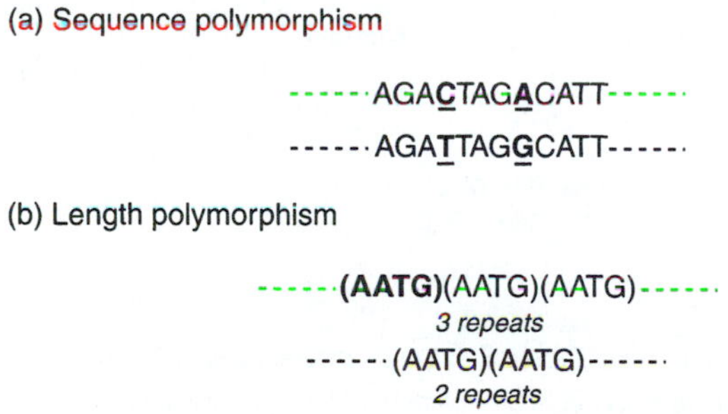

(a) Sequence polymorphism

```
------AGACTAGACATT------
------AGATTAGGCATT------
```

(b) Length polymorphism

```
------(AATG)(AATG)(AATG)------
           3 repeats
------(AATG)(AATG)------
           2 repeats
```

FIGURE 2.5

Two primary forms of variation exist in DNA: (a) sequence polymorphisms; (b) length polymorphisms. The short tandem repeat DNA markers discussed in this book are length polymorphisms.

Since it is currently not feasible in terms of time and expense to evaluate an individual's entire DNA sequence, multiple discrete locations are evaluated (Figure 2.6). The variability that is observed at these locations is used to include or exclude samples, i.e., whether they match or not. Because absolute certainty in DNA identification is not possible in practice, the next best thing is to claim virtual certainty due to the extreme small probability of a coincidental (random) match.

DNA searches can be narrowed down by comparing multiple data points in a manner analogous to the way in which the U.S. Postal Service delivers mail. The entire United States has over 300 million individuals but by including the zip code, state, city, street, street number, and name on an envelope, a letter can be delivered to a single, unique individual. Likewise, more and more information from DNA markers can be used to narrow a search down to a single individual. If marker 1, marker 2, marker 3, and so on match on a DNA profile between crime scene evidence and a suspect, one becomes more confident that the two DNA types are from the same source. The likelihood increases with each marker match.

Genetic variability

Large amounts of genetic variability exist in the human population. This is evidenced by the fact that, with the exception of identical twins, we all appear

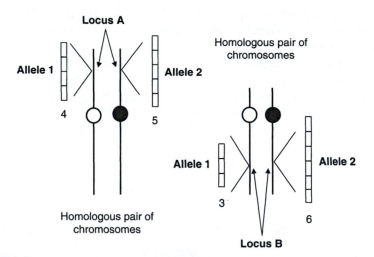

FIGURE 2.6

Schematic representation of two different STR loci on different pairs of homologous chromosomes. The chromosomes with the open circle centromeres are paternally inherited, while the solid centromere chromosomes are maternally inherited. Thus, this individual received the four repeat allele at locus A and the three repeat allele at locus B from his or her father, and the five repeat allele at locus A and the six repeat allele at locus B from his or her mother.

different from each other. Hair color, eye color, height, and shape all represent alleles in our genetic makeup. To gain a better appreciation for how the numbers of alleles present at a particular locus impact the variability, consider the ABO blood group. Three alleles are possible: A, B, and O. These three alleles can be combined to form three possible homozygous genotypes (AA, BB, and OO) and three heterozygous genotypes (AO, BO, and AB). Thus, with three alleles there are six possible genotypes. However, because AA and AO are phenotypically equal as are BB and BO, there are only four phenotypically expressed blood types: A, B, AB, and O.

With larger numbers of alleles for a particular DNA marker, a greater number of genotypes result. In general, if there are n alleles, there are n homozygous genotypes and $n(n - 1)/2$ heterozygous ones. Thus, a locus with 10 possible alleles would exhibit 10 homozygous possibilities plus $[10 \times (10 - 1)]/2$ heterozygous possibilities or $10 + 45 = 55$ total genotypes. A locus with 20 possible alleles would exhibit $20 + (20 \times 19)/2 = 210$ genotypes. A combination of 10 loci with 10 alleles in each locus would have over 2.5×10^{17} possible genotypes ($55 \times 55 \times 55 \times \ldots$), whereas the use of four loci with 30 alleles in each locus would have 465 genotypes each and 4.7×10^{10} possible genotypes ($465 \times 465 \times 465 \times 465$). The number of observed alleles per locus and the number of loci per DNA test both help produce a larger number of genetically possible genotypes.

Recombination: shuffling of genetic material

Recombination is the process by which progeny derive a combination of genes different from that of either parent. During the process of meiosis or gamete cell production, each reproductive cell receives at random one representative of each pair of chromosomes, or 23 in all. Because there are two chromosomes in each pair, meiosis results in 2^{23}, or about 8.4 million, different possible combinations of chromosomes in human eggs or sperm cells. The union of egg and sperm cells therefore results in over 70 trillion ($2^{23} \times 2^{23}$) different possible combinations—each one representing half of the genetic material from the father and half from the mother. In this manner, human genetic material is effectively shuffled with each generation producing the diversity seen in the world today.

GenBank: a database of DNA sequences

Genetic variation from DNA sequence information around the world is cataloged in a large computer database known as GenBank. GenBank is maintained by the National Center for Biotechnology Information (NCBI), which is part of the National Library of Medicine within the U.S. National Institutes of Health. The NCBI was established in 1988 as a national resource for molecular biology information to improve understanding of molecular processes affecting human health and disease. As of February 2008, GenBank contained over 85 trillion nucleotide bases from more than 80 billion different records. This repository of DNA sequence information is not from humans alone. Over 260,000 different species are represented in GenBank. GenBank DNA sequences may be viewed and retrieved over the Internet via the NCBI home page at http://www.ncbi.nlm.nih.gov.

Methods for measuring DNA variation

Techniques used by forensic DNA laboratories for human identity testing purposes are based on the same fundamental principles and methods used for medical diagnostics and gene mapping. A person's genetic makeup can be directly determined from very small amounts of DNA present in bloodstains, saliva, bone, hair, semen, or other biological material. Because all the cells in the human body descend by successive divisions from a single fertilized egg, the DNA material is (barring mutations) identical in all cells collected from that individual and, therefore, all nucleated cells provide the same forensic information.

Primary approaches for performing DNA typing can be classified into restriction fragment length polymorphism (RFLP) methods and polymerase chain reaction (PCR)-based methods. Some of the characteristics of these techniques are compared in Table 2.2. RFLP and PCR methods will be examined more

Table 2.2 Comparison of RFLP and PCR-based DNA typing methods.

Characteristic	RFLP Methods	PCR Methods
Time required to obtain results	6–8 weeks with radioactive probes; ~1 week with chemiluminescent probes	1–2 days
Amount of DNA needed	50–500 ng	0.1–1 ng
Condition of DNA needed	High-molecular-weight, intact DNA	May be highly degraded
Capable of handling sample mixtures	Yes (single-locus probes)	Yes
Allele identification	Binning required since a distribution of sizes are observed	Discrete alleles obtained
Form used in analysis	DNA must be double stranded for restriction enzymes to work	DNA can be either single stranded or double stranded
Power of discrimination	~1 in 1 billion with 6 loci	~1 in 1 billion with 8 to 13 loci (requires more loci)
Automatable and capable of high-volume sample processing	No	Yes

fully in Chapter 3. PCR-based methods largely supplanted RFLP methods due to the ability of PCR to handle forensic samples that are of low quantity and of poor quality. The desire for a rapid turnaround time and the capabilities for high-volume sample processing also drove the acceptance of PCR-based methods and markers. The most widely used forensic DNA markers today are short tandem repeats (STRs) due to a number of advantages.

This book covers the use of short tandem repeat DNA markers for human identity testing. STR markers have become popular for forensic DNA typing because they are PCR based and highly sensitive, enabling them to work with low-quantity DNA templates or degraded DNA samples. STR typing methods are amenable to automation and involve sensitive fluorescent detection, which enables scientists to collect data quickly from these markers. When sites on multiple chromosomes are examined, STRs are highly discriminating between unrelated and even closely related individuals. Finally, discrete alleles make results easier to interpret and to compare through the use of computerized DNA databases than RFLP-based systems where similar DNA sizes were grouped together.

INTRODUCTORY GENETIC PRINCIPLES

Genetics involves the study of patterns of inheritance of specific traits between parents and offspring. Rather than study inheritance patterns in single families, much of genetics today involves examining populations. *Populations* are groups of individuals, and they are often classified by grouping together those sharing a common ancestry. Population genetics assesses variation in the specific traits under consideration (e.g., STR alleles) among a group of individuals residing in a given area at a given time. Thus, *population genetics* is the study of inherited variation and its modulation in time and space. It is an attempt to quantify the variation observed within a population group or among different population groups in terms of allele and genotype frequencies.

Great genetic variation exists within species at the individual nucleotide level. For example, in humans several million nucleotides can differ between individuals. In addition, recent comparative genomic studies have revealed that entire sections of chromosomes can be deleted or duplicated. The genetic difference between individuals within human population groups is usually much greater than the average difference between populations.

Laws of Mendelian genetics

Gregor Mendel (1822–1884) is credited with being the 'father of modern genetics' for his mid-19th-century studies tracking multiple characteristics of pea plants through several successive generations (D.N.A. Box 2.2). Mendel correctly determined that each individual has two forms of each trait (gene or DNA sequence)—one coming from each parent. The observations of heredity that Mendel first described are now commonly referred to as Mendel's laws of heredity or *Mendelian inheritance*. These two laws are the law of segregation and the law of independent assortment.

These basic laws or principles of genetics first described by Mendel form the foundation for interpretation of DNA evidence. The *law of segregation* states that the two members of a gene pair segregate (separate) from each other during sex-cell formation (meiosis), so that one-half of the sex cells carry one member of the pair and the other one-half of the sex cells carry the other member of the gene pair. In other words, chromosome pairs separate during meiosis so that the sex cells (gametes) become haploid and possess only a single copy of a chromosome.

Figure 2.7 illustrates the chromosomes present in the human genome and the maternal and paternal contributions to a child's full genome. A mother contributes a single member of each of the 22 autosomal chromosomes, an X chromosome, and her mitochondrial DNA (mtDNA). A father contributes

---

D.N.A. Box 2.2 Gregor Mendel's Pea Experiments: Discovering Basic Rules for Genetic Inheritance

Gregor Mendel, an Austrian monk who lived from 1822 to 1884 in what is now the Czech Republic, is widely considered the father of modern genetics for his scientific experiments and observations regarding genetic inheritance of pea plants. Between 1856 and 1863, Mendel meticulously cultivated and tracked approximately 29,000 pea plants (*Pisum sativum*). He studied the following seven characteristics in his pea plants: (1) color and smoothness of the seeds (gray and round or white and wrinkled), (2) color of the cotyledons (yellow or green), (3) color of the flowers (white or violet), (4) shape of the pods (full or constricted), (5) color of unripe pods (yellow or green), (6) position of flowers and pods on the stems (axial or terminal), and (7) height of the plants (short or tall). Essentially, Mendel was studying seven different genetic loci, each possessing two different alleles.

Mendel's work found that hybridization of plants possessing dominant and recessive traits (alleles) produced a ratio of one-quarter purebred dominant, one-half hybrid, and one-quarter purebred recessive traits in their offspring. The dominant trait hid the recessive trait in plants containing hybrid traits. If a dominant trait is represented by the capital letter 'A' and a recessive trait by the lowercase letter 'a,' then a hybrid is represented by an 'Aa.'

In February and March 1865, Mendel described his experiments in a two-part paper titled 'Experiments on Plant Hybridization' that he read to the Natural History Society of Brno. Mendel's paper was published in German the following year in the proceedings of the society with the title 'Versuche über Pflanzen-Hybriden.' His work was ignored for 35 years until it was rediscovered in 1900 by three European scientists. Thomas Hunt Morgan later connected Mendel's theories with his chromosomal inheritance theory and thus brought Mendel's work into the mainstream of modern genetics.

Sources:
http://www.mendelweb.org/Mendel.html
http://en.wikipedia.org/wiki/mendelian_inheritance

a single member of each of the 22 autosomal chromosomes and either an X or a Y chromosome (and no mtDNA). Thus, the sex chromosome from the father's sperm (X or Y) when it combines with the mother's egg (containing an X) determines the sex of the zygote—either X,X for female or X,Y for male.

The *law of independent assortment* states that different segregating gene pairs behave independently due to recombination where genetic material is shuffled between generations. The law of segregation and the law of independent assortment are the basis for linkage equilibrium and Hardy–Weinberg equilibrium that are tested for when examining DNA population databases (see Chapter 11).

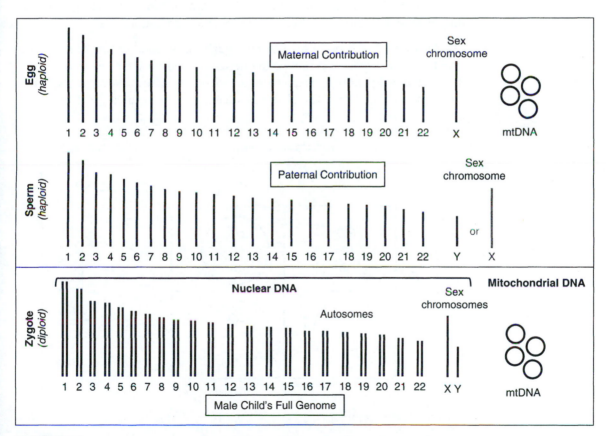

FIGURE 2.7

Human genome and inheritance. The haploid complement of chromosomes from a female's egg combines with the haploid chromosomal complement of a male's sperm to create a fully diploid zygote, which eventually develops into a child whose nongamete cells each contain the same genome. Half of the 22 autosomes come from each parent, while mtDNA is inherited only from the mother. The father's contribution of either an X or a Y chromosome determines the child's sex.

Hardy–Weinberg equilibrium and linkage equilibrium

For a genetic marker with two alleles A and a in a random-mating population, the expected genotype frequencies of AA, Aa, and aa are given by p^2, $2pq$, and q^2, where p and q are the allele frequencies of A and a, respectively, with $p + q = 1$. (Note that the use of 'p' and 'q' for allele frequencies should not be confused with the 'p' and 'q' labels used for chromosomal positions.) Figure 2.8 illustrates these principles, which constitute Hardy–Weinberg equilibrium (HWE). This graphical representation of the cross between alleles A and a from both parents is referred to as a *Punnett square*. Godfrey Hardy (1877–1947) and Wilhelm Weinberg (1862–1937) both independently discovered the mathematics for independent assortment that is now associated with their names as the Hardy–Weinberg principle. HWE proportions of genotype frequencies can be reached in a single generation of random mating. HWE is simply a way to relate allele frequencies to genotype frequencies.

Checking for HWE is performed by taking the observed allele frequencies and calculating the expected genotype frequencies based on the allele frequencies. If the observed genotype frequencies are close to the expected genotype frequencies calculated from the observed allele frequencies, then the population

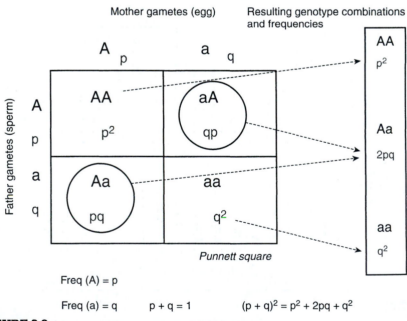

FIGURE 2.8

A cross-multiplication (Punnett) square showing Hardy–Weinberg frequencies resulting from combining two alleles 'A' and 'a' with frequencies 'p' and 'q,' respectively. Note that p + q = 1 and that the Hardy–Weinberg genotype proportions are simply a binomial expansion of $(p + q)^2$, or $p^2 + 2pq + q^2$.

is in Hardy–Weinberg equilibrium and allele combinations are assumed to be independent of one another.

One of the principal implications of HWE is that the allele and genotype frequencies remain constant from generation to generation. Another implication is that when an allele is rare, the population contains more heterozygotes for the allele than it contains homozygotes for the same allele.

Genes (or genetic markers like STR loci) that are in random association are said to be in a state of *linkage equilibrium*, while those genes or segments of the genome that are not in random association (i.e., are inherited together as a block) are said to be in *linkage disequilibrium*. Computer programs that check for linkage equilibrium are used to verify that a genetic marker is independent of other genetic markers being examined.

Relationship between allele frequency and genotype frequency

Allele frequency refers to the number of copies of an allele in a tested group of individuals divided by the total number of all alleles observed in this population. *Genotype frequency* refers to the number of individuals with a particular genotype divided by the total number of individuals examined. Figure 2.9 depicts the relationships between allele frequencies and genotype frequencies. The sum of the genotype frequencies always adds up to 100%. Thus, if the

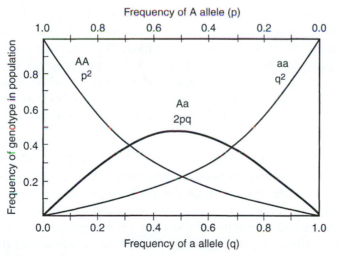

FIGURE 2.9

Graph depicting genotype frequencies for AA, Aa, and aa when Hardy–Weinberg equilibrium conditions are met. The highest proportion of heterozygotes Aa is observed when allele frequencies for both A and a are 0.5. Adapted from Hartl and Clark (1997).

genotype Aa is seen in 50% of the individuals examined, then genotype AA and genotype aa would each be expected to occur in 25% of the population (see center of Figure 2.9).

With genetic markers such as STR loci that possess more than two alleles where n alleles exist, $n(n + 1)/2$ genotypes are possible. The alleles (A and a) and genotypes (AA, Aa, and aa) represented in Figure 2.8 depict the frequency of occurrence of alleles with individuals as well as in the general population.

Diploid individuals have two copies of each autosomal gene (or DNA marker): one of paternal origin (sperm) and one of maternal origin (egg). If the alleles obtained from the sperm and the egg differ, then they are termed *heterozygous* for that locus, whereas if the individual received two identical alleles from both parents they are described as being *homozygous*.

Variability within a locus has to be stable enough to accurately pass the allele to the next generation (i.e., possess a low mutation rate) yet not be too stable or else only a few alleles would exist over time and the locus would not be as informative (i.e., useful in human identity testing applications). The simplest description of variation is the frequency distribution of genotypes. A measure of this variation is the number of heterozygote individuals present in a population or the *heterozygosity* of the genetic marker.

Genetic pedigrees: a method to represent inheritance in families

Inheritance patterns are typically represented with pedigrees that are drawn to reflect family relationships. Figure 2.10 shows a three-generation pedigree with the results from a single genetic marker. The oldest generation, in this case the grandparents, is shown at the top of a genetic pedigree. Males are represented as squares and females as circles. A horizontal line connects two biological parents. A vertical line connects offspring to their parents. A diagonal line through a square or circle indicates that the individual depicted is deceased (e.g., individual #17).

The genotypes from a single genetic marker—in this case, the STR locus FGA—are shown within the squares and circles representing the family members in this pedigree. People represented on this pedigree are labeled from #1 through #17 with the small number to the upper left-hand corner of each square or circle. Individual #2 (the grandmother) has a genotype of '23.2,25.' The '23.2' is a variant allele that typically occurs in less than 0.3% of the population. Note that this 23.2 allele is transmitted to her son (individual #3), but not to her two daughters (individuals #4 and #5). They get her other allele—the '25,' which typically occurs around 7% of the time in Caucasian individuals. Children will get either one or the other of their parent's two alleles at every

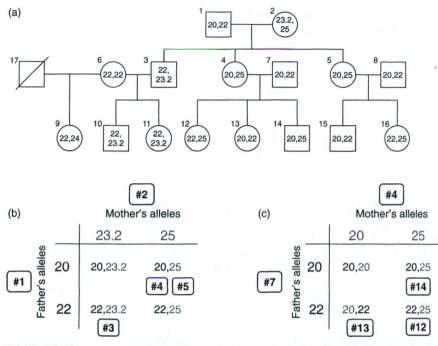

FIGURE 2.10

(a) A three-generation family pedigree with results from a single genetic locus (STR marker FGA). Squares represent males and circles females. (b) A Punnett square showing the possible allele combinations for offspring of individuals #1 and #2 in the pedigree. Individual #3 is 22,23.2 and inherited the 22 allele from his father and the 23.2 allele from his mother. (c) A Punnett square for one of the families in the second generation showing possible allele combinations for offspring of individuals #4 and #7.

locus (Figure 2.10b). Note also that the grandmother's '23.2' allele was passed on to her grandson (individual #10) and her granddaughter (individual #11). However, her other grandchildren (individuals #12 through #16) did not receive the 23.2 because neither of their parents had that particular allele.

Inheritance patterns for the three children of individuals #4 and #7 can be seen in Figure 2.10c. In this situation, all three children (#12, #13, and #14) have different genotype combinations. As can be seen with this example, if the children's genotypes are known, then it is possible to determine the parent's alleles and genotypes. This is how parentage testing and other kinship analyses are performed as will be described in Chapter 17.

Points for Discussion

- How can denaturation and hybridization of complementary DNA strands be controlled?

■ What impact has the Human Genome Project had on medicine and health? On forensic DNA testing?

■ Why is it important to understand the variation at specific genetic markers across many individuals in a population?

■ Why are some DNA markers named one way (e.g., TH01, VWA, etc.), whereas others are named with D-S designations (e.g., D3S1358)?

■ Why are Hardy–Weinberg equilibrium and linkage equilibrium important in forensic genetics?

READING LIST AND INTERNET RESOURCES

Basic DNA Principles

Primrose, S. B. (1998). *Principles of genome analysis: A guide to mapping and sequencing DNA from different organisms* (2nd ed.). Malden, MA: Blackwell Science.

Tagliaferro, L., & Bloom, M. V. (1999). *The complete idiot's guide to decoding your genes.* New York: Alpha Books.

Chromosomes, Genes, and DNA Markers

Cantor, C. R., & Smith, C. L. (1999). *Genomics: The science and technology behind the human genome project.* New York: John Wiley & Sons.

Jobling, M. A., Hurles, M. E., & Tyler-Smith, C. (2004). *Human evolutionary genetics: Origins, peoples, and diseases.* New York: Garland Science.

Ridley, M. (1999). *Genome: The autobiography of a species in 23 chapters.* New York: HarperCollins Publishers.

Watson, J. D., & Berry, A. (2003). *DNA: The secret of life.* New York: Alfred A. Knopf Publisher.

Human Genome Project and Beyond

Collins, F. S., et al. (2004). Finishing the euchromatic sequence of the human genome. *Nature, 431,* 931–945.

International HapMap Consortium. (2005). A haplotype map of the human genome. *Nature, 437,* 1229–1320.

Lander, E. S., et al. (2001). Initial sequencing and analysis of the human genome. *Nature, 409,* 860–921.

Levy, S., et al. (2007). The diploid genome sequence of an individual human. *PLoS Biology, 4; 5* (10), e254.

Mikkelsen, T. S., et al. (2005). Initial sequence of the chimpanzee genome and comparison with the human genome. *Nature, 437,* 69–87.

National Human Genome Research Institute. http://www.genome.gov

Wheeler, D. A., et al. (2008). The complete genome of an individual by massively parallel DNA sequencing. *Nature, 452,* 872–877.

Venter, J. C. (2007). *A life decoded: My genome, my life*. New York: Viking Adult.

Venter, J. C., et al. (2001). The sequence of the human genome. *Science, 291,* 1304–1351.

Population Variation

Barbujani, G., et al. (1997). An apportionment of human DNA diversity. In: *Proceedings of the National Academy of Sciences of the United States of America, 94,* 4516–4519.

Cavalli-Sforza, L. L., et al. (1994). *The history and geography of human genes*. Princeton, NJ: Princeton University Press.

GenBank. http://www.ncbi.nlm.nih.gov/GenBank

Introductory Genetic Principles

Cavalli-Sforza, L. L., & Bodmer, W. F. (1971). *The genetics of human populations*. Mineola, NY: Dover Publications.

Crow, J. F. (1999). Hardy, Weinberg and language impediments. *Genetics, 152,* 821–825.

Gonick, L., & Wheelis, M. (1983). *The cartoon guide to genetics* (updated ed.). New York: HarperCollins Publishers.

Hardy, G. H. (1908). Mendelian proportions in a mixed population. *Science, 17,* 49–50.

Hartl, D. L., & Clark, A. G. (1997). *Principles of population genetics* (3rd ed.). Sunderland, MA: Sinauer Associates.

Hartl, D. L., & Jones, E. W. (1998). *Genetics: Principles and analysis* (4th ed.). Sudbury, MA: Jones and Bartlett Publishers.

CHAPTER 3

Historical Methods

If you want to understand today, you have to search yesterday.
—Pearl Buck, from http://www.quotegarden.com/history.html

Before STRs became widely used at the end of the 1990s, a number of other serological and DNA testing techniques and markers were utilized as touched on in Chapter 1. This chapter explores more of the history behind these previous methods and how they served as a foundation for the field as it exists today.

A COMPARISON OF DNA TYPING METHODS

Technologies used for performing forensic DNA analysis differ in their ability to differentiate two individuals and in the speed with which results can be obtained. The speed of forensic DNA analysis has dramatically improved over the years. DNA testing that previously took 6 or 8 weeks can now be performed in a few hours.

The human identity testing community has used a variety of techniques including single-locus probe and multi-locus probe restriction fragment length polymorphism (RFLP) methods and more recently polymerase chain reaction (PCR)-based assays. Numerous advances have been made in the last quarter of a century in terms of sample processing speed and sensitivity. Instead of requiring large bloodstains with well-preserved DNA, tiny amounts of sample—as little as a few cells in some forensic cases—can yield a useful DNA profile.

The gamut of DNA typing technologies used during the past several decades for human identity testing is compared in Figure 3.1. The various DNA markers have been divided into four quadrants based on their power of discrimination, that is, their ability to discern the difference between individuals, and

Contribution of the National Institute of Standards and Technology, 2010.

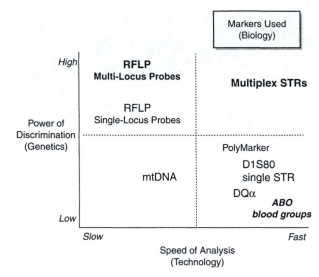

FIGURE 3.1

Comparison of DNA typing technologies. Forensic DNA markers are plotted in relationship to four quadrants defined by the power of discrimination for the genetic system used and the speed at which the analysis for that marker may be performed. Note that this diagram does not reflect the usefulness of these markers in terms of forensic cases.

the speed at which they can be analyzed. New and improved methods have developed over the years such that tests with a high degree of discrimination can now be performed in a few hours.

An ABO blood group determination, which was the first genetic tool used for distinguishing between individuals, can be performed in a few minutes but is not very informative. There are only four possible groups that are typed—A, B, AB, and O—and typically more than 80% of the population is either type O or type A. Thus, while the ABO blood groups are useful for excluding an individual from being the source of a crime scene sample, the test is not very useful when an inclusion has been made, especially if the sample is type O or type A.

On the other extreme, multi-locus RFLP probes are highly variable between individuals but require a great deal of labor, time, and expertise to produce and interpret a DNA profile. Analysis of multi-locus probes (MLP) cannot be easily automated, a fact that makes them undesirable as the demand for processing large numbers of DNA samples has increased. Deciphering sample mixtures, which are common in forensic cases, is also a challenge with MLP RFLP methods, which is the primary reason that laboratories turned to single-locus RFLP probes used in serial fashion.

The best solution in the search for a high power of discrimination and a rapid analysis speed has been achieved with short tandem repeat (STR) DNA markers, shown in the upper right quadrant of Figure 3.1. Because STRs by definition are short, three or more can be analyzed at a time. Multiple STRs can be examined in the same DNA test, or 'multiplexed.' Multiplex STRs are valuable because they can produce highly discriminating results and can successfully measure sample mixtures and biological materials containing degraded DNA molecules. This method can significantly reduce the amount of DNA required for analysis, thereby conserving more of the irreplaceable DNA collected from forensic evidence for use by scientists from opposing counsel or for additional specialized DNA testing. In addition, the detection of multiplex STRs is automated, which is an important benefit as demand for DNA testing increases.

Note that Figure 3.1 does not fully reflect the usefulness of these markers in terms of forensic cases. Mitochondrial DNA (mtDNA), which is shown in the quadrant with the lowest power of discrimination and longest sample processing time, can be very helpful in forensic cases involving severely degraded DNA samples or when associating maternally related individuals. There are instances when nuclear DNA is either so degraded or present in such low amounts in forensic evidence samples (e.g., hair shafts or putrefied bones or teeth) that it is either untestable or undetectable and mtDNA is the only viable alternative forensic DNA technology that can produce interpretable data for forensic comparisons. In other cases, such as the identification of skeletal remains, mtDNA is often the preferred method for comparing DNA from the bone evidence to the known reference mtDNA from potential family members to determine whether the mtDNA matches. In many situations, multiple technologies may be used to help resolve an important case or identify victims of mass fatalities, such as those from the World Trade Center collapse.

There has been a gradual evolution in adoption of the various DNA typing technologies shown in Figure 3.1. When early methods for DNA analysis are superseded by new technologies, there is usually some overlap as forensic laboratories implement the new technology. Validation of the new methods is crucial to maintaining high-quality results.

The purpose of the information in this chapter is to briefly review the historical methods mentioned above and to discuss the advantages and limitations of each technology. By seeing how the field has progressed during the past few decades, we can perhaps gain a greater understanding of where the field of forensic DNA typing is today and where it may be headed in the future.

THE PRE-DNA YEARS (1900–1985)

As mentioned in Chapter 1, the use of DNA for forensic and human identification purposes began with the work of Alec Jeffreys in the early 1980s.

However, prior to DNA being available, forensic laboratories utilized other genetic markers to try to assess whether or not someone could be excluded as the contributor to evidence recovered from a crime scene. While these methods may seem crude by today's standards, it is important to keep in mind that they were the best available at the time. Although the early methods had a very low power of discrimination, they were still quite capable of excluding individuals who did not match when the question (Q) and known (K) samples were compared.

Blood group testing

In 1900, Karl Landsteiner, an Austrian researcher at the University of Vienna, discovered that blood would sometimes agglutinate (i.e., clump together) when blood from different people was mixed together. His work, which resulted in the 1930 Nobel Prize in Medicine, eventually identified four blood types: O, A, B, and AB. Although there is some fluctuation between different population groups, generally speaking type O is observed about 43% of the time, type A 42% of the time, type B 12%, and type AB 3%. As anyone who has received a blood transfusion knows, the donor and recipient must have compatible ABO blood types to avoid transfusion reactions, such as clumping of incompatible red blood cells, which can be fatal.

Blood groups are related to antigen polymorphisms present on the surface of red blood cells. These antigens may be protein, carbohydrate, glycoprotein, or glycolipid differences that exist between people. The antigens are inherited from an individual's parents and therefore can be used to track paternity (Figure 3.2). Antibody-based serological tests can be developed to decipher the various blood group antigenic alleles.

ABO blood types became the first genetic evidence used in court. Leone Lattes, a professor at the Institute of Forensic Medicine in Turin, Italy, developed methods for typing dried bloodstains with antibody tests for the ABO blood groups and first used this genetic data in Italian courts starting around 1915. Over the next few decades, the use of ABO typing in paternity disputes and forensic cases spread to England, other countries in Europe, and the United States.

Another early genetic blood typing system developed was the MN system, which was discovered in 1927. Roughly 30% of the population is M, 22% N, and 48% MN so it can be helpful in differentiating among some people. Alexander Weiner (along with Karl Landsteiner who had moved to the Brooklyn Jewish Hospital in New York City) discovered the Rh factor in 1937 while working with *rhe*sus monkeys. Individuals are typically classified as 'Rh+' or 'Rh−' depending on their exposure to the Rh(D) antigen. Eventually

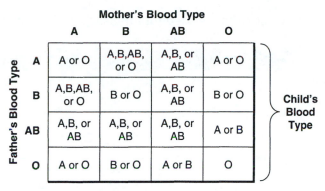

FIGURE 3.2

Blood type table showing phenotypic inheritance patterns of ABO blood groups.

other Rh factors were discovered—permitting many more allelic combinations (haplotypes) to be studied in tested individuals.

Today, the International Society of Blood Transfusion recognizes 30 major blood group systems that include the ABO, MN, and Rh systems. The genes responsible for the blood group antigens have been located and numerous alleles characterized. DNA typing assays have been reported for the genetic variants of many blood groups although these are not used routinely.

Serology is a term used to describe laboratory tests that examine specific antigen–antibody interactions. Immunological assays enable rapid screening for particular antigens (usually glycoproteins or glycolipids) with monoclonal antibodies. Serological tests can be used in detecting the various alleles of ABO and other blood groups. They are also used to perform forensic biology characterization assays of semen, saliva, sperm, and blood (see Chapter 4).

Forensic protein profiling

Amino acid sequences in some proteins vary among individuals in the human population. The use of multiple protein polymorphisms can lead to modest powers of discrimination where the chance of two unrelated people matching is one in several hundred. Prior to DNA testing becoming available in the mid- to late 1980s, protein profiling was performed in forensic biology laboratories as a crude way to potentially distinguish Q from K samples.

The human red blood cell (erythrocyte) as well as blood serum has a number of isoenzymes. These *isoenzymes* are multiple forms of a protein enzyme that can catalyze the same biochemical reaction in spite of slightly different amino acid sequences. However, there are typically only two or three forms of each isoenzyme, making them fairly poor at indicating differences between people.

Table 3.1 Characteristics of some of the isoenzymes used for forensic protein profiling in the early 1980s.

Erythrocyte Isoenzyme	Protein Symbol	Number of Alleles	Discrimination Potential
Phosphoglucomutase	PGM	2 (4 alleles with IEF)	10 phenotypes possible with IEF
Erythrocyte acid phosphatase	ACP/EAP	3	0.67
Esterase D	ESD	2	0.27
Adenylate kinase	AK	2	0.25
Glyoxalase I	GLO	2	0.57
Adenosine deaminase	ADA	2	0.06

Information from Li, R. (2008). Forensic biology, Boca Raton, FL: CRC Press, p. 169; and Ballantyne, J. (2000). 'Serology,' in Encyclopedia of forensic sciences, San Diego: Academic Press.
Key: IEF: isoelectric focusing.

Table 3.1 lists a few of the isozymes used during the 1970s and 1980s to perform forensic protein profiling.

Starch gel, agarose gel, and polyacrylamide gel electrophoresis were used early on to separate these proteins into distinguishable alleles. By the early 1980s many labs began using isoelectric focusing (IEF) polyacrylamide gel electrophoresis, which is capable of higher resolving power than protein electrophoresis because it produces sharper bands. Combined with silver staining (the same detection technique used a decade later with D1S80 and early STR systems; see below), IEF can detect fairly low levels of proteins in forensic samples. Nevertheless, proteins are not as variable as DNA nor are they as stable in forensic evidence.

THE FIRST DECADE OF DNA TESTING (1985–1995)

Alec Jeffreys' three *Nature* publications in 1985, showing that repeated DNA sequences in humans could be used to track genetic inheritance and differentiate between people, are considered by most people to mark the beginning of routine restriction fragment length polymorphism (RFLP) DNA testing. A few years earlier Wyman and White had shown that an RFLP marker was polymorphic and demonstrated Mendelian inheritance across three generations, but it was Jeffreys's work with variable number of tandem repeats (VNTRs) that enabled RFLP DNA testing to take hold.

The results with Jeffreys's multi-locus probes looked similar to bar codes (Figure 3.3). The patterns produced were termed *DNA fingerprints* because they were so variable among the individuals tested that the patterns were thought to be unique. Realizing the value to human identification work,

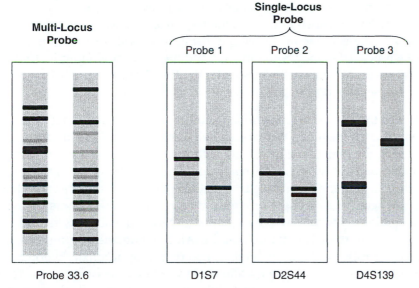

FIGURE 3.3

Illustration of patterns that might be seen with two DNA samples using multi-locus versus single-locus VNTR probes. Multi-locus probes produce a more complex pattern than the sequentially processed single-locus probes.

Jeffreys teamed up with Peter Gill and David Werrett of the British Home Office/Forensic Science Service to publish the first forensic application of 'DNA fingerprints' in December 1985.

About this same time another technique for analyzing DNA was being developed at Cetus Corporation near San Francisco, California. Kary Mullis had invented the polymerase chain reaction (PCR) as a means to make copies of any desired region of DNA. PCR enables sensitive detection that is needed for forensic applications. However, in the mid-1980s, there were no polymorphic genetic marker systems characterized yet for use with the amplification power of PCR. It would take several years before PCR-based methods came to the forensic laboratory and the courtroom.

RFLP-BASED DNA TESTING

The original RFLP process often took several weeks to complete. First, a sample of blood or some other biological material was collected. The DNA was then extracted from the cells by breaking open the cell membranes and removing the protein packaging around the DNA. Next, a restriction enzyme was added to cut the long, extracted DNA molecules into smaller pieces— much like a pair of scissors that was capable of finding and cutting specific

DNA sequences. The most commonly used restriction enzyme in the United States was *Hae*III, which recognizes the sequence GG/CC. Every time 'GGCC' appears in the genome of the sample being processed, two DNA fragments will be produced—one ending in 'GG' and the other beginning in 'CC' (the reverse would be true on the other strand). The chopped-up DNA fragments were then separated by fragment size on an agarose gel.

Following the DNA size separation, a Southern blot was performed. Here, the separated DNA fragments were transferred from the gel to a nylon membrane by placing the membrane in contact with the gel. By using a highly alkaline solution, the DNA strands were rendered single stranded. One of the strands was then fixed to the membrane by crosslinking the DNA onto the membrane with UV light (or by using a positively charged membrane). A radioactive or chemiluminescent probe, which contained a VNTR sequence, was then allowed to hybridize to the DNA attached on the nylon membrane at complementary sequence positions. Stringent binding occurred at appropriate hybridization temperature and ionic strength—allowing the labeled probe to find its complementary sequence with complete fidelity. Excess probe was then removed with several washes of the membrane. Finally, the location of the probe was noted by placing the membrane in contact with x-ray film. The resulting positions of the bands in the autoradiogram were then recorded through scanning the 'autorad' and comparing band positions to relative molecular mass markers analyzed in parallel (Figure 3.4).

For each additional VNTR probe being detected, the membrane would be stripped with alkaline solution washes to remove the previously bound probe and the process of rehybridizing another probe would be repeated. Since it took several days to a week to develop the banding patterns for each VNTR probe, the entire RFLP process could involve a month or longer.

Multi-locus VNTR probes

In the original Jeffreys method, a single probe labeled multiple VNTR loci. These multi-locus probes bound to various regions in the human genome under low hybridization stringency conditions and generated a complex pattern resembling the bar codes used in supermarkets (Figure 3.3). As noted above, this process was originally referred to as 'DNA fingerprinting' due to the ability to individualize someone with the multi-banded patterns. However, in forensic samples, where there is a possibility of mixtures from multiple contributors, a multiple-locus system could generate patterns that would be difficult to fully interpret. Thus, most RFLP typing moved to single-locus probes, where only one (a homozygote) or two (a heterozygote) alleles were detected at each VNTR locus (Figure 3.3).

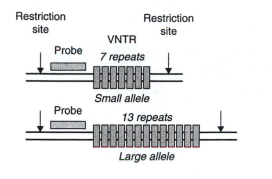
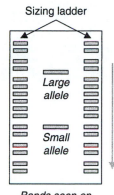

FIGURE 3.4

Illustration of the key processes with RFLP analysis. DNA from an individual, possessing two different size alleles at a single VNTR locus, is digested with a restriction enzyme. Arrows indicate restriction sites around a small and a large VNTR allele that varies in size due to the number of repeat units. The digested DNA is separated in terms of size via gel electrophoresis and transferred to a nylon membrane via Southern blotting. The membrane is washed with a radioactive or chemiluminescent probe that binds at a single probe site on each allele. A sizing ladder is run in adjacent lanes on the gel in order to estimate the VNTR allele sizes. The DNA fragments are placed into bins based on their size and then compared to other samples. The first probe is then removed and another probe is hybridized to the membrane and the process repeated to obtain results from typically four to six probes.

Single-locus VNTR probes

Table 3.2 lists six of the single-locus probe RFLP markers used extensively in the United States and Canada during the late 1980s and throughout the 1990s. Each of these RFLP markers had a large number of alleles that were classified operationally as 'bins' based on their size relative to sizing standards run simultaneously on the gel. With the exception of D17S79, all of the RFLP loci have heterozygosities of around 90% or greater. In other words, these loci are highly variable among tested individuals. The VNTR repeat unit for these various loci ranged from 9 bp (D1S7) to 38 bp (D17S79). The *Hae*III restriction enzyme typically digested the DNA fragments containing the VNTR loci to sizes of less than 12,000 bp, which helps the alleles to be better resolved from one another during electrophoresis.

Restriction enzyme differences between laboratories

Restriction enzymes are proteins discovered in various bacteria that function as smart biological scissors cutting DNA molecules precisely at specific sequence patterns. These patterns are referred to as *palindromic sequences* because they

Table 3.2 Characteristics of single-locus VNTR probes and RFLP markers widely used in North America during the late 1980s and 1990s.

Chromosome Designation	VNTR Probe	Number of Bins	Heterozygosity	HaeIII Fragment Size (kb)	Repeat Unit Length (bp)
D1S7	MS1	28	0.945	0.5–12	9
D2S44	yNH24	26	0.926	0.7–8.5	31
D4S139	pH30	19	0.899	2–12	31
D10S28	pTBQ7	24	0.943	0.4–10	33
D14S13	pCMM101	30	0.899	0.7–12	15
D17S79	V1	19	0.799	0.5–3	38

Adapted from Budowle, B., et al. (2000). DNA typing protocols: Molecular biology and forensic analysis, Natick, MA: Eaton Publishing; NIJ. The future of forensic DNA testing: Predictions of the research and development working group.
Key: *kb: kilobase pairs; bp: base pairs.*

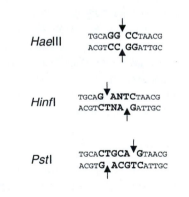

FIGURE 3.5
Restriction enzyme cut sites for HaeIII, HinfI, and PstI. The FBI and most North American labs use HaeIII. Cellmark Diagnostics and most European labs use HinfI. Lifecodes use PstI. Because each enzyme recognizes and cuts different sequences, the RFLP DNA fragment sizes cannot be compared between methods.

read the same in both directions (5′-to-3′ on the top strand and 5′-to-3′ on the bottom strand of DNA). Restriction enzymes cut both strands of DNA to generate either 'sticky' ends, which have an overhang of a few nucleotides, or 'blunt' ends.

Figure 3.5 shows the recognition and cut sites for three different restriction enzymes: *Hae*III, *Hinf*I, and *Pst*I. Early on in the application of RFLP testing, decisions were made regarding which restriction enzyme to use that led to the inability to compare results between laboratories.

Cellmark Diagnostics (a private U.S. company located near Washington, DC) and most European laboratories, including the UK's Forensic Science Service, performed their RFLP testing with *Hinf*I digestion. *Hinf*I recognizes the five nucleotides GANTC where 'N' can be any one of the four possible bases A, T, C, or G. Lifecodes Corporation (another private U.S. company located near New York City) used *Pst*I to digest their DNA samples.

Starting in the mid-1980s, before public crime labs got up to speed with DNA testing, both Cellmark and Lifecodes performed most of the early RFLP casework in the United States. When the FBI Laboratory started performing RFLP testing in late 1988, a decision was made to use a different restriction enzyme: *Hae*III. Because each restriction enzyme recognizes and cuts different sequences, the RFLP DNA fragment sizes will differ and thus alleles will be different sizes even if the same VNTR probes are used (see Figure 3.4). The public forensic laboratories in the United States and Canada followed the FBI's lead, which meant that previously tested RFLP cases performed by Cellmark or Lifecodes could not be compared with future forensic work by labs using different restriction enzymes.

The overall size of the fragments generated from a restriction digest depends on the size of the pattern recognized by the restriction enzyme. 'Four-base cutters,' like *Hae*III, target a specific four-base DNA sequence (e.g., GGCC) that should occur on average every 256 nucleotides—or ~11 million times in the human genome. 'Six-base cutters,' like *Pst*I, target a specific six-base sequence (e.g., CTGCAG) that should occur on average every 4096 nucleotides—or ~700,000 times in the human genome. Thus, four-base cutters will create smaller DNA fragments because they cut more often on average across the human genome. VNTR alleles from smaller DNA fragments can be more easily separated and sized during gel electrophoresis. The decision to use a different restriction enzyme led to a technical separation between public and private labs within the United States and prevented data compatibility between U.S. and European DNA laboratories.

During the years when RFLP was used, a number of interlaboratory studies were conducted to demonstrate comparability and reproducibility of results. Many of these studies were conducted by the National Institute of Standards and Technology (NIST), and a Standard Reference Material (SRM 2390) was produced to aid measurement assurance between forensic laboratories.

Speed and sensitivity

Because it required lots of DNA (>50 ng) as well as intact high-molecular-weight (>12-kb) DNA molecules, RFLP was quickly discovered to have severe limitations with many forensic cases. Degraded DNA samples of limited amounts that are often present with forensic cases did not work well with

RFLP methods. In addition, the desire to speed up sample processing led to some attempts to improve RFLP methods with chemiluminescent detection.

Chemiluminescent detection

In addition to great development speed, concerns over the cost and care required for dealing with radioactive phosphorous probes encouraged development of chemiluminescent detection methods by Life Technologies (Gaithersburg, MD) and Promega Corporation (Madison, WI). However, by the time chemiluminescent detection entered the arena in the mid-1990s, PCR-based methods, which had an improved ability to handle low amounts of, as well as degraded, DNA, were beginning to be widely used. Within a few years, everyone moved to fluorescent detection of multiplexed STR markers.

Long-range PCR

In the late 1990s, an attempt was made to develop the ability to use PCR amplification of the entire VNTR region in order to improve sensitivity while maintaining compatibility of results with previous RFLP DNA test results. This technique, known as long-range PCR, involved amplifying the VNTR region with a mixture of the *Taq* polymerase (commonly used with regular PCR) and a thermostable proofreading enzyme. Unfortunately, the sensitivity gains hoped for were not seen. In addition, problems with susceptibility of the target genomic DNA to degradation and preferential amplification of the smaller allele sometimes caused widespread heterozygotes to be inaccurately classified as homozygotes.

Regardless of small advances seen with long-range PCR and chemiluminescence, the paucity of validated VNTR loci and characteristics of these extremely multi-allelic systems made the transition to STRs inevitable.

Quality concerns and 'the DNA wars'

Beginning in the late 1980s, a number of vocal academic critics attacked many of the underlying assumptions and aspects of RFLP DNA typing. Concern had arisen from poor-quality work being performed with nonstandardized interpretation guidelines as well as subpar statistical support for assigning weight to the occurrence of a match between two DNA samples.

After a lengthy pretrial hearing regarding the admissibility of DNA in the 1989 *New York v. Castro* case, the court threw out DNA evidence of a match because of concerns over data quality and claims that the private forensic laboratory had not followed generally accepted standards for testing procedures and results interpretation.

Eric Lander, a scientist at MIT's Whitehead Institute in Boston, Massachusetts, who would later play a major role in the Human Genome Project, attacked how RFLP DNA testing was being performed and interpreted in the late 1980s.

In the *United States v. Yee* case heard in Cleveland, Ohio, the year after the *Castro* case, 12 expert witnesses were called to testify in the pretrial admissibility hearing including Eric Lander (MIT), Daniel Hartl (Harvard), and Richard Lewontin (Harvard), who were all 'heavyweights' in the population genetics arena. Despite their academic concerns, the DNA evidence was ruled admissible for consideration by the jury and the defendant was convicted. In December 1991, the prestigious journal *Science* published an article critical of forensic DNA testing by Hartl and Lewontin. Kenneth Kidd (Yale) and Ranajit Chakraborty (University of Texas) countered in an accompanying article. Hartl and Lewontin wanted more studies performed on various subpopulations to see if statistical assumptions of independence between loci could hold up.

Eric Lander published an article in the *American Journal of Human Genetics* in 1991 where he noted that during the vigorous discussion over the issue of possible population substructure, three schools of thought emerged: (1) the 'keep-it-simple' school, (2) the 'statistical' school, and (3) the 'empirical' school. For the most part, the community went along with the statistical approach of studying population samples of broad racial groups and applying statistical tests of Hardy–Weinberg equilibrium (HWE) and linkage equilibrium (LE) to try to detect substructure. This approach led to a proliferation of population studies looking at allele frequencies in the various genetic systems being used in forensic DNA analysis. In the end, many of these statistical tests have insufficient statistical power to detect whether or not any deviations from HWE or LE are present. Nevertheless, a direct outcome of some of these arguments in the early 1990s is the large number of DNA population studies that have been published or submitted to forensic science journals over the past decade or so.

Concern over quality issues caused the National Academy of Science's National Research Council to convene a Committee on DNA Technology in Forensic Science. This group published their thoughts on the issue of data quality concerns and statistical calculations needed. This 1992 NRC report, titled *DNA Technology in Forensic Science*, is commonly referred to as 'NRC I.' An outcry arose regarding some of the conclusions (particularly the application of a so-called 'ceiling principle' that was thought to be overly conservative), and a new committee was formed to revisit many of the statistical issues. *The Evaluation of Forensic DNA Evidence* that was published in 1996 has become known as 'NRC II.' The NRC II recommendations for statistical calculations in handling potential subpopulation structure are still used today in the United States.

In the fall of 1994, largely because of the media coverage of the O.J. Simpson trial and its use of DNA testing with such intensity in 1994–1995, Eric Lander (lead critic) and Bruce Budowle (lead FBI scientist) coauthored an article in the prominent journal *Nature* entitled 'DNA Fingerprinting Dispute Laid to Rest.' Extensive VNTR population data had been gathered and collated by the

FBI to show that subpopulation effects were not as substantial as originally claimed. In addition, quality assurance measures were being put into place in forensic laboratories that satisfied most critics. The so-called 'DNA wars' were over (although minor skirmishes continue to be fought today).

EARLY PCR-BASED DNA TESTING

As will be described in further detail in Chapter 7, the polymerase chain reaction provides the capability to copy and label a specific DNA sequence (or multiple sequences simultaneously) in order to make that sequence detectable. Over the years, a number of PCR-based tests have been developed to help differentiate individuals tested.

HLA DQ alpha/DQA1

The first PCR-based DNA test kit was for detecting sequence variation at the Human Leukocyte Antigen (HLA) DQA1 gene found on chromosome 6. Cetus Corporation (later purchased by Perkin-Elmer/Roche) released the DQ Alpha AmpliType Kit in 1990.

This kit utilized sequence-specific oligonucleotide (SSO) probes bound at specific locations on a test strip composed of nylon membrane (Figure 3.6). Denatured PCR products were annealed to the SSO probes in a water bath at a specific temperature. Following a colorimetric development process, light blue dots would form on the white background of the test strip where the PCR products bound to the immobilized SSO probes. The first DQ alpha kit could distinguish six different alleles: 1.1, 1.2, 1.3, 2, 3, and 4. With these six alleles, it was possible to define 21 genotypes.

The original DQ alpha test strip contained a total of 9 SSO probes and had the following 'dots' for differentiating the various alleles: 1, 2, 3, 4, 1.1, (1.2/1.3/4), 1.3 (all but 1.3), and a C or control dot (Figure 3.7a). The 'C' dot provided DNA analysts with a measure of confidence in their results. If it was not detected, then too little DNA was being tested to provide a reliable result. Perkin-Elmer/Roche later released a slightly more sophisticated kit called DQA1 that contained 11 SSO probes, which was capable of distinguishing the '4.1' subtype from the other allele '4' subtypes, thus providing a slight improvement over the original DQ alpha reverse dot blot test (Figure 3.7b). With an extra allele (4.1 vs. 4.2/4.3) being differentiated, the DQA1 test was able to determine 28 genotypes.

PolyMarker (PM+DQA1)

Recognizing the need for a greater power of discrimination than could be provided by the 28 detectable genotypes with DQA1, Perkin-Elmer/Roche

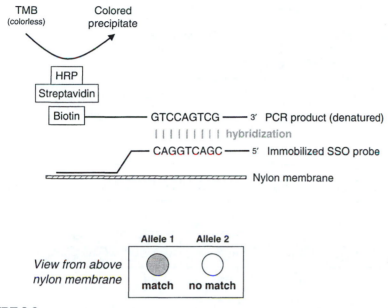

FIGURE 3.6

Reverse dot blot detection. Sequence-specific oligonucleotides (SSO) probes are attached (in the shape of a circle) to a nylon membrane. Multiple alleles are represented next to one another with different SSO probes. A denatured biotin-labeled PCR product is washed over the membrane under controlled temperature conditions where it will hybridize to the matching SSO probe(s). A streptavidin-horseradish peroxidase complex binds to the biotin and is processed with a color development substrate TMB (tetramethylbenzidine). A light blue colored precipitate results from a bound PCR product.

developed the AmpliType PM+DQA1 kit. This kit, also referred to as Poly-Marker, coamplified a portion of the HLA DQ alpha gene along with five other DNA segments located on human chromosomes 4, 7, 11, and 19 (Table 3.3). Although this PCR-based test was fairly sensitive, the five additional Poly-Marker loci utilized simple sequence polymorphisms with only two or three alleles possible for each locus. Thus, it was only capable of a power of discrimination in the range of 1 in 10,000 unrelated individuals. Problems were also noted with the potential for PCR product renaturation that sometimes impacted the ability to obtain reliable results. While PolyMarker and DQ alpha tests helped introduce PCR-based methods into the U.S. court system, they were insufficient in terms of their ability to differentiate people on a scale large enough to be useful in a national DNA database.

D1S80: a PCR-amplified VNTR

While European and U.S. laboratories were beginning to use DQ alpha and PolyMarker reverse dot blot tests, the FBI Laboratory and others began working with several-length polymorphism loci that could be PCR amplified.

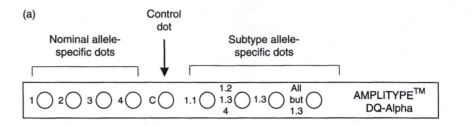

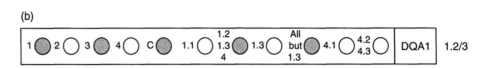

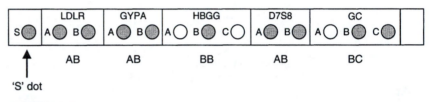

FIGURE 3.7

Reverse dot blot tests: (a) original AmpliType DQ alpha with 9 probes to detect 6 alleles and (b) the AmpliType PM+ DQA1 kit released a few years later with expanded DQA1 probes and the additional five PolyMarker loci. The control and 'S' dot serve as positive controls to test that the sample is above the PCR stochastic threshold and allele dropout should not be an issue. In (b) the DQA1 and PolyMarker genotypes for the standard cell line 9948 are illustrated: 1.2/3, AB, AB, BB, AB, BC.

Table 3.3 Characteristics of DQA1 and PolyMarker loci used in the AmpliType PM kit in the 1990s.

Locus	Gene Product	Chromosomal Location	Number of Alleles	Heterozygosity	PCR Product Size (bp)
DQA1	HLA-DQA1	6p21.3	7	0.828	242/239
LDLR	Low-density lipoprotein receptor	19p13.1–13.3	2	0.493	214
GYPA	Glycophorin A	4q28–31	2	0.498	190
HBGG	Hemoglobin G gammaglobulin	11p15.5	3	0.508	172
D7S8	—	7q22–31.1	2	0.476	151
GC	Group-specific component	4q11–13	3	0.592	138

Adapted from Budowle, B., et al. (2000). DNA typing protocols: Molecular biology and forensic analysis, Natick, MA: Eaton Publishing; NIJ. The future of forensic DNA testing: Predictions of the research and development working group.

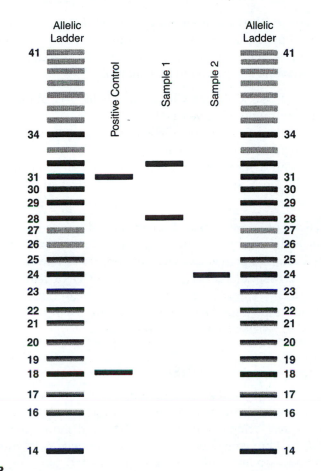

FIGURE 3.8

Illustration of a D1S80 gel image. Allelic ladders (ranging from 14 to 41 repeats) bracket a positive control sample with an 18,31 genotype and two samples (1= 28,32 and 2= 24,24). Some bands are darker in color suggesting that they contain a high amount of DNA relative to the lighter colored bands.

The amplified fragment length polymorphism, or AMP-FLP, that gained the greatest use in the early to mid-1990s was D1S80, a minisatellite on chromosome 1 containing a 16-bp repeat unit and alleles spanning the range of 14 to 41 repeat units. The PCR products from D1S80 ranged from approximately 400 to 800 bp and were typically separated on a vertical polyacrylamide gel followed by silver-stain detection (Figure 3.8). The preparation of these gels was labor intensive and time consuming because it required frequent user intervention with loading samples on the gel and performing the silver-stain development. Thus, the overall DNA analysis steps could not be automated, which prevented the high-throughput processing that would be required as the criminal justice community began to embrace DNA testing.

Perkin-Elmer/Roche released the AmpliType D1S80 kit in 1994. This kit continued to be sold by Applied Biosystems and used for about a decade by the forensic community before it was no longer considered commercially viable to stock since everyone had moved to STR analysis.

The commercial D1S80 kits came with an allelic ladder composed of rungs containing the commonly observed D1S80 alleles. By simultaneous analysis of samples in adjacent lanes to the allelic ladder on the polyacrylamide gel, D1S80 allele assignments could be made (Figure 3.8). In some cases, D1S80 was combined with a sex-typing marker named amelogenin that coamplified fragments of the X and Y chromosome with sizes of 212 and 218bp, respectively.

Because the alleles of D1S80 spanned such a large size range (400 to 800bp), it could not be easily combined with other AMP-FLPs nor did it handle highly damaged DNA samples particularly well. In addition, preferential amplification of smaller D1S80 alleles occurred with lower DNA template amounts when there was a large spread in the alleles being PCR amplified. Even though it was not a final stop along the way to the forensic DNA technology widely used today, D1S80 provided a useful stepping stone.

Short tandem repeats (STRs)

In the late 1980s, at about the same time as D1S80 and other minisatellite loci were discovered, microsatellites—better known today as short tandem repeats (STRs)—were being reported. These STRs had shorter repeat units, in the range of 2 to 7bp, compared to the approximately 8- to 100-bp repeat units found in minisatellite genetic markers (Figure 3.9).

By the mid-1990s, as DNA typing was entering its second decade of service to the criminal justice system, it was becoming apparent that STRs would be the genetic marker of choice in the future. A number of STR loci had been discovered from genomic sequencing work and were being widely utilized for genetic mapping studies. As will be described in later chapters, the United Kingdom's Forensic Science Service launched the first national DNA database in April 1995 using six STR loci. In November 1997, the FBI Laboratory selected 13 core STR loci as the basic currency for data sharing throughout the United States. More information on these core STRs can be found in Chapter 8.

The first commercial STR kit capable of multiplex amplification became available from the Promega Corporation in 1994 for silver-stain analysis. This kit consisted of the STR loci CSF1PO, TPOX, and TH01 and is often referred to as the 'CTT' triplex using the first letter in each locus (Figure 3.10). The CTT triplex only had a matching probability of ~1 in 500 but was still widely used in the United States in the mid-1990s because it was the first available STR multiplex kit and could be performed with a fairly low start-up cost.

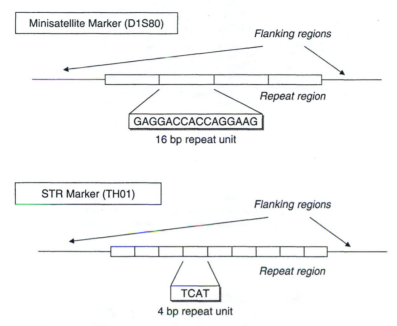

FIGURE 3.9

Schematic of minisatellite and microsatellite (STR) DNA markers. PCR primers are designed to target invariant flanking sequence regions. The number of tandem repeat units in the repeat regions varies among individuals, making them useful markers for human identification.

Table 3.4 describes some of the characteristics of D1S80 and the early STRs used in the triplex assay with silver-stain detection. Note that while a large number of D1S80 alleles exist it has a heterozygosity similar to STRs like VWA with fewer alleles. This apparent discrepancy between the number of alleles and the heterozygosity occurs because many of the D1S80 alleles are fairly rare, with alleles 18 and 24 occurring regularly in some population groups.

THE SECOND DECADE OF DNA TESTING (1995–2005)

In the mid-1990s, there were a number of different DNA testing methods under evaluation and in active use by forensic DNA laboratories. In April 1995, the United Kingdom launched their national DNA database with six STR markers using fluorescence detection—and thus led the way to where the world is today in terms of standardized sets of STR markers.

Within the United States, RFLP with single-locus probe VNTRs was still performed by the FBI Laboratory (and would be until 2000) as well as a number of other forensic labs. Many labs had also adopted and validated the reverse dot blot DQA1/PolyMarker system. Still others were using D1S80 and triplex

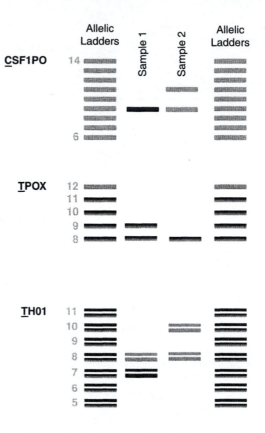

FIGURE 3.10

Illustration of a silver-stain gel image with the CTT triplex. Allelic ladders for the three STRs THO1, TPOX, and CSF1PO bracket two different samples: sample 1 = THO1-7,8; TPOX-8,9; CSF1PO-9,9; and sample 2 = THO1-8,10; TPOX-8,8; CSF1PO-9,11. Note the double bands for each allele with THO1. The forward and reverse strands of each PCR product separate from one another and are detected. This phenomenon is not as apparent with the other two loci because they are larger in size and not as well resolved on the gel.

STR assays with silver-stain detection methods. After a few years of using silver-stain detection, most labs around the world converted to STR markers with fluorescence detection.

Silver-staining STR kits

Although not as commonly used today, silver-staining procedures were used for the first commercially available STR kits from the Promega Corporation (see Table 3.4). Promega still supports silver-stain gel users although most of their customer base now uses fluorescent STR systems. Silver-stain detection methods are still quite effective for laboratories that want to perform DNA typing for a much smaller start-up cost. No expensive instruments are needed—simply a gel box for electrophoresis and some silver nitrate and other developing chemicals.

Table 3.4 List of silver-stain AmpFLP and GenePrint kits available circa 1993 to 2003. D1S80 was a stand-alone kit supplied by Perkin-Elmer. Promega supplied the following triplexes: CTT (CSF1PO, TPOX, TH01), FFv (F13A01, FES/FPS, vWA), and SilverSTR III (D16S539, D7S820, D13S317).

Kit/Locus	PCR Product Sizes (bp)	Chromosomal Location	Repeat Size (bp)	Number of Alleles	Heterozygosity
D1S80	369–801	1p	16	>30	0.82
TH01	179–203	11p15.5	4	8	0.76
TPOX	224–252	2p23–2pter	4	8	0.65
CSF1PO	295–327	5q33.5–34	4	10	0.75
F13A1	281–331	6p24–25	4	14	0.76
F13B	169–193	1q31–q32.1	4	6	0.75
LPL	105–133	8p22	4	10	0.77
FES/FPS	222–250	15q25-qter	4	6	0.69
vWA	131–171	12p12-pter	4	10	0.83

Heterozygosities from Caucasian database in Creacy, S. D., et al. (1995). In: Proceedings of the sixth international symposium on human identification, (pp. 28–31) Madison, WI: Promega.

Silver staining is performed by transferring the gel between pans filled with various solutions that expose the DNA bands to a series of chemicals for staining purposes. First, the gel is submerged in a pan of 0.2% (mass concentration) silver nitrate solution. The silver binds to the DNA and is then reduced with formaldehyde to form a deposit of metallic silver on the DNA molecules in the gel. A photograph is then taken of the gel to capture images of the silver-stained DNA strands and to maintain a permanent record of the gel. Alternatively, the gels themselves may be sealed and preserved.

Silver staining is less hazardous than radioactive detection methods used with RFLP analysis although not as convenient as fluorescence methods. Most reagents for silver staining are relatively harmless and thus require no special precautions for handling. The primary advantage of silver staining is that the technique is inexpensive. The developing chemicals are readily available at low cost. The PCR products do not need any special labels, such as fluorescent dyes. The staining may be completed within half an hour and with a minimal number of steps. Sensitivity is approximately 100 times higher than that obtained with ethidium bromide staining. However, a major disadvantage to data interpretation is that both DNA strands may be detected in a denaturing environment leading to two bands for each allele (see Figure 3.10). In addition, only one 'color' exists, which makes PCR product size differences the only method for multiplexing STR markers.

Fluorescent detection STR kits

The capability of simultaneously detecting STR alleles in the same size range was enabled by labeling the potentially overlapping PCR products with different colored fluorescent dyes. Chapters 9 and 10 contain more information on fluorescence detection and other technologies used for typing STR markers today.

Table 3.5 shows some of the early fluorescent STR multiplex systems developed in the mid-1990s. In 1991, Al Edwards and Tom Caskey from Baylor College of Medicine published the first article on fluorescent detection of STR markers. Edwards and Caskey patented their work and later licensed it to Promega Corporation and Applied Biosystems. Caskey's early work was followed up by the Forensic Science Service, the Royal Canadian Mounted Police, and FBI Laboratory publications involving fluorescent STR analysis.

One of the first STR multiplexes to be developed was a quadruplex created by the Forensic Science Service that comprised the four loci TH01, FES/FPS, VWA, and F13A1. This so-called 'first-generation multiplex'—sometimes termed the *British Home Office Quadruplex*—had a matching probability of approximately 1 in 10,000. The FSS followed with a second-generation multiplex (SGM) made up of six polymorphic STRs and a gender identification marker. The six STRs in SGM were TH01, VWA, FGA, D8S1179, D18S51, and D21S11. Results from these loci provided a matching probability of approximately 1 in 50 million. Today multiplex PCR assays capable of 15 or more STRs are used routinely by forensic laboratories to produce DNA profiles with matching probabilities of 1 in a trillion or greater.

MITOCHONDRIAL DNA SEQUENCING

During the same time in the early to mid-1990s that STR typing was beginning to utilize fluorescent labeling and detection technology, mitochondrial

Table 3.5 Early fluorescent STR multiplex systems available during the 1990s as either lab-built assays or precursors to today's commercially available STR typing kits.

Assay/Kit	Lab or Supplier	STR Loci
British Home Office Quadruplex	Forensic Science Service	TH01, VWA, F13A1, FES/FPS
Second-generation multiplex (SGM)	Forensic Science Service	TH01, VWA, FGA, D8S1179, D18S51, D21S11, amelogenin
CTTv	Promega Corporation	CSF1PO, TPOX, TH01, VWA
FFFL	Promega Corporation	F13A1, F13B, FES/FPS, LPL
GammaSTR	Promega Corporation	D16S539, D13S317, D7S820, D5S818
AmpISTR Blue	Applied Biosystems	D3S1358 VWA, FGA
AmpISTR Green	Applied Biosystems	CSF1PO, TPOX, TH01, amelogenin

DNA (mtDNA) sequencing was developed to enable recovery of DNA results from bones, hair, and teeth. As will be discussed further in Chapter 16, mtDNA has a greater number of copies per cell, which enables recovery of DNA information from difficult samples.

While STRs measure variation in the overall length of a PCR product, mtDNA analysis involves DNA sequencing (Figure 3.11). This primer extension method of sequencing is known as 'Sanger sequencing' for the Nobel laureate Fred Sanger, who first described it in 1977.

The process involves the polymerase incorporation of dideoxyribonucleotide triphosphates (ddNTPs) as chain terminators followed by a separation step capable of single-nucleotide resolution. There is no hydroxyl group at the 3′ end of the DNA nucleotide with a ddNTP and therefore chain growth terminates when the polymerase incorporates a ddNTP into the synthesized strand. Extendable dNTPs and ddNTP terminators are both present in the reaction mix so that some portions of the DNA molecules are extended. At the end of the sequencing reaction, a series of molecules are present that differ by one base from one another.

Each DNA strand is sequenced in separate reactions with a single primer. Often either the forward or reverse PCR primers are used for this purpose.

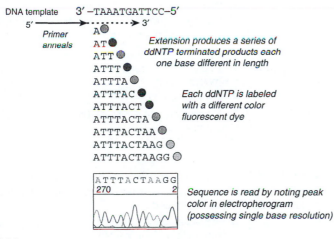

FIGURE 3.11

DNA sequencing process with fluorescent ddNTPs. A primer that has been designed to recognize a specific region of a DNA template anneals and is extended with a polymerase. Because a mixture of dNTPs and ddNTPs exist for each of the four possible nucleotides, some of the extension products are halted by incorporation of a ddNTP while other molecules continue to be extended. Each ddNTP is labeled with a different dye that enables each extension product to be distinguished by color. A size-based separation of the extension products permits the DNA sequence to be read provided that sufficient resolution is present to clearly see each base.

Four different colored fluorescent dyes are attached to the four different ddNTPs. Thus, ddTTP (thymine) is labeled with a red dye, ddCTP (cytosine) is labeled with a blue dye, ddATP (adenine) is labeled with a green dye, and ddGTP (guanine) is labeled with a yellow dye although it is typically displayed in black for easier visualization. These are similar to the fluorescent dyes used for STR detection. DNA sequencing may be reliably performed on a variety of platforms including the ABI 310, ABI 3100, and ABI 3130xl that are widely used for STR typing.

ADVANTAGES AND LIMITATIONS OF DNA TYPING METHODS

Table 3.6 summarizes the advantages and limitations associated with each of the methods reviewed in this chapter. Each of the earlier methods served to help the forensic DNA field get where it is today with multiplex STR analysis.

Table 3.6 A summary of advantages and limitations of each technique reviewed. See also NIJ (2000), *The Future of Forensic DNA Testing*.

Advantage	Limitation
Blood Group Typing	
1. Rapid, simple tests. 2. Only test available for many years.	1. Poor power of discrimination (~1 in 10) with such few alleles (i.e., inclusions are not very meaningful).
Protein Profiling	
1. Improved power of discrimination over blood group typing.	1. Poor power of discrimination (~1 in 100) even with multiple systems. 2. Poor sensitivity. 3. Proteins are not always stable in forensic stains or found in every sample.
RFLP with Single-Locus VNTR Probes	
1. Excellent powers of discrimination (~1 in millions or greater with four loci). 2. Large number of alleles (20 to 30 bins) at each locus which facilitates mixed-sample analysis.	1. Limited sensitivity (>50 to 500 ng required). 2. Time-consuming process (days to weeks) that cannot be automated. 3. Not suitable with degraded DNA samples due to high molecular weight needed. 4. Essentially continuous allele sizes, which requires grouping alleles into bins. Binning introduces statistical complications and sometimes difficulties of interpretation. 5. Limited number of validated loci (4 to 6 loci commonly used), which meant that these VNTRs were of limited value in distinguishing between siblings.

(Continued)

Table 3.6 Continued

Advantage	Limitation
DQA1+PM	
1. Fast, simple method (compared to RFLP). 2. Capable of analyzing small or degraded samples because it uses PCR. 3. No instrumentation needed after PCR.	1. Poor power of discrimination (~1 in 1000) with only six loci developed each containing only a few alleles. 2. Mixture interpretation difficult with limited number of alleles per locus.
D1S80	
1. Improved sensitivity compared to RFLP because it uses PCR. 2. Many alleles, which facilitates mixed-sample analysis. 3. Discrete allele calling possible using allelic ladder, which also simplifies statistical interpretation.	1. Large allele range, making it difficult to multiplex with other loci and giving rise to preferential amplification of smaller alleles. 2. Poor power of discrimination as a single locus (~1 in 50). 3. Allele dropout seen with highly degraded DNA. 4. Gel separation and silver-stain detection not amenable to automation or high-throughput sample processing.
Silver-Stained STRs	
1. Sensitive due to PCR. 2. Relatively rapid process (a day or two). 3. Works well with degraded DNA samples since shorter fragments of DNA can be analyzed (compared to D1S80). 4. A lower start-up cost compared to fluorescent STRs.	1. Because only a single 'color' channel is available, multiplex amplification and detection are limited to 3 to 4 loci. 2. Both strands of DNA are detected, leading to double bands with some loci that can complicate interpretation.
Fluorescent STRs	
1. Sensitive due to PCR (single-cell analysis has been demonstrated). 2. Relatively rapid process (can be completed in a few hours or at most a day or two). 3. Works fairly well with degraded samples since shorter fragments of DNA can be analyzed (compared to D1S80). miniSTRs have extended the capabilities for degraded sample analysis. 4. Multiplex PCR amplification and multi-color fluorophore labeling and detection enable examining 15 or more loci simultaneously, which provides excellent powers of discrimination (~1 in billions or greater with 8 to 9 or more STR loci). 5. Standardized sets of core loci are widely used with availability of commercial STR kits. 6. Automated detection enables high-throughput sample processing. 7. The potential number of loci is very large, which is important if siblings or other relatives are involved.	1. Less discrimination power per locus compared to VNTRs due to a smaller number of alleles and less heterozygosity per locus. 2. The possibility of contamination from stray DNA is increased because of the PCR amplification process. 3. Expensive equipment required for detection. 4. Stutter products and unbalanced peak heights may occur and make the interpretation of mixtures more difficult. 5. Data interpretation must account for artifacts such as dye blob, electrophoretic spikes, etc.

(Continued)

Table 3.6 Continued

Advantage	Limitation
Mitochondrial DNA Sequencing	
1. Excellent sensitivity and success with limited or badly damaged samples due to large number of mtDNA molecules per cell and the fact that the small mtDNA molecule is more robust than nuclear DNA.	1. Since all descendants through the female line are identical, mtDNA analysis cannot be used to distinguish among members of a sibship or maternal relatives.
2. Maternal transmission from a mother to all of her children extends possible reference sample providers and enables tracing family lineages.	2. Without recombination, the discrimination power of mtDNA is limited by the size of the population database used.
3. A majority of mtDNA haplotypes occur only once in a population database making its power of discrimination better than a single nuclear locus.	3. Heteroplasmy (the occurrence of more than one mtDNA type in a single cell or person) can complicate the analysis.
	4. Because the entire mtDNA molecule is inherited as a unit, it is equivalent to a single nuclear locus. Hence, the discrimination power is limited by the size of the database.

Overall, PCR-based methods have greatly enabled forensic DNA analysis for the following reasons:

- Very small amounts of DNA template may be used—even as little as from a single cell.
- DNA degraded to fragments only a few hundred base pairs in length can serve as an effective template for amplification.
- Large numbers of copies of specific DNA sequences can be amplified simultaneously with multiplex PCR reactions.
- Contaminant DNA, such as from fungal and bacterial sources, will not amplify because human-specific primers are used.
- Commercial kits are now available for easy PCR reaction setup and amplification.

With all of these advantages, there are three potential pitfalls that could be considered disadvantages of PCR-based techniques:

1. The target DNA template may not amplify due to the presence of PCR inhibitors in the extracted DNA.
2. Amplification may fail due to sequence mutations in the primer-binding region of the genomic DNA template—something often referred to as a 'null allele.'
3. Contamination from other human DNA sources besides the forensic evidence at hand or previously amplified DNA samples is possible

without the use of careful laboratory technique and validated protocols.

A note on history, name changes, and product unavailability

Many of the companies described as DNA test providers or commercial product suppliers no longer exist or have stopped providing the products and services listed in this historical section. In fact, since most of these technologies and marker systems are now obsolete, it is not possible to obtain commercial reagents any longer to perform the historical tests today. Applied Biosystems (who supplied Perkin-Elmer/Roche kits to the forensic community) stopped selling D1S80 and PM+DQA1 kits several years ago due to lack of demand with the transition to the now universally used STR typing kits. Fortunately, it is unlikely that a need would exist for back-compatibility with historical tests since STR profiles are now the common currency of DNA typing. (However, uncovering an old cold case with only RFLP data and no additional DNA sample could make retesting problematic!)

Many of the companies have changed names—some of them multiple times—since their products and services were utilized a decade or two ago. For example, Life Technologies was purchased by Invitrogen in 2002 and ceased to exist. Yet Invitrogen and Applied Biosystems merged in late 2008 to form a new 'Life Technologies' corporation. In the past decade Applied Biosystems, Inc., has been named Perkin-Elmer, PE Biosystems, PE Applied Biosystems, Applied Biosystems (a division of Applera), and is currently Applied Biosystems (a division of Life Technologies).

The two original RFLP testing companies in the United States—Lifecodes and Cellmark Diagnostics—were both purchased by Orchid BioSciences Inc. in the early 2000s and became Orchid Cellmark.

Points for Discussion

- Why were single-locus probes preferred over multi-locus probes for RFLP testing?
- Why did STRs replace RFLP as the method of choice in modern forensic DNA analysis?
- Discuss the advantages and disadvantages of short tandem repeat (STR) markers relative to other potential genetic loci that could be used for DNA testing.
- What is the difference between a minisatellite and a microsatellite?
- Why are fluorescence detection methods for STR typing preferred over silver-stain methods?

D.N.A. Box 3.1 DNA Evidence and Monica Lewinsky's Blue Dress

Can a simple DNA test have the power to impact world events? In 1998, independent counsel Kenneth Starr was investigating allegations that then U.S. President William Jefferson Clinton had a sexual relationship with a young White House intern, Monica Lewinsky. President Clinton had publicly denied the allegations quite emphatically and at that time there was no concrete evidence to the contrary.

During the course of the investigation, a dark blue dress belonging to Monica Lewinsky was brought to the FBI Laboratory for examination. Semen was identified on evidence item Q3243, as the dress was cataloged. The unknown semen stain was quickly examined with seven RFLP single-locus probes. Late on the evening of 3 August 1998, a reference blood sample was drawn from President Clinton for comparison purposes (Woodward, 1999).

As in the O.J. Simpson case (see D.N.A. Box 4.2), conventional RFLP markers were used to match the sample of President Clinton's blood to the semen stain on Monica Lewinsky's dress. At the time these samples were analyzed in the FBI Laboratory (early August 1998), STR typing methods were being validated but were not yet in routine use within the FBI's DNA Analysis Unit. High-molecular-weight DNA from the semen stain (FBI specimen Q3243-1) and President Clinton's blood (FBI specimen K39) was digested with the restriction enzyme *Hae*III. A seven-probe match was obtained at all seven RFLP loci examined.

This match was reported in the following manner: 'Based on the results of these seven genetic loci, specimen K39 (CLINTON) is the source of the DNA obtained from specimen Q3243-1, to a reasonable degree of scientific certainty.' The random match probability was calculated to be on the order of 1 in 7.8 trillion when compared to a Caucasian population database.

When faced with this indisputable DNA evidence, President Clinton found himself in a tight spot. Earlier statements that he had not had 'sexual relations' with Miss Lewinsky were now in doubt. The DNA results along with other evidence and testimony resulted in the impeachment of President Clinton on 19 December 1998—only the second president in U.S. history to be impeached. This physical evidence played an important role in demonstrating that a sexual relationship had existed between Miss Lewinsky and President Clinton. Although during the Senate impeachment trial, it was determined that his deeds were not serious enough for him to be removed from office, President Clinton's career will always be tainted by the semen stain on the now famous blue dress.

Sources:
Woodward, B. (1999). *Shadow: Five presidents and the legacy of Watergate.* New York: Simon & Schuster.
Grunwald, L., & Adler, S. J. (Eds.), (1999). *Letters of the century: America 1900–1999.* New York: The Dial Press, p. 673.

READING LIST AND INTERNET RESOURCES

Historical Perspectives

Ad Hoc Committee on Individual Identification by DNA Analysis, The American Society of Human Genetics. (1990). Individual identification by DNA analysis: Points to consider. *American Journal of Human Genetics, 46,* 631–634.

Aronson, J. D. (2007). *Genetic witness: Science, law, and controversy in the making of DNA profiling.* New Brunswick, NJ: Rutgers University Press.

Ballantyne, J., Sensabaugh, G., & Witkowski, J. (Eds.), (1989). *DNA technology and forensic science.* Cold Spring Harbor, NY: Cold Spring Harbor Laboratory Press. Banbury Report 32.

Inman, K., & Rudin, N. (2001). *Principles and practice of criminalistics: The profession of forensic science.* Boca Raton, FL: CRC Press.

Lee, H. C., et al. (1994). DNA typing in forensic science: I. Theory and background. *American Journal of Forensic Medicine and Pathology, 15,* 269–282.

National Institute of Justice (2000). *The future of forensic DNA testing: Predictions of the research and development working group*. Washington, DC: National Institute of Justice.

National Research Council (1992). *DNA technology in forensic science*. Washington, DC: National Academy Press (commonly called 'NRC I').

National Research Council (1996). *The evaluation of forensic DNA evidence*. Washington, DC: National Academy Press (commonly called 'NRC II').

Tamaki, K., & Jeffreys, A. J. (2005). Human tandem repeat sequences in forensic DNA typing. *Legal Medicine, 7*, 244–250.

U.S. Congress, Office of Technology Assessment (1990). *Genetic witness: Forensic uses of DNA tests*. Washington, DC: U.S. Government Printing Office.

Serology Methods

Ballantyne, J. (2000). Serology: Overview. In J.A. Siegel, et al. (Eds.), *Encyclopedia of forensic sciences, 3*, 1322–1331.

Camp, F. R. (1980). Forensic serology in the United States—I. Blood grouping and blood transfusion: Historical aspects. *American Journal of Forensic Medicine and Pathology, 1*, 47–55.

Federal Bureau of Investigation (1983). In: *Proceedings of a forensic science symposium on the analysis of sexual assault evidence*. Washington, DC: U.S. Government Printing Office.

Federal Bureau of Investigation (1984). In: *Proceedings of the international symposium on the forensic applications of electrophoresis*. Washington, DC: U.S. Government Printing Office.

Gaensslen, R. E. (1983). *Sourcebook in forensic serology, immunology, and biochemistry*. Washington, DC: U.S. Government Printing Office.

Li, R. (2008). *Forensic biology*. Boca Raton, FL: CRC Press.

Patzelt, D. (2004). History of forensic serology and molecular genetics in the sphere of activity of the German Society for Forensic Medicine. *Forensic Science International, 144*, 185–191.

Sensabaugh, G. F. (1982). Biochemical markers of individuality. In R. Saferstein (Ed.), *Forensic Science Handbook* (pp. 338–415). Englewood Cliffs, NJ: Prentice Hall.

Yuasa, I., & Umetsu, K. (2005). Molecular aspects of biochemical markers. *Legal Med, 7*, 251–254.

Blood Group Loci

The Blood Group Antigen Gene Mutation Database. http://www.ncbi.nlm.nih.gov/gv/mhc

Daniels, G. L., et al. (2004). Blood group terminology 2004 from the International Society of Blood Transfusion committee on terminology for red cell surface antigens. *Vox Sanguinis, 87*, 304–316.

Inagaki, S., et al. (2004). A new 39-plex analysis method for SNPs including 15 blood group loci. *Forensic Science International, 144*, 45–57.

Iwamoto, S. (2005). Molecular aspects of Rh antigens. *Legal Medicine, 7*, 270–273.

Owen, R. (2000). Karl Landsteiner and the first human marker locus. *Genetics, 155*, 995–998.

Rosenfield, R. E., et al. (1973). Genetic model for the Rh blood-group system. In: *Proceedings of the National Academy of Sciences of the United States of America, 70,* 1303–1307.

Stedman, R. (1972). Human population frequencies in twelve blood grouping systems. *Journal of the Forensic Science Society, 12,* 379–413.

Storry, J. R., & Olsson, M. L. (2004). Genetic basis of blood group diversity. *British Journal of Haematology, 126,* 759–771.

Yamamoto, F., et al. (1990). Molecular genetic basis of the histo-blood group ABO system. *Nature, 345,* 229–233.

Protein Profiling

Bissbort, S., et al. (1978). PGM1 subtyping by means of acid starch gel electrophoresis. *Human Genetics, 45,* 175–177.

Budowle, B., et al. (1985). Population data on the forensic genetic markers: phosphoglucomutase-1, esterase D, erythrocyte acid phosphatase and glyoxylase I. *Forensic Science International, 28,* 77–81.

Budowle, B. (1985). An agarose gel electrophoretic method for typing phosphoglucomutase-1, esterase D, or glyoxalase I. *Journal of Forensic Sciences, 30,* 1216–1220.

Budowle, B., & Eberhardt, P. (1986). Ultrathin-layer polyacrylamide gel isoelectric focusing for the identification of hemoglobin variants. *Hemoglobin, 10,* 161–172.

Carracedo, A., et al. (1983). Silver staining method for the detection of polymorphic proteins in minute bloodstains after isoelectric focusing. *Forensic Science International, 23,* 241–248.

Murch, R. S., & Budowle, B. (1986). Applications of isoelectric focusing in forensic serology. *Journal of Forensic Sciences, 31,* 869–880.

RFLP

Adams, D. E., et al. (1989). DNA analysis in the FBI laboratory. In: *Proceedings of the international symposium on the forensic aspects of DNA analysis* (pp. 173–177). Washington, DC: U.S. Government Printing Office.

Kirby, L. T. (1990). *DNA fingerprinting: An introduction.* New York: Stockton Press.

Technology Involved

Jeffreys, A. J., et al. (1985). Hypervariable 'minisatellite' regions in human DNA. *Nature, 314,* 67–73.

Southern, E. M. (1975). Detection of specific sequences among DNA fragments separated by gel electrophoresis. *Journal of Molecular Biology, 98,* 503–517.

Wyman, A. R., et al. (1980). A high polymorphic locus in human DNA. In: *Proceedings of the National Academy of Sciences of the United States of America, 77,* 6754–6758.

Multi-Locus VNTR Probes

Gill, P., et al. (1985). Forensic application of 'DNA fingerprints'. *Nature, 318,* 577–579.

Jeffreys, A. J., et al. (1985). Individual-specific fingerprints of human DNA. *Nature, 316*, 76–79.

Jeffreys, A. J., et al. (1985). Positive identification of an immigration test-case using human DNA fingerprints. *Nature, 317*, 818–819.

Jeffreys, A. J., et al. (1986). DNA 'fingerprints' and segregation analysis of multiple markers in human pedigrees. *American Journal of Human Genetics, 39*, 11–24.

Jeffreys, A. J., et al. (1991). The efficiency of multilocus DNA fingerprint probes for individualization and establishment of family relationships, determined from extensive casework. *American Journal of Human Genetics, 48*, 824–840.

Single-Locus VNTR Probes

Adams, D., et al. (1991). Deoxyribonucleic acid (DNA) analysis by restriction fragment length polymorphisms of blood and other body fluid stains subjected to contamination and environmental insults. *Journal of Forensic Sciences, 36*, 1284–1298.

Akane, A., et al. (1990). Paternity testing: Blood group systems and DNA analysis by variable number of tandem repeat markers. *Journal of Forensic Sciences, 35*, 1217–1225.

Budowle, B., et al. (1990). *Hae*III—a suitable restriction endonuclease for restriction fragment length polymorphism analysis of biological evidence samples. *Journal of Forensic Sciences, 35*, 530–536.

Evett, I. W., & Gill, P. (1991). A discussion of the robustness of methods for assessing the evidential value of DNA single locus probes in crime investigations. *Electrophoresis, 12*, 226–230.

Federal Bureau of Investigation (1989). *Proceedings of the international symposium on the forensic aspects of DNA analysis*. Washington, DC: U.S. Government Printing Office.

Markowicz, K. R., et al. (1990). Use of deoxyribonucleic acid (DNA) fingerprints for identity determination: comparison with traditional paternity testing methods—Part II. *Journal of Forensic Sciences, 35*, 1270–1276.

Nakamura, Y., et al. (1987). Variable number tandem repeat (VNTR) markers for human gene mapping. *Science, 235*, 1616–1622.

Tonelli, L. A., et al. (1990). Use of deoxyribonucleic acid (DNA) fingerprints for identity determination: Comparison with traditional paternity testing methods—Part I. *Journal of Forensic Sciences, 35*, 1265–1269.

Waye, J. S., & Fourney, R. M. (1993). Forensic DNA typing of highly polymorphic VNTR loci. In R. Saferstein (Ed.), *Forensic Science Handbook: Vol. III* (pp. 358–415). Englewood Cliffs, NJ: Prentice Hall.

Chemiluminescence Detection

Giusti, A., et al. (1995). A chemiluminescence-based detection system for human DNA quantitation and restriction fragment length polymorphism (RFLP) analysis. *Applied and Theoretical Electrophoresis, 5*, 89–98.

Klevan, L., et al. (1995). Chemiluminescent detection of DNA probes in forensic analysis. *Electrophoresis, 16*, 1553–1558.

Sprecher, C. J., et al. (1993). The GenePrint Light™ method for Southern transfer and chemiluminescent detection of human genomic DNA. *Biotechniques, 14*, 278–283.

Long-Range PCR

Cheng, S., et al. (1994). Long PCR. *Nature, 369,* 684–685.

Jeffreys, A. J., et al. (1988). Amplification of human minisatellites by the polymerase chain reaction: Towards DNA fingerprinting of single cells. *Nucleic Acids Research, 16,* 10953–10971.

Richie, K., et al. (1999). Long PCR for VNTR analysis. *Journal of Forensic Sciences, 44,* 1176–1185.

Interlab Comparisons

Duewer, D. L., et al. (1995). Interlaboratory comparison of autoradiographic DNA profiling measurements. 2. Measurement uncertainty and its propagation. *Analytical Chemistry, 67,* 1220–1231.

Duewer, D. L., et al. (1997). Interlaboratory comparison of autoradiographic DNA profiling measurements. 4. Protocol effects. *Analytical Chemistry, 69,* 1882–1892.

Duewer, D. L., et al. (1998). Interlaboratory comparison of autoradiographic DNA profiling measurements: Precision and concordance. *Journal of Forensic Sciences, 43,* 465–471.

Duewer, D. L., et al. (2000). RFLP band size standards: Cell line K562 values from 1991–1997 proficiency studies. *Journal of Forensic Sciences, 45,* 1106–1118.

Duewer, D. L., et al. (2000). RFLP band size standards: NIST Standard Reference Material 2390. *Journal of Forensic Sciences, 45,* 1093–1105.

Mudd, J. L., et al. (1994). Interlaboratory comparison of autoradiographic DNA profiling measurements: 1. Data and summary statistics. *Analytical Chemistry, 66,* 3303–3317.

Stolorow, A. M., et al. (1996). Interlaboratory comparison of autoradiographic DNA profiling measurements. 3. Repeatability and reproducibility of RFLP band sizing, particularly bands of molecular size > 10 k base pairs. *Analytical Chemistry, 68,* 1941–1947.

Quality Concerns

Lander, E. S. (1989). DNA fingerprinting on trial. *Nature, 339,* 501–505.

Lander, E. S. (1991). Invited editorial: Research on DNA typing catching up with courtroom application. (A number of letters to the editor were published in response— see *49,* 891–903.) *American Journal of Human Genetics, 48,* 819–823.

Lander, E. S., & Budowle, B. (1994). DNA fingerprinting dispute laid to rest. *Nature, 371,* 735–738.

National Research Council (1992). *DNA technology in forensic science.* Washington, DC: National Academy Press (commonly referred to as 'NRC I').

National Research Council (1996). *The evaluation of forensic DNA evidence.* Washington, DC: National Academy Press (commonly called 'NRC II').

Early PCR Systems

Inman, K., & Rubin, N. (1997). *An introduction to forensic DNA analysis.* Boca Raton, FL: CRC Press.

Reynolds, R., et al. (1991). Analysis of genetic markers in forensic DNA samples using the polymerase chain reaction. *Analytical Chemistry, 63*, 2–15.

HLA-DQA1

Blake, E., et al. (1992). Polymerase chain reaction (PCR) amplification and human leukocyte antigen (HLA)-DQα oligonucleotide typing on biological evidence samples: Casework experience. *Journal of Forensic Sciences, 37*, 700–726.

Comey, C. T., & Budowle, B. (1991). Validation studies on the analysis of the HLA-DQ alpha locus using the polymerase chain reaction. *Journal of Forensic Sciences, 36*, 1633–1648.

Comey, C. T., et al. (1993). PCR amplification and typing in the HLA DQ alpha gene in forensic samples. *Journal of Forensic Sciences, 38*, 239–249.

Erlich, H. A. (1992). HLA DQ alpha typing of forensic specimens. *Forensic Science International, 53*, 227–228.

Saiki, R., et al. (1986). Analysis of enzymatically amplified B-globin and HLA-DQa DNA with allele-specific oligonucleotide probes. *Nature, 324*, 163–166.

Saiki, R. K., et al. (1989). Genetic analysis of amplified DNA with immobilized sequence-specific oligonucleotide probes. In: *Proceedings of the National Academy of Sciences of the United States of America, 86*, 6230–6234.

Schneider, P. M., et al. (1993). Experience with the PCR-based HLA-DQA1 DNA typing system in routine forensic casework. *International Journal of Legal Medicine, 105*, 295–299.

Walsh, P. S., et al. (1991). Report of the blind trial of the Cetus AmpliType HLA DQα forensic deoxyribonucleic acid (DNA) amplification and typing kit. *Journal of Forensic Sciences, 36*, 1551–1556.

Wilson, R. B., et al. (1994). Guidelines for internal validation of the HLA-DQA1 typing system. *Forensic Science International, 66*, 9–22.

AmpliType PM (Polymarker) Kit

Budowle, B., et al. (1995). Validation and population studies of the loci LDLR, GYPA, HBGG, D7S8, and Gc (PM loci), and HLA-DQ alpha using a multiplex amplification and typing procedure. *Journal of Forensic Sciences, 40*, 45–54.

Fildes, N., & Reynolds, R. (1995). Consistency and reproducibility of AmpliType PM results between seven laboratories: Field trial results. *Journal of Forensic Sciences, 40*, 279–286.

Gross, A. M., & Guerrieri, R. A. (1996). HLA DQA1 and Polymarker validations for forensic casework: Standard specimens, reproducibility, and mixed specimens. *Journal of Forensic Sciences, 41*, 1022–1026.

Grow, M., et al. (1996). Post-amplification primer extension of heat-denatured AmpliType PCR products: Effects on typing results. *Journal of Forensic Sciences, 41*, 497–502.

Hochmeister, M. N., et al. (1995). A method for the purification and recovery of genomic DNA from an HLA DQA1 amplification product and its subsequent amplification and typing with the AmpliType PM PCR Amplification and Typing Kit. *Journal of Forensic Sciences, 40*, 649–653.

Perkin Elmer Corporation. (1994). AmpliType PM PCR Amplification and Typing Kit.

Sensabaugh, G. F., & Blake, E. T. (1993). DNA analysis in biological evidence: Applications of the polymerase chain reaction. In R. Saferstein (Ed.), *Forensic Science Handbook: Vol. III* (pp. 416–452). Englewood Cliffs, NJ: Prentice Hall.

Tomsey, C. S., et al. (1999). Use of combined frequencies for RFLP and PCR based loci in determining match probability. *Journal of Forensic Sciences, 44,* 385–388.

D1S80 and Other Amp-FLPs

Baechtel, F. S., et al. (1993). Multigenerational amplification of a reference ladder for alleles at locus D1S80. *Journal of Forensic Sciences, 38,* 1176–1182.

Budowle, B., et al. (1991). Analysis of the variable number of tandem repeats locus D1S80 by the polymerase chain reaction followed by high resolution polyacrylamide gel electrophoresis. *American Journal of Human Genetics, 48,* 137–144.

Budowle, B., et al. (1996). Multiplex amplification and typing procedure for the loci D1S80 and amelogenin. *Journal of Forensic Sciences, 41,* 660–663.

Cosso, S., et al. (1995). Validation of the AmpliFLP D1S80 amplification kit for forensic casework analysis according to TWGDAM guidelines. *Journal of Forensic Sciences, 40,* 424–434.

Duncan, G. T., et al. (1996). Microvariation at the human D1S80 locus. *International Journal of Legal Medicine, 110,* 150–154.

Kasai, K., et al. (1990). Amplification of a variable number of tandem repeats (VNTR) locus (pMCT118) by the polymerase chain reaction (PCR) and its application to forensic science. *Journal of Forensic Sciences, 35,* 1196–1200.

Kloosterman, A. D., et al. (1993). PCR-amplification and detection of the human D1S80 VNTR locus: Amplification conditions, population genetics and application in forensic analysis. *International Journal of Legal Medicine, 105,* 257–264.

Nakamura, Y., et al. (1988). Isolation and mapping of a polymorphic DNA sequence (pMCT118) on chromosome 1p (D1S80). *Nucleic Acids Research, 16,* 9364.

Perkin Elmer Corporation. (1994). AmpliFLP D1S80 PCR Amplification Kit.

Sullivan, K. M., et al. (1992). Automated DNA profiling by fluorescent labeling of PCR products. *PCR Methods and Applications, 2,* 24–40.

Tully, G., et al. (1993). Analysis of 6 VNTR loci by 'multiplex' PCR and automated fluorescent detection. *Human Genetics, 92,* 554–562.

Short Tandem Repeats

STRBase. http://www.cstl.nist.gov/biotech/strbase

Silver-Stain Detection

Bassam, B. J., et al. (1991). Fast and sensitive silver staining of DNA in polyacrylamide gels. *Analytical Biochemistry, 196,* 80–83.

Budowle, B., et al. (1997). Validation studies of the CTT multiplex system. *Journal of Forensic Sciences, 42,* 701–707.

Hochmeister, M. N., et al. (1995). Confirmation of the identity of human skeletal remains using multiplex PCR amplification and typing kits. *Journal of Forensic Sciences, 40,* 701–705.

Hochmeister, M. N., et al. (1996). Using multiplex PCR amplification and typing kits for the analysis of DNA evidence in a serial killer case. *Journal of Forensic Sciences, 41*, 155–162.

Kline, M. C., et al. (1997). Interlaboratory evaluation of short tandem repeat triplex CTT. *Journal of Forensic Sciences, 42*, 897–906.

Lins, A. M., et al. (1996). Multiplex sets for the amplification of polymorphic short tandem repeat loci—silver stain and fluorescence detection. *BioTechniques, 20*, 882–889.

Puers, C., et al. (1993). Identification of repeat sequence heterogeneity at the polymorphic short tandem repeat locus HUMTH01 [AATG]n and reassignment of alleles in population analysis by using a locus-specific allelic ladder. *American Journal of Human Genetics, 53*, 953–958.

Sprecher, C. J., et al. (1996). General approach to analysis of polymorphic short tandem repeat loci. *BioTechniques, 20*, 266–276.

Fluorescent Detection

Caskey, C. T., & Edwards, A. O. (1994). DNA typing with short tandem repeat polymorphisms and identification of polymorphic short tandem repeats. U.S. Patent 5,364,759.

Edwards, A., et al. (1991). DNA typing and genetic mapping with trimeric and tetrameric tandem repeats. *American Journal of Human Genetics, 49*, 746–756.

Fregeau, C. J., & Fourney, R. M. (1993). DNA typing with fluorescently tagged short tandem repeats: A sensitive and accurate approach to human identification. *BioTechniques, 15*, 100–119.

Hammond, H. A., et al. (1994). Evaluation of 13 short tandem repeat loci for use in personal identification applications. *American Journal of Human Genetics, 55*, 175–189.

Hammond, H. A., & Caskey, C. T. (1994). Human DNA fingerprinting using short tandem repeat loci. *Methods in Molecular Cell Biology, 5*, 78–86.

Hochmeister, M. N., et al. (1994). Swiss population data on three tetrameric short tandem repeat loci—VWA, HUMTH01, and F13A1—derived using multiplex PCR and laser fluorescence detection. *International Journal of Legal Medicine, 107*, 34–36.

Kimpton, C. P., et al. (1993). Automated DNA profiling employing multiplex amplification of short tandem repeat loci. *PCR Methods and Applications, 3*, 13–22.

Kimpton, C. P., et al. (1994). Evaluation of an automated DNA profiling system employing multiplex amplification of four tetrameric STR loci. *International Journal of Legal Medicine, 106*, 302–311.

Mayrand, P. E., et al. (1992). The use of fluorescence detection and internal lane standards to size PCR products automatically. *Applied and Theoretical Electrophoresis, 3*, 1–11.

Oldroyd, N. J., et al. (1995). A highly discriminating octoplex short tandem repeat polymerase chain reaction system suitable for human individual identification. *Electrophoresis, 16*, 334–337.

Promega Corporation. (1995). GenePrint™ fluorescent STR and sex identification systems datasheet.

Robertson, J. M., et al. (1995). Forensic applications of a rapid, sensitive, and precise multiplex off lysis of the four short tandem repeat loci HUMVWF31/A, HUMTH01, HUMF13A1, and HUMFES/FPS. *Electrophoresis, 16*, 1568–1576.

Urquhart, A., et al. (1994). Variation in short tandem repeat sequences—a survey of twelve microsatellite loci for use as forensic identification markers. *International Journal of Legal Medicine, 107*, 13–20.

Urquhart, A., et al. (1995). Highly discriminating heptaplex short tandem repeat PCR system for forensic identification. *BioTechniques, 18*, 116–121.

Ziegle, J. S., et al. (1992). Application of automated DNA sizing technology for genotyping microsatellite loci. *Genomics, 14*, 1026–1031.

Mitochondrial DNA

Fourney, R. M. (1998). Mitochondrial DNA and forensic analysis: A primer for law enforcement. *Canadian Society of Forensic Science Journal, 31*, 45–53.

Ginther, C., et al. (1992). Identifying individuals by sequencing mitochondrial DNA from teeth. *Nature Genetics, 2*, 135–138.

Holland, M. M., et al. (1993). Mitochondrial DNA sequence analysis of human skeletal remains: Identification of remains from the Vietnam War. *Journal of Forensic Sciences, 38*, 542–553.

Hopgood, R., et al. (1992). Strategies for automated sequencing of human mitochondrial DNA directly from PCR products. *Biotechniques, 13*, 82–92.

Mitochondrial DNA information on STRBase. http://www.cstl.nist.gov/biotech/strbase/mtDNA.htm

Sanger, F., et al. (1977). DNA sequencing with chain-terminating inhibitors. In: *Proceedings of the National Academy of Sciences of the United States of America, 74*, 5463–5467.

Wilson, M. R., et al. (1993). Guidelines for the use of mitochondrial DNA sequencing in forensic science. *Crime Laboratory Digest, 20*, 68–77.

Wilson, M. R., et al. (1995). Extraction, PCR amplification and sequencing of mitochondrial DNA from human hair shafts. *Biotechniques, 18*, 662–669.

Wilson, M. R., et al. (1995). Validation of mitochondrial DNA sequencing for forensic casework analysis. *International Journal of Legal Medicine, 108*, 68–74.

CHAPTER 4

Sample Collection, Storage, and Characterization

...The blood or semen that [the perpetrator of a crime] deposits or collects—all these and more bear mute witness against him. This is evidence that does not forget.... Physical evidence cannot be wrong; it cannot perjure itself; it cannot be wholly absent.... Only human failure to find, study and understand it can diminish its value.

—Paul Kirk, *Crime Investigation*, 1953

Before a DNA test can be performed on a sample, it must be collected and the DNA isolated and put in the proper format for further characterization. This chapter covers the important topics of sample collection and preservation. These steps are vital to obtaining a successful result regardless of the DNA typing procedure used. If the samples are not handled properly in the initial stages of an investigation, then no amount of hard work in the final analytical or data interpretation steps can compensate.

SAMPLE COLLECTION

DNA sample sources

DNA is present in every nucleated cell and is therefore present in biological materials left at crime scenes. DNA has been successfully isolated and analyzed from a variety of biological materials. Introduction of the polymerase chain reaction (PCR), which is described in Chapter 7, has extended the range of possible DNA samples that can be successfully analyzed because PCR enables many copies to be made of the DNA markers to be examined. While the most common materials tested in forensic laboratories are typically bloodstains and semen stains, Table 4.1 includes a listing from one laboratory of over 100 unusual casework exhibit materials that yielded successful DNA

Contribution of the National Institute of Standards and Technology, 2010.

79

profiles. DNA molecules are amazingly durable and in many cases can yield DNA typing results even when subjected to extreme conditions such as irradiation (see D.N.A. Box 4.1).

Biological evidence at crime scenes

The different types of biological evidence collected at a crime scene (e.g., Table 4.1) can be used to associate or to exclude an individual from involvement with a crime. In particular, the direct transfer of DNA from one individual to another individual or to an object can be used to link a suspect to a crime scene. As noted by Henry Lee of the Connecticut State Forensic Laboratory, this direct transfer could involve:

1. the suspect's DNA deposited on the victim's body or clothing,

2. the suspect's DNA deposited on an object,

3. the suspect's DNA deposited at a location,

4. the victim's DNA deposited on a suspect's body or clothing,

5. the victim's DNA deposited on an object,

6. the victim's DNA deposited at a location,

7. the witness's DNA deposited on the victim or suspect, or

8. the witness's DNA deposited on an object or at a location.

DNA evidence collection from a crime scene must be performed carefully and a chain of custody established in order to produce DNA profiles that are meaningful and legally accepted in court. DNA testing techniques have become so sensitive that biological evidence too small to be easily seen with the naked eye can be used to link suspects to crime scenes. The evidence must be carefully collected, preserved, stored, and transported prior to any analysis conducted in a forensic DNA laboratory. The National Institute of Justice has produced a brochure entitled 'What Every Law Enforcement Officer Should Know About DNA Evidence' (now available as online training as well; see http://www.dna.gov) that contains helpful hints for law enforcement personnel who are the first to arrive at a crime scene.

Evidence collection and preservation

The importance of proper DNA evidence collection cannot be overemphasized. If the DNA sample is contaminated from the start, obtaining unambiguous

Table 4.1 Some sources of biological materials used for PCR-based DNA typing. This listing of exhibits produced successful DNA profiles in the Canadian RCMP Forensic Biology Laboratories.

DNA Source: Hands		
Arm-rest (automobile)	Electrical cord	Paper (hand-folded)
Baseball cap (brim)	Envelope (self-adhesive)	Pen (bank robbery—roped pen owned by bank)
Binder twine	Expended .22 caliber cartridge	Plastic bag handles
Bottle cap	Fingerprint (single)	Pry bar with shoulder straps
Chocolate bar (handled end)	Gauze and tape (to cover fingertips)	Remote car starter
Cigarette lighter	Gloves (interior and exterior)	Rope
Cigarette paper	Hammer (head and handle)	Screwdriver handle
Signal light control level (automobile)	Handcuffs	Seat belt buckle (automobile)
Credit card (ATM card)	Hash-like ball (1 cm & hand-rolled)	Shoe laces
Detachable box magazine (pistol)	Hold-up note	Steering wheel
Dime	Ignition switch	Tape on club handle (exposed surface and initial start under layers)
Door bell	Keys	Toy gun
Door pull	Knife handle	Wiener (hot dog)
Drug syringe barrel exterior	Magazine (from handgun)	
DNA Source: Mouth and Nose		
Air bag (vehicle)	Envelope	Stamps (including self-adhesive)
Apple core—bite marks	Glass rim	Straw (from drinking glass)
Balaclava (knitted cap)	Gum	Telephone receiver
Bile on sidewalk	Ham (bite mark)	Thermos (cup attached)
Bite marks	Inhaler (inside mouthpiece)	Tooth
Bottle top	Lipstick (top surface and outside surface of lipstick case)	Toothbrush
Buccal stick only (swab cut off)	Nasal secretions (tissue)	Toothpick
Cake (bite mark)	Peach strudel	Utensils (fork, spoon, etc.)
Cheesecake (bite mark)	Pop cans/bottles	Vomit (bile-like sputum/liquid)
Chicken wing	Popsicle stick	Welding goggles (rim of eye/nose)
Chocolate bar (bite mark)	Salami (bite mark)	
Cigarette butt	Ski coat collar	

(Continued)

Table 4.1 Continued

DNA Source: General Body		
Baseball cap/cowboy hat (swab of inside rim)	Eyeglasses (ear and nose pieces)	Tears (on tissue)
Bullet hole in wall and bullet	Hair	Tissue paper wiping of underarms of shirt (sweat)
Buried remains	Hair comb (for head hair)	Socks
Burned remains	Head-rest (automobile)	Toilet—knife found in 'toilet trap'
Contact lens fragments (from vacuum cleaner bag)	Hood (attached to back of jacket)	Urine in snow
Dandruff (and cellular debris) from balaclava/toque	Paraffin-embedded tissue	Water—'S' trap of shower
Embryonic (umbilical) cord embedded in paraffin	Razor (disposable type/blade and plastic cap)	

Adapted from Kuperus, et al. (2003). Canadian Society of Forensic Science Journal 36(1), 19–28.

information becomes a challenge at best and an important investigation can be compromised (see D.N.A. Box 4.2).

Samples for collection should be carefully chosen as well to prevent needless redundancy in the evidence for a case. The following suggestions may be helpful during evidence collection to preserve it properly:

- Avoid contaminating the area where DNA might be present by not touching it with your bare hands or sneezing or coughing over the evidence.

- Use clean latex gloves for collecting each item of evidence. Gloves should be changed between handling of different items of evidence.

- Each item of evidence must be packaged separately.

- Bloodstains, semen stains, and other types of stains must be thoroughly air dried prior to sealing the package.

- Samples should be packaged in paper envelopes or paper bags after drying. Plastic bags should be avoided because water condenses in them, especially in areas of high humidity, and water can speed the degradation of DNA molecules. Packages should be clearly marked with case number, item number, collection date, and initialed across the package seal in order to maintain a proper chain of custody.

D.N.A. Box 4.1 DNA Recovery from Irradiated Samples

The U.S. Postal Service began using electron-beam irradiation of mail (for some ZIP postal codes in Washington, DC) as a protective measure against terrorism with biological agents following the anthrax attacks on the Senate Office Building in October 2001. The irradiation is performed at levels demonstrated to cleave microbial DNA and prevent passage of harmful materials such as anthrax.

However, recovering human DNA and developing a DNA profile from licked stamps and envelope flaps can sometimes be important in tracing the origin of threatening letters. Two studies have been published examining the effects of electron-beam irradiation on buccal-cell DNA. Both studies concluded that while electron-beam irradiation reduces the yields and quality of DNA extracted from buccal-cell collections, the short tandem repeat DNA typing systems used in human identity testing could still be successfully amplified.

Sources:
Castle, P. E., et al. (2003). Effects of electron-beam irradiation on buccal-cell DNA. *American Journal of Human Genetics, 73,* 646–651.
Withrow, A. G., et al. (2003). Extraction and analysis of human nuclear and mitochondrial DNA from electron beam irradiated envelopes. *Journal of Forensic Sciences, 48,* 1302–1308.

■ Stains on unmovable surfaces (such as a table or floor) may be transferred with sterile cotton swabs and distilled water. Rub the stained area with the moist swab until the stain is transferred to the swab. Allow the swab to air dry without touching any others. Store each swab in a separate paper envelope.

One of the most common methods for optimally collecting cellular material is the so-called double swab technique where a moist swab is followed by a dry one. The wet swab, which has been moistened by dipping it in sterile, distilled water, is first brushed over a surface to loosen any cells present and to rehydrate them. The second swab, which is initially dry, then helps collect additional cells from the surface. It is thought that the rehydrated cells following the first swab then adhere more easily to the second swab. Since both swabs are collected from the same sample, they are usually combined to maximize the yield of collected cellular material.

Collection of reference DNA samples

To perform comparative DNA testing with evidence collected from a crime scene, biological samples must also be obtained from suspects or convicted felons. Family reference samples may be used in missing persons investigations, paternity testing, and mass disaster victim identifications. It is advantageous to obtain these reference DNA samples as rapidly and painlessly as possible. Thus, many laboratories often use buccal cell collection rather than

D.N.A. Box 4.2 Importance of Carefully Collecting DNA Evidence: The O.J. Simpson Case

On the night of 12 June 1994, Nicole Brown Simpson and Ronald Goldman were found brutally murdered at Ms. Simpson's home. A few days later Ms. Simpson's ex-husband, Orenthal James (O.J.) Simpson, was picked up by Los Angeles police officers and became the chief suspect in the murder investigation. Due to O.J. Simpson's successful football career and popularity, the case immediately drew the public's attention. Over 100 pieces of biological evidence were gathered from the crime scene consisting primarily of blood droplets and stains. DNA samples were sent to three laboratories for testing. Over the summer months of 1994, the Los Angeles Police Department (LAPD) DNA Laboratory, the California Department of Justice (CA DOJ) DNA Laboratory in Berkeley, and a private contract laboratory from Maryland named Cellmark Diagnostics performed the DNA testing using both RFLP and PCR techniques. A number of RFLP and PCR markers were examined in this high-profile case. However, no STRs were typed.

The so-called 'Trial of the Century,' *People of the State of California v. Orenthal James Simpson*, began in the fall of 1994. O.J. Simpson hired a legal 'dream team,' which worked hard to acquit their client. O.J.'s defense team knew that the DNA evidence was the most powerful thing going against the football star and vigorously attacked the collection of the biological material from the crime scene. Through accusations of improper sample collection and handling as well as police conspiracies and laboratory contamination, the defense team managed to introduce a degree of 'reasonable doubt.' After a lengthy and exhausting trial, the jury acquitted O.J. Simpson on 3 October 1995.

Seven sets of bloodstains were collected by the LAPD and analyzed by the three DNA laboratories mentioned above. These sets of samples are reviewed below along with the challenges put forward by the defense team. For each sample, the statistics for the odds of a random match ranged from 1 in 40 when only PCR testing with the DQ-alpha marker was evaluated to more than 1 in 40 billion when all RFLP markers were examined.

To gain a better understanding of the magnitude of the DNA testing conducted in the O.J. Simpson case, 61 items of evidence were received by CA DOJ from LAPD (Sims et al., 1995). From these evidence items, 108 samples were extracted in 22 sets and tested alongside 21 quality control samples that were

coextracted and 24 extraction reagent blanks. These extraction reagent blanks were performed to verify that no contamination was introduced in the CA DOJ laboratory.

From a scientific point of view, the results from the three testing laboratories agreed and more than a score of DNA markers were examined with no exclusions between the crime scene samples and Mr. Simpson. The acquittal verdict goes to show that DNA evidence is not always understood and can be quite complex to explain to the general public. Expert witnesses have the challenge of presenting the difficult subjects of DNA biology, technology, and genetics, and jury members must make sense of concepts such as contamination and mixture analysis that can be fairly complex.

To their credit, the defense team focused on the evidence collection and preservation as the most important issues in the trial rather than attacking the validity of DNA testing. They implicated the LAPD in planting some of O.J. Simpson's liquid blood reference sample collected on 13 June—the day after the murders took place. Furthermore, the defense attacked the manner in which the evidence was handled in the LAPD DNA laboratory and alleged that contamination of the evidence samples by O.J.'s reference blood sample resulted from sloppy work and failure to maintain sterile conditions in the laboratory.

The contamination allegation became the focus of their arguments because much of the evidence had been handled, opened, and supposedly contaminated in the LAPD lab before it was packed up and sent to other laboratories for further testing. Thus, according to the defense, no matter how carefully the samples were handled by the California Department of Justice DNA Laboratory or Cellmark Diagnostics, their testing results would not reflect the actual evidence from the crime scene. Since the samples were supposedly tainted by the LAPD laboratory, the defense argued that the evidence should not be considered conclusive. However, the sheer number of DNA samples that typed to O.J. makes it hard to believe that some random laboratory error made it possible to obtain such overwhelmingly incriminating results.

Since the conclusion of the O.J. Simpson trial in 1995, forensic DNA laboratories have improved their vigilance in conducting DNA evidence collection and performing the testing in a manner that is above reproach. Because PCR is an extremely sensitive technology, laboratories practicing the technique need to take extraordinary measures to prevent contamination in the laboratory. Hence, the value of laboratory accreditation and routine proficiency tests to verify that a laboratory is conducting its investigations in a proper and professional manner is clear (see Chapter 13).

The issuance of the DNA Advisory Board (DAB) Quality Assurance Standards (see Chapter 13) has helped raise the professional status of forensic DNA testing. It is noteworthy that in a systematic analysis of circumstances normally encountered during casework, no PCR contamination was ever noted according to a 1999 study (Scherczinger *et al.*, 1999). Significant contamination occurred only with gross deviations from basic preventive protocols, such as those outlined in the DAB Standards, and could not be generated by simple acts of carelessness. Arguably the most important outcome of the O.J. Simpson trial was the renewed emphasis placed on DNA evidence collection.

Samples/Location (Date Collected)	Number of Samples Collected	DNA Match	Defense Challenge
Blood drops at Nicole Brown's home (13 June)	5 drops leading away from house	Simpson	Heavy degradation of the 'real' killer's DNA; tampering with evidence 'swatches' sample contamination during laboratory investigation
Stains on rear gate at Brown's home (3 July)	3 stains	Simpson	Samples planted by rogue police officers prior to collection
Stains in O.J.'s Bronco (14 June)	5 stains around vehicle; bloody footprint; stain on center console	Simpson in 5 stains; Brown in footprint; Simpson/Goldman mixture on console	Simpson's DNA present for reasons unrelated to the crime; Detective Mark Fuhrman planted the blood footprint; laboratory controls failed on console mixture analysis
Second collection of stains in O.J.'s Bronco (26 August)	3 stains	Mixture of Simpson, Brown, and Goldman	Blood planted in the vehicle between the crime and the collection
Stains at Simpson's home (13 June)	2 drops in driveway, 1 in foyer, 1 in master bedroom	Simpson	Simpson bled at these locations for reasons unrelated to the crime
Socks found in Simpson's bedroom (13 June)	Multiple stains	Simpson and Brown	Blood planted after the socks were collected
Bloody glove found on the grounds of Simpson's home (13 June)	15 stains identified	Goldman, Simpson, and Brown alone or as mixture	Glove was removed from murder scene and planted by Detective Mark Fuhrman; Simpson's DNA was present because of laboratory contamination

Sources:

Levy, H. (1996). O.J. Simpson: What the blood really showed. In H. Levy (Ed.), *And the blood cried out* (pp. 157–188). New York: Basic Books.

Scherczinger, C. A., et al. (1999). A systematic analysis of PCR contamination. *Journal of Forensic Sciences, 44*(5), 1042–1045.

Sims, G., et al. (1995). The analysis of serological evidence by the California Department of Justice DNA Laboratory in the case of *People v. Simpson.* In: *Proceedings of the sixth international symposium on human identification.* Madison, WI: Promega Corporation (pp. 116–117).

Weir, B. S. (1995). DNA statistics in the Simpson matter. *Nature Genetics, 11,* 365–368.

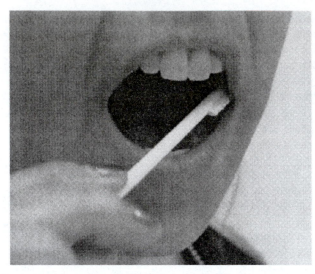

FIGURE 4.1
Photo of cheek swab being rubbed on the inside of an individual's mouth for buccal cell DNA collection.

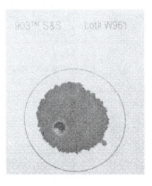

FIGURE 4.2
Photo of a bloodstain card showing a hole in the lower left-hand corner of the circle where a punch removed a portion of the sample for DNA extraction and testing purposes. The remainder of the sample is stored for future testing if needed.

drawing blood. Buccal cell collection involves wiping a small piece of filter paper or a cotton swab similar to a Q-tip against the inside cheek of an individual's mouth to collect some skin cells (Figure 4.1). The swab is then air dried or can be pressed against a treated collection card to transfer epithelial cells for storage purposes.

Bode Technology Group (Lorton, VA) has produced a simple Buccal DNA Collector that is widely used for direct collection of buccal cell samples. This collection system also comes with a transport pouch containing a desiccant to keep the sample dry and has a unique bar code on each DNA collector to enable automated sample tracking.

If a liquid blood sample is collected, then typically a few drops of blood are spotted onto a piece of treated or untreated filter paper (Figure 4.2). Blood samples are advantageous in that it is easy to visually see that a sample has been collected (versus a colorless swab from a saliva sample).

SAMPLE STORAGE

Carelessness or ignorance of proper handling procedures during storage and transport of DNA from the crime scene to the laboratory can result in a specimen unfit for analysis. For example, bloodstains should be thoroughly dried prior to transport to prevent mold growth. A recovered bloodstain on a cotton swab should be air dried in an open envelope before being sealed for transport. DNA can be stored as nonextracted tissue or as fully extracted DNA. Normally, however, DNA samples are not extracted until they reach the laboratory.

Most biological evidence is best preserved when stored dry and cold. These conditions reduce the rate of bacterial growth and degradation of DNA. Samples should be packaged carefully and hand carried or shipped using overnight delivery to the forensic laboratory conducting the DNA testing. Some laboratories will supply cardboard evidence collection boxes to crime scene investigators to enable simple shipping and handling of bloodstains and other crime scene evidence.

Inside the laboratory, DNA samples are extracted and then either stored in a refrigerator at 4°C or a freezer at −20°C (Figure 4.3). For long-term storage, extracted DNA samples may even be stored at −70°C.

DNA molecules survive best if they are dry (to prevent base hydrolysis) and protected from DNA digesting enzymes called DNases. A common method of storing DNA reference samples is on bloodstain cards. This method involves adding a few drops of liquid blood to a cellulose-based filter paper and then air drying the bloodstain before storing it. Some bloodstain cards have been treated with chemicals to enhance DNA longevity. The dried bloodstain card can also be vacuum sealed with a desiccant to prevent humidity from breaking the stored DNA molecules into smaller pieces and destroying the ability to recover a full DNA profile.

FIGURE 4.3
Photo of samples in a freezer for long-term storage purposes.

Many police evidence lockers and storage vaults that hold crime scene evidence have freezers to enable storage of rape kits or other material containing biological evidence. Storage and availability of this evidence after, in some cases, many years has enabled postconviction DNA testing of individuals incarcerated prior to the availability of DNA testing (see D.N.A. Box 1.1). Large-scale DNA reference sample collection has been performed by the U.S. military since the early 1990s in an effort to be able to identify all recovered remains of military casualties to prevent there ever being another 'unknown soldier' (D.N.A. Box 4.3).

D.N.A. Box 4.3 Long-Term DNA Storage: The U.S. Military Sample Repository

Probably the largest repository of biological samples for identification purposes is the Armed Forces Repository of Specimen Samples for the Identification of Remains (AFRSSIR), which is located just outside of Washington, DC, in Gaithersburg, Maryland. Since the early 1990s, the U.S. military has maintained a databank of bloodstain cards from all service members in order to help identify any military casualties so that there will be no more unknown soldiers. These bloodstains are typically obtained from fingerpricks during the service member's entry medical exam. Thousands of samples are shipped each month to the repository from multiple collection sites.

As of 2008, AFRSSIR contained over 5 million bloodstain cards of which only a few thousand samples have been processed for DNA typing purposes in order to identify remains recovered from military casualties. DNA specimens are also collected from civilian government employees and civilian contractors who support military missions and may be in hostile foreign environments. Samples are kept for 50 years unless the donor requests destruction of the specimen following completion of his or her military service.

For many years the bloodstain cards have been maintained in large freezers at –20°C inside of vacuum-sealed foil pouches containing a desiccant to help keep the samples dry. Since it is expensive to maintain large freezers, which also have a limited storage space, studies have been performed to evaluate the impact of room-temperature storage on DNA preservation. It has been shown that dry samples can be successfully stored and yield full DNA profiles even after 20 years or more without the advantages of a freezer environment. This should not be surprising since DNA results have been successfully obtained from properly preserved biological samples that may even be thousands of years old (e.g., Egyptian mummies and Neanderthal skeletons).

Sources:

Armed Forces Repository of Specimen Samples for the Identification of Remains (AFRSSIR). http://www.afip.org/consultation/AFMES/AFDIL/AFRSSIR/index.html

Coble, M. D., et al. (2008). A ten year study of DNA blood references collected on untreated filter paper and stored at room temperature. In: *Proceedings of the American Academy of Forensic Sciences, 14,* 90–91.

Kline, M. C., et al. (2002). Polymerase chain reaction amplification of DNA from aged blood stains: Quantitative evaluation of the 'suitability for purpose' of four filter papers as archival media. *Analytical Chemistry, 74,* 1863–1869.

Every effort should be made to avoid completely consuming or destroying evidence so that a portion is available for future testing if needed. As the NRC II report states: 'The ultimate safeguard against error due to sample mixup is to provide an opportunity for retesting' (p. 81).

SAMPLE CHARACTERIZATION

When crime scene evidence is first received into a laboratory, it is usually evaluated to see if any biological material is present. Some laboratories perform both *preliminary tests* and *confirmatory tests* prior to sending a cutting or swab for DNA testing in an effort to develop a DNA profile. A presumptive test, which really serves as a preliminary evaluation or examination, may be followed by a confirmatory test to verify the results of the first test.

Forensic serology: presumptive and confirmatory tests

Forensic evidence from crime scenes comes in many forms. For example, a bed sheet may be collected from the scene of a sexual assault. This sheet will have to be carefully examined in the forensic laboratory before selecting the area to sample for further testing. Prior to making the effort to extract DNA from a sample, *presumptive tests* are often performed to indicate whether or not biological fluids such as blood or semen are present on an item of evidence (e.g., a pair of pants). Locating a blood or semen stain on a soiled undergarment can be a trying task. Primary stains of forensic interest come from blood, semen, and saliva. Identification of vaginal secretions, urine, and feces can also be important to an investigation.

Serology is the term used to describe a broad range of laboratory tests that utilize antigen and serum antibody reactions. For example, the ABO blood group types discussed in Chapter 3 are determined using anti-A and anti-B serums and examining agglutination when mixed with a blood sample. Serology still plays an important role in modern forensic biology but has taken a backseat to DNA in many respects since presumptive tests do not have the ability to individualize a sample like a DNA profile can.

Presumptive tests should be simple, inexpensive, safe, and easy to perform. They should use only a small amount of material and have no adverse effect on any downstream DNA testing that might be conducted on the evidentiary material. Besides helping to locate the appropriate material for DNA analysis, stain characterization can in some cases provide probative value to a case (e.g., semen in a victim's mouth as evidence of an oral sexual assault).

The primary providers for presumptive forensic serology tests are Abacus Diagnostics (West Hills, CA) and Seratec (Goettingen, Germany). Their *in vitro* diagnostic tests, which appear very similar to home pregnancy tests, involve applying a small aliquot of a sample to a cartridge with a membrane containing specific antibodies. The presence of the appropriate molecules (e.g., hemoglobin with a blood test) on this immunochromatographic strip test will be detected as a colored line. Internal standards are run to verify that the test is working properly. Independent Forensics (Hillside, IL) has released confirmatory tests for blood, saliva, urine, semen, and sperm with their Rapid Stain Identification products (http://www.ifi-test.com/rsid.php). These tests are designed to not crossreact with other human body fluids or body fluids of other animals like some of the presumptive tests do.

Bloodstains

Blood is composed of liquid plasma and serum with solid components consisting of red blood cells (erythrocytes), white blood cells (leukocytes), and platelets (thrombocytes). Most presumptive tests for blood focus on detecting the presence of hemoglobin molecules, which are found in the red blood cells and used for transport of oxygen and carbon dioxide. A simple immunochromatographic test for identification of human blood is available from Abacus Diagnostics (West Hills, CA) as the ABAcard HemaTrace kit. This test has a hemoglobin limit of detection of 0.07 μg/mL and shows specificity for human blood along with higher primate and ferret blood.

Luminol is another presumptive test for identification of blood that has been popularized by the TV series *CSI: Crime Scene Investigation*. The luminol reagent is prepared by mixing 0.1 g 3-amino-phthalhydrazide and 5.0 g sodium carbonate in 100 mL of distilled water. Before use, 0.7 g of sodium perborate is added to the solution. Large areas can be rapidly evaluated for the presence of bloodstains by spraying the luminol reagent onto the item under investigation. Objects that have been sprayed need to be located in a darkened area so that the luminescence can be more easily viewed.

Luminol can be used to locate traces of blood that have been diluted up to 10 million times. The use of luminol has been shown to not inhibit DNA testing of STRs that may need to be performed on evidence recovered from a crime scene. Demonstration that presumptive tests do not interfere with subsequent DNA testing can be important when making decisions on how biological evidence is processed in a forensic laboratory.

Saliva stains

A presumptive test for amylase is used for indicating the presence of saliva, which is especially difficult to see since saliva stains are nearly invisible to the naked eye. Two common methods for estimating amylase levels in forensic samples include the Phadebas test and the starch iodine radial diffusion test. Saliva stains may be found on bite marks, cigarette butts, and drinking vessels. A molecular biology approach using messenger RNA profiling is also being taken to develop sensitive and specific tests for various body fluids including saliva (D.N.A. Box 4.4). Such a molecular biology test should be able to assay blood, semen, and saliva simultaneously with great specificity and sensitivity.

Semen stains

Almost two-thirds of cases pursued with traditional forensic DNA testing involve sexual assault evidence. Hundreds of millions of sperm are typically ejaculated in several milliliters of seminal fluid. Semen stains can be characterized with visualization of sperm cells, acid phosphatase (AP), or prostate specific antigen (PSA or p30) tests.

D.N.A. Box 4.4 RNA-Based Assays to Aid Forensic Stain Characterization

Another method for body fluid identification that has seen recent research activity is the monitoring of cell-specific gene expression through the analysis of ribonucleic acid (RNA). Conventional methods for body-fluid identification often involve labor-intensive, diverse approaches that are performed sequentially rather than simultaneously. Both time and sample are lost when many of these older characterization assays are performed. Research on RNA techniques has shown that although less stable than DNA (due to its single-stranded structure and often rapid destruction from digesting enzymes), RNA is able to help with stain identification. Multiple RNA transcripts have been detected with reverse-transcriptase PCR followed by gel or capillary electrophoresis or real-time PCR. Blood, semen, saliva, menstrual blood, and vaginal secretions have been simultaneously identified with some of these assays. The quantitation of RNA degradation has also been used in an effort to determine postmortem intervals and to determine the age of bloodstains.

Sources:
Anderson, S., et al. (2005). A method for determining the age of a bloodstain. *Forensic Science International, 148,* 37–45.
Bauer, M. (2007). RNA in forensic science. *Forensic Science International: Genetics, 1,* 69–74.
Juusola, J., & Ballantyne, J. (2003). Messenger RNA profiling: A prototype method to supplant conventional methods for body fluid identification. *Forensic Science International, 135,* 85–96.
Noreault-Conti, T. L., & Buel, E. (2008) Development of an RNA-based screening assay for forensic stain identification. In: *Proceedings of the 19th international symposium on human identification.* Available at http://www.promega.com/geneticidproc/ussymp19proc/oralpresentations/Buel.pdf

A microscopic examination to look for the presence of spermatozoa is performed in some laboratories on sexual assault evidence. However, aspermic or oligospermic males have either no sperm or a low sperm count in their seminal fluid ejaculate. In addition, vasectomized males will not release sperm. Therefore, tests that can identify semen-specific enzymes are helpful in verifying the presence of semen in sexual assault cases.

Acid phosphatase (AP) is an enzyme secreted by the prostate gland into seminal fluid and found in concentrations up to 400 times greater in semen than in other body fluids. A purple color with the addition of a few drops of sodium alpha naphthylphosphate and Fast Blue B solution or the fluorescence of 4-methyl umbelliferyl phosphate under a UV light indicates the presence of AP. Large areas of fabric can be screened by pressing the garment or bed sheet against an equal sized piece of moistened filter paper and then subjecting the filter paper to the presumptive tests. Alternatively, systematic searches can be done over sections of the fabric under examination to narrow the location of the semen stain with each successive test.

Prostate specific antigen was discovered in the 1970s and shown to have forensic value with the identity of a protein named p30 due to its apparent 30,000 molecular weight. Protein p30 was initially thought to be unique to seminal fluid although it has been reported at lower levels in breast milk and other fluids. PSA varies in concentration from approximately 300 to 4200 ng/mL in semen.

Laboratory reports where presumptive tests for semen were performed may indicate that an item was found to be 'AP positive' or 'p30 positive'—in other words, semen was detected, implying some form of sexual contact on the evidentiary item.

Direct observation of sperm

Many forensic laboratories like to observe spermatozoa as part of confirming the presence of semen in an evidentiary sample. A common method of doing this is to recover dried semen evidence from fabric or on human skin with a deionized water-moistened swab. A portion of the recovered cells is then placed onto a microscope slide and fixed to the slide with heat. The immobilized cells are stained with a 'Christmas Tree' stain consisting of aluminum sulfate, nuclear fast red, picric acid, and indigo carmine. The stained slide is then examined under a light microscope for sperm cells with their characteristic head and long tail. The Christmas Tree stain marks the anterior sperm heads light red or pink, the posterior heads dark red, the spermatozoa's midpieces blue, and the tails yellowish green.

Independent Forensics (Hillside, IL) recently released the SPERM HY-LITER PLUS kit that enables detection of even a single human sperm head in the presence of an overwhelming amount of epithelial cells. Development of sample characterization tools that utilize fluorescently tagged monoclonal antibodies, such as the SPERM HY-LITER kit, represents a major advancement and should enable much faster and accurate processing of sexual assault evidence.

Points for Discussion

- Why should forensic evidence be retained and stored even after a case has been closed?

- What advantages exist for conducting presumptive testing prior to full DNA analysis?

- What is the difference between a presumptive test and a confirmatory test?

- What advantages might RNA-based assays bring to sample characterization?

READING LIST AND INTERNET RESOURCES

Sample Collection

Benecke, M. (2005). Forensic DNA samples—collection and handling. In J. Fuchs & M. Podda (Vol. Eds.), *Encyclopedia of diagnostic genomics and proteomics: Vol. 1* (pp. 500–504). New York: Marcel Dekker. Available at http://www.benecke.com/dnacollection.html

Bond, J. W. (2007). Value of DNA evidence in detecting crime. *Journal of Forensic Sciences, 52,* 128–136.

Bond, J. W., & Hammond, C. (2008). The value of DNA material recovered from crime scenes. *Journal of Forensic Sciences, 53,* 797–801.

DNA Sample Sources

Bär, W., et al. (1988). Postmortem stability of DNA. *Forensic Science International, 39,* 59–70.

Kuperus, W. R., et al. (2003). Crime scene links through DNA evidence: The practical experience from Saskatchewan casework. *Canadian Society of Forensic Science Journal, 36,* 19–28.

McNally, L., et al. (1989). Evaluation of deoxyribonucleic acid (DNA) isolated from human bloodstains exposed to ultraviolet light, heat, humidity, and soil contaminations. *Journal of Forensic Sciences, 34,* 1059–1069.

Biological Evidence at Crime Scenes

Crime Scene and DNA Basics. http://dna.gov/training/evidence

Lee, H.C. (1996). Collection and preservation of DNA evidence. In: *Proceedings of the seventh international symposium on human identification* (pp. 39–45). Available at http://www.promega.com/geneticidproc

What every law enforcement officer should know about DNA evidence: First responding officers and investigators and evidence technicians. http://dna.gov/training/letraining

Evidence Collection

Lee, H. C., et al. (1998). Forensic applications of DNA typing: Part 2: Collection and preservation of DNA evidence. *American Journal of Forensic Medicine and Pathology, 19,* 10–18.

Lee, H. C., & Ladd, C. (2001). Preservation and collection of biological evidence. *Croatian Medical Journal, 42,* 225–228.

Pang, B. C., & Cheung, B. K. (2007). Double swab technique for collecting touched evidence. *Legal Medicine (Tokyo), 9,* 181–184.

Sweet, D., et al. (1997). An improved method to recover saliva from human skin: The double swab technique. *Journal of Forensic Sciences, 42,* 320–322.

Reference Sample Collection

Bode Technology Buccal DNA Collector. http://www.bodetech.com/solutions/collection-products

Burger, M. F., et al. (2005). Buccal DNA samples for DNA typing: New collection and processing methods. *BioTechniques, 39,* 257–261.

Zamir, A., et al. (2004). A possible source of reference DNA from archived treated adhesive lifters. *Journal of Forensic Sciences, 49,* 68–70.

Sample Storage

Graham, E. A. M., et al. (2008). Room temperature DNA preservation of soft tissue for rapid DNA extraction: An addition to the disaster victim identification investigators toolkit? *Forensic Science International: Genetics, 2,* 29–34.

Kline, M. C., et al. (2002). Polymerase chain reaction amplification of DNA from aged blood stains: Quantitative evaluation of the 'suitability for purpose' of four filter papers as archival media. *Analytical Chemistry, 74,* 1863–1869.

Sigurdson, A. J., et al. (2006). Long-term storage and recovery of buccal cell DNA from treated cards. *Cancer Epidemiology Biomarkers & Prevention, 15,* 385–388.

Sample Characterization

Ballantyne, J., et al. (2000). Serology. In J. A. Siegel (Ed.), *Encyclopedia of forensic sciences* (pp. 1322–1331). San Diego: Academic Press.

Fourney, R.M., et al. (2007). Recent progress in processing biological evidence and forensic DNA profiling: A review 2004 to 2007. In *Interpol 15th international forensic science symposium* (pp. 635–719). Available at http://www.cstl.nist.gov/biotech/strbase/tools/IFSS07-BioReview.pdf

Independent Forensics Rapid Stain Identification Series. http://www.ifi-test.com/rsid.php

Jones, E. L. (2004). The identification of semen and other body fluids. In R. Saferstein (Ed.), *Forensic science handbook: Vol. II* (2nd ed.) (pp. 329–399). Upper Saddle River, NJ: Pearson Prentice Hall.

Testing of Body Fluids and Tissues. http://dna.gov/training/forensicbiology

Li, R. (2008). *Forensic biology.* Boca Raton, FL: CRC Press.

Saferstein, R. (2001). *Criminalistics: An introduction to forensic science* (Chaps. 12 and 13, pp. 320–394) (7th ed.). Upper Saddle River, NJ: Prentice Hall.

Shaler, R. C. (2002). Modern forensic biology. In R. Saferstein (Ed.), *Forensic science handbook: Vol. I* (2nd ed.) (pp. 525–613). Upper Saddle River, NJ: Prentice Hall.

Vandenberg, N., & van Oorschot, R. A. (2006). The use of Polilight in the detection of seminal fluid, saliva, and bloodstains and comparison with conventional chemical-based screening tests. *Journal of Forensic Sciences, 51,* 361–370.

Bloodstains

Abacus Diagnostics ABAcard HemaTrace kit. http://www.abacusdiagnostics.com/blood.htm

Hochmeister, M. N., et al. (1999). Validation studies of an immunochromatographic 1-step test for the forensic identification of human blood. *Journal of Forensic Sciences, 44,* 597–602.

Independent Forensics Rapid Stain Identification Blood. http://www.ifi-test.com/rsid_blood.php

Johnson, S., et al. (2003). Validation study of the Abacus Diagnostics ABAcard HemaTrace membrane test for the forensic identification of human blood. *Canadian Society of Forensic Science Journal, 36*(3), 173–183.

Schweers, B. A., et al. (2008). Developmental validation of a novel lateral flow strip test for rapid identification of human blood (Rapid Stain Identification™-Blood). *Forensic Science International: Genetics, 2,* 243–247.

Tobe, S. S., et al. (2007). Evaluation of six presumptive tests for blood, their specificity, sensitivity, and effect on high molecular-weight DNA. *Journal of Forensic Sciences, 52,* 102–109.

Webb, J. L., et al. (2006). A comparison of the presumptive Luminol test for blood with four non-chemiluminescent forensic techniques. *Luminescence, 21,* 214–220.

Saliva Stains

Abacus Diagnostics SALIgAE saliva identification kit. http://www.abacusdiagnostics.com/saliva.htm

Abaz, J., et al. (2002). Comparison of the variables affecting the recovery of DNA from common drinking containers. *Forensic Science International, 126,* 233–240.

Auvdel, M. J. (1986). Amylase levels in semen and saliva stains. *Journal of Forensic Sciences, 31,* 426–431.

Hochmeister, M. N., et al. (1998). PCR analysis from cigarette butts, postage stamps, envelope sealing flaps, and other saliva-stained material. *Methods in Molecular Biology, 98,* 27–32.

Independent Forensics Rapid Stain Identification Saliva. http://www.ifi-test.com/rsid_saliva.php

Myers, J. R., & Adkins, W. K. (2008). Comparison of modern techniques for saliva screening. *Journal of Forensic Sciences, 53,* 862–867.

Phadebase Amylase Products. http://www.phadebas.com/applications/forensic

Whitehead, P. H., & Kipps, A. E. (1975). The significance of amylase in forensic investigations of body fluids. *Journal of Forensic Sciences, 6,* 137–144.

Urine Stains

Independent Forensics Rapid Stain Identification Urine. http://www.ifi-test.com/rsid_urine.php

Semen Stains

Abacus Diagnostics ABAcard p30 kit. http://www.abacusdiagnostics.com/semen.htm

Hochmeister, M. N., et al. (1999). Evaluation of prostate-specific antigen (PSA) membrane test assays for the forensic identification of seminal fluid. *Journal of Forensic Sciences, 44,* 1057–1060.

Independent Forensics Rapid Stain Identification Semen. http://www.ifi-test.com/rsid_semen.php

Sato, I., et al. (2002). Use of the 'SMITEST' PSA card to identify the presence of prostate-specific antigen in semen and male urine. *Forensic Science International, 127,* 71–74.

Sensabaugh, G. F. (1978). Isolation and characterization of a semen-specific protein from human seminal plasma: A potential new marker for semen identification. *Journal of Forensic Sciences, 23*, 106–115.

Seratec PSA Semiquant kit. http://www.seratec.com

Simich, J. P., et al. (1999). Validation of the use of a commercially available kit for the identification of prostate specific antigen (PSA) in semen stains. *Journal of Forensic Sciences, 44*, 1229–1231.

Sperm Detection

Herr, J. (2007). *SpermPaint optimization and validation*. NIJ Grant 2000-IJ-CX-K013 Report. Available at http://www.ncjrs.gov/pdffiles1/nij/grants/220289.pdf

Independent Forensics SPERM HY-LITER PLUS kit. http://www.spermhy-liter.com

CHAPTER 5

DNA Extraction

DNA evidence can be infuriating, particularly if you're a criminal defendant.

—Henry Lee and Frank Tirnady,
Blood Evidence, 2003

DNA EXTRACTION

A biological sample obtained from a crime scene in the form of a blood or semen stain or a tissue (blood or buccal swab) sample from a known individual contains a number of substances besides DNA. DNA molecules must be separated from other cellular material before they can be examined. Cellular proteins that package and protect DNA in the environment of the cell can inhibit the ability to analyze the DNA. Therefore, DNA extraction methods have been developed to separate proteins and other cellular materials from the DNA molecules. The quantity and quality of DNA often need to be measured prior to proceeding further with analytical procedures to ensure optimal results. This chapter will focus on the DNA extraction process while the following chapter will cover assessment of DNA quantity and quality prior to further sample processing.

Several primary techniques for DNA extraction are used in today's forensic DNA laboratory: organic extraction, Chelex extraction, and FTA or solid-phase extraction (Figure 5.1). The exact extraction or DNA isolation procedure varies depending on the type of biological evidence being examined. For example, whole blood must be treated differently from a bloodstain or a bone fragment.

Organic extraction, sometimes referred to as phenol-chloroform extraction, has been in use for the longest period of time and may be used for situations where either RFLP or PCR typing is performed. High-molecular-weight DNA,

Contribution of the National Institute of Standards and Technology, 2010.

99

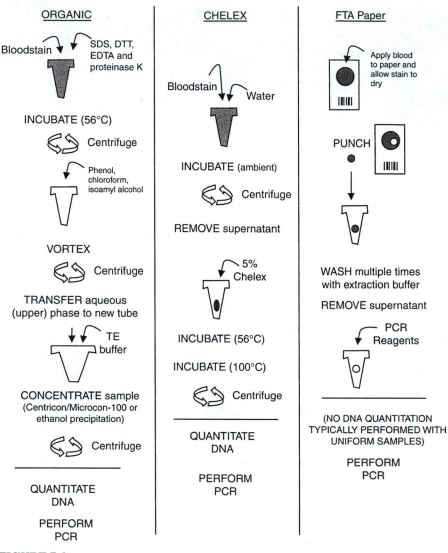

FIGURE 5.1

Schematic of commonly used DNA extraction processes.

which was essential for early RFLP methods, may be obtained most effectively with organic extraction.

The Chelex method of DNA extraction is more rapid than the organic extraction method. In addition, Chelex extraction involves fewer steps and thus fewer opportunities for sample-to-sample contamination. However, it produces single-stranded DNA as a result of the extraction process and therefore is only useful for PCR-based testing procedures.

Table 5.1 Typical DNA amounts that may be extracted from biological materials (Lee and Ladd, 2001). Both quality and quantity of DNA recovered from evidentiary samples can be significantly affected by environmental factors.

Type of Sample	Amount of DNA
Liquid blood	20,000–40,000 ng/mL
Bloodstain	250–500 ng/cm^2
Liquid semen	150,000–300,000 ng/mL
Postcoital vaginal swab	10–3000 ng/swab
Plucked hair (with root)	1–750 ng/root
Shed hair (with root)	1–10 ng/root
Liquid saliva	1000–10,000 ng/mL
Oral swab	100–1500 ng/swab
Urine	1–20 ng/mL
Bone	3–10 ng/mg
Tissue	50–500 ng/mg

All samples must be carefully handled regardless of the DNA extraction method to avoid sample-to-sample contamination or introduction of extraneous DNA. The extraction process is probably where the DNA sample is more susceptible to contamination in the laboratory than at any other time in the forensic DNA analysis process. For this reason, laboratories usually process the evidence samples at separate times and sometimes even different locations from the reference samples.

For many years, a popular method for preparation of reference samples was to make a bloodstain by applying a drop of blood on to a cotton cloth, referred to as a swatch, to produce a spot about 1 cm^2 in area. Ten microliters of whole blood, about the size of a drop, contains approximately 70,000 to 80,000 white blood cells and should yield approximately 500 ng of genomic DNA. The actual yield will vary with the number of white blood cells present in the sample and the efficiency of the DNA extraction process. The typical amounts of DNA extracted from various biological materials is shown in Table 5.1.

Extracted DNA is typically stored at −20°C, or even −80°C for long-term storage, to prevent nuclease activity. *Nucleases* are protein enzymes found in cells that degrade DNA to allow for recycling of the nucleotide components. Nucleases need magnesium to work properly so one of the measures to prevent them from digesting DNA in blood is the use of purple-topped tubes containing a blood preservative known as EDTA. The EDTA chelates, or binds up, most of the free magnesium and thus helps prevent the nucleases from destroying the DNA in the collected blood sample.

Organic (phenol-chloroform) extraction

Organic extraction was for many years the most widely used method for DNA extraction. In the past decade, new extraction methods have been developed that use chemicals which are far less toxic than phenol.

Organic extraction involves the serial addition of several chemicals. First sodium dodecylsulfate (SDS) and proteinase K are added to break open the cell walls and to break down the proteins that protect the DNA molecules while they are in chromosomes. Next a phenol-chloroform mixture is added to separate the proteins from the DNA. The DNA is more soluble in the aqueous portion of the organic–aqueous mixture. When centrifuged, the unwanted proteins and cellular debris are separated away from the aqueous phase and double-stranded DNA molecules can be cleanly transferred for analysis.

Some initial protocols involved a Centricon 100 (Millipore, Billerica, MA) dialysis and concentration step in place of the ethanol precipitation to remove heme inhibitors. While the organic extraction method works well for recovery of high-molecular-weight DNA, it is time consuming, involves the use of hazardous chemicals, and requires the sample to be transferred between multiple tubes (which increases the risk of error or contamination).

Chelex extraction

An alternative and inexpensive procedure for DNA extraction that has become popular among forensic scientists is the use of a chelating-resin suspension that can be added directly to the sample (e.g., blood, bloodstain, or semen). Introduced in 1991 to the forensic DNA community, Chelex 100 (Bio-Rad Laboratories, Hercules, CA) is an ion-exchange resin that is added as a suspension to the samples.

Chelex is composed of styrene divinylbenzene copolymers containing paired iminodiacetate ions that act as chelating groups in binding polyvalent metal ions such as magnesium. Like iron filings to a magnet, the magnesium ions are drawn in and bound up. By removing the magnesium from the reaction, DNA-destroying nuclease enzymes are inactivated and the DNA molecules are thus protected.

In most protocols, biological samples such as bloodstains are added to a 5% Chelex suspension and boiled for several minutes to break open the cells and release the DNA. An initial, prior wash step is helpful to remove possible contaminants and inhibitors such as heme and other proteins. The exposure to

100°C temperatures denatures the DNA as well as disrupt the cell membranes and destroy the cell proteins. After a quick spin in a centrifuge to pull the Chelex resin and cellular debris to the bottom of the tube, the supernatant is removed and can be added directly to the PCR amplification reaction.

Chelex extraction procedures for recovering DNA from bloodstains or semen-containing stains are not effective for RFLP typing because Chelex denatures double-stranded DNA and yields single-stranded DNA from the extraction process. Thus, it can only be followed by PCR-based analyses. However, Chelex extraction is an advantage for PCR-based typing methods because it removes inhibitors of PCR and uses only a single tube for the DNA extraction, which reduces the potential for laboratory-induced contamination.

The addition of too much whole blood or too large a bloodstain to the Chelex extraction solution can result in some PCR inhibition. The AmpF*l*STR kit manuals recommend 3 μL whole blood or a bloodstain approximately 3 mm × 3 mm.

FTA™ paper

Another approach to DNA extraction involves the use of FTA paper. In the late 1980s, FTA paper was developed by Lee Burgoyne at Flinders University in Australia as a method for storage of DNA. FTA originally stood for 'Fitzco/Flinder Technology Agreement.' FTA paper is an absorbent cellulose-based paper that contains four chemical substances to protect DNA molecules from nuclease degradation and preserve the paper from bacterial growth. As a result, DNA on FTA paper is stable at room temperature over a period of several years. However, a 2002 study evaluating FTA and three other commercial papers as DNA storage media found little difference in their ability to obtain typeable STR results after 19 months of storage.

Use of FTA paper simply involves adding a spot of blood to the paper and allowing the stain to dry. The cells are lysed upon contact with the paper, and DNA from the white blood cells is immobilized within the matrix of the paper. A small punch of the paper is removed from the FTA card bloodstain and placed into a tube for washing. The bound DNA can then be purified by washing it with a solvent to remove heme and other inhibitors of the PCR reaction. This purification of the paper punch can be seen visually because as the paper is washed, the red color is removed with the supernatant. The clean punch is then added directly to the PCR reaction. Alternatively, some groups have performed a Chelex extraction on the FTA paper punch and used the supernatant in the PCR reaction.

A major advantage of FTA paper is that consistent results may be obtained without quantification. Furthermore, the procedure may be automated on a robotic workstation. For situations where multiple assays need to be run on the same sample, a bloodstained punch may be reused for sequential DNA amplifications and typing. Unfortunately, dry paper punches do not like to stay in their assigned tubes and due to static electricity can 'jump' between wells in a sample tray. Thus, this method is not as widely used today as was once envisioned. However, due to its preservation and storage capabilities, efforts have been made to use FTA cards for more widespread collection of crime scene evidence.

SOLID-PHASE DNA EXTRACTION METHODS

With the desire to automate more steps in DNA analysis, many laboratories have moved to various forms of solid-phase extraction where DNA is selectively bound to a substrate such as silica particles and then released following stringent washes that purify the bound DNA molecules away from proteins and other cellular components. The most widely used solid-phase extraction methods are Qiagen columns, DNA IQ, and PrepFiler.

Qiagen extraction chemistry and kits

Solid-phase extraction methods for DNA have been developed in recent years in formats that enable high-throughput DNA extractions. One of the most active efforts in this area is with silica-based extraction methods and products from Qiagen, Inc. (Valencia, CA). For more than a decade, QIAamp spin columns have proven effective as a means of DNA isolation.

In this approach, nucleic acids selectively absorb to a silica support, such as small glass beads, in the presence of high concentrations of chaotropic salts such as guanidine hydrochloride, guanidine isothiocyanate, sodium iodide, and sodium perchlorate. These chaotropic salts disrupt hydrogen-bonding networks in liquid water and thereby make denatured proteins and nucleic acids more thermodynamically stable than their native folded or structured counterparts.

If the solution is more acidic than pH 7.5, DNA adsorption to the silica is typically around 95% and unwanted impurities can be washed away. Under alkaline conditions and low salt concentrations, the DNA will efficiently elute from the silica material. This solid-phase extraction approach can be performed with centrifugation or vacuum manifolds in single tube or 96-well plate formats and is even being developed into formats that will work on a microchip. Several robotic platforms have been developed to enable automated processing of Qiagen DNA extractions including the EZ1, M48, and QIAcube.

DNA IQ

Another solid-phase extraction approach is the DNA IQ™ system marketed by Promega Corporation (Madison, WI). The DNA IQ system, which stands for 'isolation' and 'quantitation,' utilizes the same silica-based DNA binding and elution chemistries as Qiagen kits but with silica-coated paramagnetic resin. With this approach, DNA isolation can be performed in a single tube by simply adding and removing solutions.

First, the DNA molecules are reversibly bound to the magnetic beads in solution with a solution pH more acidic than pH 7.5 (the same as noted previously for the Qiagen chemistry). A magnet is used to draw the silica-coated magnetic beads to the bottom or side of the tube leaving any impurities in solution. These solution impurities (proteins, cell debris, etc.) are easily removed by drawing the liquid off of the beads. The magnetic particles with DNA attached can be washed multiple times to more thoroughly clean the DNA. Finally, a defined amount of DNA can be released into solution via heating for a few minutes.

The quantity of DNA isolated with this approach is based on the number and capacity of the magnetic particles used. Since flow-through vacuum filtration or centrifugation steps are not used, magnetic bead procedures enable simple, rapid, and automated methods. This extraction method has been automated on the Beckman 2000 robot workstation and implemented into forensic casework by the Virginia Department of Forensic Science and a growing number of other crime labs.

PrepFiler

In 2008 Applied Biosystems released a magnetic particle–based DNA extraction technology named PrepFiler™ that is similar to DNA IQ. PrepFiler enables isolation of high-quality DNA from forensic samples in high yields. Up to 96 samples can be processed at a time in under 2.5 hours using the Tecan Freedom EVO® automated liquid-handling workstation.

DIFFERENTIAL EXTRACTION

Differential extraction is a modified version of the organic extraction method that separates epithelial and sperm cells (Figure 5.2). Differential extraction was first described in 1985 by Peter Gill and coworkers. This method is commonly used today by the FBI Laboratory and other forensic crime laboratories to isolate the female and male fractions in sexual assault cases that contain a mixture of male and female DNA. By separating the male fraction away from the victim's DNA profile, it is much easier to interpret the perpetrator's DNA profile in a rape case.

The differential extraction procedure involves preferentially breaking open the female epithelial cells with incubation in an SDS/proteinase K mixture. Sperm nuclei are subsequently lysed by treatment with an SDS/proteinase

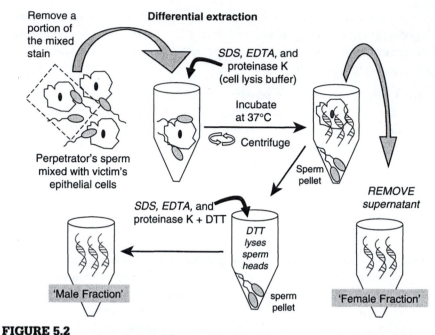

FIGURE 5.2

Schematic of differential extraction process used to separate male sperm cells from female epithelial cells.

K/dithiothreitol (DTT) mixture. The DTT breaks down the protein disulfide bridges that make up sperm nuclear membranes. Differential extraction works because sperm nuclei are impervious to digestion without DTT. The major difference between the regular version of organic extraction described earlier and differential extraction is the initial incubation in SDS/proteinase K without DTT present.

Differential extraction works well in most sexual assault cases to separate the female and male fractions from one another. Unfortunately, some perpetrators of sexual assaults have had a vasectomy in which case there is an absence of spermatozoa. Azoospermic semen (i.e., without sperm cells) cannot be separated from the female fraction with differential extraction. In the case of azoospermic perpetrators, the use of Y-chromosome–specific markers permits male DNA profiles to be deduced in the presence of excess female DNA. Failure to separate the male and female portions of a sexual assault sample results in a mixture of both the perpetrator's and the victim's DNA profiles.

Methods for directly capturing sperms cells have been developed including laser capture microdissection (D.N.A. Box 5.1). By physically separating the perpetrator's sperm cells from the victim's epithelial cells, the perpetrator's DNA can be enriched and isolated even from an excessive amount of the victim's cells.

D.N.A. Box 5.1 Laser Capture Microdissection: Selective Capture of Useful Cells

Sperm cells can be selectively captured using a clinical procedure known as *laser capture microdissection* (LCM), which is commonly used to select tumor cells from surrounding tissue on microscope slides. Sperm cells from sexual assault evidence spread on microscope slides can be collected with LCM to perform reliable STR testing. When sperm cells are observed in the field of view of the microscope, a tiny laser is activated, and a thin plastic film placed over the slide melts at the specific point of laser light contact to capture or embalm the cell of interest. By moving the microscope slide around, dozens of sperm cells are collected onto this thin film that sits directly above the sample. The collection film is then transferred to a tube where DNA from the isolated sperm can be extracted and amplified using the polymerase chain reaction. Other LCM methods catapult identified cells directly into a collection tube.

Sources:

Anslinger, K., et al. (2007). Sex-specific fluorescent labeling and laser capture microdissection of male cells. *International Journal of Legal Medical, 121,* 54–56.

Elliott, K., et al. (2003). Use of laser microdissection greatly improves the recovery of DNA from sperm on microscope slides. *Forensic Science International, 137,* 28–36.

Sanders, C. T., et al. (2006). Laser microdissection separation of pure spermatozoa from epithelial cells for short tandem repeat analysis. *Journal of Forensic Sciences, 51,* 748–757.

PCR INHIBITORS AND DNA DEGRADATION

When extracting biological materials for the purpose of forensic DNA typing, it is important to try to avoid further degradation of the DNA template as well as to remove inhibitors of the polymerase chain reaction (PCR) where possible. The presence of inhibitors or degraded DNA can manifest themselves by complete PCR amplification failure or a reduced sensitivity of detection usually for the larger PCR products.

Two PCR inhibitors commonly found in forensic cases are hemoglobin and indigo dyes from denim. Melanin found in hair samples can be a source of PCR inhibition when trying to amplify mitochondrial DNA. These inhibitors likely bind in the active site of the Taq DNA polymerase and prevent its proper functioning during PCR amplification.

DNA degrades through a variety of mechanisms including both enzymatic and chemical processes. Once a cell (or organism) dies, its DNA molecules face cellular nucleases followed by bacterial, fungal, and insect onslaughts depending on the environmental conditions. In addition, hydrolytic cleavage and oxidative base damage can limit successful retrieval and amplification of DNA. The main target for hydrolytic cleavage is the glycosidic base sugar bond. Breakage here leads to nucleobase loss and then a single-stranded 'nick' at the abasic site.

If a sufficient number of DNA molecules in the biological sample break in a region where primers anneal or between the forward and reverse primers, then PCR amplification efficiency will be reduced or the target region may fail to be amplified at all. Thus, heat and humidity, which speed up hydrolytic cleavage, are enemies of intact DNA molecules. Furthermore, UV irradiation (e.g., direct sunlight) can lead to crosslinking of adjacent thymine nucleotides on the DNA molecule, which will prevent passage of the polymerase during PCR.

Points for Discussion

- Would there be advantages to direct sample testing without DNA extraction?
- What is the purpose of DTT in an extraction procedure?
- Describe some situations where differential extraction will help separate mixture components in a sexual assault case.
- Why are PCR inhibitors problematic?

READING LIST AND INTERNET RESOURCES

General Information

Allard, J. E., et al. (2007). A comparison of methods used in the UK and Ireland for the extraction and detection of semen on swabs and cloth samples. *Science & Justice, 47*, 160–167.

DNA Extraction and Quantitation. http://dna.gov/training/extraction

Hoff-Olson, P., et al. (1999). Extraction of DNA from decomposed human tissue: An evaluation of five extraction methods for short tandem repeat typing. *Forensic Science International, 105*, 171–183.

Kobilinsky, L. (1992). Recovery and stability of DNA in samples of forensic significance. *Forensic Science Review, 4*, 68–87.

Lee, H. C., & Ladd, C. (2001). Preservation and collection of biological evidence. *Croatian Medical Journal, 42*, 225–228.

Organic Extraction

Comey, C. T., et al. (1994). DNA extraction strategies for amplified fragment length polymorphism analysis. *Journal of Forensic Sciences, 39*, 1254–1269.

Vandenberg, N., et al. (1997). An evaluation of selected DNA extraction strategies for short tandem repeat typing. *Electrophoresis, 18*, 1624–1626.

Chelex Extraction

Walsh, P. S., et al. (1991). Chelex 100 as a medium for simple extraction of DNA for PCR-based typing from forensic material. *BioTechniques, 10*, 506–513.

Willard, J. M., et al. (1998). Recovery of DNA for PCR amplification from blood and forensic samples using a chelating resin. *Methods in Molecular Biology, 98*, 9–18.

FTA Paper

Belgrader, P., et al. (1995). Automated DNA purification and amplification from blood-stained cards using a robotic workstation. *BioTechniques, 19*, 427–432.

Burger, M. F., et al. (2005). Buccal DNA samples for DNA typing: New collection and processing methods. *BioTechniques, 39,* 257–261.

Burgoyne, L. A. (1996). Solid medium and method for DNA storage. U.S. Patent 5,496,562.

Kline, M. C., et al. (2002). Polymerase chain reaction amplification of DNA from aged blood stains: Quantitative evaluation of the 'suitability for purpose' of four filter papers as archival media. *Analytical Chemistry, 74,* 1863–1869.

Solid-Phase Extraction

Qiagen

Anslinger, K., et al. (2005). Application of the BioRobot EZ1 in a forensic laboratory. *Legal Medicine (Tokyo), 7,* 164–168.

Duncan, E., et al. (2003). Isolation of genomic DNA. In B. Bowien & P. Dürre (Vol. Eds.), *Nucleic acids isolation methods* (pp. 7–19). Stevenson Ranch, CA: American Scientific Publishers.

Greenspoon, S. A., et al. (1998). QIAamp spin columns as a method of DNA isolation for forensic casework. *Journal of Forensic Sciences, 43,* 1024–1030.

Kishore, R., et al. (2006). Optimization of DNA extraction from low-yield and degraded samples using the BioRobot EZ1 and BioRobot M48. *Journal of Forensic Sciences, 51,* 1055–1061.

Montpetit, S. A., et al. (2005). A simple automated instrument for DNA extraction in forensic casework. *Journal of Forensic Sciences, 50,* 555–563.

DNA IQ

Greenspoon, S. A., et al. (2004). Application of the BioMek 2000 Laboratory Automation Workstation and the DNA IQ System to the extraction of forensic casework samples. *Journal of Forensic Sciences, 49,* 29–39.

Tereba, A. M., et al. (2004). Simultaneous isolation and quantitation of DNA. U.S. Patent 6,673,631.

PrepFiler

Applied Biosystems. http://marketing.appliedbiosystems.com

Differential Extraction

Gill, P., et al. (1985). Forensic application of DNA 'fingerprints.' *Nature, 318,* 577–579.

PCR Inhibitors and DNA Degradation

Lee, H. C., & Ladd, C. (2001). Preservation and collection of biological evidence. *Croatian Medical Journal, 42,* 225–228.

Lindahl, T. (1993). Instability and decay of the primary structure of DNA. *Nature, 362,* 709–715.

Poinar, H. N. (2003). The top 10 list: Criteria for authenticity for DNA from ancient and forensic samples. *Progress in Forensic Genetics, 9,* 575–579.

CHAPTER 6

DNA Quantitation

The little things are infinitely the most important.

—Sherlock Holmes, *A Case of Identity*

WHY QUANTIFY DNA?

When biological evidence from a crime scene is processed to isolate the DNA present, all sources of DNA are extracted and are present in the samples to be examined. Thus, nonhuman DNA, such as bacterial, fungal, plant, or animal material, may also be present in the total DNA recovered from the sample along with the relevant human DNA of interest.

To ensure that DNA recovered from an extraction is human rather than from another source such as bacteria, the FBI's quality assurance standards (Standard 9.4) require human-specific DNA quantitation. Only after DNA in a sample has been isolated can its quantity and quality be reliably assessed. The primary purpose of DNA quantitation is to determine the appropriate amount of DNA template to include in future tests, such as will be described in Chapters 7 and 8.

Determination of the amount of DNA in a sample is essential for most polymerase chain reaction (PCR)-based assays because a narrow concentration range works best with multiplex short tandem repeat (STR) typing. Typically 0.5 to 2.0 ng of input human DNA is optimal with current commercial STR kits.

Too much DNA results in overblown electropherograms that make interpretation of results more challenging and time consuming to review. Too little DNA can result in loss of alleles due to stochastic amplification and failure to equally sample the STR alleles present in the sample. Figure 6.1 illustrates

Contribution of the National Institute of Standards and Technology, 2010.

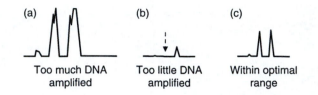

(a) Too much DNA amplified

(b) Too little DNA amplified

(c) Within optimal range

FIGURE 6.1

Illustration of STR typing results at a single heterozygous locus for a single-source sample with (a) too much DNA template showing off-scale, split peaks; (b) too little DNA template where the arrow points to allele dropout due to stochastic effects; or (c) just the right amount so that two allele peaks are balanced and on-scale.

the 'Goldilocks' principle of not wanting too much or too little DNA in a PCR reaction to produce an STR profile.

If the amount of DNA in a sample is outside of the target range for creating a 'just right' DNA profile, then the DNA amount must be adjusted prior to putting it into the PCR reaction. The process of achieving a DNA concentration that fits the optimal window for analysis is called *normalization*. This involves diluting the sample down to the desired range or concentrating it by removing excess fluid.

Evaluation of human DNA quantity in a sample can be used to screen which samples should be sent forward through the DNA testing process. When having to wade through a large number of samples (D.N.A. Box 6.1), a sample screening process, based on the amount of human DNA present, can be very helpful and cost effective. DNA quantitation that is done well can save time and preserve the often-limited DNA extracted from biological evidence.

DNA QUANTITIES USED

PCR amplification is dependent on the quantity of template DNA molecules added to the reaction. Based on the amount of DNA determined to be in a sample with a quantitation method, the extracted DNA for each sample is adjusted to a level that will work optimally in the PCR amplification reaction. As mentioned above, commercial STR typing kits work best with an input DNA template of around 1 ng.

A quantity of 1 ng of human genomic DNA corresponds to approximately 303 copies of each locus that will be amplified (D.N.A. Box 6.2). There are approximately 6 pg (one millionth of one millionth of a gram or 10^{-12} grams) of genomic DNA in each cell containing a single diploid copy of the human genome. Thus, a range of typical DNA quantities from 0.1 to 25 ng would involve approximately 30 to 8330 copies of every nuclear DNA sequence to be examined.

D.N.A. Box 6.1 The Pickton Pig Farm Case: Canada's Largest Sample Collection Effort

Project Even Handed began in November 2000 with a mandate to investigate the disappearances of 27 drug-addicted sex trade workers who had gone missing in the time frame of 1984 to 1999 from the city of Vancouver in Canada's province of British Columbia. This project was later renamed the Joint Missing Women's Task Force. In February 2002, while performing a search warrant in relationship to an illegal weapons possession, items related to some of the missing women were discovered in the residence of Robert William Pickton, who lived in a trailer on a 17-acre pig farm near Vancouver. A new search warrant was obtained and within a short while the largest crime scene in Canada was established.

The Royal Canadian Mounted Police (RCMP) set up an on-site evidence recovery unit and more than 100 crime scene investigators worked from February 2002 to November 2003 to carefully examine the entire farm. Remains of victims were found in buckets in Pickton's barns. Freezers in his garage were covered with blood spatter. The entire 17-acre farm was subdivided into 20-meter by 20-meter grids. The topsoil across the entire farm was removed down to a depth of 2 or 3 feet (~1 m), and sometimes as deep as 18 feet (~3 m), and carefully sifted through in search of human bone fragments or tissue. In total, more than half a million samples were collected of which >240,000 were processed for DNA. Robotic workstations to aid DNA extraction using Promega's DNA

IQ chemistry were validated and put into use in April 2004. Human-specific DNA quantitation with Applied Biosystems' Quantifiler kit was then performed to see if samples should be processed further to try to obtain a DNA profile. The human DNA quantitation served as an important screening step in the DNA analysis process. From the nearly quarter million soil samples and swabs collected, 944 biology reports were issued with 299 submissions yielding DNA profiles for comparison purposes to victim reference samples. More than a million pages of notes from approximately 110,000 documents were released to the defense as part of disclosure.

While sufficient evidence had been identified to charge Mr. Pickton with 27 counts of first-degree murder, his defense team successfully lobbied to have the charges divided. The trial of Robert William Pickton began January 22, 2007, with an indictment on six accounts of first-degree murder. The prosecution called 98 witnesses. The initial verdict reached by the court for Canada's most prolific serial killer was 'guilty of second degree murder' on all six counts. Both the prosecution and defense have appealed the verdict, which will be heard in April 2009.

Source:
Horley, K. (October 2008). Royal Canadian Mounted Police, Presentation at the 19th *International symposium on human identification*, Hollywood, CA.

D.N.A. Box 6.2 Calculation of DNA Quantities in Genomic DNA

1. Molecular weight of a DNA base pair = 618 g/mol

   A = 313 g/mol; T = 304 g/mol; A-T base pairs = 617 g/mol; G = 329 g/mol; C = 289 g/mol; G-C base pairs = 618 g/mol

2. Molecular weight of DNA = 1.98×10^{12} g/mol

   There are 3.2 billion base pairs in a haploid cell $\sim 3.2 \times 10^9$ bp

   $(\sim 3.2 \times 10^9 \text{ bp}) \times (618 \text{ g/mol/bp}) = 1.98 \times 10^{12}$ g/mol

3. Quantity of DNA in a haploid cell = 3 picograms

   1 mole = 6.02×10^{23} molecules

$(1.98 \times 10^{12}$ g/mol$) \times (1$ mole/6.02×10^{23} molecules$)$

= 3.3×10^{-12} g = 3.3 picograms (pg)

A diploid human cell contains ~6.6 pg genomic DNA

4. One nanogram of human DNA comes from ~152 diploid cells

   1 ng genomic DNA (1000 pg)/6.6 pg/cell = ~303 copies of each locus

   (2 per 152 diploid genomes)

DNA QUANTITATION METHODS

A number of DNA quantitation tests have been used over the years to aid estimation of the amount of total DNA or human DNA present in a sample. These DNA quantitation tests, which will be discussed briefly below, include UV absorbance, yield gels, slot blot, PicoGreen, AluQuant, end-point PCR, and real-time quantitative PCR. Early assays were 'home-brew' (i.e., prepared by the laboratory performing the test) while most forensic DNA quantitation is now performed using commercial kits from suppliers such as Applied Biosystems or Promega Corporation.

UV absorbance and yield gels

Early methods for DNA quantitation typically involved either measurement of absorbance at a wavelength of 260 nm or fluorescence after staining a yield gel with ethidium bromide. Unfortunately, because these approaches are not very sensitive, they consume valuable forensic specimens that are irreplaceable. In addition, absorbance measurements are not specific for DNA, and contaminating proteins or phenol left over from the extraction procedure can give falsely high signals. To overcome these problems, several methods have been developed for DNA quantitation purposes. These include the slot blot procedure and fluorescence-based microtiter plate assays as well as so-called real-time or quantitative PCR approaches.

Slot blot

The most commonly used method in forensic labs during the late 1990s and beginning years of the 21st century for genomic DNA quantitation was the so-called slot blot procedure. This test was specific for human and other primate DNA due to a 40-bp probe that bound to a region on chromosome 17 called D17Z1. The slot blot assay was first described with radioactive probes, but was later modified and commercialized with chemiluminescent or colorimetric detection formats.

Slot blots involved the capture of genomic DNA on a nylon membrane followed by addition of a human-specific probe. Chemiluminescent or colorimetric signal intensities were then compared between a set of standards and the samples (Figure 6.2).

As with almost all DNA quantitation methods, the slot blot procedure involved a relative measurement that compared unknown samples to a set of standards. These standard samples were prepared via a serial dilution from a DNA sample of known concentration. The comparison between the standards and unknowns was usually performed visually—and therefore influenced by the subjectivity of the analyst. However, digital capture and quantification

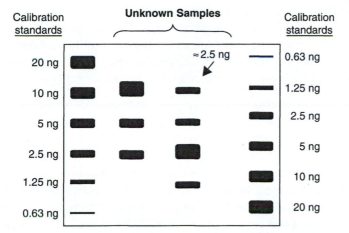

FIGURE 6.2

Illustration of a human DNA quantitation result with the slot blot procedure. A serial dilution of a human DNA standard is run on either side of the slot blot membrane for comparison purposes. The quantity of each of the unknown samples is estimated by visual comparison to the calibration standards. For example, the sample indicated by the arrow is closest in appearance to the 2.5-ng standard.

of slot blot images was also an option using a charge-coupled device (CCD) camera imaging system.

Up to 30 samples could be tested on a slot blot membrane with 6 to 8 standard samples run on each side of the membrane for comparison purposes. For example, the standards might be a serial dilution of human DNA starting with 20, 10, 5, 2.5 ng, and so forth. Typically about 5 μL of DNA extract from each sample was consumed in order to perform this DNA quantitation test.

The slot blot assay took several hours to perform and could detect both single-stranded and double-stranded DNA down to levels of approximately 150 pg. Even when no results were seen with this hybridization assay, some forensic scientists still went forward with DNA testing and often obtained a successful STR profile. Thus, the slot blot assay was not as sensitive as would have been preferred. In addition, as with most 'human-specific' tests, primate samples, such as chimpanzees and gorillas, also produced signal due to similarities in human and other primate DNA sequences.

In 2006, Applied Biosystems (Foster City, CA), the final commercial source for slot blot assay reagents, stopped selling the QuantiBlot Human DNA Quantitation Kit. Thus, this assay is now a thing of the past.

PicoGreen microtiter plate assay

As higher throughput methods for DNA determination are being developed, more automated procedures are needed for rapid assessment of extracted

DNA quantity prior to DNA amplification. To this end, in the mid-1990s, the Forensic Science Service (Birmingham, England) developed a PicoGreen assay that is capable of detecting as little as 250 pg of double-stranded DNA in a 96-well microtiter plate format. PicoGreen is a fluorescent interchelating dye whose fluorescence is greatly enhanced when bound to double-stranded DNA.

To perform this microtiter plate assay, 5 μL of sample are added to 195 μL of a solution containing the PicoGreen dye. Each sample is placed into an individual well on a 96-well plate and then examined with a fluorometer. A 96-well plate containing 80 individual samples and 16 calibration samples can be analyzed in under 30 minutes. The DNA samples are quantified through comparison to a standard curve. This assay has been demonstrated to be useful for the adjustment of input DNA into the amplification reaction of STR multiplexes. It has been automated on a robotic workstation as well. Unfortunately, this assay quantifies total DNA in a sample and is not specific for human DNA.

AluQuant human DNA quantitation system

Around 2000, the Promega Corporation developed a human DNA quantitation system, known as AluQuant, that enabled fairly sensitive detection of DNA using *Alu* repeats that are in high abundance in the human genome. Probe-target hybridization initiated a series of enzymatic reactions that ended in oxidation of luciferin with production of light. The light intensity was then read by a luminometer with the signal being proportional to the amount of DNA present in the sample. Sample quantities were determined by comparison to a standard curve. The AluQuant assay possesses a range of 0.1 to 50 ng for human DNA and can be automated on a robotic liquid-handling workstation. While this assay was used for several years by laboratories such as the Virginia Department of Forensic Sciences, it has been made obsolete with the introduction of real-time quantitative PCR assays. *Note that further information on PCR is available in the sections below and in the next chapter.*

End-point PCR

A less elegant (and less expensive than qPCR) approach for testing the 'amplifiability' of a DNA sample is to perform an end-point PCR test. In this approach a single STR locus or other region of the human genome, such as an *Alu* repeat, is amplified along with DNA samples of known concentrations. A standard curve can be generated from the samples with known amounts to which samples of unknown concentration are compared.

A fluorescent intercalating dye such as SYBR Green can be used to detect the generated PCR products. Based on the signal intensities resulting from amplification of the single STR marker or *Alu* repeat region, the level of DNA can be adjusted prior to amplifying the multiplex set of DNA markers in order to obtain the optimal results. This method is a functional test because it also monitors the level of PCR inhibitors present in the sample. In the end, each of the DNA quantitation methods described here has advantages and disadvantages and could be used depending on the equipment available and the needs of the laboratory.

Real-time quantitative PCR (qPCR)

The primary purpose in performing a DNA quantification test is to determine the amount of 'amplifiable' DNA. A PCR amplification reaction may fail due to the presence of coextracted inhibitors, highly degraded DNA, insufficient DNA quantity, or a combination of all of these factors. Thus, a test that can accurately reflect both the quality and the quantity of the DNA template present in an extracted sample is beneficial to making decisions about how to proceed. 'Real-time' PCR assays provide such an assessment.

Instruments and assays are now available that can monitor the PCR process as it is happening, enabling 'real-time' data collection. Real-time PCR, which was first described by Higuchi and coworkers at the Cetus Corporation in the early 1990s, is sometimes referred to as quantitative PCR or 'kinetic analysis' because it analyzes the cycle-to-cycle change in fluorescence signal resulting from amplification of a target sequence during PCR. This analysis is performed without opening the PCR tube and therefore can be referred to as a closed-tube or homogeneous detection assay.

Several approaches to performing real-time PCR homogeneous detection assays have been published. The most common approaches utilize either the fluorogenic 5' nuclease assay—better known as TaqMan—or use of an intercalating dye, such as SYBR Green, that is highly specific for double-stranded DNA molecules. The TaqMan approach monitors change in fluorescence due to displacement of a dual dye-labeled probe from a specific sequence within the target region while the SYBR Green assay detects formation of any PCR product.

The 5' nuclease assay (TaqMan)

TaqMan probes are labeled with two fluorescent dyes that emit at different wavelengths (Figure 6.3). The probe sequence is intended to hybridize specifically in the DNA target region of interest between the two PCR primers. Typically the probe is designed to have a slightly higher annealing temperature compared to the PCR primers so that the probe will be hybridized when extension (polymerization) of the primers begins. A minor groove binder is sometimes used near the 3'-end of TaqMan probes to enable the use of shorter sequences that still have high annealing temperatures.

The 'reporter' (R) dye is attached at the 5' end of the probe sequence while the 'quencher' (Q) dye is synthesized on the 3' end. A popular combination

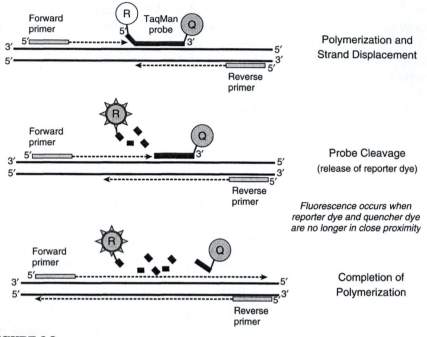

FIGURE 6.3

Schematic of TaqMan (5′ nuclease) assay.

of dyes is FAM or VIC for the reporter dye and TAMRA for the quencher dye. When the probe is intact and the reporter dye is in close proximity to the quencher dye, little to no fluorescence will result because of suppression of the reporter fluorescence due to an energy transfer between the two dyes.

During polymerization, strand synthesis will begin to displace any TaqMan probes that have hybridized to the target sequence. The Taq DNA polymerase used has a 5′ exonuclease activity and therefore will begin to chew away at any sequences in its path (i.e., those probes that have annealed to the target sequence). When the reporter dye molecule is released from the probe and is no longer in close proximity to the quencher dye, it can begin to fluoresce (Figure 6.3). An increase in the fluorescent signal results if the target sequence is complementary to the TaqMan probe.

Some assays, such as the Quantifiler kit, include an internal PCR control (IPC) that enables verification that the polymerase, the assay, and the detection instrumentation are working correctly. In this case, the IPC is labeled with a VIC (green) reporter dye and hybridizes to a synthetic template added to each reaction. The TaqMan probe for detecting the target region of interest is labeled with a FAM (blue) reporter dye and therefore is spectrally resolvable from the green VIC dye. Instruments such as the ABI Prism 7000 or 7500

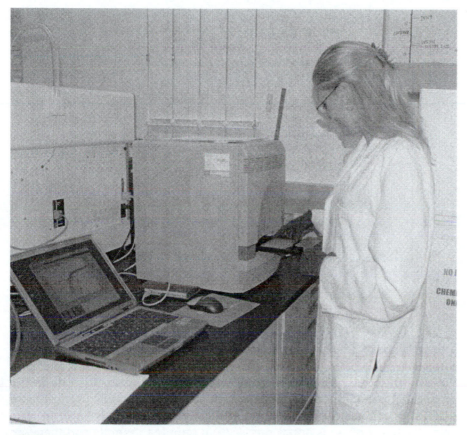

FIGURE 6.4
ABI 7500 Real Time PCR System used for quantitation of DNA samples.

Real Time PCR System (Figure 6.4) enable another dye like ROX (red dye) to be placed in each well to adjust for well-to-well differences across a plate through background subtraction.

Real-time PCR analysis

Three distinct phases define the PCR process: geometric or exponential amplification, linear amplification, and the plateau region. These regions can be seen in a plot of fluorescence versus PCR cycle number (Figure 6.5). During exponential amplification, there is a high degree of precision surrounding the production of new PCR products. When the reaction is performing at close to 100% efficiency, then a doubling of amplicons occurs with each cycle. A plot of cycle number versus a log scale of the DNA concentration should result in a linear relationship during the exponential phase of PCR amplification.

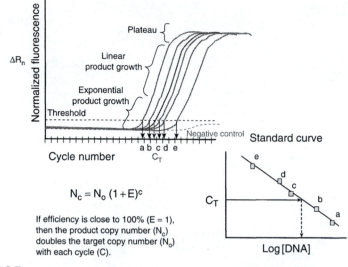

FIGURE 6.5

Real-time PCR output and example standard curve used to determine quantity of input DNA.

A linear phase of amplification follows the exponential phase as one or more components fall below a critical concentration and amplification efficiency slows down to an arithmetic increase rather than the geometric one in the exponential phase. Since components such as deoxynucleotide triphosphates (dNTPs) or primers may be used up at slightly different rates between reactions, the linear phase is not as precise from sample to sample and therefore is not as useful for comparison purposes.

The final phase of PCR is the plateau region where accumulation of PCR product slows to a halt as multiple components have reached the end of their effectiveness in the assay. The fluorescent signal observed in the plateau phase levels out. The accumulation of PCR product generally ceases when its concentration reaches approximately 10^{-7} mol/L.

The optimal place to measure fluorescence versus cycle number is in the exponential phase of PCR where the relationship between the amount of product and input DNA is more likely to be consistent. Real-time PCR instruments use what is termed the cycle threshold (C_T) for calculations. The C_T value is the point in terms of PCR amplification cycles when the level of fluorescence exceeds some arbitrary threshold, such as 0.2, that is set by the real-time PCR software to be above the baseline noise observed in the early stages of PCR. The fewer cycles it takes to get to a detectable level of fluorescence (i.e., to cross the threshold set by the software), the greater the initial number of DNA molecules put into the PCR reaction. Thus a plot of the log of DNA concentrations versus the C_T value for each sample results in a linear relationship with a negative slope (Figure 6.5).

The cleavage of TaqMan probes or binding of SYBR Green intercalating dye to double-stranded DNA molecules results in an increase in fluorescence signal. This rise in fluorescence can be correlated to the initial DNA template amounts when compared with samples of known DNA concentration. For example, in Figure 6.5, five samples (a, b, c, d, e) are used to generate a standard curve based on their measured C_T values. Provided that there is good sample-to-sample consistency and precision, a sample with an unknown DNA quantity can be compared to this standard curve to calculate its initial DNA template concentration.

Several real-time PCR assays have been developed with the human identity testing market in mind. Commercial kits for detecting human DNA as well as a real-time PCR assay for determining the amount of human Y-chromosome DNA present in a sample are now available. These kits include Quantifiler, Quantifiler Y, and Quantifiler Duo from Applied Biosystems and Plexor HY from Promega Corporation.

COMPARISON OF METHODS

Several interlaboratory tests to evaluate DNA quantification methods have been conducted by the U.S. National Institute of Standards and Technology (NIST) to better understand the measurement variability seen with various techniques. A 10-fold range of reported concentrations was observed in one study. Most DNA quantitation measurements are precise to within a factor of two if performed properly. While this degree of imprecision may seem excessive, quantitation results are usually sufficiently valid to estimate DNA template amounts that will enable optimal PCR amplification.

Points for Discussion

- What is the optimal quantity of DNA for most commercial STR kits? What is the effect of too much or too little DNA being amplified?

- What problems might exist with having quantitation assays that are less sensitive than downstream DNA testing methods?

- Why is qPCR a preferred technique over slot blot methods?

- How can reliable DNA quantitation aid decisions in terms of what route to take?

READING LIST AND INTERNET RESOURCES

Quantitation Methods

DNA Extraction and Quantitation. http://dna.gov/training/extraction

Nicklas, J. A., & Buel, E. (2003). Quantification of DNA in forensic samples. *Analytical and Bioanalytical Chemistry, 376,* 1160–1167.

PicoGreen Assay

Ahn, S. J., et al. (1996). PicoGreen quantitation of DNA: Effective evaluation of samples pre- or post-PCR. *Nucleic Acids Research, 24,* 2623–2625.

Hopwood, A., et al. (1997). Rapid quantification of DNA samples extracted from buccal scrapes prior to DNA profiling. *BioTechniques, 23,* 18–20.

Slot Blot

Budowle, B., et al. (1995). DNA protocols for typing forensic biological evidence: Chemiluminescent detection for human DNA quantitation and restriction fragment length polymorphism (RFLP) analyses and manual typing of polymerase chain reaction (PCR) amplified polymorphisms. *Electrophoresis, 16,* 1559–1567.

Budowle, B., et al. (2001). Using a CCD camera imaging system as a recording device to quantify human DNA by slot blot hybridization. *BioTechniques, 30,* 680–685.

Walsh, P. S., et al. (1992). A rapid chemiluminescent method for quantitation of human DNA. *Nucleic Acids Research, 20,* 5061–5065.

Waye, J. S., et al. (1989). A simple and sensitive method for quantifying human genomic DNA in forensic specimen extracts. *BioTechniques, 7,* 852–855.

AluQuant Kit

Greenspoon, S. A., et al. (2006). Automated PCR setup for forensic casework samples using the normalization wizard and PCR setup robotic methods. *Forensic Science International, 164,* 240–248.

Hayn, S., et al. (2004). Evaluation of an automated liquid hybridization method for DNA quantitation. *Journal of Forensic Sciences, 49,* 87–91.

Mandrekar, M. N., et al. (2001). Development of a human DNA quantitation system. *Croatian Medical Journal, 42,* 336–339.

End-Point PCR

Allen, R. W., & Fuller, V. M. (2006). Quantitation of human genomic DNA through amplification of the amelogenin locus. *Journal of Forensic Sciences, 51,* 76–81.

Fox, J. C., et al. (2003). Development, characterization, and validation of a sensitive primate-specific quantification assay for forensic analysis. *BioTechniques, 34,* 314–322.

Real-Time Quantitative PCR (qPCR)

AAFS 2008 qPCR Workshop. http://www.cstl.nist.gov/biotech/strbase/training/AAFS2008_qPCRworkshop.htm

Alonso, A., et al. (2004). Real-time PCR designs to estimate nuclear and mitochon-drial DNA copy number in forensic and ancient DNA studies. *Forensic Science International, 139*, 141–149.

Andreasson, H., et al. (2002). Real-time DNA quantification of nuclear and mitochon-drial DNA in forensic analysis. *BioTechniques, 33*, 402–411.

Higuchi, R., et al. (1992). Simultaneous amplification and detection of specific DNA sequences. *Biotechnology, 10*, 413–417.

Higuchi, R., et al. (1993). Kinetic PCR analysis: Real-time monitoring of DNA amplifi-cation reactions. *Biotechnology, 11*, 1026–1030.

Horsman, K. M., et al. (2006). Development of a human-specific real-time PCR assay for the simultaneous quantitation of total genomic and male DNA. *Journal of Forensic Sciences, 51*, 758–765.

Hudlow, W. R., et al. (2008). A quadruplex real-time qPCR assay for the simultaneous assessment of total human DNA, human male DNA, DNA degradation and the presence of PCR inhibitors in forensic samples: A diagnostic tool for STR typing. *Forensic Science International: Genetics, 2*, 108–125.

Nicklas, J. A., & Buel, E. (2003). Development of an Alu-based, real-time PCR method for quantitation of human DNA in forensic samples. *Journal of Forensic Sciences, 48*, 936–944.

Nicklas, J. A., & Buel, E. (2006). Simultaneous determination of total human and male DNA using a duplex real-time PCR assay. *Journal of Forensic Sciences, 51*, 1005–1015.

Niederstätter, H., et al. (2007). A modular real-time PCR concept for determining the quantity and quality of human nuclear and mitochondrial DNA. *Forensic Science International: Genetics, 1*, 29–34.

Shewale, J. G., et al. (2007). Human genomic DNA quantitation system, h-quant: Development and validation for use in forensic casework. *Journal of Forensic Sciences, 52*, 364–370.

Swango, K. L., et al. (2006). A quantitative PCR assay for the assessment of DNA deg-radation in forensic samples. *Forensic Science International, 158*, 14–26.

Swango, K. L., et al. (2007). Developmental validation of a multiplex qPCR assay for assessing the quantity and quality of nuclear DNA in forensic samples. *Forensic Science International, 170*, 35–45.

Timken, M. D., et al. (2005). A duplex real-time qPCR assay for the quantification of human nuclear and mitochondrial DNA in forensic samples: Implications for quantifying DNA in degraded samples. *Journal of Forensic Sciences, 50*, 1044–1060.

Walker, J. A., et al. (2005). Multiplex polymerase chain reaction for simultaneous quantitation of human nuclear, mitochondrial, and male Y-chromosome DNA: Application in human identification. *Analytical Biochemistry, 337*, 89–97.

Quantifiler Kit

Green, R. L., et al. (2005). Developmental validation of the quantifiler real-time PCR kits for the quantification of human nuclear DNA samples. *Journal of Forensic Sciences, 50*, 809–825.

Koukoulas, I., et al. (2008). Quantifiler observations of relevance to forensic casework. *Journal of Forensic Sciences, 53*, 135–141.

Westring, C. G., et al. (2007). Validation of reduced-scale reactions for the quantifiler human DNA kit. *Journal of Forensic Sciences, 52*, 1035–1043.

Quantifiler Duo Kit

Barbisin, M., et al. (2009). Development validation of the quantifiler duo DNA quantification kit for simultaneous quantification of total human and human male DNA and detection of PCR inhibitors in biological samples. *Journal of Forensic Sciences, 54*, 305–319.

Quantifiler Duo. http://duo.appliedbiosystems.com

Plexor HY Kit

Krenke, B. E., et al. (2008). Developmental validation of a real-time PCR assay for the simultaneous quantification of total human and male DNA. *Forensic Science International: Genetics, 3*, 14–21.

Plexor HY. http://www.promega.com/plexorhy

Comparison of Methods

Duewer, D. L., et al. (2001). NIST mixed stain studies #1 and #2: Interlaboratory comparison of DNA quantification practice and short tandem repeat multiplex performance with multiple-source samples. *Journal of Forensic Sciences, 46*, 1199–1210.

Kline, M. C., et al. (2003). NIST mixed stain study 3: DNA quantitation accuracy and its influence on short tandem repeat multiplex signal intensity. *Analytical Chemistry, 75*, 2463–2469.

Kline, M. C., et al. (2005). Results from the NIST 2004 DNA quantitation study. *Journal of Forensic Sciences, 50*, 571–578.

Nielsen, K., et al. (2008). Comparison of five DNA quantification methods. *Forensic Science International: Genetics, 2*, 226–230.

CHAPTER 7

DNA Amplification (The Polymerase Chain Reaction)

Out of a natural laziness, I always start with the easiest possible protocol and work from there. Better yet, I suggest that someone start from there, and I come back in a month to see how things worked out.

—Kary Mullis, inventor of PCR

Forensic science and DNA typing laboratories have greatly benefited from the discovery of a technique known as the polymerase chain reaction, or PCR. First described in 1985 by Kary Mullis and members of the Human Genetics group at the Cetus Corporation (now Roche Molecular Systems), PCR has revolutionized molecular biology with the ability to make hundreds of millions of copies of a specific sequence of DNA in a matter of only a few hours. The impact of PCR has been such that its inventor, Kary Mullis, received the Nobel Prize in Chemistry in 1993—less than 10 years after it was first described.

Without the ability to make copies of DNA molecules, many forensic samples would be impossible to analyze. DNA from crime scenes is often limited in both quantity and quality and obtaining a cleaner, more concentrated sample is normally out of the question (most perpetrators of crimes are not surprisingly unwilling to donate more evidence material to aid in their prosecution). The PCR DNA amplification technology is well suited to analysis of forensic DNA samples because it is sensitive, rapid, and not limited by the quality of the DNA as are the restriction fragment length polymorphism (RFLP) methods.

POLYMERASE CHAIN REACTION (PCR) PROCESS

PCR is an enzymatic process in which a specific region of DNA is replicated over and over again to yield many copies of a particular sequence. This molecular

Contribution of the National Institute of Standards and Technology, 2010.

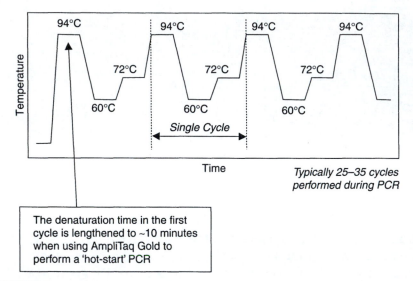

The denaturation time in the first cycle is lengthened to ~10 minutes when using AmpliTaq Gold to perform a 'hot-start' PCR

FIGURE 7.1

Thermal cycling temperature profile for PCR. Thermal cycling typically involves three different temperatures that are repeated over and over again 28 to 32 times. At 94°C, the DNA strands separate, or 'denature.' At 60°C, primers bind or 'anneal' to the DNA template and target the region to be amplified. At 72°C, the DNA polymerase extends the primers by copying the target region using the deoxynucleotide triphosphate building blocks. The entire PCR process is about 3 hours in duration with each cycle taking ~5 minutes on conventional thermal cyclers: 1 minute each at 94°, 60°, and 72°C and about 2 minutes ramping between the three temperatures.

'Xeroxing' process involves heating and cooling samples in a precise thermal cycling pattern over ~30 cycles (Figure 7.1). During each cycle, a copy of the target DNA sequence is generated for every molecule containing the target sequence (Figure 7.2). The boundaries of the amplified product are defined by oligonucleotide primers that are complementary to the 3' ends of the sequence of interest.

In an ideal situation, after 32 cycles approximately a billion copies of the target region on the DNA template have been generated (Table 7.1). This PCR product, sometimes referred to as an 'amplicon,' is then in sufficient quantity that it can be easily measured by a variety of techniques that will be discussed in more detail in Chapter 9.

PCR is commonly performed with a sample volume in the range of 5 to 100 μL. At such low volumes, evaporation can be a problem and accurate pipetting of the reaction components can become a challenge. On the other hand, larger solution volumes lead to thermal equilibrium issues for the reaction mixture because it takes longer for an external temperature change to be transmitted to the center of a larger solution than a smaller one. Therefore,

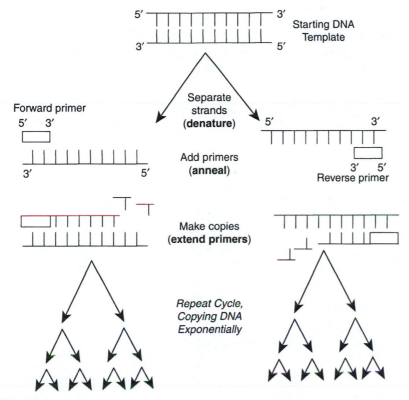

FIGURE 7.2

DNA amplification process with the polymerase chain reaction. In each cycle, the two DNA template strands are first separated (denatured) by heat. The sample is then cooled to an appropriate temperature to bind (anneal) the oligonucleotide primers. Finally the temperature of the sample is raised to the optimal temperature for the DNA polymerase and it extends the primers to produce a copy of each DNA template strand. For each cycle, the number of DNA molecular fragments (with the sequence between the two PCR primers) doubles.

longer hold times are needed at each temperature, which leads to longer over-all thermal cycling times. Most molecular biology protocols for PCR are thus in the 20- to 50-μL range.

The sample is pipetted into a variety of reaction tubes designed for use in PCR thermal cyclers. The most common tube in use with 20- to 50-μL PCR reactions is a thin-walled 0.2-mL tube. These 0.2-mL tubes can be purchased as individual tubes with and without attached caps or as 'strip-tubes' with 8 or 12 tubes connected together in a row. In higher throughput labs, 96-well or 384-well plates are routinely used for PCR amplification.

PCR has been simplified in recent years by the availability of reagent kits that allow a forensic DNA laboratory to simply add a DNA template to a premade

Table 7.1 Number of target DNA molecules created by PCR amplification (if reaction is working at 100% efficiency). The target PCR product is not completely defined by the forward and reverse primers until the third cycle. The bold font is to draw attention to common end points of 28, 32, or 34 cycles.

Cycle Number	Number of Double-Stranded Target Molecules (Specific PCR Product)
1	0
2	0
3	2
4	4
5	8
6	16
7	32
8	64
9	128
10	256
11	512
12	1024
13	2048
14	4096
15	8192
16	16,384
17	32,768
18	65,536
19	131,072
20	262,144
21	524,288
22	1,048,576
23	2,097,152
24	4,194,304
25	8,388,608
26	16,777,216
27	33,554,432

(Continued)

Table 7.1 (Continued)

Cycle Number	Number of Double-Stranded Target Molecules (Specific PCR Product)
28	67,108,864
29	134,217,728
30	268,435,456
31	536,870,912
32	1,073,741,824
33	2,147,483,648
34	4,294,967,296

PCR mix containing all the necessary components for the amplification reaction. These kits are optimized through extensive research efforts on the part of commercial manufacturers. The kits are typically prepared so that a user adds an aliquot of the kit solution to a particular amount of genomic DNA. The best results with these commercial kits are obtained if the DNA template is added in an amount that corresponds to the concentration range designed for the kit. Hence the need for DNA quantitation and sample quantity normalization described in Chapter 6.

PCR components

A PCR reaction is prepared by mixing several individual components and then adding deionized water to achieve the desired volume and concentration of each of the components. Commercial kits with premixed components may also be used for PCR. These kits have greatly simplified the use of PCR in forensic DNA laboratories.

The most important components of a PCR reaction are the two primers, which are short DNA sequences that precede or 'flank' the region to be copied. A primer acts to identify or 'target' the portion of the DNA template to be copied. It is a chemically synthesized oligonucleotide that is added in a high concentration relative to the DNA template to drive the PCR reaction. Some knowledge of the DNA sequence to be copied is required in order to select appropriate primer sequences.

The other components of a PCR reaction consist of template DNA that will be copied, dNTP building blocks that supply each of the four nucleotides, and a DNA polymerase that adds the building blocks in the proper order based on the template DNA sequence. The various components and their optimal concentrations are listed in Table 7.2. Thermal stable polymerases that do not

Table 7.2 Typical components for PCR amplification.

Reagent	Optimal Concentration
Tris-HCl, pH 8.3 (25°C)	10–50 mM
Magnesium chloride	1.2–2.5 mM
Potassium chloride	50 mM
Deoxynucleotide triphosphates (dNTPs)	200 μM each dATP, dTTP, dCTP, dGTP
DNA polymerase, thermal stable[a]	0.5–5 U
Bovine serum albumin (BSA)	100 μg/mL
Primers	0.1–1.0 μM
Template DNA	1–10 ng genomic DNA

[a]*Taq and TaqGold are the two most common thermal stable polymerases used for PCR.*

fall apart during the near-boiling denaturation temperature steps have been important to the success of PCR. The most commonly used thermal stable polymerase is *Taq*, which comes from a bacterium named *Thermus aquaticus* that inhabits hot springs.

When setting up a set of samples that contain the same primers and reaction components, it is common to prepare a 'master mix' that can then be dispensed in equal quantities to each PCR tube. This procedure helps to ensure relative homogeneity among samples. Also by setting up a larger number of reactions at once, small pipetting volumes can be avoided, which improves the accuracy of adding each component (and thus the reproducibility of one's method). When performing a common test on a number of different samples, the goal should be to examine the variation in the DNA samples, *not* variability in the reaction components used and the sample preparation method.

Controls used to monitor PCR

Controls are used to monitor the effectiveness of the chosen experimental conditions and/or the technique of the experimenter. These controls typically include a 'negative control,' which is the entire PCR reaction mixture without any DNA template. The negative control usually contains water or buffer of the same volume as the DNA template, and it is useful for assessing whether or not any of the PCR components have been contaminated by DNA (e.g., by you or someone else in your lab). An extraction 'blank' is also useful to verify that the reagents used for DNA extraction are clean of any extraneous DNA templates.

A 'positive control' is a valuable indicator of whether or not any of the PCR components have failed or were not added during the reaction setup phase of experiments conducted. A standard DNA template of known sequence with good-quality DNA should be used for the positive control. This DNA template should be amplified with the same PCR primers that are used on the rest of the samples in the batch that is being amplified. The purpose of a positive control is to ensure confidence that the reaction components and thermal cycling parameters are working for amplifying a specific region of DNA.

Stochastic effects from low levels of DNA template

Forensic DNA specimens often possess low levels of DNA. When amplifying very low levels of DNA template, a phenomenon known as *stochastic fluctuation* can occur. Stochastic effects, which are an unequal sampling of the two alleles present from a heterozygous individual, result when only a few DNA molecules are used to initiate PCR. PCR reactions involving DNA template levels below approximately 100 pg of DNA, or about 15 diploid copies of genomic DNA, have been shown to exhibit allele dropout. False homozygosity results if one of the alleles fails to be detected.

Stochastic artifacts can be avoided by adjusting the cycle number of the PCR reaction such that approximately 20 or more copies of target DNA are required to yield a successful typing result. However, efforts have been made to obtain results with low copy number (LCN) DNA testing. The challenges of LCN work and trying to interpret data obtained with less than 100 pg of DNA template will be addressed in Chapter 14 and the *Advanced Topics* volume. Whole genome amplification prior to PCR and locus-specific amplification also have the same issues in terms of stochastic fluctuations with low levels of DNA (D.N.A. Box 7.1).

Thermal cycling parameters

A wide range of PCR cycling protocols have been used for various molecular biology applications. To serve as an example of PCR cycling conditions commonly used by forensic DNA laboratories, Table 7.3 contains the parameters used with the PowerPlex STR kits from Promega Corporation and the AmpFlSTR kits from Applied Biosystems. The primary reason that PCR protocols vary is that different primer sequences have different hybridization properties and thus anneal to the DNA template strands at different rates.

Thermal cyclers

The instrument that heats and cools a DNA sample in order to perform the PCR reaction is known as a *thermal cycler*. Precise and accurate sample heating

D.N.A. Box 7.1 Whole Genome Amplification

A common challenge with forensic casework is the recovery of limited quantities of DNA from evidentiary samples. Within the past few years a new DNA enrichment technology has been developed known as whole genome amplification (WGA). WGA involves a different DNA polymerase than the TaqGold enzyme commonly used in forensic DNA analysis. WGA amplifies the entire genome using random hexamers as priming points. The WGA enzymes work by multiple displacement amplification (MDA), which is sometimes referred to as rolling circle amplification. MDA is isothermal with an incubation temperature of 30°C and requires no heating and cooling like PCR.

Qiagen (Valencia, CA) and Sigma-Aldrich (St. Louis, MO) both offer phi29 DNA polymerase cocktails for performing WGA. The kit sold by Qiagen is called REPLI-g while Sigma-Aldrich's kit is GenomePlex. Yields of 4–7 μg of amplified genomic DNA are possible from as little as 1 ng of starting material. The phi29 enzyme has a high processivity and can amplify fragments of up to 100 kb because it displaces downstream product strands, enabling multiple concurrent and overlapping rounds of amplification. In addition, phi29 has a higher replication fidelity compared to *Taq* polymerase due to 3′–5′ proofreading activity.

While all of these characteristics make WGA seem like a possible solution to the forensic problem of limited DNA starting material, studies have found that stochastic effects at low levels of DNA template prevent WGA from working reliably (Schneider *et al.*, 2004). Allele dropouts from STR loci were observed at 50- and 5-pg levels of starting material (Schneider *et al.*, 2004) just as are seen with current low copy number DNA testing (see Chapter 14). Work with 'molecular crowding' materials such as polyethylene glycol, where the amount of DNA is enriched in localized areas of a sample, has shown improved success with STR typing from low amounts of DNA (Ballantyne *et al.*, 2006). While it is possible that WGA may play a limited role in enriching samples for archiving purposes that are in the low nanogram range, it will probably not be the end-all solution to low copy number DNA samples.

Sources:

Ballantyne, K. N., et al. (2006). Molecular crowding increases the amplification success of multiple displacement amplification and short tandem repeat genotyping. *Analytical Biochemistry, 355,* 298–303.
http://www.qiagen.com/Products/wholeGenomeAmplification/
http://www.sigmaaldrich.com/life-science/molecular-biology/automation/whole-genomeamplification.html
Schneider, P. M., et al. (2004). Whole genome amplification—The solution for a common problem in forensic casework? *Progress in Forensic Genetics 10, ICS 1261,* 24–26.

and cooling are crucial to PCR in order to guarantee consistent results. There are a wide variety of thermal cycler options available from multiple manufacturers. These instruments vary in the number of samples that can be handled at a time, the size of the sample tube and volume of reagents that can be handled, and the speed at which the temperature can be changed. Prices for thermal cycling devices range from a few thousand dollars to more than $10,000.

Perhaps the most prevalent thermal cycler in forensic DNA laboratories is the GeneAmp 9700 (Figure 7.3) from Applied Biosystems (Foster City, CA). The '9700' can heat and cool 96 samples in an 8×12-well microplate format at a rate of approximately 1°C per second. The 9700 uses 0.2-mL tubes with tube caps. These tubes may be attached together in strips of 8 or 12, in which case they are referred to as 'strip-tubes' (Figure 7.4a). Alternatively, plastic 'plates' containing 96 'wells' can be used that are covered or sealed once the PCR reaction mix has been added (Figure 7.4b). Some work has also been performed with PCR amplification off of sample spots on microscope slides (D.N.A. Box 7.2).

Table 7.3 Thermal cycling parameters used to amplify short tandem repeat DNA markers with commercially available PCR amplification kits. Cycling parameters differ because reaction components, in particular the primer concentrations and sequences, vary between the different manufacturers' kits.

Step in Protocol	AmpF/STR Kits (Applied Biosystems)	PowerPlex STR Kits (Promega Corporation)
Initial incubation	95°C for 11 minutes	95°C for 11 minutes
Thermal cycling	28 cycles	30 cycles[a]
Denature	94°C for 1 minute	94°C for 30 seconds (cycles 1–10)
		90°C for 30 seconds (cycles 11–30)
Anneal	59°C for 1 minute	60°C for 30 seconds
Extend	72°C for 1 minute	70°C for 45 seconds
Final extension	60°C for 45 minutes	60°C for 30 minutes
Final soak	25°C (until samples removed)	4°C (until samples removed)

[a]*The first 10 cycles are run with a denaturation temperature of 94°C and the last 20 cycles are run at 90°C instead. The Promega PowerPlex 1.1, 2.1, and 16 kits also use specific ramp times between the different temperature steps that differ from the conventional 1°C/second.*

Modern thermal cyclers use a heated lid to keep the PCR reagents from condensing at the top of the tube (or sealed plate sample well) during the temperature cycling. However, for a number of years there were some forensic laboratories that used an older model thermal cycler called the DNA Thermal Cycler 480. Samples amplified in the 480 required an overlay of a drop of mineral oil on top of the PCR reaction mix in order to prevent evaporation since there is no heated lid.

Thermal cyclers capable of amplifying 384 samples or more at one time are now available. The Dual 384-well GeneAmp® PCR System 9700 can run 768 reactions simultaneously on two 384-well sample blocks. Thermal cyclers capable of high sample volume processing are valuable in production settings but are not widely used in forensic DNA laboratories.

Hot-start PCR

Regular DNA polymerases exhibit some activity below their optimal temperature, which for *Taq* polymerase is 72°C. Thus, primers can anneal nonspecifically to the template DNA at room temperature when PCR reactions are being set up and nonspecific products may result. It is also possible at a low

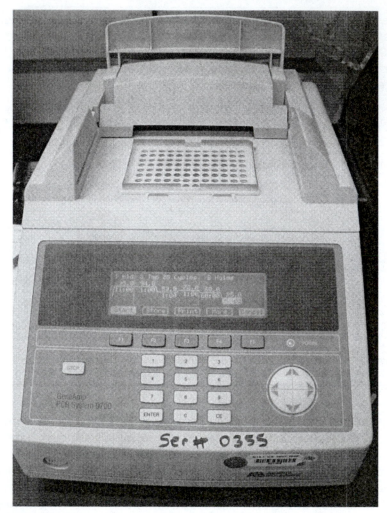

FIGURE 7.3
Photograph of a GeneAmp 9700 thermal cycler.

temperature for the primers to bind to each other, creating products called 'primer dimers.' These are a particular problem because their small size relative to the PCR products means that they will be preferentially amplified.

Once low-temperature nonspecific priming occurs, these undesirable products will be efficiently amplified throughout the remaining PCR cycles. Because the polymerase is busy amplifying these competing products, the target DNA region will be amplified less efficiently. If this happens, you will get less of what you are looking for and you may not have enough specific DNA to run your other tests.

(a)

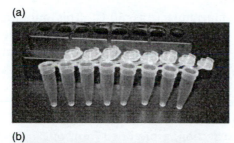

(b)

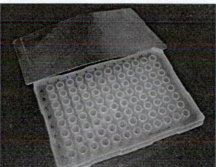

FIGURE 7.4

Photographs of (a) a set of eight PCR strip-tubes and (b) a 96-well plate with foil cover.

D.N.A. Box 7.2 Low-Volume On-Chip PCR Amplification

To scale down biochemical reactions and provide capabilities for single-cell analysis, a German company named Advalytix (Munich) has developed an on-chip PCR platform involving a microscope slide containing 48 hydrophilic spots (although earlier versions had 60 spots). Each 'anchor' spot on this AmpliGrid holds 1 μL of solution containing the reaction components necessary for PCR. Because of the chemical nature of the hydrophilic spots, liquid is attracted to the defined positions and forms a small bead, which can then be covered with 5 μL of mineral oil before thermal cycling is performed in order to prevent evaporation. The entire chip is then placed in a thermal cycler with an *in situ* adapter for the PCR heating and cooling steps.

Full DNA profiles down to 32 pg of DNA template have been achieved with a commercial STR typing kit. Although it is challenging to pipet the small volumes necessary to perform this work, this technique is cost effective due to reduced reagent consumption.

Sources:
http://www.advalytix.com/index.htm
Schmidt, U., et al. (2006). Low-volume amplification on chemically structured chips using the PowerPlex 16 DNA amplification kit. *International Journal of Legal Medicine, 120,* 42–48.

Low-temperature mispriming can be avoided by initiating PCR at an elevated temperature, a process usually referred to as 'hot-start' PCR. Hot-start PCR may be performed by introducing a critical reaction component, such as the polymerase, after the temperature of the sample has been raised above the desired annealing temperature (e.g., 60°C). This minimizes the possibility of mispriming and misextension events by not having the polymerase present during reaction setup. However, this approach is cumbersome and time consuming when working with large numbers of samples. Perhaps a more important disadvantage is the fact that the sample tubes must be opened at the thermal cycler to introduce the essential component, which gives rise to a greater opportunity for cross-contamination between samples. As will be discussed in the next section, a modified form of *Taq* DNA polymerase has been developed that requires thermal activation and thus enables closed-tube hot-start PCR. This enzyme, named AmpliTaq Gold, has greatly benefited the specificity of PCR amplifications.

AmpliTaq Gold DNA polymerase

AmpliTaq Gold™ DNA polymerase is a chemically modified enzyme that is rendered inactive until heated. An extended preincubation of 95°C, usually for 10 or 11 minutes, is used to activate the AmpliTaq Gold. The chemical modification involves a derivitization of the epsilon-amino groups of the lysine residues. At a pH below 7.0 the chemical modification moieties fall off and the activity of the polymerase is restored.

The pH of the Tris buffer in the PCR reaction varies with temperature; higher temperatures cause the solution pH to go down by approximately 0.02 pH units with every 1°C. A Tris buffer with pH 8.3 at 25°C will go down to pH ~6.9 at 95°C. Thus, not only is the template DNA well denatured but the polymerase is activated just when it is needed, and not in a situation where primer dimers and mispriming can occur as easily.

Other DNA polymerases have been developed recently that are rendered active for hot-start PCR with shorter times (e.g., 1–2 minutes instead of 10–11 minutes). These enzymes can help reduce the overall time for PCR amplification and enable rapid PCR efforts (D.N.A. Box 7.3).

PCR primer design

Well-designed primers are probably the most important components of a good PCR reaction. The target region on the DNA template is defined by the position of the primers. PCR yield is directly affected by the annealing characteristics of the primers. For the PCR to work efficiently, the two primers must be specific to the target region, possess similar annealing temperatures, not interact significantly with each other or themselves to form 'primer dimers,' and be structurally compatible. Likewise, the sequence region to which the primers bind must be fairly well conserved because if the sequence changes from one DNA template to the next, then the primers will not bind appropriately. The general guidelines to optimal PCR primer design are listed in Table 7.4.

D.N.A. Box 7.3 Rapid PCR

The current forensic DNA typing process takes about 8 to 10 hours. The longest single step in this process is multiplex PCR amplification, which requires approximately 3 hours using manufacturer-supplied protocols for commercial STR typing kits. There is great interest in developing portable, rapid DNA typing devices for a number of applications. For example, the ability to perform multiplex PCR amplification with commonly used STR markers in a few minutes rather than hours could open new potential biometric applications for DNA testing including analysis of individuals while they wait at a country border or an airport.

STR kit manufacturers have validated their kits with 1°C/second temperature ramp rates and dwell times of around 1 minute per temperature step. The time required for 28 to 32 cycles is typically 2.5 to 3 hours. Part of this time is a 10-minute front-end hot start to activate the AmpliTaq Gold DNA polymerase. A 30- to 60-minute 60°C soak is used at the end of thermal cycling to enable full adenylation of the PCR products produced.

Using different DNA polymerases and a faster temperature ramp rate, PCR amplifications of STR typing kits have been reduced to approximately 35 minutes on a conventional GeneAmp 9700 thermal cycler, which can change temperatures at a maximum rate of 4°C/second. With faster ramp rate cyclers, STR typing results have been obtained in as little as 15 minutes.

Source:
Vallone, P. M., et al. (2008). Demonstration of rapid multiplex PCR amplification involving 16 genetic loci. *Forensic Science International: Genetics, 3,* 42–45.

Table 7.4 General guidelines for PCR primer design.

Parameter	Optimal Values
Primer length	18–30 bases
Primer T_m (melting temperature)	55–72°C
Percentage GC content	40–60%
No self-complementarity (hairpin structure)	≤3 contiguous bases
No complementarity to other primer (primer dimer)	≤3 contiguous bases (especially at the 3' ends)
Distance between two primers on target sequence	<2000 bases apart
Unique oligonucleotide sequence	Best match in BLAST[a] search
T_m difference between forward and reverse primers in pair	≤5°C
No long runs with the same base	<4 contiguous bases

[a]*A BLAST search examines the similarity of the primer to other known sequences that may result in multiple binding sites for the primer and thus reduce the efficiency of the PCR amplification reaction. BLAST searches may be conducted via the Internet: http:// www.ncbi.nlm.nih.gov/BLAST*

A number of primer design software packages are commercially available including Primer Express (Applied Biosystems, Foster City, CA) and Oligo (Molecular Biology Insights, Cascade, CO). These programs use thermodynamic 'nearest neighbor' calculations to predict annealing temperatures and primer interactions with themselves or other possible primers.

The Internet has become a valuable resource for tools that aid primer selection. For example, a primer design program called Primer 3 is available on the World Wide Web through the Whitehead Institute (http://frodo.wi.mit.edu/). With Primer 3, the user inputs a DNA sequence and specifies the target region within that sequence to be amplified. Parameters such as PCR product size, primer length, and desired annealing temperature may also be specified by the user. The program then ranks the best PCR primer pairs and passes them back to the user over the Internet. Primer 3 works well for quickly designing singleplex primer pairs that amplify just one region of DNA at a time.

The National Center of Biotechnology Information recently released a combined Primer-BLAST tool that enables finding specific PCR primers through combining the features of Primer3 and BLAST (see http://www.ncbi.nlm.nih.gov).

MULTIPLEX PCR

The polymerase chain reaction permits more than one region to be copied simultaneously by simply adding more than one primer set to the reaction mixture. The simultaneous amplification of two or more regions of DNA is commonly known as multiplexing or multiplex PCR (Figure 7.5). For a multiplex reaction to work properly, the primer pairs need to be compatible. In other words, the primer annealing temperatures should be similar and excessive regions of complementarity should be avoided to prevent the formation of primer dimers that will cause the primers to bind to one another instead of the template DNA. The addition of each new primer in a multiplex PCR reaction exponentially increases the complexity of possible primer interactions.

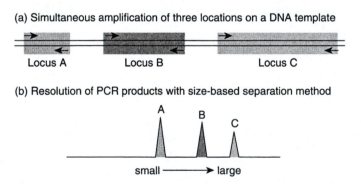

(a) Simultaneous amplification of three locations on a DNA template

Locus A   Locus B   Locus C

(b) Resolution of PCR products with size-based separation method

A   B
            C

small ———→ large

FIGURE 7.5

Schematic of multiplex PCR. A multiplex PCR makes use of two or more primer sets within the same reaction mix. (a) Three sets of primers, represented by arrows, are shown here to amplify three different loci on a DNA template. (b) The primers were designed so that the PCR products for locus A, locus B, and locus C would be different sizes and therefore resolvable with a size-based separation system.

Each new PCR application is likely to require some degree of optimization in either the reagent components or thermal cycling conditions. Multiplex PCR is no exception. In fact, multiplex PCR optimization is more of a challenge than singleplex reactions because so many primer-annealing events must occur simultaneously without interfering with each other. Extensive optimization is normally required to obtain a good balance between the amplicons of the various loci being amplified.

The variables that are examined when trying to obtain optimal results for a multiplex PCR amplification include many of the reagents listed earlier in Table 7.2 as well as the thermal cycling temperature profile. Primer sequences and concentrations along with magnesium concentrations are usually the most crucial to multiplex PCR. Extension times during thermal cycling are often increased for multiplex reactions in order to give the polymerase time to fully copy all of the DNA targets. Obtaining successful coamplification with well-balanced PCR product yields sometimes requires redesign of primers and tedious experiments with adjusting primer concentrations.

Primer design for the STR DNA markers that are discussed in Chapter 8 include some additional challenges. Primers need to be adjusted on the STR markers to achieve good size separation between loci labeled with the same fluorescent dye. In addition, the primers must produce robust amplifications with good peak height balance between loci as well as specific amplification with no nonspecific products that might interfere with proper interpretation of a sample's DNA profile. Finally, primers should produce a maximal non-template-dependent '+A' addition to all PCR products to ease data interpretation (see Chapter 10).

Multiplex PCR optimization

Obtaining a nicely balanced multiplex PCR reaction with each PCR product having a similar yield is a challenging task. With the widespread availability of commercial kits, individual forensic laboratories rarely perform PCR optimization experiments any more. Rather, internal validation studies focus on performance of the multiplex with varying conditions around the optimal parameters supplied with the kit protocol. For example, PCR product yields in the form of STR peak heights produced by a commercial kit might be evaluated at the optimal annealing temperature (e.g., 59°C) and 2° and 4°C higher and lower (e.g., 55°, 57°, 61°, and 63°C). Differences, if any, would then be noted relative to the optimal annealing temperature supplied in the kit protocol.

The development of an efficient multiplex PCR reaction requires careful planning and numerous tests and efforts in the area of primer design and balancing reaction components. Various thermal cycling parameters including annealing temperatures and extension times are often examined in developing the final protocol. Primer concentrations are one of the largest factors in a multiplex PCR reaction determining the overall yield of each amplicon. Repeated experiments and primer titrations are usually performed to achieve an optimal balance. Concentrations of magnesium chloride and deoxynucleotide triphosphates are typically increased slightly relative to singleplex reactions. A thorough evaluation of performance for a multiplex will also involve addition and removal of primer sets to see if overall balance in other amplification targets are affected.

The availability of 5-dye detection systems has enabled development of multiplexes capable of amplifying and analyzing in excess of 20 short tandem repeat loci (see Figure 15.1).

PCR INHIBITION

As mentioned at the end of Chapter 5, the PCR amplification process can be affected by substances known as 'inhibitors,' which interfere or prevent the DNA amplification process from occurring properly. These inhibitors can be present in DNA samples collected from crime scenes. Outdoor crimes may leave body fluid such as blood and semen on soil, sand, wood, or leaf litter that contain substances which may coextract with the perpetrator's DNA and prevent PCR amplification. Textile dyes, leather, and wood surfaces from interior crime scenes may also contain DNA polymerase inhibitors.

Inhibitors can (1) interfere with the cell lysis necessary for DNA extraction, (2) interfere by nucleic acid degradation or capture, and (3) inhibit polymerase activity, thus preventing enzymatic amplification of the target DNA. Occasionally substances such as textile dyes from clothing or hemoglobin from red blood cells can remain with the DNA throughout the sample preparation process and interfere with the polymerase to prevent successful PCR amplification.

The result of amplifying a DNA sample containing an inhibitor such as hematin is a loss of the alleles from the larger sized STR loci or even complete failure of all loci. Some examples of PCR inhibitors and their sources are found in Table 7.5.

In some cases, PCR inhibitors may be removed during DNA extraction or through additional DNA purification steps. A common solution to overcoming or reducing PCR inhibition is to dilute the genomic DNA template, which also dilutes the effective concentration of the PCR inhibitor. Additives to PCR reactions, such as bovine serum albumin (BSA), have been shown to prevent or reduce PCR inhibition. Thus, BSA is a common ingredient in most STR typing kits.

Table 7.5 Some PCR inhibitors and their sources.

PCR Inhibitor	Possible Source
Heme (hematin)	Blood
Melanin	Tissue and hair
Polysaccharides	Feces
Bile salts	Feces
Humic compounds	Soil
Urea	Urine
Textile dyes (denim)	Clothing (blue jeans)

PRECAUTIONS AGAINST CONTAMINATION

The sensitivity of PCR necessitates constant vigilance on the part of the laboratory staff to ensure that contamination does not affect DNA typing results. Contamination of PCR reactions is always a concern because the technique is very sensitive to low amounts of DNA. A scientist setting up the PCR reaction can inadvertently add his or her own DNA to the reaction if he or she is not careful. Likewise, the police officer or crime scene technician collecting the evidence can contaminate the sample if proper care is not taken. For this reason, each piece of evidence should be collected with clean tweezers or handled with disposable gloves that are changed frequently.

To aid discovery of laboratory contamination, everyone in a forensic DNA laboratory is typically genotyped in order to have a record of possible contaminating DNA profiles. This is often referred to as a staff elimination database. Laboratory personnel should be appropriately gowned during interactions with samples prior to PCR amplification. The appropriate covering includes lab coats and gloves as well as facial masks and hairnets to prevent skin cells or hair from falling into the amplification tubes. These precautions are especially critical when working with minuscule amounts of sample or sample that has been degraded.

Some tips for avoiding contamination with PCR reactions in a laboratory setting include:

- Pre- and post-PCR sample processing areas should be physically separated. Usually a separate room or a containment cabinet is used for setting up the PCR amplification reactions.

- Equipment, such as pipettors, and reagents for setting up PCR should be kept separate from other laboratory supplies, especially those used for analysis of PCR products.

- Disposable gloves should be worn and changed frequently.

- Reactions may also be set up in a laminar flow hood, if available.

- Aerosol-resistant pipette tips should be used and changed on every new sample to prevent cross-contamination during liquid transfers.

- Reagents should be carefully prepared to avoid the presence of any contaminating DNA or nucleases.

- Ultraviolet irradiation of laboratory PCR setup space when the area is not in use and cleaning workspaces and instruments with isopropanol and/or 10% bleach solutions help to ensure that extraneous DNA molecules are destroyed prior to DNA extraction or PCR setup.

PCR product carryover results from amplified DNA contaminating a sample that has not yet been amplified. Because the amplified DNA is many times more concentrated than the unamplified DNA template, it will be preferentially copied during PCR and the unamplified sample will be masked. The inadvertent transfer of even a very small volume of a completed PCR amplification to an unamplified DNA sample can result in the amplification and detection of the 'contaminating' sequence. For this reason, the evidence samples are typically processed through a forensic DNA laboratory prior to the suspect reference samples to avoid any possibility of contaminating the evidence with the suspect's amplified DNA.

Pipette tips should never be reused. Even a tiny droplet of PCR product left in a pipette tip may contain millions of copies of the amplifiable sequence. By comparison, a nanogram of human genomic DNA contains only about 300 copies of single-copy DNA markers (see D.N.A. Box 6.2).

Points for Discussion

- What challenges exist with designing multiplex PCR primers?

- What are the advantages of a thermal stable, hot-start DNA polymerase?

- Why is it important to separate pre-PCR and post-PCR processes?

- What is the purpose of a negative amplification control? A positive amplification control?

- What are some effective means to prevent contamination?

- What are some effective means to clean up following a contamination event?

- What are 'stochastic effects' and why are they important to forensic DNA analysis?

- Why are PCR inhibitors problematic with forensic cases and what are some ways they can be overcome?

READING LIST AND INTERNET RESOURCES

General PCR Information

Bloch, W. (1991). A biochemical perspective of the polymerase chain reaction. *Biochemistry, 30,* 2735–2747.

Mullis, K. (1987). Process for amplifying nucleic acid sequences. Cetus Corporation. U.S. patent 4,683,202.

Mullis, K. B. (Ed.), et al. (1994). *The polymerase chain reaction.* Boston: Birkhäuser.

Weissensteiner, T., Griffin, H. G., & Griffin, A. (Eds.), (2004). *PCR technology: Current innovations* (2nd ed.). Boca Raton, FL: CRC Press.

Early Papers

Mullis, K., et al. (1986). Specific enzymatic amplification of DNA *in vitro*: The polymerase chain reaction. *Cold Spring Harbor Symposia on Quantitative Biology, 51,* 263–273.

Mullis, K. B., & Faloona, F. A. (1987). Specific synthesis of DNA *in vitro* via a polymerase-catalyzed chain reaction. *Methods in Enzymology, 155,* 335–350.

Mullis, K. B. (1990). The unusual origin of the polymerase chain reaction. *Scientific American, 262,* 56–65.

Saiki, R. K., et al. (1985). Enzymatic amplification of beta-globin genomic sequences and restriction site analysis for diagnosis of sickle cell anemia. *Science, 230,* 1350–1354.

Saiki, R. K., et al. (1988). Primer-directed enzymatic amplification of DNA with a thermostable DNA polymerase. *Science, 239,* 487–491.

Stochastic Effects with Low DNA

Gill, P., et al. (2000). An investigation of the rigor of interpretation rules for STRs derived from less than 100 pg of DNA. *Forensic Science International, 112,* 17–40.

Walsh, P. S., et al. (1992). Preferential PCR amplification of alleles: Mechanisms and solutions. *PCR Methods and Applications, 1,* 241–250.

AmpliTaq Gold DNA Polymerase

Birch, D. E., et al. (1996). Simplified hot start PCR. *Nature, 381,* 445–446.

D'Aquila, R. T., et al. (1991). Maximizing sensitivity and specificity of PCR by preamplification heating. *Nucleic Acids Research, 19,* 3749.

Innis, M. A., Gelfand, D. H., & Sninsky, J. J. (Eds.), (1999). *PCR applications: Protocols for functional genomics.* San Diego: Academic Press.

Moretti, T., et al. (1998). Enhancement of PCR amplification yield and specificity using AmpliTaq Gold™ DNA polymerase. *BioTechniques, 25,* 716–722.

PCR Primer Design

Dieffenbach, C. W., et al. (1993). General concepts of PCR primer design. *PCR Methods and Applications, 3,* S30–S37.

Rozen, S., & Skaletsky, H. J. (2000). Primer3 on the WWW for general users and for biologist programmers. In S. Krawetz & S. Misener (Vol. Eds.), *Bioinformatics methods and protocols: Methods in molecular biology* (pp. 365–386). New York: Humana Press/Springer.

Rychlik, W., & Rhoads, R. E. (1989). A computer-program for choosing optimal oligonucleotides for filter hybridization, sequencing and *in-vitro* amplification of DNA. *Nucleic Acids Research, 17*, 8543–8551.

Multiplex PCR

Butler, J. M. (2005). Constructing multiplex STR assays. *Methods in Molecular Biology, 297*, 53–66.

Chamberlain, J. S., et al. (1988). Deletion screening of the Duchenne muscular dystrophy locus via multiplex DNA amplification. *Nucleic Acids Research, 16*, 11141–11156.

Edwards, M. C., & Gibbs, R. A. (1994). Multiplex PCR: Advantages, development, and applications. *PCR Methods and Applications, 3*, S65–S75.

Henegariu, O., et al. (1997). Multiplex PCR: Critical parameters and step-by-step protocol. *BioTechniques, 23*, 504–511.

Hill, C. R., et al. (2009). A new 26plex assay for use in human identity testing. *Journal of Forensic Sciences*, (in press). Information available at http://www.cstl.nist.gov/biotech/strbase/str2bplex.htm

Kimpton, C. P., et al. (1994). Evaluation of an automated DNA profiling system employing multiplex amplification of four tetrameric STR loci. *International Journal of Legal Medicine, 106*, 302–311.

Schoske, R., et al. (2003). Multiplex PCR design strategy used for the simultaneous amplification of 10 Y chromosome short tandem repeat (STR) loci. *Analytical and Bioanalytical Chemistry, 375*, 333–343.

PCR Inhibitors

Abu Al-Soud, W., & Radstrom, P. (1998). Capacity of nine thermostable DNA polymerases to mediate DNA amplification in the presence of PCR-inhibiting samples. *Applied and Environmental Microbiology, 64*, 3748–3753.

Akane, A. (1996). Hydrogen peroxide decomposes the heme compound in forensic specimens and improves the efficiency of PCR. *BioTechniques, 21*, 392–394.

Bourke, M. T., et al. (1999). NaOH treatment to neutralize inhibitors of Taq polymerase. *Journal of Forensic Sciences, 44*, 1046–1050.

Comey, C. T., et al. (1994). DNA extraction strategies for amplified fragment length polymorphism analysis. *Journal of Forensic Sciences, 39*, 1254–1269.

Eckhart, L., et al. (2000). Melanin binds reversibly to thermostable DNA polymerase and inhibits its activity. *Biochemical and Biophysical Research Communications, 271*, 726–730.

Rädström, P., et al. (2004). Pre-PCR processing: Strategies to generate PCR-compatible samples. *Molecular Biotechnology, 26*, 133–146.

Wilson, I. G. (1997). Inhibition and facilitation of nucleic acid amplification. *Applied and Environmental Microbiology, 63*, 3741–3751.

Contamination Precautions

Frégeau, C. J., et al. (2008). Automated processing of forensic casework samples using robotic workstations equipped with nondisposable tips: Contamination prevention. *Journal of Forensic Sciences, 53,* 632–651.

Kemp, B. M., & Smith, D. G. (2005). Use of bleach to eliminate contaminating DNA from the surface of bones and teeth. *Forensic Science International, 154,* 53–61.

Kwok, S., & Higuchi, R. (1989). Avoiding false positives with PCR. *Nature, 339,* 237–238.

Port, N. J., et al. (2006). How long does it take a static speaking individual to contaminate the immediate environment? *Forensic Science, Medicine and Pathology, 2,* 157–163.

Rutty, G. N., et al. (2003). The effectiveness of protective clothing in the reduction of potential DNA contamination of the scene of crime. *International Journal of Legal Medicine, 117,* 170–174.

Sarkar, G., & Sommer, S. S. (1990). Shedding light on PCR contamination. *Nature, 343,* 27.

Sarkar, G., & Sommer, S. S. (1993). Removal of DNA contamination in polymerase chain reaction reagents by ultraviolet irradiation. *Methods in Enzymology, 218,* 381–388.

Tamariz, J., et al. (2006). The application of ultraviolet irradiation to exogenous sources of DNA in plasticware and water for the amplification of low copy number DNA. *Journal of Forensic Sciences, 51,* 790–794.

Whole Genome Amplification

Ballantyne, K. N., et al. (2006). Molecular crowding increases the amplification success of multiple displacement amplification and short tandem repeat genotyping. *Analytical Biochemistry, 355,* 298–303.

Ballantyne, K. N., et al. (2007). Comparison of two whole genome amplification methods for STR genotyping of LCN and degraded DNA samples. *Forensic Science International, 166,* 35–41.

Ballantyne, K. N., et al. (2007). Decreasing amplification bias associated with multiple displacement amplification and short tandem repeat genotyping. *Analytical Biochemistry, 368,* 222–229.

Barber, A. L., & Foran, D. R. (2006). The utility of whole genome amplification for typing compromised forensic samples. *Journal of Forensic Sciences, 51,* 1344–1349.

Bergen, A. W., et al. (2005). Comparison of yield and genotyping performance of multiple displacement amplification and OmniPlex whole genome amplified DNA generated from multiple DNA sources. *Human Mutation, 26,* 262–270.

Dean, F. B., et al. (2002). Comprehensive human genome amplification using multiple displacement amplification. In: *Proceedings of the National Academy of Sciences of the United States of America, 99,* 5261–5266.

Hanson, E. K., & Ballantyne, J. (2005). Whole genome amplification strategy for forensic genetic analysis using single or few cell equivalents of genomic DNA. *Analytical Biochemistry, 346,* 246–257.

Hosono, S., et al. (2003). Unbiased whole-genome amplification directly from clinical samples. *Genome Research, 13,* 954–964.

Lizardi, P.M. (2000). Multiple displacement amplification. U.S. Patent 6,124,120.

Schneider, P. M., et al. (2004). Whole genome amplification—The solution for a common problem in forensic casework?. *Progress in Forensic Genetics 10, ICS 1261*, 24–26.

Sun, G., et al. (2005). Whole-genome amplification: Relative efficiencies of the current methods. *Legal Medicine, 7*, 279–286.

Zhang, L., et al. (1992). Whole genome amplification from a single cell: Implications for genetic analysis. In: *Proceedings of the National Academy of Sciences of the United States of America, 89*, 5847–5851.

On-Chip Low-Volume PCR

Lutz-Bonengel, S., et al. (2007). Low volume amplification and sequencing of mitochondrial DNA on a chemically structured chip. *International Journal of Legal Medicine, 121*, 68–73.

Schmidt, U., et al. (2006). Low-volume amplification on chemically structured chips using the PowerPlex 16 DNA amplification kit. *International Journal of Legal Medicine, 120*, 42–48.

Rapid PCR

Vallone, P. M., et al. (2008). Demonstration of rapid multiplex PCR amplification involving 16 genetic loci. *Forensic Science International: Genetics, 3*, 42–45.

CHAPTER 8

Short Tandem Repeat Markers

Ever since their discovery in the early 1980s, the ubiquitous occurrence of microsatellites—also referred to as short tandem repeats (STRs) or simple sequence repeats (SSRs)—has puzzled geneticists.... [Understanding STRs] is important if we wish to understand how genomes are organized and why most genomes are filled with sequences other than genes.

—Hans Ellegren, 2004

GENETIC MARKERS AND REPEATED DNA SEQUENCES

Because more than 99.7% of the human genome is the same from individual to individual, regions that differ need to be found in the remaining 0.3% in order to tell people apart at the genetic level. There are many repeated DNA sequences scattered throughout the human genome. Because these repeat sequences are typically located between genes, they can vary in size from person to person without impacting the genetic health of the individual.

Eukaryotic genomes are full of repeated DNA sequences. These repeated DNA sequences come in all types of sizes and are typically designated by the length of the core repeat unit and the number of contiguous repeat units or the overall length of the repeat region. Long repeat units may contain several hundred to several thousand bases in the core repeat.

These regions are often referred to as *satellite* DNA and may be found surrounding the chromosomal centromere. The term *satellite* arose because frequently one or more minor 'satellite bands' were seen in early experiments involving equilibrium density gradient centrifugation.

Contribution of the National Institute of Standards and Technology, 2010.

147

The core repeat unit for a medium-length repeat, sometimes referred to as a *minisatellite* or a VNTR (variable number of tandem repeats), is in the range of approximately 8 to 100 bases in length. As noted in Chapter 3, the previously used forensic DNA marker D1S80 is a minisatellite with a 16-bp repeat unit.

DNA regions with repeat units that are 2 to 7 bp in length are called *microsatellites*, *simple sequence repeats* (SSRs), or most usually *short tandem repeats* (STRs). STRs have become popular DNA repeat markers because they are easily amplified by the polymerase chain reaction (PCR) without the problems of differential amplification. This is because both alleles from a heterozygous individual are similar in size since the repeat size is small. The number of repeats in STR markers can be highly variable among individuals, which make these STRs effective for human identification purposes.

Literally thousands of polymorphic microsatellites have been characterized in human DNA and there may be more than a million microsatellite loci present depending on how they are counted. Regardless, microsatellites account for approximately 3% of the total human genome. STR markers are scattered throughout the genome and occur on average every 10,000 nucleotides.

Computer searches of the recently available human genome reference sequence have cataloged the number and nature of STR markers in the genome. A large number of STR markers have been characterized by academic and commercial laboratories for use in disease gene location studies. For example, the Marshfield Medical Research Foundation in Marshfield, Wisconsin (http://research.marshfieldclinic.org/genetics) has gathered genotype data on over 8000 STRs that are scattered across the 23 pairs of human chromosomes for the purpose of developing human genetic maps (see Chapter 17).

To perform analysis on STR markers, the invariant flanking regions surrounding the repeats must be determined. Once the flanking sequences are known, then PCR primers can be designed and the repeat region amplified for analysis (Figure 8.1). New STR markers are usually identified in one of two ways: (1) searching DNA sequence databases such as GenBank for regions with more than six or so contiguous repeat units or (2) performing molecular biology isolation methods. The availability of a reference human genome sequence now makes the first option a viable and productive one, and more than 20,000 tetranucleotide STR repeats have been located throughout the human genome. However, when the core STR loci that are widely used today were selected back in the mid-1990s, only a handful of STR loci were known and characterized.

Types of STR markers

STR repeat sequences are named by the length of the repeat unit. Dinucleotide repeats have two nucleotides repeated next to each other over and over again.

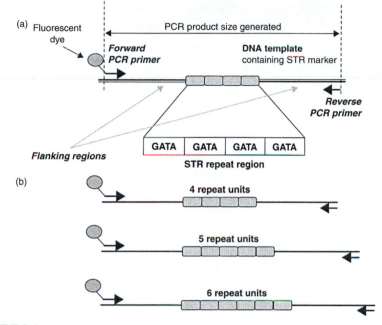

FIGURE 8.1

(a) PCR primers anneal to unique, consistent sequences in the flanking regions that bracket the variable STR repeat region. (b) The overall sizes of STR alleles typically differ by the size of the inserted repeat unit.

Trinucleotides have three nucleotides in the repeat unit, tetranucleotides have four, pentanucleotides have five, and hexanucleotides have six repeat units in the core repeat. Theoretically, there are 4, 16, 64, 256, 1024, and 4096 possible motifs for mono-, di-, tri-, tetra-, penta-, and hexanucleotide repeats, respectively. However, because microsatellites are tandemly repeated, some motifs are actually equivalent to others (D.N.A. Box 8.1). For reasons that will be discussed below, tetranucleotide repeats have become the most popular STR markers for human identification.

STR sequences not only vary in the length of the repeat unit and the number of repeats but also in the rigor with which they conform to an incremental repeat pattern. STRs are often divided into several categories based on the repeat pattern. *Simple repeats* contain units of identical length and sequence, *compound repeats* comprise two or more adjacent simple repeats, and *complex repeats* may contain several repeat blocks of variable unit length as well as variable intervening sequences. *Complex hypervariable repeats* also exist with numerous nonconsensus alleles that differ in both size and sequence and are therefore challenging to genotype reproducibly. This last category of STR markers is not commonly used in forensic DNA typing due to difficulties with allele nomenclature and measurement variability between laboratories,

D.N.A. Box 8.1 List of Possible Microsatellite Motifs

Theoretically, there are 4, 16, 64, 256, 1024, and 4096 possible motifs for mono-, di-, tri-, tetra-, penta-, and hexanucleotide repeats, respectively. However, because microsatellites are tandemly repeated, some motifs are actually equivalent to others. Two rules can be used to identify whether motif A is equivalent to motif B. Motif A is considered equivalent to motif B when (1) motif A is inversely complementary to motif B, or (2) motif A is different from motif B or the inversely complementary sequence of motif B by frameshift. For example,

$(GAAA)_n$ is equivalent to $(AGAA)_n$, $(AAGA)_n$, $(AAAG)_n$, $(TTTC)_n$, $(TTCT)_n$, $(TCTT)_n$, and $(CTTT)_n$. Note that $(AGAG)_n$ is considered a dinucleotide repeat instead of a tetranucleotide motif.

Because of this equivalence in repeat motif structure there are only 2, 4, 10, 33, 102, and 350 possible motifs for mono-, di-, tri-, tetra-, penta-, and hexanucleotide repeats, respectively (see below).

Mononucleotide repeats (2):									
A	C								
Dinucleotide repeats (4):									
AC	AG	AT	CG						
Trinucleotide repeats (10):									
AAC	AAG	AAT	ACC	ACG	ACT	AGC	AGG	ATC	CCG
Tetranucleotide repeats (33):									
AAAC	AAAG	AAAT	AACC	AACG	AACT	AAGC	AAGG	AAGT	AATC
AATG	AATT	ACAG	ACAT	ACCC	ACCG	ACCT	ACGC	ACGG	ACGT
ACTC	ACTG	AGAT	AGCC	AGCG	AGCT	AGGC	AGGG	ATCC	ATCG
ATGC	CCCG	CCGG	the AGAT (or GATA) motif is the most common motif for STR loci used by forensic scientists						

Penta- (102) and hexanucleotide (350) repeats are not shown due to the sheer number of motifs possible.

Source:
Jin, L., Zhong, Y., & Chakraborty, R. (1994). The exact numbers of possible microsatellite motifs [letter]. *American Journal of Human Genetics, 55,* 582–583.

although two commercial kits now include the complex hypervariable STR locus SE33, sometimes called ACTBP2.

Not all alleles for an STR locus contain complete repeat units. Even simple repeats can contain nonconsensus alleles that fall in between alleles with full repeat units. *Microvariants* are alleles that contain incomplete repeat units.

Perhaps the most common example of a microvariant is the allele 9.3 at the TH01 locus, which contains nine tetranucleotide repeats and one incomplete repeat of three nucleotides because the seventh repeat is missing a single adenine out of the normal AATG repeat unit.

STRs used in forensic DNA typing

For human identification purposes it is important to have DNA markers that exhibit the highest possible variation or a number of less polymorphic markers that can be combined in order to obtain the ability to discriminate between samples. As will be discussed further in Chapter 14, forensic specimens are often challenging to PCR amplify because the DNA in the samples may be severely degraded (i.e., broken up into small pieces). Mixtures are prevalent as well in some forensic samples, such as those obtained from sexual assault cases containing biological material from both the perpetrator and victim.

As noted in Chapter 3, the small size of STR alleles (~100 to 400 bp) compared to minisatellite VNTR alleles (~400 to 1000 bp) makes the STR markers better candidates for use in forensic applications where degraded DNA is common. PCR amplification of degraded DNA samples can be better accomplished with smaller product sizes. These reduced-size STR amplicons are often referred to as *miniSTRs*. Allelic dropout of larger alleles in minisatellite markers caused by preferential amplification of the smaller allele is also a significant problem with minisatellites. There are multiple reasons why the smaller STRs are advantageous compared to the larger minisatellite VNTRs.

Among the various types of STR systems, tetranucleotide repeats have become more popular than di- or trinucleotides. Penta- and hexanucleotide repeats are less common in the human genome but are being examined by some laboratories. As discussed in Chapter 10, a biological phenomenon known as 'stutter' results when STR alleles are PCR amplified. *Stutter products* are amplicons that are typically one repeat unit less in size than the true allele and arise during PCR because of strand slippage. STR product amounts vary depending on the STR locus but are usually less than 15% of the allele product quantity with tetranucleotide repeats. With di- and trinucleotides, the stutter percentage can be much greater (30% or more), making it difficult to interpret sample mixtures. In addition, the four-base spread in alleles with tetranucleotides makes closely spaced heterozygotes easier to resolve with size-based electrophoretic separations compared to alleles that could be two or three bases different in size with dinucleotides and trinucleotide markers, respectively.

STR allele nomenclature

To aid in interlaboratory reproducibility and comparisons of data, a common nomenclature has been developed in the forensic DNA community. DNA

⟶

```
          1     2     3     4     5     6
5'-TTTCCC TCAT TCAT TCAT TCAT TCAT TCAT TCACCATGGA-3'
3'-AAAGGG AGTA AGTA AGTA AGTA AGTA AGTA AGTGGTACCT-5'
          6     5     4     3     2     1
```

⟵

FIGURE 8.2

Example of the DNA sequence in a STR repeat region. Note that using the top strand versus the bottom strand results in different repeat motifs and starting positions. In this example, the top strand has 6 TCTA repeat units while the bottom strand has 6 TGAA repeat units. Under ISFG recommendations, the top strand from GenBank should be used. Thus, this example would be described as having [TCAT] as the repeat motif. Repeat numbering, indicated above and below the sequence, proceeds in the 5'-to-3' direction as illustrated by the arrows.

results cannot be effectively shared unless all parties are speaking the same language and referring to the same conditions. (It would do little good to describe the recipe for baking a cake in a language that is not understood by both the recipe giver and the chef. For example, if the recipe says to turn the oven on to 450°F and the chef uses 450 Kelvin [~250°F], the results would be vastly different.)

If one laboratory calls a sample 15 repeats at a particular STR locus and the same sample is designated 16 repeats by another laboratory, a match would not be considered, and the samples would be assumed to come from separate sources. As will be discussed in Chapter 12, the advent of national DNA databases with many laboratories contributing information to those databases has made it crucial to have internationally accepted nomenclature for designating STR alleles.

A repeat sequence is named by the structure (base composition) of the core repeat unit and the number of repeat units. However, because DNA has two strands, either of which may be used to designate the repeat unit for a particular STR marker, more than one choice is available and confusion can arise without a standard format. Also, where an individual starts counting the number of repeats can also make a difference. With double-stranded DNA sequences being read in the 5' to 3' direction, the choice of the strand impacts the sequence designation. For example, the 'top' strand for an STR marker may be 5'-...(GATA)$_n$...-3' while the 'bottom' strand for the same sequence would be 5'-...(TATC)$_n$...-3'. Depending on the sequence surrounding the repeat region, the core repeat could be shifted relative to the other strand (Figure 8.2).

Allelic ladders

An allelic ladder is an artificial mixture of the common alleles present in the human population for a particular STR marker. They are generated with

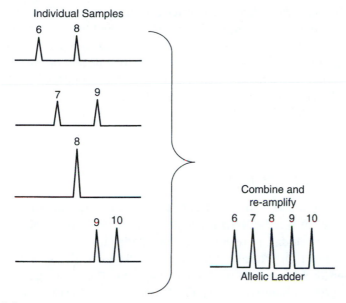

FIGURE 8.3

Principle of allelic ladder formation. STR alleles from a number of samples are analyzed and compared to one another. Samples representing the common alleles for the locus are combined and reamplified to generate an allelic ladder. Each allele in the allelic ladder is sequenced since it serves as the reference material for STR genotyping. Allelic ladders are included in commercially available STR kits.

the same primers as tested samples and thus provide a reference DNA size for each allele included in the ladder. Allelic ladders have been shown to be important for accurate genotype determinations. These allelic ladders serve as a standard like a measuring stick for each STR locus. They are necessary to adjust for different sizing measurements obtained from different instruments and conditions used by various laboratories.

Allelic ladders are constructed by combining genomic DNA or locus-specific PCR products from multiple individuals in a population, which possess alleles that are representative of the variation for the particular STR marker. The samples are then coamplified to produce an artificial sample containing the common alleles for the STR marker (Figure 8.3). Allele quantities are balanced by adjusting the input amount of each component so that the alleles are fairly equally represented in the ladder. For example, to produce a ladder containing five alleles with 6, 7, 8, 9, and 10 repeats, individual samples with genotypes of (6,8), (7,10), and (9,9) could be combined. Alternatively, the combination of genotypes could be (6,9), (7,8), and (10,10) or (6,6), (7,7), (8,8), (9,9), and (10,10).

Additional quantities of the same allelic ladder (second- and third-generation ladders) may be produced by simply diluting the original ladder 1/1000 to

1/1,000,000 parts with deionized water and then reamplifying it using the same PCR primers. It is imperative that allelic ladders be generated with the same PCR primers as those used to amplify unknown samples so that the allele 'rungs' on the ladder will accurately line up with that of the repeat number of the unknown sample when the unknown is compared to the ladder. Commercial manufacturers now provide allelic ladders in their STR typing kits so that individual laboratories do not have to produce their own allelic ladders.

CORE STR MARKERS

For DNA typing markers to be effective across a wide number of jurisdictions, a common set of standardized markers must be used. The STR loci that are commonly used today were initially characterized and developed either in the laboratory of Dr. Thomas Caskey at the Baylor College of Medicine or at the Forensic Science Service (FSS) in England. The Promega Corporation (Madison, WI) initially commercialized many of the Caskey markers, while Applied Biosystems (Foster City, CA) incorporated the FSS STR loci and also developed some new markers.

Today both Applied Biosystems and the Promega Corporation have STR kits that address the needs of the DNA typing community and cover a common set of STR loci. The availability of STR kits that permit robust multiplex amplification of eight or more STR markers has truly revolutionized forensic DNA analysis. Matching probabilities that exceed one in a billion are possible in a single amplification with 1 ng (or less) of DNA sample. Just as impressive is the fact that results can be obtained today in only a few hours compared to the weeks that restriction fragment length polymorphism (RFLP) methods took just a few years ago (see Chapter 3).

The 13 CODIS STR Loci

In the United States, utilization of STRs initially lagged behind that of Europe, especially the efforts of the Forensic Science Service in the United Kingdom. However, beginning in 1996, the FBI Laboratory sponsored a community-wide forensic science effort to establish core STR loci for inclusion within the national DNA database known as CODIS (Combined DNA Index System).

Chapter 12 covers CODIS and DNA databases in more detail. This STR project beginning in April 1996 and concluding in November 1997 involved 22 DNA typing laboratories and the evaluation of 17 candidate STR loci. The evaluated STR loci were CSF1PO, F13A01, F13B, FES/FPS, FGA, LPL, TH01, TPOX, VWA, D3S1358, D5S818, D7S820, D8S1179, D13S317, D16S539, D18S51, and D21S11.

At the STR project meeting on 13–14 November 1997, 13 core STR loci were chosen to be the basis of the future CODIS national DNA database. The 13 CODIS core loci are CSF1PO, FGA, TH01, TPOX, VWA, D3S1358, D5S818, D7S820, D8S1179, D13S317, D16S539, D18S51, and D21S11. Table 8.1 lists the original references in the literature for these 13 STRs. When all 13 CODIS core loci are tested, the average random match probability is rarer than one in a trillion among unrelated individuals. Chapter 11 provides more information on the calculation of random match probability and evaluation of the rarity of DNA profiles from the 13 CODIS STRs in various populations.

Table 8.1 Original reference describing each of the 13 CODIS STR loci and the gender identification marker amelogenin. Cooperative Human Linkage Center information is available via the Internet at http://www.chlc.org.

Locus	Reference Name
CSF1PO	Hammond, H. A., Jin, L., Zhong, Y., Caskey, C. T., & Chakraborty, R. (1994). Evaluation of 13 short tandem repeat loci for use in personal identification applications. *American Journal of Human Genetics, 55,* 175–189.
FGA	Mills, K. A., Even, D., & Murray, J. C. (1992). Tetranucleotide repeat polymorphism at the human alpha fibrinogen locus (FGA). *Human Molecular Genetics, 1,* 779.
TH01	Polymeropoulos, M. H., Xiao, H., Rath, D. S., & Merril, C. R. (1991). Tetranucleotide repeat polymorphism at the human tyrosine hydroxylase gene (TH). *Nucleic Acids Research, 19,* 3753.
TPOX	Anker, R., Steinbrueck, T., & Donis-Keller, H. (1992). Tetranucleotide repeat polymorphism at the human thyroid peroxidase (hTPO) locus. *Human Molecular Genetics, 1,* 137.
VWA	Kimpton, C. P., Walton, A., & Gill, P. (1992). A further tetranucleotide repeat polymorphism in the vWF gene. *Human Molecular Genetics, 1,* 287.
D3S1358	Li, H., Schmidt, L., Wei, M.-H., Hustad, T., Lerman, M. I., Zbar, B., & Tory, K. (1993). Three tetranucleotide polymorphisms for loci: D3S1352, D3S1358, D3S1359. *Human Molecular Genetics, 2,* 1327.
D5S818	Cooperative Human Linkage Center GATA3F03.512.
D7S820	Cooperative Human Linkage Center GATA3F01.511.
D8S1179	Cooperative Human Linkage Center GATA7G07.37564.
D13S317	Cooperative Human Linkage Center GATA7G10.415.
D16S539	Cooperative Human Linkage Center GATA11C06.715.
D18S51	Staub, R. E., Speer, M. C., Luo, Y., Rojas, K., Overhauser, J., Otto, L., & Gilliam, T. C. (1993). A microsatellite genetic linkage map of human chromosome 18. *Genomics, 15,* 48–56.
D21S11	Sharma, V., & Litt, M. (1992). Tetranucleotide repeat polymorphism at the D21S11 locus. *Human Molecular Genetics, 1,* 67.
Amelogenin	Sullivan, K. M., Mannucci, A., Kimpton, C. P., & Gill, P. (1993). A rapid and quantitative DNA sex test: fluorescence-based PCR analysis of X-Y homologous gene amelogenin. *BioTechniques, 15,* 637–641.

Table 8.2 Information on commonly used autosomal STR loci. The 13 CODIS core loci are highlighted in bold font.

Locus (UniSTS)[a]	Chromosomal Location	Physical Position (May 2004; NCBI Build 35)	GenBank Accession (Allele Repeat No.)	Category and Repeat Motif	Allele Range
TPOX (240638)	2p25.3 thyroid peroxidase, 10th intron	Chr 2 1.472 Mb	M68651 (11)	Simple GAAT	4–16
D2S1338 (30509)	2q35	Chr 2 218.705 Mb	AC010136 (20)	Compound TGCC/TTCC	15–28
D3S1358 (148226)	3p21.31	Chr 3 45.557 Mb	AC099539 (16)	Compound TCTG/TCTA	8–21
FGA (240635)	4q31.3 alpha fibrinogen, 3rd intron	Chr 4 155.866 Mb	M64982 (21)	Compound CTTT/TTCC	12.2–51.2
D5S818 (54700)	5q23.2	Chr 5 123.139 Mb	AC008512 (11)	Simple AGAT	7–18
CSF1PO (156169)	5q33.1 c-fms proto-oncogene, 6th intron	Chr 5 149.436 Mb	X14720 (12)	Simple TAGA	5–16
SE33 (ACTBP2) (none reported)	6q14 beta-actin-related pseudogene	Chr 6 89.043 Mb	V00481 (26.2)	Complex AAAG	4.2–37
D7S820 (74895)	7q21.11	Chr 7 83.433 Mb	AC004848 (13)	Simple GATA	5–16
D8S1179 (83408)	8q24.13	Chr 8 125.976 Mb	AF216671 (13)	Compound TCTA/TCTG	7–20
TH01 (240639)	11p15.5 tyrosine hydroxylase, 1st intron	Chr 11 2.149 Mb	D00269 (9)	Simple TCAT	3–14
VWA (240640)	12p13.31 von Willebrand factor, 40th intron	Chr 12 5.963 Mb	M25858 (18)	Compound TCTG/TCTA	10–25
D13S317 (7734)	13q31.1	Chr 13 81.620 Mb	AL353628 (11)	Simple TATC	5–16
Penta E (none reported)	15q26.2	Chr 15 95.175 Mb	AC027004 (5)	Simple AAAGA	5–24
D16S539 (45590)	16q24.1	Chr. 16 84.944 Mb	AC024591 (11)	simple GATA	5–16

(Continued)

Table 8.2 (Continued)

Locus (UniSTS)[a]	Chromosomal Location	Physical Position (May 2004; NCBI Build 35)	GenBank Accession (Allele Repeat No.)	Category and Repeat Motif	Allele Range
D18S51 (44409)	18q21.33	Chr 18 59.100 Mb	AP001534 (18)	Simple AGAA	7–40
D19S433 (33588)	19q12	Chr 19 35.109 Mb	AC008507 (16)	Compound AAGG/TAGG	9–17.2
D21S11 (240642)	21q21.1	Chr 21 19.476 Mb	AP000433 (29)	Complex TCTA/ TCTG	12–41.2
Penta D (none reported)	21q22.3	Chr 21 43.880 Mb	AP001752 (13)	Simple AAAGA	2.2–17

Adapted from Butler, J. M. (2006). Genetics and genomics of core short tandem repeat loci used in human identity testing. Journal of Forensic Sciences, 51, 253–265.
[a]*UniSTS is a comprehensive database of sequence tagged sites (STSs) available on the NCBI Web site: http://www.ncbi.nlm.nih. gov/entrez/query.fcgi?db=unists*

The three most polymorphic markers are FGA, D18S51, and D21S11, while TPOX shows the least variation between individuals. A summary of information on the 13 STRs is contained in Table 8.2, which describes the chromosomal location and physical location on the human genome reference sequence, the repeat motif, allele range, and GenBank accession number where the DNA sequence for a reference allele may be found. The chromosomal locations for these STRs have been updated on the completed human genome reference sequence.

Using the previously described classification scheme for categorizing STR repeat motifs, the 13 CODIS core STR loci can be divided up into four categories:

1. simple repeats consisting of one repeating sequence: TPOX, CSF1PO, D5S818, D13S317, D16S539;

2. simple repeats with nonconsensus alleles (e.g., 9.3): TH01, D18S51, D7S820;

3. compound repeats with nonconsensus alleles: VWA, FGA, D3S1358, D8S1179; and

4. complex repeats: D21S11.

European forensic DNA laboratories utilize many of the same STR loci as used in the United States. In 2006, several new European STR loci were recommended for inclusion in future STR typing kits. These include D2S441, D10S1248, D22S1045, D1S1656, and D12S391.

COMMERCIALLY AVAILABLE STR KITS

A number of kits are available for single or multiplex PCR amplification of STR markers used in DNA typing. Two primary vendors for STR kits used by the forensic DNA community exist: the Promega Corporation and Applied Biosystems. These companies have expended a great deal of effort during the past decade or so to bring STR markers to forensic scientists in kit form. More recently in Europe, companies such as Serac (Bad Homburg, Germany) and Biotype (Dresden, Germany) have begun offering commercial STR kits, but due to patent and licensing issues some of these kits have limited distribution.

The technology evolved quickly in the late 1990s for more sensitive, rapid, and accurate measurements of STR alleles. At the same time, the number of STRs that can be simultaneously amplified has increased from three or four with silver-stained systems to over 15 STRs using multiple-color fluorescent tags. The commercially available STR multiplexes from Promega and Applied Biosystems are listed in Table 8.3.

The adoption of the 13 core loci for CODIS in the United States has led to development of STR multiplexes that cover these markers. At the turn of the century, two PCR reactions were required to obtain information from all of the 13 STRs: either PowerPlex 1.1 and PowerPlex 2.1 or Profiler Plus and COfiler. As an internal check to reduce the possibility of mixing up samples, both manufacturers included overlapping loci in their kits that should produce concordant data between samples amplified from the same biological material. The Profiler Plus and COfiler kits have the loci D3S1358 and D7S820 (and the sex-typing marker amelogenin) in common while the PowerPlex 1.1 and PowerPlex 2.1 have the loci TH01, TPOX, and VWA in common.

Since 2000, both Promega and Applied Biosystems have marketed multiplex PCR reactions that permit coamplification of all 13 STRs in a single reaction along with the amelogenin sex-typing marker and two additional STR loci (Figure 8.4). Figure 8.5 displays electropherograms with size-separated PCR products for Promega's PowerPlex 16 kit as color-separated panels of loci or as an overlay of all colors. The allelic ladders for the Applied Biosystems' AmpFlSTR Identifiler kits are displayed in Figure 8.6.

When they were first developed, some of the PowerPlex kits were created to work with the Hitachi FMBIO scanner (see D.N.A. Box 9.2). However, today STR kits are developed with capillary electrophoresis instruments in mind for detection.

Commercial manufacturers of STR kits have spent a great deal of research effort defining which markers would be included in each kit as well as verifying if primer pairs are compatible and work well in combination with each

Table 8.3 Summary of available commercial STR kits that are commonly used.

Kit Name	STR Loci Included	Random Match Probability with Author's Profile[a]
Promega Corporation		
PowerPlex 1.1 and 1.2	CSF1PO, TPOX, TH01, VWA, D16S539, D13S317, D7S820, D5S818	7.4×10^{-10}
PowerPlex 2.1 (for Hitachi FMBIO users)	D3S1358, TH01, D21S11, D18S51, VWA, D8S1179, TPOX, FGA, Penta E	3.4×10^{-11}
PowerPlex ES	FGA, TH01, VWA, D3S1358, D8S1179, D18S51, D21S11, SE33, amelogenin	1.3×10^{-10}
PowerPlex 16	CSF1PO, FGA, TPOX, TH01, VWA, D3S1358, D5S818, D7S820, D8S1179, D13S317, D16S539, D18S51, D21S11, Penta D, Penta E, amelogenin	1.2×10^{-18}
PowerPlex 16 BIO (for Hitachi FMBIO users)	CSF1PO, FGA, TPOX, TH01, VWA, D3S1358, D5S818, D7S820, D8S1179, D13S317, D16S539, D18S51, D21S11, Penta D, Penta E, amelogenin	1.2×10^{-18}
PowerPlex S5	FGA, TH01, D18S51, D8S1179, amelogenin	1.0×10^{-5}
Applied Biosystems		
AmpF*l*STR Blue	D3S1358, VWA, FGA	1.0×10^{-3}
AmpF*l*STR Green I	Amelogenin, TH01, TPOX, CSF1PO	7.8×10^{-4}
AmpF*l*STR COfiler	D3S1358, D16S539, amelogenin, TH01, TPOX, CSF1PO, D7S820	2.0×10^{-7}
AmpF*l*STR Profiler Plus	D3S1358, VWA, FGA, amelogenin, D8S1179, D21S11, D18S51, D5S818, D13S317, D7S820	2.4×10^{-11}
AmpF*l*STR Profiler Plus ID[b]	D3S1358, VWA, FGA, amelogenin, D8S1179, D21S11, D18S51, D5S818, D13S317, D7S820	2.4×10^{-11}
AmpF*l*STR Profiler	D3S1358, VWA, FGA, amelogenin, TH01, TPOX, CSF1PO, D5S818, D13S317, D7S820	9.0×10^{-11}
AmpF*l*STR SGM Plus	D3S1358, VWA, D16S539, D2S1338, amelogenin, D8S1179, D21S11, D18S51, D19S433, TH01, FGA	4.5×10^{-13}
AmpF*l*STR SEfiler	FGA, TH01, VWA, D3S1358, D8S1179, D16S539, D18S51, D21S11, D2S1338, D19S433, SE33, amelogenin	5.1×10^{-15}
AmpF*l*STR Identifiler	CSF1PO, FGA, TPOX, TH01, VWA, D3S1358, D5S818, D7S820, D8S1179, D13S317, D16S539, D18S51, D21S11, D2S1338, D19S433, amelogenin	7.2×10^{-19}
AmpF*l*STR MiniFiler	CSF1PO, FGA, D7S820, D16S539, D13S317, D18S51, D21S11, D2S1338, amelogenin	1.1×10^{-11}

Adapted from Butler, J. M. (2006). Genetics and genomics of core short tandem repeat loci used in human identity testing. Journal of Forensic Sciences, 51, 253–265.
[a]*Allele frequencies used for random match probability calculations (to unrelated individuals) from U.S. Caucasian population data associated with Butler et al. (2003), Reid et al. (2003), and Levadokou et al. (2001). Subpopulation structure adjustments (theta corrections) were not made with these calculations (i.e., only p^2 and $2pq$ were used).*
[b]*Profiler Plus ID includes an additional D8S1179 reverse primer to permit amplification when a primer binding site mutation occurs.*

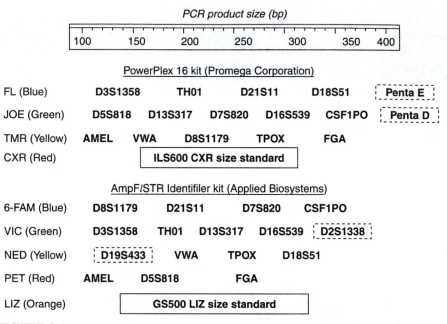

FIGURE 8.4

Commercially available STR kit solutions for a single amplification of the 13 CODIS core loci. General size ranges and dye-labeling strategies are indicated. The PowerPlex 16 kit uses four dyes while the Identifiler kit uses five dyes. Loci located within dashed boxes are additional loci specific to each kit.

other during multiplex PCR conditions. Promega has published and patented its PCR primer sequences whereas Applied Biosystems has kept its primer sequences proprietary although some information has been revealed regarding the use of degenerate primers (see D.N.A. Box 10.3). The issue over failure to disclose kit primer sequences impacted several court cases early on in the legal acceptance of STR technology but appears to have been resolved now (D.N.A. Box 8.2).

Most laboratories do not have the time or resources to design primers, optimize PCR multiplexes, and quality control primer synthesis. The convenience of using ready-made kits is augmented by the fact that widely used primer sets and conditions allow improved opportunities for sharing data between laboratories without fear of possible null alleles (see D.N.A. Box 10.3). Available STR multiplex sets vary based on which STR loci are included, the fluorescent dye combinations, the DNA strand that is labeled, allelic ladders present in kits, and, most importantly, the primer sequences utilized for PCR amplification. It is important to keep in mind that commercially available kits quickly dictate which STRs will be used by the vast majority of forensic laboratories.

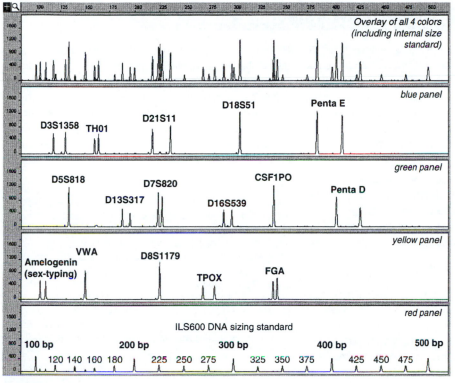

FIGURE 8.5

PowerPlex 16 result from 1 ng genomic DNA.

Commercial allelic ladders

Each manufacturer of STR kits provides allelic ladders that may be used for accurate genotyping. Kits from the Promega Corporation and Applied Biosystems for comparable STR markers often contain different alleles in their allelic ladders. For example, the PowerPlex 1.1 kit from Promega contains alleles 7 to 15 in its D5S818 allelic ladder, while the Profiler Plus kit from Applied Biosystems contains alleles 7 to 16 in its D5S818 allelic ladder. By having an allele present in the ladder, a laboratory can be more confident of a call from an unknown sample that is being analyzed.

In the D5S818 example listed here, one would be more confident typing an observed allele 16 when using the Applied Biosystems kit than the Promega kit because the D5S818 allelic ladder has an allele 16 in the ABI kit. Some of the more recent kits come with an amazing number of alleles in their ladders. For example, the Identifiler kit from Applied Biosystems contains 205 alleles (Figure 8.6). The Promega PowerPlex 16 kit has 209 alleles in its allelic ladders. Putting together and mass producing such a large set of alleles is an impressive feat.

D.N.A. Box 8.2 Disclosure of STR Kit Primer Sequences

During the early adoption of STR typing technology in U.S. court systems, three cases ruled that DNA results would not be permissible as evidence because the commercial STR kit PCR primer sequences and developmental validation studies were not public information. These cases were *People v. Bokin* (San Francisco, California, May 1999), *People v. Shreck* (Boulder, Colorado, April 2000), and *State v. Pfenning* (Grand Isle, Vermont, April 2000).

Shortly after the Pfenning case, the Promega Corporation made the decision to publish their STR kit primer sequences (see news in *Nature*, 27 July 2000 issue, Vol. 406, p. 336) and have done so since (Masibay et al., 2001; Krenke et al., 2002), along with obtaining several patents in the area of multiplex amplification of STR loci.

Applied Biosystems has repeatedly refused to release the primer sequences present in their STR kits claiming that this information is proprietary. The company is concerned that they would lose revenue if generic brand products were produced by other entities using the revealed primer information. However, in at least 16 cases, the primer sequences for the ProfilerPlus and COfiler kits have been supplied by Applied Biosystems under a protective court order.

Numerous publications since 2000 have demonstrated the reliable use of Applied Biosystems STR kits including detailed validation studies (see Holt et al., 2002). The arguments that not enough information exists to support the reliable use of commercial STR kits whose every component is not public knowledge have fallen by the wayside as millions of DNA profiles have been reliably generated with these kits in the past few years.

Sources:

Holt, C. L., et al. (2002). TWGDAM validation of AmpF*l*STR PCR amplification kits for forensic DNA casework. *Journal of Forensic Sciences, 47*, 66–96.

http://www.scientific.org/archive/archive.html

http://www.denverda.org/html_website/denver_da/DNA_resources.html

http://www.denverda.org/legalResource/ABSequencecaselist.pdf

Krenke, B. E., et al. (2002). Validation of a 16-locus fluorescent multiplex system. *Journal of Forensic Sciences, 47*, 773–785.

Masibay, A., et al. (2000). Promega Corporation reveals primer sequences in its testing kits [letter]. *Journal of Forensic Sciences, 45*, 1360–1362.

AmpF*l*STR Identifiler kit innovations

Applied Biosystems introduced two new technologies with their AmpF*l*STR Identifiler kit when it was released in 2001. The first, and most obvious, involves the use of five-dye detection systems where four different dyes (6FAM, VIC, NED, and PET) are used to label the PCR products rather than the traditional three dyes (5FAM, JOE, NED or FL, JOE, TMR) used with the previous AmpF*l*STR or PowerPlex kits. As described in Chapter 10, a single dye detection channel is always used for an internal size standard to correlate electrophoretic mobilities to an apparent PCR product size. Thus, the fifth dye (LIZ) in five-dye detection and the fourth dye (ROX or CXR) in four-dye detection are used for labeling the internal size standard. The extra dye channel for labeling PCR products enables smaller PCR products to be generated and placed in a separate dye channel rather than extending the size range for amplicons (see Figure 8.4).

The second technology introduced with the Identifiler kit involves mobility-modifying nonnucleotide linkers. The mobility modifier is composed of hexaethyleneoxide (HEO) that imparts a shift of approximately 2.5 nucleotides with each additional HEO unit. This nonnucleotide linker is synthesized

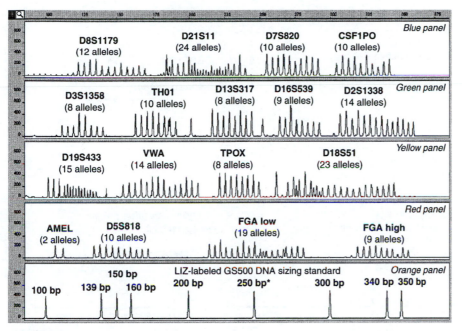

FIGURE 8.6

AmpFISTR Identifiler allelic ladders (Applied Biosystems). A total of 205 alleles are included in this set of allelic ladders used for genotyping a multiplex PCR reaction involving 15 STR loci and the amelogenin sex-typing test.

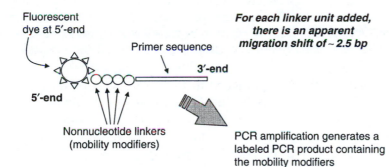

FIGURE 8.7

Illustration of mobility modifiers used in Applied Biosystems' Identifiler STR kit. Nonnucleotide linkers are synthesized into the primer between the fluorescent dye and 5' end of the primer sequence. During PCR amplification, the dye and linker are incorporated into the amplicon. With the added nonnucleotide linker, the mobility of the generated STR allele will be shifted to a larger apparent size during electrophoresis. This shift of STR alleles for a particular locus then enables optimal interlocus spacing for STR loci labeled with the same fluorescent dye without having to alter the PCR primer binding positions (see Figure 8.8).

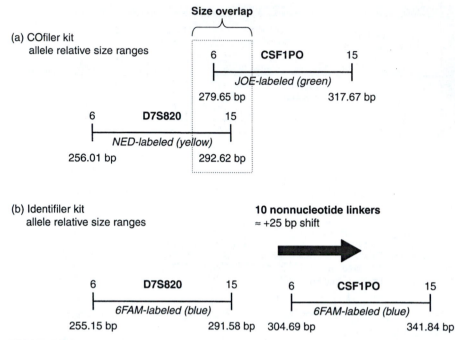

FIGURE 8.8

Illustration of how nonnucleotide linkers attached to CSF1PO PCR products in the Identifiler STR kit help with interlocus spacing between D7S820 and CSF1PO. (a) In the COfiler kit, CSF1PO and D7S820 are labeled with different colored fluorescent labels and thus do not interfere with one another. However, (b) in the Identifiler kit, both D7S820 and CSF1PO are labeled with the same dye and would therefore have overlapping STR alleles unless primer positions were changed or mobility modifiers were used. An ≈25-bp shift of the CSF1PO PCR products is accomplished by the addition of 10 nonnucleotide linkers. PCR product sizes for allelic ladder ranges displayed here are from the COfiler and Identifiler kit user's manuals. Note that sizes for D7S820 alleles do not match exactly because different dye labels are used with both the PCR products and the internal size standard, thus impacting their relative mobilities.

into the 5′ end of the PCR primer so that when the PCR product is created it contains these extra molecules on one end (Figure 8.7). By incorporating nonnucleotide linkers, mobilities for amplified alleles from one member of a pair of closely spaced STR loci can be shifted relative to the other. Thus, overlapping size ranges can be prevented (Figure 8.8).

The primary reason for introducing mobility modifiers is to permit continued use of the same PCR primers for amplifying STR loci and still have optimal interlocus spacing within the various color channels. For example, if the loci D7S820 and CSF1PO, which are labeled with two different fluorophores in the COfiler kit and therefore do not interfere with one another, were labeled with the same colored fluorescent label (e.g., 6FAM) as they are in the Identifiler STR kit, the allelic ladder products would have overlapped by ~13 bp (see Figure 8.8). To prevent this overlap in allele size ranges, either

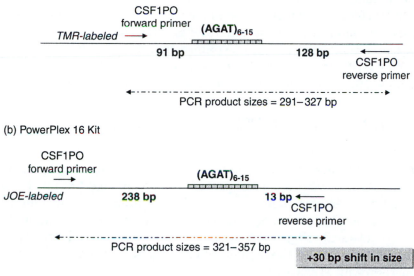

(a) PowerPlex 1.1 Kit

CSF1PO
forward primer   (AGAT)$_{6-15}$
TMR-labeled ⟶

91 bp   **128 bp**
                                    CSF1PO
                                    reverse primer

PCR product sizes = 291–327 bp

(b) PowerPlex 16 Kit

CSF1PO
forward primer
⟶
                        (AGAT)$_{6-15}$
JOE-labeled   **238 bp**   **13 bp** ⟵
                                    CSF1PO
                                    reverse primer

PCR product sizes = 321–357 bp
                                    +30 bp shift in size

FIGURE 8.9

Variation in CSF1PO primer positions between (a) PowerPlex 1.1 and (b) PowerPlex 16 STR kits. The base pair (bp) numbers in bold indicate the distance between the repeat region and 3' end of the pertinent primer. The overall PCR product size for CSF1PO is shifted +30 bp with the primer changes from Power-Plex 1.1 to PowerPlex 16. Note that the primer lengths, which contribute to the overall PCR product size, are not included.

PCR primer binding sites must be altered to change the overall size of the PCR product or mobility modifiers can be introduced to shift the apparent relative molecular mass of the larger PCR product to an even larger size. In the case of the Identifiler kit, the locus CSF1PO was shifted by approximately 25 bp—through the addition of 10 HEO nonnucleotide linkers to the 5' end of the labeled PCR primer. Nonnucleotide linkers are also present on four other loci in the Identifiler kit: D2S1338, D13S317, D16S539, and TPOX.

Promega has changed primer sequences for a few of the loci between PowerPlex versions. For example, between the PowerPlex 1.1 and PowerPlex 16 kits, the CSF1PO primer positions were drastically altered in order to achieve a 30-bp shift in PCR product size between the two kits (Figure 8.9). This primer change and subsequent PCR product shift were instituted so that CSF1PO and D16S539 loci could be labeled with the same dye in the PowerPlex 16 kit. Note that if the original CSF1PO primers had been kept, there would have been a 13-bp overlap between D16S539 allele 15 (304 bp) and CSF1PO allele 6 (291 bp), making these systems incompatible in the same dye color without altering the PCR product size (i.e., primer positions) for one of them.

Different primer positions have the potential to lead to allele dropout if a primer binding site mutation impacts one of the primer pairs (see D.N.A. Box 10.3). Hence concordance studies are needed between various STR kits to assess the level of potential allele dropout. On the other hand, Applied Biosystems has maintained the same primers over time and through their various AmpF*l*STR kits by introducing five-dye chemistry and mobility modifiers for products that would normally overlap with one another (see Figure 8.8).

GENDER IDENTIFICATION WITH AMELOGENIN

The ability to designate whether a sample originated from a male or a female source is useful in many sexual assault cases, where distinguishing between the victim and the perpetrator's evidence is important. Likewise, missing persons and mass disaster investigations can benefit from gender identification of the remains. Over the years a number of gender identification assays have been demonstrated using PCR methods. By far the most popular method for sex typing today is the amelogenin system because it can be performed in conjunction with STR analysis.

Amelogenin is a gene that codes for proteins found in tooth enamel. The British Forensic Science Service was the first to describe the particular PCR primer sets that are used so prevalently in forensic DNA laboratories today. These primers flank a 6-bp deletion within intron 1 of the amelogenin gene on the X homologue (Figure 8.10). PCR amplification of this area with their primers results in 106- and 112-bp amplicons from the X and Y chromosomes, respectively. Primers that yield a 212-bp X-specific amplicon and a 218-bp Y-specific product by bracketing the same 6-bp deletion were also described in the original amelogenin paper and have been used in conjunction with the D1S80 VNTR system.

An advantage with the above approach, that is, using a single primer set to amplify both chromosomes, is that the X-chromosome product itself plays a role as a positive control. This PCR-based assay is extremely sensitive. Mannucci and coworkers were able to detect as little as 20 pg (~3 diploid copies) as well as sample mixtures where female DNA was in 100-fold excess of male DNA.

Other regions of the amelogenin gene have size differences between the X and Y homologues and may be exploited for sex-typing purposes. For example, Eng and coworkers (1994) used a single set of primers that generated a 977-bp product for the X chromosome and a 788-bp fragment for the Y chromosome. In this case, a 189-bp deletion in the Y relative to the X chromosome was used to differentiate the two chromosomes.

A careful study found that 19 regions of absolute homology, ranging in size from 22 to 80 bp, exist between the human amelogenin X and Y genes that

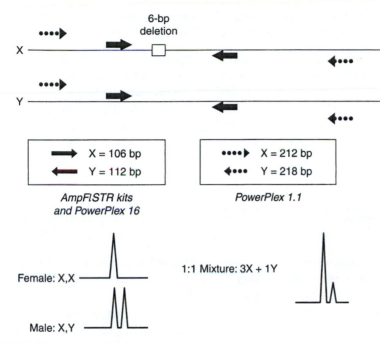

FIGURE 8.10

Schematic of the amelogenin sex-typing assay. The X and Y chromosomes contain a high degree of sequence homology at the amelogenin locus. The primer sets depicted here target a 6-bp deletion that is present only on the X chromosome. The presence of a single peak indicates that the sample comes from a female while two peaks identify the sample's source as male. The primers to amplify the 106/112-bp fragments are used in the AmpFlSTR kits and PowerPlex 16 kit while the PowerPlex 1.1 kit uses the larger primer set.

can be used to design a variety of primer sets. Thus, by spanning various deletions of the X and/or Y chromosome, it is possible to generate PCR products from the X and Y homologues that differ in size and contain size ranges that can be integrated into future multiplex STR amplifications.

Anomalous amelogenin results

While amelogenin is an effective method for sex-typing biological samples in most cases, the results are not foolproof. A rare deletion of the amelogenin gene on the Y chromosome can cause the Y-chromosome amplicon to be absent. In such a case, a male sample would falsely appear as female. It appears that this deletion of the Y-chromosome amelogenin region is more common in Indian populations than those of European or African origin. A study of almost 30,000 males in the Austrian national DNA database revealed that only six individuals lacked the amelogenin Y-amplicon. These individuals were verified to be male by testing Y-STRs and through amplification of the SRY region. More information on anomalous amelogenin results may be found on STRBase: http://www.cstl.nist.gov/biotech/strbase/Amelogenin.htm.

Amelogenin X allele dropout has also been observed in males. In this case only the amelogenin Y-amplicon is present. This phenomenon was observed only three times out of almost 7000 males examined and likely results from a rare polymorphism in the primer binding sites for the amelogenin primers used in commercial STR kits. A different set of amelogenin primers targeting the same 6-bp deletion on the X chromosome amplified both the X and Y alleles of amelogenin.

STRBASE: A HELPFUL SOURCE OF INFORMATION ON STRS

The rapid growth of the human identification applications for STR loci ensures that static written materials, such as this book, will quickly become out of date. New alleles are constantly being discovered (including 'off-ladder' microvariant alleles), additional STR markers are being developed, and population data increases with each month of published journals. Indeed, a growing list of publications describing the application of STR loci to forensic DNA typing has exceeded 3000 references.

The growth of the Internet now permits dynamic sources of information to be widely available. Several years ago a Web site was created to enable forensic scientists to keep abreast with the rapidly evolving field of DNA typing. In anticipation of the impact of STR markers on DNA typing and the need for a common source of information that could evolve as the process improved, an Internet-accessible informational database was created in early 1997. STRBase was officially launched in July 1997 and is maintained by the Applied Genetics Group of the U.S. National Institute of Standards and Technology. STRBase can be reached via the following URL: http://www.cstl.nist.gov/biotech/strbase. A portion of the home page for STRBase is shown in Figure 8.11.

STRBase contains a number of useful elements. Continually updated information includes the listing of references related to STRs and DNA typing (over 3000 references), addresses for scientists working in the field, microvariant or 'off-ladder' STR alleles, triallelic patterns, and numerous PowerPoint files and articles to aid understanding of STR typing. Other information that is updated less frequently includes STR fact sheets, links to other Web pages, a review of technology used for DNA typing as well as published primer sequence information, and population data for STR markers.

STR markers have become important tools for human identity testing. Commercially available STR kits are now widely used in forensic and paternity

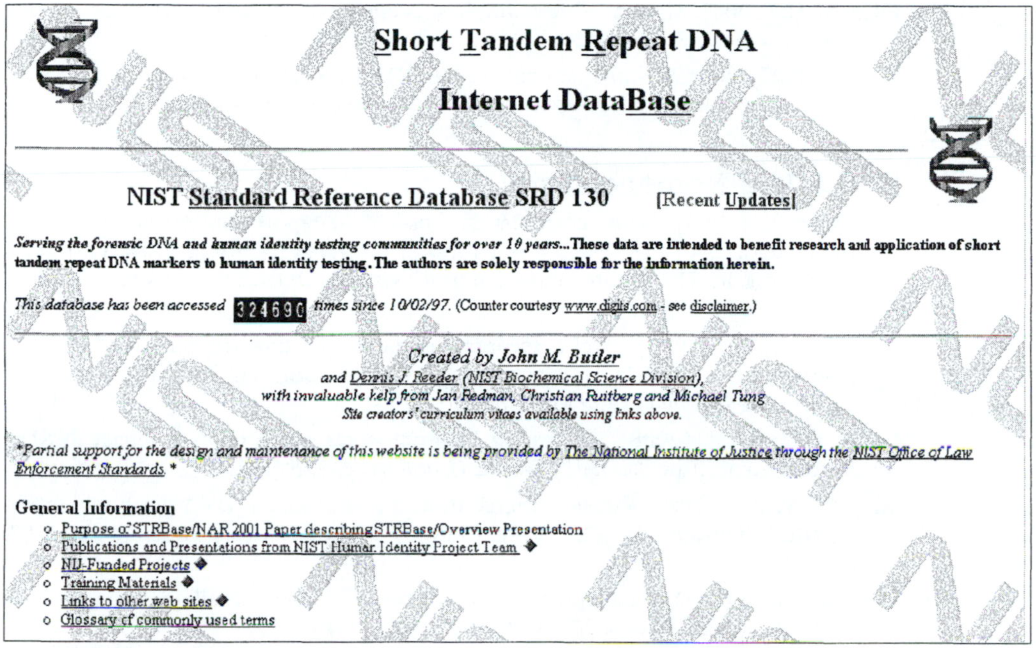

FIGURE 8.11

Home page for STRBase, an Internet-accessible database of information on STR markers used in forensic DNA typing. STRBase may be accessed via the URL http://www.cstl.nist.gov/biotech/strbase and contains, among other things, a comprehensive listing of all papers relating to STR typing for human identity testing purposes, now numbering over 3000 references.

testing laboratories. The adoption of the 13 CODIS core loci for the U.S. and other national DNA databases ensures that these STR markers will be used for many years to come.

Points for Discussion

- What are some benefits of standardizing the DNA tests used in the forensic community to a common set of STR markers?

- How do allelic ladders enable reliable STR typing?

- What are some advantages and disadvantages to using commercial STR typing kits?

READING LIST AND INTERNET RESOURCES

General Information

Butler, J. M. (2007). Short tandem repeat typing technologies used in human identity testing. *BioTechniques, 43*(4), Sii–Sv.

Ellegren, H. (2004). Microsatellites: Simple sequences with complex evolution. *Nature Reviews Genetics, 5,* 435–445.

Gill, P. (2002). Role of short tandem repeat DNA in forensic casework in the UK—Past, present, and future perspectives. *BioTechniques, 32,* 366–372.

STR Allele Nomenclature

Bär, W., et al. (1994). DNA recommendations—1994 report concerning further recommendations of the DNA Commission of the ISFH regarding PCR-based polymorphisms in STR (short tandem repeat) systems. *International Journal of Legal Medicine, 107,* 159–160.

Bär, W., et al. (1997). DNA recommendations—Further report of the DNA Commission of the ISFH regarding the use of short tandem repeat systems. *International Journal of Legal Medicine, 110,* 175–176.

Butler, J. M., et al. (2008). Addressing Y-chromosome short tandem repeat (Y-STR) allele nomenclature. *Journal of Genetic Genealogy, 4,* 125–148.

Gill, P., et al. (1997). Considerations from the European DNA profiling group (EDNAP) concerning STR nomenclature. *Forensic Science International, 87,* 185–192.

Gill, P., et al. (1997). Development of guidelines to designate alleles using an STR multiplex system. *Forensic Science International, 89,* 185–197.

Tautz, D. (1993). Notes on definitions and nomenclature of tandemly repetitive DNA sequences. In D. J. Pena, et al. (Eds.), *DNA fingerprinting: State of the science* (pp. 21–28). Basel: Birkhauser Verlag.

Allelic Ladders

Baechtel, F. S., et al. (1993). Multigenerational amplification of a reference ladder for alleles at locus D1S80. *Journal of Forensic Sciences, 38,* 1176–1182.

Griffiths, R. A., et al. (1998). New reference allelic ladders to improve allelic designation in a multiplex STR system. *International Journal of Legal Medicine, 111,* 267–272.

Kline, M. C., et al. (1997). Interlaboratory evaluation of short tandem repeat triplex CTT. *Journal of Forensic Sciences, 42,* 897–906.

Puers, C., et al. (1993). Identification of repeat sequence heterogeneity at the polymorphic short tandem repeat locus HUMTH01 [AATG]n and reassignment of alleles in population analysis by using a locus-specific allelic ladder. *American Journal of Human Genetics, 53,* 953–958.

Sajantila, A., et al. (1992). Amplification of reproducible allele markers for amplified fragment length polymorphism analysis. *Biotechniques, 12,* 16–22.

Smith, R. N. (1995). Accurate size comparison of short tandem repeat alleles amplified by PCR. *Biotechniques, 18,* 122–128.

Forensic STR Markers

Budowle, B., et al. (1998). CODIS and PCR-based short tandem repeat loci: Law enforcement tools. In: *Proceedings of the second european symposium on human identification* (pp. 73–88). Madison, WI: Promega Corporation. Available at http://www.promega.com/geneticidproc/eusymp2proc/17.pdf

Butler, J. M. (2006). Genetics and genomics of core short tandem repeat loci used in human identity testing. *Journal of Forensic Sciences, 51*, 253–265.

Carracedo, A., & Lareu, M. V. (1998). Development of new STRs for forensic casework: Criteria for selection, sequencing and population data and forensic validation. In: *Proceedings of the ninth international symposium on human identification* (pp. 89–107). Madison, WI: Promega Corporation. Available at http://www.promega.com/geneticidproc

Chakraborty, R., et al. (1999). The utility of short tandem repeat loci beyond human identification: Implications for development of new DNA typing systems. *Electrophoresis, 20*, 1682–1696.

Edwards, A., et al. (1991). DNA typing and genetic mapping with trimeric and tetrameric tandem repeats. *American Journal of Human Genetics, 49*, 746–756.

Gill, P., et al. (1996). A new method of STR interpretation using inferential logic—Development of a criminal intelligence database. *International Journal of Legal Medicine, 109*, 14–22.

Gill, P., et al. (2006). The evolution of DNA databases—Recommendations for new European STR loci. *Forensic Science International, 156*, 242–244.

Gill, P., et al. (2006). New multiplexes for Europe—Amendments and clarification of strategic development. *Forensic Science International, 163*, 155–157.

Kimpton, C. P., et al. (1993). Automated DNA profiling employing multiplex amplification of short tandem repeat loci. *PCR Methods and Application, 3*, 13–22.

Kimpton, C. P., et al. (1996). Validation of highly discriminating multiplex short tandem repeat amplification systems for individual identification. *Electrophoresis, 17*, 1283–1293.

Urquhart, A., et al. (1994). Variation in short tandem repeat sequences—A survey of twelve microsatellite loci for use as forensic identification markers. *International Journal of Legal Medicine, 107*, 13–20.

Population Data

Butler, J. M., et al. (2003). Allele frequencies for 15 autosomal STR loci on U.S. Caucasian, African American, and Hispanic populations. *Journal of Forensic Sciences, 48*, 908–911.

Reid, T. M., et al. (2003). Distribution of HUMACTBP2 (SE33) alleles in three North American populations. *Journal of Forensic Sciences, 48*, 1422–1423.

Levadokou, E. N., et al. (2001). Allele frequencies for fourteen STR loci of the PowerPlex 1.1 and 2.1 multiplex systems and Penta D locus in Caucasians, African-Americans, Hispanics, and other populations of the United States of America and Brazil. *Journal of Forensic Sciences, 46*, 736–761.

Commercial STR Kits

Buse, E. L., et al. (2003). Performance evaluation of two multiplexes used in fluorescent short tandem repeat DNA analysis. *Journal of Forensic Sciences, 48*, 348–357.

Butler, J. M., et al. (2001). Comparison of primer sequences used in commercial STR kits. Presented at *Proceedings of the 53th American Academy of Forensic Sciences,*

Seattle, WA. Available at http://www.cstl.nist.gov/biotech/strbase/pub_pres/AAFS_Feb2001.pdf

Collins, P. J., et al. (2004). Developmental validation of a single-tube amplification of the 13 CODIS STR loci, D2S1338, D19S433, and amelogenin: The AmpF*l*STR Identifiler PCR Amplification Kit. *Journal of Forensic Sciences, 49*, 1265–1277.

Holt, C. L., et al. (2002). TWGDAM validation of AmpF*l*STR PCR amplification kits for forensic DNA casework. *Journal of Forensic Sciences, 47*, 66–96.

Krenke, B. E., et al. (2002). Validation of a 16-locus fluorescent multiplex system. *Journal of Forensic Sciences, 47*, 773–785.

LaFountain, M. J., et al. (2001). TWGDAM validation of the AmpF*l*STR Profiler Plus and AmpF*l*STR COfiler STR multiplex systems using capillary electrophoresis. *Journal of Forensic Sciences, 46*, 1191–1198.

Leibelt, C., et al. (2003). Identification of a D8S1179 primer binding site mutation and the validation of a primer designed to recover null alleles. *Forensic Science International, 133*, 220–227.

Masibay, A., et al. (2000). Promega Corporation reveals primer sequences in its testing kits [letter]. *Journal of Forensic Sciences, 45*, 1360–1362.

Wallin, J. M., et al. (2002). Constructing universal multiplex PCR systems for comparative genotyping. *Journal of Forensic Sciences, 47*, 52–65.

Mobility Modifiers

Applied Biosystems. (2001). AmpF*l*STR identifiler PCR amplification kit user's manual.

Grossman, P. D., et al. (1994). High-density multiplex detection of nucleic acid sequences: Oligonucleotide ligation assay and sequence-coded separation. *Nucleic Acids Research, 22*, 4527–4534.

Gender Identification with Amelogenin

Eng, B., et al. (1994). Anomalous migration of PCR products using nondenaturing polyacrylamide gel electrophoresis: The amelogenin sex-typing system. *Journal of Forensic Sciences, 39*, 1356–1359.

Haas-Rochholz, H., & Weiler, G. (1997). Additional primer sets for an amelogenin gene PCR-based DNA-sex test. *International Journal of Legal Medicine, 110*, 312–315.

Mannucci, A., et al. (1994). Forensic application of a rapid and quantitative DNA sex test by amplification of the X-Y homologous gene amelogenin. *International Journal of Legal Medicine, 106*, 190–193.

Sullivan, K. M., et al. (1993). A rapid and quantitative DNA sex test: Fluorescence-based PCR analysis of X-Y homologous gene amelogenin. *BioTechniques, 15*, 637–641.

Amelogenin Anomalies

Cadenas, A. M., et al. (2007). Male amelogenin dropouts: Phylogenetic context, origins and implications. *Forensic Science International, 166*, 155–163.

Chang, Y. M., et al. (2007). A distinct Y-STR haplotype for Amelogenin negative males characterized by a large Y(p)11.2 (DYS458-MSY1-AMEL-Y) deletion. *Forensic Science International, 166*, 115–120.

Jobling, M. A., et al. (2007). Structural variation on the short arm of the human Y chromosome: Recurrent multigene deletions encompassing Amelogenin Y. *Human Molecular Genetics, 16*, 307–316.

Oz, C., et al. (2008). A Y-chromosome STR marker should be added to commercial multiplex STR kits. *Journal of Forensic Sciences, 53*, 858–861.

Santos, F. R., et al. (1998). Reliability of DNA-based sex tests. *Nature Genetics, 18*, 103.

Shewale, J. G., et al. (2000). Anomalous amplification of the amelogenin locus typed by AmpF*l*STR Profiler Plus amplification kit. *Forensic Science Communications, 2*(4). Available at http://www.fbi.gov/hq/lab/fsc/backissu/oct2000/shewale.htm

Steinlechner, M., et al. (2002). Rare failures in the amelogenin sex test. *International Journal of Legal Medicine, 116*(2), 117–120.

Thangaraj, K., et al. (2002). Is the amelogenin gene reliable for gender identification in forensic casework and prenatal diagnosis?. *International Journal of Legal Medicine, 116*(2), 121–123.

STRBase

Butler, J. M., et al. (1997). STRBase: A short tandem repeat DNA Internet-accessible database. In: *Proceedings of the eighth international symposium on human identification.* (pp. 38–47). Madison, WI: Promega Corporation. Available at http://www.promega.com/geneticidproc/ussymp8proc

Butler, J. M. (2007). STRBase: 10 years and beyond—New internet resources for the human identity testing community. Poster presentation at *Eighteenth international symposium on human identification*, Hollywood, CA, October 2–3, 2007. Available at http://www.cstl.nist.gov/biotech/strbase/NISTpub.htm

Butler, J. M. (2008). New resources for the forensic genetics community available on the NIST STRBase Web site. *Forensic Science International: Genetics Supplement Series (Progress in Forensic Genetics 12), 1*(1), 97–99.

Ruitberg, C. M., et al. (2001). STRBase: A short tandem repeat DNA database for the human identity testing community. *Nucleic Acids Research, 29*, 320–322.

STRBase. http://www.cstl.nist.gov/biotech/strbase

CHAPTER 9

Fundamentals of DNA Separation and Detection

It is a capital mistake to theorize before one has data. Insensibly one begins to twist facts to suit theories, instead of theories to suit facts.
—Sherlock Holmes, *A Scandal in Bohemia*

DNA SEPARATION

The need for DNA separations

A polymerase chain reaction (PCR) in which short tandem repeat (STR) alleles are amplified produces a mixture of DNA molecules that present a challenging separation problem. A multiplex PCR can produce 20 or more different-sized DNA fragments representing different alleles that must be resolved from one another. In addition, single-base resolution is required to distinguish between closely spaced alleles (e.g., TH01 alleles 9.3 and 10). The typical separation size range where this single-base resolution is needed is between 100 and 400 bp. Additionally, it is important that the separation method be reproducible and yield results that can be compared among laboratories.

To distinguish the various molecules from one another, a separation step is required to pull the different-sized fragments apart. The separation is typically performed by a process known as electrophoresis and is either conducted in a slab-gel or capillary environment. This chapter will discuss the theory and background information on separation methods and will cover how the bands in gel electrophoresis and the peaks in capillary electrophoresis are actually generated and detected.

Electrophoresis

PCR products from short tandem repeat DNA must be separated in a fashion that allows each allele to be distinguished from other alleles. Heterozygous

Contribution of the National Institute of Standards and Technology, 2010.

alleles are resolved in this manner with a size-based separation method known as electrophoresis. The separation medium may be in the form of a slab gel or a capillary.

The word *electrophoresis* comes from the Greek *electron* (charge) and the Latin *phore* (bearer). Thus, the process of electrophoresis refers to electrical charges carried by the molecules. In the case of DNA, the phosphate groups on the backbone of the DNA molecule readily give up their H^+ ions leaving the DNA fragments negatively charged in most buffer systems. Under the influence of an electric field, DNA molecules in these buffers will migrate away from the negative electrode, known as the cathode, and move toward the positive electrode, or anode. The higher the voltage, the greater the force felt by the DNA molecules and the faster the DNA moves.

The movement of ions in an electric field generates heat. This heat must be dissipated or it will be absorbed by the system. Excessive heat can cause a slab gel to generate bands that 'smile' or in very severe cases the gel can literally melt and fall apart. Performing electrophoresis in a capillary is an advantage because heat can be more easily dissipated from the capillary, which has a high surface area-to-volume ratio.

Slab gels

Slab gels consist of a microporous matrix through which the DNA molecules pass during electrophoresis. Gel materials are mixed together and poured into a mold to define the structure of the slab gel. A sample 'comb' is placed into the gel such that the teeth of the comb are embedded in the gel matrix. After the gel has solidified, the comb is removed, leaving behind wells that are used for loading the DNA samples. The basic format for a gel electrophoresis system is shown in Figure 9.1.

Types of gels

Two types of gels are commonly used in molecular biology and forensic DNA laboratories today to achieve DNA separations. Agarose gels have fairly large pore sizes and are used for separating larger DNA molecules, while polyacrylamide gels are used to obtain high-resolution separations for smaller DNA molecules, usually below 500 or 1000 bp.

Over the years, forensic DNA typing methods have used both types of gels. Restriction fragment length polymorphism (RFLP) methods used agarose gels to separate DNA fragments ranging in size from ~600 to ~23,000 bp. Low relative molecular mass DNA molecules are not well separated with agarose slab gels. On the other hand, PCR-amplified STR alleles, which range in size from ~100 to ~400 bp, are better served by polyacrylamide gels. In the case

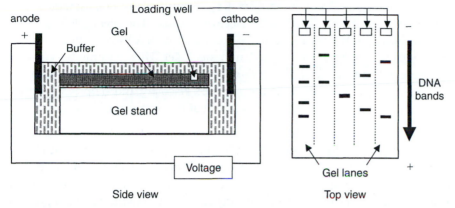

FIGURE 9.1

Schematic of a gel electrophoresis system. The horizontal gel is submerged in a tank full of electrophoresis buffer. DNA samples are loaded into wells across the top of the gel. These wells are created by a 'comb' placed in the gel while it is forming. When the voltage is applied across the two electrodes, the DNA molecules move toward the anode and separate by size. The number of lanes available on a gel is dependent on the number of teeth in the comb used to define the loading wells. At least one lane on each gel is taken up by a relative molecular mass size standard that is used to estimate the sizes of the sample bands in the other lanes.

of some STR loci that contain microvariants, the high-resolution capability of polyacrylamide gels is essential for separating closely sized DNA molecules that may only differ by a single nucleotide.

Agarose gels

Agarose is basically a form of seaweed and contains pores that are on the order of 2000 angstroms (Å) (200 nm) in diameter. Agarose gels are easily prepared by weighing out a desired amount of agarose powder and mixing it with the electrophoresis buffer. This mixture can be quickly brought to a boil by microwaving the solution whereupon the agarose powder goes into solution. After the solution cools down slightly, it is poured into a gel box to define the gel shape and thickness.

A comb is added to the liquid agarose before it cools to form wells with its teeth in the jelly-like substance that results after the gel 'sets.' Once the agarose has gelled, the comb is removed, leaving behind little wells that can hold 5 to 10 μL of sample or more, depending on the size of the teeth and the depth at which they were placed in the agarose gel. The comb teeth define the number of samples that can be loaded onto the gel as well as where the lanes will be located. There are predominantly two types of combs: square-tooth and sharks-tooth.

Electrophoresis buffer is poured over the gel until it is fully submerged. Two buffers are commonly used with electrophoresis, Tris-acetate-EDTA (TAE) and Tris-borate-EDTA (TBE). Samples are mixed with a loading dye and carefully pipetted into each well of the submerged gel. This loading dye contains a mixture of bromophenol blue, a dark blue dye that helps the analyst see the sample, and sucrose to increase the sample's viscosity and help it stay in the well prior to turning on the voltage and initiating electrophoresis.

The number of samples that can be run in parallel on the gel is defined by the number of teeth on the comb added to the gel before it sets (and hence the number of wells that will be created). Typically between 8 and 24 samples are run at a time on an agarose gel. Relative molecular mass standards are run in some of the lanes that provide an internal ruler to enable estimation of the size of each DNA sample following electrophoresis.

After the samples are loaded, a cover is placed over the gel box containing the submerged gel and the electrodes on either end of the gel are plugged into a power source. The anode (positive electrode) is placed on the end of the gel farthest from the wells to draw the DNA molecules through the gel material. Typically 100 to 600 volts (V) are placed across agarose gels, which are 10 to 40 cm in length, creating electric field strengths of approximately 1 to 10 V/cm.

As the DNA molecules are drawn through the gel, they are separated by size—the smaller ones moving more quickly and easily through the gel pores. It might help to think of the DNA molecules as marathon runners with different abilities. They all start together at the beginning and then separate during the 'race' through the gel. The smaller DNA molecules move more quickly than the larger ones through the obstacles along the gel 'race course' and thus are farther along when the voltage is turned off and the 'runners' freeze where they are. When the separation is completed, the gel is scanned or photographed to record the results for examination and comparison. In the case of capillary electrophoresis as will be described below, the DNA detection is performed at a fixed point and thus is even more analogous to the marathon race because each molecule will eventually pass a 'finish line' and have its time from start to finish recorded.

Polyacrylamide gels

Polyacrylamide (PA) gels have much smaller pore sizes (~100 to 200 Å) than agarose gels (~1500 to 2000 Å). The average pore size of a gel is an important factor in determining the ability of a slab gel to differentiate or resolve two similarly sized DNA fragments. PA gels may be run in either a horizontal or a vertical format. The type of gel box defines the running format. Detection of DNA bands in polyacrylamide gels may be performed with fluorescent dyes or silver staining (see Chapter 3).

Native versus denaturing electrophoresis conditions

Under normal conditions, the two complementary strands of DNA will remain together. Electrophoresis systems that perform the DNA separation while keeping the complementary strands together as double-stranded DNA are often referred to as 'native' or 'nondenaturing'. On the other hand, a separation system that possesses an environment capable of keeping the DNA strands apart as single-stranded DNA is usually referred to as a 'denaturing' system.

Generally better resolution between closely sized DNA molecules can be achieved with denaturing systems. This improved resolution is achieved because single-stranded DNA is more flexible than double-stranded DNA and therefore interacts with the sieving medium more effectively, allowing closely sized molecules to be differentially separated.

To achieve a denaturing environment, chemicals, such as formamide and urea, may be used to keep the complementary strands of DNA apart from one another. The addition of saturated solutions of urea is a common technique for making a denaturing gel. Formamide and urea form hydrogen bonds with the DNA bases and prevent the bases from interacting with their complementary strands. The temperature of the separation or the pH of the solution may also be raised to aid in keeping the complementary strands of DNA apart.

A popular method for achieving denatured DNA strands (prior to electrophoresis) is to dilute the samples in 100% formamide. The samples are then heated to 95°C to denature the DNA strands, and then 'snap cooled' on ice by bringing them from the heated 95°C environment immediately to 0°C by placing them on ice. Even though these heating and snap-cooling steps are typically performed in many labs, DNA samples are usually sufficiently denatured when simply placed in high-quality formamide at room temperature.

Problems with gels

The process of preparing a polyacrylamide gel involves a number of steps including cleaning and preparing the gel plates, combining the gel materials, pouring the gel, waiting for it to set up, and finally removing the comb. These steps are time consuming and rather labor intensive and represent mundane tasks in the laboratory. In addition, the acrylamide gel materials are known neurotoxins and need to be handled with extreme care.

The availability of precast gels has greatly reduced the time and labor involved in the process. However, one still has to load the DNA samples very carefully into each well (to prevent contamination from adjacent wells). Capillary electrophoresis, which is routinely used in most laboratories today, has eliminated the tedious processes of gel pouring and sample loading, and has greatly automated electrophoretic separations.

Capillary electrophoresis

Capillary electrophoresis (CE) is a relatively new addition to the electrophoresis family. The first CE separations of DNA were performed in the late 1980s. Since the introduction of new CE instrumentation in the mid-1990s, the technique has gained rapidly in popularity for routine forensic analyses. While slab-gel electrophoresis has been a proven technique for over 40 years, there are a number of advantages to analyzing DNA in a capillary format.

Advantages of CE over slab gels

First and foremost, the injection, separation, and detection steps can be fully automated, permitting multiple samples to be run unattended by CE. In addition, only tiny quantities of sample are consumed in the injection process, leaving enough sample to be easily retested if needed. This is an important advantage for precious forensic specimens that often cannot be easily replaced.

Separation in capillaries may be conducted in minutes rather than hours due to higher voltages that are permitted with improved heat dissipation from capillaries. Another advantage is that CE instruments are designed such that quantitative information is readily available in an electronic format following the completion of a run. No extra steps such as scanning the gel or taking a picture of it are required. Lane tracking is not necessary since the sample is contained within the capillary, nor is there fear of cross-contamination from samples leaking over from adjacent wells with CE.

Disadvantages of CE

Until recently, the major disadvantage of CE instruments was the time required to run multiple samples in a given time. The rate at which samples can be processed is called *throughput*. Since samples are analyzed sequentially, one at a time, single capillary instruments are not easily capable of processing high numbers of samples compared to a gel that can run several samples at once. This limitation in CE was lifted with the development of capillary array systems that can run multiple samples simultaneously, thus vastly improving sample throughput.

Another disadvantage of CE technology is that instruments require a higher start-up cost (currently more than $50,000) than slab-gel electrophoresis systems, and this fact prohibits some laboratories from using them. Nevertheless, because of their automation and ease of use, CE instruments are now the principal workhorses in almost all forensic DNA typing laboratories. For this reason, analysis by CE will be described in much greater detail than gels.

Components of CE

The primary elements of a basic CE instrument include a narrow capillary, two buffer vials, and two electrodes connected to a high-voltage power supply.

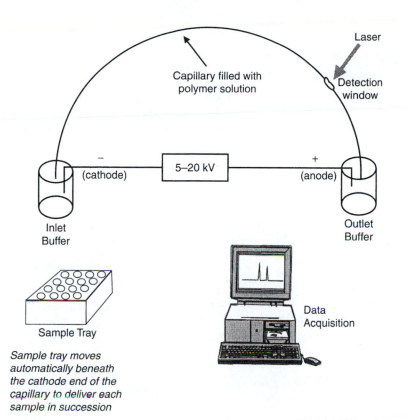

FIGURE 9.2

Schematic of capillary electrophoresis instruments used for DNA analysis. The capillary is a narrow glass tube approximately 50 cm long and 50 μm in diameter. It is filled with a viscous polymer solution that acts much like a gel in creating a sieving environment for DNA molecules. Samples are placed into a tray and injected onto the capillary by applying a voltage to each sample sequentially. A high voltage (e.g., 15,000 volts) is applied across the capillary after the injection in order to separate the DNA fragments in a matter of minutes. Fluorescent dye-labeled products are analyzed as they pass by the detection window and are excited by a laser beam. Computerized data acquisition enables rapid analysis and digital storage of separation results.

CE systems also contain a laser excitation source, a fluorescence detector, an autosampler to hold the sample tubes, and a computer to control the sample injection and detection (Figure 9.2). CE capillaries are made of glass and typically have an internal diameter of 50 μm (similar to the thickness of a human hair) and a length of approximately 25 to 75 cm.

The same buffers that are used in gel electrophoresis may also be used with CE. However, instead of a gel matrix through which the DNA molecules pass, a viscous polymer solution serves as the sieving medium. Linear, flexible polymer

D.N.A. Box 9.1 Early CE DNA work

The first capillary electrophoresis (CE) separations of short tandem repeat (STR) alleles were performed in late 1992 using nondenaturing conditions with the polymerase chain reaction (PCR) products in a double-stranded form. Fluorescent intercalating dyes were used to visualize the DNA with laser-induced fluorescence detection and to promote the resolution of closely spaced alleles. Internal standards were used to bracket the alleles in order to perform accurate STR genotyping. An allelic ladder was first run with the internal standards to calibrate the DNA migration times followed by analysis of the samples with the same internal standards (see image below). This internal sizing standard method involving a single fluorescent wavelength detector had to be used because multicolor fluorescence CE instruments were not yet available. With the commercialization of the ABI 310 in 1995 and the ABI 3100 series in 2001, internal standards labeled with a different color compared to the STR alleles are now used to perform the DNA size determinations and subsequent correlation to obtain the STR genotype (see Chapter 10).

Sources:
Butler, J. M., et al. (1994). Rapid analysis of the short tandem repeat HUMTH01 by capillary electrophoresis. *BioTechniques, 17,* 1062–1070.
Butler, J. M. (1995). *Sizing and quantitation of polymerase chain reaction products by capillary electrophoresis for use in DNA typing.* PhD Dissertation, University of Virginia, Charlottesville.
McCord, B. R., et al. (1993). High resolution capillary electrophoresis of forensic DNA using a non-gel sieving buffer. *Journal of Liquid Chromatography, 16,* 1963–1981.
McCord, B. R., et al. (1993). Capillary electrophoresis of PCR-amplified DNA using fluorescence detection with an intercalating dye. *Journal of Chromatography A, 652,* 75–82.

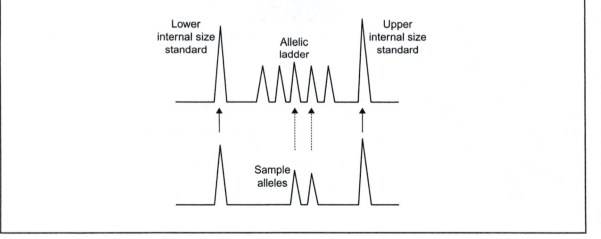

chains in the solution act as obstacles to be navigated by the negatively charged DNA fragments on their way to the positive electrode. As with gels, the larger DNA molecules are slowed down more than the smaller, more agile DNA fragments, thus again separating the different 'runners' based on their speed through the 'race course.'

Prior to injecting each sample, a new gel is 'poured' by filling the capillary with a fresh aliquot of the polymer solution. The CE capillary can be thought of as one lane in a gel that is only wide enough for one sample at a time. Different DNA samples are mixed with a constant set of DNA fragments of known size

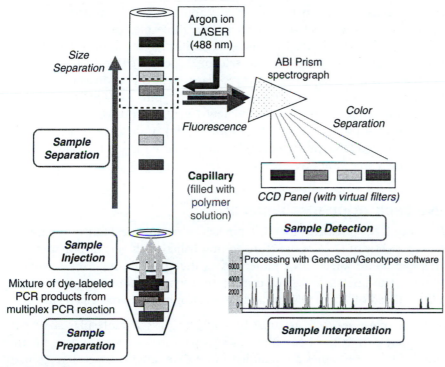

FIGURE 9.3

Schematic illustration of the separation and detection of STR alleles with an ABI Prism 310 Genetic Analyzer.

that serve as internal size standards in order to correlate results from run to run (D.N.A. Box 9.1). An important difference between CE and gels is that the electric fields are on the order of 10 to 100 times stronger with CE (i.e., 300 V/cm instead of 10 V/cm), which results in much faster run times for CE.

Detection of the sample is performed automatically by the CE instrument through measuring the time span from sample injection to sample detection with a laser placed near the end of the capillary. Laser light is shined on to the capillary at a fixed position where a window has been burned into the coating of the capillary. DNA fragments are illuminated as they pass by this window. As with gels, the smaller molecules will arrive at the detection point first followed by the larger molecules. Data from CE separations are plotted as a function of the relative fluorescence intensity observed from fluorescence emission of dyes passing the detector. The fluorescent emission signals from dyes attached to the DNA molecules can then be used to detect and quantify the DNA molecules passing the detector (Figure 9.3).

CE electrokinetic injection

To get DNA molecules onto the CE capillary, an electric voltage is applied while the end of the capillary is immersed into the liquid DNA sample. The flow of current generated by the voltage applied and the resistance experienced will pull the negatively charged DNA molecules onto the end of the capillary. Unfortunately, PCR products, in addition to the fluorescently labeled DNA molecules, also contain small salt ions, such as chloride, that compete with the DNA to be loaded onto the capillary. The PCR products created from amplifying a genomic DNA sample with an STR typing kit (see Chapter 8) are typically diluted to levels of approximately 1 in 10 with deionized formamide (e.g., $1\,\mu L$ PCR product into $9\,\mu L$ of formamide) both to help denature the double-stranded DNA molecules and to help reduce the salt levels and aid the electrokinetic injection process.

DNA separation mechanisms

To resolve DNA fragments that differ in size, a sieving mechanism is required. The separation of DNA is therefore accomplished with gels or polymer solutions that retard larger DNA molecules as they pass through the separation medium. The smaller molecules can slip through the gel pores faster and thus migrate ahead of longer DNA strands as electrophoresis proceeds (Figure 9.4).

In the simplest sense, a gel may be considered as a molecular sieve with 'pores' that permit the DNA molecules to pass in a size-dependent manner because larger molecules are retarded more than smaller ones. Two primary mechanisms for DNA separations through gel pores have been described: the Ogston model and reptation. These two theories are complementary because they operate in different size regimes. The Ogston model describes the behavior of DNA molecules that are smaller than the gel pores, while reptation describes the movement of larger DNA molecules (Figure 9.4b).

Ogston sieving

The Ogston model regards the DNA molecule as a spherical particle or coil like a small tangle of thread that is tumbling through the pores formed by the gel. Molecules move through the gel in proportion to their ability to find pores that are large enough to permit their passage. Smaller molecules migrate faster because they can pass through a greater number of pores. When DNA molecules are much larger than the mesh size of the gel-sieving medium, the Ogston model predicts that the mobility (movement) of the molecules will go to zero.

Reptation

Gel separations have been demonstrated with DNA fragments that are much larger than the predicted pore size of the gel. The reptation model for DNA separations views the DNA molecule as moving like a snake through the gel pores. DNA molecules become elongated like a straight length of thread and enter the

(a)

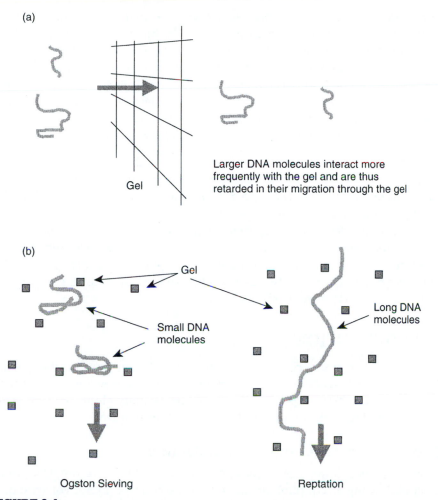

Larger DNA molecules interact more frequently with the gel and are thus retarded in their migration through the gel

Gel

(b)

Gel

Small DNA molecules

Long DNA molecules

Ogston Sieving   Reptation

FIGURE 9.4

Illustration of DNA separation modes in gel electrophoresis. (a) Separation according to size occurs as DNA molecules pass through the gel, which acts as a molecular sieve. (b) Ogston sieving and reptation are the two primary mechanisms used to describe the movement of DNA fragments through a gel.

gel matrix end on. Separation of sample components, such as two STR alleles, occurs as the DNA winds its way through the pores of the gel matrix.

DNA fragment sizing and resolution

Electrophoresis is a relative rather than an absolute measurement technique. The position of a DNA band on a gel has no meaning without reference to a size standard containing material with known DNA fragment sizes. Thus, samples are run on a gel side by side with relative molecular mass markers.

For example, a DNA restriction digest might be used with a half-dozen or more fragments ranging in size from 100 to 1000 bp. A visual comparison can then be made to estimate the fragment size of the unknown sample based on which band it comes closest to since the samples were subjected to identical electrophoretic conditions. Alternatively, in multicolor fluorescent CE systems, as will be described below, an internal sizing standard labeled with a different colored dye can be run with each sample to calibrate the migration times of the DNA fragments of interest with a sample of known size (see Chapter 10).

The separation media that the DNA passes through, as well as the overall shape of the molecule and the electric field applied to the sample, influences the molecular movement (i.e., speed of separation for each component). The exact technique that one uses to separate the DNA molecules in a particular sample is dependent on the resolution required. The resolution capability of a separation system is dependent on a number of factors including the type of separation medium used and the voltage applied. Generally speaking CE with a sieving polymer solution serves quite well to fully resolve even slightly different-sized STR alleles from one another.

DNA DETECTION

As noted earlier in this chapter, signal from fluorescent dyes attached to the DNA molecules can be used to detect and quantify the relative amounts of DNA molecules being separated during gel or capillary electrophoresis. This next section describes methods and means for detecting DNA.

Methods for detecting DNA molecules

Over the years a number of methods have been used for detecting DNA molecules following electrophoretic separation. Early techniques involved radioactive labels and autoradiography. These methods were sensitive and effective but time consuming. In addition, the use of radioisotopes was expensive due to the need for photographic films and supplies and the extensive requirements surrounding the handling and disposal of radioactive materials.

Since the late 1980s, methods such as silver staining and fluorescence techniques have gained in popularity for detecting STR alleles due to their low cost, in the case of silver staining, and their capability of automating the detection, in the case of fluorescence. Table 9.1 reviews the various methods and instruments that have been used for detecting STR alleles. The following sections will focus on fluorescence detection since it is now the dominant method utilized by the forensic DNA community. Almost all commercially available STR typing kits today involve the use of fluorescently labeled PCR primers. A historical perspective on the previously used silver-staining methods is given in Chapter 3.

Table 9.1 Detection methods and instruments used for analysis of STR alleles. A wide variety of fluorescence detection instrument platforms are listed.

Technique/Instrumentation	Comments	Reference
Fluorescence/ABI 373 or 377	Four different color dyes are used to label PCR products; peaks are measured during electrophoresis as they pass a laser that is scanning across the gel.	Frazier et al. (1996), Fregeau et al. (1999)
Fluorescence/ABI 310	Four ABI dyes are used to label PCR products; capillary electrophoresis version of ABI 377; most popular method in use today among forensic labs.	Buel et al. (1998), Lazaruk et al. (1998)
Fluorescence/ABI 3100 and ABI 3100 Avant	Five-dye colors available for detection with either 4 capillaries or 16 capillaries in parallel.	Sgueglia et al. (2003), Butler et al. (2004)
Fluorescence/FMBIO scanner	Gel is scanned following electrophoresis with a 532-nm laser; typically used with three different dyes and PowerPlex STR kits.	Micka et al. (1999), Greenspoon et al. (2004)
Fluorescence/ALF sequencer	Automated detection similar to the ABI 377 but with only single color capability.	Decorte & Cassiman (1996)
Fluorescence/LICOR	Near-IR dyes are used to label PCR products for automated detection similar to the ABI 377.	Roy et al. (1996)
Fluorescence/scanner	SYBR Green stain (intercalating dye) of gel following electrophoresis; gel is scanned with 488-nm laser.	Morin & Smith (1995)
Fluorescence/Beckman CE	PCR products are labeled with an intercalating dye during CE separation for single color detection.	Butler et al. (1994)
Fluorescence/capillary arrays	Laser scans across multiple capillaries to detect fluorescently labeled PCR products.	Wang et al. (1995), Mansfield et al. (1998)
Silver staining	Following electrophoresis, gel is soaked in silver nitrate solution; silver is reduced with formaldehyde to stain DNA bands.	Budowle et al. (1995), Micka et al. (1996)
Direct blotting electrophoresis	Following run, gel bands are blotted onto a nylon membrane, fixed with UV light, and detected with digoxygenin.	Berschick et al. (1993)
Autoradiography	P32-labeled dCTP incorporated into PCR products	Hammond et al. (1994)

Key: IR: infrared; UV: ultraviolet.

Fluorescence detection

Fluorescence-based detection assays are widely used in forensic laboratories due to their capabilities for multicolor analysis as well as rapid and easy-to-use formats. In the application to DNA typing with STR markers, the fluorescent dye is attached to a PCR primer that is incorporated into the amplified target region of DNA. Amplified STR alleles are visualized as bands on a gel or represented by peaks on an electropherogram. In this section, we first discuss some of the basics surrounding fluorescence and then follow with a review of the methods used today for labeling DNA molecules, specifically the PCR products produced from STR markers.

Basics of fluorescence

Fluorescence measurements involve exciting a dye molecule and then detecting the light that is emitted from the excited dye. A molecule that is capable of fluorescence is called a *fluorophore*. Fluorophores come in a variety of shapes, sizes, and abilities. The ones that are primarily used in DNA labeling are dyes that fluoresce in the visible region of the spectrum, which consists of light emitted in the range of approximately 400 to 600 nm.

The fluorescence process is shown in Figure 9.5. In the first step, a photon ($h\nu_{ex}$) from a laser source excites a fluorophore electron from its ground energy state

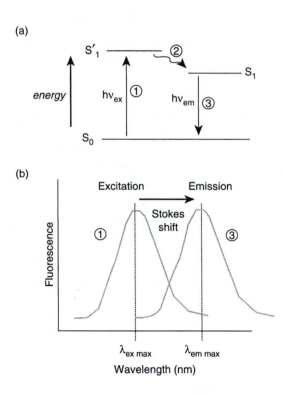

FIGURE 9.5

Illustration of the fluorescence process and excitation/emission spectra. (a) In the first step of the fluorescence process, a photon ($h\nu_{ex}$) from a laser source excites the fluorophore (dye molecule) from its ground energy state (S_0) to an excited transition state (S'_1). The fluorophore then undergoes conformational changes and interacts with its environment resulting in the relaxed singlet excitation state (S_1). During the final step of the process, a photon ($h\nu_{em}$) is emitted at a lower energy. Because energy and wavelength are inversely related to one another, the emission photon has a longer wavelength than the excitation photon. (b) Excitation and emission spectra differ in wavelength by an amount known as the 'Stokes shift.'

(S_0) to an excited transition state (S'_1). This electron then undergoes conformational changes and interacts with its environment, resulting in the relaxed singlet excitation state (S_1). During the final step of the process, a photon ($h\nu_{em}$) is emitted at a lower energy when the excited electron falls back to its ground state. Because energy and wavelength are inversely related to one another, the emission photon has a longer wavelength than the excitation photon.

The difference between the apex of the absorption and emission spectra is called the *Stokes shift*. This shift permits the use of optical filters to separate excitation light from emission light. Fluorophores have characteristic light absorption and emission patterns that are based on their chemical structure and the environmental conditions. With careful selection and optical filters, fluorophores may be chosen with emission spectra that are resolvable from one another. This capability permits the use of multiple fluorophores to measure several different DNA molecules simultaneously. The rate at which samples can be processed is much greater with multiple fluorophores than measurements involving a single fluorophore.

There are a number of factors that affect how well a fluorophore will emit light, or *fluoresce*. These factors include the following:

- *Molar extinction coefficient:* the ability of a dye to absorb light;

- *Quantum yield:* the efficiency with which the excited fluorophore converts absorbed light to emitted light;

- *Photo stability:* the ability of a dye to undergo repeated cycles of excitation and emission without being destroyed in the excited state, or experiencing 'photobleaching'; and

- *Dye environment:* factors that affect fluorescent yield include pH, temperature, solvent, and the presence of quenchers, such as hemoglobin.

The overall fluorescence efficiency of a dye molecule depends on a combination of these four factors.

Selecting the optimal fluorophore for an application

Optimal dye selection requires consideration of the spectral properties of fluorescent labels in relation to the characteristics of the instrument used for detection. The intensity of the light emitted by a fluorophore is directly dependent on the amount of light that the dye has absorbed. Thus, the excitation source is very important in the behavior of a fluorophore. Other important instrument parameters to be considered include optical filters used for signal discrimination and the sensitivity and spectral response of the detector.

Lasers are an effective excitation source because the light they emit is very intense and at primarily one wavelength. The argon ion gas laser (Ar^+) produces a blue light with dominant wavelengths of 488 and 514.5 nm. This laser is by far the most popular for applications involving fluorescent DNA labeling because a number of dyes are available that closely match its excitation capabilities.

A significant advantage of fluorescent labeling over other methods is the ability to record two or more fluorophores separately using optical filters. The signal produced has to be spectrally resolved and this is performed with a fluorophore color separation algorithm known as a *matrix*, which is sometimes referred to as a 'spectral calibration.' With this multicolor capability, components of complex mixtures can be labeled individually and identified separately in the same sample.

A fluorescence detector is a photosensitive device that measures the light intensity emitted from a fluorophore. Detection of low-intensity light may be accomplished with a photomultiplier tube (PMT) or a charge-coupled device (CCD). The action of a photon striking the detector is converted to an electric signal. The strength of the resultant current is proportional to the intensity of the emitted light. This light intensity is typically reported in arbitrary units, such as relative fluorescence units (RFUs).

Methods for labeling DNA

Fluorescent labeling of PCR products may be accomplished in one of three ways: (1) using a fluorescent intercalating dye to bind to the DNA, (2) incorporating fluorescently labeled deoxynucleotides (dNTPs) into the PCR product, or (3) incorporating a fluorescent dye into the amplicon through a 5′ end labeled oligonucleotide primer. These three methods are illustrated in Figure 9.6.

Each method of labeling DNA has advantages and disadvantages. Intercalating dyes may be used following PCR and are less expensive than the other two methods. However, they can only be used to analyze DNA fragments in a single color, which means that all of the molecules must be able to be clearly separated in terms of size. When fluorescent dNTPs are incorporated into a PCR product, both strands will be labeled in a single dye color as will all molecules being amplified.

Dye-labeled PCR primers are popular because only a single strand of a PCR product is labeled. This simplifies data interpretation because the complementary DNA strand is not visible to the detector. In addition, dye-labeled primers enable multiple PCR products to be labeled simultaneously in an independent fashion, thus increasing throughput capabilities because amplicons of overlapping size can be distinguished from one another by their dye label.

The addition of a fluorescent dye to a DNA fragment impacts the DNA molecule's electrophoretic mobility. This is because the physical size and shape of the dye change the overall size of the dye-DNA conjugate. The ionic charge, which is present on the dye, also alters the charge-to-size ratio of the nucleic

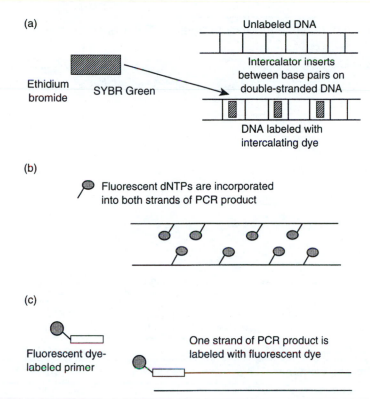

(a)

Unlabeled DNA

Ethidium bromide   SYBR Green

Intercalator inserts between base pairs on double-stranded DNA

DNA labeled with intercalating dye

(b)

Fluorescent dNTPs are incorporated into both strands of PCR product

(c)

Fluorescent dye-labeled primer

One strand of PCR product is labeled with fluorescent dye

FIGURE 9.6

Methods for fluorescently labeling DNA fragments. (a) Double-stranded DNA molecules may be labeled with fluorescent intercalating dyes. The fluorescence of these dyes is enhanced upon insertion between the DNA bases. (b) Alternatively a fluorescent dye may be attached to a nucleotide triphosphate and incorporated into the extended strands of a PCR product. (c) The most common method of detecting STR alleles is the use of fluorescent dye-labeled primers. These primers are incorporated into the PCR product to fluorescently label one of the strands.

acid conjugate. Fluorescent dyes that are covalently coupled to STR primers slightly alter the electrophoretic mobility of an STR allele PCR product moving through a gel or capillary. However, software corrections are used to mitigate this problem. In addition, genotyping of alleles is always performed relative to allelic ladders that are labeled with the *same* fluorescent dye so that differences in dye mobilities do not impact allele calls.

Fluorescent dyes used for STR allele labeling

Table 9.2 lists a number of fluorescent dyes that are commonly used to label PCR products for genotyping applications. The chemical names for the dyes are listed along with their excitation and emission wavelengths. Note that many of the chemical names and structures for these widely used fluorescent dyes are proprietary to the company that developed them.

Table 9.2 Characteristics of commonly used fluorescent dyes in STR kits and other genotyping applications.

Dye	Chemical Name	Excitation Maximum (nm)	Emission Maximum (nm)
5-FAM	5-carboxy fluorescein	493	522
JOE	6-carboxy-2',7'-dimeoxy-4',5'- dichlorofluorescein	528	554
VIC	*Proprietary to Applied Biosystems*	538	554
NED	*Proprietary to Applied Biosystems*	546	575
PET	*Proprietary to Applied Biosystems*	558	595
LIZ	*Proprietary to Applied Biosystems*	638	655
ROX (CXR)	6-carboxy-X-rhodamine	587	607
Fluorescein (FL)	Fluorescein	490	520
TMR (TAMRA)	N,N,N',N'-tetramethyl-6-carboxyrhodamine	560	583
TET	4,7,2',7'-tetrachloro-6-carboxyfluorescein	522	538
HEX	4,7,2',4',5',7'-hexachloro-6-carboxyfluorescein	535	553
Rhodamine Red	Rhodamine Red-X (Molecular Probes)	580	590
Texas Red	Texas Red-X (Molecular Probes)	595	615
SYBR Green (intercalator)	*Proprietary to Molecular Probes*	497	520

The fluorescent emission spectra of the four ABI dyes, 5-FAM, JOE, NED, and ROX, are shown in Figure 9.7. Each of the fluorescent dyes emits its maximum fluorescence at a different wavelength. This fact is used to collect the emitted light at specific wavelengths, in what is often referred to as a *virtual filter*, to capture the representative signal from each dye color channel. The approximate wavelengths of light used to separate the various colors are shown in Figure 9.7 as boxes centered on each of the four dye spectra. Note that there is considerable overlap in color between several of the dyes in the filter regions. Blue and green have an especially high degree of overlap. This overlap influences the degree of 'pull-up' that can occur between two or more dye detection channels (see Chapter 10).

Spectral calibration

In order for the computer software that is used for data analysis to know with what dye color a detected DNA fragment is labeled, the instrument detector and data collection software need to be calibrated. A multicomponent spectral calibration is performed by testing a standard set of DNA fragments labeled with each individual dye, known as matrix standard samples. The term 'matrix'

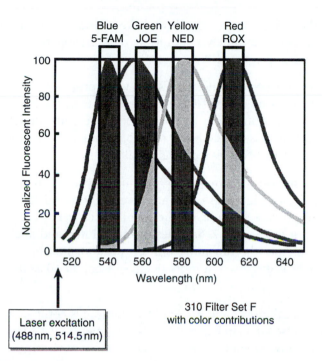

FIGURE 9.7

Fluorescent emission spectra of ABI dyes used with AmpFlSTR kits. The virtual filters for ABI 310 Filter Set F are represented by the four boxes centered on each of the four dye spectra. Each dye filter contains color contributions from adjacent overlapping dyes that must be removed by a matrix deconvolution. The dyes are excited by an argon ion laser, which emits light at 488 and 514.5 nm.

comes from the use of multiple equations (e.g., samples labeled with a single dye) being used to solve multiple unknowns (e.g., the amount of fluorescent signal contribution from each dye color in other dye color channels) in the form of a mathematical matrix (e.g., 4×4 with four dye colors).

Computer software provided with the CE instrument then analyzes the data from each of the dyes and creates a matrix or spectral calibration file to reflect the color overlap between the various fluorescent dyes. These matrix files are a summary or template of how much overlap one should expect to see just by virtue of the dyes themselves given a particular instrument and environmental conditions. The difference between these matrix values and what is actually observed in the raw data becomes part of the data set.

Spectral calibration is unique to each instrument due to the laser and detector employed and other environmental conditions. This calibration needs to be performed on a regular basis because instrument and environmental conditions, such as laser excitation power, temperature, and solution pH, can drift over time and impact the fluorescence intensity of the dyes. A spectral calibration should be performed any time a new laser or detector is installed.

As long as the electrophoresis conditions are constant from run to run, then the emission spectra of the dyes should be reproducible and spectral overlap can be accurately deciphered.

If the matrix color deconvolution does not work properly to separate spectral overlap of the dyes used for STR allele detection, then the baseline analytical signal from the instrument can be uneven or a phenomenon known as 'pull-up' can occur. *Pull-up* is the result of a color bleeding from one spectral channel into another, usually because of off-scale peaks.

The most common occurrence of pull-up involves small green peaks showing up under blue peaks that are several thousand RFUs in signal or off-scale. This occurs because of the significant overlap of the blue and green dyes seen in Figure 9.7. Samples can be diluted and analyzed again to reduce or eliminate the offending pull-up peak(s). Pull-up, also known as 'bleed-through,' is discussed in more detail in Chapter 10 as it relates to data interpretation.

Raw data from a fluorescently labeled DNA sample is compared to the color-separated processed data in Figure 9.8. DNA fragments labeled with the yellow dye are commonly shown in black to make them more visible.

The multicapillary ABI 3100 series instruments (see below) automatically apply a spectral calibration to the CE-separated fluorescence data as it is being collected such that there is no longer any 'raw data' generated by these instruments. Thus, if the color separation is not working properly, then new spectral calibration standards will have to be run and the previously poorly performing samples (i.e., those exhibiting excessive pull-up) will have to be reinjected in order to obtain higher quality data.

Summary of fluorescence detection

A laser strikes a fluorophore (dye) that is attached to the end of a DNA fragment. The fluorophore absorbs laser energy and then emits light at a lower energy (longer wavelength). Filters are used to collect only emitted light at a particular wavelength or range of wavelengths. The emitted light energy is converted to an electronic signal that is proportional to the amount of light emitted due to the number of dye-labeled molecules present. These signals are measured in relative fluorescence units (RFUs) and make up the peaks seen in capillary electropherograms or bands on a gel image.

Use of different colored fluorescent dyes has made it possible to analyze many different STR loci simultaneously, each with its own color label. However, analyzing the resulting data requires a different mind-set than that used originally on silver-stained slab gels. Instead of seeing a monochrome set of peaks that can be easily measured next to a standard, fluorescent methods now permit

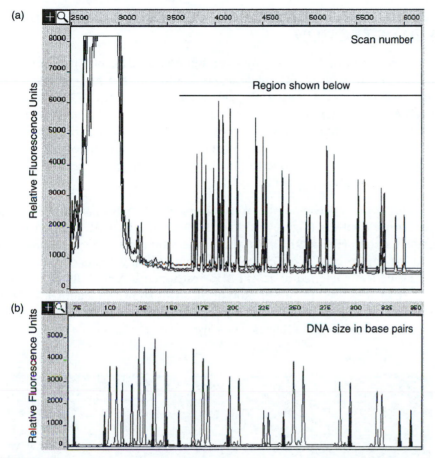

FIGURE 9.8

STR data from ABI Prism 310 Genetic Analyzer. This sample was amplified with the AmpFlSTR SGM Plus kit. (a) Raw data prior to color separation compared with (b) GeneScan 3.1 color-separated allele peaks. The red-labeled peaks are from the internal sizing standard GS500-ROX.

many more peaks of different colors to be detected, many of which overlap with one another (Figure 9.8a). With this overlapping may come a partial mixing of the dye colors and it becomes necessary to determine which color should be associated with each peak observed.

A first step in addressing this color separation challenge is the measurement of the intensity of light over defined wavelength ranges that correspond to each dye color at its maximum fluorescence. However, within those filtered ranges, there is still some significant overlap of dye colors (see Figure 9.7), which must be removed in order to separate the observed signal into the appropriate color channels. A spectral calibration enables the data analysis software to place signal from an electropherogram into the appropriate dye color.

INSTRUMENT PLATFORMS FOR DNA SEPARATION AND DETECTION

As seen earlier in Table 9.1, a number of fluorescence detection platforms exist and have been used for STR allele determination. In the mid- to late 1990s when STR typing first started, the gel-based ABI 373 and 377 instruments were the instrumental workhorses for both DNA typing and DNA sequencing. Capillary electrophoresis has now replaced slab gel systems throughout the forensic DNA community because of its ease of use, automated data collection, and labor reduction due to not having to clean gel plates and prepare polyacrylamide gels or carefully load samples onto a gel.

The most popular detection platforms today for STR analysis are the ABI Prism 310 Genetic Analyzer (Figure 9.9) and the ABI 3100 Genetic Analyzer multicapillary system (Figure 9.10). Variants of the 3100 include the 4-capillary ABI 3130 and the 16-capillary ABI 3130xl. These multicapillary systems are sometimes generically referred to as ABI 31xx instruments. A close-up of the array of 16 capillaries used in an ABI 3100 or 3130xl is shown in Figure 9.11. More details on the ABI 310 and 31xx instruments are included in the accompanying volume *Advanced Topics in Forensic DNA Typing, 3rd Edition*.

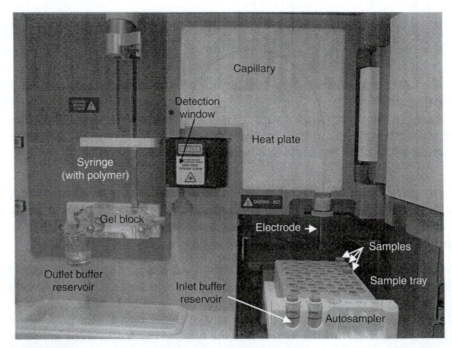

FIGURE 9.9
Photograph of ABI Prism 310 Genetic Analyzer with a single capillary.

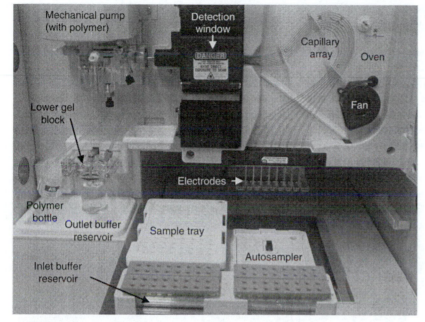

FIGURE 9.10

Photograph of ABI 3130xl Genetic Analyzer with a 16-capillary array.

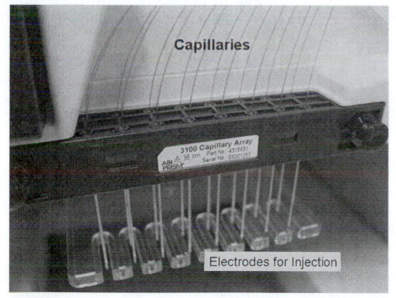

FIGURE 9.11

Photograph of a 3100 capillary array illustrating the 16 glass capillaries (top) and the electrodes surrounding the capillaries (bottom) that enable electrokinetic injection of DNA samples from two columns of an 8×12 96-well microtiter plate.

D.N.A. Box 9.2 FMBIO Gel Imager

For about a decade, gel electrophoresis followed by imaging with a Hitachi FMBIO scanner was used in many forensic laboratories including the Virginia Department of Forensic Sciences to perform STR typing (as of 2009, all of these labs have now switched to using the more automated ABI 3130xl platform). With the FMBIO II or other gel scanning systems, detection is performed following electrophoresis. Thus, many gels can be run in separate gel boxes and detected via rapid scanning on a single FMBIO fluorescence imaging system. The Promega Corporation (Madison, WI) created several multiplex STR kits to work with the FMBIO II detection platform: PowerPlex 1.1, PowerPlex 2.1, and PowerPlex 16 BIO (see image below). These kits enable amplification of the 13 core CODIS STR loci with either the combination of PowerPlex 1.1 and 2.1 or PowerPlex 16 BIO, which amplifies all 13 CODIS loci plus Penta D and Penta E in a single multiplex reaction.

When separation and detection are separate steps, as with the FMBIO gel scanner, DNA fragments of different sizes travel different distances through the gel. Smaller relative molecular mass PCR products (e.g., VWA) travel farther through the gel and are thus better resolved from one another compared to the higher relative molecular mass species (e.g., FGA) that only move a short distance through the gel before the electrophoresis is stopped and the gel is scanned.

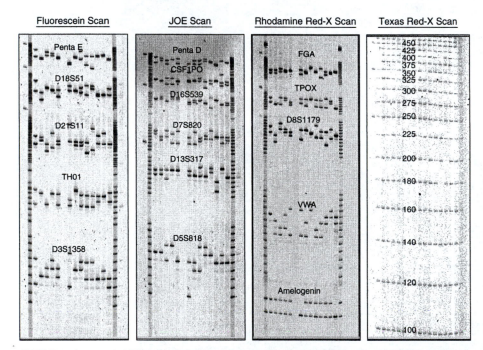

FMBIO III+ color-separated STR data collected from four scans of a gel containing PowerPlex 16 BIO PCR-amplified samples. Allelic ladders are included on the far left and right of each scan. Figure courtesy of Margaret Kline, NIST. For more information, see Greenspoon, S.A., et al. (2004) Validation and implementation of the PowerPlex 16 BIO System STR multiplex for forensic casework. Journal of Forensic Sciences, 49, 71–80.

With the single-capillary ABI 310 or multicapillary ABI 31xx, detection is performed during electrophoresis as fluorescently labeled DNA molecules pass a fixed-point detector (see Figure 9.3). As noted in D.N.A. Box 9.2, Promega Corporation for many years supported STR typing kits for gel electrophoresis followed by subsequent scanning on a Hitachi FMBIO detection platform. All widely used STR typing kits today, including Identifiler and PowerPlex 16, have been designed to work on the industry standard CE instruments, the ABI 310 or 31xx systems.

Overview of sample processing steps

Both the single-capillary ABI 310 and multicapillary ABI 31xx perform DNA separations with multiple-color fluorescence detection and provide the capability of unattended operation. An operator prepares a batch of samples and then loads them in the instrument 'autosampler,' enters the name and well position in the autosampler tray for each sample into the data collection software, places a capillary and a syringe full of polymer solution in the instrument (or capillary array and bottle of polymer solution in the case of the ABI 3130xl), and starts the 'run.'

For the ABI 310, the data are serially processed at the rate of approximately one sample every 30 minutes of operation. Run times are usually slightly longer with the ABI 31xx (e.g., 35 to 45 minutes) but with the advantage of being able to collect information on either 4 or 16 samples simultaneously, depending on the number of capillaries present in the array. A major advantage of the technique for forensic laboratories is that the DNA sample is not fully consumed and may be retested if need be. In many cases, retesting is as simple as reinjecting the already prepared DNA samples.

Sample preparation

Following PCR amplification of forensic DNA samples using a commercially available STR typing kit, the resulting fluorescently labeled STR alleles need to be separated, sized, and genotyped. Samples are prepared for the ABI 310 by diluting them in a denaturant solution of deionized formamide that helps disrupt the hydrogen bonds between the complementary strands of the PCR products. This dilution does two things. First, the high concentration of formamide helps keep the DNA strands denatured. Second, by diluting the PCR sample the salts are also diluted, which aids in the sample injection process. An internal standard is also added to each sample for sizing purposes. The samples are then heat denatured to separate the two strands of each PCR product and then loaded in the instrument for analysis.

The end result of the STR allele separation and detection steps described in this chapter is an electronic data file containing an electropherogram with many peaks. This electropherogram must be interpreted to determine the STR alleles present in the DNA sample being analyzed—the topic for Chapter 10.

Points for Discussion

■ Why is capillary electrophoresis a preferred method today over gel electrophoresis?

■ What component of a PCR reaction is labeled with a fluorescent dye to enable detection of amplified STR alleles?

■ What are the primary differences between an ABI 310 and ABI 3100 series Genetic Analyzer?

READING LIST AND INTERNET RESOURCES

DNA Separations

Amplified DNA Product Separation. http://dna.gov/training/separation

Slab Gel Electrophoresis

Bassam, B. J., et al. (1991). Fast and sensitive silver staining of DNA in polyacrylamide gels. *Analytical Biochemistry, 196,* 80–83.

Lins, A. M., et al. (1996). Multiplex sets for the amplification of polymorphic short tandem repeat loci—silver stain and fluorescence detection. *BioTechniques, 20,* 882–889.

Martin, R. (1996). *Gel electrophoresis: Nucleic acids.* Oxford: Bios Scientific Publishers.

Sprecher, C. J., et al. (1996). General approach to analysis of polymorphic short tandem repeat loci. *BioTechniques, 20,* 266–276.

Capillary Electrophoresis

Butler, J. M., et al. (2004). Forensic DNA typing by capillary electrophoresis using the ABI Prism 310 and 3100 genetic analyzers for STR analysis. *Electrophoresis, 25,* 1397–1412.

Madabhushi, R. S. (1998). Separation of 4-color DNA sequencing extension products in noncovalently coated capillaries using low viscosity polymer solutions. *Electrophoresis, 19,* 224–230.

Madabhushi, R. (2001). DNA sequencing in noncovalently coated capillaries using low viscosity polymer solutions. *Methods in Molecular Biology, 163,* 309–315.

McCord, B. R. (2003). Troubleshooting capillary electrophoresis systems. *Profiles in DNA, 6*(2), 10–12. Available at http://www.promega.com/profiles

Rosenblum, B. B., et al. (1997). Improved single-strand DNA sizing accuracy in capillary electrophoresis. *Nucleic Acids Research, 25,* 3925–3929.

Wenz, H. M., et al. (1998). High-precision genotyping by denaturing capillary electrophoresis. *Genome Research, 8,* 69–80.

Early Work

Butler, J. M., et al. (1994). Rapid analysis of the short tandem repeat HUMTH01 by capillary electrophoresis. *BioTechniques, 17*, 1062–1070.

Butler, J. M., et al. (1995). Application of dual internal standards for precise sizing of polymerase chain reaction products using capillary electrophoresis. *Electrophoresis, 16*, 974–980.

Isenberg, A. R., et al. (1998). Analysis of two multiplexed short tandem repeat systems using capillary electrophoresis with multiwavelength florescence detection. *Electrophoresis, 19*, 94–100.

DNA Separation Mechanisms

Barron, A. E., & Blanch, H. W. (1995). DNA separations by slab gel and capillary electrophoresis. *Separation Purification Methods, 24*, 1–118.

Grossman, P. D. (1992). Capillary electrophoresis in entangled polymer solutions. In P. D. Grossman & J. C. Colburn (Vol. Eds.), *Capillary electrophoresis: Theory and practice* (pp. 215–233). San Diego: Academic Press.

Ogston, A. G. (1958). The spaces in a uniform random suspension of fibres. *Transactions of the Faraday Society, 5*, 1754–1757.

Slater, G. W., et al. (2000). Theory of DNA electrophoresis: A look at some current challenges. *Electrophoresis, 21*, 3873–3887.

Viovy, J.-L., & Duke, T. (1993). DNA electrophoresis in polymer solutions: Ogston sieving, reptation and constraint release. *Electrophoresis, 14*, 322–329.

DNA Detection

Amplified DNA Product Separation. http://dna.gov/training/separation

Fluorescence Detection

Mansfield, E. S., & Kronick, M. N. (1993). Alternative labeling techniques for automated fluorescence based analysis of PCR products. *BioTechniques, 15*, 274–279.

Singer, V. L., & Johnson, (1997). Fluorophore characteristics: Making intelligent choices in application-specific dye selection. In: *Proceedings of the eighth international symposium on human identification* (pp. 70–77). Madison, WI: Promega Corporation.

Zipper, H., et al. (2004). Investigations on DNA intercalation and surface binding by SYBR Green I: Its structure determination and methodological implications. *Nucleic Acids Research, 32*, e103.

Energy Transfer Dyes

Ju, J., et al. (1995). Design and synthesis of fluorescence energy transfer dye-labeled primers and their application for DNA sequencing and analysis. *Analytical Biochemistry, 231*, 131–140.

Ju, J. Y., et al. (1996). Energy transfer primers: A new fluorescence labeling paradigm for DNA sequencing and analysis. *Nature Medicine, 2*, 246–249.

Rosenblum, B. B., et al. (1997). New dye-labeled terminators for improved DNA sequencing patterns. *Nucleic Acids Research, 25*, 4500–4504.

Yeung, S. H. I., et al. (2008). Fluorescence energy transfer-labeled primers for high-performance forensic DNA profiling. *Electrophoresis, 29*, 2251–2259.

Instrument Platforms
ABI 373 and 377

Frazier, R. R. E., et al. (1996). Validation of the Applied Biosystems Prism™ 377 automated sequencer for forensic short tandem repeat analysis. *Electrophoresis, 17,* 1550–1552.

Fregeau, C. J., et al. (1999). Validation of highly polymorphic fluorescent multiplex short tandem repeat systems using two generations of DNA sequencers. *Journal of Forensic Sciences, 44,* 133–166.

FMBIO Gel Imager

Greenspoon, S. A., et al. (2004). Validation and implementation of the PowerPlex 16 BIO System STR multiplex for forensic casework. *Journal of Forensic Sciences, 49,* 71–80.

Levedakou, E. N., et al. (2002). Characterization and validation studies of PowerPlex 2.1, a nine-locus short tandem repeat (STR) multiplex system and Penta D monoplex. *Journal of Forensic Sciences, 47,* 757–772.

Micka, K. A., et al. (1999). TWGDAM validation of a nine-locus and a four-locus fluorescent STR multiplex system. *Journal of Forensic Sciences, 44,* 1243–1257.

Tereba, A., et al. (1998). Reuse of denaturing polyacrylamide gels for short tandem repeat analysis. *Biotechniques, 25,* 892–897.

ABI Prism 310 Genetic Analyzer

Buel, E., et al. (1998). Capillary electrophoresis STR analysis: Comparison to gel-based systems. *Journal of Forensic Sciences, 43,* 164–170.

Butler, J. M., et al. (2004). Forensic DNA typing by capillary electrophoresis using the ABI Prism 310 and 3100 genetic analyzers for STR analysis. *Electrophoresis, 25,* 1397–1412.

Lazaruk, K., et al. (1998). Genotyping of forensic short tandem repeat (STR) systems based on sizing precision in a capillary electrophoresis instrument. *Electrophoresis, 19,* 86–93.

Moretti, T. R., et al. (2001). Validation of short tandem repeats (STRs) for forensic usage: Performance testing of fluorescent multiplex STR systems and analysis of authentic and simulated forensic samples. *Journal of Forensic Sciences, 46,* 647–660.

Moretti, T. R., et al. (2001). Validation of STR typing by capillary electrophoresis. *Journal of Forensic Sciences, 46,* 661–676.

ABI 3100

Koumi, P., et al. (2004). Evaluation and validation of the ABI 3700, ABI 3100, and the MegaBACE 1000 capillary array electrophoresis instruments for use with short tandem repeat microsatellite typing in a forensic environment. *Electrophoresis, 25,* 2227–2241.

Sgueglia, J. B., et al. (2003). Precision studies using the ABI prism 3100 genetic analyzer for forensic DNA analysis. *Analytical and Bioanalytical Chemistry, 376,* 1247–1254.

Stewart, J. E., et al. (2003). Evaluation of a multicapillary electrophoresis instrument for mitochondrial DNA typing. *Journal of Forensic Sciences, 48,* 571–580.

LICOR Infrared Sequencer
Roy, R., et al. (1996). Producing STR locus patterns from bloodstains and other forensic samples using an infrared fluorescent automated DNA sequencer. *Journal of Forensic Sciences, 41,* 418–424.

ALF Sequencer
Decorte, R., & Cassiman, J.-J. (1996). Evaluation of the ALF DNA sequencer for high-speed sizing of short tandem repeat alleles. *Electrophoresis, 17,* 1542–1549.

Fluorescent Scanner
Morin, P. A., & Smith, D. G. (1995). Nonradioactive detection of hypervariable simple sequence repeats in short polyacrylamide gels. *Biotechniques, 19,* 223–228.

Early Capillary Array Systems
Gill, P., et al. (2001). Sizing short tandem repeat alleles in capillary array gel electrophoresis instruments. *Electrophoresis, 22,* 2670–2678.

Mansfield, E. S., et al. (1996). Sensitivity, reproducibility, and accuracy in short tandem repeat genotyping using capillary array electrophoresis. *Genome Research, 6,* 893–903.

Wang, Y., et al. (1995). Rapid sizing of short tandem repeat alleles using capillary array electrophoresis and energy-transfer fluorescent primers. *Analytical Chemistry, 67,* 1197–1203.

Silver Stain Gels
Budowle, B., et al. (1995). DNA protocols for typing forensic biological evidence: Chemiluminescent detection for human DNA quantitation and restriction fragment length polymorphism (RFLP) analyses and manual typing of polymerase chain reaction (PCR) amplified polymorphisms. *Electrophoresis, 16,* 1559–1567.

Micka, K. A., et al. (1996). Validation of multiplex polymorphic STR amplification sets developed for personal identification applications. *Journal of Forensic Sciences, 41,* 582–590.

Direct Blotting Electrophoresis
Berschick, P., et al. (1993). Analysis of the short tandem repeat polymorphism SE33: A new high resolution separation of SE33 alleles by means of direct blotting electrophoresis. In: *Proceedings of the fourth international symposium on human identification* (pp. 201–204). Madison, WI: Promega Corporation.

Autoradiography
Hammond, H. A., et al. (1994). Evaluation of 13 short tandem repeat loci for use in personal identification applications. *American Journal of Human Genetics, 55,* 175–189.

CHAPTER 10

STR Genotyping and Data Interpretation

The technology for DNA profiling and the methods for estimating frequencies and related statistics have progressed to the point where the reliability and validity of properly collected and analyzed DNA should not be in doubt.

—NRC II Report, p. 2

In Chapter 9, we discussed how short tandem repeat (STR) amplification products labeled with fluorescent dyes are separated and detected. We also examined several commonly used instrument approaches for collecting the STR data. The data collection process leaves the analyst with only a series of peaks in a CE electropherogram (or bands on a gel). The peak information (DNA size and quantity) must be converted into a common language that will allow data to be compared between laboratories. This common language is the STR genotype. This chapter reviews the process of taking multicolor fluorescent peak information and converting it into STR genotypes.

An *STR genotype* is the allele, in the case of a homozygote, or alleles, in the case of a heterozygote, present in a sample for a particular locus and is normally reported as the number of repeats present in the allele. *A full sample genotype or STR profile is produced by the combination of all of the locus genotypes into a single series of numbers.* This profile is what is entered into a case report or a DNA database for comparison purposes to other samples. Chapter 11 will cover how statistical calculations, such as random match probabilities, are performed using the STR genotypes present in a DNA profile.

STR alleles from the same sample that are amplified with different primer sets or analyzed by different detection platforms will differ in size. However, by using locus-specific allelic ladders (prepared with the same PCR primer set), allele peak sizes may be accurately converted into genotypes. These genotypes then provide the universal language for comparing STR profiles.

Contribution of the National Institute of Standards and Technology, 2010.

STEPS IN STR GENOTYPING AND DATA INTERPRETATION

Sample data collected from the ABI 310 or other instruments described in Chapter 9 are usually represented in the form of peaks on an electropherogram that correspond to the various STR alleles amplified from the DNA sample. These peaks are present at various locations in a sample's electropherogram and are usually plotted as fluorescent signal intensity versus time passing the detector on a capillary electrophoresis system (or position on a gel once electrophoresis has been halted and the gel scanned). The steps for converting those fluorescent peaks into a descriptive number known as an 'allele call' are shown in Figure 10.1. Computer programs, such as those listed on the right side of Figure 10.1, play an important role in this process. Expert systems, which are computer programs that can rapidly and accurately process data without human intervention, are discussed in Chapter 13.

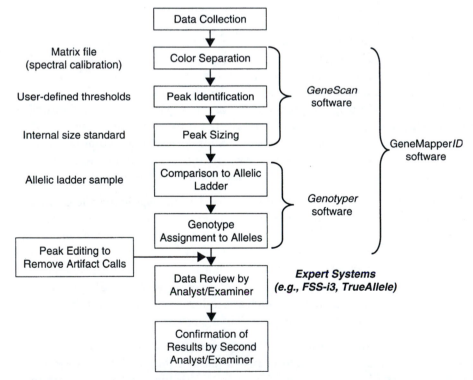

FIGURE 10.1

Steps involved in the genotyping process for STR profile determination. Software packages for DNA fragment analysis and STR genotyping perform much of the actual analysis, but extensive review of the data by trained analysts/examiners is often required.

The multiplex STR kits in use today take advantage of multiple fluorescent dyes that can be spectrally resolved. The various dye colors are separated, and the peaks representing DNA fragments are identified and associated with the appropriate color. The DNA fragments are then sized by comparison to an internal sizing standard. Finally, the PCR product sizes for the questioned sample are correlated to an allelic ladder that has been sized in a similar fashion with internal standards. The allelic ladder contains alleles of known repeat content and is used much like a measuring ruler to correlate the PCR product sizes to the number of repeat units present for a particular STR locus. From this comparison of the unknown sample with the known allelic ladder, the unknown alleles can be determined and the genotype ascertained.

Peak detection and interpretation thresholds

Data produced in any analytical instrument will contain baseline 'noise' like static on a radio. In the case of a radio signal, the message cannot be clearly understood unless it is louder than the static. In forensic DNA, the signal observed must be loud and clear and reliably reflect the DNA molecules present in the sample being tested.

Peak detection thresholds are set on capillary electrophoresis instruments below which any data is considered unreliable. A common peak detection threshold is 50 relative fluorescence units (RFUs). Only peaks above this user-defined *analytical threshold* are considered an analytical signal and thus recorded by the data analysis software. Current software only permits a single threshold to be applied across the entire electropherogram.

Figure 10.2 illustrates that a second threshold, called an *interpretation threshold*, is used in many forensic DNA laboratories. This interpretation threshold is sometimes referred to as the *stochastic threshold*, a point above which there is a low probability that the second allele in a truly heterozygous sample has not dropped out. If all observed peaks at an STR locus are above the interpretation threshold, then there is confidence that all amplified alleles are being detected. For more information on thresholds and how they are used in data interpretation, see the *Advanced Topics* volume.

Peak sizing: From data point (time) to DNA size (bp)

Once peaks have been characterized as being real data because they are above the analytical threshold, they are converted from data points in time-space (usually minutes) to DNA size-space (base pairs, bp) so results can be compared between separate runs. The fluorescently labeled DNA fragments represented by peaks in capillary electropherograms (or bands on a gel) are sized relative to an internal size standard that is mixed with the DNA samples prior to analysis (Figure 10.3).

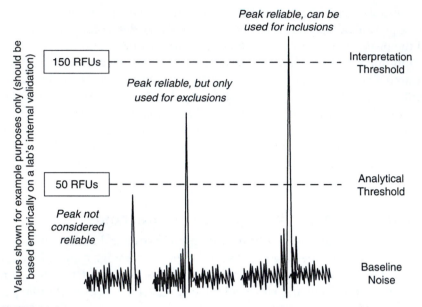

FIGURE 10.2

Two peak detection thresholds are used by many forensic DNA laboratories. Below the analytical threshold, signal observed is not considered reliable and not recorded as a peak by the data analysis software. A peak with a height in relative fluorescence units (RFUs) above the interpretation threshold is used for inclusionary (statistical) purposes. A peak above the analytical but below the interpretation threshold is only used for exclusionary purposes. Some labs set their interpretation threshold to be equal to their analytical threshold.

The internal size standard is labeled with a different colored dye so that it can be spectrally distinguished from the DNA fragments of unknown size. A calibration curve is established with each sample using the known sizes of the internal size standard. Data points from peaks in the electropherogram are then transformed into DNA sizes relative to the internal size standard calibration curve (Figure 10.3b). A method known as Local Southern sizing is commonly used to perform this time-to-size transformation.

In the case of the ABI 310 and four-dye chemistry AmpF*l*STR kits, the internal standard is usually the GS500-ROX (Figure 10.3a). This size standard contains 16 DNA fragments, ranging in size from 35 to 500 bp, that have been labeled with the red fluorescent dye ROX. Alternatively, for five-dye chemistries the DNA fragments are labeled with the orange dye LIZ to create the GS500-LIZ internal size standard.

More recently, Applied Biosystems has released a GS600-LIZ size standard, which contains 36 DNA fragments ranging in size from 20 to 600 bp. The presence of additional internal size standard peaks can lead to more precise sizing when environmental temperatures (and hence CE instrument temperatures) are not optimally consistent. For PowerPlex kit users, the internal lane

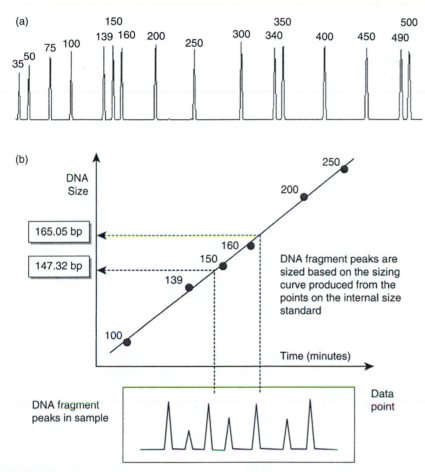

FIGURE 10.3

Peak sizing with DNA fragment analysis. (a) An internal size standard, such as GS500-ROX, is analyzed along with the DNA sample and (b) used to calibrate the peak data points to their DNA size. This standard is labeled with a different color fluorescent dye, in this case ROX (detected as red), so that it can be spectrally distinguished from the STR alleles that are labeled in other colors.

standard ILS 600 is commonly employed. This size standard contains 22 DNA fragments, ranging in size from 60 to 600 bp, that have been labeled with the red fluorescent dye CXR. The ILS 600 size marker is commonly used with the PowerPlex 16 and PowerPlex Y kits from Promega.

STR genotyping: from DNA size (bp) to allele call (# repeats)

Following the sizing of all peaks above the analytical threshold, the peaks in each sample are converted from DNA size to STR allele through the use of

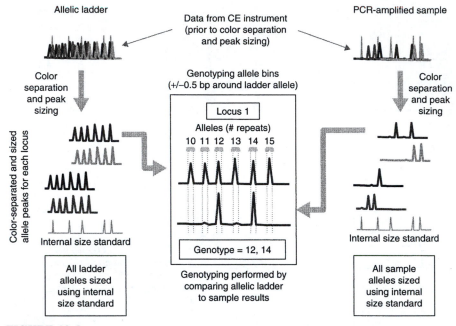

FIGURE 10.4

Genotyping is performed through a comparison of sized peaks from PCR-amplified samples to allele size bins. These allele bins are defined with the genotyping software using size information from an allelic ladder run with each batch of samples. Any peak falling in a particular dye color and allele bin size range is designated as an allele for that locus. Peaks in both the allelic ladder and the PCR-amplified samples are sized using the same internal size standard so that they may be compared to one another.

allelic ladders (Figure 10.4). As noted in Chapter 8, these allelic ladders are provided by the commercial kit providers (although a laboratory could prepare its own ladder by gathering alleles from a diverse set of samples). The ladders are prepared with commonly observed STR alleles usually spaced a single repeat unit apart from one another. The ladder alleles are PCR-amplified with the same primers as provided in the STR typing kit for testing unknown samples. Thus, samples amplified with a kit will produce alleles that are the same size as an allele in the allelic ladder.

Each allele or 'rung' of an allelic ladder has been characterized in terms of the number of repeats it contains through DNA sequencing. The STR kit manufacturer supplies information to the users regarding the allele nomenclature and number of repeats present in each allele in the ladder. The data analysis software enables a conversion of all peaks in samples being processed from DNA size (relative to a common internal size standard) to repeat number. The DNA sizes of the allelic ladder alleles are used to calibrate size ranges for allele classification. A common size range for the genotyping allele bins is ±0.5 bp around each allele. This size range enables PCR products that are 1 bp different from one another to be differentiated. Due to slight changes in instrument environmental conditions over time, allelic ladders are run regularly (typically with every batch of samples) in order to keep the size-to-allele conversion process well calibrated.

Any peak with the same dye-color label that is sized within half a base pair of an allelic ladder is designated by the STR genotyping software as being that allele. An analyst, while performing DNA profile review, assesses whether or not the labeled peak is truly an allele or an artifact, such as a stutter product or pull-up of signal from another dye color. Occasionally so-called *variant* or *microvariant alleles* are observed that are 'off-ladder' and do not have sizes that fall within the typical ±0.5 bp window around the allelic ladder alleles (D.N.A. Box 10.1).

DNA fragment analysis and genotyping software

Fairly sophisticated software has been developed to take sample electrophoretic data rapidly through the genotyping process just described. When the ABI 310 was first released in the mid-1990s, sample processing was performed in two steps by two different software programs: GeneScan and Genotyper. The GeneScan software was used to spectrally resolve the dye colors for each peak, to label peaks above a minimum analytical threshold, and to size the DNA fragments in each sample. The resulting electropherograms were then imported into a second software program where genotyping was performed. The Genotyper program determined each sample's genotype by comparing the sizes of alleles observed in a standard allelic ladder sample to those obtained at each locus tested in the DNA sample. The user could select allele calling ranges utilizing the allelic ladder allele DNA size information based on the specific STR kit in use.

These older programs have now been replaced by a software package called GeneMapper*ID* that combines the functions of GeneScan and Genotyper with additional quality scores for the data. 'Bins' and 'panels' are created by the user or provided by the STR kit manufacturer that enable the electrophoretic peaks to be designed as STR alleles for each tested locus.

After the data has been processed, the analyst examines the peaks that have been called and based on experience and laboratory protocol may or may not edit the calls made by the software. Decisions to edit a software-designated peak come from an understanding of biological or instrumental artifacts that will be discussed later in this chapter. Any editing of the data is usually documented either in an analyst's case notes or in comments made in the electronic or paper printouts of the STR data. An allele table may then be created from the edited allele calls. Prior to finalizing the DNA profile results, a second

D.N.A. Box 10.1 Variant Alleles

Occasionally a sample may contain an allele that does not fall within 0.5 bp of an allele from the corresponding locus-specific allelic ladder. These alleles are designated as 'off-ladder' alleles or variant alleles. The off-ladder allele peak may be larger or smaller than the alleles spanning the allelic ladder range or it may fall in between the rungs of the allelic ladder.

If the allele is sized to be less than the ladder, it may be designated as smaller than the smallest allele in the ladder used for genotyping purposes. For example, a CSF1PO allele sized below allele 6, which is the smallest in the ladder, would be designated CSF1PO <6. Likewise, an allele sized above allele 15, the largest in the ladder, would be designated CSF1PO >15. Because the alleles in allelic ladders differ between manufacturers, an allele designation of '>15' from an amplification using one STR kit could be equivalent to an allele designation '16' from another.

For further information, see http://www.cstl.nist.gov/biotech/strbase/var_tab.htm

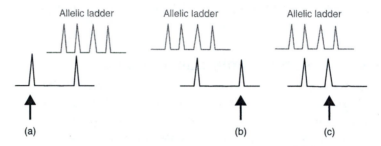

Three types of 'off-ladder' or 'variant' alleles: (a) below-ladder alleles, (b) above-ladder alleles, and (c) between-ladder alleles.

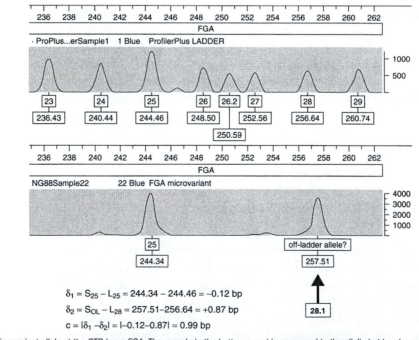

$$\delta_1 = S_{25} - L_{25} = 244.34 - 244.46 = -0.12 \text{ bp}$$
$$\delta_2 = S_{OL} - L_{28} = 257.51 - 256.64 = +0.87 \text{ bp}$$
$$c = |\delta_1 - \delta_2| = |-0.12 - 0.87| = 0.99 \text{ bp}$$

Detection of a microvariant allele at the STR locus FGA. The sample in the bottom panel is compared to the allelic ladder shown in the top panel using Genotyper software. Peaks are labeled with the allele category and the calculated fragment sizes using the internal sizing standard GS500-ROX.

reviewer performs a confirmatory review to verify all results as part of the quality assurance process (see Chapter 13).

The allele calls produced by the GeneScan/Genotyper or GeneMapper*ID* software may be exported to a spreadsheet program, such as Microsoft Excel, for further data analysis. Data uploaded into a DNA database are converted to a common format to be compatible with previously uploaded DNA typing information.

Manual intervention in STR genotype determinations

While STR allele calls may be made in an automated fashion with data analysis software, the resulting genotype information needs to be manually examined by experienced analysts. As described in Chapter 13, genotyping computer programs known as *expert systems* have also been developed to perform automated STR data review according to user-defined criteria. Data analysis and review are essential for confirming STR results prior to making final reports.

Software algorithms follow set parameters and criteria and hence can never be as effective at making difficult calls as a trained analyst. Strict guidelines for data interpretation should be in place to avoid problems with individual bias when the data is reviewed. However, there is always enough variation between data sets that it is difficult to cover every situation with a predetermined rule.

Laboratories typically have two independent reads of the data by different operators. The genotypes must agree with each other before results will be reported in a case report or uploaded to a DNA database. Likewise, a match between two samples is only reported if the two DNA profiles display the same STR allele calls.

FACTORS AFFECTING GENOTYPING RESULTS

There are a number of issues that are important to obtaining accurate genotype results. Some issues are biology related and some are technology related. For example, the amount of stutter or incomplete 3′ nucleotide addition present is a biology issue related to the amount of DNA template, the primer sequences, and the PCR conditions utilized. On the other hand, 'pull-up' artifacts result from the fluorescent technology and spectral calibration used when genotyping the samples.

Three parts of the genotyping process illustrated in Figure 10.1 are crucial to the success of genotyping samples. These include the matrix file, the internal size standard, and the allelic ladder sample.

The *matrix file* (sometimes termed a *spectral calibration*) is critical for proper color separation in an electropherogram. If the observed peaks are not associated with the proper dye label, then the sample genotype cannot be correctly determined. As noted in Chapter 9, matrix files are established by running samples that contain each of the dyes individually. The results of the individual dye runs are combined to form a mathematical matrix that is used to subtract the contribution of other colors in the overlapping spectra. A matrix is most accurate under consistent environmental conditions. Thus, if the instrument laser is changed, a new matrix should be established in order to obtain the most accurate color deconvolution between the different dyes.

The *internal size standard* is necessary for proper sizing of DNA fragment peaks detected in an electropherogram. If any of the peaks in the size standard are below the peak detection threshold established in the data collection and analysis software, then the sizing algorithms will not work properly and STR alleles may be sized incorrectly. As part of data quality assurance, an analyst checks to make sure that the internal size standard peaks were all detected properly before proceeding to genotype the STR alleles in a sample.

The *allelic ladder* is the standard to which STR alleles are compared to obtain the sample genotype. The alleles in an allelic ladder need to be resolved from one another and above the peak detection threshold of the data collection and analysis software in order to correctly call STR alleles in unknown samples. The sizes obtained for each allele in the allelic ladder are used to make the final genotype determination in the unknown samples. Therefore, they must be determined correctly.

The importance of precision in accurate genotyping

STR genotyping is performed by comparison of the size of a sample's alleles to size of alleles in allelic ladders for the same loci being tested in the sample (see Figure 10.4). A high degree of precision is needed between multiple runs in order to make an accurate comparison of data from two runs, where one run is the allelic ladder standard and the other run is the questioned sample. The precision for a measurement system is determined by analyzing replicate samples or allelic ladders under normal operating conditions.

Precision for the separation and detection platform must be less than ± 0.5 bp to accurately distinguish between microvariant (partial repeat) alleles and complete repeat alleles that differ by a single nucleotide. For single capillary CE instruments, there is a reliance on a high degree of precision for run-to-run comparisons since a number of samples are run in a sequential fashion through the capillary between each injection of the allelic ladder. This same principle applies for multicapillary array systems.

The DNA sizing precision on CE instruments is typically better than 0.1 bp. However, a laboratory temperature variation of as little as 2° or 3°C over the course of a number of runs can cause allele peaks to migrate slightly differently from the internal sizing standard and therefore size differently over time. To alleviate this problem, the allelic ladder may be run more frequently (e.g., every 10 injections instead of every 20 injections), and the samples can be typed to the allelic ladder sample that was injected nearest in time to them.

Sizing algorithm issues

The sizing of DNA fragments with internal standards is performed as illustrated earlier in Figure 10.3. The most common algorithm used for determining the DNA fragment size is known as the Local Southern method (the 'Southern' portion of the technique's name refers to Ed Southern, the same English scientist who developed the Southern blotting technique for RFLP described in Chapter 3). This method uses the size of two peaks on either side of the unknown one being measured in order to make the calculations. Using the example in Figure 10.3, the 165.05-bp peak size is determined with Local Southern sizing by the position of the 150- and 160-bp peaks on the lower side and the position of the 200- and 250-bp peaks on the upper side.

The Local Southern method works very well for accurate sizing of DNA fragments over the 100- to 450-bp size range necessary for STR alleles—primarily because in this size range DNA molecules migrate during electrophoresis with an approximately linear relationship between size and separation time. However, there are some caveats that should be kept in mind that depend on the internal size standard used. Within the GS500-ROX and GS500-LIZ size standard, the 250-bp peak (and sometimes the 340-bp peak as well) does not size reproducibly, especially when there are temperature fluctuations across or between runs. Therefore, the 250-bp peak is typically left out of analyses by not designating it as a standard peak.

It is important to realize that unknown DNA fragment peaks that are larger than the peaks present (or designated by the software) in the internal sizing standard cannot be accurately determined. Peaks that fall near the edge of the region defined by the internal sizing standard are less accurately sized since only one—not two—size standard DNA fragment is available. The Local Southern sizing algorithm requires two peaks from the size standard on either side of the unknown peak.

Therefore, with the GS500-ROX internal standard commonly used in conjunction with the AmpF*l*STR kits, any unknown peaks falling above 490 bp or below 50 bp will not be sized with the Local Southern method. Likewise, if the signal intensity for any of the calibration peaks in the internal sizing standard is too weak, then unknown peaks in that region will not be sized accurately. For this reason it is important to check that all peaks in the internal sizing standard are above the relative fluorescence threshold to be called as peaks and that these peaks are accurately designated by the software.

Several studies have found that a different sizing algorithm called the Global Southern method works well and maintains a better precision than Local Southern sizing in situations where temperature fluctuations can occur. Global Southern involves fitting a larger number of the peaks in the size standard to form a best-fit size calibration line rather than just using the two peaks above and below the peak of interest as is done with Local Southern. Regardless of which method is used, it must be consistently applied to both the allelic ladders and samples being typed so that equivalent size comparisons may be made.

Off-ladder alleles

Off-ladder alleles (see D.N.A. Box 10.1) can be verified by rerunning the amplified product, reamplifying the sample, or by amplifying the sample with single-locus primers. Heterozygous samples with one 'normal' allele and one microvariant allele make it easy to confirm the microvariant. In this particular case, the normal allele with a full-length repeat sequence will fall in an allele bin from the allelic ladder, while the microvariant allele possessing a partial repeat sequence will fall between the allele bins created by the allelic ladder. New microvariants are constantly being discovered as more samples are being analyzed at various STR loci around the world. As of December 2008, more than 475 variant 'off-ladder' alleles have been reported for all 13 of the CODIS core STR loci (see http://www.cstl.nist.gov/biotech/strbase/var_tab.htm).

Partial STR profiles

If the genomic DNA in a sample is severely degraded or PCR inhibitors are present, only a partial STR profile may be obtained. Usually the larger STR loci in a multiplex reaction, such as D18S51 and FGA, will be the first to fail on a degraded DNA sample. When only a partial profile is obtained, the significance of a match will decrease because there are fewer loci to compare. However, the use of miniSTRs with smaller PCR product sizes than those used in commercial STR kits can be used to recover information lost at the larger loci (see Chapter 14).

Mixture interpretation

Mixtures of DNA from two or more individuals are common in some forensic cases and must be dealt with in the interpretation of the DNA profiles. In evaluating the evidence, an analyst must decide whether the source of the DNA in the questioned sample is from a single individual or more than one person. This may be accomplished by examination of the number of alleles detected at each locus as well as severely imbalanced peak height ratios or pronounced peaks in the stutter position (see Chapter 14). Occasionally, as discussed in the next section, extra peaks occur in the data that should not be confused with true alleles.

EXTRA PEAKS OBSERVED IN THE DATA

Electropherograms may contain peaks other than the primary target alleles of interest. These peaks can arise from a number of sources related to the biology of STRs and the technology of detecting fluorescently labeled amplification products. Experienced analysts recognize these peaks and edit them out of the data before final genotypes are determined in order to avoid making an incorrect exclusion because of the presence of spurious peaks in either the known (K) or the question (Q) sample.

A laboratory needs to establish criteria to identify a true allele because a DNA typing analyst must decide which peaks contribute to a donor(s) profile(s) and which are due to an artifact. The following material reviews some of the commonly seen artifacts (Figure 10.5), but should not be considered a comprehensive list for troubleshooting purposes. Additional information on these biology and technology artifacts is found in the *Advanced Topics* volume.

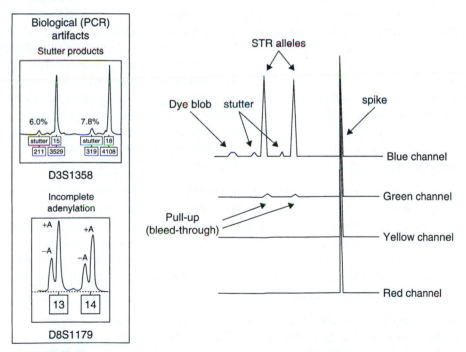

FIGURE 10.5

Hypothetical electropherogram displaying several artifacts often observed with STR typing. Two primary biological artifacts of the PCR amplification process with STRs are stutter and incomplete adenylation, which causes split peaks (inset).

Biology-related artifact peaks

Stutter products are the most common source of additional peaks in an electropherogram of an STR sample. When STR loci are PCR-amplified, a minor product peak four bases ($n-4$) shorter than the corresponding main allele peak is commonly observed in tetranucleotide repeats (see Figure 10.5). Validation studies conducted in a laboratory help define maximum percent stutter for each locus. However, if the target allele peak is off-scale, then the stutter product can appear larger than it really is in relationship to the corresponding allele peak. For data interpretation, an upper-limit stutter percentage interpretational threshold may be set for each locus as three standard deviations above the highest stutter percentage normally observed at that locus. Alternatively, some laboratories prefer to apply a universal stutter filter, usually in the range of 10% to 20%. A genotyping software-implemented stutter filter then automatically removes the peak labels on any peaks found within the designated size range (e.g., 4 bp $\pm$ 0.25 bp) and relative height (e.g., 10% to 20%) of the STR allele peaks.

Incomplete 3′ (+A) nucleotide addition results with amplifications containing too much DNA template or thermal cycling conditions that affect the optimization of the PCR reaction. The *Taq* DNA polymerase used for amplifying STR loci will catalyze the addition of an extra nucleotide, usually an 'A' (adenine), on the 3′ end of double-stranded PCR products. The commercially available multiplex STR kits have been optimized to favor complete adenylation (i.e., adding an extra 'A'). However, when incomplete 3′ nucleotide addition occurs, 'split peaks' will result (see Figure 10.5), sometimes referred to as $+/-A$, or N and $N+1$ peaks. In these cases, the allele of interest will be represented by two peaks 1 bp apart. Genotyping software may inadvertently call one of these peaks an 'off-ladder' (microvariant) allele that the analyst will have to edit it out of the electropherogram so that it does not appear in the allele table.

Triallelic patterns result from extra chromosomal fragments being present in a sample or the DNA sequence where the primers anneal being duplicated on one of the chromosomes. These rare anomalies are detected by an extra peak at a single locus, as opposed to multiple loci as would likely be seen in a mixture. The three peaks can either be of approximate equal intensity or possess peak heights such that two of the peaks sum up to approximately the height of the third allele (D.N.A. Box 10.2).

Mixed sample results are observed if more than one individual contributed to the DNA profile. Mixtures are readily apparent when multiple loci are examined. An analyst looks for higher-than-expected stutter levels, more than two peaks at a locus of equivalent intensity, or a severe imbalance in heterozygote peak intensities. It is usually difficult to detect the minor contributor below a level of 1:10 compared to the major donor in the DNA profile. Full

D.N.A. Box 10.2 Triallelic Patterns

Triallelic patterns are sometimes observed at a single locus in a multiplex STR profile. These extra peaks are not a result of a mixture but are reproducible artifacts of the sample itself. Extra chromosomal occurrences (e.g., Down syndrome) or primer point mutations have been known to occur and result in a three-banded pattern. For example, three-banded patterns have been observed in the 9948 cell line with CSF1PO and in the K562 cell line with D21S11 (see D.N.A. Box 14.3).

More than 175 different triallelic patterns have been reported at all 13 CODIS STR loci with most of them being seen at TPOX, D18S51, D21S11, VWA, and FGA. A frequently updated listing of triallelic patterns can be found on the STRBase Web site (http://www.cstl.nist.gov/biotech/strbase/tri_tab.htm).

Source:
Clayton, T. M., et al. (2004). A genetic basis for anomalous band patterns encountered during DNA STR profiling. *Journal of Forensic Sciences, 49,* 1207–1214.

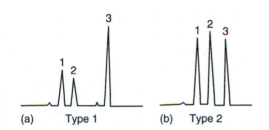

(a)   Type 1   (b)   Type 2

Triallelic patterns are sometimes observed at a single locus in a multiplex STR profile. They may be classified into one of two different groups based on relative peak heights: (a) 'Type 1' where the sum of two peak heights is almost equal to the third (1 + 2 ≈ 3) or (b) 'Type 2' where fairly balanced peak heights are observed (1 ≈ 2 ≈ 3).

deconvolution may not be possible depending on the alleles present from the contributors (see Chapter 14).

Technology-related artifact 'peaks'

Matrix (multicomponent) failure, sometimes referred to as 'pull-up,' is a result of the inability of the detection instrument to properly resolve the dye colors used to label STR amplicons. This phenomenon is due to spectral overlap as noted in Chapter 9. A peak of another color is 'pulled up' or 'bleeds through' (see Figure 10.5) as a result of exceeding the linear range of detection for the instrument (i.e., sample overloading). A matrix failure is observed as a peak-beneath-a-peak or as an elevation of the baselines for any color. Matrix standards may need to be rerun for spectral calibration purposes with the latest set of conditions and a new matrix generated by the software to correct this problem.

Dye blobs occur when fluorescent dyes come off of their respective primers and migrate independently through the capillary. Most dye artifacts, which are created through incomplete attachment of the fluorescent dye during oligonucleotide (primer) synthesis, are typically removed or significantly reduced through primer purification performed by the STR kit manufacturer. If a particular batch of STR primers has a significant level of dye blobs, these artifacts can be removed by the end user following PCR using filtration columns. Dye blob peaks are fairly broad and possess the spectrum (dye color label) of one of the dyes used for genotyping (see Figure 10.5). Dye artifacts can be most easily seen in PCR negative controls and will migrate through the CE capillary at characteristically consistent sizes. For example, there is a prominent fluorescein dye blob that sizes, depending on electrophoresis conditions, at around 120 bp.

Air bubbles, urea crystals, or *voltage spikes* can give rise to a false peak in an ABI 310 or other CE instrument. These peaks are usually sharp and appear equally intense throughout all four colors (see Figure 10.5). These peaks are not reproducible and should not appear in the same position if the sample is reinjected onto the capillary.

Sample contaminants, materials that fluoresce in the visible region of the spectrum (~500 to 600 nm), may interfere with DNA typing when using fluorescent scanners or a fluorescence detection CE system by appearing as identifiable peaks in the electropherogram. In some early studies conducted by the U.K.'s Forensic Science Service, a number of fluorescent compounds were examined to determine their apparent mobility when electrophoresed in a polyacrylamide gel. All of the compounds studied, which included antibiotics, vitamins, polycyclic aromatics, fluorescent brighteners, and various textile dyes, could be removed with an organic extraction (i.e., phenol/chloroform, as is commonly used to extract DNA from cells). Fortunately, these interfering peaks were usually wide and possessed a broader fluorescent spectrum, which made it fairly easy to distinguish them from the fluorescent dye-labeled PCR products.

DEVELOPING AN INTERPRETATION STRATEGY

A forensic DNA laboratory should develop its own STR interpretation guidelines based on its own validation studies. Information from STR kit and instrument manufacturers and results reported in the literature can also be helpful. Practical experience with instrumentation and results from performing casework are also important factors in developing an interpretation strategy.

Validation studies define observed stutter ratios for each locus, establish minimum peak height thresholds for detecting reliable data, and define expected heterozygous peak ratios within a locus. When in doubt on a sample's correct result, the sample should be retested. This may be as simple as reinjecting it on a CE instrument. Even if sample retesting involves reextracting and/or reamplifying the 'problem' sample, it is worthwhile in order to obtain an accurate result.

A match or not a match: That is the question …

Generally, the process of comparing two or more samples is limited to one of three possible outcomes that are submitted in a case report:

1. *Inclusion (match):* Peaks between the compared STR profiles have the same genotypes and no unexplained differences exist between the samples. Statistical evaluation of the significance of the match is usually cited in the match report. Alternatives for presentation of a match range from statements of identity, to computations of the likelihood ratio for the hypothesis that the defendant is the source, to descriptions of random-match probabilities in various populations, to a simple qualitative report of a match with no statistics behind its significance.

2. *Exclusion (nonmatch):* The genotype comparison shows profile differences that can only be explained by the two samples originating from different sources.

3. *Inconclusive:* The data does not support a conclusion as to whether the profiles match. This finding might be reported if two analysts remain in disagreement after review and discussion of the data and it is felt that insufficient information exists to support any conclusion.

If a match is observed between a suspect (known sample 'K') and crime scene evidence (question sample 'Q'), then three possibilities exist: (1) the suspect deposited the sample, (2) the suspect did not provide the sample but has the profile by chance, or (3) the suspect did not provide the sample and the matching result is a false positive due to laboratory error. The first explanation is the basis behind the use of DNA testing in the criminal justice system. The second possibility depends on population genetics principles, covered in Chapter 11, from which the probability of a random match is determined. The third explanation of why a match might occur concerns the possibility of laboratory mistakes. Chapter 13 discusses quality assurance measures that are in place to prevent or reduce the possibility of error in performing DNA testing. Generally speaking, a great deal of effort goes into ensuring reliable forensic DNA testing.

When utilizing data comparisons with DNA databases that may have data coming from many sources, it is important to recognize that different PCR primer sets can give rise to allele dropout relative to one another due to possible primer binding site mutations (D.N.A. Box 10.3).

In forensic DNA analysis, if any STR locus fails to match when comparing the genotypes between two or more samples, then the comparison of profiles between the questioned and reference sample is usually declared a nonmatch, regardless of how many other loci match. As noted in Chapter 17, paternity

D.N.A. Box 10.3 Null Alleles

When amplifying DNA fragments that contain STR repeat regions, it is possible to have a phenomenon known as *allele dropout*. Sequence polymorphisms are known to occur within or around STR repeat regions. These variations can occur in three locations (relative to the primer binding sites): within the repeat region, in the flanking region, or in the primer binding region. If a base pair change occurs in the DNA template at the PCR primer binding region, the hybridization of the primer can be disrupted, resulting in a failure to amplify and, therefore, failure to detect an allele that exists in the template DNA. More simply, the DNA template exists for a particular allele but fails to amplify during PCR due to primer hybridization problems. This phenomenon results in what is known as a *null allele*. Fortunately null alleles are rather rare because the flanking sequence around STR repeats is fairly stable and consistent between samples.

Allele dropout may occur due to mutations (variants) at or near the 3′ end of a primer binding site and thus produce little or no extension during PCR. Null alleles have been 'discovered' by the observation of different typing results when utilizing independent STR primer sets. During a comparison of STR typing results on 600 population samples at the VWA locus, one sample typed 16,19 with Promega's PowerPlex 1.1 kit and 16,16 with Applied Biosystem's AmpF*l*STR Blue kit (Kline et al., 1998). In this case, the VWA allele 19 was present in the sample but failed to be amplified by one of the primer sets. It was later reported that the null allele resulted from a rare A–T nucleotide change in the DNA template at the second base from the 3′ end of the AmpF*l*STR VWA forward primer (Walsh, 1998).

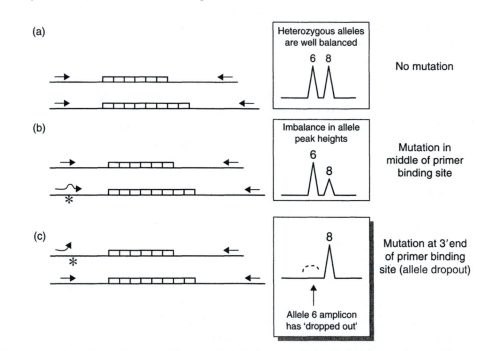

Impact of a sequence polymorphism in the primer binding site illustrated with a hypothetical heterozygous individual possessing a '6,8' genotype. Arrows represent PCR primers in different positions around the STR repeat region. Heterozygous allele peaks may be (a) well-balanced, (b) imbalanced, or (c) exhibit allele dropout. A 'null allele,' such as that shown in (c), can be detected through use of different PCR primers.

No primer set is completely immune to the phenomenon of null alleles. However, when identical primer sets are used to amplify evidence samples and suspect reference samples, full concordance is expected from biological materials originating from a common source. If the DNA templates and PCR conditions are identical between two samples from the same individual, then identical DNA profiles should result regardless of how well or poorly the PCR primers amplify the DNA template.

The potential of null alleles is not a problem within a laboratory that uses the same primer set to amplify a particular STR marker. However, with the emergence of national and international DNA databases, which store only the genotype information for a sample, allele dropout could potentially result in a false negative or incorrect exclusion of two samples that come from a common source. To overcome this potential problem, the matching criteria in database searches can be made less stringent when searching a crime stain sample against the DNA database of convicted offender profiles (see Chapter 12). That is, the database search might be programmed to return any profiles with a match at 25 out of 26 alleles instead of 26 out of 26.

When primers are selected for amplification of STR loci, candidate primers are evaluated carefully to avoid primer binding site mutations. Sequence analysis of multiple alleles is performed, family inheritance studies are conducted, within-locus peak signal ratios for heterozygous samples are examined, apparent homozygous samples are reamplified with lower annealing temperatures, and statistical analysis of observed versus expected homozygosity is performed on population databases. It is truly a challenge to design multiplex STR primer sets in which primer binding sites are located in sequence regions that are as highly conserved as possible and yet do not interfere with primers amplifying other loci.

In some cases, STR kit manufacturers have added an additional PCR primer to the assay that can hybridize properly to the alternative allele when it exists in a sample. This has been the preferred solution for Applied Biosystems, while Promega has sometimes moved their primers to overcome allele dropout problems. According to their publications, Applied Biosystems has added an additional primer to correct for single-point mutations in AmpF*l*STR primer binding sites for D16S539 (Wallin et al., 2002), VWA (Lazaruk et al., 2001), and D8S1179 (Leibelt et al., 2003).

Sources:
Kline, M. C., et al. (1998). Non-amplification of a vWA allele. *Journal of Forensic Sciences, 43*(1), 250.
Lazaruk, K., et al. (2001). Sequence variation in humans and other primates at six short tandem repeat loci used in forensic identity testing. *Forensic Science International, 119*, 1–10.
Leibelt, C., et al. (2003). Identification of a D8S1179 primer binding site mutation and the validation of a primer designed to recover null alleles. *Forensic Science International, 133*, 220–227.
STRBase Null Allele Report. http://www.cstl.nist.gov/biotech/strbase/NullAlleles.htm
Wallin, J. M., et al. (2002). Constructing universal multiplex PCR systems for comparative genotyping. *Journal of Forensic Sciences, 47*, 52–65.
Walsh, S. (1998). Commentary on Kline, M.C., Jenkins, B., Rogers, S. Non-amplification of a vWA allele. *Journal of Forensic Sciences, 43*(1), 250. *Journal of Forensic Sciences, 43*, 1103–1104.

testing is an exception to this 'single mismatch leads to exclusion' rule because of the possibility of mutational events. When analyzing and reporting the results of parentage cases, an allowance for one or even two possible mutations is often made. In other words, if 13 loci are used and the questioned parentage is included for all but one locus, the data from the noninclusive allele is usually attributed to a possible mutation.

In the end, interpretation of results in forensic casework is a matter of professional judgment and expertise. Interpretation of results within the context of a case is the responsibility of the case analyst with supervisors or technical leaders conducting a follow-up verification of the analyst's interpretation of the data as part of the technical and administrative review process. When coming to a final conclusion regarding a match or exclusion between two or more DNA profiles, laboratory interpretation guidelines should be adhered to by both the case analyst and the supervisor. However, as experience using various analytical procedures grows, interpretation guidelines may evolve and improve. These guidelines should always be based on the proper use of controls and validated methods.

Points for Discussion

- Is it better to prevent or promote nontemplate addition? Explain your reasons.
- What are some approaches to dealing with the possibility of allele dropout due to PCR primer binding site mutations?
- What observations indicate that a peak in an electropherogram is a spike as opposed to DNA?
- What steps are typically taken to confirm the presence of an off-ladder allele?
- Why are mutations and mutation rates a concern with parentage and kinship analysis but not with forensic DNA testing?

READING LIST AND INTERNET RESOURCES

Data Analysis and Interpretation

Butler, J. M., & McCord, B. R. (2008). Workshop on troubleshooting common laboratory problems presented at the *19th international symposium on human identification*. http://www.cstl.nist.gov/biotech/strbase/training.htm

STR Data Analysis and Interpretation. http://dna.gov/training/strdata

DNA Sizing

Elder, J. K., & Southern, E. M. (1983). Measurement of DNA length by gel-electrophoresis. 2. Comparison of methods for relating mobility to fragment length. *Analytical Biochemistry, 128,* 227–231.

Hartzell, B., et al. (2003). Response of short tandem repeat systems to temperature and sizing methods. *Forensic Science International, 133,* 228–234.

Klein, S. B., et al. (2003). Addressing ambient temperature variation effects on sizing precision of AmpF*l*STR profiler plus alleles detected on the ABI Prism 310 genetic analyzer. *Forensic Science Communication, 5*(1). Available at http://www.fbi.gov/hq/lab/fsc/backissu/jan2003/klein.htm

Mayrand, P. E., et al. (1992). The use of fluorescence detection and internal lane standards to size PCR products automatically. *Applied and Theoretical Electrophoresis, 3,* 1–11.

Smith, R. N. (1995). Accurate size comparison of short tandem repeat alleles amplified by PCR. *Biotechniques, 18,* 122–128.

Genotyping

Leclair, B., et al. (2004). Precision and accuracy in fluorescent short tandem repeat DNA typing: Assessment of benefits imparted by the use of allelic ladders with the AmpF*l*STR profiler plus kit. *Electrophoresis, 25*, 790–796.

Dye Blobs

Butler, J. M., et al. (2003). The development of reduced size STR amplicons as tools for analysis of degraded DNA. *Journal of Forensic Sciences, 48*(5), 1054–1064.

Other Artifacts

Hartzell, B., & McCord, B. (2005). Effect of divalent metal ions on DNA studied by capillary electrophoresis. *Electrophoresis, 26*, 1046–1056.

Murphy, K. M., et al. (2005). Capillary electrophoresis artifact due to eosin: Implications for the interpretation of molecular diagnostic assays. *Journal of Molecular Diagnostics, 7*, 143–148.

Sparkes, R., et al. (1996). The validation of a 7-locus multiplex STR test for use in forensic casework. (II), artefacts, casework studies and success rates. *International Journal of Legal Medicine, 109*, 195–204.

Urquhart, A., et al. (1994). Multiplex STR systems with fluorescent detection as human identification markers. In: *Proceedings from the fifth international symposium on human identification* (pp. 73–83). Madison, WI: Promega Corporation.

Stutter Products

Applied Biosystems (1998). *AmpF*l*STR PCR amplification kit user's manual.* Profiler Plus Foster City, CA: Applied Biosystems.

Blackmore, V. L., et al. (2000). Preferential amplification and stutter observed in population database samples using the AmpF*l*STR profiler multiplex system. *Canadian Society of Forensic Science Journal, 33*, 23–32.

Gibb, A. J., et al. (2009). Characterization of forward stutter in the AmpF*l*STR SGM Plus PCR. *Science & Justice, 49*, 24–31.

Hauge, X. Y., & Litt, M. (1993). A study of the origin of 'shadow bands' seen when typing dinucleotide repeat polymorphisms by the PCR. *Human Molecular Genetics, 2*, 411–415.

Leclair, B., et al. (2004). Systematic analysis of stutter percentages and allele peak height and peak area ratios at heterozygous STR loci for forensic casework and database samples. *Journal of Forensic Sciences, 49*, 968–980.

Schlötterer, C., & Tautz, D. (1992). Slippage synthesis of simple sequence DNA. *Nucleic Acids Research, 20*, 211–215.

Walsh, P. S., et al. (1996). Sequence analysis and characterization of stutter products at the tetranucleotide repeat locus vWA. *Nucleic Acids Research, 24*, 2807–2812.

Nontemplate Addition

Brownstein, M. J., et al. (1996). Modulation of non-templated nucleotide addition by Taq DNA polymerase: Primer modifications that facilitate genotyping. *Biotechniques, 20*, 1004–1010.

Clark, J. M. (1988). Novel non-templated nucleotide addition reactions catalyzed by prokaryotic and eukaryotic DNA polymerases. *Nucleic Acids Research, 16*, 9677–9686.

Kimpton, C. P., et al. (1993). Automated DNA profiling employing multiplex amplification of short tandem repeat loci. *PCR Methods and Applications, 3*, 13–22.

Magnuson, V. L., et al. (1996). Substrate nucleotide-determined non-templated addition of adenine by Taq DNA polymerase: implications for PCR-based genotyping and cloning. *Biotechniques, 21*, 700–709.

Variant Alleles

Allor, C., et al. (2005). Identification and characterization of variant alleles at CODIS STR loci. *Journal of Forensic Sciences, 50*, 1128–1133.

Crouse, C. A., et al. (1999). Analysis and interpretation of short tandem repeat microvariants and three banded patterns using multiple allele detection systems. *Journal of Forensic Sciences, 44*, 87–94.

Grubwieser, P., et al. (2005). Unusual variant alleles in commonly used short tandem repeat loci. *International Journal of Legal Medicine, 119*, 164–166.

Heinrich, M., et al. (2005). Characterisation of variant alleles in the STR systems D2S1338, D3S1358 and D19S433. *International Journal of Legal Medicine, 119*, 310–313.

Huel, R., et al. (2007). Variant alleles, triallelic patterns, and point mutations observed in nuclear short tandem repeat typing of populations in Bosnia and Serbia. *Croatian Medical Journal, 48*(4), 494–502.

Moller, A., et al. (1994). Different types of structural variation in STRs: HumFES/FPS, HumVWA and HumD21S11. *International Journal of Legal Medicine, 106*, 319–323.

Puers, C., et al. (1993). Identification of repeat sequence heterogeneity at the polymorphic short tandem repeat locus HUMTH01 [AATG]n and reassignment of alleles in population analysis by using a locus-specific allelic ladder. *American Journal of Human Genetics, 53*, 953–958.

STRBase Variant Allele Reports. http://www.cstl.nist.gov/biotech/strbase/var_tab.htm

Triallelic Patterns

Clayton, T. M., et al. (2004). A genetic basis for anomalous band patterns encountered during DNA STR profiling. *Journal of Forensic Sciences, 49*, 1207–1214.

Crouse, C. A., et al. (1999). Analysis and interpretation of short tandem repeat microvariants and three banded patterns using multiple allele detection systems. *Journal of Forensic Sciences, 44*, 87–94.

Lane, A. B. (2008). The nature of tri-allelic TPOX genotypes in African populations. *Forensic Science International: Genetics, 2*, 134–137.

Lukka, M., et al. (2006). Triallelic patterns in STR loci used for paternity analysis: evidence for a duplication in chromosome 2 containing the TPOX STR locus. *Forensic Science International, 164*, 3–9.

STRBase Tri-Allelic Pattern Catalog. http://www.cstl.nist.gov/biotech/strbase/tri_tab.htm

Zamir, A., et al. (2002). Presentation of a three-banded pattern—analysis and interpretation. *Journal of Forensic Sciences, 47*, 824–826.

Null Alleles

Budowle, B., et al. (2001). STR primer concordance study. *Forensic Science International, 124*, 47–54.

Butler, J. M. (2006). Genetics and genomics of core STR loci used in human identity testing. *Journal of Forensic Sciences, 51*, 253–265.

Clayton, T. M., et al. (2004). Primer binding site mutations affecting the typing of STR loci contained within the AMPF*l*STR SGM plus kit. *Forensic Science International, 139*, 255–259.

Delamoye, M., et al. (2004). False homozygosities at various loci revealed by discrepancies between commercial kits: Implications for genetic databases. *Forensic Science International, 143*, 47–52.

Hill, C. R., et al. (2007). Concordance study between the AmpF*l*STR MiniFiler PCR amplification kit and conventional STR typing kits. *Journal of Forensic Sciences, 52*, 870–873.

Kline, M. C., et al. (1998). Non-amplification of a vWA allele. *Journal of Forensic Sciences, 43*(1), 250.

Lazaruk, K., et al. (2001). Sequence variation in humans and other primates at six short tandem repeat loci used in forensic identity testing. *Forensic Science International, 119*, 1–10.

Leibelt, C., et al. (2003). Identification of a D8S1179 primer binding site mutation and the validation of a primer designed to recover null alleles. *Forensic Science International, 133*, 220–227.

Nelson, M. S., et al. (2002). Detection of a primer-binding site polymorphism for the STR locus D16S539 using the PowerPlex 1.1 system and validation of a degenerate primer to correct for the polymorphism. *Journal of Forensic Sciences, 47*, 345–349.

Ricci, U., et al. (2007). A single mutation in the FGA locus responsible for false homozygosities and discrepancies between commercial kits in an unusual paternity test case. *Journal of Forensic Sciences, 52*, 393–396.

STRBase Null Allele Report. http://www.cstl.nist.gov/biotech/strbase/NullAlleles.htm

Vanderheyden, N., et al. (2007). Identification and sequence analysis of discordant phenotypes between AmpF*l*STR SGM plus and PowerPlex 16. *International Journal of Legal Medicine, 121*(4), 297–301.

Wallin, J. M., et al. (2002). Constructing universal multiplex PCR systems for comparative genotyping. *Journal of Forensic Sciences, 47*, 52–65.

Walsh, S. (1998). Commentary on Kline, M. C., Jenkins, B., Rogers, S. Non-amplification of a vWA allele. *Journal of Forensic Sciences, 43*(1), 250. *Journal of Forensic Sciences, 43*, 1103–1104.

Interpretation Guidelines

Scientific Working Group on DNA Analysis Methods. (2000). Short tandem repeat (STR) interpretation guidelines. *Forensic Science Communication, 2*(3). Available at http://www.fbi.gov/hq/lab/fsc/backissu/july2000/strig.htm

CHAPTER 11

Statistical Interpretation: Evaluating the Strength of Forensic DNA Evidence

It would not be scientifically justifiable to speak of a match as proof of identity in the absence of underlying data that permit some reasonable estimate of how rare the matching characteristics actually are.

—NRC II, p. 192

In Chapter 10 on short tandem repeat (STR) data interpretation, we concluded with a section entitled 'To match or not to match: That is the question.' If a DNA profile from a suspect does not match the evidence from a crime scene (and the testing has been performed properly), then we can reliably conclude that the individual in question did not contribute the biological sample recovered from the crime scene.

However, the more interesting outcome of a DNA profile comparison is what to conclude when the profiles between suspect and evidence match. Are they from the same individual or is there someone else out there who might just happen to match the evidence in question? Since we do not have the luxury of access to DNA profiles of everyone living on planet Earth, we must use smaller population data sets to extrapolate the possibility of a random match.

To estimate this match probability, allele frequencies are collected from various ethnic/racial sample sets. Based on their allele frequencies from validated databases, population genetic principles are applied to infer how reasonable it is that a random, unrelated individual could have contributed the DNA profile in question (Figure 11.1).

It is important to distinguish between unrelated and related individuals in assumptions being made for the calculations that follow. Obviously related individuals have DNA profiles that are more similar than unrelated individuals who are compared. In most equations that will be used in this chapter,

Contribution of the National Institute of Standards and Technology, 2010.

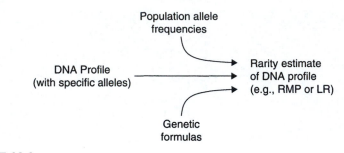

FIGURE 11.1

The rarity estimate for a specific DNA profile (in the form of a random match probability, RMP, or likelihood ratio, LR) is determined based on the alleles present in the profile, the population allele frequencies used, and genetic formulas that account for population substructure or degree of relatedness.

we will be assuming that unrelated individuals are involved. In Chapter 17, applications are considered where assumptions are made that individuals are related, such as paternity testing and disaster victim identification using biological relatives.

Of the three possible outcomes of a DNA test—'exclusion,' 'inconclusive,' or 'inclusion' between samples examined—only the third requires statistics. Statistics attempt to provide meaning to the match. These match statistics are usually provided in the form of an estimate of the random match probability or, in other words, the frequency for the particular genotype (DNA profile) in a population. However, different approaches may be taken in stating rarity of a match between a questioned (Q) and known (K) sample.

This chapter discusses basic principles that are important when considering statistical interpretation of forensic DNA profiles and estimating the rarity of a particular set of STR alleles. Example equations are examined and discussed using the population allele frequency information contained in Table 11.1. The goal is not to perform an in-depth examination of each genetic and statistical principle but rather to keep things in an understandable format for beginners in the field. Those readers desiring more extensive information on the topics discussed within this book may refer to additional references listed at the end of this chapter or to the accompanying volume, *Advanced Topics in Forensic DNA Typing, 3rd Edition*. Appendix 3 at the back of this book also covers basic principles of probability and statistics.

POPULATION DATA

To assess how common or rare a particular allele and allele combination are, data is gathered from representative groups of individuals. It is possible to run a small subset of the population and reliably predict allele and genotype

Table 11.1 STR allele frequencies from Caucasian and African American U.S. population samples.

Allele	Caucasian (N = 302)	African American (N = 258)
CSF1PO		
7	—	0.05253
8	0.00497*	0.06031
9	0.01159	0.03696
10	0.21689	0.25681
11	0.30132	0.24903
12	0.36093	0.29767
13	0.09603	0.03696
14	0.00828	0.00973
FGA		
18	0.02649	0.00194*
18.2	—	0.01163
19	0.05298	0.06202
20	0.12748	0.05620
21	0.18543	0.11628
22	0.21854	0.19574
22.2	0.01159	0.00388*
23	0.13411	0.17054
23.2	0.00331*	0.00194*
24	0.13576	0.12209
25	0.07119	0.12403
26	0.02318	0.08140
27	0.00331*	0.02326
28	—	0.01163
TH01		
6	0.23179	0.12403
7	0.19040	0.42054
8	0.08444	0.19380
9	0.11424	0.15116

(Continued)

Table 11.1 Continued

Allele	Caucasian (N = 302)	African American (N = 258)
9.3	0.36755	0.10465
10	0.00828	0.00194*
TPOX		
6	0.00166*	0.10078
7	—	0.01744
8	0.53477	0.37209
9	0.11921	0.17829
10	0.05629	0.08915
11	0.24338	0.21899
12	0.04139	0.02132
VWA		
14	0.09437	0.07752
15	0.11093	0.18605
16	0.20033	0.24806
17	0.28146	0.24225
18	0.20033	0.15504
19	0.10430	0.06202
20	0.00497*	0.01550
D3S1358		
14	0.10265	0.08915
15	0.26159	0.30233
16	0.25331	0.33527
17	0.21523	0.20543
18	0.15232	0.06008
19	0.01159	0.00388*
D5S818		
8	0.00331*	0.04845
9	0.04967	0.03876
10	0.05132	0.06977
11	0.36093	0.23256

Table 11.1 Continued

Allele	Caucasian (*N* = 302)	African American (*N* = 258)
12	0.38411	0.35271
13	0.14073	0.23837
14	0.00662*	0.01550
D7S820		
7	0.01821	0.01550
8	0.15066	0.23643
9	0.17715	0.10853
10	0.24338	0.33140
11	0.20695	0.20349
12	0.16556	0.08721
13	0.03477	0.01357
D8S1179		
8	0.01159	0.00194*
9	0.00331*	0.00581*
10	0.10099	0.02907
11	0.08278	0.04457
12	0.18543	0.14147
13	0.30464	0.21705
14	0.16556	0.30039
15	0.11424	0.18411
16	0.03146	0.06977
D13S317		
8	0.11258	0.03295
9	0.07450	0.03295
10	0.05132	0.02326
11	0.33940	0.30620
12	0.24834	0.42442
13	0.12417	0.14535
14	0.04801	0.03488
15	0.00166*	—

(Continued)

Table 11.1 Continued

Allele	Caucasian (N = 302)	African American (N = 258)
D16S539		
8	0.01821	0.03876
9	0.11258	0.19574
10	0.05629	0.11628
11	0.32119	0.31783
12	0.32616	0.19574
13	0.14570	0.11822
14	0.01987	0.01744
D18S51		
10	0.00828	0.00584*
11	0.01656	0.00195*
12	0.12748	0.07782
13	0.13245	0.05253
14	0.13742	0.07198
15	0.15894	0.16148
16	0.13907	0.15759
17	0.12583	0.15175
18	0.07616	0.12257
19	0.03808	0.09922
20	0.02152	0.06420
21	0.00828	0.00973
22	0.00828	0.00584*
D21S11		
27	0.02649	0.07752
28	0.15894	0.25775
29	0.19536	0.19767
30	0.27815	0.17442
30.2	0.02815	0.00969
31	0.08278	0.08140
31.2	0.09934	0.04651
32	0.00662*	0.00775*

Table 11.1 Continued

Allele	Caucasian (*N* = 302)	African American (*N* = 258)
32.2	0.08444	0.05814
33	0.00166*	0.00581*
33.2	0.02649	0.03488
34	—	0.00581*
34.2	0.00497*	—
35	0.00166*	0.02326
36	—	0.00969

Reported in Butler, J.M., et al. (2003). Allele frequencies for 15 autosomal STR loci on U.S. Caucasian, African American, and Hispanic populations. Journal of Forensic Sciences, 48, 908–911; Genotypes for the individuals used to generate these allele frequencies are available on STRBase at http://www.cstl.nist.gov/biotech/strbase/NISTpop.htm

Note: Allele frequencies denoted with an asterisk (*) are below the 5/2N minimum allele threshold recommended by the NRC II report. Some additional rare alleles were removed to save space.

frequencies in the entire population—much like a telephone survey of several hundred individuals is used to try to predict the outcome of a political election. The key is collecting information from enough individuals to reliably estimate the frequency of the major alleles for a genetic locus.

The primary goal of generating a population database is to find all 'common' alleles and sample these alleles multiple times in order to reliably estimate the frequency of alleles present in the population under consideration. It is worth noting that some alleles, particularly variant alleles, have only been observed a few times and are therefore rather rare. Table 11.1 lists allele frequencies for U.S. Caucasian and African American populations at the 13 core STR loci used in the United States. These allele frequencies are used throughout the book in calculations made for various purposes.

Generating a population database

The primary steps in generating and testing a population database are illustrated in Figure 11.2. A laboratory must first decide on the number of samples that will be tested and what particular ethnic/racial groups are relevant to estimating DNA profile frequencies that might be encountered by the lab. Population databases are often generated by gathering a set of biological samples in the form of liquid blood from a local hospital or blood bank. Usually the individuals selected are healthy and, it is hoped, unrelated to one another so that they reliably represent the population of interest. These 'convenience' samples are deemed reliable since they are similar to other data sets from

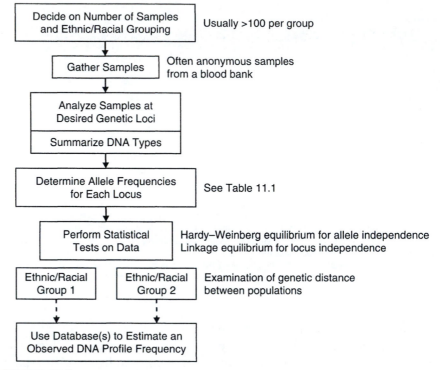

FIGURE 11.2

Steps in generating and validating a population database that can then be used to estimate the frequency of an observed DNA profile in the population.

similar population groups. Usually the individual samples are devoid of identifiers that could be used to link the DNA typing results back to the donor.

After the samples have been gathered, they are extracted, PCR-amplified, and genotyped at the STR loci of interest, such as the 13 core loci used in the FBI's Combined DNA Index System (CODIS). These single-source samples are typically processed using commercial STR kits and standard interpretation guidelines to designate alleles.

Following the gathering of the genotype data, the information is converted into allele frequencies by counting the number of times each allele is observed. D.N.A. Box 11.1 shows an example of allele counting with the STR locus D13S317 used to determine the Caucasian data in Table 11.1.

Allele frequency information allows for more compact data storage and enables Hardy–Weinberg equilibrium testing. Typically the sample genotypes and allele frequencies associated with a particular ethnic/racial group are segregated to enable both intragroup and intergroup comparisons.

D.N.A. Box 11.1 Converting Collected STR Genotypes into Observed Allele Frequencies

Following the gathering of the genotype data at each STR locus, the information is converted into allele frequencies by counting the number of times each allele is observed. The table below shows an example of allele counting for the locus D13S317 used to determine the Caucasian data in Table 11.1.

The observed alleles, ranging from 8 to 15 repeats, are listed across the top and down the left side. At the intersection of the rows and columns, the numbers of observed genotypes are listed. For example, starting in the top left-hand corner, the genotype 8,8 is seen 9 times in the set of 302 individuals examined, while the genotype 11,14 is seen 12 times. On the right side, the numbers of observed alleles are counted by summing the row and column containing the allele of interest. Thus, the number of chromosomes containing allele 8 is equal to 68 from 9 + 9 + 1 + 17 + 13 + 10 + 0 + 0 for the row containing allele 8 plus 9 for the column with the

8,8 genotype. The number of 8,8 genotypes is counted twice since both chromosomes contain an allele 8 at the D13S317 marker. The frequency for allele 8 is determined by dividing 68 into the total number of chromosomes, which are 604 since there are two chromosomes for each of the 302 individuals typed. Note that there is only one allele 15 observed in this study, which comes from a 10,15 genotype. The frequency for allele 15 is marked with an asterisk since it is observed only once and falls below the minimum allele frequency of $5/2N$ or 0.00828, where $N = 302$ individuals tested.

Source:

Butler, J. M., et al. (2003). Allele frequencies for 15 autosomal STR loci on U.S. Caucasian, African American, and Hispanic populations: All allele frequencies and genotypes. *Journal of Forensic Sciences*, 48, 908–911. Available at http://www.cstl.nist.gov/biotech/strbase/NISTpopdata/JFS2003IDresults.xls

Genotype Array	8	9	10	11	12	13	14	15		Allele Count	Observed Frequency
	8,8	8,9	8,10	8,11	8,12	8,13	8,14	8,15			
8	9	9	1	17	13	10	0	0	8	68	0.11258
		9,9	9,10	9,11	9,12	9,13	9,14	9,15			
9		1	2	15	10	4	3	0	9	45	0.07450
			10,10	10,11	10,12	10,13	10,14	10,15			
10			2	12	6	3	2	1	10	31	0.05132
				11,11	11,12	11,13	11,14	11,15			
11				37	54	21	12	0	11	205	0.33940
					12,12	12,13	12,14	12,15			
12					21	18	7	0	12	150	0.24834
						13,13	13,14	13,15			
13						7	5	0	13	75	0.12417
							14,14	14,15			
14							0	0	14	29	0.04801
								15,15			
15								0	15	1	0.00166*
										Total = 604	

Sample sizes used for allele frequency estimation

Most published population data include on the order of 100 to 200 STR types per locus per population examined. In a key paper in 1992 entitled 'Sample size requirements for addressing the population genetic issues of forensic use of DNA typing,' Ranajit Chakraborty concluded that 100 to 150 individuals per population could provide an adequate sampling for a genetic locus provided that allele frequencies below 1% were not used in forensic calculations. Others have arrived at similar conclusions; namely, that 100 to 120 individuals per locus per population are sufficient for robust likelihood calculations. Collecting information from more samples usually only improves the accuracy of frequency estimates for rare alleles. Comparisons of data collected with typical population sizes versus thousands of individuals show similar allele frequency results (D.N.A. Box 11.2).

Population comparison DNA databases are often generated by individual forensic laboratories to assess variations in common local populations. This is particularly important to locales that may have an isolated population within its jurisdiction. For example, in Arizona it would be helpful to have a population database involving Native Americans such as Apaches and Navajos since they live in fairly close-knit communities within Arizona and would be expected to have different genotype frequencies compared to Caucasians or African Americans living in Arizona.

Minimum allele frequency

To obtain a reliable estimate of an allele frequency, it is important to collect more than one data point for that allele. A conservative minimum allele frequency is used to ensure that an allele has been sampled sufficiently to be used reliably in statistical tests. The 1996 National Research Council report (NRC II) states that an estimate of an allele frequency can be very inaccurate if the allele is so rare that it is represented only once or a few times in a database, and some rare alleles might not be represented at all. Thus, it is recommended that each allele be observed at least five times to be included in reliable statistical calculations. The minimum allele frequency is therefore $5/(2N)$, where N is the number of individuals sampled from a population and $2N$ is the number of chromosomes counted because autosomes are in pairs due to inheritance of one allele from one's mother and one from one's father.

When an observed allele frequency falls below the minimum allele frequency of $5/2N$, such as the D13S317 allele 15 in D.N.A. Box 11.1, then the minimum allele frequency is used instead. Thus, with the D13S317 allele 15 example, a value of 0.00828 ($5/[2 \times 302]$) would be used in allele frequency

D.N.A. Box 11.2 Comparison of STR Allele Frequencies from a 'Normal' versus a Larger Population Study

Most population data sets used in estimating STR allele frequencies come from roughly a hundred to a few hundred individuals. To demonstrate that collection of data from a few hundred individuals can provide reliable STR allele frequency estimates, comparisons of individual allele frequencies can be made to much larger data sets. In the table below, a comparison of a typical population study with a few hundred individuals (Butler et al., 2003) is made to a much larger study involving thousands of samples (Einum & Scarpetta, 2004). In both African American and Caucasian data sets, most of the allele frequencies are very similar. For example, D13S317 allele 12 in African Americans was seen in 42.9% with the 7833 sample study and 42.4% with the 258 sample study. Note that with the larger sample set, more rare alleles were observed (e.g., alleles 7 and 16).

D13S317	African American		Caucasian	
Alleles	$N = 7833$	$N = 258$	$N = 7814$	$N = 302$
7	0.0001	—	0.0003	—
8	0.0260	0.0330	0.1200	0.1126
9	0.0218	0.0330	0.0754	0.0745
10	0.0273	0.0233	0.0618	0.0513
11	0.2940	0.3062	0.3110	0.3394
12	0.4290	0.4244	0.2830	0.2483
13	0.1520	0.1454	0.1040	0.1242
14	0.0486	0.0349	0.0443	0.0480
15	0.0010	—	0.0014	0.0017
16	0.0002	—	—	—
Minimum allele frequency (5/2N)	0.0003	0.0096	0.0003	0.0083

Sources:
Butler, J. M., et al. (2003). Allele frequencies for 15 autosomal STR loci on U.S. Caucasian, African American, and Hispanic populations. *Journal of Forensic Sciences, 48*, 908–911.

Einum, D. D., & Scarpetta, M. A. (2004). Genetic analysis of large data sets of North American Black, Caucasian, and Hispanic populations at 13 CODIS STR loci. *Journal of Forensic Sciences, 49*, 1381–1385.

calculations rather than the 0.00166 actually reported in the study described in D.N.A. Box 11.1.

Sources of samples for population databases

Individuals whose DNA profiles will be used to construct a population database for allele frequency estimation purposes should be selected without prior knowledge of genotypes at the loci under examination to ensure randomness of the samples. A frequent practice is to collect samples from blood donors or hospital volunteers. For example, the samples used to generate the STR typing data used in Table 11.1 were purchased from two different blood banks and represent anonymous blood donors with self-identified ethnicities. Well-characterized population samples with anthropological descriptions would be desirable in many cases to carefully define population groups but are not necessary to obtain valid information in forensic DNA population databases. Self-declaration of ethnicity can be a suitable method of categorizing samples on the basis of ethnicity.

Broad racial/ethnic categories are usually adequate for most forensic population databases, unless an isolated population is of interest, such as an Amish community. It is also desirable to use unrelated individuals in creating a population database in order to improve the precision of allele frequency estimates by increasing the number of independent alleles sampled.

Statistical tests on population data

Once STR genotypes have been generated from population samples, the data are typically evaluated with statistical tests to ensure that the allele frequencies are reasonable based on genetic inheritance principles (D.N.A. Box 11.3). Computer programs are used to conduct statistical tests for Hardy–Weinberg equilibrium (HWE) and linkage equilibrium in order to assess independence of alleles and loci (Figure 11.3).

With the assumption of independence, it then becomes possible to equate the overall match probability with the product of the locus-specific match probabilities. This combination of locus-specific match probabilities is referred to as the *product rule*. In other words, the match probability for the STR locus D13S317 can be combined with additional STR loci such as TH01 and D18S51 to decrease the odds of a random match to an unrelated individual.

GENETIC FORMULAS

Most of the examples that are worked in this chapter utilize the simple HWE model for the genetic formulas applied (i.e., 2pq for heterozygotes and p^2 for homozygotes). However, real-world populations often need adjustments to correct for what is known as *population substructure*.

Genetic mixing of alleles is not completely random because parents often share some common ancestry. The consequence of this nonrandom mating is that there is usually a decrease in heterozygotes and an increase in homozygotes. This population substructure can be adjusted for with the use of a correction factor referred to as theta (θ). The National Research Council (NRC II) report

D.N.A. Box 11.3 Hardy–Weinberg Equilibrium Testing

STR alleles are inherited by an individual from his or her mother and father in a Mendelian fashion and frequencies of occurrence follow a predictable pattern of probability. If two alleles A and a occur with frequencies p and q in the population, then the genotype AA (a homozygote) should occur p^2 and the genotype Aa (heterozygote) should occur with frequency 2pq. Allele frequencies are used to generate expected genotype frequencies that are then compared to the observed genotype frequencies. If observed and expected values are similar, then it is assumed that alleles within the genetic locus are stable or in other words 'in equilibrium.'

Hardy–Weinberg equilibrium (HWE) predicts the stability of allele and genotype frequencies from one generation to the next. The primary purpose in testing for HWE is to determine if alleles within a locus are independent of each other. Frequencies should not change over the course of many generations if the locus is genetically stable. However, natural populations usually violate HWE to some degree and thereby cause allele frequencies to change over time.

HWE assumes a random mating population of infinite size with no migration or mutation to introduce new alleles, which of course does not exist in real human populations.

The reasons for each of these HWE assumptions are listed below:

If minor departures are seen from HWE, there is generally no major cause for concern with using a particular database. Some authors will do little more than note that there is a statistically significant departure from HWE for a particular locus in their population data set. It is important to keep in mind that there are three principal reasons for observations of major differences (departures) from Hardy–Weinberg equilibrium: (1) Parents might be related, leading to inbreeding and a higher than expected number of homozygotes; (2) population substructure; and (3) selection because persons with different genotypes might survive and reproduce at different rates.

Another purpose of performing an HWE test is to look for any indications of excess homozygosity. The primary explanation for excess homozygosity is allelic dropout or 'null alleles' (see D.N.A. Box 10.3) where only one allele is observed from a truly heterozygous individual.

Source:
National Research Council Committee on DNA Forensic Science (1996). *The evaluation of forensic DNA evidence.* Washington, DC: National Academy Press.

The Assumption	The Reason
Large population	Lots of possible allele combinations
No natural selection	No restriction on mating so all alleles have equal chance of becoming part of next generation
No mutation	No new alleles being introduced
No immigration/emigration	No new alleles being introduced or leaving
Random mating	Any allele combination is possible

entitled *The Evaluation of Forensic DNA Evidence* discusses issues that surround population structure. The NRC II report makes several recommendations for taking population substructure into account.

The NRC II Recommendation 4.1 substructure adjustments replace p^2 for homozygote calculations with $p^2 + p(1 - p)\theta$, where θ is an empirically

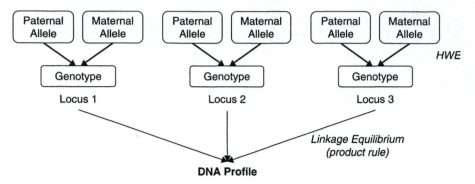

FIGURE 11.3

A DNA profile is made up of genotypes from individual genetic loci. The genotype at each locus results from inheritance of paternal and maternal alleles. Hardy–Weinberg equilibrium (HWE) tests evaluate the independence of alleles within a genetic locus, while linkage equilibrium tests ascertain the independence of alleles between loci. Independent loci and alleles enable use of the product rule.

determined measure of population subdivision. A conservative value for θ is 0.01 for typical at-large populations and 0.03 with smaller, isolated, and more inbred groups of people. A number of studies have demonstrated that θ = 0.01 is a reliable and conservative estimate of population substructure with extensive population data.

The impact of these recommendations on homozygote and heterozygote frequency calculations is illustrated in Table 11.2. Examples are given with a TH01 homozygote 6,6 and a D13S317 heterozygote 11,14.

Impact of relatives on STR profile frequency estimates

If the suspect and the true perpetrator of a crime are related, then their genotype frequencies are not independent and a different calculation is required. Since STR profiles from relatives are expected to be more similar to the individual in question than a random, unrelated individual, NRC II Recommendation 4.4 covers probability calculations from various scenarios of individuals related to the suspect. These calculations are discussed in the companion volume *Advanced Topics in Forensic DNA Typing, 3rd Edition.*

If the possibility exists that a close relative of the accused had access to the crime scene and may have been a contributor of the evidence, then the best action is usually to obtain a reference sample from the relative. For example, a scenario involving a brother as a potential evidence contributor should be sufficient probable cause for obtaining a reference sample from the brother and typing it with the same STR markers as used for the evidence. This information could then be used to resolve the question of whether or not the relative carries the same DNA profile as the accused.

Table 11.2 Comparison of statistical treatment for homozygotes and heterozygotes under different assumptions.

	Under HWE	Unconditional (NRC II Recommendation 4.1)	Conditional with Substructure Adjustment
			(NRC II Recommendation 4.10a)
Homozygote	p_i^2	$p_i^2 + p_i(1-p_i)\theta$	$\dfrac{[p_i(1-\theta) + 2\theta][p_i(1-\theta) + 3\theta]}{(1+\theta)(1+2\theta)}$
TH01 **6,6** $p_i = 0.23$ $\theta = 0.01$	$(0.23)^2 = \mathbf{0.053}$	$(0.23)^2 + (0.23)$ $(1-0.23)(0.01)$ $= 0.053 + 0.0018$ $= \mathbf{0.055}$	$[(0.23)(1-0.01) + 2(0.01)][(0.23)(1-0.01)$ $+ 3(0.01)] (1+0.01)(1+2(0.01))$ $= (0.2477)(0.2577)/(1.01)(1.02)$ $= \mathbf{0.062}$
			(NRC II Recommendation 4.10b)
Heterozygote	$2p_i\,p_j$	$2p_i\,p_j$	$\dfrac{2[p_i(1-\theta) + \theta][p_j(1-\theta) + \theta]}{(1+\theta)(1+2\theta)}$
D13S317 **11,14** $p_i = 0.34$ $p_j = 0.05$ $\theta = 0.01$	$2(0.34)(0.05) = \mathbf{0.0340}$	$2(0.34)(0.05) = \mathbf{0.0340}$	$2[(0.34)(1-0.01) + 0.01][(0.05)$ $(1-0.01) + 0.01] (1+0.01)(1+2(0.01))$ $= 2(0.3466)(0.0595)/(1.01)(1.02)$ $= \mathbf{0.0400}$

Note: Allele frequency values (p_i, p_j) for the TH01 and D13S317 example data are from Table 11.1 (U.S. Caucasians). Note that if θ is zero, then unconditional and conditional formulas collapse to their Hardy–Weinberg equilibrium (HWE) functions.

METHODS FOR STATING THE RARITY OF A DNA PROFILE

When a match is observed between an evidence sample (the 'unknown' or questioned sample—Q) and a reference sample (the 'known'—K), then statistical methods are typically invoked to provide information regarding the relevance of this match (see Figure 11.1). The prosecution argues that the Q and K samples have a common source, while the defense typically argues that the samples happen to match by chance. The possibility of another *unrelated* individual pulled at random from the population possessing an identical genotype can be determined by calculating the frequency with which the observed genotype occurs in a representative population database. When a DNA profile is fairly common, then it is easier to imagine that the suspect might not be connected to the crime scene. If, on the other hand, the genotype is found to be extremely rare, then the evidence is stronger that the suspect contributed the crime scene sample in question.

A number of population databases have been generated in recent years to which a DNA profile may be compared. Some basic U.S. population allele frequencies, which are listed in Table 11.1, will be used to illustrate how profile frequencies are determined. For calculations performed in one's own laboratory, a relevant population database, usually specific to possible populations in one's local area, would be used instead.

It is important to keep in mind that methods for reporting DNA evidence vary between laboratories. Some laboratories present random match probabilities that are based on genotype frequency estimates. Another approach is to report likelihood ratios to convey relative support for the weight of DNA evidence under the hypothesis that the defendant is the source of the DNA profile versus an unrelated individual from the population at large. The FBI Laboratory has opted for a source attribution approach when random match probabilities are sufficiently rare. In the following sections, we will discuss the issues surrounding each approach and go through the statistical calculations performed with each method.

FREQUENCY ESTIMATE CALCULATIONS

DNA profile frequency estimates are calculated by first considering the genotype frequency for each locus and then multiplying the frequencies across all loci. The most effective method to understand how the probability of a random match is calculated is to work through an example.

The frequency for any DNA profile can be calculated with knowledge of the alleles from the DNA profile and allele frequencies seen in a population database. Of course, a different size database or one with different allele frequencies can result in a different expected genotype frequency for each tested locus and hence a different DNA profile frequency. It is therefore important that the database used is large enough and representative of the population of the suspect(s). Frequencies from multiple populations are typically reported to provide a range of possibilities since the population of the true perpetrator is unknown.

In Table 11.3 and Table 11.4 the DNA profile frequencies for 13 STR loci are determined using allele frequencies from the two different population groups listed in Table 11.1. One database contains allele frequencies from DNA profiles generated from 302 U.S. Caucasians or 604 measured alleles. The other set of allele frequencies in Table 11.1 comes from 258 African Americans or 516 measured alleles. The DNA profile in question contains the following alleles: 11 and 14 at D13S317 (heterozygous), 6 at TH01 (homozygous), and 14 and 16 at D18S51 (heterozygous).

In the population sample of 604 alleles (302 U.S. Caucasian individuals), allele 11 for D13S317 was observed 205 times, which is 0.33940 or approximately 34% of the time (see D.N.A. Box 11.1 and Table 11.1). In other words, we can assume that there is a 34% chance that any particular D13S317 allele

Table 11.3 Random match probability for a 13-locus STR profile using the U.S. Caucasian allele frequencies found in Table 11.1.

	Allele 1	Allele 2	Allele 1 Frequency (p)	Allele 2 Frequency (q)	Formula	Expected Genotype Frequency
D13S317	11	14	0.33940	0.04801	2pq	0.0326
TH01	6	6	0.23179		p^2	0.0537
D18S51	14	16	0.13742	0.13907	2pq	0.0382
D21S11	28	30	0.15894	0.27815	2pq	0.0884
D3S1358	16	17	0.25331	0.21523	2pq	0.1090
D5S818	12	13	0.38411	0.14073	2pq	0.1081
D7S820	9	9	0.17715		p^2	0.0314
D8S1179	12	14	0.18543	0.16556	2pq	0.0614
CSF1PO	10	10	0.21689		p^2	0.0470
FGA	21	22	0.18543	0.21854	2pq	0.0810
D16S539	9	11	0.11258	0.32119	2pq	0.0723
TPOX	8	8	0.53477		p^2	0.2860
VWA	17	18	0.28146	0.20033	2pq	0.1128
AMEL	X	Y				
Product rule						1.20×10^{-15}
Combined frequency						1 in 8.37×10^{14}

selected at random from an unrelated individual will be an 11. In the same manner, the chance for observing an allele 14 in a Caucasian population is q = 0.04801 since this allele was seen 29 times in 604 allele measurements (see D.N.A. Box 11.1 and Table 11.1).

If the individual with the 11,14 D13S317 genotype received these alleles at random from each of his parents, then the chance of receiving an 11 from his mother and a 14 from his father is pq and of receiving the 14 from his mother and the 11 from his father is another pq. With either combination possible, the probability to be 11,14 by chance is pq + pq or 2pq.

Plugging the frequency values of p = 0.33940 and q = 0.04801 into the formula 2pq ($2 \times 0.33940 \times 0.04801$) results in an estimated genotype frequency of 0.0326 or, in other words, approximately 3% of people from a Caucasian population are expected to have an 11,14 genotype at the D13S317 locus. Conducting the same analysis with an African American population database will result in a similar genotype frequency of 0.0214 or 2% (Table 11.4).

Table 11.4 Random match probability calculations for the same 13-locus STR profile shown in Table 11.3 but using the African American allele frequencies found in Table 11.1.

	Allele 1	Allele 2	Allele 1 Frequency (p)	Allele 2 Frequency (q)	Formula	Expected Genotype Frequency
D13S317	11	14	0.30620	0.03488	2pq	0.0214
TH01	6	6	0.12403		p^2	0.0154
D18S51	14	16	0.07198	0.15759	2pq	0.0227
D21S11	28	30	0.25775	0.17442	2pq	0.0899
D3S1358	16	17	0.33527	0.20543	2pq	0.1377
D5S818	12	13	0.35271	0.23837	2pq	0.1682
D7S820	9	9	0.10853		p^2	0.0118
D8S1179	12	14	0.14147	0.30039	2pq	0.0850
CSF1PO	10	10	0.25681		p^2	0.0660
FGA	21	22	0.11628	0.31783	2pq	0.1244
D16S539	9	11	0.19574	0.32119	2pq	0.0723
TPOX	8	8	0.37209		p^2	0.1385
VWA	17	18	0.24225	0.15504	2pq	0.0751
AMEL	X	Y				
Product rule						6.04×10^{-17}
Combined frequency						1 in 1.66×10^{16}

With the TH01 locus, a homozygous allele 6 was observed (Table 11.3). The same comparison of the profile's observed allele to a measured allele frequency in a population database is performed with TH01 but in this case the combined probability of inheriting allele 6 from both parents is pp or p^2 (see Figure 2.8). Since allele 6 was observed 140 times out of 604 allele measurements in U.S. Caucasians, $p = 0.23179$ and $p^2 = 0.0537$ (Table 11.3). Using the African American allele frequency for TH01 allele 6 (Table 11.1), $p = 0.12403$ and $p^2 = 0.0154$ (Table 11.4). Thus, allele is more rare in African Americans.

Since these two STR loci are on separate chromosomes (e.g., chromosome 13 for D13S317 and chromosome 11 for TH01), they will segregate independently during meiosis, allowing the genotype frequencies to be multiplied. In the case of a U.S. Caucasian population, the chance of a person having the combined genotype of 11,14 at D13S317 and 6,6 at TH01 is 5% of 3% (i.e., 0.0537×0.0326) or 0.175%.

D.N.A. Box 11.4 Names of Big Numbers with Their Corresponding Scientific Notation

10^6	Million	10^{39}	Duodecillion
10^9	Billion	10^{42}	Tredecillion
10^{12}	Trillion	10^{45}	Quattuordecillion
10^{15}	Quadrillion	10^{48}	Quindecillion
10^{18}	Quintillion	10^{51}	Sexdecillion
10^{21}	Sextillion	10^{54}	Septendecillion
10^{24}	Septillion	10^{57}	Octodecillion
10^{27}	Octillion	10^{60}	Novemdecillion
10^{30}	Nonillion	10^{63}	Vigintillion
10^{33}	Decillion	10^{100}	Google
10^{36}	Undecillion		

Source:
http://www.sizes.com/numbers/big_numName.htm

Similar calculations for the D18S51 locus with alleles 14 and 16 result in an estimated genotype frequency of 3.82% (see Table 11.3). The combined profile frequency with these three loci thus becomes 0.000067—the product of the three individual genotype frequencies ($0.0326 \times 0.0537 \times 0.0382$) or about 1 in 15,000. Note that when using the African American allele frequencies, the DNA profile frequency in this example drops to 0.0000076 ($0.0214 \times 0.0154 \times 0.0227$) or about 1 in 131,000 individuals (see Table 11.4). Because the alleles observed in the specific STR profile under consideration in Table 11.4 are rarer in an African American population, the profile has a rarer frequency estimate.

Working through the rest of the STR loci in Table 11.3 and Table 11.4, the final combined frequency estimate for the DNA profile in question is 1 in 837 trillion (8.37×10^{14}) using Caucasian allele frequencies (Table 11.3) and 1 in 16.6 quadrillion (1.66×10^{16}) using African American allele frequencies (Table 11.4).

Often the rarity of a calculated DNA profile goes beyond one in billions (10^9) or trillions (10^{12}) to numbers that are not frequently used because they are so large. A list of some big number names is contained in D.N.A. Box 11.4 to aid in verbal descriptions of rare DNA profiles. For example, the inverted value of 1.20×10^{-15} is 1 in 8.37×10^{14} or 0.84×10^{15} (one in 0.84 quadrillion).

D.N.A. Box 11.5 OmniPop: Calculating STR Profile Frequencies against Multiple Population Databases

The ability to determine simultaneously the frequency for a particular STR profile in multiple population databases was recently made easier with the development of a Microsoft Excel macro called OmniPop. Below the cumulative profile frequency range is calculated for the particular STR profile listed against 202 published population studies involving Profiler Plus kit loci and 120 published reports containing all 13 CODIS core loci. The cumulative profile frequencies obtained with U.S. Caucasian allele frequencies presented in the Table 11.1 data set are listed as well.

These profile frequencies were all calculated with a theta value of 0.01. When using a theta value of 0.03 as recommended by NRC II for more inbred populations, the range for the computed profile with all 13 STR loci across the 120 published population data sets is 1.19×10^{14} to 1.27×10^{21}.

It is worth noting that the computed profile is part of the U.S. Caucasian data set used to generate the allele frequencies described in Table 11.1 and thus this database would be expected to compute fairly conservative values for this particular 13-locus STR profile as demonstrated below.

STR Locus	Profile Computed	Number of Populations Used	Cumulative Profile Frequency Range (1 in ...)	Cumulative Profile Frequency against U.S. Caucasians (Table 11.1)
D3S1358	16,17	202	4.53 to 62.6	9.19
VWA	17,18	202	37.6 to 1,080	81.8
FGA	21,22	202	737 to 119,000	1,010
D8S1179	12,14	202	8,980 to 5,430,000	16,400
D21S11	28,30	202	165,000 to 248,000,000	186,000
D18S51	14,16	202	3.85×10^6 to 2.68×10^{10}	4.88×10^6
D5S818	12,13	202	2.28×10^7 to 4.22×10^{11}	4.51×10^7
D13S317	11,14	202	4.32×10^8 to 1.69×10^{13}	1.38×10^9
D7S820	9,9	202	1.17×10^{10} to 2.98×10^{16}	4.22×10^{10}
D16S539	9,11	120	3.14×10^{11} to 1.11×10^{18}	5.82×10^{11}
TH01	6,6	120	3.53×10^{12} to 1.45×10^{19}	1.05×10^{13}
TPOX	8,8	120	9.13×10^{12} to 1.54×10^{20}	3.63×10^{13}
CSF1PO	10,10	120	1.42×10^{14} to 2.65×10^{21}	7.43×10^{14}

Source:
OmniPop 200.1 was used for these calculations. Created by Brian Burritt of the San Diego Police Department and freely available at http://www.cstl.nist.gov/biotech/strbase/populationdata.htm

As more and more loci match during a Q and K sample comparison, it becomes less and less likely that an *unrelated*, random person in the population contributed the crime scene sample. Thus, either the suspect contributed the evidence or a very unlikely coincidence occurred.

Impact of various population databases

From the combined STR profile frequencies calculated in Tables 11.3 and 11.4, it is apparent that different populations can yield different frequency estimates due to variations in allele frequencies in these populations. A calculation of the same STR profile as used in the previous examples against 202 different published population databases (including the two present in Table 11.1) found that the cumulative profile frequency ranged from 1 in 3.43×10^{14} to 1 in 2.65×10^{21} (D.N.A. Box 11.5).

It is probably worth noting that the final calculated value in the far right column of D.N.A. Box 11.5 (1 in 7.43×10^{14}) differs slightly from that determined in Table 11.3 (1 in 8.37×10^{14}) due to the number of significant figures carried throughout the calculations. Thus, to obtain consistent frequency estimates with the same allele frequency information, it is essential to maintain the same significant figures between calculations.

Another source of population databases that enables an online search is the European Network of Forensic Science Institutes (ENFSI) DNA Working Group STR Population Database located at http://www.str-base.org/index.php. An estimated random match probability for a DNA profile of interest can be calculated using allele frequencies produced from 5700 profiles covering 24 European populations that have been generated with the SGM Plus loci.

General match probability

DNA profile probabilities can be calculated for a variety of scenarios. There are five different sets of people and possible relationships to a suspect: (1) the suspect's siblings, (2) his other relatives, (3) other members of his subpopulation, (4) other members of his racial group, and (5) everyone else.

Instead of having to calculate all of these case-specific match probabilities, some authors have proposed using general match probabilities that have been calculated from the theoretically most conservative method involving the most two common alleles for each locus (D.N.A. Box 11.6). The primary advantage of this approach is that repeated calculations are not required for each profile observed. Rather the general match probability is provided in court as being a very conservative estimate on the rarity of the observed DNA profile. Another reason that this approach is advocated is that some statisticians feel that it is difficult to provide any sound statistical support for probabilities of

D.N.A. Box 11.6 General Match Probability Values

In a paper performing statistical analyses to support forensic interpretation of the 10 loci present in the SGM Plus kit, Foreman and Evett (2001) advocate the use of general probability values when reporting full-matching STR profiles. With the 10 STR loci present in the SGM Plus kit used in the United Kingdom and Europe, the probabilities are shown in the table below (see Foreman & Evett, 2001, Table 4).

They argue that adoption of such figures would eliminate the need to perform case-specific match probabilities making it much easier to present information to the court. The match probabilities for specific STR profiles are typically several orders of magnitude smaller than those given above, which were calculated from the theoretically most common SGM Plus profile. Thus, these probabilities should provide a fair and reasonable assessment of the weight of DNA evidence for each category and in the end would probably be favorable to the suspect (defendant).

A similar calculation for a full match with the 13 CODIS loci using the most common alleles observed in U.S. population databases, such as Table 11.1, would result in even higher general match probability values since more STR loci are being examined.

Sources:
Balding, D. J. (1999). When can a DNA profile be regarded as unique. *Science & Justice, 39,* 257–260.
Foreman, L. A., & Evett, I. W. (2001). Statistical analyses to support forensic interpretation for a new 10-locus STR profiling system. *International Journal of Legal Medical, 114,* 147–155.

Relationship with suspect	Match probability
Sibling	1 in 10 000
Parent/child	1 in 1 million
Half-sibling or uncle/nephew	1 in 10 million
First cousin	1 in 100 million
Unrelated	1 in 1 billion

such a small magnitude (e.g., 10^{-21}) given the limited sampling that has been performed.

What a random match probability is not

It is important to realize what a random match probability is not. It is not the chance that someone else is guilty or that someone else left the biological material at the crime scene. Likewise, it is not the chance of the defendant not being guilty or the chance that someone else in reality would have that same genotype. Rather a *random match probability* is simply the estimated frequency at which a particular STR profile would be expected to occur in a population. This random match probability may also be thought of as the theoretical chance that if you sample one person at random from the population he or she will have the particular DNA profile in question.

Switching the language and meaning of a random match probability is something referred to as the *prosecutor's fallacy* or the fallacy of the transposed conditional. Statements such as 'there is only a 1 in 15,000 chance that the DNA profile came from someone else' or 'there is only a 1 in 15,000 chance that the defendant is not guilty' are examples of the prosecutor's fallacy. A correct statement would be 'the probability of selecting the observed profile from a population of random unrelated individuals is expected to be 1 in 15,000 based on the alleles present in this sample….' Note that with a 13 STR locus-match instead of just the three used in the above example the random match probabilities are in the range of trillions, quadrillions, and beyond.

The *defense attorney's fallacy* is equally problematic where the assumption is made that everyone else with the same genotype has an equal chance of being guilty or that every possible genotype in a mixture has an equal chance of having committed the crime. Access to the crime scene, motive, and legitimate alibis all play a role in an investigation, suggesting that it is unwise to consider DNA evidence and corresponding frequency estimates in a vacuum devoid of other information. A suspect is usually under suspicion and investigation prior to his DNA profile being known, and thus the DNA results are most often used to corroborate and connect a criminal perpetrator to his crime scene rather than as the sole evidentiary material.

LIKELIHOOD RATIO

When matching STR profiles are obtained between a suspect (known sample, K) and the crime scene evidence (question sample, Q), it is necessary to quantify the evidentiary value of this match. Another approach in assessing the weight of the Q-K comparison besides the match probability profile frequency estimate just described is the use of a likelihood ratio (LR). LRs involve a comparison of the probabilities of the evidence under two alternative propositions. These mutually exclusive hypotheses represent the position of the prosecution—namely, that the DNA from the crime scene originated from the suspect—and the position of the defense—that the DNA just happens to coincidently match the defendant and is instead from an unknown person out in the population at large.

A likelihood ratio is a ratio of two probabilities of the same evidence under different hypotheses (see Appendix 3). For example, if a DNA profile generated from a crime scene evidence sample matches a suspect's DNA profile, then there are generally two possible hypotheses for why the profiles match each other: (1) the suspect matches because he left his biological sample at the crime scene or (2) the true perpetrator is still at large and just happens to match the suspect at the DNA markers examined.

Typically, the first hypothesis (and that championed by the prosecution) is placed in the numerator of the likelihood ratio while the second hypothesis—that someone else other than the defendant committed the crime (which is of course the defense's position)—is placed in the denominator. Thus, in mathematical terms:

$$LR = \frac{H_p}{H_d}$$

or verbally the likelihood ratio equals the hypothesis of the prosecution divided by the hypothesis of the defense. Since the hypothesis of the prosecution is that the defendant committed the crime, then $H_p = 1$ (assumes 100% probability). On the other hand, the hypothesis of the defense that the profile originated from someone else can be calculated from the genotype frequency of the particular STR profile. If the STR typing result is heterozygous, then this probability would be $2pq$, where p is the frequency of allele 1 and q is the frequency of allele 2 in the relevant population for the locus in question. Alternatively, for a homozygous STR type the H_d would be p^2. Therefore,

$$LR = \frac{H_p}{H_d} = \frac{1}{2pq}$$

If the STR type in question was D13S317 alleles 11 and 14, then p is 0.3394 and q is 0.04801 for the Caucasian population (Table 11.1). The likelihood ratio for the D13S317 genotype match then becomes

$$LR = \frac{H_p}{H_d} = \frac{1}{2pq} = \frac{1}{2(0.33940)(0.04801)} = \frac{1}{0.03259} = 30.7$$

If the value for a likelihood ratio is greater than one, then it provides support to the prosecution's case. If on the other hand, the LR is less than one, then the defense's case is supported. In the example shown here, if there is a match between a crime stain possessing D13S317 alleles 11 and 14 and the suspect who also possesses a D13S317 genotype of 11,14, then it is 30.7 times more likely that the suspect left the evidence than that it came from some unknown person out of the general Caucasian population.

Note that the rarer the particular STR genotype is, the higher the likelihood ratio will be since there is a reciprocal relationship. In its simplest form, an LR is the inverse of the estimated genotype frequency for each locus, and if discrete alleles and independent marker systems are utilized, then the LR is simply the inverse of the relative frequency of the observed genotype in the relevant population. Of course, LRs can become much more complicated if mixtures or alternative scenarios for the evidence are possible. The product of all locus-specific LRs results in the full profile LR, which in the example of the Caucasian data shown in Table 11.3 comes to 8.37×10^{14} (the inverse of 1.20×10^{-15}).

When considering the strength of a likelihood ratio in terms of supporting the prosecution's position, the following guidelines have been suggested:

If likelihood ratio is...	Then the evidence provides...
1 to 10	limited support...
10 to 100	moderate support...
100 to 1000	moderately strong support...
1000 to 10,000	strong support...
10,000 or greater	very strong support...

With a 13-locus STR match likelihood ratio of 8.37×10^{14} based on a full profile with unambiguous results (e.g., no mixture present), the evidence has extremely strong support from the proposition that the suspect supplied the evidentiary sample.

SOURCE ATTRIBUTION

With average random match probabilities for unrelated individuals of less than one in a trillion using the 13 core STR loci, there comes within the context of a particular case and Q-K comparison a high degree of confidence that an individual is the source of an evidentiary DNA sample with reasonable degree of scientific certainty. When the rarity of a specific DNA profile (based on frequency estimates) exceeds a predefined threshold (D.N.A. Box 11.7), a laboratory may set a policy to declare that the Q sample can be attributed to the K reference sample. Such a declaration is known as *source attribution*.

Even with very small probabilities, it is important to keep in mind that absolute certainty is outside the realm of scientific inquiry. Yet a high degree of confidence in individualization of a DNA profile can be obtained when the rarity of a profile exceeds the world population many fold. For this reason, the FBI Laboratory adopted a policy in 2000 that when a specific profile's probability was less than a thousand times the U.S. population size, the sample's questioned source (Q sample) was attributed to the reference known (K sample).

A statement provided with a report involving a source attribution might include the following words: 'In the absence of identical twins or close

D.N.A. Box 11.7 Source Attribution

Many laboratories in the United States use a source attribution statement when a DNA profile frequency estimate exceeds a predefined threshold. The logic for this approach, as described by Budowle et al. (2000), is discussed next.

If p_x is the random match probability for a given evidentiary profile X, then $(1 - p_x)^N$ is the probability of not observing the particular profile in a sample of N *unrelated* individuals.

When this probability is greater than or equal to a $1 - \alpha$ confidence level (with α being 0.01 for 99%), then

$(1 - p_x)^N \geq 1 - \alpha$ or $p_x \leq 1 - (1 - \alpha)^{1/N}$, which enables the calculation that if N is approximately the size of the U.S. population ($N = 300{,}000{,}000$), then a random match probably of less than 3.35×10^{-11} will confer at least 99% confidence that the evidentiary profile is unique in the population. The table below lists the random match probability thresholds for various population sizes and confidence levels:

Random match probability thresholds for source attribution at various population sizes and confidence levels. With a random match probability of 1.20×10^{-15} in U.S. Caucasians, the example STR profile would be considered 'unique.'

	Sample Size (N)	Confidence Levels (1 − α)			
		0.90	0.95	0.99	0.999
	2	5.13×10^{-2}	$2.53 \infty 10^{-2}$	$5.01 \infty 10^{-3}$	5.00×10^{-4}
	3	3.45×10^{-2}	1.70×10^{-2}	3.34×10^{-3}	3.33×10^{-4}
	4	2.60×10^{-2}	1.27×10^{-2}	2.51×10^{-3}	2.50×10^{-4}
	5	2.09×10^{-2}	1.02×10^{-2}	2.01×10^{-3}	2.00×10^{-4}
	10	1.05×10^{-2}	5.12×10^{-3}	1.00×10^{-3}	1.00×10^{-4}
	25	4.21×10^{-3}	2.05×10^{-3}	4.02×10^{-4}	4.00×10^{-5}
	50	2.10×10^{-3}	1.03×10^{-3}	2.01×10^{-4}	2.00×10^{-5}
	100	1.05×10^{-3}	5.13×10^{-4}	1.00×0^{-4}	1.00×10^{-5}
	1000	1.05×10^{-4}	5.13×10^{-5}	1.01×10^{-5}	1.00×10^{-6}
	100,000	1.05×10^{-6}	5.13×10^{-7}	1.01×10^{-7}	1.00×10^{-8}
	1,000,000	1.05×10^{-7}	5.13×10^{-8}	1.01×10^{-8}	1.00×10^{-9}
	10,000,000	1.05×10^{-8}	5.13×10^{-9}	1.01×10^{-9}	1.00×10^{-10}
	50,000,000	2.11×10^{-9}	1.03×10^{-9}	2.01×10^{-10}	2.00×10^{-11}
U.S. (1999)	260,000,000	4.05×10^{-10}	1.97×10^{-10}	3.87×10^{-11}	3.85×10^{-12}
U.S. (2005)	300,000,000	3.51×10^{-10}	1.71×10^{-10}	3.35×10^{-11}	3.33×10^{-12}
	1,000,000,000	1.05×10^{-10}	5.13×10^{-11}	1.01×10^{-11}	1.00×10^{-12}
World pop	6,000,000,000	1.76×10^{-11}	8.55×10^{-12}	1.68×10^{-12}	1.67×10^{-13}

Source:
Budowle, B., et al. (2000). Source attribution of a forensic DNA profile. *Forensic Science Communication, 2*(3). Available at http://www.fbi.gov/hq/lab/fsc/backissu/july2000/source.htm

relatives, it can be concluded to a reasonable scientific certainty that the DNA from (Q) and from (K) came from the same individual' or 'Reasonable scientific certainty means that you are (x%) certain that you would not see this profile in a sample of (y) unrelated individuals.'

ADDITIONAL STATISTICAL CALCULATIONS

The previous sections have all focused on different approaches to providing statistical interpretation on single-source autosomal STR data. A number of other scenarios may exist, however, for which a forensic scientist might need to provide statistical support for a DNA result. Several of these other scenarios are briefly discussed below. Greater detail on these topics may be found by consulting the articles or texts cited in the reference list for this chapter. These topics are also discussed in greater detail in the *Advanced Topics of Forensic DNA Typing, 3rd Edition*.

Database match probability

As noted in Chapter 12, the development of national DNA databases filled with profiles from both convicted offenders and unsolved casework samples permits searches for matches between evidentiary and database profiles. To calculate what might be termed a *database match probability*, NRC II Recommendation 5.1 advocates that the random match probability be multiplied by N, the number of persons in the database. The FBI's DNA Advisory Board in their February 2000 recommendations on statistical approaches endorsed this NRC II report recommendation.

Mixture statistics

When mixed DNA profiles are observed, several approaches are taken for statistical evaluation of the strength of the evidence. These include likelihood ratios and combined probabilities of inclusion/exclusion. A worked example using the combined probability of exclusion can be found in D.N.A. Box 14.2. The combined probability of exclusion is sometimes referred to as the 'random man not excluded' (RMNE) approach.

The DNA Advisory Board in their 2000 recommendations on statistical approaches noted that both the probability of exclusion and likelihood ratio calculations are acceptable and recommended that 'one or both calculations be carried out whenever feasible and a mixture is indicated.' The DNA Commission of the International Society of Forensic Genetics (ISFG) in their 2006 recommendations on mixture interpretation emphasized the value of likelihood ratios.

Lineage markers and the counting method

As noted in Chapter 16, lineage markers include mitochondrial DNA and Y-chromosome haplotypes that are transferred directly from generation to generation either from mother to child in the case of mitochondrial DNA or from father to son in the case of the Y chromosome. The counting method in conjunction with an upper bound confidence limit is typically used when estimating the rarity of a mtDNA or Y-chromosome haplotype. The counting method relies on the size of the database and involves counting the number of times the profile (haplotype) has been observed within the database. A frequency estimate with a confidence interval is then made based on this count. Worked examples for Y-STRs and mtDNA are found in D.N.A. Boxes 16.2 and 16.3.

Points for Discussion

- What might be some of the advantages and disadvantages of combining population databases (i.e., having a universal or mixed ethnicity database)?
- Why is the counting method used for estimating Y-STR and mtDNA haplotype frequencies rather than a random match probability calculation using the product rule?

READING LIST AND INTERNET RESOURCES

General Information

Balding, D. J. (2005). Weight-of-evidence for forensic DNA profiles. Hoboken, NJ: John Wiley & Sons.

Buckleton, J., Triggs, C. M., & Walsh, S. J. (Eds.), (2005). *Forensic DNA evidence interpretation*. Boca Raton, FL: CRC Press.

Brenner, C. H. (2003). Forensic genetics: Mathematics. In D. N. Cooper (Ed.), *Nature encyclopedia of the human genome: Vol. 2* (pp. 513–519). New York: Macmillan Publishers Ltd., Nature Publishing Group.

DNA Advisory Board. (2000). Statistical and population genetic issues affecting the evaluation of the frequency of occurrence of DNA profiles calculated from pertinent population database(s). *Forensic Science Communications, 2*(3). Available at http://www.fbi.gov/programs/lab/fsc/backissu/july2000/dnastat.htm

Evett, I. W., & Weir, B. S. (1998). *Interpreting DNA evidence: Statistical genetics for forensic scientists*. Sunderland, MA: Sinauer Associates.

Fung, W. K., & Hu, Y.-Q. (2008). *Statistical DNA forensics: Theory, methods and computation*. Hoboken, NJ: John Wiley & Sons.

National Research Council Committee on DNA Forensic Science (1996). *The evaluation of forensic DNA evidence*. Washington, DC: National Academy Press.

Population Genetics

Gonick, L., & Wheelis, M. (1983). *The cartoon guide to genetics* (updated ed.). New York: HarperCollins Publishers.

Hartl, D. L., & Clark, A. G. (1997). *Principles of population genetics* (3rd ed.). Sunderland, MA: Sinauer Associates.

Weir, B. S. (1996). *Genetic data analysis II: Methods for discrete population genetic data.* Sunderland, MA: Sinauer Associates.

Statistics

Lucy, D. (2005). *Introduction to statistics for forensic scientists.* Hoboken, NJ: John Wiley & Sons.

Tracey, M. (2001). Short tandem repeat-based identification of individuals and parents. *Croatian Medical Journal, 42,* 233–238.

Weir, B. S. (2003). DNA evidence: Inferring identity. In D. N. Cooper (Ed.), *Nature Encyclopedia of the human genome: Vol. 2* (pp. 85–88). New York: Macmillan Publishers Ltd., Nature Publishing Group.

Weir, B. S., et al. (2006). Genetic relatedness analysis: Modern data and new challenges. *Nature Reviews Genetics, 7,* 771–780.

Weir, B. S. (2007). Forensics. In D. J. Balding, M. Bishop, & C. Cannings (Vol. Eds.), *Handbook of statistical genetics* (3rd ed.) (pp. 1368–1392). Hoboken, NJ: John Wiley & Sons.

Population Databases

Butler, J. M., et al. (2003). Allele frequencies for 15 autosomal STR loci on U.S. Caucasian, African American, and Hispanic populations. *Journal of Forensic Sciences, 48,* 908–911.

Chakraborty, R. (1992). Sample size requirements for addressing the population genetic issues of forensic use of DNA typing. *Human Biology, 64,* 141–159.

Devlin, B. (1993). Forensic inference from genetic markers. *Statistical Methods in Medical Research, 2,* 241–262.

Einum, D. D., & Scarpetta, M. A. (2004). Genetic analysis of large data sets of North American Black, Caucasian, and Hispanic populations at 13 CODIS STR loci. *Journal of Forensic Sciences, 49,* 1381–1385.

Fung, W. K. (1996). Are convenience DNA samples significantly different? *Forensic Science International, 82,* 233–241.

Profile frequency estimates

Balding, D. J., & Nichols, R. A. (1994). DNA profile match probability calculation: How to allow for population stratification, relatedness, database selection and single bands. *Forensic Science International, 64,* 125–140.

Balding, D. J. (1999). When can a DNA profile be regarded as unique? *Science & Justice, 39,* 257–260.

Curran, J. M., et al. (2007). Empirical testing of estimated DNA frequencies. *Forensic Science International: Genetics, 1,* 267–272.

Likelihood ratios

Evett, I. W., & Weir, B. S. (1998). *Interpreting DNA evidence: Statistical genetics for forensic scientists.* Sunderland, MA: Sinauer Associates.

Evett, I. W. (2000). The impact of the principles of evidence interpretation on the structure and content of statements. *Science & Justice, 40*, 233–239.

Source attribution

Budowle, B., et al. (2000). Source attribution of a forensic DNA profile. *Forensic Science Communications, 2*(3). Available at http://www.fbi.gov/hq/lab/fsc/backissu/july2000/source.htm

Subpopulation issues

Buckleton, J. S., et al. (2006). How reliable is the sub-population model in DNA testimony? *Forensic Science International, 157*, 144–148.

Curran, J. M., et al. (2003). What is the magnitude of the subpopulation effect? *Forensic Science International, 135*, 1–8.

Prosecutor's fallacy

Balding, D. J., & Donnelly, P. (1994). The prosecutor's fallacy and DNA evidence. *Criminal Law Reviews, 1994*, 711–721.

Leung, W. C. (2002). The prosecutor's fallacy—A pitfall in interpreting probabilities in forensic evidence. *Medicine, Science, and the Law, 42*, 44–50.

Thompson, W. C., & Schumann, E. L. (1987). Interpretation of statistical evidence in criminal trials: The prosecutor's fallacy and the defense attorney's fallacy. *Law & Human Behavior, 11*, 167–187.

CHAPTER 12

DNA Databases

I think that everyone should give a DNA sample.... Frankly, the remote possibility that Big Brother will one day be perusing my genetic fingerprint for some nefarious end worries me less than the thought that tomorrow a dangerous criminal may go free—perhaps only to do further evil—or an innocent individual may languish in prison for want of a simple DNA test.

—James Watson, 2003, DNA: *The Secret of Life*, p. 290

On 13 October 1998, the Federal Bureau of Investigation (FBI) officially launched its nationwide DNA database for NDIS-participating law enforcement agencies. As this chapter is being written more than a decade later, the U.S. National DNA Index System (NDIS) database of the Combined DNA Index System (CODIS) contains over 6.5 million short tandem repeat (STR) profiles and links all 50 states in the United States with the capability to search criminal DNA profiles. Since the first national DNA database was established in the United Kingdom in April 1995, DNA databases around the world have revolutionized the ability to use DNA profile information to link crime scene evidence to perpetrators.

These databases are effective because a majority of crimes are committed by repeat offenders. Studies have shown that more than 60% of those individuals put in prison for violent offenses and subsequently released are rearrested for a similar offense in less than 3 years. Serious serial crimes can be connected and their perpetrators stopped through matching biological evidence between crime scenes and offenders. This chapter discusses the DNA databases being used in the United States and throughout the world to stop violent criminals, as evidenced by the introductory case reviewed in Chapter 1. Issues surrounding the use and potential expansion of DNA databases are also covered.

Contribution of the National Institute of Standards and Technology, 2010.

VALUE OF DNA DATABASES

Information sharing has always been crucial to successful law enforcement. Good information can solve crimes and ultimately save lives. Of anything related to forensic DNA typing, DNA databases have arguably had the greatest impact on the criminal justice system in recent years. Serial crimes have been connected and solved. Perpetrators in cases without initial suspects have been brought to justice. The innocence of unjustly incarcerated individuals has been verified when postconviction evidence has matched another offender.

DNA databases have demonstrated their ability to serve as valuable tools in aiding law enforcement investigations. Their effectiveness continues to grow as the size of the databases gets larger. These databases can be used to locate suspects in violent crime cases that would otherwise never have been solved, such as the sexual assault case described at the beginning of this book. As noted in Chapter 1, without the Virginia DNA database, Montaret Davis would probably have avoided detection and prosecution for his sexual assault. However, with the growth and success of DNA databases, privacy concerns have been raised regarding the use and potential expansion of DNA databases, as discussed later in the chapter.

An important role that DNA databases can serve is to make associations between groups of unsolved cases. Criminals do not honor the same geographical boundaries that law enforcement personnel do. Crimes committed in Florida can be linked to those committed in Virginia through an effective national DNA database.

DNA profile information must be in the database for it to be of value. For many years, tremendous sample backlogs have existed in the United States— meaning that samples have been collected from either crime scenes or qualifying offenders but are awaiting analysis and entry into the DNA database. To try to alleviate this sample backlog, hundreds of millions of dollars have been poured into U.S. forensic DNA laboratories since U.S. Attorney General John Ashcroft announced the President's DNA Initiative in March 2003. For more information on this initiative and results, see http://www.dna.gov.

The result of this influx of substantial funding has been the rapid expansion of the DNA database size in the United States. Yet sample backlogs still exist because the success of DNA testing has encouraged more sample submissions. In addition, expanded laws enable a wider collection of qualified offenders, which translates to larger numbers of DNA samples that must be processed. Many U.S. states now have laws requiring those arrested for any felony offense to have their DNA collected and submitted to a DNA database.

The establishment of an effective DNA database requires time and full cooperation between forensic DNA laboratories, the law enforcement community, and government policymakers. An analysis of the return on this investment illustrates the worth of this work to society and especially to victims of crime (D.N.A. Box 12.1).

D.N.A. Box 12.1 The Business Case for Using Forensic DNA Technology

National DNA databases, such as the Combined DNA Index System (CODIS), have opened an entirely new avenue of identifying repeat offenders and assisting in 'no suspect' sexual assault investigations. With limited budgets and difficult decisions being made by lawmakers on how best to prioritize funds to aid society, a business analysis of the expected return on an investment in forensic DNA technology was presented at the 2004 Annual Meeting of the American Academy of Forensic Sciences in Dallas, Texas. The numbers below come from this analysis by Ray Wickenheiser, then director of the Acadiana Criminalistics Laboratory (New Iberia, LA) and now director of the Montgomery County Crime Laboratory (Rockville, MD).

Within the United States, there are 366,460 sexual assaults reported each year (1992 to 2000 average). Since only 1/3 to 1/20 of sexual assaults are reported to the police, this number is quite conservative. Approximately 34% of sexual assaults are committed by a stranger and would thus be termed 'no suspect.' These cases are normally unsolved without the power of DNA testing.

Studies have shown that 2/3 of offenders are repeat offenders. The average serial rapist commits eight sexual assaults prior to apprehension. Thus, seven of these offenses would be preventable if crime scene DNA testing was done on every case and the rapist's profile was in the DNA database to make the hit to the first sexual assault.

The cost of these crimes per offense committed is approximately $111,238 (adjusted from 1995 study to 2003 dollars). This figure includes the physical injury, hospitalization, lost time at work, counseling, and 'pain and suffering' incurred by the victim. The cost of investigating the crime and prosecuting and incarcerating the offender is not included in this number so it too is quite conservative.

There is approximately a 47.58% success rate of finding sperm and recovering a foreign DNA profile from sexual assault victims.

The Forensic Science Service in England has demonstrated that when a DNA database is sufficiently populated with criminal DNA profiles, a 42% hit rate can be obtained where a hit is made from a 'no suspect' case on a known offender present in the database.

Working through these numbers gives the following cost to crime:

$366,460 \times 34\% = 124,596$ reported 'no suspect' sexual assaults

$124,596 \times 2/3 = 83,056$ of 'no suspect' sexual assaults are committed by repeat offenders

$83,056 \times 7 = 581,392$ future sexual assaults that are preventable

$581,392 \times 47.58\% = 276,626$ unnecessary victims of preventable sexual assaults

$276,626 \times 42\% = 116,183$ estimated sexual assaults could be solved with DNA database hits

$116,183 \times \$111,238 = $ **$12.9 billion saved** in terms of costs from prevented crimes

The cost to perform sexual assault testing in every case is approximately $366 million assuming a cost of $1000 per case and working all 366,460 sexual assaults. Thus, the return on investment is over 3500%. For every dollar invested in forensic DNA testing, this analysis shows over $35 would be saved in terms of expense to victims and society.

Source:
Ray Wickenheiser presentation at February 2004 American Academy of Forensic Sciences meeting (Dallas, TX). Wickenheiser, R. A. (2004). The business case for using forensic DNA technology to solve and prevent crime. *Journal of Biolaw & Business, 7*(3), 34–50.

Definitions: Database vs. Databank

It is helpful to define several terms as we will use them in the course of this book: database, databank, and population database. A *database* is a collection of computer files containing entries of DNA profiles that can be searched to look for potential matches. In the case of essentially all forensic laboratories today, a DNA profile consists of a listing of STR genotypes produced through the process outlined in Figure 1.3 and described in the previous chapters. However, because each country may choose to use a different set of core STR markers, not all data will be compatible between countries or laboratories if there was ever a desire to search someone else's database with your unknown crime scene profile. The need for a compatible currency of data exchange is the reason that the 13 CODIS core STR loci were selected in the United States in November 1997, as noted in Chapter 8, almost a year before launching NDIS in October 1998.

The samples from which STR profiles are generated are usually from forensic casework or a criminal offender who has been deemed to legally qualify for entry into the database. A *databank*, as the term will be used in this book, is a collection of the actual samples—usually in the form of a blood sample or buccal swab or their DNA extracts. Most jurisdictions permit the retention of the biological specimen even after the STR typing results have been obtained and the DNA profile entered into the database. This sample retention is for quality control purposes (including hit confirmation) and enables testing of additional STRs or other genetic loci should a new technology be developed in the future. However, as will be discussed later in the chapter, sample retention is one of the first points raised by critics as inappropriate due to their fear that other genetic data will be collected from these samples.

Finally, as discussed in the previous chapter, information on allele frequencies from a group or groups of representative samples is included in a *population database*. Again, as a database, this refers to a collection of DNA profiles. However, this population database is not used for any kind of sample matching purposes. Rather it is used to estimate random match probabilities based on allele frequency measurements from a group of usually 100 or more individuals selected to represent a specific group of interest. The individuals from which DNA profiles are generated for use in a population database are completely anonymous and only classified and grouped by their self-identified ethnicity. Within the CODIS software, a computer program known as PopStats performs the match probability calculations using allele frequencies from a previously typed set of samples whose STR profiles comprise the various classifications of the population database (e.g., African American, Caucasian).

ASPECTS OF A NATIONAL DNA DATABASE

Implementing an effective national DNA database is an enormous task. A number of components must be in place before the database can be established and actually be effective. These include:

- A commitment on the part of each state (and local) government to provide samples for the DNA database—both offender and crime scene samples;
- A common set of DNA markers or standard core set so that results can be compared between all samples entered into the database;
- Standard software and computer formats so that data can be transferred between laboratories and a secure computer network to connect the various sites involved in the database (if more than one laboratory is submitting data); and
- Quality standards so that everyone can rely on results from each laboratory.

The technology of forensic DNA databases basically involves three parts: (1) collecting specimens from known criminals or other qualifying individuals as defined by law, (2) analyzing those specimens and placing their DNA profiles in a computer database, and (3) subsequently comparing unknown or 'Q' profiles obtained from crime scene evidence with the known or 'K' profiles in the computer database. This last part often requires laboratories to work cases without suspects in order to put the crime scene DNA profiles into the database. A DNA database then enables a massive Q-K comparison. Using these DNA databases, law enforcement agencies have been successful in identifying suspects in cases that would likely be unsolvable by any other means.

Within the United States, all 50 states have enacted legislation to establish a DNA database containing profiles from individuals convicted of specific crimes. The laws vary widely across the states concerning the scope of crimes requiring sample collection for DNA databank entry. Almost all of the states now collect samples from all felons and a growing fraction are even entering DNA profiles from those arrested of certain violent crimes. The trend toward broader coverage of criminal DNA databases will likely continue as these resources demonstrate their value to the criminal justice system.

NATIONAL DNA DATABASES AROUND THE WORLD

A number of countries around the world have started national DNA databases. The first national DNA database, and so far the most effective (and aggressive in its application), was created in the United Kingdom in April 1995.

The UK National DNA Database (NDNAD)

On 10 April 1995 the world's first national DNA database, often referred to as NDNAD, was launched by the United Kingdom's Home Office. This database originally stored data from only six STR loci from the Second Generation Multiplex (SGM) consisting of FGA, TH01, VWA, D8S1179, D18S51, and D21S11. In 1999, an expansion was made to 10 STR loci (the six SGM loci plus D3S1358, D16S539, D2S1338, and D19S433) using the SGM Plus kit from Applied Biosystems. Plans for a potential future Pan-European database will likely expand the number of required loci to as many as 15 STRs.

In its first five years (1995–2000), more than 500,000 DNA profiles were entered into the database and more than 50,000 criminal investigations were aided. As of 2008, the NDNAD contains more than 4 million profiles and regularly aids U.K. law enforcement personnel in resolving thousands of crimes each year. A survey in 2004 showed that, at the time, the NDNAD was delivering more than 1700 crime scene-to-crime scene or suspect-to-crime scene hits per week! The U.K. government invested more than £182 million into NDNAD in the first 10 years of its existence, which equates to approximately $5 per citizen invested in DNA databasing.

Other national DNA databases around the world

National DNA databases are being used in many countries around the world, and a number of other nations are in the early stages of building their own DNA databases. The same STR markers are being used in many instances. For example, there are eight STR loci (FGA, TH01, VWA, D3S1358, D8S1179, D16S539, D18S51, and D21S11) that overlap between European and U.S. DNA database collection efforts. This fact will permit international collaborations on cases that warrant them, although having more loci in common would be beneficial as the various DNA databases continue to grow in size. Some countries, such as Germany, use STR markers (e.g., the highly polymorphic STR locus SE33) that are not as widely applied in other national DNA databases. Therefore, information from additional genetic markers like SE33 cannot be used in linking potential cross-border crime since it would not be available in data sets from both countries.

Canada, New Zealand, Australia, Japan, and a number of countries in Europe besides the United Kingdom have developed successful DNA databases. The European Network of Forensic Science Institutes (ENFSI) provides periodic surveys and information on DNA databases and database laws in Europe on their Web site (see http://www.enfsi.eu). Each country has different laws regarding reasons for obtaining a DNA profile, when a profile would be expunged from the database, whether or not a DNA sample will be stored following analysis, and which STR loci are included. Most countries within the

European Union have standardized on use of the AmpF*l*STR SGM Plus kit, which will enable fruitful collaboration of criminal DNA information in the future. China and India, the two nations with the largest populations on earth, have also begun efforts to produce DNA databases.

A minimal standard set of loci have been adopted by the European community known as the European Standard Set (ESS). The current ESS includes the seven STR loci FGA, TH01, VWA, D3S1358, D8S1179, D18S51, and D21S11. Interpol has adopted the ESS along with the sex-typing marker amelogenin as additional optional information. Plans have been proposed to expand this core set with additional STR loci including five STRs that will likely be part of future commercial STR kits: D12S391, D1S1656, D2S441, D10S1248, and D22S1045. For more information on core STR loci used by various countries, see http://www.cstl.nist.gov/biotech/strbase/coreSTRs.htm.

International data comparison

Several approaches have been taken to permit examination of data across international borders. These include (1) having a network of individual DNA databases that can be queried by all approved personnel, (2) sending a query profile (typically a crime scene profile from an unknown source) to another country's DNA database administrator and requesting them to search it against the country's index of crime scene profiles and/or index of offender profiles, and (3) some kind of combination of either #1 or #2. Differences in legislation between countries prevent DNA databases from being unified—instead data is exchanged between countries based on agreements made and legislature authorizing such communication.

Interpol has established a platform for exchange of data called the 'Interpol Gateway.' In addition, several European countries have signed what is known as the Prüm treaty to facilitate DNA profile data exchange. Many countries use a stand-alone version of the CODIS software (see next section), which could help unify and standardize data storage and exchange formats.

THE U.S. NATIONAL DNA DATABASE

The U.S. Congress authorized the FBI Laboratory to establish and oversee a U.S. national DNA database with the DNA Identification Act of 1994. However, the FBI had started a pilot project several years earlier with 14 state and local crime laboratories to see how effective a DNA database could be. It took several years to gather enough DNA profiles from convicted offenders to reach the critical mass necessary to obtain matches for crime scene evidence. During the 1990s, the number of samples in CODIS grew to several hundred thousand. In addition, the number of laboratories submitting data increased.

When NDIS was launched in October 1998, only nine states participated. As state laws were passed permitting DNA data collection, the number of participating states grew. Since July 2004, all 50 states within the United States have participated in NDIS as do the FBI Laboratory, the U.S. Army Criminal Investigation Laboratory (USACIL), and the Bureau of Alcohol, Tobacco, and Firearms (ATF) Laboratory on a federal level.

The National DNA Index System (NDIS) manages nationwide information in a single repository maintained by the FBI Laboratory. Participating states submit their DNA profiles in order to have searches performed on a national level. The role of NDIS is to search casework and offender indices, manage candidate matches, and return results of matches to the local and/or state level.

Local, state, and national levels

The U.S. national DNA database is composed of three tiers: local, state, and national (Figure 12.1). All three levels contain the convicted offender and casework indexes and the population data file. The software is configurable to support any RFLP or PCR DNA markers, although since 2000 only STR data has been added. At the local level, or Local DNA Index System (LDIS), investigators can input their DNA profiles and search for matches with local cases. Forensic DNA records that originate at the local level are 'uploaded' or transmitted to the state and national levels.

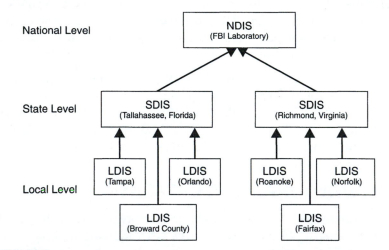

FIGURE 12.1

Schematic of the three tiers in the Combined DNA Index System (CODIS). DNA profile information begins at the local level, or Local DNA Index System (LDIS), and then can be uploaded to the state level, or State DNA Index System (SDIS), and finally to the national level, or National DNA Index System (NDIS). Each local or state laboratory maintains its portion of CODIS while the FBI Laboratory maintains the national portion (NDIS).

Each participating state within the United States has a single laboratory that functions as the State DNA Index System (SDIS) to manage information at the state level. SDIS enables exchange and comparison of DNA profiles within a state and is usually operated by the agency responsible for maintaining a state's convicted offender DNA database program.

Combined DNA Index System (CODIS) software

As noted previously, CODIS stands for the Combined DNA Index System and represents the software used to connect laboratories housing U.S. DNA data at the local, state, or national level in LDIS, SDIS, or NDIS. These U.S. sites are all networked together on the CJIS WAN (Criminal Justice Information Systems Wide Area Network), a stand-alone law enforcement computer network that operates in a similar fashion to the Internet. The software is the same at all sites with various configurations that permit different levels of access (LDIS, SDIS, or NDIS). Software versions are updated periodically and provided to all CODIS laboratories.

As of December 2008, CODIS software was installed in 180 U.S. laboratories representing all 50 states as well as the FBI Laboratory, U.S. Army Crime Lab, and Puerto Rico. This software enables NDIS participating laboratories to submit DNA profiles for the 13 CODIS core STR loci to the U.S. national DNA database. Of the 180 sites where CODIS software is installed, 127 are LDIS and 53 are SDIS (the FBI is the only NDIS site).

The FBI has also provided a stand-alone version of the CODIS software to 44 laboratories in 30 different countries to aid the DNA database work in these countries. These countries include Belgium, Bosnia, Botswana, Canada, Cayman Islands, Chile, Colombia, Croatia, Czech Republic, Denmark, Estonia, Finland, France, Greece, Hong Kong, Hungary, Iceland, Israel, Italy, Latvia, Lithuania, Netherlands, Norway, Poland, Portugal, Singapore, Slovakia, Spain, Sweden, and Switzerland. *However, it is important to note that the DNA databases using the CODIS software in these countries are for their own DNA database initiatives and are not connected to the national, state, or local DNA databases in the United States.*

Each year, usually in October or November, the FBI Laboratory sponsors a National CODIS Conference to inform CODIS users regarding relevant issues and updates to the software and its use. Information on this conference is available at http://www.fbi.gov/hq/lab/html/codis1.htm.

CJIS WAN: The computer network of CODIS

Public crime laboratories in the United States are connected via the FBI's Criminal Justice Information Services Wide Area Network (CJIS WAN) through

T1 lines capable of transmitting 1.5 megabytes of information per second. CJIS WAN provides Internet-like connectivity but without the security risk. This network is an intranet with access only granted to participating laboratories.

Each state pays for its end of the system. The computer equipment for a state system costs around $15,000 to $25,000. The FBI Laboratory provides the CODIS software and maintains the equipment for the national system. SDIS and LDIS laboratories sign memoranda of understanding with the FBI. CODIS users agree to adhere to FBI-issued quality assurance standards (and accreditation) and to submit to NDIS audits.

Information storage categories

Data stored in the U.S. national DNA database is maintained in one of several categories, termed indexes or indices. The convicted offender index and the forensic index are the two largest groups of sample data. The *convicted offender index* (sometimes shortened here to *offender index*) contains DNA profiles from individuals convicted of crimes such as sexual assault, murder, burglary, etc. The *forensic index* on the other hand comes from crime scene evidence without a suspect (if a suspect exists for a particular crime and matches the evidence, there is no need for a DNA database search regarding this particular crime). Thus, in a sense, the offender index serves as the 'known' sample in the Q-K comparison described in Chapter 1, while the forensic index provides 'question' samples.

With the passage of federal and state laws enabling DNA to be collected from individuals who are arrested of crimes (prior to conviction), an *arrestee index* was established a few years ago. When state laws permit collection of DNA samples prior to conviction, these DNA profiles are housed in the arrestee index.

A national missing persons program (see Chapter 17) is supported with several separate indices in NDIS. DNA profiles from missing persons, unidentified human remains, and biological relatives of missing persons can be stored and searched against one another to try to find a direct or kinship match.

Numbers of DNA profiles

When NDIS was first activated in October 1998, there were 119,000 offender profiles and 5,000 forensic casework profiles from nine states. By December 1999, a little over a year later, 21 states and the FBI had input 211,673 offender profiles and 11,112 forensic profiles.

While many of the original DNA profiles were from RFLP markers, forensic DNA laboratories in the United States have now converted completely to the 13 core STR loci. Presumably all samples for the foreseeable future will be

Table 12.1 Growth in samples present in various NDIS indices (cumulative totals by year).

Year Ending December 31	Convicted Offender	Forensic	Arrestee
2000	460,365	22,484	–
2001	750,929	27,897	–
2002	1,247,163	46,177	–
2003	1,493,536	70,931	–
2004	2,038,514	93,956	–
2005	2,826,505	126,315	–
2006	3,977,433	160,582	54,313
2007	5,287,505	203,401	85,072
2008	6,398,874	248,943	140,719

Source: CODIS brochure available at http://www.fbi.gov/hq/lab/pdf/codisbrochure2.pdf and FBI Laboratory's CODIS Unit.

typed with these STRs. In October 2008, the total number of offender STR profiles stood at almost 6.5 million with around 240,000 forensic profiles present in NDIS. Table 12.1 shows the growth in the number of samples at NDIS in offender, forensic, and arrestee indices from 2000 to 2008. Arrestee data have only been allowed at NDIS since 2005.

An examination of the numbers of samples in these various categories over the past several years shows several trends. First, there has been tremendous growth in the numbers of DNA profiles submitted to NDIS. This is due to increased funding and expansion of DNA database laws. Second, a much smaller number of forensic samples is being submitted. The primary reason for the smaller number of crime scene samples is that it is much harder to process crime scene samples than single-source DNA samples of high quality and quantity from offenders and arrestees. Convicted offender and arrestee samples of high quality and quantity are also in the same format (i.e., liquid blood or DNA extracted from buccal swabs), which improves the ability to automate the DNA typing process. On the other hand, forensic cases can involve the examination of a dozen or more pieces of biological evidence from a variety of formats (e.g., semen stains, bloodstains, etc.), which makes them much more challenging to process, especially if DNA degradation is found or mixtures are present.

What information is stored

Since they were selected in November 1997, the 13 CODIS core STR loci have been required for data entry into the national level of the U.S. DNA database.

These 13 STR markers provide a random match probability of approximately 1 in 100 trillion (assuming unrelated individuals).

While a complete DNA profile for the 13 core STR loci (or four RFLP markers initially) is required for the convicted offender index, a minimum of 10 of the 13 CODIS STR (previously at least three CODIS RFLP loci) is needed for forensic casework index information before uploading to NDIS. Fewer core STR loci were originally acceptable at the state and local level. The lower number of loci needed for casework DNA profiles comes from recognition that degraded DNA samples obtained from forensic cases may not yield results at every marker. Effort is also made to avoid putting mixtures onto the database.

CODIS is not a criminal history information database but rather a system of pointers that provides only the information necessary for making Q-K comparisons and matches. CODIS information on each DNA sample includes four pieces of data: (1) an identifier for the submitting agency, (2) the specimen ID, (3) the STR profile itself, and (4) an identifier for the analyst responsible for the profile. As can be seen with the example in Table 12.2, there are no names associated with the STR profile stored in the CODIS software indices. No personal information, criminal history information, or case-related information is contained within CODIS.

As noted in Chapter 8, the 13 CODIS STR loci are not from gene coding regions (i.e., exons) nor are any of them trinucleotides, which can be prone to expansions that cause genetic defects. An STR profile is simply a string of numbers that provides a unique genetic identifier to a tested sample.

How data quality is maintained

The old adage of 'garbage in, garbage out' applies with any database containing information that will be probed regularly. If the DNA profiles entered into a DNA database are not accurate, then they will be of little value for making a meaningful match. The high quality of data going into a DNA database is ensured by requiring laboratories to follow quality assurance standards, by also requiring them to submit to audits of their procedures, and by conducting regular proficiency tests of analysts as described in Chapter 13.

In order for a state to have its DNA profiles included in the national DNA index system, a memorandum of understanding must be signed whereby the state DNA laboratories agree to adhere to the FBI-issued Quality Assurance Standards (QAS) and undergo regular audits to evaluate compliance of NDIS-participating laboratories to the forensic and databasing QAS in accordance with federal law. The original forensic QAS were adopted in October 1998 (April 1999 for convicted offender QAS). Revised QAS were implemented in July 2009 for both forensic and DNA databasing laboratories.

Table 12.2 Example of the STR profile information stored in the CODIS DNA database for a single sample.

Agency ID	Sample ID	Analyst ID	Category	
VADFS-N	1999082605	JMB	Convicted offender	
Marker	**Allele 1**	**Allele 2**	**Date**	**Time**
AMEL	X	Y	15-FEB-2000	17:38:30
CSF1PO	10	10	15-FEB-2000	17:38:30
D13S317	11	14	15-FEB-2000	17:38:30
D16S539	9	11	15-FEB-2000	17:38:30
D18S51	14	16	15-FEB-2000	17:38:30
D21S11	28	30	15-FEB-2000	17:38:30
D3S1358	16	17	15-FEB-2000	17:38:30
D5S818	12	13	15-FEB-2000	17:38:30
D7S820	9	9	15-FEB-2000	17:38:30
D8S1179	12	14	15-FEB-2000	17:38:30
FGA	21	22	15-FEB-2000	17:38:30
TH01	6	6	15-FEB-2000	17:38:30
TPOX	8	8	15-FEB-2000	17:38:30
VWA	17	18	15-FEB-2000	17:38:30

Note: There is no personal information that can be used to link an individual to his or her DNA profile. The two alleles for each STR marker are placed in separate columns labeled allele 1 and allele 2. For markers with homozygous results, both allele 1 and allele 2 are the same (e.g., CSF1PO). The information in the 'sample ID' field can be related to a known individual only by the originating forensic DNA laboratory. The date and time stamp are included to illustrate when the DNA profile was uploaded to LDIS.

Audits are conducted annually for each NDIS-participating laboratory and DNA analysts undergo semiannual proficiency tests. Failure to pass this audit can result in a laboratory being disconnected from NDIS. Likewise, proficiency tests must be successfully completed in order for an analyst to be able to continue to submit data to LDIS, SDIS, and NDIS.

Who inputs data

For a criminal DNA database to be successful, convicted offender DNA samples must be entered and crime scene material from cases where there is no suspect must be tested. Because the demand for DNA testing often surpasses the ability of public forensic laboratories to perform the tests, private contract laboratories have been used to reduce the sample backlogs for convicted offender as well as for some forensic casework samples. Much of this work in the United States is being performed with federal government financial assistance through grant programs administered by the National Institute of Justice.

Currently, pursuant to federal law, only government law enforcement forensic DNA laboratories that comply with the QAS have access to CODIS. Therefore, while data may be generated by a private laboratory through outsourcing from a public forensic lab, the STR typing data must be evaluated by the public laboratory who assumes ownership of the data. Only then, after quality of the STR typing data is confirmed, can it be uploaded by the public laboratory to LDIS, SDIS, and ultimately NDIS.

During the past decade, contract laboratories have collectively generated millions of STR profiles and directly aided the rapid growth of the U.S. national DNA database. During this same time, with federal grant programs for capacity building, many government forensic laboratories have been working to build up their own capacity in order to be able to do all of their sample testing in-house. Improved automation through robotic sample handling and multicapillary CE systems have simplified the process of DNA typing and aided sample throughput. In addition, several expert systems have been approved for reviewing single-source DNA databasing profiles.

How success of a DNA database is measured

The purpose of DNA databases is to solve crimes that would otherwise be unsolvable. A common method of measuring the effectiveness of CODIS or any other DNA database is in what is referred to as a 'hit.' A hit is a confirmed match between two or more DNA profiles discovered by the database search. Within CODIS, hits may occur at a local (LDIS), state (SDIS), or national (NDIS) level. Sometimes hits are distinguished as *cold* or *warm* depending on how much previous information is available when performing the search. A *cold hit* is one made without any prior investigative leads between the matching samples.

Hits fall into two different categories. A *forensic hit* occurs when two or more forensic casework samples are linked at LDIS, SDIS, or NDIS. These types of hits are sometimes called case-to-case hits and are especially important to solving serial crimes. An *offender hit* occurs when one or more forensic samples are linked to a convicted offender sample. These types of hits are sometimes referred to as case-to-offender hits. Either type of hit contributes to the bottom-line performance metric of a DNA database—the number of criminal *investigations aided*. 'Investigations aided' is defined as the number of criminal investigations where CODIS has added value to the investigative process (CODIS can only aid an investigation one time). In the first 5 years of operation (1998–2003), the CODIS system aided more than 11,000 investigations

Table 12.3 Hit counting statistics (cumulative totals by year). Most offender hits (~87%) are intrastate rather than interstate (national).

Year Ending December 31	Investigations Aided	Forensic Hits	Offender Hits	Within-State Hits (~87%)	National Offender Hits
2000	1,573	507	731	705 (97%)	26
2001	3,635	1,031	2,371	2,204 (93%)	167
2002	6,670	1,832	5,032	4,394 (87%)	638
2003	11,220	3,004	8,269	7,118 (86%)	1,151
2004	20,788	5,147	13,855	11,991 (87%)	1,864
2005	30,455	7,071	21,519	18,664 (87%)	2,855
2006	43,156	9,529	32,439	28,163 (87%)	4,276
2007	62,059	11,750	49,813	43,305 (87%)	6,508
2008	80,948	14,122	66,783	58,304 (87%)	8,479

Source: CODIS brochure available at http://www.fbi.gov/hq/lab/pdf/codisbrochure2.pdf and FBI Laboratory's CODIS Unit.

in the United States. Through December 2008, more than 80,000 investigations had been aided using CODIS, allowing thousands of crimes to be linked and solved around the United States.

Table 12.3 summarizes the growth of forensic and offender hits over the past few years. Note that almost 90% of the time, offender hits are occurring within states rather than between states, which emphasizes the value of DNA databases on a local level.

Because the number of hits is largely related to the size of the database, as CODIS continues to grow, so will its value. The U.K.'s NDNAD maintains close to a 40% chance of obtaining a match between a crime scene profile and a 'criminal justice' (arrestee or suspect) profile loaded into the database.

What searches are conducted to obtain hits

Figure 12.2 illustrates the primary searches conducted with the three largest indices of the U.S. national DNA database and the types of 'hits' or matches that can occur. An offender hit is produced when a match occurs between a DNA profile on the convicted offender or arrestee index during a search of offenders or arrestee DNA profiles against the crime scene DNA profiles present in the forensic index. As noted previously, a forensic hit results from searching DNA profiles in the forensic index against other crime scene DNA profiles—essentially an effective method to look for crimes committed by a serial offender.

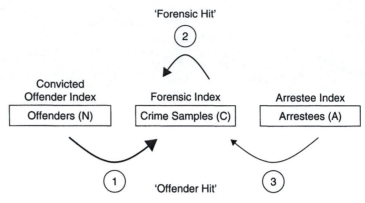

FIGURE 12.2

Primary searches conducted with the three largest indices of the U.S. national DNA database. (1) 'Offender hit' produced by conducting a search of offenders against the crime scene samples present in the forensic index. (2) 'Forensic hit' from searching DNA profiles in the forensic index against other crime scene profiles looking for serial crimes. (3) Arrestee search against forensic index—usually classified as 'offender hit.'

There is another possible search not illustrated in Figure 12.2, which is not currently performed at the national level but could be at a local or state level for quality assurance purposes. A search of offenders against other offenders can be a useful tool at the local or state level to check for DNA profile duplicates. If an offender used different aliases when being processed through the criminal justice system on separate occasions, then the DNA profile records would match and could be consolidated if desired. Of course, identical twins, who by definition possess identical STR profiles, would also match in such a search. This type of search can help verify that the search algorithms are working properly and matching when they should be.

Although these offender-offender searches can help maintain data quality and prevent unnecessary duplicates in the database, they can become taxing on the search algorithm used and computer time required to search due to the sheer volume of comparisons required. With a million samples in a state DNA database, almost half a trillion STR profile comparisons are required. As DNA databases grow in size, they become more valuable as an intelligence tool, but they also become more of a challenge to search rapidly.

Search stringency used

The capability of having search strategies that permit two DNA profiles to 'match' without 100% allele agreement is necessary because the various laboratories submitting data to the DNA database can use different STR kits. The STR kits produced by the various manufacturers may have different primer binding regions for the same loci—and allele dropout could result with one primer set and not the other due to primer binding site mutations as noted previously in Chapter 10. This would result in an apparent discrepancy between DNA profile genotype results obtained with one STR kit versus another. In addition, some results from forensic specimens may be from unresolved mixtures requiring that multiple possibilities be permitted in matching.

Lower-stringency search algorithms may be used to address this issue. For example, the CODIS search algorithm and match criteria can be loosened on a search permitting a match at 25 out of 26 possible alleles instead of requiring that all 26 possible alleles from the 13 STRs match between the two samples being compared. Such a 'moderate' stringency search takes longer.

There are three levels of search stringency possible in the CODIS software: high, moderate, and low stringency. With *high stringency*, all available alleles are the same or match between the two DNA profiles. A *moderate stringency* requires all available alleles to match, but the two profiles can contain a different number of alleles. For example, the forensic index profile may include alleles 9,10,12 (from a mixture), while the candidate offender match has only alleles 9,12 (from a single source). A *low-stringency* match occurs when one or more alleles match when the two profiles are compared at a given STR locus. Thus, a low-stringency match would exist between profiles containing alleles 8,11 and 11,14 at a given STR locus because the '11' is common to the two profiles.

Follow-up to database 'cold hits'

When a potential match is identified by the CODIS software, the laboratories responsible for the matching profiles are notified. They then contact each other to validate or refute the match. After the match has been confirmed by qualified DNA analysts, which involves retesting of the matching convicted offender DNA sample, laboratories may exchange additional information, such as names and phone numbers of criminal investigators and case details. A hit is only counted once the candidate match is confirmed and determined that the match provided additional information to the case.

If a match is obtained with the convicted offender index, the identity and location of the convicted offender are determined and an arrest warrant procured but, as noted above, only after the hit is confirmed by retesting the offender sample. This retesting or 'hit confirmation' is an added quality assurance measure to verify that no sample switches accidently occurred during the sample accession at the crime lab or throughout the DNA testing process.

PopStats: A tool for estimating DNA profile rarity

As noted previously in the chapter, there is a population database provided to CODIS users with allele frequency information from anonymous persons intended to represent major population groups found in the United States. These databases are used to estimate statistical frequencies of DNA profiles using the program *PopStats*. Caucasians, African Americans, Southeast Hispanics, and Southwest Hispanics are the typical groups reported when estimating the rarity of a particular DNA profile. The STR allele frequencies used in PopStats were published in the May 2001 issue of the *Journal of Forensic Sciences* by Bruce Budowle and FBI colleagues in an article entitled 'CODIS STR loci data from 41 sample populations.'

Missing persons

DNA databases can also play an important role in helping to identify missing individuals and aiding mass disaster reconstruction following a plane crash or terrorist activity (see Chapter 17). In these cases, DNA samples are often obtained from biological relatives that can be searched against DNA of remains recovered from a missing individual or a disaster site. Many states within the United States and nations around the world are beginning to establish missing persons databases to enable matching of recovered remains to their family members.

CODIS also has several indices to aid missing-person investigations that can store DNA profiles from both recovered remains and family samples that serve as references. Much of the data from missing-person investigations is in the form of mitochondrial DNA sequences since this information can be successfully recovered from highly degraded samples. As noted in Chapter 16, use of mitochondrial DNA also enables access to a larger number of reference samples from maternal relatives of a victim.

NDIS Procedures Board

Operational procedures are set by an NDIS Procedures Board that meets several times each year. The NDIS Procedures Board is currently composed of six state and local representatives, a representative elected by the state CODIS administrators, the chair of the Scientific Working Group on DNA Analysis Methods (SWGDAM), and six FBI Laboratory representatives. The state and local representatives are selected based on region of the country, laboratory size, and the number of searchable DNA records contributed to NDIS.

DNA DATABASE LAWS IN THE UNITED STATES

DNA databases work because most criminals are repeat offenders. If their DNA profiles can be entered into the system early in their criminal careers, then they can be identified when future crimes are committed. Serial crimes can also be linked effectively with a computerized DNA database. Ultimately,

Table 12.4 A brief review of the history of federal U.S. laws on DNA databases.

Legislation	What Was Authorized
DNA Identification Act of 1994	FBI receives authority to establish a National DNA Index System (NDIS); NDIS becomes operational in October 1998 with nine states participating
DNA Analysis Backlog Elimination Act of 2000	Authorizes collection of DNA samples from federal convicted offenders
Justice for All Act of 2004	Indicted persons permitted at NDIS, one-time 'keyboard' search authorized; accreditation and audit for labs required; expansion to all felonies for federal convicted offenders; requires notification of Congress if new core loci desired
DNA Fingerprint Act of 2005	Arrestees and legally collected samples permitted at NDIS; elimination of one-time 'keyboard' search; expansion to arrestees and detainees for federal offenders

the value of the DNA database is in its ability to apprehend criminals who are not direct suspects in a case and to prevent further victims from crimes committed by those individuals. Within the United States, both federal and state laws impact the use of DNA databases.

Federal laws

As mentioned earlier in the chapter, the FBI Laboratory received congressional authority to establish NDIS with the DNA Identification Act of 1994. NDIS became operational in October 1998 with nine states participating. Table 12.4 summarizes several federal laws since 1994 that have authorized expanded sample collection. These expansions include DNA samples from federal convicted offenders as well as arrestees and other legally collected samples as deemed by state and federal laws.

Crimes for inclusion in a state DNA database

As of June 1998, all 50 states in the United States had passed legislation requiring convicted offenders to provide samples for DNA databasing. However, each state has different requirements as to what types of offenses are considered for DNA sample collection. In many states these requirements are changing over time to include more and more criminal offenses.

The requirements for having to donate a DNA sample range from arrestees to all felons to strictly sex offenses. The trend has been to enact laws that require a DNA sample submission for any felony crime and is now expanding in many cases to arrested individuals. Table 12.5 includes a summary list of the qualifying offenses for entry into a state's DNA database and the number of states within the United States that fall into each category as of 1999, 2004, and 2008.

Table 12.5 Summary of U.S. state DNA database laws and qualifying offenses for DNA collection as of 1999, 2004, and 2008.

Offenses	Number of States		
	1999	2004	2008
Sex crimes	50	50	50
All violent crimes	36	48	50
Burglary	14	47	50
All felons	5	37	47
Juveniles	24	32	32
Arrestees/suspects	1	4	14

Source and information on up-to-date data: http://www.dnaresource.com. See also http://www.ncsl .org/programs/cj/dnadatabanks.htm

Some state DNA database statutes specify exactly how the sample will be taken while others simply require any biological sample containing DNA. A 1999 survey of state laws found that California required two specimens of blood, a saliva sample, and right thumb and full palm print impressions for verifying identity of the submitting convicted offender while South Carolina only asked for 'a suitable sample' from which DNA may be obtained.

The ability of state and local forensic DNA laboratories to improve their capabilities for DNA analysis, especially with the STR technology described in this book, has been greatly aided by federal funding. The DNA Identification Act of 1994 provided approximately $40 million in federal matching grants to aid states in DNA analysis activities. The Debbie Smith Act, part of the President's DNA Initiative, has brought hundreds of millions of dollars of funding to U.S. forensic DNA laboratories since 2004. This funding has been a great benefit to forensic DNA laboratories, which are often understaffed and underfunded. As noted in D.N.A. Box 12.1, society benefits from this investment in forensic DNA technology. Progress on legislation regarding the use of DNA is available through the Web site http://www.dnaresource.com.

ISSUES AND CONCERNS WITH DNA DATABASES

There are a number of important issues for DNA databases. These issues include security of the information contained in them, the ability to perform rapid searches and effective matches from large numbers of entries, ensuring that high-quality data is submitted for both offender and forensic data, maintaining the quality of the input data, and handling changes in technology.

Both computer and DNA technologies are constantly improving at a rapid rate. DNA databases have to be flexible enough to handle this change. Legacy data must be maintained, or the value of the database will be diminished. If different genetic markers are universally used at some time in the future, then previously collected data would be inaccessible unless there was some kind of overlap or compatibility in results demonstrated. It would be an expensive and time-consuming proposition to retype previously tested samples, which may amount to millions of samples, with new genetic markers. As discussed in Chapter 18, several possible ways forward exist for maintaining core loci while adding supplementary information to established DNA databases.

Privacy concerns

One of the major challenges for maintaining a DNA database is the issue of privacy and security of the information stored in the database of profiles and the corresponding databank of samples. DNA samples contain genetic information that could be used against an individual or his or her family if not handled properly.

The issue of privacy is approached in two ways. First, the DNA markers, such as the 13 CODIS core STR loci, are in noncoding regions of the DNA and are not known to have any association with a genetic disease or any other genetic predisposition. Thus, the information in the database is only useful for human identity testing.

Second, no names of individuals or other characterizing data is stored with the DNA profiles. The National DNA Index System of CODIS only references the sources of the DNA profiles, such as Orange County Sheriff's Office or Palm Beach County Crime Laboratory. Specific case data is secured and controlled by the law enforcement agencies submitting the data. Thus, only the crime laboratory that submitted the DNA profile has the capability to link the DNA results with a known individual.

Another important facet to the privacy and security of the information in DNA databases is that access to CODIS is solely for law enforcement purposes. There are strict penalties for anyone using the information or samples for any purpose other than law enforcement including a $250,000 fine for unauthorized disclosure of information on any sample.

During the time period from 1990 to 2008 in the United States, there have been over 170 cases brought to court relating to the constitutionality of federal and state DNA databank sample collection and DNA database searches. Time after time the constitutionality of criminal DNA databases and databanks has been upheld. These challenges are usually unsuccessful because people who have been convicted of committing a crime have lost many of their rights.

Likewise, there is not any expectation of privacy for genetic material discarded at a crime scene.

The Genetic Information Nondiscrimination Act (GINA) was signed into U.S. law in May 2008 and provides protection of genetic information in relationship to medical testing. It provides an exception for DNA data collected in relationship to law enforcement or human remains identification work that is used for quality assurance purposes.

Thus, there are several important policies in place to help maintain privacy. First, genetic markers have been selected that are located in noncoding regions of the human genome and not known to have any medical implications. Second, offender profiles are uploaded to the DNA database with only agency, sample, and analyst identifiers. There are no names directly associated with a DNA profile in the database. Third, data are encrypted and shared through a secure network only accessible to state and local CODIS administrators. Fourth, federal and state laws harshly penalize improper use of criminal DNA samples including fines and possible imprisonment.

Sample collection from convicted offenders

One of the aspects about DNA databanks that is often overlooked is the sample collection process. Law enforcement personnel have to extract blood or obtain a saliva sample from incarcerated felons who are not always cooperative. In some cases, extraordinary efforts including force may be required to persuade felons to submit to sample collection. Collecting the actual samples can be a challenge considering the fact that the convicted offender likely knows his blood or saliva could be used to catch him committing another crime in the future or match him to a previous unsolved crime that he committed.

Sample retention

Critics of DNA databases and databanks are concerned that DNA samples from offenders are retained after a DNA profile has been generated from the sample with STR markers. As has already been noted, the justification for retaining these samples is twofold. First and foremost, because samples are retested following an offender hit, it is necessary to have the original sample to confirm its profile. This hit confirmation is an important quality control measure and helps prevent any kind of potential error during laboratory processing from causing a lead to be followed and a warrant to be issued for the wrong person. Another reason to retain sample specimens is to enable analyses using technology advancements in the future. If new genetic markers or assays are developed in the future to enable better recovery of information from forensic samples, then previously examined offender samples would need to be retested with the new genetic markers/technology in order to permit a comparison between offender and forensic results.

WHAT IF THERE ARE NO HITS AFTER A DATABASE SEARCH?

If a perpetrator of a particular crime has not been arrested or convicted of another crime (and had a DNA sample previously collected and uploaded to a DNA database), then no amount of searching the database with a particular crime scene profile will help solve the case. Searching the database again at a future date may be helpful if the perpetrator has been included in the meantime for another crime. However, in order to keep the case active, other measures are often required. For example, in order to stop the clock on the statute of limitations for filing a grievance on a particular case, 'John Doe warrants' have been used in a number of cases (D.N.A. Box 12.2). This action can then extend the time frame for possibly solving a case.

Additional efforts or strategies are sometimes considered to help obtain a question-to-known-sample match, especially in particularly heinous crimes. Each of these involves casting a wider net through use of currently available DNA profiles or collecting additional samples.

D.N.A. Box 12.2 The 'John Doe' Warrant

The capabilities of forensic DNA testing have generated new legal issues for prosecutors. The sensitivity of the polymerase chain reaction enables DNA profiles to be obtained from previously intractable evidence. Furthermore, the existence of DNA databases now permits matches between perpetrators of crimes spanning jurisdictions and 'cold hits' on unsolved crimes many years after they occurred.

Many states have *statutes of limitations*, meaning that after a certain period of time a crime cannot be prosecuted. If DNA evidence exists from a crime scene yet no suspect has been located to be charged with the crime, a 'John Doe' warrant may be issued based solely on the assailant's genetic code. In September 1999 Norman Gahn, assistant district attorney from Milwaukee County, Wisconsin, filed the first warrant for the arrest of 'John Doe,' an unknown male who could be identified by his DNA profile. This approach has been successful in stopping the ticking clock of a crime's statute of limitations, making it possible to prosecute the crime when the assailant is identified through a DNA database cold hit in the future. Several of these 'John Does'

have been subsequently identified with DNA database cold hits and successfully prosecuted for the crimes they committed.

Wisconsin law governing the statute of limitations was amended in September 2001 to provide for the use of DNA profiles from individuals unknown to the prosecution at the time the warrant for arrest is issued. The new legislation creates an exception to the time limits for prosecuting sexual assault crimes if the state has DNA evidence related to the crime. John Doe warrants have also been issued in other states.

Sources:

Gahn, N. (2000). John Doe: D1S7, D2S44, D5S110, D10S28, D17S79, charged with rape (interview). *Profiles in DNA, 3*(3), 8–9. Available at http://www.promega.com/profiles/303/ProfilesinDNA_303_08.pdf

Gahn, N. A. (2002). From John Doe to known offender: DNA profile arrest warrants. *Silent Witness, 7*(1). Available at http://www.ndaa.org/apri/programs/dna/newsletter.html

See also: http://www.denverda.org/DNA/John_Doe_DNA_Warrants.htm http://www.dna.gov/uses/solving-crimes/cold_cases/identifying_analyzing_prioritizing/johndoewarrant http://www.dna.gov/statutes-caselaw/caselaw/john-doe-caselaw

Partial matches and familial searching

In a May 2006 *Science* article entitled 'Finding criminals through DNA of their relatives,' the authors propose that if a crime stain does not match anyone in the offender database that there is a chance that a relative might be in the database. Since relatives will have similar DNA to one another, loosening the search stringency to permit partial matches rather than full high-stringency matches (where every allele in an STR profile must match) may return a list of results that could include a brother or other close relative. This list of potential relatives could be narrowed through further testing with Y-chromosome markers, which would require all of the potential relatives plus the crime scene sample to be examined with the additional genetic markers. In theory with this approach, the database is effectively enlarged to include close relatives of criminals whose profiles are already on the DNA database.

The United Kingdom pioneered this partial matching technique, better known as 'familial searching,' and has used it to solve a number of cases—but not without controversy. It is worth noting that during routine searches of a DNA database, partial matches can result from samples that have common STR alleles—particularly with moderate or low stringency searches. Generally speaking, a familial search is a second deliberate search looking for relatives.

Privacy rights groups feel that familial searching is going too far. In March 2008, the FBI Laboratory organized a meeting held in Washington, DC, to discuss the advantages and concerns with familial searching. Scientists, lawyers, and legal scholars presented their points of view. Although no formal proceedings were published from this meeting (as of late 2008), the forum permitted a vigorous discussion of the issues by proponents and opponents of familial searching. Only time will tell how far the general public and policymakers will permit DNA databases to extend.

DNA dragnets through mass screens

There have been instances in the past when a DNA dragnet was instituted if a DNA database search did not link any offenders on the database to a particular crime scene sample(s). Prior to the availability of national DNA databases, these DNA mass screens were more common.

The first use of forensic DNA testing involved a genetic dragnet of over 4,000 adult males in the Narborough, England, area. Samples that failed to be excluded from the crime scene sample with traditional blood typing were subjected to 'DNA fingerprinting' or multilocus RFLP testing. Colin Pitchfork was eventually apprehended based on this mass DNA intelligence screen and additional police work (see D.N.A. Box 1.2). However, challenges have been raised to the cost effectiveness of this mass screening approach. For example, Colin

Pitchfork was apparently the 4583rd male tested for the mass screen described in Joseph Wambaugh's *The Blooding*.

DNA intelligence or 'mass' screens to aid identification of a perpetrator and exclusion of innocent individuals in no-suspect cases have been successfully used many times by the U.K's Forensic Science Service and other law enforcement agencies. In these mass screens, the police ask individuals within a predetermined group (e.g., males 18 to 35 years old within a defined location) to voluntarily provide DNA samples in an effort to identify the perpetrator of a crime or a series of crimes that have been linked by DNA evidence. Within the United States, these types of DNA dragnets raise constitutional concerns such as violation of Fourth Amendment rights that protect an individual's privacy until evidence is produced and a warrant obtained that would compel an invasive search.

The largest mass screen conducted to date by the U.K's Forensic Science Service was in conjunction with the investigation of the murder of Louise Smith, whose body was found near Chipping Sodbury, England, in 1996. Over 4500 samples from local volunteers were analyzed at an expense of over 1 million pounds. Eventually police realized that one of the potential suspects had since moved to South Africa. He was tracked down and his DNA sample taken, which was found to match an evidentiary STR profile recovered from the crime scene. David Frost in now serving time for the crime he committed and fled from, hoping to escape justice.

In probably the largest genetic screening effort ever conducted within the United States, over 2100 individuals in the Dade County (Miami), Florida, area were typed with AmpliType PM and HLA-DQA1 during the fall of 1994. Tested individuals were primarily selected based on a prior arrest record for soliciting a prostitute because six homicide victims had been prostitutes who were killed within a 3-mile radius between September 1994 and January 1995. During the course of the investigation, 3 of the 2100 individuals tested matched with the PM + DQA1 screening assay, but subsequently were excluded by follow-up RFLP analysis, which (as noted in Chapter 3) has a higher power of discrimination. In the end, the serial rapist/murderer was caught when a potential victim freed herself and police were called. Thus, while the perpetrator's DNA was found to match DNA evidence from the previous six crime scenes (and this information was used in his prosecution), the mass screen was not responsible for his apprehension.

Of course, this type of effort and expense is not conducted in every case, but it has proven useful in some situations. However, collecting samples from every individual fitting a particular description or living in a particular geographical region is not always greeted fondly by the general public. Questions about genetic privacy and civil liberties are often raised, particularly in the United States, when mass screens are initiated.

In April 2004, a DNA dragnet was conducted in Charlottesville, Virginia, to try to stop a rapist who had attacked at least six women between 1997 and 2003. Community concerns that black men were being targeted led police in Charlottesville to eventually suspend the mass screen after only collecting and analyzing samples from about 200 men. The perception of being 'guilty' before proven 'innocent' through DNA testing is an issue often raised by critics of DNA dragnets—particularly in the United States where the goal is always to be 'innocent until proven guilty.'

A September 2004 report that surveyed DNA mass screens conducted in the United States over the previous two decades found these efforts to be 'extremely unproductive' in identifying the true perpetrator. This report recommended that police not conduct DNA mass screens based on general descriptions of criminal suspects. On the other hand, a study presented to the European Network of Forensic Science Institutes (ENFSI) DNA Working Group in April 2006 found that 315 out of 439 mass screens conducted in Europe were successful in identifying the perpetrator. The 72% success rate in Europe illustrates that DNA intelligence-led screens can be helpful in solving crimes when other efforts have failed—although the approach may not be well accepted by the public in some areas. *It is hoped that the proper balance can be found in the future to fully utilize the power of DNA testing and yet preserve the privacy and civil liberties of innocent citizens.*

Points for Discussion

- What challenges exist in establishing a national DNA database?
- How have DNA databases helped the criminal justice system?
- What are some of the primary privacy concerns raised by critics of DNA databases?

READING LIST AND INTERNET RESOURCES

General Information

Bille, T. W. (1999). DNA analysis: A powerful investigative tool. *Profiles in DNA, 3*(2), 8–9. Available at http://www.promega.com/profiles

Butler, J. M. (2006). Genetics and genomics of core short tandem repeat loci used in human identity testing. *Journal of Forensic Sciences, 51*, 253–265.

Gill, P., et al. (2004). An assessment of whether SNPs will replace STRs in national DNA databases—Joint considerations of the DNA working group of the European Network of Forensic Science Institutes (ENFSI) and the Scientific Working Group on DNA Analysis Methods (SWGDAM). *Science & justice, 44*, 51–53.

Langan, P. A., & Levin, D. J. (2002). *Recidivism of prisoners released in 1994*. Washington, DC: Bureau of Justice Statistics, U.S. Department of Justice. Available at http://www.ojp.usdoj.gov/bjs/abstract/rpr94.htm

Langan, P. A., et al. (2003). *Recidivism of sex offenders released from prison in 1994.* Washington, DC: Bureau of Justice Statistics, U.S. Department of Justice. Available at http://www.ojp.usdoj.gov/bjs/abstract/rsorp94.htm

Lovirich, N.P., et al. (2004). *National Forensic DNA Study Report.* Available at http://www.ojp.usdoj.gov/nij/pdf/dna_studyreport_final.pdf

National Commission on the Future of DNA Evidence (2000). *The future of forensic DNA testing: Predictions of the research and development working group.* Washington, DC: National Institute of Justice. Available at http://www.ojp.usdoj.gov/nij/pubs-sum/183697.htm

Wickenheiser, R. A. (2004). The business case for using forensic DNA technology to solve and prevent crime. *Journal of Biolaw & Business, 7,* 34–50.

International DNA Efforts

Asplen, C. H. (2004). International perspectives on forensic DNA databases. *Forensic Science International, 146S,* S119–S121.

European Network of Forensic Science Institutes (ENFSI) DNA Working Group Document on DNA Databases in Europe: http://www.enfsi.eu/get_doc.php?uid=227

Gill, P., et al. (2006). The evolution of DNA databases—Recommendations for new European STR loci. *Forensic Science International, 156,* 242–244.

Gill, P., et al. (2006). New multiplexes for Europe—Amendments and clarification of strategic development. *Forensic Science International, 163,* 155–157.

Harbison, S. A., et al. (2001). The New Zealand DNA databank: Its development and significance as a crime solving tool. *Science & Justice, 41,* 33–37.

Interpol Handbook on DNA Data Exchange and Practice. http://www.interpol.int/Public/Forensic/dna/HandbookPublic.pdf

Martin, P. D., et al. (2001). A brief history of the formation of DNA databases in forensic science within Europe. *Forensic Science International, 119,* 225–231.

Martin, P. D. (2004). National DNA databases—Practice and practicability. A forum for discussion. *Progress in Forensic Genetics, 10,* ICS 1261, 1–8.

Schneider, P. M., & Martin, P. D. (2001). Criminal DNA databases: The European situation. *Forensic Science International, 119,* 232–238.

Walsh, S. J. (2004). Recent advances in forensic genetics. *Expert Review of Molecular Diagnostics, 4,* 31–40.

U.K. National Database (NDNAD)

Asplen, C.H. (2004). The application of DNA technology in England and Wales. Available at http://www.ojp.usdoj.gov/nij/pdf/uk_finaldraft.pdf

Association of Chief Police Officers of England, Wales and Northern Ireland. http://www.acpo.police.uk/policies.asp

Forensic Science Service Annual Reports. http://www.forensic.gov.uk

Gill, P., et al. (1996). A new method of STR interpretation using inferential logic—development of a criminal intelligence database. *International Journal of Legal Medicine, 109,* 14–22.

Home Office. http://www.homeoffice.gov.uk/science-research/using-science/dna-database

LGC Forensics. http://www.lgcforensics.com

The National DNA Database (2006). Parliament Office of Science and Technology, Postnote 258. Available at http://www.parliament.uk/documents/upload/postpn258.pdf

Werrett, D. J. (1997). The National DNA Database. *Forensic Science International, 88,* 33–42.

Werrett, D. J., & Sparkes, R. (1998). 300 matches per week—the effectiveness and future development of DNA intelligence databases—parts 1 and 2. In: *Proceedings of the ninth international symposium on human identification* (pp. 55–62). Available at http://www.promega.com/geneticidproc

Canadian DNA Database

Kuperus, W. R., et al. (2003). Crime scene links through DNA evidence: The practical experience from Saskatchewan casework. *Canadian Society of Forensic Science Journal, 36,* 19–28.

Lalonde, S. A. (2006). Canada's national DNA data bank: A success story. *Canadian Society of Forensic Science Journal, 39,* 39–46.

Royal Canadian Mounted Police. (2007). National DNA Data Bank Advisory Committee 2006–2007 Annual Report. Available at http://www.rcmp-grc.gc.ca/dna_ac/annualreport_e.htm

U.S. National Database

Budowle, B., et al. (1998). CODIS and PCR-based short tandem repeat loci: Law enforcement tools. In: *Proceedings of the second european symposium on human identification* (pp. 73–88). Madison, WI: Promega Corporation. Available at http://www.promega.com/geneticidproc

Budowle, B., & Moretti, T.R. (1998). Examples of STR population databases for CODIS and for casework. In: *Proceedings of the ninth international symposium on human identification.* Available at http://www.promega.com/geneticidproc/

Budowle, B., et al. (2001). CODIS STR loci data from 41 sample populations. *Journal of Forensic Sciences, 46,* 453–489.

Hoyle, R. (1998). The FBI's national DNA database. *Nature Biotechnology, 16,* 987–987.

Niezgoda, S. & Brown, B. (1995). The FBI Laboratory's Combined DNA Index System program. In: *Proceedings of the sixth international symposium on human identification.* Available at http://www.promega.com/geneticidproc

Niezgoda, S. (1997). CODIS program review. In: *Proceedings of the eighth international symposium on human identification.* Available at http://www.promega.com/geneticidproc

Pederson, J. (1999). DNA typing in action: Databasing in the Commonwealth of Virginia. *Profiles in DNA, 3*(1), 3–7. Available at http://www.promega.com/profiles

DNA Database Laws

DNA Resource.com (information on the latest developments in forensic DNA policy). http://www.dnaresource.com

Herkenham, D. (2002). DNA database legislation and legal issues Madison, WI: Promega Corporation. *Profiles in DNA*, *5*(1), 6–7. Available at http://www.promega.com/profiles

McEwen, J. E., & Reilly, P. R. (1994). A review of state legislation on DNA forensic data banking. *American Journal of Human Genetics*, *54*, 941–958.

McEwen, J. E. (1995). Forensic DNA data banking by state crime laboratories. *American Journal of Human Genetics*, *56*, 1487–1492.

National Conference of State Legislatures (state laws on DNA data banks, qualifying offenses, others who must provide sample, summary as of July 2008). http://www.ncsl.org/programs/cj/dnadatabanks.htm

Palmer, L. J. (2004). *Encyclopedia of DNA and the United States criminal justice system.* London: McFarland.

Spalding, V. B. (1995). DNA databanking laws: The North Carolina experience and a national review of laws and challenges. In: *Proceedings of the sixth international symposium on human identification* (pp. 137–148). Madison, WI: Promega Corporation. Available at http://www.promega.com/geneticidproc

Williams, R., & Johnson, P. (2005). *Forensic DNA databasing: A European perspective* (interim report). http://www.dur.ac.uk/resources/sass/WilliamsandJohnsonInterimReport2005-1.pdf

Willing, R. (2006). Many DNA matches aren't acted on. *USA Today*. November 20, 2006. Available at http://www.usatoday.com/news/nation/2006-11-20-dna-matches_x.htm

Privacy and Ethical Concerns

Gene Watch. http://www.gene-watch.org/DNADatabases

Gamero, J. J., et al. (2008). A study of Spanish attitudes regarding the custody and use of forensic DNA databases. *Forensic Science International: Genetics*, *2*, 138–149.

Guillén, M., et al. (2000). Ethical-legal problems of DNA databases in criminal investigation. *Journal of Medical Ethics*, *26*, 266–271.

Kaye, D. H. (2006). Who needs special needs?: On the constitutionality of collecting DNA and other biometric data from arrestees. *Journal of Law Medicine & Ethics*, *34*, 188–198.

Kaye, J. (2006). Police collection and access to DNA samples. *Genomics, Society & Policy*, *2*, 16–27. Available at http://www.gspjournal.com

Nuffield Council on Bioethics (2007). *The forensic use of bioinformation: Ethical issues.* Available at http://www.nuffieldbioethics.org

Privacy International. http://www.privacyinternational.org

Rothstein, M. A., & Talbott, M. K. (2006). The expanding use of DNA in law enforcement: What role for privacy? *Journal of Law Medicine & Ethics*, *34*, 153–164.

Simoncelli, T. (2006). Dangerous excursions: The case against expanding forensic DNA databases to innocent persons. *Journal of Law Medicine & Ethics*, *34*, 390–397.

Simoncelli, T., & Krimsky, S. (2007). A new era of DNA collections: At what cost to civil liberties? An issue brief available at http://www.acslaw.org/node/5338

Williams, R., & Johnson, P. (2006). Inclusiveness, effectiveness and intrusiveness: Issues in the developing uses of DNA profiling in support of criminal investigations. *Journal of Law Medicine & Ethics*, *34*, 234–247.

Sample Retention

Gaensslen, R. E. (2006). Should biological evidence or DNA be retained by forensic science laboratories after profiling? No, except under narrow legislatively-stipulated conditions. *Journal of Law Medicine & Ethics, 34*, 375–379.

Herkenham, M. D. (2006). Retention of offender DNA samples necessary to ensure and monitor quality of forensic DNA efforts: Appropriate safeguards exist to protect the DNA samples from misuse. *Journal of Law Medicine & Ethics, 34*, 380–384.

Familial Searching

Bieber, F. R., et al. (2006). Finding criminals through DNA of their relatives. *Science, 312*, 1315–1316.

Bieber, F. R. (2006). Turning base hits into earned runs: Improving the effectiveness of forensic DNA data bank programs. *Journal of Law Medicine & Ethics, 34*, 222–233.

Curran, J. M., & Buckleton, J. S. (2008). Effectiveness of familial searches. *Science & Justice, 48*, 164–167.

Fu, J., et al. (2007). Considerations for the interpretation of STR results in cases of questioned half-sibship. *Transfusion, 47*, 515–519.

Greely, H. T., et al. (2006). Family ties: The use of DNA offender databases to catch offenders' kin. *Journal of Law Medicine & Ethics, 34*, 248–252.

Grimm, D. J. (2007). The demographics of genetic surveillance: Familial DNA testing and the Hispanic community. *Columbia Law Review, 107*, 1164–1194.

Reid, T. M., et al. (2004). Specificity of sibship determination using the ABI Identifiler multiplex system. *Journal of Forensic Sciences, 49*, 1262–1264.

Reid, T. M., et al. (2008). Use of sibling pairs to determine the familial searching efficiency of forensic databases. *Forensic Science International: Genetics, 2*(4), 340–342.

DNA Dragnets through Mass Screens

Hansen, M. (2004). DNA dragnet. *American Bar Association Journal, 90*, 38–43. Available at http://www.abajournal.com/magazine/dna_dragnet

http://www.forensic.gov.uk

http://www.washingtonpost.com (14, 15, and 17 April 2004)

Kahn, R., et al. (1996). AmpliType PM testing of potential perpetrators on a massive scale. In: *Proceedings of the American Academy of Forensic Sciences*, p. 52.

Kaye, D. H. (2009). Rounding up the usual suspects: A legal and logical analysis of DNA trawling cases. *North Carolina Law Review, 87*(2), 425–503.

Szibor, R., et al. (2006). Forensic mass screening using mtDNA. *International Journal of Legal Medicine, 120*, 372–376.

Walker, S. (2004). Police DNA 'sweeps' extremely unproductive: A national survey of police DNA 'sweeps.' A report by the Police Professionalism Initiative. Available at http://www.unomaha.edu/criminaljustice/PDF/dnareport.pdf

Wenzel, R. (2007). Report on criminal cases in Europe solved by ILS (DNA mass testing) for the European Network of Forensic Science Institutes DNA Working Group. Available at http://www.enfsi.eu

John Doe Warrants

Denver DA John Doe Case Filings. http://www.denverda.org/DNA/John_Doe_DNA_Warrants.htm

DNA.gov. http://www.dna.gov/uses/solving-crimes/cold_cases/identifying_analyzing_prioritizing/johndoewarrant

Gahn, N. (2000). John Doe: D1S7, D2S44, D5S110, D10S28, D17S79, charged with rape (interview). *Profiles in DNA*, *3*(3), 8–9. Available at http://www.promega.com/profiles/303/ProfilesinDNA_303_08.pdf

Cold Hits, Partial Matches within Databases, and Database Match Probability

Balding, D. J. (2002). The DNA database search controversy. *Biometrics*, *58*, 214–244.

Budowle, B., *et al.* (2006). Clarification of statistical issues related to the operation of CODIS. In: *Proceedings of the seventeenth international symposium on human identification*. Promega Corporation. Available at http://www.promega.com/geneticidproc/ussymp17proc

Budowle, B., et al. (2009). Partial matches in heterogeneous offender databases do not call into question the validity of random match probability calculations. *International Journal of Legal Medicine*, *123*, 59–63.

DNA Advisory Board. (2000). Statistical and population genetic issues affecting the evaluation of the frequency of occurrence of DNA profiles calculated from pertinent population database(s). *Forensic Sciences Communications*, *2*(3). Available at http://www.fbi.gov/hq/lab/fsc/backissu/july2000/dnastat.htm

Meester, R., & Sjerps, M. (2003). The evidentiary value in the DNA database search controversy and the two-stain problem. *Biometrics*, *59*, 727–732.

Rudin, N., & Inman, K. (2007). A frosty debate: The chilling effect of a 'cold hit.' *CACNews* 1st Quarter 2007, pp. 31–35. Available at http://www.cacnews.org or http://www.forensicdna.com/Articles.htm

Troyer, K., et al. (2001). A nine STR locus match between two apparently unrelated individuals using AmpF*l*STR Profiler Plus and COfiler. In: *Proceedings of the twelfth international symposium on human identification*. Madison, WI: Promega Corporation. Available at http://www.promega.com/geneticidproc/ussymp12proc/abstracts.htm

Weir, B. S. (2004). Matching and partially-matching DNA profiles. *Journal of Forensic Sciences*, *49*, 1009–1014.

CHAPTER 13

Quality Assurance

Laboratories should adhere to high quality standards (such as those defined by TWGDAM and the DNA Advisory Board) and make every effort to be accredited for DNA work (by such organizations as ASCLD-LAB).

—NRC II Report, Recommendation 3.1, p. 4

IMPORTANCE OF QUALITY ASSURANCE

Any scientific test that results in information that may lead to the loss of liberty of an individual accused of a crime needs to be performed with utmost care. DNA typing is no exception. It is a multistep, technical process that needs to be performed by qualified and effectively trained personnel to ensure that accurate results are obtained and interpreted correctly. When the process is conducted properly, DNA testing is a capable investigative tool for the law enforcement community with results that stand up to legal scrutiny in court. When laboratories have not followed validated protocols or have not had adequately trained personnel, problems have arisen in the past (D.N.A. Box 13.1).

Two topics are commonly referred to when discussing the importance of maintaining good laboratory practices to obtain accurate scientific results: quality assurance and quality control. *Quality assurance* (QA) refers to those planned or systematic actions necessary to provide adequate confidence that a product or service will satisfy given requirements for quality. *Quality control* (QC), on the other hand, usually refers to the day-to-day operational techniques and the activities used to fulfill requirements of quality.

Thus, an organization plans QA measures and performs QC activities in the laboratory. The forensic DNA community has long recognized the importance of quality results and, since early in the development of forensic DNA

Contribution of the National Institute of Standards and Technology, 2010.

D.N.A. Box 13.1 'Houston, We Have a Problem...': The Importance of Quality DNA Results

An alarming audit of the Houston Police Department (HPD) Crime Laboratory in December 2002 found that problems abounded in this unaccredited laboratory. In a poorly funded and managed environment, laboratory personnel were not adequately trained, evidence was often consumed, and the roof in the evidence storage area leaked from rain damage. The city of Houston shut down operations in the HPD laboratory and outsourced hundreds of cases for review to a private Houston-based laboratory named Identigene. While most of the retesting supported the original conclusions that the suspect in a case could be included in contributing the crime sample, unfortunately errors in data interpretation by the HPD laboratory led to the false conviction and incarceration of a young man accused of a 1998 rape.

In March 2003 Josiah Sutton's case made national headlines when it was revealed that DNA tests performed by Identigene found that he could not have committed the crime for which he had been incarcerated for more than 4 years based on DNA evidence originally analyzed by HPD. With this news also came the stigma that DNA testing was fallible.

It is important to note that many of the problematic tests performed by the HPD laboratory involved DNA mixtures and the use of an earlier, low-resolution PCR-based test known as HLA-DQA1 rather than the current and more precise method of STR typing. Since only six alleles are possible with DQA1 typing, it is inherently poor at separating mixture components.

More than $4.6 million were allocated for retesting of samples from almost 400 cases originally handled by the HPD laboratory. Thus, failure to achieve laboratory accreditation, properly train personnel, maintain adequate facilities, and follow guidelines for data interpretation can cost significantly more than just a laboratory's reputation. In June 2007, the HPD crime laboratory was granted accreditation following an ASCLD/LAB inspection. It is hoped that the HPD laboratory will maintain its status as an accredited laboratory and conduct quality forensic DNA testing.

The FBI DNA Laboratory has also come under fire in recent years largely due to the deceitful actions of a forensic biologist named Jacqueline Blake. Ms. Blake apparently ran over 100 cases in the FBI's DNA Analysis Unit I without performing testing of her negative control samples—and then falsified documents to make it appear as though she had followed the standard operating procedure. The Department of Justice's Office of the Inspector General issued a report in May 2004 reviewing the protocol and practice vulnerabilities of the FBI DNA Laboratory to ensure that this type of failure is not observed again.

It is important to keep in mind that these two cases represent the rare exception rather than the rule because the vast majority of forensic laboratories work hard to be accredited, maintain analyst training and proficiency, carefully validate methods, and follow standard operating procedures. The science itself is sound and reliable when performed correctly. These situations simply illustrate the need for consistent internal quality assurance and external oversight to ensure procedural accuracy within a laboratory.

Sources:
Houston Chronicle. http://www.chron.com
http://www.hpdlabinvestigation.org
U.S. Department of Justice Office of the Inspector General. (2004, May). The FBI DNA Laboratory: A review of protocol and practice vulnerabilities. Available at http://www.usdoj.gov/oig/special/0405/final.pdf

technology, has established organizations to recommend and oversee quality assurance guidelines and quality control measures.

Organizations involved

A number of organizations exist around the world that work on a local, national, or international level to aid in quality assurance work and to ensure that DNA testing is performed properly. The organizations are made up primarily of working scientists who want to coordinate their efforts to benefit the DNA typing community as a whole.

The *International Society of Forensic Genetics* (ISFG), which was founded in 1968 and formerly known as the International Society of Forensic Haemogenetics (ISFH), today represents a group of approximately 1100 scientists from more than 60 countries. Meetings are held biannually to discuss the latest topics in forensic genetics. Conference volumes were originally published under the title *Advances in Forensic Haemogenetics*, but are now titled *Progress in Forensic Genetics*. The 2007 ISFG meeting proceedings (*Progress in Forensic Genetics 12*) were published online as part of the *Forensic Science International: Genetics Supplement Series* (http://www.fsigeneticssup.com).

Every few years, as a specific need arises, a *DNA Commission of the ISFG* is formed and makes recommendations on the use of genetic markers. These publications are available at http://www.isfg.org/Publications/DNA+Commission and include the following topics (with their publication year): DNA polymorphisms (1989), PCR-based polymorphisms (1992), naming variant STR alleles (1994), STR repeat nomenclature (1997), mitochondrial DNA (2000), Y-STR use in forensic analysis (2001), additional information on Y-STRs including nomenclature (2006), mixture interpretation (2006), disaster victim identification (2007), and biostatistics for paternity testing (2008). For additional information on ISFG, visit its Web site at http://www.isfg.org

The *International Organization for Standardization* (ISO) issues guidance documents on a variety of topics. ISO 17025:2005 entitled *General Requirements for the Competence of Testing and Calibration Laboratories* is the standard to which many DNA testing laboratories seek to be accredited to by accrediting organizations, such as ASCLD/LAB or FQS-I (see below). For more information on ISO, see http://www.iso.org

The *Technical Working Group on DNA Analysis Methods* (TWGDAM) was established in November 1988 under FBI Laboratory sponsorship to aid forensic DNA scientists throughout North America. Since 1998, TWGDAM has been known as SWGDAM, which stands for the *Scientific Working Group on DNA Analysis Methods*. SWGDAM is a group of approximately 50 scientists representing federal, state, and local forensic DNA laboratories in the United States and Canada. Meetings are held twice a year, usually in January and July. Public meetings have also been held in conjunction with scientific meetings such as the International Symposium on Human Identification, sponsored each fall by the Promega Corporation. Since 2006 a public SWGDAM meeting has been held as part of the FBI-sponsored National CODIS Conference.

During the past two decades, five individuals have served as TWGDAM or SWGDAM chairs: James Kearney (FBI), Bruce Budowle (FBI), Richard

Guerrieri (FBI), David Coffman (Florida Department of Law Enforcement), and Ted Staples (Georgia Bureau of Investigation). Several TWGDAM or SWGDAM subcommittees have operated to bring recommendations before the entire group. These subcommittees have included restriction fragment length polymorphism (RFLP), polymerase chain reaction (PCR), Combined DNA Index System (CODIS), mitochondrial DNA, short tandem repeat (STR) interpretation, training, validation, Y chromosome, expert systems, missing persons/mass disasters, mixture interpretation, and quality assurance. TWGDAM issued guidelines for quality assurance in DNA analysis in 1989, 1991, and 1995. Revised SWGDAM validation guidelines were published in 2004. Several ad hoc subcommittees have produced recommendations on such topics as review of outsourced data and handling partial matches.

The *DNA Advisory Board* (DAB) was a congressionally mandated organization that was created and funded by the U.S. Congress's DNA Identification Act of 1994. The first meeting of the DAB was held on 12 May 1995, and chaired by Nobel laureate Dr. Joshua Lederberg. The DAB consisted of 13 voting members that included scientists from state, local, and private forensic laboratories; molecular geneticists and population geneticists not affiliated with a forensic laboratory; a representative from the National Institute of Standards and Technology; the chair of TWGDAM; and a judge.

The DAB was created for a 5-year period to issue standards for the forensic DNA community. When the DAB's responsibilities ended in 2000, SWGDAM took over operation as the group responsible for offering recommendations to the forensic community within the United States. In 2007 SWGDAM revised the *Quality Assurance Standards for Forensic Caseworking Laboratories* and the *Quality Assurance Standards for DNA Databasing Laboratories*. These revised standards went into effect 1 July 2009 after being approved by the FBI Laboratory's director.

The *American Society of Crime Laboratory Directors* (ASCLD) and its Laboratory Accreditation Board (ASCLD/LAB) play an important role in the United States as well as internationally for laboratory accreditation programs. The ASCLD/LAB motto is 'quality assurance through inspection.' The Crime Laboratory Accreditation Program is a voluntary program in which any crime laboratory may participate to demonstrate that its management, operations, personnel, procedures, and instruments meet stringent standards. The goal of accreditation is to improve the overall service of forensic laboratories to the criminal justice system. If a forensic laboratory is intersted in becoming accredited, an ASCLD/LAB accreditation manual is available from the executive secretary for a fee. As of December 2008, a total of 356 crime laboratories had been accredited by ASCLD/LAB although not all of them are doing DNA testing. For additional information on ASCLD/LAB, visit its Web site at http://www.ascld-lab.org

Forensic Quality Services (FQS) and *Forensic Quality Services—International* (FQS-I) are not-for-profit organizations established in 2003 by the National Forensic Science Technology Center (NFSTC), which is located in Largo, Florida. FQS-I accredits forensic laboratories to ISO 17025. As of December 2008, a total of 53 labs had been accredited by FQS-I. For additional information on FQS and FQS-I, visit their Web site at http://www.forquality.org

The *American Association of Blood Banks* (AABB) sets standards for laboratories performing DNA parentage or relationship testing. AABB provides accreditation for paternity testing laboratories. As of December 2008, there were 40 accredited paternity testing laboratories in the United States. For more information on AABB, visit its Web site at http://www.aabb.org

American Board of Criminalistics (ABC) offers voluntary levels of certification for forensic scientists. Exams are given on a regular basis to test general understanding or specific knowledge in an area of forensic science such as molecular biology or drug analysis. Two levels of certification can be achieved: Diplomat (D-ABC) and Fellow (F-ABC). For more information on ABC, visit its Web site at http://www.criminalistics.com

The *European Network of Forensic Science Institutes* (ENFSI) was started in 1995 to set standards for exchange of data between European member states and to be an accrediting body through conducting laboratory audits. Within the ENFSI, there is a DNA working group that meets twice a year to discuss forensic DNA protocols and research in much the same fashion as SWGDAM does within North America. For additional information on ENFSI, visit its Web site at http://www.enfsi.eu

The European forensic DNA community has another organization similar to SWGDAM named EDNAP (*European DNA Profiling Group*). EDNAP, which first began meeting in October 1988, is effectively a working group of the International Society of Forensic Genetics and consists of representatives from more than a dozen European nations. EDNAP has conducted a series of interlaboratory studies on various STR markers to investigate the reproducibility of multiple laboratories in testing the same samples. These studies have demonstrated that with the proper quality control measures excellent reproducibility can be seen between forensic laboratories. EDNAP typically meets twice a year in conjunction with the ENFSI DNA working group meetings. For additional information on EDNAP, visit its Web site at http://www.isfg.org/EDNAP

LEVELS OF QA/QC

Table 13.1 summarizes the overall quality assurance measures utilized within the United States, from the community level down to the individual case, that are in place to help provide confidence in the results produced by laboratories. Each of these levels will be covered in more depth in subsequent sections.

Table 13.1 Quality assurance/quality control (QA/QC) measures in place at each level within the forensic DNA community.

Level	QA/QC Measure
Community	Quality assurance standards
Laboratory	Accreditation and audits
Analyst	Proficiency tests and continuing education
Method/instrument	Validation of performance (along with use of traceable standard sample)
Protocol	Standard operating procedure written and followed
Data sets	Positive and negative amplification controls
Individual sample	Internal size standard present in every sample
Interpretation of result	Case review by a second qualified analyst or supervisor
Court presentation of evidence	Defense attorneys and experts with power of discovery requests

At the broadest level of the entire U.S. forensic DNA typing community, quality assurance standards have been established that require laboratories to carefully conduct their work. Exploratory interlaboratory studies, although not required, are also occasionally conducted to demonstrate that laboratories are obtaining comparable results.

At the individual laboratory level, audits are conducted regularly and accreditation granted when minimum standards are met. Proficiency testing and continuing education are required to help the individual analyst stay current in his or her work. Individual instruments and methods are validated and performance verified on a regular basis—often with traceability to a certified reference material. Each laboratory has standard operating procedures to describe the steps of the process to be followed to help ensure consistency over time and across cases within that laboratory.

At the sample batch level, positive and negative PCR amplification controls help demonstrate that sample reagents are working properly. Allelic ladders verify that all detectable STR alleles can be resolved from one another. Internal size standards are included with each sample processed for capillary electrophoresis STR allele separation and detection. Technical and administrative case review is performed to confirm the results obtained and conclusions reached. Finally, within the U.S. legal system, defendants have a right to counsel. Defense discovery requests and review of case information on evidence going to court provide additional quality checks on the DNA results.

Quality Assurance Standards

Forensic DNA laboratories in the United States are mandated by Congress to follow strict quality assurance standards. In October 1998, the FBI Laboratory's DNA Advisory Board issued *Quality Assurance Standards* (QAS) that define how forensic laboratories are required to conduct business (D.N.A. Box 13.2). These QAS were recently revised and went into effect July 2009. U.S. forensic DNA laboratories are governed by these QAS and regularly audited for their compliance with these standards.

Audits

A *laboratory audit* evaluates the entire operation of a laboratory. It is a systematic examination that may be conducted by the laboratory management or by an independent organization according to preestablished guidelines. A laboratory must possess *standard operating procedures* (SOPs) and adhere to these protocols. Likewise, instruments and other equipment vital to the successful completion of a forensic DNA case must be maintained properly, and personnel must be appropriately trained to perform their jobs.

An audit team, typically consisting of scientists from other forensic DNA laboratories, visits the lab being audited and evaluates this lab according to criteria spelled out in an audit document. Records of an audit are maintained and serve to describe the findings of the audit team and a course of action that may be taken to resolve any existing problems. If any negative findings are noted, then the lab has to take corrective action or lose accreditation.

Laboratory accreditation

Laboratory accreditation results from a successful completion of an inspection or audit by an accrediting body. The two primary accrediting organizations within the United States that are recognized by the forensic DNA community are ASCLD/LAB and FQS (and FQS-I). Accreditation requires that the laboratory demonstrate and maintain good lab practices including chain-of-custody and evidence handling procedures.

The accreditation process generally involves several steps such as a laboratory self-evaluation, filing application and supporting documents to initiate the accreditation process, on-site inspection by a team of trained auditors, an inspection report, and an annual accreditation review report. The inspection evaluates the facilities and equipment, the training of the technical staff, the written operating and technical procedures, and the casework reports and supporting documentation of the applicant laboratory.

Proficiency tests

A *proficiency test*, as it relates to the DNA typing field, is an evaluation of a laboratory analyst's performance in conducting DNA analysis procedures. These tests

D.N.A. Box 13.2 FBI's Quality Assurance Standards

The DNA Advisory Board (DAB) was established by the director of the FBI under the DNA Identification Act of 1994 to operate for a period of 5 years and consisted of 13 voting members during its 1995–2000 tenure. One of the primary purposes of the DAB was to recommend standards for quality assurance in conducting analysis of DNA and to provide guidance to forensic analysts performing those DNA analyses. The original Quality Assurance Standards (QAS) for forensic DNA testing laboratories were issued in October 1998 and were followed 6 months later by the QAS for convicted offender DNA databasing laboratories. In July 2009, the original QAS were superseded by revised Quality Assurance Standards (rQAS) for Forensic Labs and rQAS for DNA Databasing Labs based on input from the FBI-sponsored Scientific Working Group on DNA Analysis Methods (SWGDAM), a group of about 50 local, state, and federal U.S. scientists that meets semiannually to review and evaluate issues of interest to the forensic DNA community.

The following seventeen topics are covered by the rQAS (and original QAS):

1. SCOPE
2. DEFINITIONS
3. QUALITY ASSURANCE PROGRAM
4. ORGANIZATION AND MANAGEMENT
5. PERSONNEL
6. FACILITIES
7. EVIDENCE/SAMPLE CONTROL
8. VALIDATION
9. ANALYTICAL PROCEDURES
10. EQUIPMENT CALIBRATION AND MAINTENANCE
11. REPORTS/DOCUMENTATION
12. REVIEW
13. PROFICIENCY TESTING
14. CORRECTIVE ACTION
15. AUDITS
16. SAFETY
17. OUTSOURCING

As noted in the scope, the standards describe the quality assurance requirements that laboratories performing forensic DNA testing or utilizing the Combined DNA Index System (CODIS) must follow to ensure the quality and integrity of the data generated by the laboratory. These standards also apply to vendor laboratories that perform forensic DNA testing and DNA databasing in accordance with Standard 17. These standards do not preclude the participation of a laboratory, by itself or in collaboration with others, in research and development of procedures that have not yet been validated.

Sources:
http://www.fbi.gov/hq/lab/html/databasinglab.htm
http://www.fbi.gov/hq/lab/html/testinglab.htm

are performed periodically, usually on a semiannual basis, for each DNA analyst or examiner. In fact, Standard 13.1 of the Quality Assurance Standards requires that each DNA analyst undergo an external proficiency test at least twice a year. Biological specimens with a previously determined DNA profile are submitted to the laboratory personnel being tested. The purpose of the test is to evaluate their ability to obtain a concordant result using the laboratory's approved SOPs.

These proficiency tests may be administered by someone else in the laboratory (*internal proficiency test*) or by an external organization (*external proficiency test*). If the test administered by an external organization is performed such that the laboratory personnel do not know that a test is being conducted, then it is termed a *blind external proficiency test*. A blind external proficiency test is generally considered the most effective at monitoring a laboratory's abilities but can be rather expensive and time consuming to arrange and conduct. Participation in a proficiency-testing program is an essential part of a successful laboratory's

D.N.A. Box 13.3 Blind Proficiency Tests

Four models exist for blind proficiency testing: (1) blind/law enforcement, where a law enforcement agency fully disguises the test as a routine case and participates in the deception of the target laboratory; (2) blind/conduit lab, where another laboratory, perhaps one that is part of a multilaboratory state system, submits appropriate specimens for a case and is part of the deception of the target laboratory; (3) blind analyst, where only the DNA analysts are in the dark about the test while laboratory QA coordinators administer the test; and (4) random audit/reanalysis, where a reexamination of a case is performed by another analyst or an auditor external to the laboratory to review and even reanalyze the samples. Cost estimates for these various forms of blind proficiency range from $1400 to $10,000 per test with the blind analyst approach (number 3) being the least expensive and easiest to implement. Thus, running a program that tests 150 to 200 DNA laboratories in the United States with two tests per year would become rather expensive.

Another challenge besides cost is the fact that deception of the other party is necessary in an effort to create a 'real' case situation. When laboratories and law enforcement agencies are trying to build trust, deception for the purpose of quality assurance may seem a bit extreme. In addition, protection of specimen donors is important and if a 'case' is entered into CODIS, can the profiles for the innocent donors be purged? Likewise, if only a few donors are used in the proficiency test, then DNA laboratories might figure out in a short period of time which profiles are part of the blind proficiency test. Based on these and other considerations, implementation of a large national blind proficiency-testing program was not recommended in the United States.

In Europe, the German DNA profiling group (GEDNAP) has developed a blind trial concept that is really a 'graded' interlaboratory test. The primary requirement of this blind trial is that all participants receive exactly the same material to be tested, enabling a direct comparison with the known

standard as well as an interlaboratory comparison to be carried out. Samples are prepared to be as close to real casework situations as possible.

The GEDNAP trials have four purposes: (1) standardization of methods and procedures, (2) standardization of nomenclature, (3) evaluation of the competence of a laboratory to obtain the correct result, and (4) elimination of errors in typing. GEDNAP trials 22 and 23 conducted in 2001 had 122 participating laboratories from 28 European countries while participation grew to 160 laboratories for trials 26 and 27 held in 2003. Laboratories are each assigned a code number that enables anonymity throughout the interlaboratory comparison process. Typically seven samples are provided with each GEDNAP trial. When results are returned to the organizing laboratory in Münster, each allele call is classified into one of four categories: (1) no errors, (2) mixture not detected, (3) error in typing but would not be reported, and (4) error in typing which would be reported. Finally, a certificate is issued by the organizing laboratory, which states that the laboratory in question has successfully completed the blind trial for the particular loci examined.

The types of errors observed in the GEDNAP trials show that human carelessness is the predominant source of error with transposition of samples and transcription errors. The error rate over the past few years has held relatively constant at 0.4% to 0.7%.

Sources:

Peterson, J., et al. (2003). The feasibility of external blind DNA proficiency testing. I. Background and findings. *Journal of Forensic Sciences, 48,* 21–31.

Peterson, J., et al. (2003). The feasibility of external blind DNA proficiency testing. II. Experience with actual blind tests. *Journal of Forensic Sciences, 48,* 32–40.

Rand, S., et al. (2002). The GEDNAP (German DNA profiling group) blind trial concept. *International Journal of Legal Medicine, 116,* 199–206.

Rand, S., et al. (2004). The GEDNAP blind trial concept part II. Trends and developments. *International Journal of Legal Medicine, 118,* 83–89.

quality assurance effort. Forensic laboratories develop their own proficiency-testing programs or establish one in cooperation with other laboratories. The German DNA profiling group (GEDNAP) has established a successful blind proficiency-testing program (D.N.A. Box 13.3).

The purpose of proficiency testing is to evaluate the performance of an analyst using a sample or set of samples that is unknown to the analyst but known to the test provider. Recommendation 3.2 of NRC II states that: 'Laboratories should participate regularly in proficiency tests, and the results should be available for court proceedings.' Successful completion of this examination permits a degree of confidence to exist in how an analyst might perform on a real forensic case sample. Unfortunately, if analysts are aware that they are being tested, they might be more careful than they would when normally processing routine samples on a daily basis. Thus, the concept of blind proficiency has often been discussed in order to have a true test of the entire system because the analysts would not know that he or she was being tested. However, as noted in D.N.A. Box 13.3, a number of challenges and costs are associated with blind proficiency tests.

Validation

While work quality of analysts can be confirmed through proficiency tests, instruments used and methods performed are verified through validation. *Validation* refers to the process of demonstrating that a laboratory procedure is robust, reliable, and reproducible in the hands of the personnel performing the test in that laboratory.

A *robust method* is one in which successful results are obtained a high percentage of the time and few, if any, samples need to be repeated. A *reliable method* refers to one in which the obtained results are accurate and correctly reflect the sample being tested. A *reproducible method* means that the same or very similar results are obtained each time a sample is tested. All three types of methods are important for techniques performed in forensic laboratories.

There are generally considered to be two stages of validation: developmental validation and internal validation. *Developmental validation* involves the testing of new STR loci or STR kits, new primer sets, and new technologies for detecting STR alleles. *Internal validation*, on the other hand, involves verifying that established procedures examined previously under the scrutiny of developmental validation (often by another laboratory) will work effectively in one's own laboratory. Developmental validation is typically performed by commercial STR kit manufacturers and large laboratories such as the FBI Laboratory, whereas internal validation is the primary form of validation performed in smaller local and state forensic DNA laboratories. More information on validation will be provided later in this chapter.

Standard operating procedures and interpretation guidelines

Each forensic laboratory develops or adopts *standard operating procedures* (SOPs) that give a detailed listing of all the materials required to perform an assay as well as the exact steps required to successfully complete the experiment. In addition, SOPs list critical aspects of the assay that must be monitored carefully. SOPs are followed exactly when performing forensic DNA casework.

SOPs also include interpretation guidelines to aid analysts in making decisions in evaluating data. For example, should a peak observed in an electropherogram be called an allele or be removed from consideration in the DNA profile because it is an instrumental artifact (e.g., a spike) or a biological artifact (e.g., a stutter product)? These interpretation guidelines are based on internal validation studies performed by the laboratory. Usually, the more specific the interpretation guidelines are, the more consistent data review will be between analysts within a laboratory and across cases examined by the same analyst over time.

Controls for data sets and individual samples

Multiple levels of quality control are available for DNA samples being processed. Biological samples are quantified to determine the amount of human DNA present prior to PCR amplification. Reagent blanks, which are analytical control samples containing no template DNA, are carried through the DNA typing process from extraction onward to monitor potential contamination. PCR amplification positive and negative controls are amplified alongside the casework evidence or reference samples to demonstrate that the PCR reagents are working properly and are not contaminated.

Allelic ladder samples permit an evaluation of DNA separation, resolution, and sizing precision over time—particularly because multiple allelic ladders are often associated with each set of data collected. Each sample is also mixed with an internal size standard prior to being analyzed with capillary electrophoresis. These controls enable troubleshooting of the process should something go wrong during PCR amplification or data collection on the CE instrument. Proper performance of each control also provides confidence in the results obtained.

Case review

As with patients who request a second opinion when faced with a medical procedure, DNA results are reviewed by a second analyst and/or supervisor to confirm allele calls and case conclusions. Forensic DNA laboratories conduct administrative and technical reviews of case files and reports prior to releasing this information to ensure that conclusions reached are reasonable based on available data collected.

Court proceedings

A case report prepared based on the laboratory results obtained may be entered into evidence as part of court proceedings. In the U.S. legal system, defense attorneys and defense experts have the power of *discovery requests*. Under a discovery request, the forensic laboratory has to turn over the items requested so that they can be reviewed in the interest of the defendant. Thus, lab results may be scrutinized before and during a trial. This review provides another level to ensure that quality results have been obtained in the case under consideration. In addition, an analyst may be called on to testify in court to the DNA results obtained. Cross-examination by the defense team then provides the final level of review in order to confirm the DNA testing results.

VALIDATION

Validation is an important part of forensic DNA typing. Defense lawyers today rarely challenge the science behind DNA typing—rather they challenge the process by which the laboratory performs the DNA analysis. Thus, the scientific community must carefully document the validity of new techniques and technologies to ensure that procedures performed in the laboratory accurately reflect the examined samples. In addition, a laboratory must carefully document its technical procedures and policies for interpretation of data and follow them to guarantee that each sample is handled and processed appropriately.

Publication and presentation of validation results

Results of developmental validation studies are shared as soon as possible with the scientific community either through presentations at scientific professional meetings or publication in peer-reviewed journals. Rapid dissemination of information about these studies is important to the legal system that forensic science serves because the courts rely on precedence when ruling whether DNA evidence is admissible.

The most commonly used scientific journals for publishing validation studies and population results are the *Journal of Forensic Sciences*, the *International Journal of Legal Medicine*, *Legal Mediciane*, and *Forensic Science International* (and since 2007 its daughter journal *FSI Genetics*). Other forensic journals include *Science and Justice*, *Canadian Society of Forensic Science Journal*, *American Journal of Forensic Medicine and Pathology*, *Forensic Science Review*, and *Forensic Science, Medicine, and Pathology*. Forensic DNA studies have also been published in *Analytical Chemistry*, *Electrophoresis*, *Human Mutation*, *Genome Research*, and other scientific journals. The FBI Laboratory maintains an online journal entitled *Forensic Science Communications* that is published quarterly and is available at http://www.fbi.gov/hq/lab/fsc/current/index.htm. Prior to 1999, this journal was known as *Crime Laboratory Digest*.

Scientific meetings where DNA typing research and validation studies are presented include the International Symposium on Human Identification (sponsored each fall by the Promega Corporation), the American Academy of Forensic Sciences (held each February), the Congress of the International Society of Forensic Genetics (held in late summer biannually), and the International Association of Forensic Sciences (held every 3 years in the summer months).

A number of other regional meetings are also held each year. For example, in the United States, regional forensic organizations holding annual meetings include the Northeastern Association of Forensic Scientists (NEAFS), the Mid-Atlantic Association of Forensic Scientists (MAAFS), the Midwestern Association of Forensic Scientists (MAFS), the Northwestern Association of Forensic Scientists (NWAFS), the Southwestern Association of Forensic Scientists (SWAFS), the Southern Association of Forensic Scientists (SAFS), and the California Association of Criminalists (CAC).

Internal validation of established procedures

To meet DAB/SWGDAM guidelines for quality assurance, forensic DNA laboratories conduct tests as part of the process of becoming 'validated.' These studies demonstrate that DNA typing results can be consistently and accurately obtained by the laboratory personnel involved in the testing.

Validation studies are performed with each new DNA typing system that is developed and used. For example, a lab may be validated with the Profiler Plus kit but it would need to perform additional validation studies when expanding its capabilities to amplifying the STR loci included in the Identifiler kit.

Typical studies for an internal validation include reproducibility, precision measurements for sizing alleles, and sensitivity (e.g., 50 ng down to 20 pg) along with mixture analysis and nonprobative casework samples. In sizing precision studies, the calculated allele sizes in base pairs are plotted against the size deviation from the corresponding allele in the allelic ladder with which the genotype was determined. If a high degree of precision cannot be maintained due to laboratory conditions such as temperature fluctuations, then samples may not be able to be genotyped accurately.

OTHER AIDS TO QUALITY ASSURANCE

There are several other aids to quality assurance outside the realm of the levels of quality assurance mentioned earlier. These include interlaboratory tests, certified reference materials, and commercial STR kits. Automation of sample handling and tracking as well as data interpretation also aids production of high-quality DNA typing results.

Exploratory interlaboratory tests

Exploratory interlaboratory tests are one way that the forensic community uses to demonstrate that the methods used in one's own laboratory are reproducible in another laboratory and comparable results are generated by these laboratories. These tests are essential to demonstrate consistency in results from multiple laboratories especially since DNA databases are now used where many laboratories contribute to the DNA profile information.

Since 1994, the European DNA Profiling Group (EDNAP) has conducted a series of interlaboratory evaluations on various STR loci and methodologies used for analyzing them. Each study involved the examination of five to seven bloodstains that were distributed to multiple laboratories (usually a dozen or more) to test their abilities to obtain consistent results. In all cases where simple STR loci were tested, consistent results were obtained. However, in early studies, complex STR markers, such as ACTBP2 (SE33), often gave inconsistent results. Thus, at that time, STRs with complex repeat structures were not recommended for use in DNA databases in which results are submitted from multiple laboratories. The availability of commercial kits and allelic ladders that enable consistent amplification and typing of SE33 now means that obtaining reproducible results is more feasible.

In the United States several interlaboratory studies have been performed. The first large test with commercial STR typing kits was conducted by the National Institute of Standards and Technology (NIST) and involved 34 laboratories that evaluated the three STRs TH01, TPOX, and CSF1PO in a multiplex amplification format. This study concluded that as long as locus-specific allelic ladders were used, a variety of separation and detection methods could be used to obtain equivalent genotypes for the same samples.

NIST has also conducted several DNA quantitation and mixture interlaboratory studies. While instrument sensitivity differences have been observed between laboratories, these studies have demonstrated that consistent results can be obtained between participating laboratories, thus helping support the conclusion that forensic DNA typing methods are reliable and reproducible when performed properly.

Certified reference materials

One of the primary ways to support a consistent and calibrated STR allele nomenclature is to use common reference materials between DNA testing laboratories. The National Institute of Standards and Technology, which is a nonregulatory agency in the U.S. Department of Commerce, provides reference materials for a variety of fields to enable accurate and comparable measurements. NIST supplies over 1300 reference materials to industry, academia, and government laboratories to facilitate quality assurance and support measurement traceability. These Standard Reference Materials (SRMs) are certified through carefully characterizing the properties for which values are assigned.

Reference DNA samples are crucial to the validation of any DNA testing procedure. Standard 9.5.5 in the revised Quality Assurance Standards issued in July 2009 states: 'The laboratory shall check its DNA procedures annually or whenever substantial changes are made to the protocol(s) against an appropriate and available NIST standard reference material or standard traceable to a NIST standard.'

NIST supplies several DNA SRMs to enable validation of a laboratory's measurement capabilities as well as calibration of instrumentation and methods. Current SRMs used by the forensic DNA community include SRM 2391b PCR-Based DNA Profiling Standard for autosomal STR markers, SRM 2392-I Mitochondrial DNA Sequencing for mtDNA sequence information, SRM 2395 Human Y-Chromosome DNA Profiling Standard for Y-chromosome markers, and SRM 2372 Human DNA Quantitation Standard for human DNA quantitation.

Commercial STR kits

In the early days of STR typing, forensic laboratories put together their own PCR mixes, primer sets, and allelic ladders. This meant that variation existed in the materials used by various laboratories and sometimes in the interpretation of a sample's genotype. Laboratories often had to spend a significant amount of time preparing the allelic ladders and verifying that each lot of primer mix worked appropriately.

Today, commercially available STR typing kits help to maintain a high level of confidence in results and to ensure consistency in nomenclature between laboratories. Use of commercial kits does increase the cost of DNA testing but aids in overall quality assurance due to compatibility and consistency of results (both in terms of loci examined and STR allele nomenclature used). These commercial kits come with company-supplied allelic ladders, which are composed of common alleles and used in sample data interpretation to make the specific STR allele designations. Although slight differences may exist in alleles present between the various kit allelic ladders as well as the PCR primers used to target the STR locus, concordance studies have shown that equivalent results can be obtained.

AUTOMATION

As the demand for a higher volume of DNA testing has grown, laboratory automation has played an increasingly important role. Laboratories will take on more cases and have larger numbers of samples to type because of DNA database laws. The use of laboratory automation is growing in forensic DNA typing laboratories in primarily three areas: liquid handling, sample tracking, and data analysis.

Liquid-handling robots

There are a number of liquid-handling tasks performed in DNA typing laboratories during the DNA extraction, PCR setup, and PCR amplification steps. These liquid-handling tasks are typically performed with manual pipettors by a DNA technician or analyst. Small volumes of liquids are repeatedly moved from one tube to another. These repetitive tasks can lead to mistakes as laboratory personnel get tired or become distracted.

By introducing automated liquid handling with robotics, the level of human error can be greatly reduced. Computers and robotics do the same tasks the same way time after time without getting tired. The challenge though lies in setting up the automation and maintaining it. Liquid-handling automation is being used in both high-volume sample processing of convicted offender DNA samples and forensic casework.

There are a number of commercially available liquid-handling robotic systems. Among the more popular are systems from Beckman Coulter, Qiagen, and Tecan. Each robotic system has different capabilities and should be carefully assessed in order to meet the needs and goals of one's own laboratory environment. Robotic liquid handling for steps of DNA extraction, quantification, PCR amplification setup, and preparation of sample plates for STR typing will likely become more prevalent in forensic laboratories particularly as the need for higher-volume work increases.

Sample-tracking programs

Managing large amounts of data becomes a problem for many laboratories as they scale up their efforts. Computer databases are often developed to aid in tracking samples and results obtained. Sample tubes and plates can be barcoded and tracked through the analysis process. Laboratory information management systems (LIMS) are rather expensive and are typically used only by laboratories with very high sample volumes.

Commercial LIMS systems, such as the Crime Fighter B.E.A.S.T. (computerized *Bar-coded Evidence Analysis, Statistics, and Tracking LIMS*) from Porter Lee Corporation (Schaumburg, IL), are being used in a growing number of forensic laboratories to provide electronic case files and automated sample-tracking capabilities. A LIMS manufacturer typically sets up its software and customizes it to accommodate protocols and processes within each customer laboratory.

The Armed Forces DNA Identification Laboratory (AFDIL, Rockville, MD) has worked in conjunction with Future Technologies Inc. (Fairfax, VA) to develop LISA, which stands for Laboratory Information Systems Applications. LISA contains a number of subsystems that permit case accessioning and the ability to electronically track the life cycle of each evidence and reference sample. There are additional modules such as MFIMS (*Mass Fatality Incident Management System*) and ASAP (*AFDIL Statistical Application Program*) that manage victim and family reference data as well as easing the tedious process of reporting results.

STaCS (*Sample Tracking and Control System*) is a system codeveloped by forensic DNA scientists at the Royal Canadian Mounted Police (RCMP) and Anjura Technology Corporation (Ottawa, ON) that integrates robotic sample processing with custom LIMS software. STaCS monitors instrument performance and can provide a variety of operational information reports to help make the process of DNA typing more efficient. This system has been set up in several DNA databasing laboratories including the Florida Department of Law Enforcement (Tallahassee, FL) and the FBI Laboratory (Quantico, VA).

Fully integrated systems with robotic liquid handling are especially useful for DNA databasing of convicted offender samples, which are usually more uniform in nature (i.e., all bloodstains or all buccal swabs), single-source samples, and relatively concentrated in amount. In one laboratory, over 17,000 DNA samples were processed in a 20-month period using robotics and LIMS with an overall typing success rate of 99.99%. While automation is being developed and implemented to robotically process and track samples through the steps of DNA extraction, quantitation, PCR amplification, and sample setup prior to electrophoretic separation, separate computer programs commonly referred to as 'expert systems' are being constructed to enable automatic interpretation of STR alleles from the resulting electropherograms.

Expert systems for STR data interpretation

One of the highest labor efforts in the process of typing STRs is the data interpretation stage. For many high-throughput laboratories, data assessment and interpretation of STRs represent approximately 50% or more of the resource requirement to deliver final results for samples. In many cases, more time is actually spent evaluating the STR profiles than preparing and collecting the data on the sample. To reduce this resource requirement, software has been designed and implemented to replace the traditional manual assessment.

Two of the first expert systems used operationally include FSS-i[3] developed by the Forensic Science Service in England (and sold by Promega Corporation in the United States) and TrueAllele developed by Mark Perlin of Cybergenetics (Pittsburgh, PA). Applied Biosystems (Foster City, CA) has also developed GeneMapperID-X, a program that includes quality flags on data collected with the ABI 310 or 3100 Genetic Analyzers. Following validation of the software performance, DNA profiles from samples given a 'green light' are generally considered fine and therefore further manual review is not required.

These expert systems are designed to translate the electropherogram signal into a genotype compatible with a database. As these expert systems are developed and implemented, bottlenecks will shift to other areas in the DNA typing process and thus permit development of expert systems that can solve ever more complex and diverse problems. Several years ago the National Institute of Justice established an NIJ Expert System Testbed (NEST) project at Marshall University (Huntington, WV) that has evaluated the various expert system platforms for both single-source and mixture interpretation.

Points for Discussion

- Why are multiple levels of quality assurance beneficial?

- Why are blind proficiency tests so challenging to implement?

- How can robotic sample-handling, sample-tracking, and expert systems improve quality assurance?

READING LIST AND INTERNET RESOURCES

Quality Assurance

Aboul-Enein, H. Y., et al. (2001). *Quality and reliability in analytical chemistry.* Washington, DC: CRC Press.

Christian, G. D. (2004). *Analytical chemistry* (6th ed.). New York: John Wiley & Sons.

Schneider, P. M. (2007). Scientific standards for studies in forensic genetics. *Forensic Science International, 165,* 238–243.

Taylor, J. K. (1981). Quality assurance of chemical measurements. *Analytical Chemistry, 53,* 1588A–1596A.

Taylor, J. K. (1987). *Quality assurance of chemical measurements.* Chelsea, MI: Lewis Publishers.

Taylor, J. K. (1990). *Statistical techniques for data analysis.* Chelsea, MI: Lewis Publishers.

VIM. (2008). *International vocabulary of metrology—Basic and general concepts and associated terms* (3rd ed., JCGM 200:2008); also published as ISO Guide 99 (ISO/IEC Guide 99-12:2007). Available at http://www.bipm.org/utils/common/documents/jcgm/JCGM_200_2008.pdf

Standards Organizations

American National Standards Institute. http://www.ansi.org

ASTM International (formerly American Society for Testing and Materials). http://www.astm.org

Bureau International des Poids et Mesures. http://www.bipm.org

International Organization for Standardization. http://www.iso.org

Scientific Organizations

European Network of Forensic Science Institutes. http://www.enfsi.eu

International Society of Forensic Genetics. http://www.isfg.org

ISFG Guidelines/Recommendations

Bär, W., et al. (1992). Editorial: Recommendations of the DNA Commission of the International Society for Forensic Haemogenetics relating to the use of PCR-based polymorphisms. *Forensic Science International, 55,* 1–3.

Bär, W., et al. (1993). Editorial: Statement by DNA Commission of the International Society for Forensic Haemogenetics concerning the National Academy of Sciences report on DNA Technology in Forensic Science in the USA. *Forensic Science International, 59,* 1–2.

Bär, W., et al. (1994). DNA recommendations—1994 report concerning further recommendations of the DNA Commission of the ISFH regarding PCR-based polymorphisms in STR (short tandem repeat) systems. *International Journal of Legal Medicine, 107,* 159–160.

Bär, W., et al. (1997). DNA recommendations—Further report of the DNA Commission of the ISFH regarding the use of short tandem repeat systems. *International Journal of Legal Medicine, 110,* 175–176.

Brinkmann, B., et al. (1989). Editorial: Recommendations of the Society for Forensic Haemogenetics concerning DNA polymorphisms. *Forensic Science International, 43,* 109–111.

Brinkmann, B., et al. (1992). Editorial: 1991 Report concerning recommendations of the DNA Commission of the International Society for Forensic Haemogenetics relating to the use of DNA polymorphisms. *Forensic Science International, 52,* 125–130.

Carracedo, A., et al. (2000). DNA Commission of the International Society for Forensic Genetics: Guidelines for mitochondrial DNA typing. *Forensic Science International, 110,* 79–85.

Gill, P., et al. (2001). DNA Commission of the International Society of Forensic Genetics: Recommendations on forensic analysis using Y-chromosome STRs. *Forensic Science International, 124,* 5–10.

Gill, P., et al. (2006). DNA Commission of the International Society of Forensic Genetics: Recommendations on the interpretation of mixtures. *Forensic Science International, 160,* 90–101.

Gjertson, D. W., et al. (2007). ISFG: Recommendations on biostatistics in paternity testing. *Forensic Science International: Genetics, 1*(3–4), 223–231.

Gusmão, L., et al. (2006). DNA Commission of the International Society of Forensic Genetics (ISFG): An update of the recommendations on the use of Y-STRs in forensic analysis. *Forensic Science International, 157,* 187–197.

Morling, N., et al. (2002). Paternity Testing Commission of the International Society of Forensic Genetics: Recommendations on genetic investigations in paternity cases. *Forensic Science International, 129,* 148–157.

Prinz, M., et al. (2007). DNA Commission of the International Society for Forensic Genetics (ISFG): Recommendations regarding the role of forensic genetics for disaster victim identification (DVI). *Forensic Science International: Genetics, 1*(1), 3–12.

SWGDAM/TWGDAM/DAB Guidelines

Budowle, B., et al. (1995). Guidelines for a quality assurance program for DNA analysis. *Crime Laboratory Digest, 22*(2), 20–43.

DNA Advisory Board. (2000). Statistical and population genetics issues affecting the evaluation of the frequency of occurrence of DNA profiles calculated from pertinent population database(s). *Forensic Science Communications, 2*(3). Available at http://www.fbi.gov/hq/lab/fsc/backissu/july2000/dnastat.htm

Kearney, J., et al. (1989). Guidelines for a quality assurance program for DNA restriction fragment length polymorphism analysis. *Crime Laboratory Digest, 16*(2), 40–59.

Kearney, J., et al. (1991). Guidelines for a quality assurance program for DNA analysis. *Crime Laboratory Digest, 18*(2), 44–75.

SWGDAM. (2000). Short tandem repeat (STR) interpretation guidelines. *Forensic Science Communications, 2*(3). Available at http://www.fbi.gov/hq/lab/fsc/backissu/july2000/strig.htm

SWGDAM. (2001). Training guidelines. *Forensic Science Communications, 3*(4). Available at http://www.fbi.gov/hq/lab/fsc/backissu/oct2001/kzinski.htm

SWGDAM. (2003). Bylaws of the Scientific Working Group on DNA Analysis Methods. *Forensic Science Communications, 5*(2). Available at http://www.fbi.gov/hq/lab/fsc/backissu/april2003/swgdambylaws.htm

SWGDAM. (2003). Guidelines for mitochondrial DNA (mtDNA) nucleotide sequence interpretation. *Forensic Science Communications, 5*(2). Available at http://www.fbi.gov/hq/lab/fsc/backissu/april2003/swgdammitodna.htm

SWGDAM. (2003). Guidance document for implementing health and safety programs in DNA laboratories. *Forensic Science Communications, 5*(2). Available at http://www.fbi.gov/hq/lab/fsc/backissu/april2003/swgdamsafety.htm

SWGDAM. (2004). Revised validation guidelines. *Forensic Science Communications, 6*(3). Available at http://www.fbi.gov/hq/lab/fsc/backissu/july2004/standards/2004_03_standards02.htm

SWGDAM. (2004). Report on the current activities of the Scientific Working Group on DNA Analysis Methods Y-STR subcommittee. *Forensic Science Communications, 6*(3). Available at http://www.fbi.gov/hq/lab/fsc/backissu/july2004/standards/2004_03_standards03.htm

Quality Assurance Standards

Cormier, K. L., et al. (2005). Evolution of the quality assurance documents for DNA laboratories. *Forensic Magazine, 2*(1), 16–19.

Federal Bureau of Investigation. (2000). Quality assurance standards for convicted offender DNA databasing laboratories. *Forensic Science Communications.* Available at http://www.fbi.gov/hq/lab/fsc/backissu/july2000/codispre.htm

Federal Bureau of Investigation. (2000). Quality assurance standards for forensic DNA testing laboratories. *Forensic Science Communications.* Available at http://www.fbi.gov/hq/lab/fsc/backissu/july2000/codispre.htm

Presley, L. A. (1999). The evolution of quality assurance standards for forensic DNA analyses in the United States. *Profiles in DNA, 3*(2), 10–11.

Quality Assurance Standards for DNA Databasing Laboratories. (2009). http://www.fbi.gov/hq/lab/html/databasinglab.htm

Quality Assurance Standards for Forensic DNA Testing Laboratories. (2009). http://www.fbi.gov/hq/lab/html/testinglab.htm

Laboratory Accreditation

American Society of Crime Laboratory Directors—Laboratory Accreditation Board (ASCLD-LAB). http://www.ascld-lab.org

Forensic Quality Services—International (FQS-I). http://www.forquality.org

ISO/IEC 17025:2005. (2005). General requirements for the competence of testing and calibration laboratories. Available at http://www.iso.org

Malkoc, E., & Neuteboom, W. (2007). The current status of forensic science laboratory accreditation in Europe. *Forensic Science International, 167*, 121–126.

Proficiency Testing

Collaborative Testing Services. http://www.cts-interlab.com

College of American Pathologists. http://www.cap.org

National Research Council (1996). *The Evaluation of Forensic DNA Evidence.* Washington, DC: National Academy Press (commonly called 'NRC II').

Peterson, J. L., et al. (2003). The feasibility of external blind DNA proficiency testing: I. Background and findings. *Journal of Forensic Sciences, 48*, 21–31.

Peterson, J. L., et al. (2003). The feasibility of external blind DNA proficiency testing: II. Experience with actual blind tests. *Journal of Forensic Sciences, 48*, 32–40.

Rand, S., et al. (2002). The GEDNAP (German DNA profiling group) blind trial concept. *International Journal of Legal Medicine, 116*, 199–206.

Rand, S., et al. (2004). The GEDNAP blind trial concept part II. Trends and developments. *International Journal of Legal Medicine, 118*, 83–89.

Serological Research Institute. http://www.serological.com

Validation

Budowle, B., et al. (2008). Criteria for validation of methods in microbial forensics. *Applied and Environment Microbiology, 74*, 5599–5607.

Butler, J. M., et al. (2004). Can the validation process in forensic DNA typing be standardized? In: *Proceedings of the 15th international symposium on human identification.* Madison, WI: Promega Corporation. Available at http://www.promega.com/geneticidproc

Butler, J. M. (2006). Debunking some urban legends surrounding validation within the forensic DNA community. *Profiles in DNA, 9*(2), 3–6. Available at http://www.promega.com/profiles

Butler, J. M. (2007). Validation: What is it, why does it matter, and how should it be done? (Applied Biosystems), *Forensic News, 20*. See also http://www.cstl.nist.gov/biotech/strbase/pub_pres/Butler_ForensicNews_Jan2007.pdf

EURACHEM Guide. (1998). *The fitness for purpose of analytical methods: A laboratory guide to method validation and related topics.* Available at http://www.eurachem.org/guides/valid.pdf

Feinberg, M., et al. (2004). New advances in method validation and measurement uncertainty aimed at improving the quality of chemical data. *Analytical and Bioanalytical Chemistry, 380*, 502–514.

Green, J. M. (1996). A practical guide to analytical method validation. *Analytical Chemistry, 68*, 305A–309A.

Gunzler, H. (Ed.), (1996). *Accreditation and quality assurance in analytical chemistry.* New York: Springer.

Huber, L. (1999). *Validation and qualification in analytical laboratories.* Boca Raton, FL: CRC Press.

Peters, F. T., et al. (2007). Validation of new methods. *Forensic Science International, 165*, 216–224.

Promega Corporation. (2006). *Internal validation of STR systems reference manual.* Available at http://www.promega.com/techserv/apps/hmnid/referenceinformation/powerplex/ValidationManual.pdf

Scientific Working Group on DNA Analysis Methods (SWGDAM). (2004). Revised validation guidelines. *Forensic Science Communications, 6*(3). Available at http://www.fbi.gov/hq/lab/fsc/backissu/july2004/standards/2004_03_standards02.htm

Swartz, M. E., & Krull, I. S. (1997). *Analytical method development and validation.* New York: Marcel Dekker.

Taylor, J. K. (1983). Validation of analytical methods. *Analytical Chemistry, 55,* 600A–608A.

Validation information on STRBase. http://www.cstl.nist.gov/biotech/strbase/validation.htm

Interlaboratory Studies

Bjerre, A., et al. (1997). A report of the 1995 and 1996 paternity testing workshops of the English speaking working group of the International Society of Forensic Haemogenetics. *Forensic Science International, 90,* 41–55.

Carracedo, A., et al. (2001). Results of a collaborative study of the EDNAP group regarding the reproducibility and robustness of the Y-chromosome STRs DYS19, DYS389 I and II, DYS390 and DYS393 in a PCR pentaplex format. *Forensic Science International, 119,* 28–41.

Hallenberg, C., & Morling, N. (2001). A report of the 1997, 1998 and 1999 paternity testing workshops of the English speaking working group of the International Society for Forensic Genetics. *Forensic Science International, 116,* 23–33.

Hallenberg, C., & Morling, N. (2002). A report of the 2000 and 2001 paternity testing workshops of the English speaking working group of the International Society for Forensic Genetics. *Forensic Science International, 129,* 43–50.

Prieto, L., et al. (2008). 2006 GEP-ISFG collaborative exercise on mtDNA: Reflections about interpretation, artifacts, and DNA mixtures. *Forensic Science International: Genetics, 2,* 126–133.

Summary of interlaboratory studies. http://www.cstl.nist.gov/biotech/strbase/interlab.htm

Tully, G., et al. (2004). Results of a collaborative study of the EDNAP group regarding mitochondrial DNA heteroplasmy and segregation in hair shafts. *Forensic Science International, 140,* 1–11.

Reference Materials

Fregeau, C. J., et al. (1995). Characterization of human lymphoid cell lines GM9947 and GM9948 as intra- and interlaboratory reference standards for DNA typing. *Genomics, 28,* 184–197.

Kline, M.C. (2006). NIST SRM updates: Value-added to the current materials in SRM 2391b and SRM 2395. Poster presentation at 17th International Symposium on Human Identification, Nashville, TN. Available at http://www.cstl.nist.gov/biotech/strbase/pub_pres/Promega2006_Kline.pdf

Institute for Reference Materials and Measurements. http://irmm.jrc.ec.europa.eu/html/homepage.htm

May, W.E., et al. (1999). Definitions of terms and modes used at NIST for value-assignment of reference materials for chemical measurements. *NIST Special Publication 260–136*. Washington, DC: U.S. Government Printing Office. Available at http://www.cstl.nist.gov/div839/special_pubs/SP260136.pdf

National Institute of Standards and Technology. http://www.nist.gov

National Institute of Standards and Technology SRMs. http://www.nist.gov/srm

Reeder, D. J. (1999). Impact of DNA typing on standards and practice in the forensic community. *Archives of Pathology and Laboratory Medicine, 123*, 1063–1065.

Roper, P., et al. (2001). *Applications of reference materials in analytical chemistry*. Cambridge, UK: Royal Society of Chemistry.

Szibor, R., et al. (2003). Cell line DNA typing in forensic genetics—The necessity of reliable standards. *Forensic Science International, 138*, 37–43.

Automation

Hedman, J., et al. (2008). A fast analysis system for forensic DNA reference samples. *Forensic Science International: Genetics, 2*, 184-189.

Maxwell 16. http://www.promega.com/maxwell16

Parson, W., & Steinlechner, M. (2001). Efficient DNA database strategy for high-throughput STR typing of reference samples. *Forensic Science International, 122*, 1–6.

Qiagen EZ1 and other robotic systems. http://www1.qiagen.com/Products/Automation

Tecan Freedom EVO. http://www.tecan.com/freedomevo

Expert Systems

Bill, M., & Knox, C. (2005). FSS-i3 expert system. *Profiles in DNA, 8*(2), 8-10.

Frappier, R., et al. (2008 February–March). Improving forensic DNA laboratory throughput: Enhanced data analysis and expert systems capability. *Forensic Magazine*, 25–31.

FSS-i3 software (from FSS and Promega). http://www.promega.com/fssi3; http://www.forensic.gov.uk/forensic_t/i3/index.htm

GeneMapper*ID-X* (from Applied Biosystems). http://idx.appliedbiosystems.com

Kadash, K., et al. (2004). Validation study of the TrueAllele automated data review system. *Journal of Forensic Sciences, 49*, 660–667.

National Institute of Justice Expert System Testbed (NEST) Project. http://forensics.marshall.edu/NEST/NEST-Intro.html

Oldroyd, N., & Schade, L. L. (2008). Expert assistant software enables forensic DNA analysts to confidently process more samples. *Forensic Magazine, 5*(6), 25-28.

Power, T., et al. (2008). FaSTR DNA: A new expert system for forensic DNA analysis. *Forensic Science International: Genetics, 2*, 159-165.

Roby, R. K., & Christen, A. D. (2007). Validating expert systems: Examples with the FSS-i3™ expert systems software. *Profiles in DNA, 10*(2), 13-15.

TrueAllele (from Cybergenetics). http://www.cybgen.com

CHAPTER 14

Forensic Challenges: Degraded DNA, Mixtures, and LCN

It is of the highest importance in the art of detection to be able to recognize out of a number of facts, which are incidental and which vital. Otherwise your energy and attention must be dissipated instead of being concentrated.

—Sherlock Holmes, *The Reigate Puzzle*

UNIQUE NATURE OF FORENSIC SAMPLES

A forensic DNA laboratory often has to deal with DNA samples that are less than ideal. The biological material serving as evidence of a crime may have been left exposed to a harsh environment for days, months, or even years, such as in the case of an investigation into a missing person. The victims of homicides are typically taken to out of the way places where they remain until their bodies are discovered. Instead of being preserved in a freezer away from caustic chemicals that can break it down, the DNA molecules may have been left in direct sunlight or in damp woods.

Regardless of the situation, the DNA molecules from a crime scene come from a less than pristine environment than is normally found in a molecular biology laboratory. Just as important is that the retrieved biological sample may be limited in quantity. Thus, accurate sample analysis is critical since a forensic scientist may only obtain enough evidence for one attempt at analysis. In this chapter, we explore some forensic challenges including degraded DNA samples, mixtures, and low levels of DNA.

DEGRADED DNA

Environmental exposure degrades DNA molecules by randomly breaking them into smaller pieces. Enemies to the survival of intact DNA molecules

Contribution of the National Institute of Standards and Technology, 2010.

include water and enzymes called nucleases that chew up DNA. Both are ubiquitous in nature. With older technologies such as restriction fragment length polymorphism (RFLP), these severely degraded DNA samples would have been very difficult if not impossible to analyze. As described in Chapter 3, DNA molecules of high relative molecular mass need to be present in the sample in order to detect large VNTR (variable number of tandem repeats) alleles (e.g., 20,000 bp) with RFLP techniques.

An ethidium-bromide stained agarose 'yield gel' may be run to evaluate the quality of a DNA sample. Typically high relative molecular mass, high-quality genomic DNA runs as a relatively tight band of approximately 20,000 bp relative to an appropriate relative molecular mass marker. On the other hand, degraded DNA appears as a smear of DNA that is much less than 20,000 bp in size (Figure 14.1a).

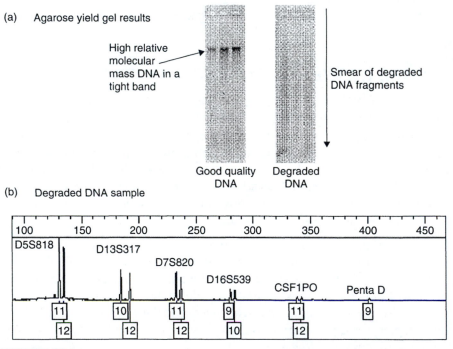

FIGURE 14.1

Impact of degraded DNA on (a) agarose yield gel results and (b) STR typing. (a) Degraded DNA is broken up into small pieces that appear as a smear on a scanned yield gel compared to good-quality DNA possessing intact high relative molecular mass DNA. (b) Signal strength is generally lost with larger-size PCR products when STR typing is performed on degraded DNA, such as is shown from the green dye-labeled loci in the PowerPlex 16 kit. Thus, 180-bp D13S317 PCR products have a higher signal than 400-bp Penta D amplicons because more DNA molecules are intact in the 200-bp versus the 400-bp size range.

Modern-day PCR methods, such as multiplex STR typing, are powerful because minuscule amounts of DNA can be measured by amplifying them to a level where they may be detected. Less than 1 ng of DNA can now be analyzed with multiplex PCR amplification of STR alleles compared to 100 ng or more that might have been required for RFLP only a few years ago. However, this sensitivity to low levels of DNA also brings the challenge of avoiding contamination from the police officer or crime scene technician who collects the biological evidence.

In order for PCR amplification to occur, the DNA template must be intact where the two primers bind as well as between the primers so that full extension can occur. Without an intact DNA strand that surrounds the STR repeat region to serve as a template strand, PCR will be unsuccessful because primer extension will halt at the break in the template. The more degraded a DNA sample becomes, the more breaks occur in the template, and fewer and fewer DNA molecules contain the full length needed for PCR amplification.

Fortunately, because STR loci can be amplified with fairly small product sizes, there is a greater chance for the STR primers to find some intact DNA strands for amplification. In addition, the narrow size range of STR alleles benefits analysis of degraded DNA samples because allele dropout via preferential amplification of the smaller allele is less likely to occur since both alleles in a heterozygous individual are similar in size.

A number of experiments have shown that there is an inverse relationship between the size of the locus and successful PCR amplification from degraded DNA samples, such as those obtained from a crime scene or a mass disaster. The STR loci with larger sized amplicons in a multiplex amplification, such as D18S51 and FGA or CSF1PO and Penta D, are the first to drop out of the DNA profile when amplifying extremely degraded DNA samples (Figure 14.1b).

PCR amplification using a damaged DNA template results in a partial profile. As seen in Figure 14.2, the impact of DNA degradation is that fewer STR loci yield results. Obtaining a partial DNA profile is analogous to only having a portion of a phone number. A full phone number might be 001-301-975-4049. If you only had '4049,' this information would be of limited value since it could match to other phone numbers from different area codes. However, in some situations, a few digits may be enough information to narrow down the possibilities in an investigation. Likewise, while full DNA profiles are preferable, partial profiles may be helpful in some instances.

Use of reduced-size PCR products (miniSTRs)

In an article entitled 'Less is more—length reduction of STR amplicons using redesigned primers,' Wiegand and Kleiber (2001) demonstrated that highly degraded DNA as well as very low amounts of DNA could be more successfully typed using some new redesigned PCR primers that were close to the

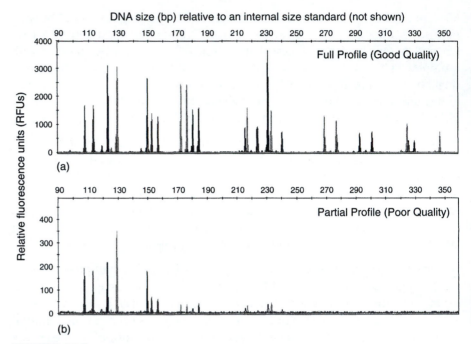

FIGURE 14.2

A comparison of DNA profiles originating from the same biological source but of different qualities. (a) Intact, good-quality DNA yields a full profile. (b) Degraded, poor-quality DNA yields a partial profile with only the lower-size PCR products producing detectable signal. With the degraded DNA sample shown in (b), information is lost at the larger-sized STR loci. Also note the lower relative fluorescence units with the poor-quality partial profile in (b). (Figure courtesy of Margaret Kline, NIST.)

STR repeat compared to the established sequences that generated longer amplicons for the same loci.

STR loci used in commercially available kits can extend past 400 bp in size. Most of this length, however, comes from the flanking sequence surrounding the STR repeat of interest. PCR primers for larger-sized STR markers have been moved away from the repeat region that imparts variability to the locus in order to fit into a desired size range for a particular multiplex assay.

Figure 14.3 illustrates this size reduction principle when creating reduced-size STR amplicons or 'miniSTRs.' It is important to keep in mind that some loci can be reduced in size more than others (Table 14.1).

Several disadvantages do exist for miniSTRs. A major disadvantage is that only a few loci can be simultaneously amplified in a multiplex because the size aspect has been removed. Large multiplex assays like PowerPlex 16 pack four or more loci into a single dye color by shifting primers away from the repeat region to make larger PCR products. Many of the research 'miniplexes'

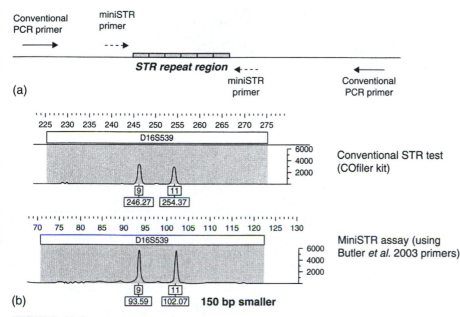

FIGURE 14.3

(a) MiniSTRs or reduced-sized amplicons for STR typing are created by designing PCR primers that anneal closer to the repeat region than conventional STR kit primers. (b) PCR product sizes, such as demonstrated here with D16S539, can be reduced by over 150 bp relative to conventional tests. MiniSTR assays can produce the same typing result as those from larger STR amplicons produced by kits often with greater success on degraded DNA samples.

created for amplifying miniSTRs have primers that are as close as possible to the repeat region and therefore typically only have one locus per dye color because all of the loci are about the same general size range of ~100 bp. However, using mobility modifiers to adjust the electrophoretically observed PCR product sizes, Applied Biosystems was able to put eight miniSTRs and amelogenin into their single-amplification MiniFiler kit.

Since different PCR primers are in use with miniSTRs compared to conventional STR megaplexes, it is important for concordance studies to be performed to verify that allele dropout from primer binding site mutations is rare or nonexistent. This is performed by examining the genotyping results to see if they are the same between the primer sets. Occasionally a point mutation or an insertion or deletion may occur in the flanking region *outside* of a miniSTR primer binding site, which can lead to a problematic (and undetectable without concordance studies) difference in a heterozygous allele call.

Regardless of these disadvantages, it is likely that miniSTRs will play a role in the future of degraded DNA analysis to help recover information that has been lost with larger loci from conventional megaplex amplification. Reduced-size

Table 14.1 PCR product size reduction obtained with new primers for several miniSTR loci.

Locus	MiniSTR Size (bp)	Allele Range	Size Reduction[a] (bp)
TH01	51–98	3–14	−105
TPOX	65–101	5–14	−148
CSF1PO	89–129	6–16	−191
VWA	88–148	10–15	−64
FGA	125–281	12.2–51.2	−71
D3S1358	72–120	8–20	−25
D5S818	81–117	7–16	−53
D7S820	136–176	5–15	−117
D8S1179	86–134	7–19	−37
D13S317	88–132	5–16	−105
D16S539	81–121	5–15	−152
D18S51	113–193	7–27	−151
D21S11	153–211	24–38.2	−33
Penta D	94–167	2.2–17	−282
Penta E	80–175	5–24	−299
D2S1338	90–142	15–28	−198

From Butler, J.M., et al. (2003), The development of reduced size STR amplicons as tools for analysis of degraded DNA. Journal of Forensic Sciences, 48(5), 1054–1064.
[a]*Compared to Applied Biosystems STR kits except for Penta D and Penta E, which are in Promega's PowerPlex 16 kit.*

STR assays have helped make possible some of the World Trade Center victim identifications from burned and damaged bone samples (see D.N.A. Box 17.4).

Even telogen hair shafts, which contain very little nuclear DNA, have sometimes been successfully typed using reduced-size STR amplicons. New STR loci besides the CODIS markers and others that are currently used in forensic DNA typing are also being examined as potential miniSTR systems with a focus on loci possessing small alleles and narrow size ranges. Thus, a battery of additional assays should be available to aid researchers and forensic practitioners in the future when working with degraded DNA specimens.

MIXTURES

Mixtures arise when two or more individuals contribute to the sample being tested. Mixtures can be challenging to detect and interpret without extensive experience and careful training. As detection technologies have become more sensitive, using PCR coupled with fluorescent measurements, the ability to see minor components in the DNA profile of mixed samples has improved dramatically over what was available with RFLP methods only a few years ago. Likewise, the theoretical aspects of statistical calculations for mixture interpretation have been examined more thoroughly. More information on mixture interpretation is available in the companion volume, *Advanced Topics in Forensic DNA Typing, 3rd Edition*.

Value of highly polymorphic markers in deciphering mixtures

The probability that a mixture will be detected improves with the use of more loci and genetic markers that have a high incidence of heterozygotes. The detectability of multiple DNA sources in a single sample relates to the ratio of DNA present from each source, the specific combinations of genotypes, and the total amount of DNA amplified. In other words, some mixtures will not be as easily detectable as are others.

Using highly polymorphic STR markers with more possible alleles translates to a greater chance of seeing differences between the two components of a mixture. For example, D18S51 has 51 possible alleles while TPOX only has 15 known alleles, making D18S51 a more useful marker for detecting mixtures. Likewise, the more markers examined (e.g., by using a multiplex STR amplification), the greater the chance of observing multiple components in a mixture.

The quantity of each component in a mixture makes a difference in the ability to detect all contributors to the mixed sample. For example, if the two DNA sources are present in similar quantities they will be much easier to detect than if one is present at only a fraction of the other. The minor component of a mixture is usually not detectable for mixture ratios below 5% or 1:20. Minor components can have their alleles masked by larger-quantity major-component alleles. Stochastic amplification can adversely affect amplification of minor-component alleles at low levels of DNA template.

Quantitative information from fluorescence measurements

The ability to obtain quantitative information from peaks in an electropherogram, using the ABI 310 or 3100 platform, permits relative peak heights or areas of STR alleles to be measured. This peak information can then be used to decipher the possible genotypes of the contributors to the mixed sample. Although peak areas were originally advocated due to peak shape variation seen in early gel systems, peak heights are now routinely used in most laboratories for mixture interpretation. The peaks produced with today's capillary electrophoresis systems are fairly symmetrical, and thus peak heights represent the relative amounts of DNA portrayed in the electropherogram pretty well. Also, since detection and interpretation thresholds are based on peak height information, it is easier to work with height rather than area data.

Distinguishing genotypes in a mixed sample

Several clues exist to help determine that a mixture is present. Answers to the following questions can help ascertain the genotypes that make up the composite DNA profile of the mixture:

- Does any of the loci show more than two peaks in the expected allele size range?
- Is there a severe peak height imbalance between heterozygous alleles at a locus?
- Does the stutter product appear abnormally high (e.g., >15% to 20%)?

If the answer to any one of these three questions is 'yes,' then the DNA profile may very well have resulted from a mixed sample.

Usually a mixture is first identified by the presence of three or more prominent peaks at one or more loci (Figure 14.4). At a single locus, a sample containing DNA from two sources can exhibit one, two, three, or four peaks due to the possible genotype combinations listed below.

Four peaks:

- heterozygote + heterozygote, no overlapping alleles (genotypes are unique)

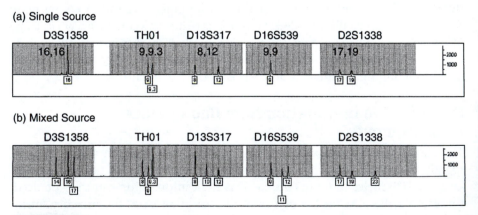

FIGURE 14.4

Comparison of alleles observed at five STR loci from (a) a single-source sample and (b) a mixture of two sources. (Figure courtesy of Becky Hill, NIST.)

Three peaks:

- heterozygote + heterozygote, one overlapping allele
- heterozygote + homozygote, no overlapping alleles (genotypes are unique)

Two peaks:

- heterozygote + heterozygote, two overlapping alleles (genotypes are identical)
- heterozygote + homozygote, one overlapping allele
- homozygote + homozygote, no overlapping alleles (genotypes are unique)

Single peak:

- homozygote + homozygote, overlapping allele (genotypes are identical)

When two contributors to a mixed stain share one or more alleles, the alleles are 'masked' and the contributing genotypes may not be easily decipherable. For example, if two individuals at the FGA locus have genotypes 23,24 and 24,24, then a mixture ratio of 1:1 will produce a ratio of 1:3 for the 23:24 peak areas. In this particular case, the mixture could be interpreted as a homozygous allele with a large stutter product without further information. However, by examining the STR profiles at other loci that have unshared alleles, that is, three or four peaks per locus, this sample may be able to be dissected or 'deconvoluted' properly into its components.

Mixture classification

Recognizing that there are differences in the types of mixtures seen in case-work evidence, the German Stain Commission, which is a group of scientists from Institutes of Legal Medicine and Forensic Science within Germany, proposed a classification scheme for mixtures. Their three categories of mixtures are labeled 'Type A', 'Type B', and 'Type C' (D.N.A. Box 14.1).

Type A mixtures have no obvious major contributor with no evidence of stochastic effects. In other words, there is plenty of DNA amplified but alleles cannot be clearly assigned to a major or minor contributor because all of the allele quantities are too similar. The result in Figure 14.4(b) is a Type A mixture. *Type B mixtures* contain clearly distinguishable major and minor DNA components with no evidence of stochastic effects. Again, there is enough DNA being amplified to have confidence that all alleles are being detected. *Type C mixtures* are low-level mixtures with no major component(s) and evidence of stochastic effects. As noted in D.N.A. Box 14.1, different statistical approaches may be taken to reporting results from these various types of mixtures.

D.N.A. Box 14.1 Mixture Classification Scheme from the German Stain Commission

Several years ago the German Stain Commission, a group of scientists from Germany's Institutes of Legal Medicine, developed a three-part classification scheme for DNA mixtures. Simple examples of what a Type A (no major contributor), Type B (major and minor contributors distinguishable), or Type C (low-level DNA with stochastic effects) mixture might look like at a single STR locus are shown below:

Type A mixtures require a biostatistical analysis that can be performed with a likelihood ratio (LR) or combined probability of exclusion (CPE), which is also known as 'random

man not excluded' (RMNE). Type B mixtures can be deconvoluted into the major and minor components, usually if they are present with consistent peak-to-height ratios of approximately 4:1. The major component following deconvolution can be treated as a single-source profile with a random match probability (RMP) being calculated. For Type C mixtures, where all alleles may not be seen due to allele dropout, a biostatistical interpretation is not appropriate, and a clear decision about whether to include or exclude a suspect may be difficult to reach.

The DNA mixture in Figure 14.4(b) would be classified as a Type A mixture. Biostatistical analysis using the combined probability of exclusion (CPE) for the mixture data in Figure 14.4 is shown in D.N.A. Box 14.2. A mixture classification flowchart is shown below based on the three types of mixtures.

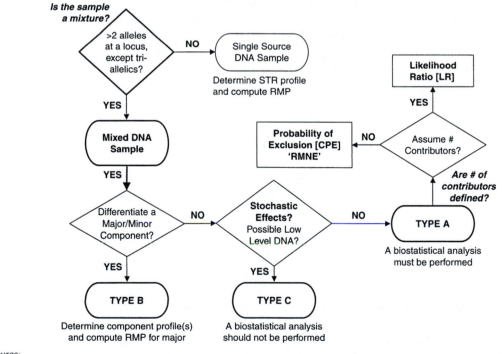

Source:
Schneider, P. M., et al. (2009). The German Stain Commission: Recommendations for the interpretation of mixed stains. *International Journal of Legal Medicine, 123*, 1–5. [Originally published in German in Rechtsmedizin (2006) *16*: 401–404.].

Mixture interpretation

The six primary steps for interpreting mixtures that were originally described in 1998 by Tim Clayton and colleagues at the Forensic Science Service are outlined in Figure 14.5.

An understanding of how nonmixtures behave is essential to being able to proceed with mixture interpretation. Mixed DNA profiles need to be interpreted against a background of biological and technological artifacts. Chapter 10 reviewed some of the prominent biological artifacts that exist for STR markers. These include stutter products and null alleles. In addition, chromosomal abnormalities, such as triallelic (three-banded) patterns resulting from trisomy (the presence of three chromosomes instead of the normal two) or duplication of specific chromosomal regions can occur.

Stutter products represent the greatest challenge in confidently interpreting a mixture and designating the appropriate alleles. It is not always possible to exclude stutters since they are allelic products and differ from their associated allele by a single repeat unit. The general guideline for stutter identification of one repeat unit less than the corresponding allele and less than 15% of that allele's peak height is typically a useful one and can be used to mark suspected stutter products.

After a mixture has been identified as such and all of the alleles have been called, the next step (Figure 14.5, step #3) is to identify the number of potential

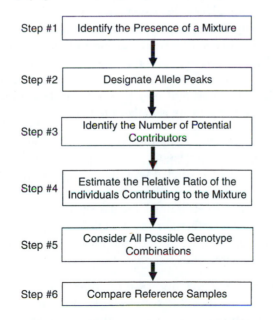

FIGURE 14.5

Steps in the interpretation of mixtures (Clayton et al., 1998).

contributors. For a two-person mixture, the maximum number of alleles at any given locus is four if both individuals are heterozygous and there is no allele overlap. Thus, if more than four alleles are observed at a locus, then a complex mixture consisting of more than two individuals is possible. Fortunately, the overwhelming majority of mixtures encountered in forensic casework involve two-person mixtures.

Mixtures can range from equal proportions of each component to one component being greatly in excess. The varying proportions of a mixture are usually referred to in a ratio format (e.g., 1:1 or 1:5). Mixtures of known quantities of DNA templates have shown that the mixture ratio is approximately preserved during PCR amplification. Thus, the peak areas and heights observed in an electropherogram can in most cases be related back to the amount of DNA template components included in the mixed sample.

An approximate mixture ratio can be best determined by considering the profile as a whole and looking at all of the information from each locus. The ratio of mixture components is most easily determined when there are no shared alleles at a locus. Thus, it is best to first examine loci with four alleles as a starting point for estimating the relative ratio of the two individuals contributing to the mixture. Determining the ratio when there are shared alleles is more complex because there may be more than one possible combination of alleles that could explain the observed peak patterns.

Mixture ratios cannot always be calculated at every locus with complete confidence, especially those with two or three peaks that have shared alleles between the contributors. Stutter products and imbalanced heterozygote peak signals make calculation of mixture ratios less accurate. Amelogenin, the sex-typing marker, can also help estimate the contributions of genetically normal male and female individuals and may be useful in determining whether the major contributor to the mixture is male or female.

The next step in examining a mixture is to consider all possible genotype combinations at each locus (Figure 14.5, step #5). Peaks representing the allele calls at each locus are labeled with the designations A, B, and so forth. Each particular combination of alleles at the different loci is considered in light of the information determined previously regarding the mixture ratio for the sample under investigation (step #4). By stepping through each STR locus in this manner, the genotypes of the major and minor contributors to the mixture can be deciphered.

The final step in the interpretation of a mixture is to compare the resultant genotype profiles for the possible components of the mixture with the genotypes of reference samples (Figure 14.5, step #6). In a sexual assault case, this reference sample could be the suspect and/or the victim. If the DNA profile from the suspect's reference sample matches the major or minor component of the mixture, then that person cannot be eliminated as a possible contributor to the mixed sample.

Statistical approaches to mixture analysis

Three different approaches are generally taken with statistical analysis of mixtures: (1) performing match probability estimates on the major contributor after deducing the possible genotypes of the contributors using, for example, the strategy outlined in the previous section; (2) calculating exclusion probabilities (D.N.A. Box 14.2); and (3) performing likelihood ratio calculations.

As the FBI's DNA Advisory Board noted in their February 2000 recommendations on statistics, 'The DAB finds either one or both [the exclusion probability or the likelihood ratio] calculations acceptable and strongly recommends that one or both calculations be carried out whenever feasible and a mixture is indicated.' More on each of these approaches is covered in the *Advanced Topics* volume.

Software for deciphering mixture components

Computer programs can be used to aid the process of deciphering mixture components and determining mixture ratios and statistical calculations. Modules exist in many of the so-called expert systems described in Chapter 13 that enable mixture calculations. However, the mixture deconvolution modules are typically thought of as 'expert assistants' because final decisions in terms of mixture interpretation still reside with the DNA analyst.

Chromosomal abnormalities

Chromosomal abnormalities do exist and can give rise to extra allele peaks at a particular STR locus. Chromosomal translocations, somatic mutations, and trisomies may occur in the cells of the donor of a forensic stain. However, the STR profile from the individual with the chromosomal abnormality would most likely show only a single extra peak and the same pattern would be present in both the forensic stain and the reference sample from the matching suspect. The rare cases where a chromosomal abnormality is observed can even help strengthen the final conclusions.

An excellent example of a chromosomal abnormality is found in the standard cell line K562. Three peaks are obtained at the D21S11 locus and at least five other STR loci have heterozygous peak patterns that are not balanced

D.N.A. Box 14.2 Combined Probability of Exclusion

When contributors to a DNA mixture profile cannot be fully distinguished (deconvoluted) into the individual contributions from the various contributors, the probability of exclusion (PE) may be used to convey the weight of the evidence based on the alleles present in the mixture. The PE provides an estimate of the portion of the population that has a genotype composed of at least one allele not observed in the mixture profile. PE calculations do not require an assumption of the number of contributors to a mixture and can be easier to explain in court compared to likelihood ratios. However, PE calculations do not take into account peak heights or DNA profile results from the victim and/or suspect(s) and therefore do not fully use all available information.

Almost always in a mixture, there are some genotypes that can be excluded from being possible contributors to the observed alleles present in the mixture. The PE can be calculated most easily by first determining the probability of inclusion (PI) at each locus. PI (not to be confused with the paternity index described in Chapter 17) is calculated from the sum of the frequencies for genotypes of all possible contributors to a DNA mixture, which is the same as the square of the sums of all observed allele frequencies. PI and PE should add up to 100% or 1. Thus, PE = 1 − PI and PI = 1 − PE. After determining the PE or PI for each individual STR locus, the results may be combined through multiplying results from unlinked loci using the following formula: $CPE = 1 − [PI_1 \times PI_2 \times PI_3 \times \ldots \times PI_n]$.

The individual locus PI and PE calculations for the five STR loci shown in the Figure 14.4(b) mixture are determined below. U.S. Caucasian allele frequencies from Butler et al. (2003) were used for these calculations.

With a combined probability of exclusion of 0.998, an estimated 99.8% of the population can be excluded from contributing to the mixture shown in Figure 14.4(b).

Sources:

Butler, J. M., et al. (2003). Allele frequencies for 15 autosomal STR loci on U.S. Caucasian, African American, and Hispanic populations. *Journal of Forensic Sciences, 48*, 908–911.

Devlin, B. (1993). Forensic inference from genetic markers. *Statistical Methods in Medical Research, 2*, 241–262.

Locus	Alleles	Frequencies	Sum	PI = Sum²	PE = (1 − PI)
D3S1358	14	0.103	0.571	0.326	0.674
	16	0.253			
	17	0.215			
TH01	8	0.084	0.566	0.320	0.680
	9	0.114			
	9.3	0.368			
D13S317	8	0.113	0.412	0.170	0.830
	10	0.051			
	12	0.248			
D16S539	9	0.113	0.76	0.578	0.422
	11	0.321			
	12	0.326			
D2S1338	17	0.182	0.414	0.171	0.829
	19	0.114			
	23	0.118			
				CPI	CPE
				0.002	0.998

D.N.A. Box 14.3 Abnormal STR Peak Heights in K562 Cell Line DNA Profile

For many years, DNA extracted from the cell line K562 was supplied as a control sample from Promega Corporation with their GenePrint STR typing kits. Back in the RFLP days of DNA testing (see Chapter 3), K562 served as a *de facto* control material in forensic laboratories. However, as can be seen from the peak profiles below, some of the STR loci exhibit imbalanced heterozygous alleles and/or multiple peaks that would make the sample appear to come from more than one source of DNA. In this particular case, these extra peaks or peak imbalances are the result of an abnormal number of chromosomes present in the sample rather than a problem with the DNA typing system. K562 cells are derived from a female human subject with a diagnosis of chronic myelogenous leukemia. Because mutant cells are present with chromosomes that possess somatic mutations that affect the number of repeats in various STR markers, the K562 cell line results do not possess the normal balance of chromosomal material seen in healthy individuals. Thus, balanced heterozygous allele peaks are not always seen. Shown below are six STR markers amplified from K562 genomic DNA that possess a significant variation in the balance of the STR allele peak heights.

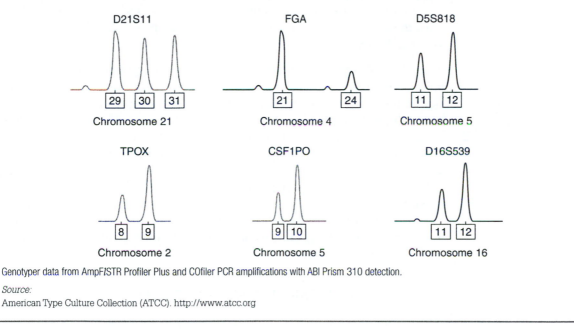

Genotyper data from AmpF*l*STR Profiler Plus and COfiler PCR amplifications with ABI Prism 310 detection.

Source:
American Type Culture Collection (ATCC). http://www.atcc.org

(D.N.A. Box 14.3). At first glance, one might suspect this sample to have arisen from more than one source rather than a sample with an abnormal number of chromosomes.

As described in Chapter 10, triallelic patterns have been reported for a number of STR loci. In fact, more than 175 different triallelic patterns have been reported spanning all 13 CODIS core loci (see http://www.cstl.nist.gov/biotech/strbase/tri_tab.htm).

Additional thoughts on interpreting mixtures

Mixed-sample stains are present in many forensic investigations and STR typing procedures have been demonstrated to be effective means of differentiating components of a mixed sample. However, a case may contain multiple stains and not all of these will be mixtures. In fact, the proportions of a mixture can vary across the forensic stain itself. Thus, if additional samples can be tested that are easier to interpret, they should be sought. As recommended by Peter Gill of the Forensic Science Service, the best advice is 'Don't do mixture interpretation unless you have to.'

As an example of the number of mixture samples encountered in typical casework, Torres et al. (2003) reviewed all of the mixture STR profiles seen in their laboratory over a 4-year time period. From 1547 criminal cases worked which involved a total of 2424 samples, only 163 (6.7%) showed a mixed profile. Depending on the type of evidence submitted to and worked by a laboratory, the number and complexity of mixtures seen may be higher than those reported by Torres et al.

Some forensic DNA laboratories may decide not to go through the trouble of fully deciphering the genotype possibilities and assigning them to the major and minor contributors. An easier approach is to simply include or exclude a suspect's DNA profile from the crime scene mixture profile. If all of the alleles from a suspect's DNA profile are represented in the crime scene mixture, then the suspect cannot be excluded as contributing to the crime scene stain and a combined probability of exclusion can be calculated (see D.N.A. Box 14.2). Likewise, the alleles in a victim's DNA profile could be subtracted from the mixture profile to simplify the alleles that need to be present in the perpetrator's DNA profile. Further details on mixture interpretation and approaches to attaching a statistical value to mixture results are presented in the *Advanced Topics* volume.

LOW COPY NUMBER DNA TESTING

Many laboratories have demonstrated the ability to obtain DNA profiles from very small amounts of sample. Low copy number (LCN) DNA testing, sometimes referred to as low-level DNA, typically refers to examination of less than 100 pg of input DNA, or about 15 diploid cells. While fluorescent multiplexes have been used to obtain STR typing results from as little as a single buccal cell, a number of challenges exist when trying to obtain results from low amounts of template DNA.

Increased number of PCR cycles

The number of PCR cycles is often increased to improve the amplification yield from samples containing extremely low levels of DNA template. For example, by increasing the PCR cycle number from 28 to 34, many more copies of DNA molecules are being generated. With 100% efficiency, 67 million copies of a target sequence are produced with 28 cycles while 4 billion copies are generated with 34 cycles (see Table 7.1). This increase in PCR amplification cycles enables STR typing to routinely obtain results with samples containing less than 100 pg of DNA template. However, application of LCN results should be approached with caution due to the possibilities of allele dropout, allele drop-in, and increased risks of collection-based and laboratory-based contamination.

Touch DNA

Remarkably, DNA profiles may be obtained from fingerprint residues due to cells that are left on the objects that are touched. DNA technology may permit the handles of tools used in crimes, such as knives or guns, to be effectively evaluated and used to link a perpetrator to his crime. In 2002, Ray Wickenheiser published a nice review of the theory and application of trace DNA detection.

It is important to realize that when trying to work with extremely low levels of DNA template, recovered DNA profiles may not be associated with the crime event itself but rather have been left innocently before the crime occurred. Secondary transfer of skin cells due to casual contact such as hand shaking has been demonstrated to occur in controlled laboratory settings. This phenomenon occurs to a variable degree depending on what kind of 'shedder' the individuals are.

Issues with LCN work

Trying to generate a reliable STR profile with only a few cells from a biological sample is similar to looking for an object in the mud or trying to decipher the image in a fuzzy photograph. Since the sensitivity of the STR typing assay is turned up so high, it is often not immediately clear if you have a reliable result or even a probative one.

When LCN testing is performed, at least three artifacts typically arise: (1) additional alleles are often observed from sporadic contamination in what is referred to as allele 'drop-in,' (2) allele 'dropout' is common where an allele fails to amplify due to stochastic effects, and (3) stutter product amounts are enhanced so that they are often higher than the typical 5% to 10% of the nominal allele. Heterozygote peak imbalance is typically exacerbated due to stochastic PCR amplification, where one of the alleles is amplified by chance during the early rounds of PCR in a preferential fashion. Allele dropout can be thought of as an extreme form of heterozygote peak imbalance.

Figure 14.6 illustrates some of the stochastic problems that can be seen with DNA template quantities below 100 pg. These stochastic effects include severe imbalance of heterozygous alleles and allele dropout.

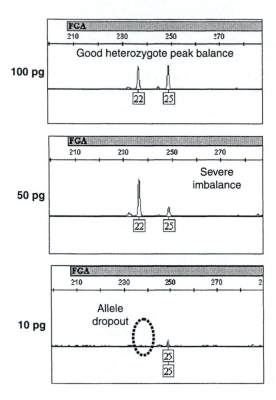

FIGURE 14.6

Signal observed for a heterozygous sample at a single STR locus (FGA) amplified from three different amplifications of low amounts of DNA template. Results produced with Identifiler STR kit using 31 cycles instead of the manufacturer-recommended 28 cycles. Note the peak imbalance at 50 pg and allele dropout of the '22' allele with the 10-pg sample. (Figure courtesy of Becky Hill, NIST.)

Precautions to ensure optimal results with low-level DNA

The allele drop-in phenomenon is usually not reproducible and can be detected through PCR amplifying a DNA sample multiple times. As noted in an early paper describing reliable genotyping of samples with very low DNA quantities, the probability of obtaining a particular extra allele (i.e., allele drop-in) does not exceed 5%, and thus the probability of obtaining this same extra allele in two independent PCR reactions is <1%. Thus, the routine application of LCN involves at least two (and more commonly three) amplifications from the same DNA extract with a rule that an allele cannot be scored unless it is present at least twice in replicate samples. The consensus or composite STR profile is then the one that is reported. This approach has been confirmed with consensus profiles from separate single-cell PCR experiments matching the actual profile of the cell donor.

It is essential that work with low amounts of DNA template be performed in a sterile environment to prevent contamination from laboratory personnel. DNA extractions and setting up PCR reactions should be performed in a dedicated laboratory similar to what is done in the 'ancient DNA' field. Laboratory personnel should wear disposable lab coats, gloves, and face masks. In addition, benches and equipment should be frequently treated with bleach to destroy any extraneous DNA. STR profile results should be compared against a staff elimination database as well as anyone who may have legitimately come into contact with the crime scene evidence prior to the DNA testing.

Additional thoughts on low-level DNA work

In practice many LCN profiles are mixtures and difficult to interpret reliably due to the issues of allele dropout and drop-in described above. The success rate for obtaining a clean profile can be poor due to the limited amount of sample available. Thus a lot of work can go into generating DNA profiles that may not be probative or useful in a particular forensic case. Although a DNA profile may be obtained, it is usually not possible to identify the types of cells from which the DNA originated or when the cells were deposited. Furthermore, with such little starting material, it may not be possible to preserve LCN evidence to enable confirmatory testing by a second laboratory should that be required. Nevertheless, even with these caveats LCN results have enabled recovery of DNA profiles from burglaries and other situations where only a few cells from the perpetrator were present and have thereby extended the power of DNA testing.

In some cases, it may be possible to obtain reliable results from low levels of DNA without having to boost the PCR cycle number and push the sensitivity of the amplification. There are several alternatives to enable boosting a signal for an STR profile without increasing the PCR cycle number and the concomitant increased risk of contamination. These include (1) reducing the PCR volume to get a more concentrated PCR product, (2) filtration of the PCR product to remove ions that compete with the STR amplicons when being injected into the capillary, (3) use of a formamide with lower conductivity, (4) adding more amplified product to the analysis tube, and (5) increasing the injection time on the capillary electrophoresis instrument.

Some important LCN reporting guidelines include (1) multiple tube PCR amplifications with demonstrated duplication of every allele before reporting results; (2) if negative controls associated with a particular batch of samples show duplicated alleles that correspond to any of the samples, then the samples should not be reported and, where possible, samples should be retested; and (3) if there is one allele in a sample that does not match the suspect's STR profile, then further testing may be pursued. Generating STR data with an increased number of PCR cycles and invoking an LCN philosophy can provide a useful lead in many instances for an investigation but it is unlikely to provide definitive probative evidence of a crime in every instance.

Points for Discussion

- What are some solutions for recovering information from degraded DNA?
- Why are more polymorphic loci useful in identifying a mixture?
- What are the benefits of using a mixture classification scheme as outlined in D.N.A. Box 14.1?
- What are some of the difficulties with low copy number DNA analysis? What kinds of checks and balances can a laboratory employ to ensure reliability of DNA profiles coming from low amounts of DNA template?

READING LIST AND INTERNET RESOURCES

General Information

Gill, P. (2002). Role of short tandem repeat DNA in forensic casework in the UK—Past, present, and future perspectives. *BioTechniques, 32*(2), 366–385.

Sparkes, R., et al. (1996). The validation of a 7-locus multiplex STR test for use in forensic casework. (I). Mixtures, ageing, degradation and species studies. *International Journal of Legal Medicine, 109*, 186–194.

Sparkes, R., et al. (1996). The validation of a 7-locus multiplex STR test for use in forensic casework. (II), Artefacts, casework studies and success rates. *International Journal of Legal Medicine, 109*, 195–204.

Degraded DNA

Kobilinsky, L. (1992). Recovery and stability of DNA in samples of forensic significance. *Forensic Science Review, 4*, 68–87.

Lindahl, T. (1993). Instability and decay of the primary structure of DNA. *Nature, 362*, 709–715.

Schneider, P. M., et al. (2004). STR analysis of artificially degraded DNA—Results of a collaborative European exercise. *Forensic Science International, 139*, 123–134.

Takahashi, M., et al. (1997). Evaluation of five polymorphic microsatellite markers for typing DNA from decomposed human tissues—Correlation between the size of the alleles and that of the template DNA. *Forensic Science International, 90*, 1–9.

Whitaker, J. P., et al. (1995). Short tandem repeat typing of bodies from a mass disaster: High success rate and characteristic amplification patterns in highly degraded samples. *Biotechniques, 18*, 670–677.

miniSTRs

Butler, J. M., et al. (2003). The development of reduced size STR amplicons as tools for analysis of degraded DNA. *Journal of Forensic Sciences, 48*(5), 1054–1064.

Chung, D. T., et al. (2004). A study on the effects of degradation and template concentration on the efficiency of the STR miniplex primer sets. *Journal of Forensic Sciences, 49*(4), 733–740.

Coble, M. D., & Butler, J. M. (2005). Characterization of new miniSTR loci to aid analysis of degraded DNA. *Journal of Forensic Sciences, 50*(1), 43–53.

Dixon, L. A., et al. (2006). Analysis of artificially degraded DNA using STRs and SNPs—Results of a collaborative European (EDNAP) exercise. *Forensic Science International, 164*, 33–44.

Drabek, J., et al. (2004). Concordance study between miniplex STR assays and a commercial STR typing kit. *Journal of Forensic Sciences, 49*(4), 859–860.

Fondevila, M., et al. (2008). Case report: Identification of skeletal remains using short-amplicon marker analysis of severely degraded DNA extracted from a decomposed and charred femur. *Forensic Science International: Genetics, 2*, 212–218.

Grubwieser, P., et al. (2006). A new "miniSTR-multiplex" displaying reduced amplicon lengths for the analysis of degraded DNA. *International Journal of Legal Medicine, 120*, 115–120.

Hellmann, A., et al. (2001). STR typing of human telogen hairs—A new approach. *International Journal of Legal Medicine, 114*(4-5), 269–273.

Hill, C. R., et al. (2007). Concordance study between the AmpF*l*STR MiniFiler PCR Amplification Kit and conventional STR typing kits. *Journal of Forensic Sciences, 52*(4), 870–873.

Hill, C. R., et al. (2008). Characterization of 26 miniSTR loci for improved analysis of degraded DNA samples. *Journal of Forensic Sciences, 53*(1), 73–80.

MiniFiler product information. http://minifiler.appliedbiosystems.com

MiniSTR timeline of events. http://www.cstl.nist.gov/biotech/strbase/miniSTR/timeline.htm

Mulero, J. J., et al. (2008). Development and validation of the AmpF*l*STR MiniFiler PCR Amplification Kit: A miniSTR multiplex for the analysis of degraded and/or PCR inhibited DNA. *Journal of Forensic Sciences, 53*, 838–852.

Müller, K., et al. (2007). Improved STR typing of telogen hair root and hair shaft DNA. *Electrophoresis, 28*(16), 2835–2842.

Opel, K. L., et al. (2006). The application of miniplex primer sets in the analysis of degraded DNA from human skeletal remains. *Journal of Forensic Sciences, 51*(2), 351–356.

Opel, K. L., et al. (2007). Developmental validation of reduced-size STR miniplex primer sets. *Journal of Forensic Sciences, 52*(6), 1263–1271.

Parsons, T. J., et al. (2007). Application of novel 'mini-amplicon' STR multiplexes to high volume casework on degraded skeletal remains. *Forensic Science International: Genetics, 1*, 175–179.

Schumm, J. W., et al. (2004). Robust STR multiplexes for challenging casework samples. *Progress in Forensic Genetics 10*, ICS 1261, 547–549.

Wiegand, P., & Kleiber, M. (2001). Less is more—Length reduction of STR amplicons using redesigned primers. *International Journal of Legal Medicine, 114*(4–5), 285–287.

Mixtures

Torres, Y., et al. (2003). DNA mixtures in forensic casework: A 4-year retrospective study. *Forensic Science International, 134*, 180–186.

Recommendations

Gill, P., et al. (2006). DNA Commission of the International Society of Forensic Genetics: Recommendations on the interpretation of mixtures. *Forensic Science International, 160*, 90–101.

Gill, P., et al. (2008). National recommendations of the technical UK DNA working group on mixture interpretation for the NDNAD and for court going purposes. *Forensic Science International: Genetics, 2*, 76–82.

Morling, N., et al. (2007). Interpretation of DNA mixtures—European consensus on principles. *Forensic Science International: Genetics, 1*, 291–292.

Schneider, P. M., et al. (2009). The German Stain Commission: Recommendations for the interpretation of mixed stains. *International Journal of Legal Medicine, 123*, 1–5.

Strategy

Buckleton, J. S., et al. (2007). Towards understanding the effect of uncertainty in the number of contributors to DNA stains. *Forensic Science International: Genetics, 1*, 20–28.

Clayton, T. M., et al. (1998). Analysis and interpretation of mixed forensic stains using DNA STR profiling. *Forensic Science International, 91*, 55–70.

Clayton, T., & Buckleton, J. (2005). Mixtures. In J. Buckleton, C. M. Triggs, & S. J. Walsh (Eds.), *Forensic DNA evidence interpretation* (Chapter 7, pp. 217–274). Boca Raton, FL: CRC Press.

Curran, J. M. (2008). A MCMC method for resolving two person mixtures. *Science & Justice, 48*, 168–177.

Gill, P., et al. (1998). Interpretation of simple mixtures when artifacts such as stutters are present—With special reference to multiplex STRs used by the Forensic Science Service. *Forensic Science International, 95*, 213–224.

Gill, P., et al. (2008). Interpretation of complex DNA profiles using empirical models and a method to measure their robustness. *Forensic Science International: Genetics, 2*, 91–103.

Leclair, B., et al. (2004). Systematic analysis of stutter percentages and allele peak height and peak area ratios at heterozygous STR loci for forensic casework and database samples. *Journal of Forensic Sciences, 49*, 968–980.

Paoletti, D. R., et al. (2005). Empirical analysis of the STR profiles resulting from conceptual mixtures. *Journal of Forensic Sciences, 50*(6), 1361–1366.

Wickenheiser, R. (2006). General guidelines for categorization and interpretation of mixed STR DNA profiles. *Canadian Society of Forensic Science Journal, 39*, 179–216.

Software

Bill, M., et al. (2005). PENDULUM—A guideline-based approach to the interpretation of STR mixtures. *Forensic Science International, 148*, 181–189.

FSS-i3 software (from FSS and Promega). http://www.promega.com/fssi3; http://www.forensic.gov.uk/forensic_t/i3/index.htm

GeneMapper*ID-X* (from Applied Biosystems). http://idx.appliedbiosystems.com

Oldroyd, N., & Schade, L. L. (2008). Expert assistant software enables forensic DNA analysts to confidently process more samples. *Forensic Magazine, 5*(6), 25–28.

TrueAllele (from Cybergenetics). http://www.cybgen.com

Wang, T., et al. (2006). Least-squares deconvolution: A framework for interpreting short tandem repeat mixtures. *Journal of Forensic Sciences, 51*(6), 1284–1297.

Statistics

Buckleton, J., & Curran, J. (2008). A discussion of the merits of random man not excluded and likelihood ratios. *Forensic Science International: Genetics, 2*(4), 343–348.

Curran, J. M., et al. (1999). Interpreting DNA mixtures in structured populations. *Journal of Forensic Sciences, 44*(5), 987–995.

DNA Advisory Board. (2000). Statistical and population genetic issues affecting the evaluation of the frequency of occurrence of DNA profiles calculated from pertinent population database(s). *Forensic Science Communications, 2*(3). Available at http://www.fbi.gov/programs/lab/fsc/backissu/july2000/dnastat.htm

Ladd, C., et al. (2001). Interpretation of complex forensic DNA mixtures. *Croatian Medical Journal, 42*(3), 244–246.

Weir, B. S., et al. (1997). Interpreting DNA mixtures. *Journal of Forensic Sciences, 42*(2), 213–222.

Interlaboratory studies

Duewer, D. L., et al. (2001). NIST mixed stain studies #1 and #2: Interlaboratory comparison of DNA quantification practice and short tandem repeat multiplex performance with multiple-source samples. *Journal of Forensic Sciences, 46*(5), 1199–1210.

Duewer, D. L., et al. (2004). NIST mixed stain study 3: Signal intensity balance in commercial short tandem repeat multiplexes. *Analytical Chemistry, 76,* 6928–6934.

Kline, M. C., et al. (2003). NIST mixed stain study 3: DNA quantitation accuracy and its influence on short tandem repeat multiplex signal intensity. *Analytical Chemistry, 75,* 2463–2469.

NIST Mixture Interpretation Study 2005 (MIX05). http://www.cstl.nist.gov/biotech/strbase/interlab/MIX05.htm

Low Copy Number (LCN) and Touch DNA Evidence

Abaz, J., et al. (2002). Comparison of the variables affecting the recovery of DNA from common drinking containers. *Forensic Science International, 126,* 233–240.

Alessandrini, F., et al. (2003). Fingerprints as evidence for a genetic profile: morphological study on fingerprints and analysis of exogenous and individual factors affecting DNA typing. *Journal of Forensic Sciences, 48,* 586–592.

Budowle, B., et al. (2001). Low copy number—Consideration and caution. In: *Proceedings of the twelfth international symposium on human identification.* Madison, WI: Promega Corporation. http://www.promega.com/geneticidproc/ussymp-12proc/contents/budowle.pdf

Buckleton, J., & Gill, P. (2005). Low copy number. In J. Buckleton, C. M. Triggs, & S. J. Walsh (Eds.), *Forensic DNA evidence interpretation* (Chapter 8, pp. 275–297). Boca Raton, FL: CRC Press.

Caddy, B., et al. (2008). Review of the science of low template DNA analysis. Available at http://police.homeoffice.gov.uk/publications/operational-policing/Review_of_Low_Template_DNA_1.pdf

Capelli, C., et al. (2003). 'Ancient' protocols for the crime scene? Similarities and differences between forensic genetics and ancient DNA analysis. *Forensic Science International, 131*, 59–64.

Evett, I. W., et al. (2002). Interpreting small quantities of DNA: The hierarchy of propositions and the use of Bayesian networks. *Journal of Forensic Sciences, 47*(3), 520–530.

Findlay, I., et al. (1997). DNA fingerprinting from single cells. *Nature, 389*, 555–556.

Forensic Science Regulator. (2008). Response to Professor Brian Caddy's review of the science of low template DNA analysis. Available at http://police.homeoffice.gov.uk/publications/operational-policing/response-caddy-dna-review

Gill, P. (2001). Application of low copy number DNA profiling. *Croatian Medical Journal, 42*(3), 229–232.

Gill, P., et al. (2000). An investigation of the rigor of interpretation rules for STRs derived from less than 100 pg of DNA. *Forensic Science International, 112*(1), 17–40.

Kloosterman, A. D., & Kersbergen, P. (2003). Efficacy and limits of genotyping low copy number (LCN) DNA samples by multiplex PCR of STR loci. *Journal de la Société de biologie, 197*(4), 351–359.

Lowe, A., et al. (2002). The propensity of individuals to deposit DNA and secondary transfer of low level DNA from individuals to inert surfaces. *Forensic Science International, 129*, 25–34.

Lowe, A., et al. (2003). Use of low copy number DNA in forensic inference. *Progress in Forensic Genetics 9, ICS 1239*, 799–801.

Murray, C., et al. (2001). Use of low copy number (LCN) DNA in forensic inference. In: *Proceedings of the twelfth international symposium on human identification*. Madison, WI: Promega Corporation. Available at http://www.promega.com/geneticidproc

Polley, D., et al. (2006). An investigation of DNA recovery from firearms and cartridge cases. *Canadian Society of Forensic Science Journal, 39*, 217–228.

Raymond, J. J., et al. (2008). Trace DNA analysis: Do you know what your neighbour is doing? A multi-jurisdictional survey. *Forensic Science International: Genetics, 2*, 19–28.

Rutty, G. N., et al. (2003). The effectiveness of protective clothing in the reduction of potential DNA contamination of the scene of crime. *International Journal of Legal Medicine, 117*, 170–174.

Schiffner, L. A., et al. (2005). Optimization of a simple, automatable extraction method to recover sufficient DNA from low copy number DNA samples for generation of short tandem repeat profiles. *Croatian Medical Journal, 46*(4), 578–586.

Taberlet, P., et al. (1996). Reliable genotyping of samples with very low DNA quantities using PCR. *Nucleic Acids Research, 24*, 3189–3194.

Van Hoofstat, D. E. O., et al. (1998). DNA typing of fingerprints and skin debris: Sensitivity of capillary electrophoresis in forensic applications using multiplex PCR. In: *Proceedings of the second european symposium on human identification*. Madison, WI: Promega Corporation (pp. 131–137). Available at http://www.promega.com/geneticidproc/eusymp2proc

Van Oorschot, R. A., & Jones, M. (1997). DNA fingerprints from fingerprints. *Nature, 387*, 767.

Walsh, P. S., et al. (1992). Preferential PCR amplification of alleles: Mechanisms and solutions. *PCR Methods and Applications, 1*, 241–250.

Whitaker, J. P., et al. (2001). A comparison of the characteristics of profiles produced with the AMPFISTR SGM Plus multiplex system for both standard and low copy number (LCN) STR DNA analysis. *Forensic Science International, 123*(2–3), 215–223.

Wickenheiser, R. A. (2002). Trace DNA: A review, discussion of theory, and application of the transfer of trace quantities of DNA through skin contact. *Journal of Forensic Sciences, 47*(3), 442–450.

CHAPTER 15

Additional Loci and Nonhuman DNA Testing

Research into the identification and validation of more and better marker systems for forensic analysis should continue with a view of making each profile unique.

—NRC II Report, Recommendation 5.3, p. 7

BEYOND THE CORE GENETIC MARKERS

In this chapter and the next one, we examine other DNA markers that are being used or being developed for forensic DNA typing purposes or other applications such as paternity testing that will be reviewed in Chapter 17. Core short tandem repeat (STR) loci are being used extensively today and will probably continue to be used for many years in the future because they are part of the DNA databases that are growing around the world. Yet forensic DNA scientists often use additional markers as the need arises to obtain further information about a particular sample.

As described in Chapter 8, sex-typing via examination of a portion of the amelogenin gene is performed in conjunction with available STR kits to provide the gender of the individual who is the source of the DNA sample in question. Additionally, in cases where samples may be extremely degraded and fail to result in useful information with conventional STR typing, mitochondrial DNA (see Chapter 16) may be used because it is present in higher copy number per cell than nuclear DNA and thus more resistant to complete sample degradation.

Y-chromosome STRs can help extract information from the male portion of a sample mixture in sexual assault cases (see Chapter 16). Information from nonhuman DNA sources has already been used to solve forensic cases and will continue to grow in value as our knowledge of genomic DNA sequence diversity in human populations as well as other organisms improves.

Contribution of the National Institute of Standards and Technology, 2010.

It is conceivable that within a few years, a wide variety of validated marker sets and technologies will exist that will provide a forensic DNA laboratory with a smorgasbord of possibilities in their arsenal of weapons that may be used to solve crimes with biological evidence.

ADDITIONAL STR LOCI

While the current core STR loci are generally sufficient for forensic matching of evidence to suspect, additional autosomal or Y-chromosomal STR loci can be beneficial or even necessary to address a variety of other human identity/relationship testing questions.

Kinship analysis such as missing persons/mass disaster sample testing, complex paternity analysis, parentage testing with only one available parent, and immigration testing can benefit from additional genetic markers. A 2007 article on immigration testing urged the use of 25 genetic loci to avoid erroneous conclusions when a limited number of reference samples are available. More STR loci can also help resolve relatives in growing national DNA databases to avoid adventitious matches. A number of additional STRs have been characterized beyond the core/common STRs that are used in commercial STR kits today.

Some desirable characteristics in potential supplemental STR loci as compared to the core loci that are now widely used include (1) a genomic location that is adequately spaced from other 'new' loci as well as current STR loci to enable independence of inheritance and permit use of the product rule in estimating the rarity of a particular profile and (2) avoiding known disease genes or linkage to disease genes to limit privacy concerns.

A multiplex PCR assay that simultaneously amplifies 25 unlinked STRs and the sex-typing marker amelogenin from as little as a 100-pg sample has been developed. This assay utilizes four dye colors and has PCR product sizes ranging from 75 to 400 bp (Figure 15.1).

SINGLE NUCLEOTIDE POLYMORPHISMS (SNPs)

A single-base sequence variation between individuals at a particular point in the genome is often referred to as a *single nucleotide polymorphism*, or SNP (pronounced 'snip'). SNPs are abundant in the human genome and, as such, are being used for linkage studies to track genetic diseases. Millions of SNPs exist per individual and thus the abundance of SNPs means that they could be used to help differentiate individuals from one another. Table 15.1 compares and contrasts SNP and STR markers.

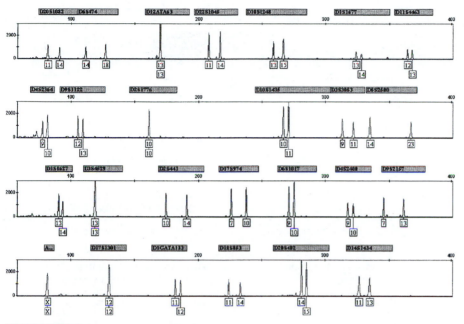

FIGURE 15.1

A 26plex assay developed with noncore markers that amplifies 25 STRs and amelogenin in a four-dye, 75- to 400-bp size range. (Figure courtesy of Becky Hill, NIST.)

Pros and cons of SNPs

SNPs have been promoted to the forensic DNA community for several reasons. First and foremost, the polymerase chain reaction (PCR) products from SNPs can be less than 100 bp in size, which means that these markers would be able to withstand degraded DNA samples better than STRs that have amplicons as large as 300 to 400 bp. Second, they can be potentially multiplexed to a higher level than STRs because some detection methods (e.g., array hybridization) are not constrained by electrophoretic space (e.g., four fluorescent dye labels and a size range of 75 to 450 bp). Third, the sample processing and data analysis may be more fully automated because a size-based separation is not needed. Fourth, there is no stutter artifact associated with each allele, which should help simplify interpretation of the allele call. Finally, the ability to predict ethnic origin and certain physical traits may be possible with careful selection of SNP markers.

The vast majority of SNPs are biallelic, meaning that they have two possible alleles and therefore three possible genotypes. For example, if the alleles for a SNP locus are A and B (where 'A' could represent a C, T, A, or G and 'B' could also be a C, T, A, or G nucleotide), then the three possible genotypes would be AA, BB, or AB. Mixture interpretation can present a challenge with SNPs

Table 15.1 Comparison of STR and SNP markers.

Characteristics	Short Tandem Repeats (STRs)	Single Nucleotide Polymorphisms (SNPs)
Occurrence in human genome	~1 in every 15 kb	~1 in every 1 kb
General informativeness	High	Low; only 20% to 30% as informative as STRs
Mutation rate	~1 in 1000	~1 in 100,000,000
Marker type	Di-, tri-, tetra-, and pentanucleotide repeat markers with many alleles	Mostly biallelic markers with six possibilities: A/G, C/T, A/T, C/G, T/G, A/C
Number of alleles per marker	Usually 5 to 20	Typically 2 (some triallelic SNPs exist)
Detection methods	Gel/capillary electrophoresis	Sequence analysis; microchip hybridization
Multiplex capability	>10 markers with multiple fluorescent dyes	Difficult to amplify more than 50 SNPs (detection of 1000s with microchips)
Amplicon size	~75 to 400 bp	Can be less than 100 bp
Ability to predict ethnicity (biogeographical ancestry)	Limited	Some SNPs associated with ethnicity
Phenotypic information	No	Possible to predict some hair colors, etc.
Major advantage for forensic application	Many alleles enabling higher success rates for detecting and deciphering mixtures	PCR products can be made small, potentially enabling higher success rates with degraded DNA samples

Note: SNPs are more common in the human genome than STRs but are not as polymorphic.

because it may be difficult to tell the difference between a true heterozygote and a mixture containing two homozygotes or a heterozygote and a homozygote. The ability to obtain quantitative information from SNP allele calls is important when attempting to decipher mixtures.

At this time, one of the biggest challenges to using SNPs in forensic DNA typing applications is the inability to simultaneously amplify enough SNPs in robust multiplexes from small amounts of DNA. Because a single biallelic SNP by itself yields less information than a multiallelic STR marker, it is necessary to analyze a larger number of SNPs in order to obtain a reasonable power of discrimination to define a unique profile. Progress is being made in the area of multiplex PCR amplification, and assays capable of amplifying and analyzing more than 50 SNPs simultaneously have been demonstrated.

Since each SNP locus typically possesses only two possible alleles, more markers are needed to obtain a high discriminatory power than for STR loci that possess multiple alleles. Computational analyses have shown that on average 25 to 45 SNP loci are needed to yield equivalent random match probabilities as the 13 core STR loci. Another study predicted that 50 SNPs possessing frequencies in the range of 20% to 50% for the minor allele can theoretically result in likelihood ratios similar to approximately 12 STR loci. The number of SNPs needed may fluctuate in practice because some SNP loci have variable allele frequencies in different population groups. Most likely a battery of 50 to 100 SNPs will be required to match the same powers of discrimination and mixture resolution capabilities now achieved with 10 to 16 STR loci.

SNP databases

Large national and international efforts have been under way over the past few years to catalog human variation found in the form of SNP markers. The SNP Consortium (TSC) was established in the spring of 1999 to create a high-density SNP map of the human genome. The TSC effort (http://snp.cshl.org) produced several million mapped and characterized human SNP markers that have been entered into public databases including dbSNP housed at the National Institutes of Health's National Center for Biotechnology Information (http://www.ncbi.nlm.nih.gov/SNP). The original TSC work became the foundation for the International HapMap project that was a follow-on to the Human Genome Project (see D.N.A. Box 2.1). The HapMap work involved typing 270 individuals from African, European, and Asian populations with several million SNPs (http://www.hapmap.org/). With these large ventures ongoing around the world, there is no shortage of available SNP markers and accompanying population data.

SNP analysis techniques

A number of SNP typing methods are available, each with its own strengths and weaknesses. Several reviews of SNP typing technologies have been published and can be consulted for a more in-depth view of methodologies. A few SNP analysis techniques are summarized in Table 15.2.

One of the important characteristics of an SNP assay is its ability to examine multiple markers simultaneously since SNPs are not as variable as STRs and typically a limited amount of DNA template is available in forensic casework. While pyrosequencing and TaqMan assays are limited in their multiplexing capabilities, Luminex and minisequencing (SNaPshot) assays enable multiplexed analysis of a dozen or more SNP markers simultaneously. A number of SNP assays for detecting mtDNA, Y-chromosome, and autosomal markers have been described in the literature using the SNaPshot approach, which is capable of being run on ABI 310 and 3100 instruments already in use in most forensic DNA laboratories.

Table 15.2 Selected SNP analysis techniques.

Method	Description	References
Reverse dot blot or linear arrays	A series of allele-specific probes are attached to a nylon test strip at separate sites; biotinylated PCR products hybridize to their complementary probes and are then detected with a colorimetric reaction and evaluated visually	Saiki et al. (1989), Kline et al. (2005)
TaqMan 5' nuclease assay	A fluorescent probe consisting of reporter and quencher dyes is added to a PCR reaction; amplification of a probe-specific product causes cleavage of the probe and generates an increase in fluorescence target, which results in fluorescence	Livak (1999)
Pyrosequencing	Sequencing by synthesis of 20 to 30 nucleotides beyond primer site; dNTPs are added in a specific order and those incorporated result in release of pyrophosphate and light through an enzyme cascade	Ahmadian et al. (2000)
Allele-specific hybridization (Luminex 100)	Dye-labeled PCR products hybridize to oligonucleotide probes (representing the various SNP types) attached to as many as 100 different colored beads; each bead is interrogated to determine its color and whether or not a PCR product is attached as the beads pass two lasers in a flow cytometer	Armstrong et al. (2000)
Minisequencing (SNaPshot assay)	Allele-specific primer extension across the SNP site with fluorescently labeled ddNTPs; mobility modifying tails can be added to the 5' end of each primer in order to spatially separate them during electrophoresis	Tully et al. (1996)

SNP markers and multiplexes

SNPs occur in noncoding regions of the genome as well as in genes (both exons and introns). Depending on the potential application, SNP markers might be selected to be away from genes or the direct cause of the gene mutation. From a forensic historical perspective, the first work with SNP typing was with the HLA-DQA1 and AmpliType PM kits. As noted in Chapter 3, these early PCR assays were sensitive but not very informative because collectively DQA1 and PolyMarker only examined six loci. In recent years, a great deal of work has been performed to characterize a number of new SNP loci and to develop useful SNP multiplex assays.

Several members of the European forensic DNA typing community launched a project in 2003 known as SNP*for*ID that worked to develop SNP assays to directly aid forensic DNA analysis. This group selected several sets of potential forensic SNP markers and developed highly multiplexed SNP assays. Population data was also gathered to measure SNP allele frequencies in various groups of interest. The SNP*for*ID Web site (http://www.snpforid.org) contains links to their publications and population data. The SNP*for*ID consortium has published a 52plex PCR and SNaPshot assay and has collaborated with Applied Biosystems to develop a 48 autosomal SNP+amelogenin sex-typing assay based on the GenPlex genotyping system.

Ken Kidd's group at Yale University has characterized allele frequencies for more than 100 SNPs in roughly 40 different global human populations in an effort to find optimal human identity SNP markers. This group has also published criteria for selecting what they term a 'universal individual identification panel' of SNPs.

SNP applications

SNP markers may be classified into four general uses: (1) human identification SNPs, (2) ancestry informative SNPs, (3) lineage informative SNPs, and (4) phenotype informative SNPs. Most of the work to date has been performed with the human ID SNPs. Some SNP detection assays have also been used for pathology and toxicology purposes.

While many more SNPs than STRs are required to obtain similar random match probabilities, SNPs have the potential to be used in other ways to aid investigations, such as predicting a perpetrator's ancestral background. SNPs have a much lower mutation rate than STRs and therefore are more likely to become 'fixed' in a population. SNPs change on the order of once every 10^8 generations while STR mutation rates are approximately one in a thousand (see D.N.A. Box 17.3). Because of their low mutation rate, SNPs and *Alu* insertions (see D.N.A. Box 15.2 later in the chapter) are often found to be population specific. These loci can thus be useful in predicting a perpetrator's ethnic origin to aid criminal investigations. In addition, SNPs can serve as supplemental markers when STR results are not definitive enough in complex relationship tests.

The presence of rare STR or SNP alleles in particular population groups can be used to estimate the ethnic origin of a sample. Although efforts have been made with STRs, estimating ethnic origin is far from foolproof. Individuals with mixed ancestral background may not possess the expected phenotypic characteristics (e.g., dark-colored skin for African Americans). Thus, results from genetic tests attempting to predict ethnic origin or ancestry should always be interpreted with caution and only in the context of other reliable evidence.

A company named DNAPrint (Sarasota, FL) provides a DNA test for estimating an individual's ethnic/racial background with a panel of SNPs. DNAPrint has targeted pigmentation and xenobiotic metabolism genes in their search for ancestrally informative SNPs. Much of their work is based on the research efforts of Dr. Mark Shriver from Penn State University (State College, PA) who is looking for ancestry informative markers (AIMs) that possess alleles with large frequency differences between populations.

D.N.A. Box 15.1 Aiding a Criminal Investigation by Predicting the Ethnic Origin of a Biological Sample

DNA typing tests with the standard 13 STRs linked five murders and rapes in the Baton Rouge, Louisiana, area that occurred over an 18-month period. Based on an eyewitness report that a white male was seen leaving one of the crime scenes in a pickup truck, a police dragnet was initiated to collect DNA samples from more than 1000 white males in the area. However, the dragnet and seven long months of investigative work failed to find the culprit.

The police then turned to DNAPrint Genomics Inc. (Sarasota, FL) to perform a genetic test with single nucleotide polymorphisms (SNPs) to predict the ethnic ancestry of the biological samples obtained from the crime scenes. The DNAPrint test revealed that the samples came from a person who had 85% African American ancestry and 15% American Indian ancestry. Authorities turned their attention to black males and within 2 months arrested Derrick Todd Lee, an African American resident in the area with an extensive criminal record. Confirmatory testing with the standard 13 STRs matched Derrick Todd Lee's DNA profile with the ones found at the crime scenes.

In the future, this type of analysis to predict ethnicities and even phenotypic characteristics of perpetrators may be used in conjunction with DNA intelligence screens (see Chapter 12) to help narrow the list of possible suspects. Currently SNP tests, like the DNAPrint assay, consume too much DNA material to be used routinely on precious crime scene samples. More validation studies will be needed in the future before such ethnicity tests become widely accepted.

Source:
Frudakis, T. N. (2008). *Molecular photofitting: Predicting ancestry and phenotype using DNA* (pp. 599–603). San Diego: Elsevier Academic Press.

'Population-specific alleles' have been found in both STR and SNP markers. Although presently used AIMs are not 100% accurate for predicting ancestral background of samples (and perhaps never will be), the DNAPrint SNP typing approach was used to aid the investigation of an important serial rapist case in 2003 demonstrating the forensic value of this type of approach (D.N.A. Box 15.1).

As more and more information is uncovered about the nature and content of the human genome, we will be able to identify the genetic variants that code for phenotypic characteristics (e.g., red hair or blue eyes). For example, several years ago the Forensic Science Service developed an SNP typing assay involving mutations in the human melanocortin 1 receptor gene that are associated with red hair phenotype. DNAPrint has developed a genetic test for inference of eye color.

Perhaps SNP sites can be identified in the future that will correlate to facial features, thus aiding investigators with information about the possible appearance of a perpetrator. However, due to the complexity of multigenic traits and outside factors such as aging and environment, it is unlikely that a few carefully chosen SNPs will present a foolproof picture of a sample's source. Research will likely continue in this area and hopefully will provide beneficial information to investigations of the future.

As noted in Chapter 18, it is unlikely that SNPs (or even other STR markers) will replace core STRs in the near- or even medium-term future as the primary source of information used in criminal investigations. Rather than replacing the millions of profiles that exist in large national DNA databases through retyping convicted offender and casework samples with new SNP markers, what is more likely is that new STRs or SNPs will be slowly added to national DNA databases as technologies are proven and costs come down.

Other biallelic markers

Another form of a biallelic (or diallelic) polymorphism is an *insertion-delet*ion or *indel*. An indel can be the insertion or deletion of a segment of DNA ranging from one nucleotide to hundreds of nucleotides, such as is seen with an *Alu* insertion (D.N.A. Box 15.2). The two alleles for diallelic indels can simply be classified as 'short' and 'long.' From a certain perspective, STR markers can be thought of as multiallelic indels since the different alleles are typically insertions or deletions of a tandem repeat unit.

Most diallelic indels exhibit allele-length differences of only a few nucleotides. James Weber and colleagues at the Marshfield Medical Research Foundation have characterized over 2000 biallelic indels in the human genome. A total of 71% of these indels possessed 2-, 3-, or 4-nucleotide length differences with only 4% having greater than a 16-nucleotide length difference. Allele frequencies for the short and long alleles have been measured in African, European, Japanese, and Native American populations. These markers can be easily typed and may prove useful for future genetic studies including human identity testing.

NONHUMAN DNA TESTING

While the vast majority of forensic DNA typing performed for criminal investigations involves human DNA, it is not the only source of DNA that may be useful in demonstrating the guilt or innocence of an individual suspected of a crime. Domestic animals such as cats and dogs live in human habitats and deposit hair that may be used to place a suspect at the crime scene. Demonstration that a botanical specimen came from a particular plant can aid the linkage of a crime to a suspect or help demonstrate that the body of a deceased victim may have been moved from the murder site. DNA testing can now be used to link sources of marijuana. A large area of future application for forensic DNA typing involves identification of bioterrorism materials such as anthrax. This section will briefly discuss each of these topics and the value of nonhuman DNA testing in forensic casework.

The American Pet Products Association reported in their 2007 and 2008 national pet owners survey that over 71 million U.S. households own a pet (see http://www.appma.org). Their survey found 88 million cats and 75 million

D.N.A. Box 15.2 *Alu* Insertion Polymorphisms

Short, interspersed nuclear elements (SINEs) are another form of repeated DNA that has been investigated for population variation studies. SINEs consist of a short, identifiable sequence inserted at a location in the genome. The best-studied SINEs are *Alu* insertion polymorphisms, which were named for an *Alu*I restriction endonuclease site typical of the sequence. *Alu* units are found in nearly 1 million copies per haploid genome (5% to 10% of the human genome) and can be found flanking genes or clustered with other interspersed repeated sequences.

The insertion of an *Alu* element at a particular locus can be regarded as a unique event. Once inserted, *Alu* elements are stable genetic markers and do not appear to be subject to loss or rearrangement. Human-specific *Alu* insertions may be typed in a biallelic fashion by using PCR, agarose gel electrophoresis, and ethidium bromide staining. The presence of the *Alu* insertion will be indicated by a 400-bp PCR product while the absence of the insertion will result in a 100-bp amplicon. Commonly used *Alu* insertion polymorphisms include APO, PV92, TPA25, FXIIIB, D1, ACE, A25, and B65.

Alu repeats have shown the potential to yield information about the geographic/ethnic origin of the sample being tested. Since many *Alu* sequences are unique to humans, it is possible to design multiplex assays that are completely human specific (i.e., no cross-reaction with even other primates). However, *Alu* repeats exhibit less variation than multiplex STR profiles and would therefore most likely be used to gain more information on an unknown sample rather than as an independent source of identification. *Alu*-based quantitative PCR assays have proven to be very effective for human DNA quantitation purposes (see Chapter 6). Quantitative PCR assays based on high copy number *Alu* insertions are much more sensitive than assays that target single-copy DNA sequences.

Sources:

Batzer, M. A., & Deininger, P. L. (1991). A human-specific subfamily of Alu sequences. *Genomics, 9,* 481–487.

Batzer, M., et al. (1993). *Alu* repeats as markers for human population genetics. In: *Fourth international symposium on human identification* (pp. 49–57). Madison, WI: Promega Corporation.

Primrose, S. B. (1998). *Principles of genome analysis: A guide to mapping and sequencing DNA from different organisms.* Malden, MA: Blackwell Science.

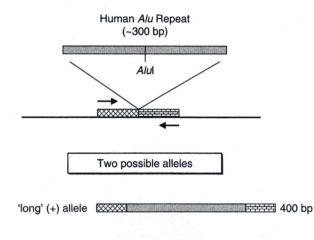

Human *Alu* Repeat
(~300 bp)

*Alu*I

Two possible alleles

'long' (+) allele ▨▨▨▨▨▨▨▨▨▨▨▨▨▨▨▨ 400 bp

'short' (–) allele ▨▨▨▨▨▨▨▨ 100 bp

Schematic of the Alu *element insertion PCR assay. The* Alu *sequence, which is approximately 300 bp in size, may either be present or absent at a particular location in the human genome. When the flanking region of the* Alu *repeat is targeted with primers, PCR amplification will result in products that are 400 bp if the* Alu *element is inserted or 100 bp if it is absent. A simple ethidium bromide–stained agarose gel may be used to genotype individuals. Individuals who are homozygous for the insertion will amplify a 400-bp DNA fragment. Those who are heterozygous for the insertion will amplify both 400- and 100-bp fragments, and individuals who are homozygous for the lack of the* Alu *insertion element will exhibit only the 100-bp DNA fragment.*

dogs in these households, which make up almost two-thirds of all U.S. residences. Since many of these domestic animals shed hair, these hairs could be picked up or left behind at the scene of a crime by a perpetrator. An assailant may unknowingly carry clinging cat hairs from a victim's cat away from the scene of a crime, or hair from the perpetrator's cat may be left at the scene.

The Veterinary Genetics Laboratory at the University of California–Davis (see http://www.vgl.ucdavis.edu/forensics) has been performing forensic animal DNA analyses since 1996. They have found that there are three types of animal DNA evidence: (1) the animal as victim, (2) the animal as perpetrator, and (3) the animal as witness.

Animal abuse cases or the theft of an animal can sometimes be benefited by the power of DNA testing. The remains of a lost pet can be positively identified through genetic analysis. Typically genetic markers like STRs and mtDNA are examined in much the same way as with human DNA.

When animals are involved in an attack on a person, DNA typing may be used to identify the animal perpetrator (e.g., a pit bull). If the victim is deceased, then DNA evidence may be the only witness that an animal in custody committed the crime. Animal DNA testing can 'exonerate' innocent animals so that they are not needlessly destroyed.

Animal DNA has been used successfully to link suspects to crime scenes (D.N.A. Box 15.3). A 1998 study on the transfer of animal hair during simulated criminal behavior found that hundreds of cat hairs or dog hairs could be transferred from the homes of victims to a burglar or an aggressor. In fact, the number of hairs found was so high that the authors of this study felt that it is almost impossible to enter a house where a domestic animal lives without being 'contaminated' by cat and/or dog hairs even when the owner describes his or her animal as a poor source of hair. Due to the fact that shed hairs often do not contain roots, nuclear DNA may not be present in sufficient quantities

D.N.A. Box 15.3 Snowball's DNA

The identity of white cat hairs found on a bloodstained leather jacket left at a murder scene became a turning point in the case of Douglas Leo Beamish versus Her Majesty The Queen in the Province of Prince Edward Island, Canada. The victim, Shirley Duguay, was discovered in a shallow grave in a wooded area 8 months after she disappeared. Beamish, her former common law husband, was charged with the crime. At the time he lived with his parents and a white cat named Snowball. Laboratory analysis of the bloodstains on the recovered jacket contained the victim's DNA profile. The white cat hairs matched Snowball at 10 STR loci. The defendant was convicted of murder based in part on this evidence.

Source:
Menotti-Raymond, M., et al. (1997). Pet cat hair implicates murder suspect. Nature, 386, 774.

for STR typing. Mitochondrial DNA may be a more viable alternative for many of these types of shed hair transfers.

Cat DNA testing

Cats have 18 pairs of autosomes and the sex chromosomes X and Y. Genetic markers have been developed on each of the *Felis catus* chromosomes. A panel of STR markers dubbed the 'MeowPlex' has been developed that contains 11 STRs on nine different autosomes. A gender identification marker was also included in this assay through the addition of PCR primers that are specific for the SRY gene on the cat Y chromosome. Population studies on over 1200 cats from 37 different breeds have been conducted by the Laboratory of Genomic Diversity at the National Cancer Institute–Frederick Cancer Research and Development Center in Frederick, Maryland. These feline STR allele frequencies from domestic cats have been collected for the purpose of demonstrating uniqueness of DNA profiles in forensic investigations, such as used in the Beamish case with his cat 'Snowball' (D.N.A. Box 15.3).

Dog DNA testing

While cat DNA testing may be involved in situations where the animal hair acts as a silent witness to connecting a perpetrator to a crime scene, evidence from dogs is more frequently linked to situations where the animal is the perpetrator. Rottweilers, German shepherds, Doberman pinschers, and pit bulls can be trained as security animals and may attack, injure, or even kill people. A number of STR markers have been mapped and characterized on the 38 pairs of autosomes and the X chromosome of *Canis familiaris*, the domestic dog. Canine mitochondrial DNA possesses two hypervariable regions (HV1 and HV2) similar to the human mtDNA described in Chapter 16. While domesticated dog mtDNA is not as variable as human mtDNA, it can still provide helpful clues in forensic cases.

Species identification

Sequence analysis of the mtDNA cytochrome b gene is effective at identifying the species of origin for a biological sample. Some tests have even been developed to simultaneously amplify both the human mtDNA control and the cytochrome b gene to enable simultaneous human and species identification. Another mtDNA region examined for species identification is the 12S ribosomal RNA gene. In one study, DNA sequence analysis of an ~150-bp fragment of the 12S rRNA mtDNA successfully identified dog, feral pig, raccoon, cat, goat, sheep, rat, and yak DNA samples in 12 different forensic cases.

Plant DNA testing

In the area of plant DNA testing, two primary areas are currently being investigated. The first is the linking of plant material to suspects or victims in order to make an association with a particular area where a crime was committed. The second is in linking marijuana to aid in forensic drug investigations.

Crimes often occur in localized areas containing a unique combination of botanical growth. If these plants, algae, or grasses are sufficiently rare, then recovery of trace evidence from the clothing of a victim or the personal property of a suspect may be helpful in making an association that can link them to a crime scene. Although plant DNA testing is not yet used routinely, it has helped link suspects to crime scenes and aided important investigations.

In the first use of forensic botanical evidence, two small seedpods from an Arizona Palo Verde tree found in the back of pickup truck were used to place an accused murderer at the crime scene. Genetic testing on the seeds showed that in a 'lineup' of 12 Palo Verde trees near the crime scene, DNA from the seeds matched only the tree under which the victim's body had been found. In *State v. Bogan*, the jury found the accused guilty based in large measure on the plant DNA evidence.

Several DNA tests have been developed for *Cannabis sativa* (marijuana) because it is an illegal substance associated with many crime scenes. Marijuana is one of the most commonly identified drugs tested by U.S. forensic laboratories (see http://www.deadiversion.usdoj.gov/nflis).

Marijuana DNA testing can link an individual to a sample, link growers, and help track distribution networks. However, it is important to keep in mind that if the marijuana plants were propagated clonally rather than by seed, then they will have identical DNA profiles. Clonal propagation in marijuana is performed by taking cuttings from a 'mother' plant and rooting them directly in the soil to create large numbers of plants having identical DNA.

A few STR markers have been characterized in *Cannabis sativa* and developed into effective DNA tests. As with human STRs, marijuana STR markers are highly polymorphic, specific to unique sites in the genome, and capable of deciphering mixtures. Efforts are under way to improve molecular techniques for identifying marijuana plants and to develop comparative databases to serve as effective tools for law enforcement purposes. To determine the possibility of a random match with marijuana seizure samples, it is important to have a database of seizure samples so their DNA profiles can be used for comparison.

Bacterial DNA in soil

Soil is filled with a variety of microscopic organisms including bacteria and fungi. It has been shown that different combinations of bacteria in soil samples from different locations can be differentiated with DNA testing.

The use of these DNA signatures from soil microbes is being explored to see if this information can be used to link individuals to a specific location based on soil found on their shoes or clothing. This type of forensic soil evaluation could then potentially link a suspect to a crime scene or identify where a victim was killed and whether the body was moved to a different location. Appropriate sampling still remains a challenge as well as overcoming PCR inhibitors present in soil, but this is an area that could bear fruit in the future.

Wildlife DNA testing

The remains of stolen animals or illegally procured meat (e.g., endangered species or poaching) can be identified through DNA testing. Genetic testing can be used to help prosecute individuals who exploit exotic or endangered animals. The U.S. Fish and Wildlife Service has a forensic laboratory in Ashland, Oregon, that does some species identification using DNA (see http://www.lab.fws.gov). Other laboratories performing similar wildlife DNA testing are located in Canada and the United Kingdom.

Challenges with presenting nonhuman DNA in court

In a 1998 article, George Sensabaugh and David Kaye considered several issues regarding whether a given application with nonhuman DNA is ready for court use. These issues include the novelty of the application, the validity of the underlying scientific theory, the validity of any statistical interpretations, and the existence of a relevant scientific community to consult in assessing the application. Many times new methods are applied for the first time in microbial forensics (D.N.A. Box 15.4) or animal or plant DNA testing that have not yet undergone the scrutiny of regular forensic DNA testing techniques. Reference

D.N.A. Box 15.4 Microbial Forensics and the Amerithrax Investigation

Microbial forensics will likely become a larger part of DNA testing in the future with the threat of terrorism and the use of biological warfare agents. Microbial evidence can be from either real terrorist events or hoaxes. The efforts in this area will likely require forensic laboratories to build strong collaborations with academic, private sector, and national laboratories. Important requirements of biothreat detection assays are high sensitivity, high specificity in complex samples, fast measurement, compact design for portability and field use, and internal calibration and reference to ensure reliable results.

In October 2001 a bioterrorism attack impacted the United States as government offices and media outlets received anthrax-laden letters sent anonymously through the postal service. This attack resulted in 22 anthrax cases and five deaths. In addition, many people were afraid to open their mail for months afterwards. In the 2 years following the attack, more than 125,000 samples were processed as part of this case, termed by the FBI as the "Amerithrax" investigation. In August 2008, almost 7 years after the anthrax attack, the FBI Laboratory announced a breakthrough with plans to charge Dr. Bruce Ivins, a scientist at the U.S. Army Medical Research Institute for Infectious Diseases (USAMRIID) in Frederick, Maryland. Dr. Ivins committed suicide before the charges could be filed.

Several challenges arise when trying to gather evidence, identify the biocrime organism(s), and trace the source of the organism(s). First responders to crime scenes where biological weapons have been dispersed have to be concerned about their own safety and the safety of others while maintaining a chain of custody of any evidence collected from the crime scene, all the while trying to prevent contamination of the evidence and the environment. Databases need to be established for intrinsic background species and biothreat strains. Reliable reference material is needed for comparison purposes. Proficiency and validation testing are necessary to estimate false-positive and false-negative rates.

The U.S. government has made a significant effort to build infrastructure to aid response to potential bioterrorism threats in the future. The FBI initiated a Scientific Working Group on Microbial Genetics and Forensics (SWGMGF) that will help develop guidelines related to the operation of microbial forensics.

Sources and additional reading:
Budowle, B., et al. (2005). Microbial forensics: The next forensic challenge. *International Journal of Legal Medicine, 119*, 317–330.

Budowle, B., et al. (2008). Criteria for validation of methods in microbial forensics. *Applied and Environmental Microbiology, 74*, 5599–5607.

FBI Amerithrax Investigation. http://www.fbi.gov/anthrax/amerithraxlinks.htm

Kiem, P. (2003). *Microbial forensics: A scientific assessment.* Washington, DC: American Academy of Microbiology. Available at http://academy.asm.org/images/stories/documents/microbialforensics.pdf

Keim, P., et al. (2008). Microbial forensics: DNA fingerprinting of *Bacillus anthracis* (Anthrax). *Analytical Chemistry, 80*, 4791–4799.

Popovic, T., & Glass, M. (2003). Laboratory aspects of bioterrorism-related anthrax—from identification to molecular subtyping to microbial forensics. *Croatian Medical Journal, 44*, 336–341.

SWGMGF. (2003). Quality assurance guidelines for laboratories performing microbial forensic work. *Forensic Science Communication, 5*(4). Available at http://www.fbi.gov/hq/lab/fsc/backissu/oct2003/2003_10_guide01.htm

U.S. Army Medical Research Institute of Infectious Diseases (USAMRIID). http://www.usamriid.army.mil

DNA databases for comparison purposes and use in calculating the probability of a chance match take time to develop and may not be in place prior to an investigation. Finding appropriate experts to review the scientific soundness of a novel application can also be challenging. Nevertheless, the power and influence of forensic DNA testing will continue to grow as it is used in more and more diverse applications to solve crimes that were previously inaccessible.

Points for Discussion

- What are some potential applications for additional STR loci?
- Why are SNPs being considered for use in human identity testing?
- What are the advantages and disadvantages of SNPs compared to currently used STR markers?
- Will SNPs replace STRs as a primary means of forensic DNA testing? Why or why not?
- Are there ethical challenges with using SNPs to predict ethnicity and physical traits? If so, what are they and how should the law enforcement community use this type of information in the future?
- What keeps forensic laboratories from performing more nonhuman DNA testing?
- What are some of the major challenges facing microbial forensics?

READING LIST AND INTERNET RESOURCES

General Information

Non-STR DNA Markers: SNPs, Y-STRs, LCN and mtDNA. http://www.dna.gov/training/markers

Additional STR Loci

Butler, J. M., et al. (2007). New autosomal and Y-chromosome STR loci: Characterization and potential uses. In: *Proceedings of the eighteenth international symposium on human identification*. Madison, WI: Promega Corporation. Available at http://www.promega.com/geneticidproc

Gill, P., et al. (2006). The evolution of DNA databases—Recommendations for new European STR loci. *Forensic Science International, 156*, 242–244.

Gill, P., et al. (2006). New multiplexes for Europe—Amendments and clarification of strategic development. *Forensic Science International, 163*, 155–157.

Grubwieser, P., et al. (2007). Evaluation of an extended set of 15 candidate STR loci for paternity and kinship analysis in an Austrian population sample. *International Journal of Legal Medicine, 121*, 85–89.

Henke, J., & Henke, L. (2005). Which short tandem repeat polymorphisms are required for identification? Lessons from complicated kinship cases. *Croatian Medical Journal, 46*, 593–597.

Henke, L., et al. (2007). Validation of a 'new' short tandem repeat (STR) fluorescent multiplex system and report of population genetic data. *Clinical Laboratory, 53*, 477–482.

Hill, C. R., et al. (2008). Characterization of 26 miniSTR loci for improved analysis of degraded DNA samples. *Journal of Forensic Sciences, 53*, 73–80.

Hou, J. Y., et al. (2008). How many markers are enough for motherless cases of parentage testing?. *Forensic Science International: Genetics Supplement, 1*, 649–651.

Karlsson, A. O., et al. (2007). DNA-testing for immigration cases: The risk of erroneous conclusions. *Forensic Science International, 172*, 144–149.

Single Nucleotide Polymorphisms

Brookes, A. J. (1999). The essence of SNPs. *Gene, 234*, 177–186.

Butler, J. M., et al. (2008). Report on ISFG SNP panel discussion. *Forensic Science International: Genetics Supplement, 1*, 471–472.

Syvanen, A. C. (2001). Accessing genetic variation: Genotyping single nucleotide polymorphisms. *Nature Reviews Genetics, 2*, 930–942.

Pros and cons

Amorim, A., & Pereira, L. (2005). Pros and cons in the use of SNPs in forensic kinship investigation: A comparative analysis with STRs. *Forensic Science International, 150*, 17–21.

Butler, J. M., et al. (2007). STRs vs SNPs: Thoughts on the future of forensic DNA testing. *Forensic Science, Medicine and Pathology, 3*, 200–205.

Chakraborty, R., et al. (1999). The utility of short tandem repeat loci beyond human identification: Implications for development of new DNA typing systems. *Electrophoresis, 20,* 1682–1696.

Gill, P. (2001). An assessment of the utility of single nucleotide polymorphisms (SNPs) for forensic purposes. *International Journal of Legal Medicine, 114,* 204–210.

Gill, P., et al. (2004). An assessment of whether SNPs will replace STRs in national DNA databases—Joint considerations of the DNA working group of the European Network of Forensic Science Institutes (ENFSI) and the Scientific Working Group on DNA Analysis Methods (SWGDAM). *Science & Justice, 44,* 51–53.

Phillips, C., et al. (2008). Resolving relationship tests that show ambiguous STR results using autosomal SNPs as supplementary markers. *Forensic Science International: Genetics, 2,* 198–204.

SNP Databases

ALFRED. http://alfred.med.yale.edu

dbSNP: http://www.ncbi.nlm.nih.gov/sites/entrez?db=snp

Park, J., et al. (2007). SNP@Ethnos: A database of ethnically variant single-nucleotide polymorphisms. *Nucleic Acids Research, 35,* D711–D715.

Smigielski, E. M., et al. (2000). dbSNP: A database of single nucleotide polymorphisms. *Nucleic Acids Research, 28,* 352–355.

SNP Consortium and now International HapMap Data. http://snp.cshl.org

SNPforID Browser. http://spsmart.cesga.es/snpforid.php

Thorisson, G. A., & Stein, L. D. (2003). The SNP Consortium Web site: Past, present and future. *Nucleic Acids Research, 31,* 124–127.

Analysis techniques

Ahmadian, A., et al. (2000). Single-nucleotide polymorphism analysis by pyrose-quencing. *Analytical Biochemistry, 280,* 103–110.

Armstrong, B., et al. (2000). Suspension arrays for high throughput, multiplexed single nucleotide polymorphism genotyping. *Cytometry, 40,* 102–108.

Budowle, B. (2004). SNP typing strategies. *Forensic Science International, 146S,* S139–S142.

Chen, X., & Sullivan, P. F. (2003). Single nucleotide polymorphism genotyping: Biochemistry, protocol, cost and throughput. *Pharmacogenomics Journal, 3,* 77–96.

Divne, A. M., & Allen, M. (2005). A DNA microarray system for forensic SNP analysis. *Forensic Science International, 154,* 111–121.

Gut, I. G. (2001). Automation in genotyping of single nucleotide polymorphisms. *Human Mutation, 17,* 475–492.

Heller, M. J., et al. (2000). Active microelectronic chip devices which utilize controlled electrophoretic fields for multiplex DNA hybridization and other genomic applications. *Electrophoresis, 21,* 157–164.

Kline, M. C., et al. (2005). Mitochondrial DNA typing screens with control region and coding region SNPs. *Journal of Forensic Sciences, 50,* 377–385.

Kwok, P. Y. (2001). Methods for genotyping single nucleotide polymorphisms. *Annual Review of Genomics and Human Genetics, 2,* 235–258.

Li, J., et al. (1999). Single nucleotide polymorphism determination using primer extension and time-of-flight mass spectrometry. *Electrophoresis, 20*, 1258–1265.

Li, L., et al. (2006). SNP genotyping by multiplex amplification and microarrays assay for forensic application. *Forensic Science International, 162*, 74–79.

Livak, K. J. (1999). Allelic discrimination using fluorogenic probes and the 5′ nuclease assay. *Genetic Analysis, 14*, 143–149.

McKeown, B., et al. (2006). Intramolecular controls for the generation of clinical-quality SNP genotypes and the assessment of normal heterozygote imbalance. *Electrophoresis, 27*, 1725–1731.

Saiki, R. K., et al. (1989). Genetic analysis of amplified DNA with immobilized sequence-specific oligonucleotide probes. In: *Proceedings of the National Academy of Sciences of the United States of America, 86*, 6230–6234.

Sobrino, B., et al. (2005). SNPs in forensic genetics: A review on SNP typing methodologies. *Forensic Science International, 154*, 181–194.

Tully, G., et al. (1996). Rapid detection of mitochondrial sequence polymorphisms using multiplex solid-phase fluorescent minisequencing. *Genomics, 34*, 107–113.

Wang, D. G., et al. (1998). Large-scale identification, mapping, and genotyping of single-nucleotide polymorphisms in the human genome. *Science, 280*, 1077–1082.

Ye, J., et al. (2002). Melting curve SNP (McSNP) genotyping: A useful approach for diallelic genotyping in forensic science. *Journal of Forensic Sciences, 47*, 593–600.

Markers and multiplexes

Budowle, B., & van Daal, A. (2008). Forensically relevant SNP classes. *Biotechniques, 44*, 603–610.

Dixon, L. A., et al. (2005). Validation of a 21-locus autosomal SNP multiplex for forensic identification purposes. *Forensic Science International, 154*, 62–77.

Kidd, K. K., et al. (2006). Developing a SNP panel for forensic identification of individuals. *Forensic Science International, 164*, 20–32.

Lee, H. Y., et al. (2005). Selection of twenty-four highly informative SNP markers for human identification and paternity analysis in Koreans. *Forensic Science International, 148*, 107–112.

Musgrave-Brown, E., et al. (2007). Forensic validation of the SNP*for*ID 52-plex assay. *Forensic Science International: Genetics, 1*, 186–190.

Pakstis, A. J., et al. (2007). Candidate SNPs for a universal individual identification panel. *Human Genetics, 121*, 305–317.

Phillips, C., et al. (2007). Evaluation of the Genplex SNP typing system and a 49plex forensic marker panel. *Forensic Science International: Genetics, 1*, 180–185.

Sanchez, J. J., et al. (2006). A multiplex assay with 52 single nucleotide polymorphisms for human identification. *Electrophoresis, 27*, 1713–1724.

Sanchez, J. J., et al. (2008). Forensic typing of autosomal SNPs with a 29 SNP-multiplex—Results of a collaborative EDNAP exercise. *Forensic Science International: Genetics, 2*, 176–183.

SNP*for*ID Project. http://www.snpforid.org

STRBase Forensic SNP Information (assays, markers, etc.). http://www.cstl.nist.gov/biotech/strbase/SNP.htm

Vallone, P. M., et al. (2005). Allele frequencies for 70 autosomal SNP loci with U.S. Caucasian, African-American, and Hispanic samples. *Forensic Science International*, *149*, 279–286.

Ethnicity estimation

Frudakis, T., et al. (2003). A classifier for the SNP-based inference of ancestry. *Journal of Forensic Sciences*, *48*, 771–782.

Frudakis, T. N. (2008). *Molecular photofitting: Predicting ancestry and phenotype using DNA.* San Diego: Elsevier Academic Press.

Pfaff, C. L., et al. (2004). Information on ancestry from genetic markers. *Genetic Epidemiology*, *26*, 305–315.

Phillips, C., et al. (2007). Inferring ancestral origin using a single multiplex assay of ancestry-informative marker SNPs. *Forensic Science International: Genetics*, *1*, 273–280.

Shriver, M. D., & Kittles, R. A. (2004). Genetic ancestry and the search for personalized genetic histories. *Nature Reviews Genetics*, *5*, 611–618.

Wetton, J. H., et al. (2005). Inferring the population of origin of DNA evidence within the UK by allele-specific hybridization of Y-SNPs. *Forensic Science International*, *152*, 45–53.

Physical traits

Branicki, W., et al. (2007). Determination of phenotype associated SNPs in the MC1R gene. *Journal of Forensic Sciences*, *52*, 349–354.

Duffy, D. L., et al. (2007). A three-single-nucleotide polymorphism haplotype in intron 1 of OCA2 explains most human eye-color variation. *American Journal of Human Genetics*, *80*, 241–252.

Frudakis, T., et al. (2003). Sequences associated with human iris pigmentation. *Genetics*, *165*, 2071–2083.

Grimes, E. A., et al. (2001). Sequence polymorphism in the human melanocortin 1 receptor gene as an indicator of the red hair phenotype. *Forensic Science International*, *122*, 124–129.

Lamason, R. L., et al. (2005). SLC24A5, a putative cation exchanger, affects pigmentation in zebrafish and humans. *Science*, *310*, 1782–1786.

Pulker, H., et al. (2007). Finding genes that underlie physical traits of forensic interest using genetic tools. *Forensic Science International: Genetics*, *1*, 100–104.

Sturm, R. A., et al. (2008). A single SNP in an evolutionary conserved region within intron 86 of the HERC2 gene determines human blue-brown eye color. *American Journal of Human Genetics*, *82*, 424–431.

Sulem, P., et al. (2007). Genetic determinants of hair, eye and skin pigmentation in Europeans. *Nature Genetics*, *39*, 1443–1452.

Tully, G. (2007). Genotype versus phenotype: Human pigmentation. *Forensic Science International: Genetics*, *1*, 105–110.

Other Biallelic Markers

Weber, J. L., et al. (2002). Human diallelic insertion/deletion polymorphisms. *American Journal of Human Genetics*, *71*, 854–862.

Nonhuman DNA

Budowle, B., et al. (2005). Recommendations for animal DNA forensic and identity testing. *International Journal of Legal Medicine, 119,* 295–302.

Coyle, H. M. (Ed.). (2008). *Nonhuman DNA typing: Theory and casework applications.* Boca Raton, FL: CRC Press.

D'Andrea, F., et al. (1998). Preliminary experiments on the transfer of animal hair during simulated criminal behavior. *Journal of Forensic Sciences, 43,* 1257–1258.

Halverson, J. L., et al. (2005). Forensic DNA identification of animal-derived trace evidence: Tools for linking victims and suspects. *Croatian Medical Journal, 46,* 598–605.

International Society of Animal Genetics (ISAG). http://www.isag.org.uk

QuestGen Forensics. http://www.questgen.biz and http://www.questgen.biz/cv.htm#casework

Sensabaugh, G., & Kaye, D. H. (1998). Nonhuman DNA evidence. *Jurimetrics Journal, 38,* 1–16.

UC-Davis Veterinary Forensic Genetics. http://www.vgl.ucdavis.edu/forensics

U.S. Fish and Wildlife Service. http://www.lab.fws.gov

Cat DNA Testing

Butler, J. M., et al. (2002). The MeowPlex: A new DNA test using tetranucleotide STR markers for the domestic cat. *Profiles in DNA, 5*(2), 7–10. Available at http://www.promega.com/profiles/502/ProfilesInDNA_502_07.pdf

Menotti-Raymond, M., et al. (1997). Genetic individualization of domestic cats using feline STR loci for forensic applications. *Journal of Forensic Sciences, 42,* 1039–1051.

Menotti-Raymond, M., et al. (1997). Pet cat hair implicates murder suspect. *Nature, 386,* 774.

Menotti-Raymond, M., et al. (2005). An STR forensic typing system for genetic individualization of domestic cat (*Felis catus*) samples. *Journal of Forensic Sciences, 50,* 1061–1070.

Menotti-Raymond, M., et al. (2008). Patterns of molecular genetic variation among cat breeds. *Genomics, 91,* 1–11.

Pet Food Institute. http://petfoodinstitute.org

STRBase Cat STRs information. http://www.cstl.nist.gov/biotech/strbase/catSTRs.htm

Dog DNA Testing

Berger, B., et al. (2008). Forensic canine STR analysis. In H. M. Coyle (Ed.), *Nonhuman DNA typing: Theory and casework applications* (Chapter 4, pp. 45–68). Boca Raton, FL: CRC Press.

Brauner, P., et al. (2001). DNA profiling of trace evidence—Mitigating evidence in a dog biting case. *Journal of Forensic Sciences, 46,* 1232–1234.

Eichmann, C., et al. (2004). Canine-specific STR typing of saliva traces on dog bite wounds. *International Journal of Legal Medicine, 118,* 337–342.

Eichmann, C., et al. (2005). Estimating the probability of identity in a random dog population using 15 highly polymorphic canine STR markers. *Forensic Science International, 151,* 37–44.

Eichmann, C., et al. (2007). Molecular characterization of the canine mitochondrial DNA control region for forensic applications. *International Journal of Legal Medicine, 121*, 411–416.

Gundry, R. L., et al. (2007). Mitochondrial DNA analysis of the domestic dog: Control region variation within and among breeds. *Journal of Forensic Sciences, 52*, 562–572.

Halverson, J., et al. (2005). A PCR multiplex and database for forensic DNA identification of dogs. *Journal of Forensic Sciences, 50*, 352–363.

Himmelberger, A. L., et al. (2008). Forensic utility of the mitochondrial hypervariable region 1 of domestic dogs, in conjunction with breed and geographic information. *Journal of Forensic Sciences, 53*, 81–89.

ISAG Canine Marker Panels. http://www.isag.org.uk/ISAG/all/2005ISAGPanelDOG.pdf

STRBase Dog STRs information. http://www.cstl.nist.gov/biotech/strbase/dogSTRs.htm

Wetton, J. H., et al. (2003). Mitochondrial profiling of dog hairs. *Forensic Science International, 133*, 235–241.

Species identification

Bataille, M., et al. (1999). Multiplex amplification of mitochondrial DNA for human and species identification in forensic evaluation. *Forensic Science International, 99*, 165–170.

Bellis, C., et al. (2003). A molecular genetic approach for forensic animal species identification. *Forensic Science International, 134*, 99–108.

Dawnay, N., et al. (2007). Validation of the barcoding gene COI for use in forensic genetic species identification. *Forensic Science International, 173*, 1–6.

Kitano, T., et al. (2007). Two universal primer sets for species identification among vertebrates. *International Journal of Legal Medicine, 121*, 423–427.

Melton, T., & Holland, C. (2007). Routine forensic use of the mitochondrial 12S ribosomal RNA gene for species identification. *Journal of Forensic Sciences, 52*, 1305–1307.

Parson, W., et al. (2000). Species identification by means of the cytochrome b gene. *International Journal of Legal Medicine, 114*, 23–28.

Unseld, M., et al. (1995). Identification of the species origin of highly processed meat products by mitochondrial DNA sequences. *PCR Methods and Applications, 4*, 241–243.

Plant DNA Testing

Howard, C., et al. (2008). Developmental validation of a *Cannabis sativa* STR multiplex system for forensic analysis. *Journal of Forensic Sciences, 53*, 1061–1067.

Miller-Coyle, H., et al. (2001). The Green Revolution: Botanical contributions to forensics and drug enforcement. *Croatian Medical Journal, 42*, 340–345.

Miller-Coyle, H., et al. (2003). An overview of DNA methods for the identification and individualization of marijuana. *Croatian Medical Journal, 44*, 315–321.

Miller-Coyle, H., et al. (2003). A simple DNA extraction method for marijuana samples used in amplified fragment length polymorphism (AFLP) analysis. *Journal of Forensic Sciences, 48*, 343–347.

Miller-Coyle, H., et al. (2005). Forensic botany: Using plant evidence to aid in forensic death investigation. *Croatian Medical Journal, 46*, 606–612.

Norris, D. O., & Bock, J. H. (2000). Use of fecal material to associate a suspect with a crime scene: Report of two cases. *Journal of Forensic Sciences, 45,* 184–187.

Virtanen, V., et al. (2007). Forensic botany: Usability of bryophyte material in forensic studies. *Forensic Science International, 172,* 161–163.

Ward, J., et al. (2005). A molecular identification system for grasses: A novel technology for forensic botany. *Forensic Sciences International, 152,* 121–131.

Yoon, C. K. (1993). Forensic science: Botanical witness for the prosecution. *Science, 260,* 894–895.

Bacterial DNA in soil

Heath, L. E., & Saunders, V. A. (2006). Assessing the potential of bacterial DNA profiling for forensic soil comparisons. *Journal of Forensic Sciences, 51,* 1062–1068.

Heath, L. E., & Saunders, V. A. (2008). Spatial variation in bacterial DNA profiles for forensic soil comparisons. *Canadian Society of Forensic Science Journal, 41,* 29–37.

Horswell, J., et al. (2002). Forensic comparisons of soils by bacterial community DNA profiling. *Journal of Forensic Sciences, 47,* 350–353.

Kang, S., & Mills, A. L. (2006). The effect of sample size in studies of soil microbial community structure. *Journal of Microbiological Methods, 66,* 242–250.

LaMontagne, M. G., et al. (2002). Evaluation of extraction and purification methods for obtaining PCR-amplifiable DNA from compost for microbial community analysis. *Journal of Microbiological Methods, 49,* 255–264.

Lerner, A., et al. (2006). Can denaturing gradient gel electrophoresis (DGGE) analysis of amplified 16s rDNA of soil bacterial populations be used in forensic investigations? *Soil Biology & Biochemistry, 38,* 1188–1192.

Schwarzenbach, K., et al. (2007). Objective criteria to assess representativity of soil fungal community profiles. *Journal of Microbiological Methods, 68,* 358–366.

Wildlife testing

Cassidy, B. G., & Gonzales, R. A. (2005). DNA testing in animal forensics. *Journal of Wildlife Management, 69,* 1454–1462.

Dawnay, N., et al. (2008). A forensic STR profiling system for the Eurasian badger: A framework for developing profiling systems for wildlife species. *Forensic Science International: Genetics, 2,* 47–53.

Jobin, R. M., et al. (2008). DNA typing in populations of mule deer for forensic use in the Province of Alberta. *Forensic Science International: Genetics, 2,* 190–197.

Jobin, R. M. (2008). Use of forensic DNA typing in wildlife investigations. In H. M. Coyle (Ed.), *Nonhuman DNA typing: Theory and casework applications* (Chapter 7, pp. 99–116). Boca Raton, FL: CRC Press.

Lorenzini, R. (2005). DNA forensics and the poaching of wildlife in Italy: A case study. *Forensic Science International, 153,* 218–221.

Tepnel Wildlife DNA Forensics. http://www.tepnel.com/ls-wildlife-forensic-applications.asp

Trent University Wildlife Forensic DNA Laboratory. http://www.forensicdna.ca

U.S. Fish and Wildlife Service Forensics Laboratory. http://www.lab.fws.gov

CHAPTER 16

Lineage Markers: Y Chromosome and mtDNA Testing

DNA is the messenger, which illuminates (our connection to the past), handed down from generation to generation, carried, literally, in the bodies of (our) ancestors. Each message traces a journey through time and space....

—Bryan Sykes, *The Seven Daughters of Eve*

LINEAGE MARKERS

Autosomal DNA markers, such as the 13 core short tandem repeat (STR) loci, are shuffled with each generation because half of an individual's genetic information comes from his or her father and half from his or her mother. However, the Y chromosome (ChrY) and mitochondrial DNA (mtDNA) markers that will be discussed in this chapter represent 'lineage markers.' They are passed down from generation to generation without changing (except for mutational events). Maternal lineages can be traced with mitochondrial DNA sequence information, whereas paternal lineages can be followed with Y-chromosome markers (Figure 16.1).

With lineage markers, the genetic information from each marker is referred to as a haplotype rather than a genotype because there is only a single allele per individual. Because Y chromosome markers are linked on the same chromosome and are not shuffled with each generation, the statistical calculations for a random match probability cannot involve the product rule. Therefore, haplotypes obtained from lineage markers can never be as effective in differentiating between two individuals as genotypes from autosomal markers that are unlinked and segregate separately from generation to generation. However, as will be discussed in this chapter, Y chromosome, X chromosome, and mitochondrial DNA markers can play an important role in forensic investigations as well as other applications.

Contribution of the National Institute of Standards and Technology, 2010.

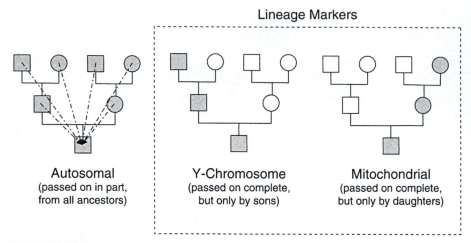

FIGURE 16.1

Illustration of inheritance patterns from recombining autosomal genetic markers and the lineage markers from the Y chromosome and mitochondrial DNA.

Y-CHROMOSOME DNA ANALYSIS

The human Y chromosome (ChrY) is the second smallest human chromosome with a length of approximately 60 million nucleotides. The tips of the Y chromosome, which are called the *pseudoautosomal regions*, recombine with their sister sex X-chromosome homologous regions. The remainder of the Y chromosome (~95%) is known as the *nonrecombining portion of the Y chromosome*, or NRY. The NRY remains the same from father to son unless a mutation occurs. Genetic polymorphisms including STRs and SNPs that occur along the NRY can be used to track male genetic pedigrees as they are passed on intact from father to son barring any mutations that may occur.

Applications of ChrY testing

Y-chromosome DNA testing is important for a number of different applications of human genetics including forensic evidence examination, paternity testing, historical investigations, studying human migration patterns throughout history, and genealogical research (Table 16.1).

The value of the Y chromosome in forensic DNA testing is that it is found only in males. The SRY (*sex-determining region of the Y*) gene determines maleness. Since a vast majority of crimes where DNA evidence is helpful, particularly sexual assaults, involve males as the perpetrators, DNA tests designed to only examine the male portion can be valuable.

With Y-chromosome tests, interpretable results can be obtained in some cases where autosomal tests are limited by the evidence, such as high levels of

Table 16.1 Areas of use in Y-chromosome testing.

Use	Advantage
Forensic casework on sexual assault evidence	Male-specific amplification (can avoid differential extraction to separate sperm and epithelial cells)
Verification of amelogenin Y–deficient males	Analysis of multiple regions along the Y chromosome that should not be affected by deletion of the amelogenin region
Paternity testing	Male children can be tied to fathers in motherless paternity cases or testing of male relatives if father is unavailable
Missing persons investigations	Patrilineal male relatives may be used for reference samples
Human migration and evolutionary studies	Lack of recombination enables comparison of male individuals separated by large periods of time
Historical and genealogical research	Surnames usually retained by males; can make links where paper trail is limited

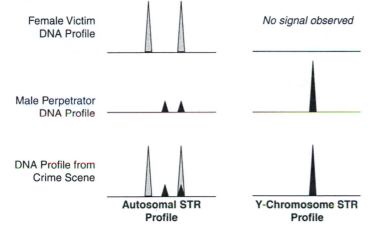

Female-Male Mixture Performance with Autosomal vs. Y-Chromosome DNA Markers

FIGURE 16.2

Schematic illustrating the types of autosomal or Y-STR profiles that might be observed with sexual assault evidence where mixtures of high amounts of female DNA may mask the STR profile of the perpetrator. Y-STR testing permits isolation of the male component without having to perform a differential lysis.

female DNA in the presence of minor amounts of male DNA (Figure 16.2). These situations include sexual assault evidence from azoospermic or vasectomized males and blood–blood or saliva–blood mixtures where the absence of sperm prevents a successful differential extraction for isolation of male DNA. In addition, the number of individuals involved in a 'gang rape' may be easier to decipher with Y-chromosome results than with highly complicated autosomal STR mixtures. The use of Y-chromosome-specific PCR primers can improve the chances of detecting low levels of the perpetrator's DNA in a high background of the female victim's DNA. Y-chromosome tests have also been used to verify amelogenin Y-deficient males.

The same feature of the Y chromosome that gives it an advantage in forensic testing, namely maleness, is also its biggest limitation. A majority of the Y chromosome is transferred directly from father to son (see Figure 16.1) without recombination to shuffle its genes and provide greater variety to future generations. Random mutations are the only mechanisms for variation over time between paternally related males. Thus, while exclusions in Y-chromosome DNA testing results can aid forensic investigations, a match between a suspect and evidence only means that the individual in question could have contributed the forensic stain—as could a brother, father, son, uncle, paternal cousin, or even a distant cousin from his paternal lineage! Needless to say, inclusions with Y-chromosome testing are not as meaningful as autosomal STR matches from a random match probability point of view.

On the other hand, the presence of relatives having the same Y chromosome (Figure 16.3) expands the number of possible reference samples in missing persons investigations and mass disaster victim identification efforts. Deficient paternity tests where the father is dead or otherwise unavailable for testing are benefited if Y-chromosome markers are used. However, an autosomal DNA test is always preferred if possible since it provides a higher power of discrimination.

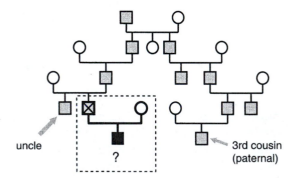

FIGURE 16.3

An example pedigree showing patrilineal inheritance where all shaded males have the same Y chromosome barring any mutations. To help identify the person in question, any of the other males with the same patrilineage could provide a reference sample to assist in a missing persons investigation, mass disaster victim identification, or deficient paternity test (boxed region) where the father is deceased or otherwise not available for testing.

The Y chromosome has also become a popular tool for tracing historical human migration patterns through male lineages. Anthropological, historical, and genealogical questions can be answered through Y-chromosome results. For example, Y-chromosome results in 1998 linked modern-day descendants of Thomas Jefferson and Eston Hemings, leading to the controversial conclusion that Jefferson fathered the slave (D.N.A. Box 16.1).

D.N.A. Box 16.1 The Thomas Jefferson–Sally Hemings Affair

In 1802, a year after becoming president of the United States, Thomas Jefferson was publicly accused by a Richmond, Virginia, newspaper of fathering a child by his slave, Sally Hemings. While it is uncertain how this accusation arose, the connection between Thomas Jefferson and his slave Sally Hemings has been a source of controversy for almost 200 years. In November 1998, the prestigious scientific journal *Nature* published a report that introduced DNA evidence into this historical controversy. The report, entitled 'Jefferson fathered slave's last child,' used Y-chromosome DNA markers to trace the Jefferson male line to a descendant of Sally Hemings's youngest son, Eston Hemings. The study involved 19 samples collected from living individuals who represented the Jefferson and Hemings line as well as other people who potentially could have been Jefferson's offspring or the father of Eston Hemings. These samples were tested at 19 different sites on the Y chromosome.

The study began in 1996 when Dr. Eugene Foster, a retired pathology professor, began tracking down living male-line relatives of President Thomas Jefferson. To show whether or not President Jefferson had fathered a child with Sally Hemings, direct male descendants were needed from both the Jefferson and the Hemings lines. Unfortunately, Jefferson's only legitimate son died in infancy. His two daughters who lived to adulthood obviously did not carry his Y chromosome and therefore their descendants were not useful in this study. There were two other possibilities for direct male-line descendants, Thomas Jefferson's brother Randolph and his father's brother Field. The last of the direct male descendants of Jefferson's brother Randolph died in the 1920s or 1930s so Dr. Foster turned to the relatives of President Jefferson's paternal uncle, Field Jefferson. Seven living descendants of Field Jefferson were located. Five of them agreed to cooperate in the study and had their blood drawn for Y-chromosome marker testing purposes.

On the Hemings side of the equation, it was even more difficult to come up with an abundance of living male relatives. Sally Hemings had at least six children: Harriet (1795–1797), Beverly (1798–post 1822), Harriet (1801–post 1822), an unnamed daughter (1799–1800), Madison (1805–1877), and Eston (1808–1856). According to the oral history of the descendants of Thomas Woodson (1790–1879), he was Sally Hemings's first child. Sally's son Beverly and daughter Harriet are listed as dying post 1822 because they disappeared into white society in the Washington, DC, area in the year 1822. Of the three known male sons from Sally Hemings, only descendants of Madison and Eston could possibly be located since Beverly's fate is unknown. Madison's Y-chromosome line ended in the mid-1800s when one of his three sons vanished into white society and the other two had no children. Thus, Eston Hemings's descendants remained the last chance to find a male-line descendant of the man who fathered Sally Hemings's children.

Eston Hemings was born on 21 May 1808, at Monticello where he lived until President Jefferson's death in 1826, at which time he was freed. Eventually he married and moved to Ohio and finally to Madison, Wisconsin, where he died and was buried in 1856. Eston assumed the surname of Jefferson when he left Virginia and gave everyone the impression that he was white because of his light skin color. Eston Hemings Jefferson had two sons and a daughter. His youngest son, Beverly Jefferson, lived from 1838–1908 and had one son. This son, Carl Smith Jefferson, lived from 1876–1941 and had two sons, William Magill Jefferson (1907–1956) and Carl Smith Jefferson, Jr. (1910–1948). Only William had a son. This son, John Weeks Jefferson, was born in 1946. As the *only* living male descendant of Eston Hemings, John Weeks Jefferson's blood was drawn to help answer the question of whether or not President Thomas Jefferson was Eston Hemings's father.

(Continued)

D.N.A. Box 16.1 (Continued)

Another important set of samples for testing was gathered from direct male-line descendants of Samuel and Peter Carr, who were Thomas Jefferson's nephews, the sons of his sister. According to Thomas Jefferson's grandchildren Thomas Jefferson Randolph and Ellen Coolidge, Samuel and Peter Carr were the fathers of the children of Sally Hemings and her sister. Dr. Foster collected three blood samples from living descendants of John Carr, the grandfather of Samuel and Peter Carr. Finally, five male descendants from several old-line Virginia families around Charlottesville were sampled to serve as control samples. These controls were tested to provide a 'background' signal with the idea that potential similarities in the Y-chromosome tests due to geographic proximity needed to be eliminated.

In all, 19 Y-chromosome markers were examined in this study. These included 11 STRs, seven SNPs, and one minisatellite MSY1, which proved to be the most polymorphic marker. All 19 regions of the Y chromosome examined in this study matched between the Jefferson and Hemings descendants.

These DNA results were viewed by Dr. Foster and his coauthors as evidence for President Thomas Jefferson fathering the last child of Sally Hemings. The John Carr lines differed significantly from the Jefferson–Hemings results with at least 7 of the 19 tested DNA markers giving different results. Thus, neither Samuel Carr nor Peter Carr was the father of Eston Hemings. The results of the Virginia old-line families were not reported, presumably because these samples served their purpose as effective controls and revealed no unusual Y-chromosome patterns.

Shortly after the results of Dr. Foster's study were announced, an alternative scenario was proposed. Could some other male Jefferson have fathered Eston Hemings? All the results in this study conclusively show is that there is a genetic match between descendants of Eston Hemings and Thomas Jefferson's uncle, Field Jefferson. Was it historically possible for another male Jefferson to have fathered Sally Hemings's children? The Thomas Jefferson Memorial Foundation, a private,

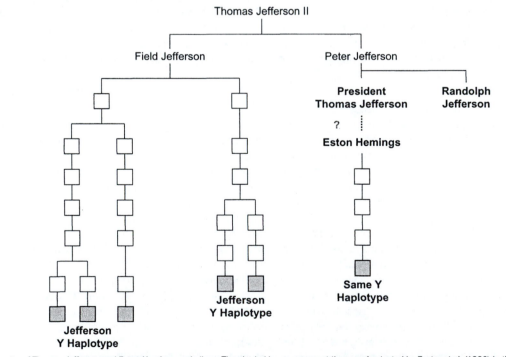

Ancestry of Thomas Jefferson and Eston Hemings male lines. The shaded boxes represent the samples tested by Foster et al. (1998) in their Jefferson Y-chromosome study. A male descendant of Eston Hemings, son of Thomas Jefferson's slave Sally Hemings, was found to have a Y-chromosome haplotype that matched male descendants of Field Jefferson, President Thomas Jefferson's uncle. Although he nor none of his descendants was tested, Randolph Jefferson, President Jefferson's brother, would also possess the same Y-chromosome haplotype.

nonprofit organization established in 1923 that owns and operates Monticello with the goal of preservation and education, conducted a yearlong investigation into the historical record.

According to this careful historical investigation, 25 adult male descendants of Thomas Jefferson's father Peter and his uncle Field lived in Virginia during the 1794–1807 period of Sally Hemings's pregnancies (Monticello, 2000). Most of them lived over 100 miles from Monticello and make no appearance in Thomas Jefferson's correspondence documents. Several male Jeffersons including President Jefferson's brother Randolph and his sons did live in the area of Monticello and visited occasionally. However, the historical records fail to indicate that any of these individuals were present at Monticello 9 months before the births of Sally Hemings's children. This information combined with the fact that Thomas Jefferson was present at Monticello during the time of conception of each of Sally Hemings's six children led to the 26 January 2000 Thomas Jefferson Memorial Foundation report that he was the father of all of Sally Hemings's children.

A more recent study by a 13-member Scholars Commission of the Thomas Jefferson Heritage Society unanimously agreed that the allegations of a relationship are 'by no means proven.' The findings of this group are reported in a 565-page report available at the Heritage Society's Web site: http://www.tjheritage.org. This report notes that the original DNA study indicated only that a Jefferson male had fathered one of Sally Hemings's children and that the available DNA evidence could not specify Thomas Jefferson as the father *to the exclusion of all other possibilities*. Thomas Jefferson's younger brother Randolph, who was known to fraternize with the Monticello slaves, is considered a likely possibility by many members of the Scholars Commission. Randolph and other family members would have visited Monticello when President Jefferson was home and therefore the circumstantial evidence of Thomas Jefferson being present on the plantation when Sally Hemings conceived might not be as strong as originally presented.

This study of Jefferson lineage DNA demonstrates one of the major disadvantages of Y-chromosome DNA testing, namely that results only indicate connection to a male lineage and are not specific to an individual like autosomal STR profiles can be. While a Jefferson Y-chromosome match exists between his descendants and those of Sally Hemings, the matter can probably never be definitely solved by Y-chromosome information alone.

Sources:

Foster, E. A., et al. (1998). Jefferson fathered slave's last child. *Nature, 396*, 27–28.

Monticello. (2000). Thomas Jefferson Memorial Foundation Research Committee Report on Thomas Jefferson and Sally Hemings, 26 January 2000. Available at http://www.monticello.org

Murray, B., & Duffy, B. (1998). *US News and World Report*, 1998, November 9. pp. 59–63.

ChrY markers

Y-chromosome DNA analysis can be performed with either Y-STRs or Y-SNPs. Since Y-STRs change more rapidly (mutation rate ~ 1 in 10^3) compared to Y-SNPs (mutation rate ~ 1 in 10^9), Y-STR results exhibit more variability and thus have greater use in forensic applications. Typically Y-STRs are described as defining haplotypes while Y-SNPs define haplogroups. Y-SNPs can be useful in DNA ancestry studies.

Although more than 400 Y-STR loci have been mapped along the human Y chromosome, only a small set of core loci are routinely analyzed. In 1997, the European forensic community settled on a core set of Y-STR markers or 'minimal haplotype.' that includes DYS19, DYS389I/II, DYS390, DYS391, DYS392, DYS393, and DYS385 a/b. Most Y-chromosome data to date has been generated with these loci. In 2003, the U.S. Scientific Working Group on DNA Analysis Methods (SWGDAM) recommended a core set of Y-STRs that includes the nine markers in the minimal haplotype plus DYS438 and DYS439. These loci are available in commercial Y-STR kits (see next section).

Although new markers will be added to databases as their value is demonstrated and they become part of commercially available kits, these 11 established markers are likely to continue to be important in future Y-STR research.

Y-STR kits

As discussed previously in Chapter 8, forensic scientists rely heavily on commercially available kits to perform DNA testing. Table 16.2 lists the loci present in the two most widely used Y-STR kits (Table 16.3): PowerPlex Y (Promega Corporation) and Yfiler (Applied Biosystems). Note that all of the European and U.S. core Y-STR loci are included in both kits with PowerPlex Y having one additional locus (DYS437) and Yfiler have six additional loci (DYS437, DYS448, DYS456, DYS458, DYS635, and GATA-H4). A Yfiler kit PCR amplification result is shown in Figure 16.4.

Table 16.2 Characteristics of commonly used Y-chromosome STR loci.

STR Marker	Position (Mb)	Repeat Motif	Allele Range	Mutation Rate
DYS393	3.19	AGAT	8–17	0.08%
DYS456	4.33	AGAT	13–18	0.72%
DYS458	7.93	GAAA	14–20	1.1%
DYS19	10.13	TAGA	10–19	0.24%
DYS391	12.61	TCTA	6–14	0.29%
DYS635	12.89	TSTA	17–27	0.42%
DYS437	12.98	TCTR	13–17	0.15%
DYS439	13.03	AGAT	8–15	0.54%
DYS389 I/II	13.12	TCTR	9–17/24–34	0.19%/0.30%
DYS438	13.38	TTTTC	6–14	0.05%
DYS390	15.78	TCTR	17–28	0.24%
GATA–H4	17.25	TAGA	8–13	0.25%
DYS385 a/b	19.26	GAAA	7–28	0.22%
DYS392	21.04	TAT	6–20	0.06%
DYS448	22.78	AGAGAT	17–24	0.18%

Adapted from Butler, J. M. (2006). Genetics and genomics of core short tandem repeat loci used in human identity testing. Journal of Forensic Sciences, 51, 253–265; Decker, A. E., et al. (2007). The impact of additional Y-STR loci on resolving common haplotypes and closely related individuals. Forensic Sciences International: Genetics, 1, 215–217; and Decker, A. E., et al. (2008). Analysis of mutations in father–son pairs with 17 Y-STR loci. Forensic Sciences International: Genetics, 2, e31–e35.

Table 16.3 Commercially available Y-STR kits. Characteristics of each locus may be found in Table 16.2.

Kit Name (Source)	Dye Color	Loci Amplified Arranged by Size
PowerPlex Y (Promega Corporation)	Blue	DYS391, DYS389I, DYS439, DYS389II
	Green	DYS438, DYS437, DYS19, DYS392
	Yellow	DYS393, DYS390, DYS385a/b
Yfiler (Applied Biosystems)	Blue	DYS456, DYS389I, DYS390, DYS389II
	Green	DYS458, DYS19, DYS385a/b
	Yellow	DYS393, DYS391, DYS439, C4, DYS392
	Red	H4, DYS437, DYS438, DYS448

Note: An internal size standard is typically run in the fourth or fifth dye position on multicolor fluorescence detection systems for allele sizing purposes. The underlined loci, such as DYS437 present in the PowerPlex Y kit, are not part of the core Y-STR loci.

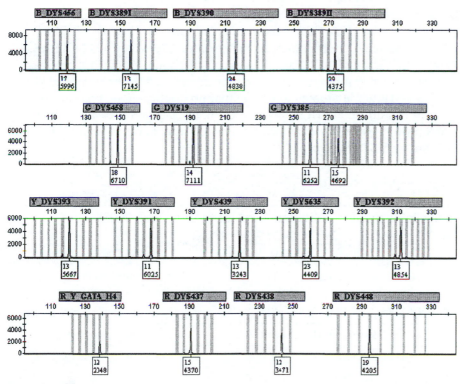

FIGURE 16.4

Yfiler result from a single-source male of European ancestry. Allele calls and peak heights are shown under each peak. (Figure courtesy of Amy Decker, NIST.)

Y-STR haplotype databases

A number of online Y-STR databases exist (Table 16.4). The forensic databases contain collections of anonymous individuals and can be used to estimate the frequency of specified Y-STR haplotypes. The genetic genealogy databases, such as Ysearch and Ybase, contain Y-STR haplotype information gathered by genetic genealogy companies with different sets of loci from males trying to make genealogical connections. Thus, the haplotypes in these genealogy databases are associated with specific individuals and family names.

The largest and most widely used forensic and general population genetics Y-STR database, known as the Y-STR Haplotype Reference Database (YHRD), was created by Lutz Roewer and colleagues at Humbolt University in Berlin, Germany, and has been available online since 2000. As of December 2008, YHRD contains results from more than 65,000 samples representing greater than 500 different groups of sample submissions from various populations around the world.

A U.S.-population-specific Y-STR Database (US Y-STR) was launched in December 2007 to enable haplotype frequency estimates on five different U.S. groups using the 11 SWGDAM recommended loci. The original version of US Y-STR contained 4796 African American profiles, 820 Asian, 5047 Caucasians, 2260 Hispanics, and 983 Native Americans. In some cases, further subdivision of these five primary groups can be examined if desired. Where possible, US Y-STR has attempted to ensure that no duplicates are present through examining autosomal STR typing results on any samples possessing the same Y-STR profile. Having both autosomal and Y-STR data can be helpful in cases of common Y-STR haplotypes.

Table 16.4 Summary of available online Y-STR databases (as of December 2008).

Database	Number of Samples (Population Groups)	Number of Y-STR Markers Tested	Web Site
Y-STR Haplotype Reference Database (YHRD)	65,165 (517 groups)	7 to 17	http://www.YHRD.org
US Y-STR Database (US Y-STR)	13,906 (5 groups)	11 to 17	http://www.usystrdatabase.org
Ysearch	65,869 (genealogists)	Up to 100	http://www.ysearch.org
Ybase	13,830 (genealogists)	Up to 49	http://www.ybase.org
Sorenson Molecular Genealogy Foundation	>30,000 (genealogists)	Up to 43	http://www.smgf.org

Note: For updated information, see http://www.cstl.nist.gov/biotech/strbase/y_strs.htm

Several genetic genealogy Y-STR haplotype databases are also available online. These databases are typically not used for Y-STR forensic haplotype frequency estimates, but could be helpful in trying to associate a family surname with a particular haplotype if this information was desired in an investigation. These genetic genealogy databases contain information from the minimal haplotype loci, a subset of the minimal haplotype loci, or additional Y-STRs, and therefore cannot always be searched across all loci of interest.

Interpretation of Y-STR results

Since the Y chromosome is passed down unchanged (except for mutations) from father to son, the observation of a match with Y-STRs does not carry the same power of discrimination and weight in court as an autosomal STR match would. The lack of recombination between Y-chromosome markers means that Y-STR results have to be combined into a haplotype for searching available databases as well as estimating the rarity of a particular haplotype.

Generally speaking there are three possible interpretations resulting from comparing Y-STR haplotypes produced from question (Q) and known (K) samples: (1) *exclusion* because the Y-STR profiles are different and could not have originated from the same source, (2) *inconclusive* where data are insufficient to render an interpretation or ambiguous results were obtained, or (3) *failure to exclude* (or *inclusion*) because the Y-STR haplotype results from the Q-K comparison are the same and could have originated from the same source.

When the Q and K samples (e.g., evidence and suspect haplotypes) do not match, then Y-STR typing is helpful in demonstrating the exclusion. However, estimating the strength of a match when a suspect's Y-STR haplotype cannot be excluded is more problematic because barring any mutations, paternal relatives (e.g., all brothers, male children, father, uncles, paternal grandfather, and paternal cousins) would be expected to have the same Y-STR profile.

Since it is common practice to place some significance on the likelihood of a random match with unrelated individuals, statistics derived from population data can be applied. Estimates for a random match with Y-STR haplotypes (and mtDNA sequence information) are done by the *counting method*, where the number of times the haplotype of interest is observed is divided by the total number of haplotypes in the database used. The size of the database used for the counting method makes a difference when trying to estimate the rarity of a Y-STR profile. The larger the number of unrelated individuals in the database (i.e., the denominator in the counting method calculation), the better the statistics will be for a random match frequency estimate.

The Y-STR profile observed earlier in Figure 16.4 is found zero times in 10, 243 17-locus haplotypes found in YHRD and zero times in 4163 17-locus

D.N.A. Box 16.2 Calculation of Y-STR Haplotype Frequency Estimates Using the Counting Method

In cases where a Y-STR haplotype is observed a particular number of times (X) in a database containing N profiles, its frequency (p) can be calculated as follows:

$$p = X/N$$

A 95% upper bound confidence interval (CI) can be placed on the profile's frequency using:

$$p + 1.96\sqrt{\frac{(p)(1-p)}{N}}$$

In cases where the profile has not been observed in a database, the upper bound CI is

$$1 - \alpha^{1/N} \quad \text{or} \quad 1 - (0.05)^{1/N}$$

where α is the confidence coefficient (0.05 for a 95% confidence interval) and N is the number of individuals in the database.

Using the haplotype results from the 17-locus Yfiler profile seen in Figure 16.4, a search was performed using the YHRD and US Y-STR databases. Subsets of the same haplotype were also searched using the Y-STR loci present in the 12-locus PowerPlex Y, 11-locus SWGDAM recommended, 9-locus European minimal haplotype, and 7-locus minimal haplotype minus DYS385 a/b.

Note that the size of the database (N)—and therefore the denominator of the counting method—changes depending on the number of Y-STR loci searched because these databases contain fewer complete 17-locus Yfiler haplotypes compared to the usual full set of minimal haplotype results. As with any investigation, the relevance of using an entire world survey of Y-STR haplotypes rather than a specific ethnic or geographic group for a population comparison must also be considered within the scope of the case. The results from several different population databases could be utilized in a case report for comparison purposes. In the end, comparisons would only be reported where results were available for both the Q and K samples.

Sources:
Y-STR Haplotype Reference Database (YHRD). http://www.yhrd.org
US Y-STR Database. http://www.usystrdatabase.org

YHRD	Search Results	Upper Bound CI	~1 in Every...
17-locus	0/10243	0.029%	3420
12-locus	3/13751	0.047%	2150
11-locus	18/36174	0.073%	1375
9-locus	307/63369	0.539%	186
7-locus	2099/65165	3.36%	30

US Y-STR	Search Results	Upper Bound CI	~1 in Every...
17-locus	0/4163	0.072%	1390
12-locus	7/10865	0.112%	892
11-locus	19/13906	0.198%	505
9-locus	128/13906	1.08%	93
7-locus	846/13906	6.48%	15

haplotypes found in US Y-STR. D.N.A. Box 16.2 works through some example calculations with searches using subsets of the 17 Yfiler loci.

Frequency estimates calculated with the counting method, while not as powerful as those produced with unlinked autosomal STRs, may nevertheless be informative in many forensic casework scenarios and provide another piece of evidence in the overall framework of a case.

MITOCHONDRIAL DNA ANALYSIS

Conventional STR typing systems do not work in every instance—even with the development of the miniSTR assays mentioned in Chapter 14. Ancient DNA specimens or samples that have been highly degraded often fail to produce results with nuclear DNA typing systems. However, recovery of DNA information from environmentally damaged DNA is sometimes possible with mitochondrial DNA (mtDNA). While a nuclear DNA test is usually more valuable, a mtDNA result is better than no result at all.

Because there are hundreds if not thousands of copies of mtDNA in each cell, the probability of obtaining a DNA typing result from mtDNA is higher than that of polymorphic markers found in nuclear DNA, particularly in cases where the amount of extracted DNA is very small, as in tissues such as bone, teeth, and hair. When remains are quite old or badly degraded, often bone, teeth, and hair are the only biological sources left from which to draw a sample.

The following sections will review the characteristics of mitochondrial DNA, the steps involved in obtaining results in forensic casework, and issues important to interpreting mtDNA results.

Characteristics of mtDNA

The primary characteristic that permits mtDNA recovery from degraded samples is the higher copy number of mtDNA in cells relative to the nuclear DNA from which STRs are amplified. In short, though nuclear DNA contains much more information, there are only two copies of it in each cell (one maternal and one paternal) while mtDNA has a bit of useful genetic information times hundreds of copies per cell. With a higher copy number, some mtDNA molecules are more likely to survive than nuclear DNA. Table 16.5 contains a comparison of some basic characteristics of nuclear DNA and mitochondrial DNA.

Location and structure of mtDNA

The vast majority of the human genome is located within the nucleus of each cell. However, there is a small, circular genome found within the mitochondria, the energy-producing cellular organelle residing in the cytoplasm. The number of mtDNA molecules within a cell can range from hundreds to thousands.

Mitochondrial DNA has approximately 16,569 base pairs; the total number of nucleotides in a mtDNA genome (mtGenome) can vary due to small mutations that are either insertions or deletions. Most of the mtGenome codes for 37 gene products used in the oxidative phosphorylation process or cellular energy production (Figure 16.5). There is also a 1122-bp 'control' region that contains the origin of replication for one of the mtDNA strands but does not code for any gene products and is therefore referred to sometimes as the 'noncoding' region.

Table 16.5 Comparison of human nuclear DNA and mitochondrial DNA markers.

Characteristics	Nuclear DNA	Mitochondrial DNA (mtDNA)
Size of genome	~3.2 billion bp	~16,569 bp
Copies per cell	2 (1 allele from each parent)	Can be >1000
Percent of total DNA	99.75%	0.25% content per cell
Structure	Linear; packaged in chromosomes	Circular
Inherited from	Father and mother	Mother
Chromosomal pairing	Diploid	Haploid
Generational recombination	Yes	No
Replication repair	Yes	No
Unique	Unique to individual (except identical twins)	Not unique to individual (same as maternal relatives)
Mutation rate	Low	At least 5–10 times nuclear DNA
Reference sequence	Described in 2001 by the Human Genome Project	Described in 1981 by Anderson and coworkers

There is an asymmetric distribution of nucleotides in the mtGenome that gives rise to a 'light' and 'heavy' strand. The 'heavy' or H-strand contains a greater number of guanine nucleotides, which have the largest relative molecular mass of the four nucleotides (A, T, C, and G), than the 'light' or L-strand. Replication of mtDNA begins with the H-strand in the noncoding 'control region,' also known as the displacement loop or D-loop.

Since the D-loop does not code for gene products, the constraints are fewer for nucleotide variability, and polymorphisms between individuals are more abundant than in similarly sized portions of the coding region. More simply, there can be differences in the D-loop region because the sequences do not code for any substances necessary for the cell's function.

Most of the focus in forensic DNA studies to date has involved two hypervariable regions within the control region commonly referred to as HVI (HV1) and HVII (HV2). Occasionally a third portion of the control region, known as HV3, is examined to provide more information regarding a tested sample.

Human mtDNA reference sequence(s)

Human mtDNA was first sequenced in 1981 in the laboratory of Frederick Sanger in Cambridge, England. For many years, the original 'Anderson' sequence

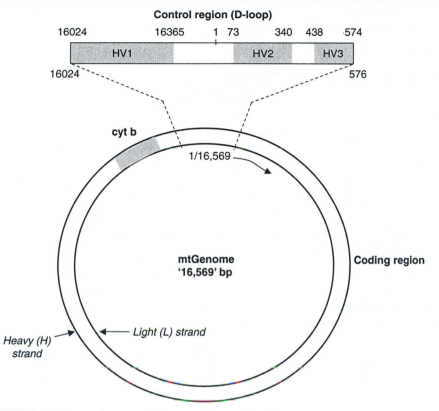

FIGURE 16.5

Illustration of the circular mitochondrial DNA genome (mtGenome). The heavy (H) strand is represented by the outside line and contains a higher number of C-G residues than the light (L) strand. Most forensic mtDNA analyses presently examine only HV1 and HV2 (and occasionally HV3) in the noncoding control region (also known as the displacement loop or D-loop) shown at the top of the figure. Due to insertions and deletions that exist around the mtGenome in different individuals, it is not always 16,569 bp in length. Sequence analysis of the cytochrome b gene (cyt b) is sometimes used for species identification.

(named after the first author listed in alphabetical order from the Sanger research group) was the reference sequence to which new sequences were compared. The Anderson sequence is also referred to as the Cambridge Reference Sequence (CRS). In 1999, the original placental material used by Anderson and coworkers to generate the CRS was resequenced. This revised Cambridge reference sequence (rCRS) is now the accepted standard for comparison.

To track work with a specific mtDNA sequence, results are commonly reported in comparison to the rCRS reference sequence. Nucleotide positions within the mtDNA molecule are numbered from 1 to 16,569 using the L-strand sequence with position 1 arbitrarily coming from a restriction enzyme site found in the control region. The HV1 region commonly used in forensic labs spans positions 16,024 to 16,365, or 342 bp, while HV2 covers positions 73 to 340, or 268 bp. Thus, use of both HV1 and HV2 provides examination of 610 bp of mtDNA sequence.

Maternal inheritance of mtDNA

Human mtDNA is considered to be inherited strictly from one's mother. At conception only the sperm's nucleus enters the egg and joins directly with the egg's nucleus. The fertilizing sperm does not contribute other cellular components. When the zygote cell divides and a blastocyst develops, the cytoplasm and other cell parts except the nucleus are consistent with the mother's original egg cell. Mitochondria with their mtDNA molecules are passed directly to all offspring independent of any male influence. Thus, barring mutation, a mother passes along her mtDNA type to her children, and therefore siblings and maternal relatives have an identical mtDNA sequence. Hence, an individual's mtDNA type is not unique to him or her.

An example family pedigree is shown in Figure 16.6 to demonstrate the inheritance pattern of mtDNA. In this example, unique mtDNA types exist solely for individuals 1, 5, 7, and 12. Note that individual 16 will possess the same mtDNA type as seven of the other represented individuals (e.g., 2, 3,

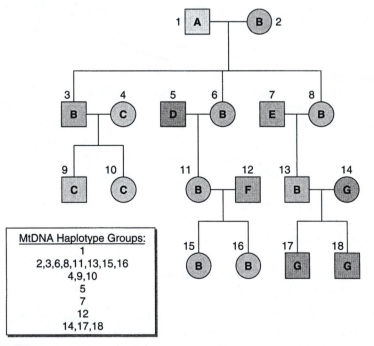

MtDNA Haplotype Groups:
1
2,3,6,8,11,13,15,16
4,9,10
5
7
12
14,17,18

FIGURE 16.6

Illustration of maternal mitochondrial DNA inheritance for 18 individuals in a hypothetical pedigree. Squares represent males and circles females. Each unique mtDNA type is represented by a different letter.

6, 8, 11, 13, and 15). This can be helpful in solving missing persons or mass disaster investigations but can reduce the significance of a match in forensic cases. Since even distantly related maternal relatives should possess the same mtDNA type, this extends the number of useful reference samples that may be used to confirm the identity of a missing person.

Steps involved in obtaining mtDNA results

The steps involved in performing mitochondrial DNA sequence comparisons are illustrated in Figure 16.7. Extraction of the mtDNA needs to be performed in a very clean laboratory environment because mtDNA is more sensitive to

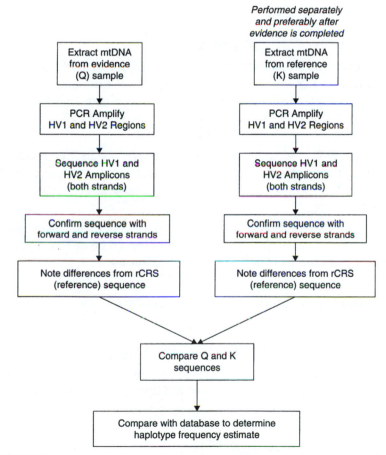

FIGURE 16.7

Process for evaluating mtDNA samples. The evidence or question (Q) sample may come from a crime scene or a mass disaster. The reference or known (K) sample may be a maternal relative or the suspect in a criminal investigation. In a criminal investigation, the victim may also be tested and compared to the Q and K results.

contamination than nuclear DNA since it is in a higher copy number per cell. Thus, it is preferable to analyze the reference samples after the evidence samples have been completely processed to avoid any potential contamination.

Mitochondrial DNA analysis is commonly performed using the Sanger sequencing chemistry introduced in Chapter 3. This DNA sequencing is performed in both the forward and reverse directions so that the complementary strands can be compared to one another for quality control purposes.

Typically laboratories report results in terms of variation compared the rCRS. Thus, the observation of a C nucleotide at position 16,126, which contains a T in the reference sequence, would be reported as 16126C. If no other nucleotide variants are reported, then it is assumed that the remaining sequence contains the same sequence as the rCRS.

Interpretation of mtDNA results

Following completion of mtDNA sequence analysis as outlined in Figure 16.7, results from the edited and reviewed sequences for a question (Q) and a known (K) sample are compared as illustrated in Figure 16.8 for a portion of HV1. All 610 nucleotides (positions 16,024–16,365 and 73–340) are normally evaluated between samples being compared.

Based on the Q-K comparison, mtDNA sequence results can generally be grouped into three categories: exclusion, inconclusive, or failure to exclude. The SWGDAM guidelines for mtDNA interpretation make the following recommendations:

- *Exclusion:* If there are two or more nucleotide differences between the questioned and known samples, the samples can be excluded as originating from the same person or maternal lineage.

(a) mtDNA Sequences Aligned with rCRS (positions 16071–16140)

```
          16090       16100       16110       16120       16130       16140

rCRS ACCGCTATGT ATTTCGTACA TTACTGCCAG CCACCATGAA TATTGTAGGG TACCATAAAT

   Q ACCGCTATGT ATCTCGTACA TTACTGCCAG CCACCATGAA TATTGTACAG TACCATAAAT

   K ACCGCTATGT ATCTCGTACA TTACTGCCAG CCACCATGAA TATTGTACAG TACCATAAAT
```

(b) Reporting Format with Differences from rCRS

Sample Q	Sample K
16093C	16093C
16129A	16129A

FIGURE 16.8

(a) Comparison of sequence alignments for hypothetical Q and K samples with (b) conversion to the revised Cambridge reference sequence (rCRS) differences for reporting purposes.

- *Inconclusive:* If there is one nucleotide difference between the questioned and known samples, the result will be inconclusive.
- *Cannot exclude (failure to exclude):* If the sequences from questioned and known samples under comparison have a common base at each position or a common length variant in the HV2 C-stretch, the samples cannot be excluded as originating from the same person or maternal lineage.

The reason that a single base difference is classified in terms of an 'inconclusive result' is that mutations have been observed between mother and children. For example, if a maternal relative is used for a reference sample, the possibility of a single base difference may exist between two samples that are in fact maternally related. Often additional samples, usually more reference samples, are run if an inconclusive result is obtained in an attempt to clarify the interpretation.

When 'failure to exclude' is the interpretation for reference and evidence samples, then a statistical estimate of the significance of a match is needed. Mitochondrial DNA is inherited in its entirety from one's mother without recombination (see Figure 16.1). Therefore, individual nucleotide positions are inherited in a block and must be treated as a single locus haplotype, the same as with Y-chromosome information discussed earlier in this chapter. The product rule applied to independently segregating STR loci found on separate chromosomes cannot be used with mtDNA polymorphisms.

As previously noted with Y-STR interpretation, the current practice of conveying the rarity of a mtDNA type among unrelated individuals involves counting the number of times a particular haplotype (sequence) is seen in a database. This approach is commonly referred to as the 'counting method' and depends entirely on the number of samples present in the database that is searched.

Population frequencies for most DNA types (around 60%) are not known presently because they occur only a single time in a database. Based on available population information, confidence intervals can be used to estimate the upper bound of a frequency calculation (D.N.A. Box 16.3). It is important to keep in mind that mtDNA can never have the power of discrimination that an autosomal STR marker can since its inheritance is uniparental.

Other issues with mtDNA

Several other issues that often arise when considering mtDNA data from forensic evidence are introduced in this section. The accompanying *Advanced Topics* volume will cover these issues in greater detail.

D.N.A. Box 16.3 Calculation of mtDNA Profile Frequency Estimates Using the Counting Method

In cases where an mtDNA profile is observed a particular number of times (X) in a database containing N profiles, its frequency (p) can be calculated as follows:

$$p = X/N$$

A 95% upper bound confidence interval can be placed on the profile's frequency using:

$$p + 1.96\sqrt{\frac{(p)(1-p)}{N}}$$

In cases where the profile has not been observed in a database, the upper bound on the confidence interval is

$$1 - \alpha^{1/N} \quad \text{or} \quad 1 - (0.05)^{1/N}$$

where α is the confidence coefficient (0.05 for a 95% confidence interval) and N is the number of individuals in the database.

For example, the mtDNA type 16129A, 263G, 309d, 315.1C occurs twice in 1148 African American profiles, twice in 1655 Caucasian profiles, and not at all in 686 Hispanic profiles when searched against the mtDNA Population Database

(Monson et al., 2002). Using the equations above, calculations for the rarity of this profile in the respective sample sets are as follows:

For African Americans: p = 2/1148 + 1.96 [(2/1148)(1 − (2/1148))/1148]$^{1/2}$ = 0.0017 + 0.002 = 0.004 = 0.4%

For Caucasians: p = 2/1655 + 1.96 [(2/1655)(1 − (2/1655))/1655]$^{1/2}$ = 0.0012 + 0.0017 = 0.0029 = 0.29%

For Hispanics: 1 − (0.05)$^{1/686}$ = 1 − 0.9956 = 0.0044 = 0.44%

These calculations demonstrate that the statistical weight can be similar whether or not a match is found to a few previously observed samples in a database.

Sources:
Evett, I. W., & Weir, B. S. (1998). *Interpreting DNA evidence.* Sunderland, MA: Sinauer Associates (p. 142).
Monson, K. L., et al. (2002). The mtDNA population database: An integrated software and database resource. *Forensic Science Communications,* 4(2). Available at http://www.fbi.gov/hq/lab/fsc/backissu/april2002/miller1.htm
Tully, G., et al. (2001). Considerations by the European DNA profiling (EDNAP) group on the working practices, nomenclature and interpretation of mitochondrial DNA profiles. *Forensic Science International,* 124, 83–91.

Heteroplasmy

Heteroplasmy is the presence of more than one mtDNA type in an individual. Two or more mtDNA populations may occur between cells in an individual, within a single cell, or within a single mitochondrion. It is now thought that all individuals are heteroplasmic at some level—many below the limits of detection in DNA sequence analysis. It is highly unlikely that millions of mtDNA molecules scattered throughout an individual's cells are completely identical given that regions of the mtGenome have been reported to evolve at 6 to 17 times the rate of single-copy nuclear genes.

Heteroplasmy may be observed in several ways: (1) Individuals may have more than one mtDNA type in a single tissue; (2) individuals may exhibit one mtDNA type in one tissue and a different type in another tissue; and/or (3) individuals may be heteroplasmic in one tissue sample and homoplasmic in another tissue sample. Given that heteroplasmy happens, interpretation guidelines must take into account how to handle differences between known and questioned samples.

Both sequence and length heteroplasmy have been reported. Length heteroplasmies often occur around the homopolymeric C-stretches in HV1 at positions 16,184 to 16,193 and HV2 at positions 303 to 310. Sequence heteroplasmy is typically detected by the presence of two nucleotides at a single site, which show up as overlapping peaks in a sequence electropherogram.

One of the major challenges of heteroplasmic samples is that the ratio of bases may not stay the same across different tissues, such as blood and hair or between multiple hairs. Some mtDNA protocols now recommend sequencing multiple hairs from an individual in order to confirm heteroplasmy. While heteroplasmy can sometimes complicate the interpretation of mtDNA results, the presence of heteroplasmy at identical sites can improve the probability of a match, such as seen in the Romanov investigation (see D.N.A. Box 16.5 later in chapter).

Sample mixtures

A major advantage of mtDNA in terms of sequencing is that it is haploid and therefore only a single type exists for analysis (barring detectable heteroplasmy). However, mixed samples from more than one biological source are commonly encountered in forensic settings. Generally attempts are not made to decipher samples containing a mixture of individuals due to the complexity of the sequencing signals that could arise. If three or more sites within the 610 bases evaluated across HV1 and HV2 are found to possess multiple nucleotides at a position (i.e., sequence heteroplasmy), then the sample can usually be considered a mixture—either by contamination or from the original source material.

Presently mixture interpretation is not routinely attempted in forensic laboratories. However, it has been demonstrated that some mtDNA mixtures can be resolved through cloning and sequencing the resulting HV1/HV2 regions from individual colonies. Denaturing HPLC has also been used to separate mtDNA amplicon mixtures.

Nuclear pseudogenes

Segments of mtDNA are present in the human nuclear genome. These 'molecular fossils' or pseudogenes are rare events caused by migration and integration of a portion of the mtDNA into nuclear DNA. These pseudogenes can create the potential for complications in mtDNA human identity testing if they are amplified instead of the intended mtDNA target when a high number of PCR cycles are invoked to try to tease out mtDNA sequence information from a particularly difficult sample. Under unique circumstances, nuclear pseudogenes could act to contaminate the true mtDNA sequence. However, with the primer sets commonly used in forensic mtDNA testing and a direct PCR with fewer than 40 cycles, nuclear DNA sequences that are similar to mtDNA rarely cause a problem because their initial copy number is so much lower than that of mtDNA.

Most common types

One of the biggest weaknesses of mtDNA analysis is that some haplotypes are rather common in various population groups. For example, in the FBI mtDNA Population Database of 1655 Caucasians there are 15 individuals who match with identical haplotypes at 263G, 315.1C, and 153 additional profiles that differ from this haplotype by only a single difference. Thus, 168 out of 1655 (10.2%) of the Caucasian database would not be able to be excluded if a sample was observed with this common mtDNA type! However, additional sequence information from polymorphic sites around the entire mtGenome has been characterized to help better resolve many of these most common types. Using this information, assays have been developed to help subdivide several most common Caucasian, African American, and Hispanic mtDNA types.

mtDNA Population Databases

Population databases play an important role in estimating the expected frequency of mtDNA haplotypes that are observed in casework when a suspect's mtDNA sequence matches that of an evidentiary sample. A great deal of effort has been expended to gather information from thousands of maternally unrelated individuals in various population groups around the world. The size of the database is important because without recombination between mtDNA molecules, an mtDNA sequence is treated as a single locus (i.e., haplotype instead of genotype). Having high-quality information in the database is also important in order to make a reliable estimate of the frequency for a random match.

FBI mtDNA Database

The FBI Laboratory has compiled an mtDNA population database with 4839 mtDNA profiles from 14 different populations. The samples have been sequenced and the electropherograms carefully reviewed across positions 16,024 to 16,365 for HV1 and positions 73 to 340 for HV2.

The FBI's mtDNA database was publicly released in April 2002 in a Microsoft Access format and can be downloaded from the FBI Web site along with an analysis tool called MitoSearch. MitoSearch examines the population data sets for specific mtDNA sequences, which are entered based on differences from the Cambridge reference sequence. The software returns the number of times that the specified profile appears in each population group. For example, the mtDNA type 16129A, 263G, 309del, 315.1C occurs twice in 1148 African American profiles, twice in 1655 Caucasian profiles, and not at all in 686 Hispanic profiles. (see D.N.A Box 16.3).

EMPOP

The European forensic mtDNA sequencing community has been actively engaged for a number of years in developing new high-quality population databases for forensic and human identity testing applications. A European DNA Profiling Group mitochondrial DNA population database project (EMPOP) has gathered thousands of mtDNA sequences and constructed a high-quality mtDNA database that can be accessed at http://www.empop .org. As of December 2008, there were 4527 'forensic' (high-quality) data that could be searched online. A majority of the current samples are classified as West Eurasian (Caucasian).

mtDNAmanager

A Korean group from Yonsei University (Seoul, Korea) has created an on-line mtDNA searchable population database called mtDNAmanager. As of December 2008, this database contained 7090 mtDNA control region sequences grouped into five subsets: African (1388), West Eurasian (2857), East Asian (1557), Oceanian (currently no samples included), and Admixed (1288). mtDNAmanager can be accessed at http://mtmanager.yonsei.ac.kr

Issues with sequence quality

Concerns with mtDNA database sequence quality and the impact that it might have on accurately estimating frequency estimates for random matches have been raised by Hans Bandelt, Peter Forster, Antonio Salas, and others in a number of publications. Using a statistical analysis tool called phylogenetics, the similarities and differences between multiple and closely related DNA sequences (i.e., from the same region) can be compared systematically. Sequence alignments are created and compared to look for samples that are extremely different. Extreme or unusual differences may be an indication that the sample was contaminated or the sequence data was incorrectly recorded. For example, a laboratory may put HV1 data for a sample with another sample's HV2 sequence and thereby create an artificial recombinant or accidental composite sequence. Thus, phylogenetic analyses can play a role in verifying sequence quality.

Errors that can creep into mitochondrial DNA population databases can be segregated into four different classes: (1) mistakes in the course of transcription of the results (i.e., clerical errors), (2) sample mix-up (e.g., putting data from HV1 on one sample together with data from HV2 on another sample), (3) contamination, and (4) use of different nomenclatures.

From a pilot collaborative study of 21 laboratories, 14 nonconcordant haplotypes (16 individual errors) were observed out of a total of 150 submitted samples/haplotypes representing the examination of approximately 150,000 nucleotides. Measures are being put into place for complete electronic transfer of data and base calling to avoid the primary problem of clerical errors when transferring information from raw sequence data to final report. In the future, mtDNA databases may require retention of raw data for population samples in order to more easily verify authenticity of results should an inquiry into the origin of sequence results be needed at a later date. Search strategies using the complete query sequence will also likely be implemented.

Laboratories performing mtDNA testing

The first efforts in mtDNA sequence analysis with a forensic applications focus were performed by the Forensic Science Service in England. Today there are a number of laboratories internationally that perform mtDNA testing. One of the most widely respected is Walther Parson's lab at the University of Innsbruck in Austria, which runs the EMPOP database. Within the United States, the Armed Forces DNA Identification Laboratory and the FBI Laboratory have led the efforts in mtDNA analysis but in slightly different arenas.

The Armed Forces DNA Identification Laboratory (AFDIL) is located in Rockville, Maryland, and is charged with identifying the remains of military personnel. Bones recovered from Vietnam, Korea, and even World War II operations have been successfully analyzed with mtDNA. AFDIL also aids mass disaster victim identification including those necessitated by U.S. airline crashes (see Chapter 17).

AFDIL has used mtDNA analysis to help link soldiers' remains to their families and solve historical puzzles such as identifying remains from the Tomb of the Unknown Soldier (D.N.A. Box 16.4) and the Romanov family (D.N.A. Box 16.5).

The FBI Laboratory focuses on the use of forensic evidence, including mtDNA, in criminal investigations. Two DNA units exist within the FBI Laboratory: DNA Unit I, which focuses exclusively on nuclear DNA, and DNA Unit II, which performs mtDNA analysis and aids missing persons investigations. The FBI Laboratory DNA Unit II has conducted mitochondrial DNA casework since June 1996. In 2005, four regional FBI-funded mtDNA laboratories became operational to conduct mtDNA casework as an extension of the FBI's own operations.

Several private laboratories in the United States have validated mtDNA procedures and offer mtDNA testing for a fee. These laboratories include Mitotyping Technologies, LLC (State College, PA), Bode Technology Group (Lorton, VA), Orchid Cellmark (Dallas, TX), and Laboratory Corporation of America (Research Triangle Park, NC). The University of North Texas Center for Human Identification (Ft. Worth, TX) is funded by the National Institute of Justice to perform mtDNA sequence analysis in aiding missing persons work (see Chapter 17).

D.N.A. Box 16.4 Identifying Remains from the Tomb of the Unknown Soldier

On 30 June 1998, U.S. Secretary of Defense William Cohen announced to the world that DNA technology had been used to identify the Vietnam Unknown in the Tomb of the Unknown Soldier located in Arlington National Cemetery. The remains of First Lieutenant Michael J. Blassie, United States Air Force, were identified through the use of mitochondrial DNA. An exact match across 610 nucleotides of the polymorphic mtDNA control region was obtained between Jean Blassie, Michael's mother, and a sample extracted from the bone fragments removed from the Tomb of the Unknown Soldier. At the same time, eight other possible soldiers were excluded because family reference samples did not match.

Michael Blassie was an Air Force Academy graduate and the oldest of five children who grew up in St. Louis, Missouri. Lieutenant Blassie arrived in Vietnam in January 1972 and was flying his 132nd mission when his A-37B attack jet was shot down on 11 May 1972, outside An Loc, a hotly contested South Vietnamese village near the Cambodian border. Intense fighting in the area prevented the site from being searched and his remains were not recovered until almost 5 months later. By this time only four ribs, the right humerus, and part of the pelvis remained along with some personal items, including Blassie's identification card. The remains were sent to the Army's Central Identification Laboratory in Hawaii where they remained for 8 years designated as 'believed to be Michael Blassie.' In 1980, a military review board changed the designation on the remains to 'unknown' and the identification card found with the body had vanished.

The Tomb of the Unknown Soldier was first opened in 1921 to honor soldiers who had died in World War I. On the tomb are inscribed the words 'Here rests in honored glory an American soldier known but to God.' Within this hallowed ground lie four servicemen, the unknown soldiers of World War I, World War II, the Korean War, and the Vietnam War. These unknown soldiers are guarded 24 hours a day at Arlington National Cemetery by a sentinel from the 3rd U.S. Infantry. The World War II and Korean War unknowns were selected from about 8500 and 800 unidentifiable remains, respectively, and were entombed on Memorial Day 1958. The Vietnam War casualty was authorized in 1973 for enshrinement, but it was not filled for 11 more years. To honor a Vietnam veteran on Memorial Day 1984 one of the few available unknown remains was selected for enshrinement and honored in a ceremony led by President Ronald Reagan. There the remains of the Vietnam Unknown lay until 14 May 1998, when they were disinterred in a solemn ceremony and transported to the Armed Forces Institute of Pathology for investigation. So sacred is the tomb and the memory of the soldiers resting there, that it has only been opened four times: in 1921 for WW I, in 1958 for WW II and Korea, in 1984 for Vietnam, and in 1998 to remove the Vietnam remains for DNA testing.

Throughout the month of June 1998, mtDNA sequence information was recovered from the skeletal material (pelvis) and analyzed by scientists at the Armed Forces DNA Identification Laboratory (AFDIL) located in Rockville, Maryland. Maternal relatives from eight possible American casualties near An Loc were also evaluated as family reference samples. The mtDNA sequence content from positions 16,024 to 16,365 (HVI) and positions 73 to 340 (HVII) on the polymorphic control region were evaluated. Only a complete match was observed between Jean Blassie (Michael's mother) and the skeletal remains disinterred from the Tomb of the Unknown Soldier. Because of this positive identification, the Blassies were permitted to bury Lieutenant Blassie's remains at Jefferson Barracks National Cemetery located in St. Louis, Missouri. This ceremony was conducted on 11 July 1998, and brought closure to the Blassie family.

Source:
Holland, M. M., & Parsons, T. J. (1999). Mitochondrial DNA sequence analysis: Validation and use for forensic casework. *Forensic Science Review, 11*, 21–50.

D.N.A. Box 16.5 Identifying the Remains of the Last Russian Czar and His Entire Family

Russian Czar (or Tsar) Nicholas II and his family were removed from power and murdered during the Bolshevik Revolution of 1918. They were shot by a firing squad, doused with sulfuric acid to render their bodies unrecognizable, and disposed of in a shallow pit under a road. Their remains were lost to history until July 1991 when nine skeletons were uncovered from a shallow grave near Ekaterinburg, Russia. A number of forensic tests were attempted involving computer-aided reconstructions and odontological analysis, but because the facial areas of the skulls were destroyed, classical facial identification techniques were difficult at best and not conclusive.

The chief forensic medical examiner of the Russian Federation turned to the Forensic Science Service in the United Kingdom to carry out DNA-based analysis of the remains for purposes of identification. Five STR markers (VWA, TH01, F13A1, FES/FPS, and ACTBP2) were used to examine the nine skeletons. Approximately 1 gram of bone from each of the skeletons yielded about 50 pg of DNA, just enough for PCR amplification of several STR markers. The remains of the Romanov family members consisting of the Tsar, the Tsarina, and three children were distinguishable from those of three servants and the family doctor by their STR genotypes. But two children were missing: their son Alexi and a daughter—thought to be Anastasia or Maria.

While the STR analysis served to establish family relationships between the remains through comparing matching alleles, a link still had to be made with a known descendant

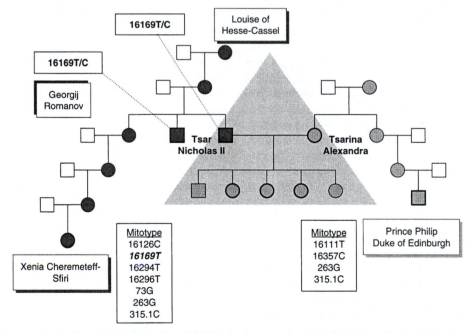

Lineage of Romanov family. The individuals represented by light shading are maternal relatives of the Tsarina Alexandra while those shown in dark shading are maternal relatives of Tsar Nicholas II. Living maternal relatives Prince Philip (for Tsarina) and Xenia Cheremeteff-Sfiri (for Tsar) served as family reference samples. The mtDNA mitotype for each reference sample is listed with the nucleotide changes relative to their position in the rCRS reference sequence. Tsar Nicholas II and his brother Georgij Romanov both exhibited a heteroplasmic T/C at mtDNA position 16169, which differed from the homoplasmic T found in Xenia Cheremeteff-Sfiri. Prince Philip's mitotype matched the remains of the Tsarina and her children while Xenia's mitotype matched the remains of the Tsar at all positions except the heteroplasmic position 16169.

of the Romanov family to verify that the remains were indeed those of the Russian royal family. Mitochondrial DNA analysis was used to answer this question.

Mitochondrial DNA was extracted from the femur of each skeleton and sequenced. Blood samples were then obtained from maternally related descendants of the Romanov family and sequenced in the same manner. His Royal Highness Prince Philip, Duke of Edinburgh and husband of the present British Queen Elizabeth, is a grand nephew of unbroken maternal descent from Tsarina Alexandra. His blood sample thus provided the comparison to confirm the sibling status of the children and the linkage of the mother to the Tsarina's family. The sequences of all 740 tested nucleotides from the mtDNA control region matched between HRH Prince Philip and the putative Tsarina and the three children.

The mtDNA sequence from the putative Tsar was compared with two relatives of unbroken maternal descent from Tsar Nicholas II's grandmother, Louise of Hesse-Cassel. The two relatives had the same mtDNA sequence as the putative Tsar with the exception of a single nucleotide at position 16169. At this position, the putative Tsar's sample had a mixture of two nucleotides (T and C), a condition known as heteroplasmy, while the blood samples of relatives had only a T nucleotide.

To further confirm the putative Tsar's remains, the remains of the brother of Nicholas II, Grand Duke of Russia Georgij

Romanov, were exhumed and tested by the Armed Forces DNA Identification Laboratory (AFDIL). Heteroplasmy was found again at the identical nucleotide site within the mtDNA sequence. Due to the extreme rarity of this heteroplasmy happening by chance between two unrelated individuals, the remains of Tsar Nicholas II and his family were declared authentic and laid to rest in St. Petersburg, Russia, with a funeral fit for a royal family on July 18, 1998 (the 80th anniversary of their murder).

In July 2007, another grave was discovered in close proximity to the original grave site for the other Romanov remains. DNA testing performed by AFDIL using autosomal mini-STRs, Y-STRs, and mtDNA all confirmed that these sets of remains—one male and one female—fit genetically as children of the Tsar and Tsarina. All members of the Romanov family have now been accounted for thanks to the power of DNA testing.

Sources:

Coble, M. D., et al. (2009). Mystery solved: The identification of the two missing Romanov children using DNA analysis. *PLoS ONE, 4,* e4838.

Gill, P., et al. (1994). Identification of the remains of the Romanov family by DNA analysis. *Nature Genetics, 6,* 130–135.

Ivanov, P. L., et al. (1996). Mitochondrial DNA sequence heteroplasmy in the Grand Duke of Russia Georgij Romanov establishes the authenticity of the remains of Tsar Nicholas II. *Nature Genetics, 12,* 417–420.

USING THE X CHROMOSOME IN IDENTITY TESTING

The X chromosome has potential forensic and human identity testing applications due to its inheritance pattern. Normal males possess one X chromosome and one Y chromosome, whereas females possess two X chromosomes although there are occasionally some irregular karyotypes, such as XXY (Klinefelter's syndrome). More than 30 STR markers have been characterized from the X chromosome and population studies have been performed with many of these X-STRs.

X-STR haplotyping can be helpful in some kinship testing particularly with deficient paternity cases where a DNA sample from one of the parents is not available for testing. For example, if a father/daughter parentage relationship is in question, X-STRs may be helpful. On the other hand, a father/son parentage question would be better suited to Y-chromosome results. The literature on the use of X-chromosome analysis is growing and more information on this topic is available in the accompanying *Advanced Topics* volume.

Points for Discussion

- Will the availability and use of Y-chromosome tests change the strategy for examining forensic DNA evidence in the future? If so, how?
- What are some of the challenges with trying to determine a reliable Y-STR profile frequency estimate when a suspect cannot be excluded from contributing to a crime scene sample?
- What are some of the situations where mtDNA may be used and some of the benefits of doing so?

READING LIST AND INTERNET RESOURCES

Lineage Markers

Non-STR DNA Markers. SNPs, Y-STRs, LCN and mtDNA. http://www.dna.gov/training/markers

Y-Chromosome and Mitochondrial DNA Workshop (John Butler and Mike Coble, November 2006). http://www.cstl.nist.gov/biotech/strbase/YmtDNAworkshop.htm

Y Chromosome

Butler, J. M. (2003). Recent developments in Y-short tandem repeat and Y-single nucleotide polymorphism analysis. *Forensic Science Review, 15*, 91–111.

Jobling, M. A., & Tyler-Smith, C. (2003). The human Y chromosome: An evolutionary marker comes of age. *Nature Reviews Genetics, 4*, 598–612.

Applications

Brown, K. (2002). Tangled roots? Genetics meets genealogy. *Science, 295*, 1634–1635.

Foster, E. A., et al. (1998). Jefferson fathered slave's last child. *Nature, 396*, 27–28.

Honda, K., et al. (1999). Male DNA typing from 25-year-old vaginal swabs using Y-chromosomal STR polymorphisms in a retrial request case. *Journal of Forensic Sciences, 44*, 868–872.

Prinz, M., et al. (2001). Validation and casework application of a Y chromosome specific STR multiplex. *Forensic Science International, 120*, 177–188.

Shewale, J. G., et al. (2003). DNA profiling of azoospermic semen samples from vasectomized males by using Y-PLEX 6 amplification kit. *Journal of Forensic Sciences, 48*, 127–129.

Wolinsky, H. (2006). Genetic genealogy goes global. *EMBO Reports, 7*, 1072–1074.

Y-STR markers

Butler, J. M. (2006). Genetics and genomics of core short tandem repeat loci used in human identity testing. *Journal of Forensic Sciences, 51*, 253–265.

Decker, A. E., et al. (2007). The impact of additional Y-STR loci on resolving common haplotypes and closely related individuals. *Forensic Science International: Genetics, 1*, 215–217.

Hanson, E. K., & Ballantyne, J. (2006). Comprehensive annotated STR physical map of the human Y chromosome: Forensic implications. *Legal Medicine (Tokyo), 8*, 110–120.

Kayser, M., et al. (2004). A comprehensive survey of human Y-chromosomal microsatellites. *American Journal of Human Genetics, 74*, 1183–1197.

Redd, A. J., et al. (2002). Forensic value of 14 novel STRs on the human Y chromosome. *Forensic Science International, 130*, 97–111.

Rodig, H., et al. (2008). Evaluation of haplotype discrimination capacity of 35 Y-chromosomal short tandem repeat loci. *Forensic Science International, 174*, 182–188.

Seo, Y., et al. (2003). A method for genotyping Y chromosome-linked DYS385a and DYS385b loci. *Legal Medicine (Tokyo), 5*, 228–232.

SWGDAM. (2004). Report on the current activities of the Scientific Working Group on DNA Analysis Methods Y-STR Subcommittee. *Forensic Science Communications, 6*(3). Available at http://www.fbi.gov/hq/lab/fsc/backissu/july2004/standards/2004_03_standards03.htm

Y-STR kits and assays

Butler, J. M., et al. (2002). A novel multiplex for simultaneous amplification of 20 Y chromosome STR markers. *Forensic Science International, 129*, 10–24.

Hanson, E. K., & Ballantyne, J. (2007). An ultra-high discrimination Y chromosome short tandem repeat multiplex DNA typing system. *PLoS ONE, 2*, e688.

Krenke, B. E., et al. (2005). Validation of male-specific, 12-locus fluorescent short tandem repeat (STR) multiplex. *Forensic Science International, 151*, 111–124.

Mayntz-Press, K. A., & Ballantyne, J. (2007). Performance characteristics of commercial Y-STR multiplex systems. *Journal of Forensic Sciences, 52*, 1025–1034.

Mulero, J. J., et al. (2006). Development and validation of the AmpF*l*STR Yfiler™ PCR Amplification Kit: A male specific, single amplification 17 Y-STR multiplex system. *Journal of Forensic Sciences, 51*, 64–75.

Parson, W., et al. (2008). Y-STR analysis on DNA mixture samples—Results of a collaborative project of the ENFSI DNA Working Group. *Forensic Science International: Genetics, 2*, 222–238.

Population databases

Fatolitis, L., & Ballantyne, J. (2008). The US Y-STR database. *Profiles in DNA, 11*(1), 13–14.

Roewer, L., et al. (2001). Online reference database of European Y-chromosomal short tandem repeat (STR) haplotypes. *Forensic Science International, 118*, 106–113.

STRBase Listing of Y-STR Databases. http://www.cstl.nist.gov/biotech/strbase/y_strs.htm

U.S. Y-STR Database. http://www.usystrdatabase.org

Willuweit, S., & Roewer, L. (2007). Y chromosome haplotype reference database (YHRD): Update. *Forensic Science International: Genetics, 1*, 83–87.

Y-Chromosome Haplotype Reference Database (YHRD). http://www.yhrd.org

Interpretation

Budowle, B., et al. (2005). Twelve short tandem repeat loci Y chromosome haplotypes: Genetic analysis on populations residing in North America. *Forensic Science International, 150,* 1–15.

Budowle, B., et al. (2008). Null allele sequence structure at the DYS448 locus and implications for profile interpretation. *International Journal of Legal Medicine, 122,* 421–427.

Butler, J. M., et al. (2005). Chromosomal duplications along the Y-chromosome and their potential impact on Y-STR interpretation. *Journal of Forensic Sciences, 50,* 853–859.

Kayser, M., et al. (2003). Y chromosome STR haplotypes and the genetic structure of U.S. populations of African, European, and Hispanic ancestry. *Genome Research, 13,* 624–634.

Redd, A. J., et al. (2006). Genetic structure among 38 populations from the United States based on 11 U.S. core Y chromosome STRs. *Journal of Forensic Sciences, 51,* 580–585.

SWGDAM. (2009). Y-STR interpretation guidelines. *Forensic Science Communications, 11*(1). Available at http://www.fbi.gov/hq/lab/fsc/backissu/jan2009/standards/2009_01_standards01.htm

Y-STR mixtures

Fukshansky, N., & Bär, W. (2005). DNA mixtures: Biostatistics for mixed stains with haplotypic genetic markers. *International Journal of Legal Medicine, 119,* 285–290.

Prinz, M., et al. (1997). Multiplexing of Y chromosome specific STRs and performance for mixed samples. *Forensic Science International, 85,* 209–218.

Joint match probabilities

Amorim, A. (2008). A cautionary note on the evaluation of genetic evidence from uniparentally transmitted markers. *Forensic Science International: Genetics, 2*(4), 376–378.

Walsh, B., et al. (2008). Joint match probabilities for Y chromosomal and autosomal markers. *Forensic Science International, 174,* 234–238.

Mutation rates

Decker, A. E., et al. (2008). Analysis of mutations in father-son pairs with 17 Y-STR loci. *Forensic Science International: Genetics, 2,* e31–e35.

Gusmão, L., et al. (2005). Mutation rates at Y chromosome specific microsatellites. *Human Mutation, 26,* 520–528.

Kayser, M., et al. (2000). Characteristics and frequency of germline mutations at microsatellite loci from the human Y chromosome, as revealed by direct observation in father/son pairs. *American Journal of Human Genetics, 66,* 1580–1588.

Use with familial searching

Bieber, F. R., et al. (2006). Finding criminals through DNA of their relatives. *Science, 312,* 1315–1316.

Sims, G., et al. (2008). The DNA partial match and familial search policy of the California Department of Justice. In: *Proceedings of the 19th International Symposium on Human Identification*. Available at http://www.promega.com/geneticidproc

Mitochondrial DNA

Bandelt, H.-J., Richards, M., & Macaulay, V. (Eds.), (2006). *Human mitochondrial DNA and the evolution of* Homo sapiens. Berlin/Heidelberg: Springer-Verlag.

Budowle, B., et al. (2003). Forensics and mitochondrial DNA: Applications, debates, and foundations. *Annual Review of Genomics and Human Genetics, 4*, 119–141.

Butler, J. M., & Levin, B. C. (1998). Forensic applications of mitochondrial DNA. *Trends in Biotechnology, 16*, 158–162.

Fourney, R. M. (1998). Mitochondrial DNA and forensic analysis: A primer for law enforcement. *Canadian Society of Forensic Science Journal, 31*, 45–53.

Characteristics

Anderson, S., et al. (1981). Sequence and organization of the human mitochondrial genome. *Nature, 290*, 457–465.

Andrews, R. M., et al. (1999). Reanalysis and revision of the Cambridge reference sequence for human mitochondrial DNA. *Nature Genetics, 23*, 147.

Chen, X. J., & Butow, R. A. (2005). The organization and inheritance of the mitochondrial genome. *Nature Reviews Genetics, 6*, 815–825.

Ingman, M., et al. (2000). Mitochondrial genome variation and the origin of modern humans. *Nature, 408*, 708–713.

Scheffler, I. E. (1999). *Mitochondria*. New York: Wiley-Liss.

Steps involved

Isenberg, A. R. (2004). Forensic mitochondrial DNA analysis. In R. Saferstein (Ed.), *Forensic science handbook: Vol. II* (2nd ed.) (pp. 297–327). Upper Saddle River, NJ: Pearson Prentice Hall.

Wilson, M. R., et al. (1995). Validation of mitochondrial DNA sequencing for forensic casework analysis. *International Journal of Legal Medicine, 108*, 68–74.

Interpretation

Carracedo, A., et al. (2000). DNA Commission of the International Society for Forensic Genetics: Guidelines for mitochondrial DNA typing. *Forensic Science International, 110*, 79–85.

Parson, W., & Bandelt, H.-J. (2007). Extended guidelines for mtDNA typing of population data in forensic science. *Forensic Science International: Genetics, 1*, 13–19.

SWGDAM. (2003). Guidelines for mitochondrial DNA (mtDNA) nucleotide sequence interpretation. *Forensic Science Communications, 5*(2). Available at http://www.fbi.gov/hq/lab/fsc/current/backissu.htm

Wilson, M. R., et al. (1993). Guidelines for the use of mitochondrial DNA sequencing in forensic science. *Crime Laboratory Digest, 20*, 68–77.

Wilson, M. R., et al. (2002). Recommendations for consistent treatment of length variants in the human mitochondrial DNA control region. *Forensic Science International, 129,* 35–42.

Heteroplasmy

Bendall, K. E., & Sykes, B. C. (1995). Length heteroplasmy in the first hypervariable segment of the human mtDNA control region. *American Journal of Human Genetics, 57,* 248–256.

Bendall, K. E., et al. (1996). Heteroplasmic point mutations in the human mtDNA control region. *American Journal of Human Genetics, 59,* 1276–1287.

Melton, T. (2004). Mitochondrial DNA heteroplasmy. *Forensic Science Review, 16,* 1–20.

Sekiguchi, K., et al. (2004). Mitochondrial DNA heteroplasmy among hairs from single individuals. *Journal of Forensic Sciences, 49,* 986–991.

Mixtures

Bever, R.A., et al. (2003). Resolution of mixtures by cloning of the mitochondrial DNA control region. In: *Proceedings of the 14th international symposium on human identification.* Available at http://www.promega.com/geneticidproc/

Danielson, P. B., et al. (2007). Resolving mtDNA mixtures by denaturing high-performance liquid chromatography and linkage phase determination. *Forensic Science International: Genetics, 1,* 148–153.

Walker, J. A., et al. (2004). Resolution of mixed human DNA samples using mitochondrial DNA sequence variants. *Analytical Biochemistry, 325,* 171–173.

Nuclear DNA pseudogenes

Zischler, H., et al. (1995). A nuclear 'fossil' of the mitochondrial D-loop and the origin of modern humans. *Nature, 378,* 489–492.

Most common types and coding region assays

Brandstätter, A., et al. (2006). Dissection of mitochondrial superhaplogroup H using coding region SNPs. *Electrophoresis, 27,* 2541–2550.

Coble, M. D., et al. (2004). Single nucleotide polymorphisms over the entire mtDNA genome that increase the power of forensic testing in Caucasians. *International Journal of Legal Medicine, 118,* 137–146.

Coble, M. D., et al. (2006). Effective strategies for forensic analysis in the mitochondrial DNA coding region. *International Journal of Legal Medicine, 120,* 27–32.

Nilsson, M., et al. (2008). Evaluation of mitochondrial DNA coding region assays for increased discrimination in forensic analysis. *Forensic Science International: Genetics, 2,* 1–8.

Parsons, T. J., & Coble, M. D. (2001). Increasing the forensic discrimination of mitochondrial DNA testing through analysis of the entire mitochondrial DNA genome. *Croatian Medical Journal, 42,* 304–309.

Vallone, P. M., et al. (2004). A multiplex allele-specific primer extension assay for forensically informative SNPs distributed throughout the mitochondrial genome. *International Journal of Legal Medicine, 118*, 147–157.

mtDNA population databases

EMPOP Mitochondrial DNA Control Region Database. http://www.empop.org

Irwin, J. A., et al. (2007). Development and expansion of high-quality control region databases to improve forensic mtDNA evidence interpretation. *Forensic Science International Genetics, 1*(2), 154–157.

Lee, H. Y., et al. (2008). mtDNAmanager: A web-based tool for the management and quality analysis of mitochondrial DNA control-region sequences. *BMC Bioinformatics, 9*, 483. Available at http://www.biomedcentral.com

MITOMAP: A human mitochondrial genome database. http://www.mitomap.org

Monson, K. L., et al. (2002). The mtDNA population database: An integrated software and database resource. *Forensic Science Communications, 4*(2). Available at http://www.fbi.gov/hq/lab/fsc/backissu/april2002/miller1.htm

mtDNAmanager. http://mtmanager.yonsei.ac.kr

Parson, W., & Dür, A. (2007). EMPOP—A forensic mtDNA database. *Forensic Science International: Genetics, 1*(2), 88–92.

Quality concerns with mtDNA data

Bandelt, H. J., et al. (2001). Detecting errors in mtDNA data by phylogenetic analysis. *International Journal of Legal Medicine, 115*, 64–69.

Bandelt, H. J., et al. (2002). The fingerprint of phantom mutations in mitochondrial DNA data. *American Journal of Human Genetics, 71*, 1150–1160.

Bandelt, H. J., et al. (2004). Artificial recombination in forensic mtDNA population databases. *International Journal of Legal Medicine, 118*, 267–273.

Brandstätter, A., et al. (2005). Phantom mutation hotspots in human mitochondrial DNA. *Electrophoresis, 26*, 3414–3429.

Parson, W., et al. (2004). The EDNAP mitochondrial DNA population database (EMPOP) collaborative exercises: Organization, results and perspectives. *Forensic Science International, 139*, 215–226.

Salas, A., et al. (2005). A practical guide to mitochondrial DNA error prevention in clinical, forensic, and population genetics. *Biochemistry and Biophysics Research Communications, 335*, 891–899.

Salas, A., et al. (2007). Phylogeographic investigations: The role of trees in forensic genetics. *Forensic Science International, 168*, 1–13.

mtDNA laboratories

Armed Forces DNA Identification Laboratory. http://www.afip.org/consultation/AFMES/AFDIL

Bode Technology Group. http://www.bodetech.com

FBI Laboratory DNA Unit II. http://www.fbi.gov/hq/lab/html/mdnau1.htm

LabCorp. http://www.labcorp.com

Mitotyping. http://www.mitotyping.com

Orchid Cellmark. http://www.orchidcellmark.com/forensicdna

University of North Texas Center for Human Identification. http://www.unthumanid.org

Forensic casework

Allen, M., et al. (1998). Mitochondrial DNA sequencing of shed hairs and saliva on robbery caps: Sensitivity and matching probabilities. *Journal of Forensic Sciences, 43,* 453–464.

Divine, A. M., et al. (2005). Forensic casework analysis using the HVI/HVII mtDNA linear array assay. *Journal of Forensic Sciences, 50,* 548–554.

Holland, M. M., et al. (1993). Mitochondrial DNA sequence analysis of human skeletal remains: Identification of remains from the Vietnam War. *Journal of Forensic Sciences, 38,* 542–553.

Melton, T., & Nelson, K. (2001). Forensic mitochondrial DNA analysis: Two years of commercial casework experience in the United States. *Croatian Medical Journal, 42,* 298–303.

Melton, T., et al. (2005). Forensic mitochondrial DNA analysis of 691 casework hairs. *Journal of Forensic Sciences, 50,* 73–80.

Nelson, K., & Melton, T. (2007). Forensic mitochondrial DNA analysis of 116 casework skeletal samples. *Journal of Forensic Sciences, 52,* 557–561.

Stone, A. C., et al. (2001). Mitochondrial DNA analysis of the presumptive remains of Jesse James. *Journal of Forensic Sciences, 46,* 173–176.

Wilson, M. R., et al. (1995). Extraction, PCR amplification and sequencing of mitochondrial DNA from human hair shafts. *Biotechniques, 18,* 662–669.

X Chromosome

Forensic X-STR Research. http://www.chrx-str.org

Krawczak, M. (2007). Kinship testing with X-chromosomal markers: Mathematical and statistical issues. *Forensic Science International: Genetics, 1,* 111–114.

Machado, F. B., & Medina-Acosta, E. (2009). Genetic map of human X-linked microsatellites used in forensic practice. *Forensic Science International: Genetics, 3,* 202–204.

Szibor, R., et al. (2003). Use of X-linked markers for forensic purposes. *International Journal of Legal Medicine, 117,* 67–74.

Szibor, R., et al. (2006). A new Web site compiling forensic chromosome X research is now online. *International Journal of Legal Medicine, 120,* 252–254.

Szibor, R. (2007). X-chromosomal markers: Past, present and future. *Forensic Science International: Genetics, 1,* 93–99.

Szibor, R. (2007). The X chromosome in forensic science: Past, present and future. In R. Rapley & D. Whitehouse (Eds.), *Molecular forensics* (pp. 103–126). Hoboken, NJ: Wiley.

Turrina, S., et al. (2007). Development and forensic validation of a new multiplex PCR assay with 12 X-chromosomal short tandem repeats. *Forensic Science International: Genetics, 1,* 201–204.

CHAPTER 17

Applications of DNA Typing

Any truth is better than indefinite doubt.

—Sherlock Holmes, *The Yellow Face*

Besides its use in criminal investigations, DNA data plays an important role in other applications such as parentage and kinship testing where DNA results from potential relatives are being compared. Different questions are usually being asked in parentage testing than in criminal casework where a direct match is being considered between evidence and suspect. Several applications exist that involve DNA evidence from related individuals. These include traditional parentage testing that usually involves addressing questions of paternity (i.e., who is the father?) and missing persons and mass disaster investigations that involve reverse parentage analysis (i.e., could these sets of remains have come from a child of these reference samples?). Immigration cases also involve kinship testing to determine if an individual could have a proposed relationship to reference samples.

PARENTAGE TESTING

Every year in the United States more than 300,000 paternity cases are performed where the identity of the father of a child is in dispute. These cases typically involve the mother, the child, and one or more alleged fathers (D.N.A. Box 17.1). In 2008, almost 1 million samples were analyzed for this purpose in the United States. Several dozen DNA laboratories have been accredited by the American Association of Blood Banks (AABB) to perform parentage testing.

The determination of parentage is made based on whether or not alleles are shared between the child and the alleged father when a number of genetic

D.N.A. Box 17.1 Anna Nicole Smith

In early 2007, the news media brought paternity testing into the forefront of the public's attention when a DNA test was conducted to find the father of a daughter born on 7 September 2006 to a model/actress named Vickie Lynn Marshall—better known as Anna Nicole Smith. Anna Nicole Smith, who had gained fame in the early 1990s as a Playboy model, died suddenly on 8 February 2007 at the age of 39 from what was deemed an accidental drug overdose. With her untimely death, attention turned to a paternity struggle over her 5-month-old daughter. The child was originally named Dannielynn Hope Marshall Stern with Anna Nicole's former lawyer turned live-in partner Howard K. Stern listed on the birth certificate as the father. However, a number of men came forward claiming to be the father of baby Dannielynn including a European prince, Anna Nicole's bodyguard, and a convict who had been a former boyfriend. A Los Angeles-based entertainment photojournalist Larry Birkhead was foremost among those who challenged having Howard Stern listed on the birth certificate as Dannielynn's father.

After a lengthy legal battle, which took place in the Bahamas where Anna Nicole Smith had been living prior to her death, DNA samples were collected and analyzed to definitively determine the paternity. On 10 April 2007, Dr. Michael Baird, the laboratory director of DNA Diagnostics Center, a paternity testing company near Cincinnati, Ohio, appeared at a Bahamian court to provide DNA testing results. These results, generated with the Identifiler STR kit, gave a probability of paternity of 99.99999% that Larry Birkhead was the biological father of Anna Nicole Smith's daughter Dannielynn. Dannielynn's birth certificate was subsequently updated and her name changed to Dannielynn Hope Marshall Birkhead.

Sources:

http://en.wikipedia.org/wiki/Anna_Nicole_Smith
http://en.wikipedia.org/wiki/Dannielynn_Birkhead_paternity_case
http://www.dnacenter.com?media/anna-nicole-dna-test.html
Personal communication from Michael Baird

markers are examined. Thus, the outcome of parentage testing is simply inclusion or exclusion. Paternity testing laboratories often utilize the same short tandem repeat (STR) multiplexes and commercial kits as employed by forensic testing laboratories. However, rather than looking for a complete one-to-one match in a DNA profile, the source of the nonmaternal or 'obligate paternal allele' at each genetic locus is under investigation.

The basis of paternity comes down to the fact that, in the absence of mutation, a child receives one allele matching each parent at every genetic locus examined (Figure 17.1). Thus, parents with genotypes 11,14 (father) and 8,12 (mother) may produce offspring with the following types: 8,11 8,14 11,12 and 12,14. Conversely, if the mother's genotype is known to be 8,12 and the children possess alleles 8, 11, 12, and 14, then we may deduce that their father contributed alleles 11 and 14—but this does not necessarily mean that one man fathered all of the children.

The obligate paternal allele for each child in this example is shown in Figure 17.1. In this particular example, the parents had nonoverlapping alleles. Paternity testing becomes more complicated when mother and father share alleles, but the logic remains the same in calculating exclusion probability and the paternity index likelihood ratio described below.

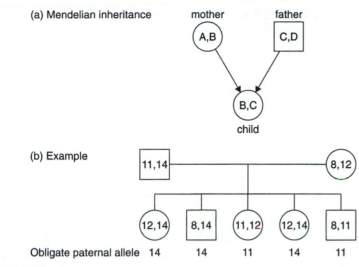

(a) Mendelian inheritance

(b) Example

Obligate paternal allele

FIGURE 17.1

(a) Mendelian inheritance patterns with a mother possessing alleles A and B contributing one of them to the child while the father who possesses alleles C and D also contributes one of his alleles to the child. (b) An example pedigree for a family where the parents possess different alleles, enabling identification of the obligate paternal allele in each of the children. This scenario can become more complicated to interpret if mutations occur or maternal and paternal alleles are shared.

Statistical calculations

If the man tested cannot be excluded as the biological father of the child in question (due to allele sharing), then statistical calculations are performed to aid in understanding the strength of the association. The most commonly applied test in this regard is the paternity index.

The *paternity index* (PI) is the ratio of two conditional probabilities where the numerator assumes paternity and the denominator assumes a random man of similar ethnic background was the father. The numerator is the probability of observed genotypes, given the tested man is the father, while the denominator is the probability of the observed genotypes, given that a random man is the father. The paternity index then is a likelihood ratio of two probabilities conditional upon different competing hypotheses. This likelihood ratio reflects how many times more likely it is to see the evidence (e.g., a particular set of alleles) under the first hypothesis compared to the second hypothesis (see Appendix 3). When mating is random, the probability that the untested alternative father will transmit a specific allele to his child is equal to the allele frequency of the specific allele under consideration.

The PI is generally represented in the formula X/Y, where X is the chance that the alleged father (AF) could transmit the obligate allele and Y is the chance

D.N.A. Box 17.2 Worked Paternity Example

A paternity trio consists of DNA samples from a child (C), a mother (M), and an alleged father (AF). Deficient paternity testing can be performed with just the C and AF samples but will not be as statistically significant without the mother's DNA profile to help ascertain the father's obligate alleles. The probability that an alleged father is the actual biological father rather than having the required alleles by coincidence (i.e., that a random man is the true father) is represented as a likelihood ratio known as the paternity index (PI). A maternity index (MI) may be calculated in the same fashion using the allele frequencies for the observed alleles in common between the mother and the child.

To perform parentage analysis, three sets of information are needed: (1) the genotypes for each of the individuals being tested, (2) the relevant allele frequencies for the genetic loci examined, and (3) the appropriate equation from 1 of 21 specific scenarios that depends on the allele combinations present in the tested individuals. The numerator, denominator, and likelihood ratios for each of these 21 scenarios are described more fully in other sources, such as Lucy (2005).

1. Genotypes present at the STR locus D13S317

   M: 8,12   C: 12,14   AF: 11,14

   Substituting the actual alleles for alphabetical symbols starting with 'P', we obtain: 8 = P; 12 = Q; 14 = R; and 11 = S. Thus, M = PQ, C = QR, and AF = SR.

2. D13S317 allele frequencies (Caucasians, $N = 302$; see Table 11.1):

   Allele 8 (p): 0.113

Allele 12 (q): 0.248

Allele 14 (r): 0.048

Allele 11 (s): 0.339

Note that by convention the allele frequencies are represented by the lowercase letter for the corresponding allele. Thus, allele 12 = Q while the frequency of allele 12 = q.

3. Specific scenario equation to be used (1/2r), where r = frequency of allele 14:

   $$PI = 1/2r = 1/(2 \times 0.048) = 10.4$$

Because the child and alleged father share allele 14, the frequency for this allele is used to determine the PI calculations for this STR marker. In the case illustrated here, the results of *the DNA testing using a single STR locus are 10.4 times more likely if the tested man is the biological father of the child than if the biological father is another man, unrelated to the tested man.*

By multiplying the various PI values for each STR marker together, the combined paternity index (CPI) might be greater than 100,000 with 13 or 15 STRs examined. The probability of parentage is calculated by using the CPI values: [CPI/(CPI+1)] × 100%. Thus, with a CPI of 100,000, the probability of paternity would be 99.999%.

Sources:

Brenner, C. H. (1997). Symbolic kinship program. *Genetics, 145,* 535–542.

Lucy, D. (2005). *Introduction to statistics for forensic scientists.* Hoboken, NJ: Wiley.

that some other man of the same race could have transmitted the allele. Typically, X is assigned the value of 1 if the AF is homozygous for the allele of interest and 0.5 if the AF is heterozygous. A population database containing frequency distributions for the various alleles at the tested genetic markers, such as Table 11.1, is used to calculate the potential of a randomly selected man passing the obligate allele to the child. D.N.A. Box 17.2 shows a worked example of a potential paternity case.

The PI is calculated for each locus and then individual PI values are multiplied together to obtain the combined paternity index (CPI) for the entire set of genetic loci examined. The generally accepted minimum standard for an inclusion of paternity is a PI of 100 or greater. A PI of 100 correlates to the probability that the alleged father has a 99 to 1 chance of being the father compared to a random man.

Another statistical test performed in paternity testing is the *exclusion probability*, which is the combined frequency of all genotypes that would be excluded if the pedigree relationships were true assuming Hardy–Weinberg equilibrium.

A number of computer programs have been used for statistical calculations in parentage testing including DNA View, familias, and EasyDNA. Jiri Drábek in a recent article describes the capabilities and cost of 13 different software programs he evaluated for calculating the likelihood ratio in parentage and kinship analysis.

Reference samples

Unfortunately, complete parentage trios are not always available. Sometimes the mother's DNA sample may not be included in a case or the father is not available for testing. The advantage of having a mother's DNA in a paternity testing case is that the obligate paternal alleles can be more easily deciphered in the child's DNA profile.

While more statistical uncertainty can arise in deficient parentage cases (where one of the parents is not tested), they can still be brought to a reasonable degree of resolution although sometimes results from additional genetic loci are needed. For example, mitochondrial DNA, Y-chromosome, or X-chromosome results can help with confirming genetic relationships between individuals. These additional loci permit evaluation of samples from different genetic angles and also extend the range of reference samples that are possible to more distantly related relatives. A combination of samples from more than one close relative can help provide greater confidence in this kinship analysis.

Impact of mutational events

Since parentage and kinship testing involve measuring genetic relationships across generations (rather than matching of direct references as in the case of forensic comparisons), mutations that may occur must be taken into account in these investigations. These mutations are *germ-line mutations* in that they occur in either the father's sperm or mother's egg cell and are passed on during zygote formation. (*Somatic mutations*, on the other hand, occur within different cells or tissues coming from the same individual, such as with cancerous tumors.)

Any time parentage testing is performed or a family reference sample is used to try to associate recovered remains during a mass disaster or missing persons investigation, mutations become an important issue because an exact match cannot be made when a mutation is present. Mutation rates for genetic markers are typically measured through analysis of many parent–offspring allele comparisons (D.N.A. Box 17.3).

D.N.A. Box 17.3 Mutation Rates for STR Loci

As with any region of DNA, mutations can and do occur at STR loci. By some not completely characterized mechanism, STR alleles can change over time. Theoretically, all of the alleles that exist today for a particular STR locus have resulted from only a few 'founder' individuals by slowly changing over tens of thousands of years. The mutational event may be in the form of a single base change or in the length of the entire repeat. The molecular mechanisms by which STRs mutate are thought to involve replication slippage or defective DNA replication repair.

Estimation of mutational events at a DNA marker may be achieved by comparison of genotypes from offspring to those of their parents. Genotype data from paternity trios involving a father, a mother, and at least one child is examined. A discovery of an allele difference between the parents and the child is seen as evidence for a possible mutation (see figure). The search for mutations in STR loci typically involves examining thousands of parent–child allele transfers because the mutation rate is rather low in many STRs.

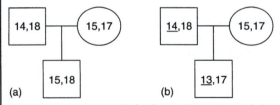

(a)   (b)

Mutational event observed in family trios. Normal transmission of alleles from an STR locus (a) is compared here to mutation of paternal allele 14 into the child's allele 13 (b).

The majority of STR mutations involve the gain or loss of a single repeat unit. Thus, a VWA allele with 14 repeats would show up as a 13 or a 15 in the next generation following a mutational event (see figure). In most studies, paternal mutations appear to be more frequent than maternal ones for STR loci. However, depending on the genotype combinations it can be difficult to ascertain from which parent the mutant allele was inherited.

The mutation rates for the 13 core STR loci have been gathered from a number of studies in the literature and are summarized in the following table. Most of these mutation rates

are on the order of 1 to 3 mutations per 1000 (0.1% to 0.3%) allele transfers or generational events. The STR loci with the lowest observed mutation rates are TH01 and TPOX. Not surprisingly, the STR loci with the highest mutation rates—D21S11, FGA, D18S51, and SE33—are among the most polymorphic and possess the highest number of observed alleles.

CSF1PO	0.16%
FGA	0.28%
TH01	0.01%
TPOX	0.01%
VWA	0.17%
D3S1358	0.12%
D5S818	0.11%
D7S820	0.10%
D8S1179	0.14%
D13S317	0.14%
D16S539	0.11%
D18S51	0.22%
D21S11	0.19%
Penta D	0.14%
Penta E	0.16%
D2S1338	0.12%
D19S433	0.11%
SE33	0.64%

Until recently, only general information on STR mutation rates was reported—namely, how many mutations occurred relative to the number of meioses measured. The realization that certain alleles are more prone to mutation than others has prompted the American Association of Blood Banks (AABB) to carefully examine *which alleles* were mutating based on records from accredited parentage testing laboratories. For example, with the STR locus FGA an apparent change from allele 24 to 25 was observed 62 times (11.7%) out of 530 total paternal mutations seen in 2002, while an apparent change from allele 19 to 20 was seen only eight times (1.5%). In general, longer alleles were seen to mutate more frequently. As this information continues to be collated in future studies, it should prove useful in refining mutation rates and aid in a better understanding of the process of STR origins and variability over human history.

Sources:
American Association of Blood Banks Annual Report Summary for Testing in 2006. http://www.aabb.org/Documents/Accreditation/Parentage_Testing_Accreditation_Program/rtannrpt06.pdf
http://www.cstl.nist.gov/biotech/strbase/mutation.htm

In paternity testing situations, a high mutation rate for an STR marker could result in a false exclusion at that locus. The American Association of Blood Banks (AABB) has issued standards for parentage testing laboratories regarding mutations. The AABB standards recognize that mutations are naturally occurring genetic events and require that the mutation frequency at a tested locus be documented. The AABB standards also emphasize that an opinion of nonpaternity shall not be rendered on the basis of an exclusion at a single DNA locus (single inconsistency). It is important to keep in mind that the more genetic systems examined, the greater the chance of a random mutation being observed. With STR analysis often examining a battery of a dozen or more loci, it is not uncommon to see two inconsistencies between a child and the true biological father.

Reverse parentage testing

In identification of remains as part of missing persons investigations or mass disaster victim identification work, the question under consideration may be whether or not a child belongs to the mother and father tested or other biological references available (Figure 17.2). This is essentially the opposite question as that asked in parentage testing, namely, given a child's genotype, who are the parents? The samples examined may be the same family trio as studied in parentage testing: alleged mother, alleged father, and child. Unfortunately, it is normally a luxury to have samples from both parents available. Typically, only a single parent or sibling samples are available, which makes the reverse parentage analysis more challenging.

DISASTER VICTIM IDENTIFICATION (DVI)

Mass diasters, whether natural or man-made, can involve loss of life for many victims of the tragedy. Efforts to identify these victims are referred to as *disaster victim identification*, or DVI.

In the United States, DNA testing has now become routine and expected in disaster victim identification in the event of a plane crash, large fire, or terrorist

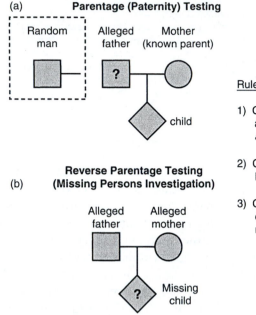

(a) **Parentage (Paternity) Testing**

Random man | Alleged father | Mother (known parent)

? child

Reverse Parentage Testing
(b) **(Missing Persons Investigation)**

Alleged father | Alleged mother

? Missing child

Rules of Inheritance

1) Child has two alleles for each autosomal marker *(one from mother and one from biological father)*

2) Child will have mother's mitochondrial DNA haplotype (barring mutation)

3) Child, if a son, will have father's Y-chromosome haplotype (barring mutation)

FIGURE 17.2

Illustration of question being asked with (a) parentage testing and (b) reverse parentage testing. The most common form of parentage testing, namely paternity testing, uses results from a mother and a child to answer the question of whether the alleged father could have fathered the child versus a random man. With a reverse parentage test, DNA types from one or both parents are used to determine whether an observed type could have resulted from a child of the alleged father and mother.

attack. Military casualties are also identified through STR typing or mitochondrial DNA sequencing by the Armed Forces DNA Identification Laboratory (AFDIL). All airplane crashes within the United States are examined by the National Transportation Safety Board (http://www.ntsb.gov), which often contracts with AFDIL to identify the air crash victims through DNA testing as part of the investigation.

Often mass disasters leave human remains that are literally in pieces or burned beyond recognition. In some cases it is possible to visually identify a victim, but body parts can be separated from one another and the remains comingled, making identification without DNA techniques virtually impossible. The use of fingerprints and dental records (odontology) still plays an important role in victim identification but these modalities obviously require a finger or an intact skull or jawbone along with previously archived fingerprint and dental records that can be made available for comparison purposes.

DNA testing has a major advantage in that it can be used to identify *each and every portion of the remains* recovered from a disaster site, provided (1) that there

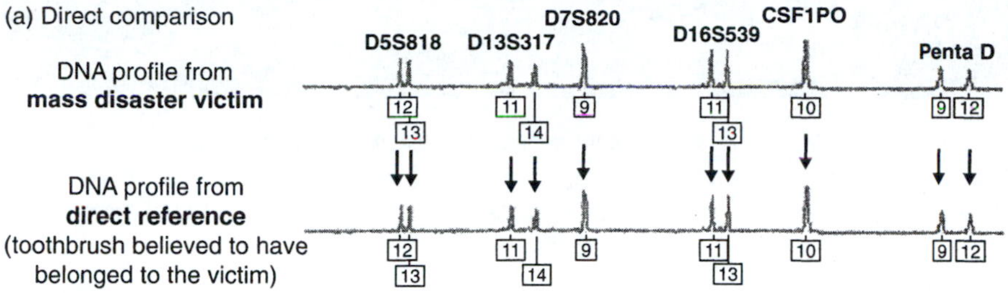

(a) Direct comparison

DNA profile from
mass disaster victim

DNA profile from
direct reference
(toothbrush believed to have
belonged to the victim)

(b) Kinship analysis

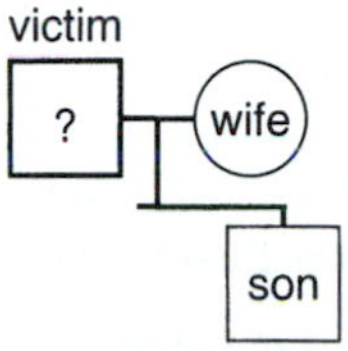

	D5S818	D13S317	D7S820	D16S539	CSF1PO	Penta D	
	11,13	8,12	8,12	8,9	10,12	8,10	wife
	11,13	8,14	8,9	9,13	10,10	9,10	son
Predicted victim profile	11,? or ?,13	?,14	9,?	?,13	?,10	9,?	**victim** (father)
Mass disaster victim profile	12,13	11,14	9,9	11,13	10,10	9,12	*actual profile*

FIGURE 17.3

Example demonstrating the use of reference samples in mass disaster victim identification using DNA typing. (a) Direct comparison involves analysis of a direct reference sample from some kind of personal effect of the victim. (b) Kinship analysis utilizes close biological relatives to reconstruct a victim's DNA profile.

is sufficient intact DNA present to obtain a DNA type and (2) a reference sample is available for comparison purposes from a surviving family member or some verifiable personal item containing biological material. Personal items from the deceased including toothbrushes, combs, razors, or even dirty laundry can provide biological material to generate a reference DNA type for the victim. The direct comparison of DNA results from disaster victim remains to DNA recovered from personal items (Figure 17.3a) represents the easiest way to obtain a match—and hence an identification—provided it is possible to verify the source (e.g., the toothbrush was not used by some other household member). The use of DNA from biological relatives (Figure 17.3b) necessitates the added complexity of kinship analysis similar to that employed for paternity or reverse parentage testing.

DVI always involves comparison of post-mortem (PM) and ante-mortem (AM) data. PM data are generated from the recovered human remains, which may be highly fragmented depending on the type of disaster. AM data come from either direct reference samples (e.g., toothbrushes or razors known to belong to the victim) or kinship comparisons to biological relatives (e.g., parent, child, or sibling).

D.N.A. Box 17.4 World Trade Center Victim DNA Identification Efforts

The terrorist attacks against the United States on 11 September 2001 left over 3000 victims in three different locations: the Pentagon in Washington, DC, a field near Shanksville (Somerset County), Pennsylvania, and the twin towers of the World Trade Center (WTC) in New York City. DNA samples from the Pentagon and Pennsylvania sites were processed by the Armed Forces DNA Identification Laboratory (AFDIL) while the WTC work was performed by the New York City Office of Chief Medical Examiner Department of Forensic Biology, the New York State Police, and a number of contract laboratories and consultants.

The DNA identification efforts for the WTC victims have become arguably the world's largest forensic case to date. More than 19,917 pieces of human remains were collected from a pile of rubble weighing over a million tons and extending more than 70 feet (21m) in height following the crushing collapse of the Twin Towers. The initial removal and sorting of human remains took place between September 2001 and May 2002. However, the primary DNA identification efforts went on for more than 3 years—almost 2.5 years after the last piece of debris had been removed from the WTC site. As of late 2008, more than 1600 victims of the 2749 present when the Twin Towers collapsed had been identified. Without the capabilities of DNA testing, there would have been only a fraction of the victims identified based on other modalities such as fingerprints and dental records.

Biological samples recovered from the WTC site had been subjected to extreme pressures with the building collapse and then subterranean fires of 1500°F (815°C) or more for the 3 months following the terrorist attack. The jet fuel from both planes that rammed the WTC towers burned intensely enough to melt the steel support beams and bring down the buildings. Thus, human remains in this pressure cooker were often comingled, very fragmented, and in many cases likely vaporized.

Several innovations came out of the 9/11 tragedy. These included new extraction methods from bone, reduced size amplicons or miniSTRs, panels of single nucleotide polymorphisms (SNPs), and high-throughput mitochondrial DNA sequencing. In addition, new software was developed to aid in matching reference samples and recovered remains as well as associating remains with the same DNA profile.

One of the largest challenges from this investigation was review of the massive amounts of data produced by contracting laboratories. More than 52,528 STR profiles, 16,938 SNP profiles, and 31,155 mtDNA sequences were generated in an effort to identify the 2749 victims of the World Trade Center collapse based on 19,917 recovered remains—truly a heroic effort. Most of the data from the recovered remains contained only partial DNA profiles, making it even more difficult to sort through and piece together sufficient information to make a reliable identification. While we hope to never see the likes of another 11 September 2001 terrorist attack, forensic DNA typing laboratories should be prepared to aid in victim identification efforts in future mass fatality incidents.

Sources:
Biesecker, L. G., et al. (2005). DNA identifications after the 9/11 World Trade Center attack. *Science, 310,* 1122–1123.
Shaler, R. C. (2005). *Who they were—Inside the World Trade Center DNA story: The unprecedented effort to identify the missing.* New York: Free Press.

DVI is much more complicated than parentage testing because so many more comparisons are being made depending on the number of victims involved. In addition, the quality of the recovered human remains may be compromised depending on the type of disaster and thus partial DNA profiles or mixtures may result. DNA statistics for DVI work are usually best represented with likelihood ratios because this permits DNA results to be combined between multiple genetic systems as well as other non-DNA evidence.

DNA testing has been used to help identify victims of numerous airline crashes, the victims of terrorist attacks (D.N.A. Box 17.4), recovered remains

D.N.A. Box 17.5 DNA Identification from Mass Graves

DNA can play an important role in identifying remains in unmarked graves. Unfortunately, there are regions of the world that have suffered severely under the hands of ruthless dictators who do not value human life. Mass graves are often the tragic trademark of such tyrants.

The former Yugoslavia contains an estimated 40,000 unidentified bodies in mass graves. The International Commission on Missing Persons (ICMP) was created in 1996 to help with identifying human remains in these mass graves. In effect, the ICMP is using DNA technology to map human genocide.

One of the major challenges for performing DNA identification from mass graves is obtaining biological reference samples from relatives. Family outreach centers take information and blood samples from living relatives such as parents or a spouse and a child of a missing loved one. These reference samples are then typed with STRs and mitochondrial

DNA sequencing to provide points of comparison to results obtained from the remains in mass graves.

Mitochondrial DNA often is the only source of successful DNA recovery from bones that have been in the ground for many years although improved DNA extraction methods have enabled successful STR typing results to be obtained in many cases. DNA often provides the only way to confirm the death of a missing person, enable return of the remains to a living relative, and help bring justice to the criminals who initiated the massacres that led to the mass grave sites.

Sources:

Huffine, E., et al. (2001). Mass identification of persons missing from the break-up of the former Yugoslavia: Structure, function, and role of the International Commission on Missing Persons. *Croatian Medical Journal, 42,* 271–275.

International Commission on Missing Persons (ICMP). http://www .ic-mp.org

---

from mass graves (D.N.A. Box 17.5), and in a more limited fashion in natural disasters like the Southeast Asia tsunami that occurred in December 2004 and Hurricane Katrina, which struck New Orleans in August 2005.

Several documents have been published with lessons learned from previous DVI work. In 2007, the International Society of Forensic Genetics (ISFG) published 12 recommendations for DVI work. More details on mass disaster victim identification and issues faced can be found in the companion *Advanced Topics* volume and through reviewing articles cited in the reference section at the end of this chapter.

MISSING PERSONS INVESTIGATIONS

An estimated 40,000 unidentified human remains have been recovered and are currently located in medical examiner and coroners' offices around the United States. Every year in the United States, tens of thousands of people become 'missing,' often under suspicious circumstances. While some of these missing persons are later located alive through law enforcement efforts, many become unidentified human remains that resulted from criminal activity, such as rape and murder. Knowledge of who the victim is can help solve these crimes and bring closure to families of the missing.

There are three categories of samples associated with missing persons cases: direct reference samples, family reference samples, and unidentified human remains (UHR) samples. The UHR samples are generally skeletal remains (bones), teeth, or tissue. Much of the data from missing person investigations is in the form of mitochondrial DNA sequences since this information can be successfully recovered from highly degraded samples. Mitochondrial DNA also enables access to a larger number of reference samples from maternal relatives of a victim.

Some possible direct reference samples include medical samples from the missing individual, such as a newborn screening bloodspot or a biopsy sample. Personal effects, such as a toothbrush or hairbrush, may also provide direct reference samples. Family reference samples can be buccal swabs from close biological relatives, such as parents, children, or siblings of the missing individual. More distant relatives, such as maternal aunts, maternal or paternal uncles, or maternal or paternal cousins, can also be useful if mitochondrial or Y-chromosome DNA testing is performed. A combination of samples from more than one close relative can help provide greater confidence in this kinship analysis (D.N.A. Box 17.6).

D.N.A. Box 17.6 Verifying the Identity of Saddam Hussein

'We've got him!' were the words of Paul Bremer, U.S. governor in Iraq, at a press conference on 14 December 2003. From the beginning of the war in Iraq in March 2003, one of the stated missions of the United States military was to kill or capture Saddam Hussein, the dictator of Iraq, in order to remove him from power after more than two decades of threatening the world and terrorizing his own people. However, Saddam was known to have many 'stunt doubles' to protect his life from assassins. Therefore, the ability to verify his identity through genetic testing was essential to knowing that the United States in fact 'had their man.' Forensic DNA testing using short tandem repeat (STR) markers played an important role in the identification effort behind the words of Paul Bremer.

Validated reference samples are required in any missing persons investigation or paternity testing when kinship is being verified through similarities in nuclear or mitochondrial DNA profiles. In this case, DNA from Saddam's two sons provided the family reference samples. Saddam's sons Uday and Qusay were killed in a gunfight near Mosul, Iraq, on 22 July 2003. DNA samples were collected from their remains shortly after they were killed for use as reference samples in verifying the identity of their father if he was ever located.

Both autosomal and Y-chromosome STR profiles were generated from Uday and Qusay's biological samples.

Shortly after Saddam was captured in a small hole underneath a farmhouse near Tikrit, Iraq, in December 2003, blood and hair samples were flown to the United States where they were immediately examined by DNA scientists at the Armed Forces DNA Identification Laboratory (AFDIL) located near Washington, DC. Working through the night, several scientists carefully extracted and then amplified the DNA sample using the autosomal STR kits Profiler Plus and COfiler to obtain a full 13-locus STR profile. These STR profiles possessed alleles in common with the previously generated DNA profiles of Saddam's two sons. Additionally, the Y-chromosome STR kit Y-PLEX 6 also showed full allele sharing between Saddam and his two sons, indicating that the sample in question was from their same paternal lineage. Saddam's capture was a great relief to many who feared his reemergence and continued terror campaign.

Sources:
Personal communication from AFDIL.
Walgate, R. (2003). Saddam's DNA (19 December 2003 daily news article). *The Scientist.*

DNA databases can play an important role in helping identify missing individuals over time. When a family member goes missing, DNA samples can be obtained from direct reference samples or biological relatives. DNA profiles from these samples would then be uploaded to the database and searched against DNA profiles from unidentified human remains in an effort to make an association to a missing individual. Many states within the United States and nations around the world are beginning to establish missing persons databases to enable matching of recovered remains to their family members. The National DNA Index System (NDIS) discussed in Chapter 12 also contains indices to help with missing persons investigations.

In an effort to help make connections between family members and their missing relatives, the U.S. government established in 2007 a National Missing and Unidentified Persons System (NamUs) Web site. As of December 2008, NamUs listed 2734 unidentified human remains cases, of which 2641 were open.

OTHER USES FOR STRs AND DNA TYPING METHODS

STR typing with the same core set of markers and commercial STR kits is being used for several other purposes besides forensic and parentage testing. These applications involve mixture detection or tracking genetic inheritance and family relationships.

Characterizing cell lines

Cell lines can, unfortunately, become contaminated by other cell lines in the laboratory, resulting in either mixtures or a complete transformation to the new cell line. Human cell line authentication is now being carried out by the American Type Culture Collection (ATCC) along with other international suppliers of cell lines.

STR typing enables rapid discovery of cross-contamination between cell lines and may serve as a universal reference standard for characterizing human cell lines. This type of analysis has been dubbed 'cell culture forensics.' Over the past several years, the ATCC has created a database of over 500 human cell lines that have been run with eight STR loci present in the PowerPlex 1.2 kit from the Promega Corporation (see http://www.atcc.org). It is important to note that cell cultures, such as K562 (D.N.A. Box 14.3), may not always have a regular diploid complement of chromosomes and thus may possess tri-allelic patterns and severe peak imbalances due to the presence of additional copies of one allele.

Detecting genetic chimeras

Chimerism, which is the presence of two genetically distinct cell lines in an organism, can be acquired through blood stem cell transplantation or blood transfusion or can be inherited. Approximately 8% of nonidentical twins can have chimeric blood. Several years ago an interesting case was reported of a phenotypically normal woman who possessed different DNA types in different body tissues due to tetragametic chimerism (D.N.A. Box 17.7).

A 2004 study with 203 matched related donor–recipient pairs ranked 27 different STRs, including the 13 CODIS core loci, in terms of their ability to detect chimeric mixtures. Not surprisingly, the loci with the highest heterozygosities, namely, Penta E, SE33, D2S1338, and D18S51, worked the best.

Monitoring transplants

Monitoring the engraftment of donor cells after bone marrow transplants or allogeneic blood stem cell transplantation is another important application of STR testing. Examination of STR profiles from transplant recipients can help diagnose graft failure or a relapse of the disease. In these cases, mixtures are detected as mixed chimerism that exists within the recipient from their own cells and those of the donor.

D.N.A. Box 17.7 Natural Mixtures and Chimeric Individuals

In May 2002, the *New England Journal of Medicine* published a report of the genetic analysis of a phenotypically normal chimeric individual who was unexpectedly identified because histocompatibility testing of family members suggested that she was not the biological mother of two of her three children. The doctors examining this chimeric individual proposed that her condition had arisen because two fertilized eggs, destined originally to be fraternal twins, had fused to form a zygote that possessed DNA of two different types. Thus, from a genetic perspective she was both her children's mother and their aunt.

Among the various genetic tests performed on this chimeric individual was analysis of 22 STR loci. All of the CODIS core loci except CSF1PO were examined in this study. This unusual patient possessed some differences in her STR profiles among various tissues tested. While the buccal and blood samples tested matched exactly, a mixture containing another type was present as the minor component in the thyroid, hair, and skin cells of this chimeric patient.

It is believed that chimeric individuals such as the one described here are most likely extremely rare in the general population. Nevertheless, it is possible in theory for DNA testing from different tissues of a chimeric individual to not match one another and thus lead to a false exclusion. The possibility of chimeric individuals may increase in frequency with the rise of *in vitro* fertilization since multiple eggs are sometimes fertilized in order to increase the success rate of the procedure.

Sources:

Baron, D. (2003). *DNA tests shed light on hybrid human*. National Public Radio—Morning Edition, August 11, 2003. Available at http://www.npr.org

Pearson, H. (2002). Human genetics: Dual identities. *Nature, 417*, 10–11.

Yu, N., et al. (2002). Disputed maternity leading to identification of tetragametic chimerism. *New England Journal of Medicine, 346*, 1545–1552.

Verifying cloning success

When an organism is cloned, STR typing using genetic markers specific to the organism tested (e.g., cat or dog) has been used in some cases to verify success of the cloning process. If an identical STR profile is not observed between the supposedly cloned animal and its originating 'parent' cells, then the cloning process was not successful. This STR typing approach was used several years ago to verify the authenticity of the cloned Korean dog 'Snuppy.'

Detecting fetal cells in mother's blood

When a mother is pregnant, some of her child's cells can be transferred through the placenta and be detected in her bloodstream. This condition, known as microchimerism, has been used to perform noninvasive prenatal paternity testing from maternal blood.

Monitoring needle sharing among drug users

In yet another application of the capability to perform mixture detection with STRs, a laboratory method was described using the CODIS STR marker D8S1179 (called D6S502 in the paper) to differentiate between single- and multiple-person use of syringes by intravenous drug users. Monitoring needle sharing can help determine the source of spreading blood-borne pathogens among drug users.

Detecting cancer tumors

Loss of heterozygosity (LOH) is a method of monitoring genetic deletions common in tumors for many types of cancers. LOH is manifested by severe allelic imbalance at a locus in a single-source DNA sample so that a true heterozygote almost appears as a homozygote since some of the chromosomes have a deletion present in the region of the locus being PCR amplified.

Probably the only time that LOH would have an impact on human identity testing is if an archived clinical specimen from a tissue biopsy was used as a reference sample to identify someone from a mass disaster. However, it is worth being aware that normal and cancerous tissue from an individual can vary fairly dramatically in some instances in terms of their STR allele peak heights. An examination of a cancer biopsy tissue specimen compared to normal tissue with the nine STR loci present in the AmpFlSTR Profiler kit found that the D13S317 locus exhibited a severe peak imbalance consistent with that seen arising from LOH. The authors suggest that this LOH might be due to a deletion of 13q21–22 seen previously with prostate cancer that is near the physical location of D13S317 on chromosome 13.

Mapping genetic diseases

Genome scans for disease gene mapping have been routinely performed with around 400 STRs covering the human genome at 5 centiMorgan (cM) to 10 cM distances. For a number of years, Marshfield Genetics (http://research .marshfieldclinic.org/genetics) and the Center for Inherited Disease Research (CIDR; http://www.cidr.jhmi.edu) performed high-volume genetic testing using hundreds of STRs per DNA sample. Studies of STR allele frequencies between normal and disease patient populations were used to help make associations with the genetic disease. When correlations were made between an STR locus and a disease gene through linkage analysis, then the known location of the STR marker could be used to help pinpoint the previously unknown location of the disease gene of interest.

Examining human population diversity and tracing human history

Tracing human migration throughout history is an interesting academic use of DNA typing. Sample sets from various groups of living individuals are gathered and examined with a number of DNA tests to try to estimate past connections between the groups based on DNA similarities or differences.

The Genographic Project is a large effort begun in 2005 to trace human history by examining Y-chromosome and mitochondrial DNA results from tens of thousands of individuals around the world. Analysis of Y-chromosome STRs and mitochondrial DNA have also been used for genetic genealogy studies. Both STR markers and single nucleotide polymorphisms (SNPs) should continue to play an important role in understanding human diversity at the genetic level.

GENETIC GENEALOGY

Genealogists in large numbers are beginning to turn to Y-chromosome DNA testing to extend their research efforts. A number of so-called genetic genealogy companies have begun offering DNA testing services to avid family historians in order to help establish links between related individuals when the paper documentary trail runs cold. The major assumption behind these efforts is that surnames, which generally are passed on from father to son, can be correlated to Y-chromosome haplotype results. An early study with four Y-STR markers found a common core haplotype in 21 out of 48 men with the Sykes surname. Unfortunately, illegitimacy, adoption, and Y-STR mutations introduce a level of ambiguity into results. Nevertheless, this field is taking off quickly with demands for higher numbers of tested markers than are currently used in the forensic DNA typing community. As these DNA testing services are offered to the general public, results from genetic genealogy labs have been used for interesting applications such as tracking sperm bank fathers using the publicly available databases (e.g., http://www.ysearch.org).

Tens of thousands of genetic genealogy tests, primarily Y-STR typing of a dozen to a few dozen loci, are being conducted each year by several commercial enterprises. These companies offer Y-STR 'surname' (paternal lineage) testing and mitochondrial DNA (maternal lineage) testing for genealogical purposes. Each company typically has its own database to enable comparisons to those with similar DNA results. The International Society of Genetic Genealogy (ISOGG) maintains a Web site at http://www.isogg.org that compares the cost and numbers of Y-STR markers analyzed by companies such as Oxford Ancestors (Oxford, England), FamilyTree DNA (Houston, TX), DNA Ancestry (Salt Lake City, UT), and DNA Heritage (Dorset, England).

Points for Discussion

- What are some of the challenges in attempting kinship associations in parentage testing, disaster victim identification, and missing persons investigations using DNA instead of direct matching as performed in forensic testing?
- Why are disaster victim identifications more challenging than missing persons investigations?
- How might genetic genealogy information intersect with forensic DNA testing in the future?

READING LIST AND INTERNET RESOURCES

Parentage Testing

AABB relationship testing annual reports. http://www.aabb.org/Content/Accreditation/Parentage_Testing_Accreditation_Program/Relationship_Testing_Annual_Reports

Buckleton, J., et al. (2007). Parentage analysis and other applications of human identity testing (Chapter 82). In I. Freckelton & H. Selby (Eds.), *Expert evidence*. North Ryde, Australia: Thomson Lawbook Co.

Gjertson, D. W., et al. (2002). Parentage testing. In T. L. Simon (Ed.), *Rossi's principles of transfusion medicine* (3rd ed.) (pp. 898–911). Philadelphia: Lippincott, Williams & Wilkins.

Gjertson, D. W., et al. (2007). ISFG: Recommendations on biostatistics in paternity testing. *Forensic Science International Genetics, 1*, 223–231.

Morling, N., et al. (2002). Paternity testing commission of the international society of forensic genetics: Recommendations on genetic investigations in paternity cases. *Forensic Science International, 129*, 148–157.

Thomson, J. A., et al. (1999). Validation of short tandem repeat analysis for the investigation of cases of disputed paternity. *Forensic Science International, 100*, 1–16.

Thomson, J. A., et al. (2001). Analysis of disputed single-parent/child and sibling relationships using 16 STR loci. *International Journal of Legal Medicine, 115*, 128–134.

Wenk, R. E. (2004). Testing for parentage and kinship. *Current Opinion in Hematology, 11*, 357–361.

Wurmb-Schwark, N., et al. (2006). Possible pitfalls in motherless paternity analysis with related putative fathers. *Forensic Science International, 159*, 92–97.

Calculations and software

Brenner, C. H. (1997). Symbolic kinship program. *Genetics, 145*, 535–542.

DNA-View. http://dna-view.com

Drabek, J. (2009). Validation of software for calculating the likelihood ratio for parentage and kinship. *Forensic Science International: Genetics, 3*, 112–118.

EasyDNA. http://www.hku.hk/statistics/EasyDNA

Eisenberg, A. (2003). Popstats relatedness statistics. *Workshop presented at 14th international symposium on human identification.* Available at http://www.promega.com/geneticidproc/ussymp14proc/stats_workshop.htm

Familias software program. http://www.math.chalmers.se/~mostad/familias

Lucy, D. (2005). *Introduction to statistics for forensic scientists.* Hoboken, NJ: Wiley.

Paternity Index. http://www.paternityindex.com

Sibship testing

Allen, R. W., et al. (2007). Considerations for the interpretation of STR results in cases of questioned half-sibship. *Transfusion, 47*, 515–519.

Gaytmenn, R., et al. (2002). Determination of the sensitivity and specificity of sibship calculations using AmpF*l*STR profiler plus. *International Journal of Legal Medicine, 116*, 161–164.

Wenk, R. E., et al. (1996). Determination of sibship in any two persons. *Transfusion, 36*, 259–262.

Mutation rates

Brinkman, B., et al. (1998). Mutation rate in human microsatellites: Influence of the structure and length of the tandem repeat. *American Journal of Human Genetics, 62*, 1408–1415.

Hohoff, C., et al. (2006). Meiosis study in a population sample from Afghanistan: Allele frequencies and mutation rates of 16 STR loci. *International Journal of Legal Medicine, 120*, 300–302.

STRBase Mutation Rates for Common Loci. http://www.cstl.nist.gov/biotech/strbase/mutation.htm

Vicard, P., et al. (2008). Estimating mutation rates from paternity casework. *Forensic Science International: Genetics, 2*, 9–18.

Disaster Victim Identification
General information

Alonso, A., et al. (2005). Challenges of DNA profiling in mass disaster investigations. *Croatian Medical Journal, 46*, 540–548.

Buckleton, J., et al. (2005). Disaster victim identification, identification of missing persons, and immigration cases. In J. Buckleton, C. M. Triggs, & S. J. Walsh (Eds.), *Forensic DNA evidence interpretation* (Chapter 11, pp. 395–437). Boca Raton, FL: CRC Press.

Corach, D., et al. (1995). Mass disasters: Rapid molecular screening of human remains by means of short tandem repeats typing. *Electrophoresis, 16*, 1617–1623.

Graham, E. A. M. (2006). Disaster victim identification. *Forensic Science Medicine and Pathology, 2*, 203–207.

Recommendations

Budowle, B., et al. (2005). Forensic aspects of mass disasters: Strategic considerations for DNA-based human identification. *Legal Medicine, 7*, 230–243.

International Criminal Police Organization, Interpol Disaster Victim Identification Guide. Available at http://www.interpol.int/Public/DisasterVictim/default.asp

Lee, J., et al. (2008). Recommendations for DNA laboratories supporting disaster victim identification (DVI) operations—Australian and New Zealand consensus on ISFG recommendations. *Forensic Science International: Genetics, 3*, 54–56.

National Institute of Justice. (2005). *Mass fatality incidents: A guide for human forensic identification*. http://www.ojp.usdoj.gov/nij/pubs-sum/199758.htm

National Institute of Justice. (2006). *Lessons learned from 9/11: DNA identifications in mass fatality incidents*. http://massfatality.dna.gov

Prinz, M., et al. (2007). DNA Commission of the international society of forensic genetics (ISFG): Recommendations regarding the role of forensic genetics for disaster victim identification (DVI). *Forensic Science International: Genetics, 1*, 3–12.

Westen, A. A., et al. (2008). Femur, rib, and tooth sample collection for DNA analysis in disaster victim identification (DVI): A method to minimize contamination risk. *Forensic Science Medicine and Pathology, 4*, 15–21.

Waco Branch Davidian fire

Clayton, T. M., et al. (1995). Identification of bodies from the scene of a mass disaster using DNA amplification and short tandem repeat (STR) loci. *Forensic Science International, 76*, 7–15.

DiZinno, J., et al. (1994). The Waco, Texas incident: The use of DNA analysis to identify human remains. In: *Proceedings from the fifth international symposium on human identification* (pp. 129–135). Madison, WI: Promega.

Airplane crashes

Ballantyne, J. (1996). Mass disaster genetics. *Nature Genetics, 15*, 329–331.

Goodwin, W., et al. (1999). The use of mitochondrial DNA and short tandem repeat typing in the identification of air crash victims. *Electrophoresis, 20*, 1707–1711.

Olaisen, B., et al. (1997). Identification by DNA analysis of the victims of the August 1996 spitsbergen civil aircraft disaster. *Nature Genetics, 15*, 402–405.

Swissair Flight 111

Fregeau, C. J., et al. (2000). The swissair flight 111 disaster: Short tandem repeat mutations observed. *Progress in Forensic Genetics 8*, 40–42.

Leclair, B., et al. (2000). Enhanced kinship analysis and STR-based DNA typing for human identification in mass disasters. *Progress in Forensic Genetics 8*, 91–93.

Leclair, B., et al. (2004). Enhanced kinship analysis and STR-based DNA typing for human identification in mass fatality incidents: The Swissair Flight 111 disaster. *Journal of Forensic Sciences, 49*, 939–953.

Southeast Asian tsunami

Brenner, C. H. (2006). Some mathematical problems in the DNA identification of victims in the 2004 tsunami and similar mass fatalities. *Forensic Science International, 157*, 172–180.

Deng, Y.-J., et al. (2005). Preliminary DNA identification for the tsunami victims in Thailand. *Genomics, Proteomics & Bioinformatics, 3*, 143–157.

Zehner, R. (2007). 'Foreign' DNA in tissue adherent to compact bone from tsunami victims. *Forensic Science International: Genetics, 1*, 218–222.

Hurricane Katrina

Donkervoort, S., et al. (2008). Enhancing accurate data collection in mass fatality kinship identifications: Lessons learned from hurricane katrina. *Forensic Science International: Genetics, 2*, 354–362.

9/11/01: Pentagon and Pennsylvania sites

Edson, S. M., et al. (2004). Naming the dead—Confronting the realities of rapid identification of degraded skeletal remains. *Forensic Science Review, 16*, 63–90.

9/11/01: World Trade Center DNA identification effort

Biesecker, L. G., et al. (2005). DNA identifications after the 9/11 World Trade Center attack. *Science, 310*, 1122–1123.

Brenner, C. H., & Weir, B. S. (2003). Issues and strategies in the identification of World Trade Center victims. *Theoretical Population Biology, 63*, 173–178.

Budimlija, Z. M., et al. (2003). World Trade Center human identification project: Experiences with individual body identification cases. *Croatian Medical Journal, 44*, 259–263.

Gill, J. R. (2006). 9/11 and the New York City Office of Chief Medical Examiner. *Forensic Science Medicine and Pathology, 2*, 29–32.

Hennessey, M. (2002). World Trade Center DNA identifications: The administrative review process. In: *Proceedings of the thirteenth international symposium on human identification.* Available at http://www.promega.com/geneticidproc/ussymp13proc/contents/hennesseyrev1.pdf

Holland, M. M., et al. (2003). Development of a quality, high throughput DNA analysis procedure for skeletal samples to assist with the identification of victims from the World Trade Center attacks. *Croatian Medical Journal, 44*, 264–272.

Leclair, B., et al. (2007). Bioinformatics and human identification in mass fatality incidents: The World Trade Center disaster. *Journal of Forensic Sciences, 52*, 806–819.

National Institute of Justice. (2006). Lessons learned from 9/11: DNA identifications in mass fatality incidents. http://massfatality.dna.gov

Shaler, R. C. (2005). *Who they were—Inside the World Trade Center DNA story: The unprecedented effort to identify the missing.* New York: Free Press.

Mass graves

Baybar, J. P. (2008). When DNA is not available, can we still identify people? Recommendations for best practice. *Journal of Forensic Sciences, 53*, 533–540.

Biruš, I., et al. (2003). How high should paternity index be for reliable identification of war victims by DNA typing? *Croatian Medical Journal, 44*, 322–326.

Cox, M., et al. (2008). *The scientific investigation of mass graves: Towards protocols and standard operating procedures.* New York: Cambridge University Press.

Davoren, J., et al. (2007). Highly effective DNA extraction method for nuclear short tandem repeat testing of skeletal remains from mass graves. *Croatian Medical Journal, 48*, 478–485.

Gornik, I., et al. (2002). The identification of war victims by reverse paternity is associated with significant risks of false inclusion. *International Journal of Legal Medicine, 116*, 255–257.

Huffine, E., et al. (2001). Mass identification of persons missing from the break-up of the former Yugoslavia: Structure, function, and role of the International Commission on Missing Persons. *Croatian Medical Journal, 42*, 271–275.

Huffine, E., et al. (2007). Developing role of forensics in deterring violence and genocide. *Croatian Medical Journal, 48*, 431–436.

International Commission on Missing Persons (ICMP). http://www.ic-mp.org

Kracun, S. K., et al. (2007). Population substructure can significantly affect reliability of a DNA-led process of identification of mass fatality victims. *Journal of Forensic Sciences, 52*, 874–878.

Primorac, D. (2004). The role of DNA technology in identification of skeletal remains discovered in mass graves. *Forensic Science International, 146S*, S163–S164.

Williams, E. D., & Crews, J. D. (2003). From dust to dust: Ethical and practical issues involved in the location, exhumation, and identification of bodies from mass graves. *Croatian Medical Journal, 44*, 251–258.

Missing Persons Investigations

FBI National Missing Persons Program. http://www.fbi.gov/wanted/kidnap/kidmiss.htm

National Center for Missing & Exploited Children. http://www.missingkids.com/

National Crime Information Center (NCIC). http://www.fbi.gov/hq/cjisd/ncic.htm

National Institute of Justice articles. http://www.dna.gov/pubs/missing

National Missing and Unidentified Persons System (NamUs). http://www.namus.gov

Holland, M. M., et al. (1993). Mitochondrial DNA sequence analysis of human skeletal remains: Identification of remains from the Vietnam War. *Journal of Forensic Sciences, 38*, 542–553.

Lorente, J. A., et al. (2002). Social benefits of non-criminal genetic databases: Missing persons and human remains identification. *International Journal of Legal Medicine, 116*, 187–190.

University of North Texas Center for Human Identification. http://www.unthumanid.org

Other Uses for STRs
Characterizing cell lines

ATCC STR Profile Database for Cell Lines. http://www.atcc.org/CulturesandProducts/CellBiology/STRProfileDatabase/tabid/174/Default.aspx

Azari, S., et al. (2007). Profiling and authentication of human cell lines using short tandem repeat (STR) loci: Report from the National Cell Bank of Iran. *Biologicals, 35,* 195–202.

Cabrera, C. M., et al. (2006). Identity tests: Determination of cell line cross-contamination. *Cytotechnology, 51,* 45–50.

Hughes, P., et al. (2007). The costs of using unauthenticated, over-passaged cell lines: How much more data do we need? *Biotechniques, 43,* 575–584.

Masters, J. R., et al. (2001). Short tandem repeat profiling provides an international reference standard for human cell lines. In: *Proceedings of the National Academy of Sciences of the United States of America, 98,* 8012–8017.

Matsuo, Y., et al. (1999). Efficient DNA fingerprinting method for the identification of cross- culture contamination of cell lines. *Human Cell, 12,* 149–154.

NIH Notice Regarding Authentication of Cultured Cell Lines. http://grants.nih.gov/grants/guide/notice-files/NOT-OD-08-017.html

O'Brien, S. J. (2001). Cell culture forensics. In: *Proceedings of the National Academy of Sciences of the United States of America, 98,* 7656–7658.

Parson, W., et al. (2005). Cancer cell line identification by short tandem repeat profiling: Power and limitations. *FASEB Journal, 19,* 434–436.

Webb, M. B., et al. (1992). Cell line characterisation by DNA fingerprinting: A review. *Developments in Biological Standardization, 76,* 39–42.

Monitoring transplants and detecting genetic chimeras

Hong, Y. C., et al. (2007). Hair follicle: A reliable source of recipient origin after allogeneic hematopoietic stem cell transplantation. *Bone Marrow Transplantation, 40,* 871–874.

Lee, K.-H., et al. (2003). Monthly prospective analysis of hematopoietic chimerism after allogeneic hematopoietic cell transplantation. *Bone Marrow Transplantation, 32,* 423–431.

Millson, A. S., et al. (2000). Comparison of automated short tandem repeat and manual variable number of tandem repeat analysis of chimerism in bone marrow transplant patients. *Diagnostic Molecular Pathology, 9,* 91–97.

Nollet, C., et al. (2001). Standardisation of multiplex fluorescent short tandem repeat analysis for chimerism testing. *Bone Marrow Transplantation, 28,* 511–518.

Spyridonidis, A., et al. (2005). Capillary electrophoresis for chimerism monitoring by PCR amplification of microsatellite markers after allogeneic hematopoietic cell transplantation. *Clinical Transplantation, 19,* 350–356.

Thiede, C., et al. (1999). Rapid quantification of mixed chimerism using multiplex amplification of short tandem repeat markers and fluorescence detection. *Bone Marrow Transplantation, 23,* 1055–1060.

Thiede, C., et al. (2001). Sequential monitoring of chimerism and detection of minimal residual disease after allogeneic blood stem cell transplantation (BSCT) using multiplex PCR amplification of short tandem repeat-markers. *Leukemia, 15,* 293–302.

Thiede, C. (2004). Diagnostic chimerism analysis after allogeneic stem cell transplantation: New methods and markers. *American Journal of Pharmacogenomics, 4*, 177–187.

Thiede, C., et al. (2004). Evaluation of STR informativity for chimerism testing—Comparative analysis of 27 STR systems in 203 matched related donor recipient pairs. *Leukemia, 18*, 248–254.

van Dijk, B. A., et al. (1996). Blood group chimerism in human multiple births is not rare. *American Journal of Medical Genetics, 61*, 264–268.

Walker, T. J. (2008). Chimaerism, mosaicism, and forensic DNA analysis. *Canadian Society of Forensic Science Journal, 41*, 21–28.

Yu, N., et al. (2002). Disputed maternity leading to identification of tetragametic chimerism. *New England Journal of Medicine, 346*, 1545–1552.

Verifying cloning success

Parker, H. G., et al. (2006). DNA analysis of a putative dog clone. *Nature, 440*, E1–E2.

Monitoring needle sharing

Shrestha, S., et al. (2000). Short tandem repeat methodology for genotypic identification of single-person versus multi-person use of syringes. *AIDS, 14*, 1507–1513.

Shrestha, S., et al. (2006). Multiperson use of syringes among injection drug users in a needle exchange program: A gene-based molecular epidemiologic analysis. *Journal of Acquired Immune Deficiency Syndromes, 43*, 335–343.

Shrestha, S., et al. (2006). Unknown biological mixtures evaluation using STR analytical quantification. *Electrophoresis, 27*, 409–415.

Detecting cancer tumors

Hyytinen, E. R., et al. (1999). Three distinct regions of allelic loss at 13q14, 13q21–22, and 13q33 in prostate cancer. *Genes, Chromosomes and Cancer, 25*, 108–114.

Rubocki, R. J., et al. (2000). Loss of heterozygosity detected in a short tandem repeat (STR) locus commonly used for human DNA identification. *Journal of Forensic Sciences, 45*, 1087–1089.

Pelotti, S., et al. (2007). Cancerous tissues in forensic genetic analysis. *Genetic Testing, 11*, 397–400.

Poetsch, M., et al. (2004). Evaluation of allelic alterations in short tandem repeats in different kinds of solid tumors—Possible pitfalls in forensic casework. *Forensic Science International, 145*, 1–6.

Vauhkonen, H., et al. (2004). Evaluation of gastrointestinal cancer tissues as a source of genetic information for forensic investigations by using STRs. *Forensic Science International, 139*, 159–167.

Detecting fetal cells in mother's blood

Wagner, J., et al. (2008). Analysis of multiple loci can increase reliability of detection of fetal Y-chromosome DNA in maternal plasma. *Prenatal Diagnosis, 28*, 412–416.

Wagner, J., et al. (2009). Non-invasive prenatal paternity from maternal blood. *International Journal of Legal Medicine, 123*, 75–79.

Mapping genetic disease

Center for Inherited Disease Research (CIDR). http://www.cidr.jhmi.edu (no longer offering STR whole genome scans—now performing SNP analysis)

Ghebranious, N., et al. (2003). STRP screening sets for the human genome at 5 cM density. *BMC Genomics, 4*(1), 6. Available at http://www.biomedcentral.com/bmcgenomics

Marshfield Genetics. http://research.marshfieldclinic.org/genetics (generated more than 68 million genotypes with STR whole genome scans between 1994 and 2006)

Examining human population diversity

Rosenberg, N. A., et al. (2002). Genetic structure of human populations. *Science, 298,* 2381–2385.

Rosenberg, N. A., et al. (2003). Informativeness of genetic markers for inference of ancestry. *American Journal of Human Genetics, 73,* 1402–1422.

Shriver, M. D., & Kittles, R. A. (2004). Genetic ancestry and the search for personalized genetic histories. *Nature Reviews Genetics, 5,* 611–618.

Helgason, A., et al. (2003). A population-wide coalescent analysis of Icelandic matrilineal and patrilineal genealogies: Evidence for a faster evolutionary rate of mtDNA lineages than Y chromosomes. *American Journal of Human Genetics, 72,* 1370–1388.

Tracing human migrations and the genographic project

Behar, D. M., et al. (2007). The genographic project public participation mitochondrial DNA database. *PLoS Genetics, 3,* e104.

Genographic Project Web site. https://www3.nationalgeographic.com/genographic

Jobling, M. A., Hurles, M. E., & Tyler-Smith, C. (2004). *Human evolutionary genetics: Origins, peoples, and diseases.* New York: Garland Science.

Olson, S. (2002). *Mapping human history.* New York: Houghton Mifflin.

Relethford, J. H. (2001). *Genetics and the search for modern human origins.* New York: Wiley-Liss.

Relethford, J. H. (2003). *Reflections of our past: How human history is revealed in our genes.* Boulder, CO: Westview Press.

Stix, G. (2008). Traces of a distant past. *Scientific American* (July), 56–63.

Underhill, P. A., & Kivisild, T. (2007). Use of Y chromosome and mitochondrial DNA population structure in tracing human migrations. *Annual Review of Genetics, 41,* 539–564.

Wells, S. (2007). *Deep ancestry: Inside the genographic project.* Washington, DC: National Geographic.

Zalloua, P. A., et al. (2008). Identifying genetic traces of historical expansions: Phoenician footprints in the Mediterranean. *American Journal of Human Genetics, 83,* 633–642.

Zerjal, T., et al. (2003). The genetic legacy of the Mongols. *American Journal of Human Genetics, 72,* 717–721.

Genetic Genealogy

Bolnick, D. A., et al. (2007). Genetics: The science and business of genetic ancestry testing. *Science, 318*, 399–400.

Brown, K. (2002). Tangled roots? Genetics meets genealogy. *Science, 295*, 1634–1635.

Butler, J. M., et al. (2008). Addressing Y-chromosome short tandem repeat (Y-STR) allele nomenclature. *Journal of Genetic Genealogy, 4*(2), 125–148. Available at http://www.jogg.info

DNA Ancestry. http://dna.ancestry.com

FamilyTree DNA. http://www.familytreedna.com

International Society of Genetic Genealogy. http://www.isogg.org

Jobling, M. A. (2001). In the name of the father: Surnames and genetics. *Trends in Genetics, 17*, 353–357.

Jobling, M. A., & Tyler-Smith, C. (2003). The human Y chromosome: An evolutionary marker comes of age. *Nature Reviews Genetics, 4*, 598–612.

Journal of Genetic Genealogy. http://www.jogg.info

King, T. E., et al. (2006). Genetic signatures of coancestry within surnames. *Current Biology, 16*, 384–388.

Smolenyak, M. S., & Turner, A. (2004). *Trace your roots with DNA: Using genetic tests to explore your family tree.* New York: Rodale.

Sorenson Molecular Genealogy Foundation. http://www.smgf.org

Sykes, B., & Irven, C. (2000). Surnames and the Y chromosome. *American Journal of Human Genetics, 66*, 1417–1419.

Wolinsky, H. (2006). Genetic genealogy goes global. *EMBO Reports, 7*, 1072–1074.

CHAPTER 18

Future Trends

640K ought to be enough for anybody.
                —Attributed to Bill Gates in 1981—he later denied ever having said it

As noted in Chapter 3, the forensic DNA field has advanced quickly over the past several decades but has now stabilized on short tandem repeat (STR) typing with capillary electrophoresis detection. Innovations continue to be made with every step along the process of producing an STR profile particularly in terms of automation for data collection and data interpretation software.

Anyone who listens to weather reports and their predictions for temperature or possible precipitation a few days in the future knows that forecasting the future is tenuous at best and not always reliable. The quote attributed to Bill Gates at the beginning of the chapter also underscores that technologies often advance beyond our ability to predict them.

As difficult as it is to predict the future, by seeing where we are today and where we have been in the recent past, it is possible to provide a few thoughts on where we are going. As an active researcher in the field attempting to develop and evaluate new technologies and implement standards and certified reference materials, I offer in this chapter my perspective on future areas of growth and applications for forensic DNA typing.

ADDITIONAL GENETIC MARKERS

A growing number of tools are available in the toolbox of forensic DNA scientists. Table 18.1 summarizes the status of various genetic markers in use as of late 2008 and some of their potential applications in the future. As noted in Chapter 15, single nucleotide polymorphisms (SNPs) are being explored for

Contribution of the National Institute of Standards and Technology, 2010.

Table 18.1 Summary of genetic markers used today.

Genetic Marker	Current Application and Likely Use in the Future
STRs	Widely used in forensic casework and national DNA databases worldwide
miniSTRs	Smaller versions of STR loci that can work well on degraded DNA
Y-STRs	Permit examination of male-only DNA and can aid familial searching
mtDNA	Used in specialty labs for highly degraded specimens or hair shafts that contain limited amounts of DNA
SNPs	Ancestry-informative SNPs show potential for identifying ethnicity of an evidence sample; lineage-informative SNPs may help missing persons investigations link relatives; phenotype-informative SNPs can provide a high probability of identifying physical features; all are being explored in research settings and likely to be limited in use

a variety of applications including estimating source ethnicity (biogeographical ancestry) of evidentiary samples. Research is also ongoing to find SNPs or other genetic markers that might help characterize the physical characteristics of the individual who left biological evidence at a crime scene. Because many physical characteristics are influenced by multiple genes (as well as an individual's environment), genetic tests for physical features will probably never be fully precise or completely predictive. Nevertheless, efforts toward correlating physical height, eye color, hair color, and skin color with DNA results are progressing.

While a variety of DNA tests could be performed to aid forensic casework, the advent of DNA databases and their ability to connect past, present, and future crimes involving biological evidence through processing large numbers of offender and casework samples is driving the genetic markers being analyzed by most forensic DNA laboratories.

Holding to the past while moving into the future

In November 2000, members of the Research and Development Working Group of the National Commission on the Future of DNA Evidence published their thoughts on where DNA testing would be in 2002, 2005, and 2010. Their work is worth reviewing and in many ways still provides a road map for the future. National DNA databases have stabilized the field through the prevalence of core STR markers as millions of profiles now exist in countries like the United States and United Kingdom. Should a change occur in the future to include different or additional genetic markers, some period of overlap in use of the two technologies would be needed in order for legacy data to not be impacted before the new genetic markers could be brought fully online.

As has been noted many times throughout this book, DNA testing is always a matter of comparing a question (Q) sample against a known (K) sample.

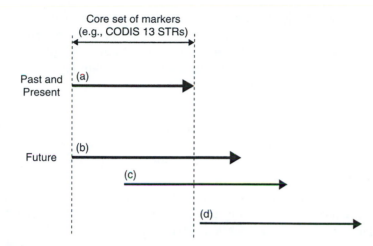

FIGURE 18.1

Possible scenarios for extending sets of genetic markers to be used in national DNA databases. (a) A core set of markers has been established for past and present DNA profiles now numbering in some cases in the millions of profiles (e.g., in the United States, 13 CODIS core STR loci). Three future scenarios exist: (b) keep all of the current core loci and add some additional supplemental loci (e.g., Identifiler or PowerPlex 16 add two additional STRs); (c) only retain some of the current core loci and add more additional supplemental loci; or (d) abandon the previous genetic markers and have no overlap with current core loci.

This Q-K comparison (Figure 1.3) requires that both samples be tested with the same genetic markers. Thus, if a new technology or set of genetic markers became available that enabled improved recovery of information from crime scene samples, it would require retroactive analysis of all previously collected and typed forensic and offender samples. Information not compatible with previously typed samples would render those existing DNA databases obsolete. Thus, what will likely happen in the future is to extend sample testing to additional loci but keep all or a portion of previously typed markers (Figure 18.1).

In many cases, the extension to additional STR loci illustrated in Figure 18.1b is already happening with analysis of STR kits like PowerPlex 16 or Identifiler that include the 13 CODIS core STR loci plus two additional ones (e.g., Penta D and Penta E with PowerPlex 16 or D2S1338 and D19S433 with Identifiler). The ability to create large multiplex PCR assays is critical to being able to extend the reach of information collected on new loci while retaining original loci.

The scenario illustrated in Figure 18.1c is also possible because some of the original core STR loci are not very informative. For example, CSF1PO, TPOX, and TH01 are not as polymorphic as most of the other core STRs used in the United States. They were originally selected more for historical reasons because they were some of the first STRs analyzed. Now that many more STR loci have been characterized with higher powers of discrimination, replacing some of those early STRs with other loci is an option worth considering. The possibility of dropping CSF1PO, TPOX, and TH01 from future multiplex STR assays of course will have to be weighed with the value of retaining a connection to previous data from these markers.

What is unlikely, at least for applications involving criminal DNA databases in the foreseeable future, is the abandonment of previously typed genetic markers in favor of a whole new set (Figure 18.1d). New loci or assays (e.g., Figure 15.1) could, however, be used in other situations, such as parentage testing or disaster victim identification. Comparisons with these applications are being made within a closed population data set rather than needing to be able to effectively communicate with a much broader past, present, and future data set like a criminal DNA database represents.

The expense of replacing previously typed samples from both offenders and crime scene evidence with new markers will likely keep most countries continuing to work with legacy sets of genetic markers and following either of the Figure 18.1b or 18.1c scenarios. New STR typing kits will most likely become available to aid forensic DNA testing of the future with an overlap of old and new STR loci.

Effort required to add additional genetic markers

Figure 18.2 shows the primary steps involved in adopting new genetic markers and assays or commercial DNA typing kits. Government-funded or private research efforts lead to new genetic markers being described. Assays are then constructed and studies performed to see how these new markers vary with various populations of interest.

After information has been gathered, decisions are made by manufacturers whether or not a particular DNA test is deemed commercially viable. If so, then kit development proceeds and eventually the kit may be beta-tested by a select group of laboratories. If the testing goes well, then the kit is released to the community. Individual forensic laboratories perform internal validation to look primarily at reproducibility and sensitivity in their own hands prior to implementing the new genetic markers into casework. Court approval may also be required if the DNA tests are viewed as substantially different from previously accepted tests.

From start to finish, this process can take several years. Commercial manufacturers may decide that proceeding with a particular assay is not in their best interest because they may feel that they cannot get a good return on their investments. Patent issues or intellectual property licensing limitations may also prevent a perfectly good DNA test from ever making it into the hands

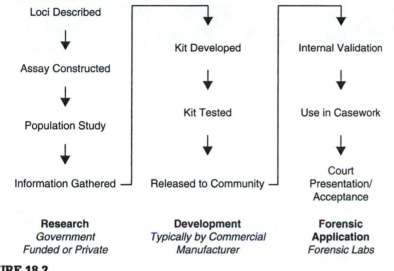

FIGURE 18.2

Primary steps in adopting new genetic markers.

of forensic DNA laboratories. Thus, many factors influence whether or not a new DNA test or technology makes it through the research and development phases and into forensic application.

NEW TECHNOLOGIES

We live in an age of rapid discovery in biotechnology, and new technologies and instruments are continually being developed. The growing toolbox for forensic DNA analysis also includes new technologies along with the additional genetic markers discussed in the previous section. Mass spectrometry, portable DNA devices utilizing rapid PCR amplification and microchip CE separations, additional laboratory automation, and improved data interpretation computer programs all represent current areas of research that could yield improved efficiencies while maintaining high-quality DNA profiles. Some of the D.N.A. boxes scattered throughout this book also discuss technological developments that are aiding DNA sample processing now and into the future. For example, next-generation DNA sequencing instruments have been used to recover information from ancient DNA samples (D.N.A. Box 18.1).

Higher resolution of STR alleles with mass spectrometry

Mass spectrometry is a versatile analytical technique that involves the detection of ions and the measurement of their mass-to-charge ratio. Since these ions are separated in a vacuum environment, the analysis times can be extremely

D.N.A. Box 18.1 Next-Generation DNA Sequencing and Ancient DNA

Next-generation DNA sequencing involves rapid, high-throughput collection of short sections of DNA. The desire for more genomic information is driving costs down with one goal of being able to obtain a full human genome sequence for $1000 or less. Because these next-generation sequencing approaches generate short sequence reads of typically 25 to 250 bases in a massively parallel fashion, it has been possible to successfully obtain sequence information from ancient DNA samples, which are normally too fragmented to sequence by traditional techniques. As of late 2008, a complete Neandertal mitochondrial genome sequence had been obtained, and researchers are attempting to sequence the entire 3 billion base pair genome of a 40,000-year-old Neandertal bone sample.

It is unclear whether or not next-generation sequencing techniques will help traditional forensic testing as they are helping ancient DNA sample sequencing. Current methods have a difficult time with repetitive sequences and thus unless future improvements are made, STR regions would probably not be able to be reliably analyzed with next-generation DNA sequencing.

Sources:

Green, R. E., et al. (2008). A complete Neandertal mitochondrial genome sequence determined by high-throughput sequencing. *Cell, 134*, 416–426.

Hert, D. G., et al. (2008). Advantages and limitations of next-generation sequencing technologies: A comparison of electrophoresis and non-electrophoresis methods. *Electrophoresis, 29*, 4618–4626.

Shendure, J., & Ji, H. (2008). Next-generation DNA sequencing. *Nature Biotechnology, 26*(10), 1135–1145.

rapid, on the order of seconds. Combined with robotic sample preparation, mass spectrometry offers the potential for processing vast numbers of DNA samples in an automated fashion.

With mass spectrometry, the actual mass of the DNA molecule is being measured, making it a more accurate technique than a relative-size measurement as in electrophoresis. To get the DNA molecules into the gas phase for analysis in the mass spectrometer, two different ionization techniques have been used: matrix-assisted laser desorption-ionization (MALDI) or electrospray ionization (ESI).

Over a decade ago, STR markers were successfully analyzed via MALDI time-of-flight mass spectrometry by redesigning the PCR primers to be closer to the repeat region, thereby reducing the size of the amplified alleles. While MALDI had a size limitations of ~100 bp, recent ESI time-of-flight techniques have extended the size range for accurate mass spectrometry measurements to ~250 bp.

By analyzing the overall mass of an STR allele or a section of mtDNA, the base composition of the measured DNA molecule can be deciphered and internal sequence differences ascertained. In this manner, STR alleles that are apparently homozygous by electrophoretic techniques have been subdivided into separate alleles if internal sequence polymorphisms exist.

The expense of mass spectrometers and expertise required to keep them running and the previous widescale acceptance of fluorescent methodologies will likely keep mass spectrometry from becoming a major player in forensic DNA analysis of STR markers. However, capabilities for mitochondrial DNA base composition analysis and SNP typing may enable mass spectrometry to play a useful role in the future of forensic DNA analysis.

Microchip CE and portable devices

The desire to take DNA testing capabilities out of the laboratory to a crime scene or close to a battlefield is propelling efforts to develop portable DNA testing devices. For example, some have claimed that a rapid DNA device might aid elimination of innocent suspects early in an investigation. Much of the work so far has been focused on miniaturizing the DNA separation steps.

Microfabrication techniques revolutionized the integrated circuit industry 20 years ago and have brought the world ever-faster and more powerful computers. These same microfabrication methods are now being applied to develop miniature, microchip-based laboratories, or so-called 'labs-on-a-chip'. Miniaturizing the sample preparation and analysis steps in forensic DNA typing could lead to devices that permit investigation of biological evidence at a crime scene or more rapid and less expensive DNA analysis in a conventional laboratory setting.

The primary advantage of analyzing DNA in a miniature capillary electrophoresis (CE) device is that shorter channels, or capillaries, lead to faster DNA separations. Separation speeds that are 10 to 100 times faster than conventional electrophoresis can be obtained with this approach. Over a decade ago, tetranucleotide STR alleles were separated in as little as 30 seconds using a 2-cm separation distance (compared to 36 cm for an ABI 310 capillary). However, routine and robust analyses of DNA with appropriate resolution of STR alleles have not yet been achieved at these speeds even though several groups are working extensively in this area.

Research is ongoing to improve separation speeds and ease of use with the hope that in the near future microchip CE devices will be used routinely for rapid DNA analyses. When portable devices become available, there will be a need for sensitivity and resolution standards to make sure that DNA separation and detection devices at multiple locations have performance similar to one another.

More automation

As noted in Chapter 13, robotic liquid-handling platforms to aid sample preparation enable higher throughput, increase laboratory efficiency, and aid quality assurance efforts. Robotic systems can reduce hands-on time for DNA analysts, enabling them to focus on other aspects of the process such as data interpretation. Potential sample contamination or mix-ups by human operators can be reduced because instruments will perform mundane tasks of sample transfers and deliver precise volumes of liquids more quickly and reliably.

As of late 2008, a variety of small-scale and large-scale liquid-handling robotic platforms were available with new ones in development. Some of the robotic systems in use by forensic DNA laboratories include the Maxwell 16 (Promega Corporation), the EZ1 and QIAcube (Qiagen), the Janus Automated Workstation (Perkin-Elmer), the Tecan Freedom EVO (Tecan), and the Biomek 2000 and Biomek FX (Beckman Coulter). New sample preparation chemistries for improved DNA extraction will likely be incorporated into these and future robotic sample workstations.

Real-time quantitative PCR (qPCR) has greatly benefited DNA quantitation both in terms of sensitivity and specificity. Assays and commercial kits capable of detecting multiple targets play an important role in deciding what path to follow in processing DNA samples. With different genetic markers like those listed in Table 18.1 ready for use in a forensic DNA laboratory, screening the quality of DNA samples can be valuable. Current qPCR assays can determine the amount of total DNA versus Y chromosome or the amount of nuclear DNA versus mtDNA. Knowing the level of degradation can also help analysts decide if a miniSTR assay should be attempted because of severe DNA degradation.

Expert systems for data analysis are beginning to be used in DNA databasing laboratories, and so-called expert assistant tools to aid in mixture interpretation have been developed to aid casework analysis. The need for computer-based tools for data interpretation and statistical interpretation of mixed DNA samples has long been recognized and will be an important area of future improvements in the forensic DNA field.

EXPANDED USES FOR DNA TESTING

The success of DNA testing in solving crimes and aiding parentage investigations over the past several decades has led to attempts to use DNA in additional areas. An interesting application is the attempt to trace ink samples by lacing them with specific synthetic DNA fragments that could then be amplified at a later date to verify the origin of the ink on a written document (D.N.A. Box 18.2). While such an application is not routinely performed today, it shows creative thinking about future possibilities for DNA analysis.

Several questions that are often asked regarding the capability of DNA testing for human identification purposes are considered in the following sections.

D.N.A. Box 18.2 DNA Traceable Ink

Among the various types of biometric personal identification systems, DNA provides the most reliable personal identification. It is intrinsically digital and unchangeable while the person is alive, and even after his or her death. Increasing the number of DNA loci examined can enhance the power of discrimination. 'DNA ink' has been developed that contains synthetic DNA mixed with printing inks.

Single-stranded DNA fragments encoding a personalized set of short tandem repeats (STR) were synthesized. The sequence was defined as follows. First, a decimal DNA personal identification (DNA-ID) was established based on the number of STRs in the locus. Next, this DNA-ID was encrypted using a binary, 160-bit algorithm, using a hashing function to protect privacy. Since this function is irreversible,

no one can recover the original information from the encrypted code. Finally, the bit series generated above is transformed into base sequences, and double-stranded DNA fragments are amplified by PCR to protect against physical attacks. Synthesized DNA was detected successfully after samples printed in DNA ink were subjected to several resistance tests used to assess the stability of printing inks. Endurance test results showed that this DNA ink would be suitable for practical use as a printing ink and was resistant to 40 hours of ultraviolet exposure.

Source:

Hashiyada, M. (2004). Development of biometric DNA ink for authentication security. *The Tohoku Journal of Experimental Medicine, 204,* 109–117.

First, is there an age limit to obtaining successful results from a sample? Second, how small a sample can be successfully analyzed? Third, are there limitations on how DNA can be used to answer questions about whether or not someone is related to a person in question? Four, how quickly can a sample be analyzed and at what cost?

As discussed throughout this book, there is a core competence that currently exists for DNA testing with STR markers. However, going beyond this core competence, either in terms of attempting to examine extremely low amounts of sample or trying to answer questions regarding extended family relationships, requires additional information (Figure 18.3). While research is ongoing in these areas, it is important not to confuse standard DNA testing with extended uses.

How old can we go?

Due to the success of DNA in solving crimes and in exonerating people (e.g., the Innocence Project; see D.N.A. Box 1.1), attempts are being made to dig back into police evidence lockers to try to help close 'cold cases.' While it is admirable to make attempts to solve crimes that happened many years ago, contamination that would invalidate results is a realistic possibility.

DNA results have been obtained from samples that are thousands of years old provided the DNA is not too badly damaged by water, heat, or UV irradiation. As with ancient DNA efforts, accidental contamination by small amounts of higher quality, more modern DNA will likely impact older samples more seriously than the DNA being completely destroyed. Bloodstains that are over

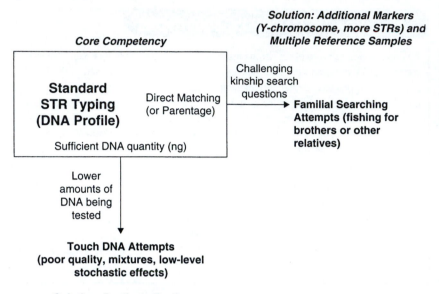

FIGURE 18.3

Beyond the current core competencies of standard STR typing. Going outside the box that represents nanogram or high-picogram quantities of DNA being testing and direct matching or first-degree relative associations requires additional testing. When looking at lower amounts of DNA, replicate amplifications are needed to ensure reliability and reproducibility. When attempting to answer challenging kinship questions, additional markers and reference samples are required to obtain meaningful results.

100 years old have yielded successful STR profiles when the analysis is performed carefully.

Issues surrounding the impact of contamination on casework reporting guidelines were explored by Peter Gill and Amanda Kirkham in a 2004 article entitled 'Development of a simulation model to assess the impact of contamination in casework using STRs.' Negative controls were used to predict the level of overall contamination in an operational DNA unit. However, because PCR contamination can be tube specific, negative controls analyzed with a batch of samples cannot provide complete confidence that the associated batch of extracted casework material is contaminant free. This study concluded that the most likely outcome of a contamination event is false exclusion because contaminating DNA material can be preferentially amplified over extremely low levels of original material present from the casework sample or may mask the perpetrator's profile in a resulting mixture.

While this contamination possibility might only rarely impact a careful forensic DNA laboratory, it can have potential significance on old cases under review including the Innocence Project. For example, if biological evidence from a 20-year-old case was handled by ungloved police officers or evidence custodians (prior to knowledge regarding the sensitivity of modern DNA testing), then the true perpetrator's DNA might be masked by contamination from the collecting officer or evidence custodian. Thus, when a DNA test is performed, the police officer's or evidence custodian's DNA would be detected rather than the true perpetrator's. In the absence of other evidence, the individual in prison might then be falsely declared 'innocent' because his DNA profile was not found on the original crime scene evidence. *This scenario emphasizes the importance of considering DNA evidence as an investigative tool within the context of a case rather than the sole absolute proof of guilt or innocence.*

How low can we go?

The polymerase chain reaction is very sensitive and STR typing results have been demonstrated from as little as a single collected cell. This capability has encouraged attempts to try to recover DNA profiles from touch evidence that might be helpful in a case. However, this low template DNA analysis can sometimes push the envelope of what constitutes reliable results unless measures are taken to demonstrate reproducibility of allele calls.

Attempts to generate results with low levels of DNA come up against a fundamental scientific barrier of stochastic amplification. The stochastic effects exist due to random selection of alleles when a diluted DNA template-to-primer-to-polymerase ratio exists. To date, whole genome amplification or other sample enrichment techniques have not successfully overcome this problem (see D.N.A. Box 7.1). Replicate amplifications are necessary to demonstrate reproducibility in STR allele calls when PCR amplifications from low-level DNA templates are being attempted.

When working with low amounts of DNA template, success rates are often poor. Dedicated 'clean' facilities and extreme care are required to avoid or at least limit contamination. Often mixtures result from touch DNA or other low-level DNA analyses that may not yield meaningful results. Finally, in the end, results may not be probative if the sample could have been deposited innocently at the crime scene before the crime even occurred. Thus, low-level DNA recovered from a crime scene may not be relevant to the committed crime.

Research and validation experiments have demonstrated successful low-template DNA analyses that track appropriately back to the sample donor. Thus, low-level DNA results can be reliable. When appropriate controls are in place and replicated results are repeatable, DNA interpretation should proceed—but cautiously.

How far out on the family tree can we go?

The possibility of linking family members with DNA testing has led to efforts in some jurisdictions of attempting familial searching with DNA databases in

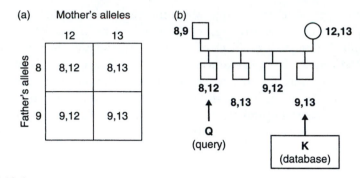

FIGURE 18.4

Problems with sibling searches illustrated with STR results from a single locus in a family pedigree containing four sons with different genotypes. (a) Genetic theory predicts that 25% of brothers will be an exact match at a locus, 50% will exhibit a partial match, but 25% will share no alleles with other brothers when the parents have different alleles. (b) If a familial search is attempted with a DNA profile from the '8,12' genotype brother, it would miss the '9,13' genotype brother searching on either alleles '8' or '12.' Collection of reference DNA from one more brother (either '8,13' or '9,12') would help extend the possible alleles available to make an association.

the hopes of making an association to a relative of the perpetrator whose profile is already on the database. While parent–child relationships are routinely performed with parentage testing due to allele sharing, siblings and more distant relatives are not expected to always share alleles. Thus, they may be undetected with a DNA database search.

Figure 18.4 illustrates the problem with sibling searches in that 25% of offspring from parents with different genotypes are not expected to match each other at the tested locus. Testing of additional markers can, however, be helpful in some cases as can DNA results from additional relatives.

Closely linked SNPs or lineage markers such as Y-STRs or mitochondrial DNA may strengthen the confidence of a kinship association. Due to their low mutation rate, SNPs or combinations of SNP loci will maintain their same allelic state for many generations. Alternatively, the collection and testing of additional samples will also be helpful to gaining a better understanding of the expected genotype for the individual in question.

When someone is immigrating to a new country, questions may arise as to the true biological relationship of the immigrant to someone already a citizen of the country being entered. In such a case, DNA testing may be requested to tell whether or not someone is a child versus a cousin or someone completely unrelated. The farther the two compared individuals are from each other biologically (i.e., parent-to-child vs. cousin-to-cousin comparison), the greater the chance of mutations occurring with the polymorphic STR markers being used. The best way to reduce the possibility of mutation problems is to collect additional reference samples from more closely related individuals. In the absence of additional reference samples, information from extra loci can help as noted earlier.

How quickly can a result be obtained and at what cost?

As of late 2008, the DNA testing process outlined in Chapters 4 through 11 could be performed in as little as 8 to 10 hours. The longest part of the process is the PCR amplification step, which takes around 3 hours with currently used DNA polymerases and thermal cycling parameters to amplify the 16 loci using an STR kit. Rapid PCR efforts using specialized DNA polymerases and faster temperature ramp rates have brought multiplex PCR amplification times down to around 30 minutes or less (see D.N.A. Box 7.3).

Efforts are under way to integrate the various steps involved in DNA extraction, amplification, and STR allele detection. Routine STR typing in less than an hour is a strong possibility in the near future. Rapid analysis of DNA could open up a whole new set of DNA biometric applications such as analysis of individuals at a point of interest like an airport or a country border. Only time will tell to what extent technology will open new doors.

DNA testing in late 2008 cost around $30 per test with high-volume single-source samples used in databasing. Forensic samples cost more due to the labor that can be involved in sample handling, data interpretation, and report writing. While STR kit reagents and other supplies contribute a significant portion to the cost, labor remains an important component of the cost. Improved automation should help reduce costs in the future.

Prosecution of property crimes

Within the United States, forensic DNA testing has primarily focused on violent criminal offenses such as sexual assaults and murder. A National Institute of Justice–funded study conducted by the Urban Institute reported in April 2008 that high-volume crime such as residential burglary, commercial burglary, and automobile theft could be successfully investigated using DNA.

More than twice as many property crime suspects were found, arrested, and prosecuted when DNA evidence was processed compared with traditional investigations. The study also found that DNA results were five times more likely to result in a suspect identification compared with fingerprints. Overall, the study concluded that a suspect was identified in 31% of cases where biological evidence was present and analyzed.

If the law enforcement and legal communities fully embraced the possibility of DNA testing on property crimes, there would be a substantial increase in the number of samples submitted to forensic DNA laboratories. For example, in 2006, there were around 110,000 rapes and murders within the United States—but more than 2 million burglaries. Without expanding laboratories' capacity to handle an increase in the numbers of submitted samples, backlogs will develop or increase in size. Thus, in some ways, DNA is at risk of becoming a victim of its own success.

Points for Discussion

- Why will core STR loci continue to be examined for the foreseeable future?
- What are some advantages of mass spectrometry over current capillary electrophoresis techniques? Disadvantages?
- How might portable DNA typing devices be used in the future?
- Should DNA testing be performed in property crime cases? If so, what are some of the challenges with implementing an expanded use of DNA testing?

READING LIST AND INTERNET RESOURCES

General Information

Advanced and Emerging DNA Techniques and Technologies. http://www.dna. gov/training/Technology

Additional Genetic Markers and Assays

Butler, J. M., et al. (2007). STRs vs. SNPs: Thoughts on the future of forensic DNA testing. *Forensic Science Medicine and Pathology, 3,* 200–205.

Gill, P., et al. (2006). The evolution of DNA databases—Recommendations for new European STR loci. *Forensic Science International, 156,* 242–244.

Hill, C. R., et al. (2008). Characterization of 26 miniSTR loci for improved analysis of degraded DNA samples. *Journal of Forensic Sciences, 53,* 73–80.

Hill, C. R., et al. (2009). A new 26plex assay for use in human identity testing. *Journal of Forensic Sciences,* (in press). Information available at http://www.cstl.nist.gov/ biotech/strbase/str2bplex.htm

National Commission on the Future of DNA Evidence (2000). *The future of forensic DNA testing: Predictions of the research and development working group.* Washington, DC: National Institute of Justice.

New Technologies

Mass spectrometry

Butler, J. M., et al. (1998). Reliable genotyping of short tandem repeat loci without an allelic ladder using time-of-flight mass spectrometry. *International Journal of Legal Medicine, 112,* 45–49.

Hall, T. A., et al. (2005). Base composition analysis of human mitochondrial DNA using electrospray ionization mass spectrometry: A novel tool for the identification and differentiation of humans. *Analytical Biochemistry, 344,* 55–69.

IBIS Biosciences. http://www.ibisbiosciences.com

Jiang, Y., et al. (2007). Mitochondrial DNA mutation detection by electrospray mass spectrometry. *Clinical Chemistry, 53*(2), 195–203.

Oberacher, H., et al. (2006). Some guidelines for the analysis of genomic DNA by PCR-LC-ESI-MS. *Journal of the American Society for Mass Spectrometry, 17*(2), 124–129.

Oberacher, H., & Parson, W. (2007). Forensic DNA fingerprinting by liquid chromatography-electrospray ionization mass spectrometry. *Biotechniques, 43*(4), vii–xiii.

Oberacher, H., et al. (2007). Liquid chromatography-electrospray ionization mass spectrometry for simultaneous detection of mtDNA length and nucleotide polymorphisms. *International Journal of Legal Medicine, 121*(1), 57–67.

Oberacher, H., et al. (2008). Increased forensic efficiency of DNA fingerprints through simultaneous resolution of length and nucleotide variability by high-performance mass spectrometry. *Human Mutation, 29*(3), 427–432.

Pitterl, F., et al. (2008). The next generation of DNA profiling—STR typing by multiplexed PCR-ion-pair RP LC-ESI time-of-flight MS. *Electrophoresis, 29*, 4739–4750.

Microchip CE and portable devices

Bienvenue, J. M., et al. (2006). Microchip-based cell lysis and DNA extraction from sperm cells for application to forensic analysis. *Journal of Forensic Sciences, 51*, 266–273.

Greenspoon, S. A., et al. (2008). A forensic laboratory tests the Berkeley microfabricated capillary array electrophoresis device. *Journal of Forensic Sciences, 53*, 828–837.

Liu, P., et al. (2007). Integrated portable polymerase chain reaction-capillary electrophoresis microsystem for rapid forensic short tandem repeat typing. *Analytical Chemistry, 79*, 1881–1889.

Liu, P., et al. (2008). Real-time forensic DNA analysis at a crime scene using a portable microchip analyzer. *Forensic Science International: Genetics, 2*(4), 301–309.

Microchip Biotechnologies Inc. http://www.microchipbiotech.com

Microlab Diagnostics. http://www.microlabdiagnostics.com

Network Biosystems. http://www.netbio.com

Schmalzing, D., et al. (1997). DNA typing in thirty seconds with a microfabricated device. In: *Proceedings of the National Academy of Sciences of the United States of America, 94*, 10273–10278.

Woolley, A. T., & Mathies, R. A. (1994). Ultra-high-speed DNA fragment separations using microfabricated capillary array electrophoresis chips. In: *Proceedings of the National Academy of Sciences of the United States of America, 91*, 11348–11352.

Woolley, A. T., et al. (1996). Functional integration of PCR amplification and capillary electrophoresis in a microfabricated DNA analysis device. *Analytical Chemistry, 68*, 4081–4086.

Yeung, S. H., et al. (2006). Rapid and high-throughput forensic short tandem repeat typing using a 96-lane microfabricated capillary array electrophoresis microdevice. *Journal of Forensic Sciences, 51*, 740–747.

Yeung, S. H., et al. (2008). Fluorescence energy transfer-labeled primers for high-performance forensic DNA profiling. *Electrophoresis, 29*, 2251–2259.

Extended Uses of DNA

Potential contamination

Gill, P., & Kirkham, A. (2004). Development of a simulation model to assess the impact of contamination in casework using STRs. *Journal of Forensic Sciences, 49*(3), 485–491.

Low-level DNA

Butler, J. M. (2007). The cutting edge of DNA testing: Mixture interpretation, miniSTRs, and low level DNA. In *Workshop at NEAFS*. Bolton Landing, NY. Available at http://www.cstl.nist.gov/biotech/strbase/pub_pres/NEAFS2007_CuttingEdgeDNA.pdf

Findlay, L., et al. (1997). DNA fingerprinting from single cells. *Nature, 389*, 555–556.

Gill, P., et al. (2002). Role of short tandem repeat DNA in forensic casework in the UK—Past, present, and future perspectives. *Biotechniques, 32*(2), 366–372.

Van Oorschot, R. A. H., et al. (2003). Are you collecting all the available DNA from touched objects? *Progress in Forensic Genetics, 10*, ICS 1239, 803–807.

Extended kinship analysis

Butler, J.M., et al. (2007). New autosomal and Y-chromosome STR loci: Characterization and potential uses. In: *Proceedings of the eighteenth international symposium on human identification*. Available at http://www.promega.com/geneticidproc

Karlsson, A. O., et al. (2007). DNA-testing for immigration cases: The risk of erroneous conclusions. *Forensic Science International, 172*, 144–149.

DNA biometrics

Johnson, P., & Williams, R. (2007). European securitization and biometric identification: The uses of genetic profiling. *Ann Ist Super Sanita, 43*(1), 36–43. Available at http://www.iss.it/publ/anna/2007/1/43136.pdf

Prosecution of property crimes

DNA and Property Crimes. http://www.ojp.usdoj.gov/nij/topics/forensics/dna/property-crime

Roman, J. K., et al. (2008). The DNA Field Experiment: Cost-effectiveness analysis of the use of DNA in the investigation of high-volume crimes. Available at http://www.ncjrs.gov/pdffiles1/nij/grants/222318.pdf

Appendix 1: Glossary of Terms

Sources for some of these definitions:

Buckleton, J., et al. (2005). *Forensic DNA evidence interpretation.* Boca Raton, FL: CRC Press.

http://www.dna.gov/glossary

Rudin, N., & Inman, K. (2002). *An introduction to forensic DNA analysis* (2nd ed.). Boca Raton, FL: CRC Press.

Strachan, T., & Read, A. P. (1999). *Human molecular genetics* (2nd ed.). New York: Wiley.

Taylor, J. K. (1987). *Quality assurance of chemical measurements.* Washington, DC: Lewis Publishers.

2p rule: a genotype probability assignment often associated with the F (allele dropout) designation; used when the genotype may contain allele p and any other allele

9947A: a female DNA sample created from a cell line that is commonly used for a positive control in commercially supplied DNA test kits; also a component of NIST SRM 2391b

9948: a male DNA sample created from a cell line that is commonly used for a positive control in commercially supplied DNA test kits; also a component of NIST SRM 2391b

007: a male DNA sample supplied by Applied Biosystems as a positive control with their STR kits that exhibits a high degree of heterozygous genotypes

3′ ('three prime'): end of a DNA or RNA molecule bearing a free hydroxyl group on the 3′-carbon of the sugar ring

5′ ('five prime'): end of a DNA or RNA molecule bearing a free hydroxyl group on the 5′-carbon of the sugar ring

ABC: American Board of Criminalistics; an organization that certifies the knowledge of forensic scientists in specific disciplines including drug analysis and forensic biology

ABI: Applied Biosystems Inc.; an instrument and reagent manufacturing company based in Foster City, California

ABI 310 Genetic Analyzer: a capillary electrophoresis instrument sold by Applied Biosystems and widely used throughout the forensic DNA community since its introduction in 1995; an ABI 310 uses a single capillary filled with a viscous polymer solution to separate DNA molecules based on their relative size; many labs have now adopted a multicapillary instrument such as the ABI 3100 or ABI 3130xl Genetic Analyzer

ABI 3100 Genetic Analyzer: a multicapillary electrophoresis instrument sold by Applied Biosystems since 2001; 4-capillary and 16-capillary versions are available; newer versions include a mechanical polymer pump instead of a syringe and are named ABI 3130 or ABI 3130xl

ABI 31xx: a shorthand abbreviation meant to include the multicapillary ABI 3100, ABI 3100 Avant, ABI 3130, and ABI 3130xl Genetic Analyzers

Accreditation: the formal process by which a laboratory is evaluated, with respect to established criteria, for its competence to perform a specified kind of measurement; the evaluation takes place through an audit by an outside, qualified agency and helps provides confidence that the laboratory meets minimum professional standards for general operations

Accuracy: the degree of agreement or conformity of a measured value with its actual (true) value

Adenine: a purine base; one of the four molecules containing nitrogen present in the nucleic acids DNA and RNA; designated by letter A

Adenylation: *see* Plus A

Admissibility: court acceptance of a particular technology used to process forensic evidence

Adventitious DNA: a term sometimes given to contaminating DNA that unintentionally becomes amplified along with the intentional template DNA obtained from evidence or reference samples

Adventitious match: a match to the profile of a person who is not the true donor of that profile; usually arises from having too few loci available from the casework (question) sample due to a degraded DNA partial profile

Allele: an alternative form of a gene or a section of DNA at a particular genetic location (locus); typically multiple alleles are possible for each STR marker

Allele frequency: the proportion of a particular allele among the chromosomes carried by individuals in a population; how often an allele is found within a particular group of individuals aids in determining the rarity of a DNA profile

Allelic drop-in: contamination from unknown source

Allelic dropout: failure to detect an allele within a sample or failure to amplify an allele during PCR; due to primer binding site mutations or stochastic effects when attempting to amplify low amounts of DNA template

Allelic ladder: a mixture of common alleles at a locus used for calibration of STR allele measurements and converting DNA fragment size to repeat number because the number of repeat units in each 'rung' of the ladder have been previously sequenced

Amelogenin: a commonly used sex-typing genetic marker because the gene, which codes for tooth enamel, occurs on both the X and Y chromosomes

Amino acid: any of a class of 20 molecules that are combined to form proteins in living things; the sequence of amino acids in a protein and hence protein function are determined by the genetic code

AmpFLPs (AMP-FLPs): amplified fragment length polymorphisms; typically thought of as VNTR (e.g., D1S80) rather than STR PCR amplification

Amplicon: the product of polymerase chain reaction (PCR) DNA amplification

Amplification: an increase in the number of copies of a specific DNA fragment; can be *in vivo* or *in vitro*

Analyst: an individual trained and qualified to report DNA results

Analytical procedure: an orderly step-by-step process designed to ensure operational uniformity and to minimize analytical drift over time and between analysts

Analytical threshold: an acceptable 'relative fluorescence units' (RFU) level determined to be appropriate for use in the PCR/STR DNA typing process; a minimum threshold for data comparison is identified by the specific forensic laboratory doing the testing through independent validation studies

Annealing: the process of two complementary DNA strands finding and binding to their matching sequence to form a double helix; portion of the PCR thermal cycling process where the oligonucleotide primers locate complementary target sequences in the template DNA

Anode: positively charged electrode; negatively charged DNA molecules will move toward the anode

Antibody: a protein produced by white blood cells in response to antigens (foreign proteins) found in the bloodstream; antibodies bind very specifically to their antigens and can be used in forensic serology to perform presumptive or confirmatory tests

Antigen: a substance, usually a protein, which prompts the generation of antibodies and creates an immune response; the target of a specific antibody

Artifact: any nonallelic product of the amplification process (stutter or minus A) or anomaly of the detection process (pull-up or spike)

ASCLD: American Society of Crime Laboratory Directors

ASCLD-LAB: American Society of Crime Laboratory Directors—Laboratory Accreditation Board

Audit: evaluation of a laboratory based on a set of criteria established by an outside, qualified agency (e.g., ASCLD-LAB)

Autosome: a chromosome not involved in sex determination; the diploid human genome consists of 46 chromosomes—22 pairs of autosomes and one pair of sex chromosomes (the X and Y chromosomes)

Base pair (bp): two complementary nucleotides joined by hydrogen bonds; base pairing occurs between A and T and between G and C

Base sequence: the order of nucleotide bases in a DNA molecule

Base sequence analysis: a method, sometimes automated, for determining the base sequence

Bayes's theorem: developed in the 1700s by British mathematician Thomas Bayes to interpret probabilities of random events; states that the posterior odds are equal to the prior odds multiplied by the likelihood ratio

Biallelic: only two alleles are observed at a genetic locus

Biochemistry: study of the nature of biologically important molecules in living systems, DNA replication and protein synthesis, and the quantitative and qualitative aspects of cellular metabolism

Biotechnology: a set of biological techniques developed through basic research and now applied to research and product development

Biparental inheritance: inheritance from both parents

Bleed-through: *see* Pull-up

Blind proficiency test: a quality assurance tool in which a sample is submitted to an analyst for analysis whose composition is known to the submitter but unknown to the analyst; in a truly blind study, the analyst does not know he or she is being evaluated

Blood group: a classification of blood types based on the presence or absence of inherited forms of antigens on the surface of red blood cells; some 30 blood groups have been characterized including the ABO system

Buccal swab: a relatively noninvasive sample collection technique of scraping the inside of a mouth to collect cells from the inner cheek lining

Calibration: comparison of a measurement standard or instrument with another standard or instrument to report or eliminate by adjustment any variation in the accuracy of the item being compared

Capillary electrophoresis (CE): an electrophoretic technique for separating DNA molecules by their size based on migration through a narrow glass capillary tube filled with a liquid polymer

Cathode: negatively charged electrode

CCD camera: a charge-coupled device detector used on the ABI 310 and 31xx instruments to collect fluorescence emissions across the visible spectrum from the electrophoretically separated, dye-labeled PCR products

cDNA: complementary DNA; DNA synthesized from an RNA template by the reverse transcriptase enzyme

CE: *see* Capillary electrophoresis

Ceiling principle: a conservative and now-defunct statistical calculation, originally endorsed by the NRC I, that estimated the frequency of a genetic profile within major population groups knowing that each is composed of a number of subpopulations; for each allele in a product calculation, the highest frequency among the groups sampled, or 5%, must be used, whichever is larger

Cell: the basic building block of an organism; humans have approximately 100 trillion cells

Cell cycle: the series of replication events leading to the division of a cell into two daughter cells; consists of four phases: G_1 (growth), S (synthesis), G_2, and M (mitosis)

Centromere: the central region of a chromosome that is involved in cell division; contains repetitive sequences referred to as 'satellite DNA'; divides the short (p) and long (q) arms of a chromosome

Certification: voluntary process of peer review by which an individual or laboratory is recognized with a certificate as having attained the professional qualifications necessary to practice

Certified reference material: a material for which values are certified by a technically valid procedure and accompanied by, or traceable to, a certificate or other documentation that is issued by a certifying body

Chain of custody: establishing a paper trail with items of physical evidence that tracks sample collection, transfer, and analysis from the time the items come into the care of a forensic laboratory; helps demonstrate integrity of the connection between the items collected and the data analyzed and presented in court

Chelex extraction: a method of DNA extraction involving Chelex resin that produces single-stranded DNA

Chimera: an organism derived from more than one zygote

Chromatin: the complex of genomic DNA and protein found in the nucleus of a cell

Chromosome: the structure by which hereditary information is physically transmitted from one generation to the next

ChrX: an abbreviation for the X chromosome

ChrY: an abbreviation for the Y chromosome

Coding region: portion of a DNA sequence that contains genes and thus is used as a template for production of proteins

Coding strand: in double-stranded DNA, the strand that has the same sequence as the resulting RNA (except thymine instead of uracil)

CODIS: Combined DNA Index System; the software architecture that runs the U.S. national DNA database under the direction of the FBI Laboratory

CODIS loci: an established set of 13 STRs required for inclusion of a DNA profile at the national level in CODIS

COfiler: a multiplex STR typing kit from Applied Biosystems that coamplifies D3S1358, D16S539, TH01, TPOX, CSF1PO, and D7S820 along with the sex-typing marker amelogenin

Cold hit: a match made between a crime scene DNA profile and a DNA profile found on a DNA database in the absence of any prior investigative leads

Complementary sequences: nucleic acid base sequences that form a double-stranded structure by matching base pairs; the complementary sequence to G-T-A-C is C-A-T-G

Complete profile: a full DNA result with values being obtained from all attempted loci

Concordance: obtaining the same value when testing multiple times

Confirmatory test: a follow-up experiment to verify results from a presumptive test; usually less sensitive but more specific than a presumptive test

Conservative: an assignment of the weight of evidence that is believed to favor the defense

Contamination: the unintentional introduction of exogenous DNA into a DNA sample or PCR reaction

Continuing education: a class, lecture, or conference that brings individuals up to date in their relevant area of knowledge

Control region: a noncoding portion of the human mitochondrial DNA molecule commonly used in forensic DNA testing; approximately 1120 bp in length that encompasses HVI and HVII; also called the D-loop

Controls: samples run in parallel with experimental samples that are used to demonstrate that a procedure is working correctly

CPE: combined probability of exclusion; produced by multiplying the probabilities of exclusion from each locus

Criminal justice system: law enforcement and legal efforts made by local or national governments to prevent or prosecute crime in order to maintain social stability

Critical reagents: components of chemical tests that are deemed by empirical studies or routine practice to be essential to the success of the test; they are typically evaluated prior to use on forensic casework samples to confirm that they are working as intended

Cytoplasm: cellular contents found between the outside cell membrane and the nuclear membrane

Cytosine: a pyrimidine base; one of the four molecules containing nitrogen present in the nucleic acids DNA and RNA; designated by letter C

D1S80: an AMP-FLP locus used for a time in the 1990s ranging in size from 400 to 800 bp with 16-bp repeat units

Daubert: reference to a 1993 U.S. Supreme Court case, *Daubert v. Merrell Dow Pharmaceuticals*, that considered when expert testimony should be admitted into court; makes judges the gatekeepers in considering if a scientific technique is valid, published, and accepted

ddNTPs: dideoxynucleotide triphosphates; used in sequencing reactions to terminate a growing DNA strand

Deconvolution/dissection: separating out one or more unknown contributors to a mixed DNA profile based on relative intensities of allele peaks present in a sample; involves using quantitative peak height information and inference of contributor mixture ratios

Deduction: inference of an unknown contributor's DNA profile after taking into consideration the contribution of the known/expected contributor's DNA profile; involves using quantitative peak height information and inference of contributor mixture ratios

Degradation: the fragmenting, or breakdown, of DNA by chemical or physical means

Denaturation: the process of splitting the complementary double strands of DNA to form single strands

Deoxyribonucleic acid (DNA): the genetic material of organisms, usually double stranded; a class of nucleic acids identified by the presence of deoxyribose, a sugar, and the four nucleobases, adenine, thymine, cytosine, and guanine

Detection limit: the smallest amount of some component of interest that can be measured by a single measurement with a stated level of confidence

Differential amplification: the selection of one target region over another during PCR; for example, with damaged DNA templates, larger molecular weight loci usually do not amplify as well as smaller sized loci; can also arise between two alleles within a single locus if one of the alleles has a mutation within a PCR primer binding site, causing this allele to be copied less efficiently because of a primer-template mismatch

Differential extraction: a DNA extraction procedure in which the sperm cells are physically separated from the DNA of other cells before the sperm DNA is isolated; generally results in a sperm and nonsperm (epithelial) fraction

Diploid: having two copies of each chromosome; the normal constitution of most human somatic cells

D-loop: *see* Control region

DNA: *see* Deoxyribonucleic acid

DNA databank: a repository of stored bloodstain cards or DNA samples used to generate DNA profiles

DNA database: a computer repository of DNA profiles

DNA fingerprinting: term coined by Sir Alec Jeffreys to describe his initial multilocus probe results that resembled a bar code–like output; this term has been replaced by DNA profiling or DNA typing

DNA profiling or typing: a method of identifying an individual through comparison of patterns arising from differences in DNA sequences; represented as a string of values (numbers or letters) compiled from the results of DNA testing at one or more genetic markers

DNA sequence: the relative order of base pairs, whether in a fragment of DNA, a gene, a chromosome, or an entire genome.

dNTPs: deoxynucleotide triphosphates; used in PCR as building blocks to construct new DNA strands

Dominant trait: an expressed trait that exerts its effect when present in an individual in just a single copy

Double helix: the native form of DNA, which looks like a twisted ladder; two linear strands of DNA assume this shape when held together by complementary base pairing (ladder rungs)

Double-stranded DNA (dsDNA): form of DNA in which the individual single strands are held together by complementary base pairing

Downstream: DNA sequence in the 3′ direction of a reference point

DQA1: a sequence polymorphism found on chromosome 6 in the human leukocyte antigen (HLA) region and developed into a commercial DNA test that was used for a time in the 1990s; also referred to as HLA DQα and has been used in transplantation biology

DTT: dithiothreitol; a chemical used during differential extraction to break protein disulfide bonds found in sperm nuclear membranes

Dye blobs: artifact peaks in capillary electropherograms arising from fluorescent dye molecules coming off their associated PCR primer during primer synthesis (and failing to be purified); generally dye blobs are wider than true STR alleles, are lower in signal intensity, and can be characteristically sized in each color channel

EDNAP: European DNA Profiling Group; a working group of the International Society of Forensic Genetics established in 1988 to coordinate research efforts with forensic DNA

EDTA: ethylenediaminetetraacetic acid; a commonly used chemical in biological buffers, which inhibits the activity of enzymes that break down DNA by sequestering magnesium ions and thus acts as a DNA preservative

Electropherogram: the graphic representation of the separation of molecules by electrophoresis in which the data appear as 'peaks' along a line

Electrophoresis: a technique in which molecules are separated by their velocity in an electric field

Elimination sample: a sample collected from an individual who had lawful access to the crime scene (e.g., the spouse of a rape victim); results from this sample may be helpful in sorting out a DNA mixture

ENFSI: European Network of Forensic Science Institutes; an organization of forensic laboratories established in 1995 to set standards for exchange of data between member states

Enzyme: a protein that can speed up a specific chemical reaction without being changed or consumed in the process

Epg: abbreviation used sometimes for electropherogram

Epithelial cells: skin cells, vaginal cells, or other cells that are normally found on an inner or outer body surface

Euchromatin: part of the chromosome that is loosely packed in the interphase portion of the cell cycle; most transcribed regions (genes) of a genome are located within the euchromatin as opposed to the heterochromatin

Eukaryote: an organism with cells containing a nucleus

Evidence sample: biological sample collected from a crime scene or people or objects associated with a crime scene; sometimes referred to as the 'Q' or question sample

Exclusion: a DNA test result indicating that an individual is excluded (does not match at the tested DNA locations) as the source of the DNA evidence; in a criminal case, 'exclusion' does not necessarily equate 'innocence'

Exon: a segment of a gene that is represented in the final mRNA product

Exonuclease: an enzyme that cleaves nucleotides one at a time from either the 3' end or 5' end of a polynucleotide chain through hydrolyzing the phosphodiester bonds

Expert system: a software program or set of software programs designed to rapidly and accurately process data without human intervention

Extension: step during PCR thermal cycling where individual nucleotides are added to an annealed primer with a DNA polymerase to create a new nucleotide strand that is complementary to the target sequence

Extraction control: a negative control set up in parallel with experimental samples during the DNA extraction process and carried through PCR amplification and analysis; contains no purposely added DNA template in order to monitor the presence of adventitious DNA within extraction reagents

F designation: used in a description of a genotype where an allele may have dropped out (e.g., when attempting to amplify low amounts of DNA template); a genotype of '16,F' implies that the true genotype may be allele 16 and anything else

FBI: Federal Bureau of Investigation; the federal police force for the United States

Federal Rules of Evidence: an admissibility standard for scientific evidence that relies on Federal Rules 702 and 403; the criteria are reliability, relevancy, and probative value

Fluorescence: the emission of light from a molecule following its excitation by light energy; in the context of DNA analysis, different fluorescent dyes permit simultaneous detection of similar size PCR products through fluorescence emission in different colors

Fluorophore: a molecule capable of fluorescence

Forensic hit: a CODIS match between two or more crime scene samples found in the forensic index; links serial crime

Forensic index: the collection of DNA profiles from crime scene samples that are stored in CODIS

Forensic science: the application of scientific knowledge to questions of civil and criminal law, typically through presentation of results from evidence in court

Frequency: rate at which an event occurs

Frye standard: an admissibility standard for scientific evidence that relies on the 1923 federal decision of *Frye v. United States*; general acceptance in the relevant scientific community is the main criterion

FSS: Forensic Science Service; now a government-owned company providing DNA testing services in the United Kingdom

Fst: the between-person inbreeding coefficient used in subpopulation corrections; commonly equated with the theta (θ) correction

FTA paper: an absorbent cellulose-based paper that contains chemicals to inhibit bacterial growth and to protect DNA from enzymatic degradation; liquid blood or saliva may be spotted onto FTA paper for room temperature storage

Gamete: a haploid reproductive cell; sperm or egg

Gel: semisolid matrix (usually agarose or acrylamide) used in electrophoresis to separate molecules

GenBank: a public repository of DNA sequences maintained by the National Center for Biotechnology Information, part of the U.S. National Institutes of Health

Gene: the basic unit of heredity; a sequence of DNA nucleotides on a chromosome

Gene diversity: a measure of the level of variability of a locus in a population

Gene frequency: the relative occurrence of a particular allele in a population

Gene mapping: determination of the relative positions of genes on a DNA molecule (chromosome or plasmid) and of the distance, in linkage units or physical units, between them

Genetic marker: *see* Marker

Genetics: the study of the patterns of inheritance of specific traits

Genome: all of the genetic material in the chromosomes of a particular organism; its size is generally given as the total number of base pairs

Genome projects: research and technology development efforts aimed at mapping and sequencing some or all of the genome of an organism

Genomic DNA: chromosomal DNA

Genotype: the genetic makeup of an organism, as characterized by its physical appearance or phenotype

Guanine: a purine base; one of the four molecules containing nitrogen present in the nucleic acids DNA and RNA; designated by the letter G

Guidelines: a set of general principles used to provide direction and parameters for decision making

Haploid: a single copy of the genome for an individual; gametes (sperm and egg) are haploid and when combined restore the zygote to a diploid complement of chromosomes

Haplotype: the genetic type from a set of linked markers in an individual, such as that found with Y-STRs or mtDNA

Hardy–Weinberg equilibrium: the observation reported independently in 1908 by Godfrey Hardy and Wilhelm Weinberg that in a large random intrabreeding population, not subjected to excessive selection or mutation, the gene and genotype frequencies will remain constant over time; the sum of $p^2+2pq+q^2$ applies at equilibrium for a single allele pair where p is the frequency of the allele A, q is the frequency of a, p^2 is the frequency of genotype AA, q^2 is the frequency of aa, and 2pq is the frequency of Aa; permits relating allele frequencies to genotype frequencies

H_d: hypothesis of the defense; denominator in a likelihood ratio

Hemizygous: having only one copy of a gene or DNA sequence in diploid cells; males are hemizygous for most genes on the X and Y sex chromosomes

Heredity: the transmission of characteristics from one generation to the next

Heterochromatin: a highly condensed part of the chromosome that remains tightly packed throughout the cell cycle and is predominantly noncoding

Heteroplasmy: the presence of more than one mtDNA type within a single individual

Heterozygosity: the presence of different alleles at one or more loci on homologous chromosomes; the probability that a given loci will be heterozygous in a randomly selected individual

Heterozygote: a diploid organism that carries different alleles at one or more genetic loci on each of the paired homologous chromosomes

Heterozygous: having different alleles at a particular locus; manifest as two distinct peaks for a locus in an electropherogram

Hit: a match between a crime scene DNA profile and a DNA profile found on a DNA database; termed a 'cold hit' if the connection made is in the absence of any prior investigative leads

Homologies: similarities in DNA or protein sequences between individuals of the same linear sequences, each derived from one parent

Homologous chromosomes: a pair of chromosomes containing the same linear gene sequences, each derived from one parent

Homoplasmy: a cell or organism having identical (indistinguishable) copies of mitochondrial DNA or other measured genetic loci

Homozygote: a diploid organism that carries two identical alleles at a particular locus on each of the paired homologous chromosomes

Homozygous: having two identical or indistinguishable alleles at a particular genetic locus; could occur because the alleles are identical by descent or identical by state; manifest as a single peak for a locus in an electropherogram

H_p: hypothesis of the prosecution; numerator in a likelihood ratio

Human leukocyte antigen (HLA): cell structures that differ among individuals and are important for acceptance or rejection of tissue grafts or organ transplants; the DNA locus for one particular class, HLA DQA1, was used for PCR-based forensic analysis in the 1990s

HVI: a section of the human mtDNA control region spanning nucleotide positions 16,024–16,365

HVII: a section of the human mtDNA control region spanning nucleotide positions 73–340

Hybridization: the binding or reassociation of complementary strands of nucleic acids or oligonucleotides

Hydrogen bonding: manner of interaction between complementary bases during nucleic acid hybridization that involves the highly directional attraction of an electropositive hydrogen atom to an electronegative oxygen or nitrogen atom; adenine forms two hydrogen bonds with thymine and cytosine forms three hydrogen bonds with guanine

Hypervariable: an area on the DNA which can have many different alleles in sequences from different people

Identical by descent (IBD): alleles in an individual or in two people that are identical because they have both been inherited from the same common ancestor

Identical by state (IBS): coincidental possession of alleles that appear identical; the alleles may or may not be truly identical

Identifiler: a multiplex STR typing kit from Applied Biosystems that coamplifies 15 STRs and the sex-typing marker amelogenin; the STR loci amplified are D8S1179, D21S11, D7S820, CSF1PO, D3S1358, TH01, D13S317, D16S539, D2S1338, D19S433, VWA, TPOX, D18S51, D5S818, and FGA

In vitro: outside a living organism; literally 'in glass' meaning biochemical reactions conducted in a test tube or other laboratory apparatus

In vivo: within the cell or organism

Inclusion: the inability to exclude an individual as a possible source of a biological sample due to a complete match between all examined regions of DNA producing a result

Inconclusive: a situation in which no conclusion can be reached regarding testing done due to one of many possible reasons (e.g., no results obtained, uninterpretable results obtained, or no reference sample available for testing)

Inhibitor: a substance that interferes with or prevents the polymerase chain reaction amplification process

Intercalating dye: a chemical that can insert itself between the stacked bases at the center of the DNA double helix; because the fluorescent properties of the dye change when bound to double-stranded DNA, these dyes can be used for DNA detection; some examples include ethidium bromide and SYBR Green

Internal size standard (ISS): specific DNA fragments of known length that are used to size other DNA fragments in a sample being measured; an ISS is commonly labeled with a different fluorescent dye not found in the sample, enabling mixing of the ISS and sample without interference in the analysis; sometimes referred to as an internal lane standard (ILS)

Interpretation/stochastic threshold: the value above which it is reasonable to assume that allelic dropout of a sister allele has not occurred; only loci with all peaks present above this threshold can be used for CPE calculations

Intimate sample: a biological sample obtained directly from a victim's body such as a vaginal swab

Intron: noncoding DNA which separates neighboring exons in a gene; intron sequences are removed during transcription (the creation of mRNA) so that only exons contribute to gene expression

ISFG: International Society of Forensic Genetics; an organization of scientists from more than 60 countries that meets biannually; conference proceedings have been entitled *Advances in Forensic Haemogenetics* or *Progress in Forensic Genetics*

Isoenzymes: enzymes that differ in amino acid sequence yet catalyze the same chemical reaction

IUPAC: International Union of Pure and Applied Chemistry

K562: name of a control DNA sample, originating from a cell line, that was widely used with RFLP analysis

Karyotype: a summary of the chromosome constitution of a cell or individual, such as 46,XY (a male with 23 pairs of chromosomes)

Kilobase (kb): unit of length for DNA fragments equal to 1000 nucleotides

Kinship analysis: DNA evaluations using biological relatives to predict expected genotypes in missing individuals; serves as an indirect form of human identification when no direct reference samples are available

Known sample: biological material whose source is established; used in a comparison to an unknown or questioned sample; abbreviated 'K'

Laboratory report: a summary of work performed and conclusions drawn in the course of evaluating evidence submitted as part of a forensic case

LCN: *see* Low-copy number

Length polymorphism: a locus that exhibits variation in length between individuals

Likelihood ratio (LR): the ratio of two probabilities of the same event under different hypotheses; typically the numerator contains the prosecution's hypothesis and the denominator the defense's hypothesis; when the evaluation is complete, the conclusion is phrased as 'the evidence is X times more likely under the numerator's proposition than under the denominator's proposition'

Limit-of-detection (LOD): the point below which is it not possible to reliably distinguish analytical signal data from background noise; typically defined as three times the standard deviation of the average background noise; *see* Analytical threshold

Limit-of-quantitation (LOQ): the point below which is it not possible to reliably quantify analytical signal data; typically defined as 10 times the standard deviation of the average background noise; *see* Analytical threshold

Lineage marker: term applied to Y-chromosome or mtDNA loci that can be used to trace paternal or maternal inheritance

Linkage: the proximity of two or more markers (genes or specific DNA sequences) on a chromosome; the closer together the markers are, the lower the probability that they will be separated during a DNA repair or replication process, and hence the greater the probability that they will be inherited together

Linkage disequilibrium (LD): particular alleles at two or more neighboring loci occurring together with frequencies significantly different from those predicted from independent assortment and individual allele frequencies; sometimes called *allelic association*

Linkage equilibrium (LE): when two or more genetic loci appear to segregate randomly in a given population; in practical terms, LE means that genotypes between the loci will be independent and will appear randomly with respect to each other

Loci: plural of locus

Locus: a unique physical location of a gene (or specific sequence of DNA) on a chromosome; the plural of locus is loci

Locus dropout: failure to obtain any measurable alleles at a locus in a particular sample

Low-copy number (LCN): analysis of a small quantity of DNA often by increasing the number of PCR amplification cycles; usually defined as less than approximately 100 pg or about 15 human diploid cells

Major contributor or component: the individual who donated the highest portion of material to a DNA mixture; the DNA profile which can account for the predominance of the mixture ratio

Marker: a gene or specific DNA sequence of known location on a chromosome; used as a point of reference in the mapping of other loci

Match: when genetic profiles show the same types at all loci tested and no unexplainable differences exist

Match criteria: a set of empirically derived, laboratory-specific data that is used to set limits on the amount of allowable difference within two DNA fragments in order to be considered the same size in RFLP or STR analysis

Maternal inheritance: inheritance from the mother

Matrix calibration: the process of establishing the color separation on an ABI 310 or 3100 Genetic Analyzer; also known as spectral calibration

Matrix failure: failure of the detection instrumentation and software to properly separate the dye colors used to label the PCR products being analyzed; *see* Pull-up

Megabase (Mb): unit of length for DNA fragments equal to 1 million nucleotides

Meiosis: the process of cell division in sex cells or gametes to the point where each possesses a haploid set of chromosomes

Melting temperature (T_m): temperature at which 50% of the DNA molecules for a specific sequence are separated from one another due to heat denaturation

Mendelian inheritance: reference to the basic principles that govern transmission of genetic traits from parents to offspring discovered by Gregor Mendel in the late 19th century

Methodology: an assembly of measurement techniques and the order in which they are used; the analytical processes and procedures used to support a DNA typing technology

Microsatellite DNA: *see* Short tandem repeats (STRs)

Minisatellite DNA: *see* Variable number of tandem repeats (VNTRs)

Minor contributor or component: the individual who donated the lesser portion of material to a two-person DNA mixture; the genotype portion of a DNA mixture that is lower in amount

Minus A (−A): form of a PCR product that does not possess an extra nucleotide at the 3' end; sometimes referred to as $n-1$

Mismatch: one or more nucleotides in a double-stranded DNA molecule are not complementary and do not base pair; for mismatches to be tolerated, the hybridization (annealing) temperature must be sufficiently below the sequence melting temperature; mismatches between template DNA and PCR primers can result in a null allele due to failure of the primer to hybridize and amplify the target sequence

Mitochondria: organelles found in eukaryotes (including humans) that provide the energy for the cell; singular form = mitochondrion

Mitochondrial DNA (mtDNA): a small, circular DNA molecule located in the mitochondria that contains approximately 16,500 nucleotides; the abundance of hundreds of copies of mtDNA in each cell make it useful with samples originating from limited or damaged biological material

Mitosis: the process of nuclear division in cells that produces daughter cells, which are genetically identical to each other and to the parent

Mitotype: a summary of the typing or sequencing results from mtDNA

Mixture: a sample resulting from the combination of biological material from two or more contributors

Mixture profile: a DNA profile originating from a combination of more than one contributor; usually distinguishable from a single source sample by the presence of more than two alleles from at least one locus and/or imbalance in peak height ratios dependant upon the mixture ratio of the contributors

Mixture ratio: relative contributions of components to the mixture as determined by the use of quantitative peak height information and peak height ratios; also referred to as mass ratio

MLP: *see* Multilocus probes

Molar extinction coefficient: a measure of the ability of a fluorescent dye to absorb light

Molecular biology: study of the theories, methods, and techniques used in the analysis of gene structure, organization, and function

mtDNA: *see* Mitochondrial DNA

Multilocus probes: a form of RFLP testing developed by Alec Jeffreys with two VNTR probes 33.15 and 33.6, which visualized many loci simultaneously with a bar code–like image containing 30 or more bands per individual; *see* DNA fingerprinting

Multiplex PCR: coamplification of multiple regions of a genome with more than one set of primers; enables information from the different target sequences to be collected simultaneously

Mutation: any inheritable change in DNA sequence; an alteration or change of an allele at a genetic locus resulting in genetic inconsistency between a biological parent and offspring

Mutation rate: a measure of the frequency at which mutations have been observed at a specific genetic locus

Nanogram (ng): one billionth of a gram

NCBI: National Center of Biotechnology Information; home of GenBank, PubMed, and other resources

NDIS: National DNA Index System; the highest tier of CODIS in the United States

Negative control: a sample consisting of only PCR amplification reagents without the addition of template DNA

Nested PCR: a two-stage amplification procedure where an aliquot from an initial PCR amplification is used as a template for the second, which may use different primers and conditions; an extremely sensitive technique that is prone to contamination

NIH: National Institutes of Health

NIJ: National Institute of Justice

NIST: National Institute of Standards and Technology

No results: no data (peaks) detected above the analytical threshold

Noise: background signal detected by a data collection instrument; signal above the limit of detection or three times the average noise level is considered analytical data (i.e., true allele or artifact)

Noncoding region: a region of DNA that lacks the capacity to produce a protein (gene product)

Nonconsensus: a repeat unit that differs in structure from the main repeating sequence (e.g., TH01 allele 9.3 contains a nonconsensus '-CAT' in the middle of its normal TCAT repeats)

Nonsperm cell fraction: the portion of a sample produced during differential extraction containing DNA from nonsperm cells; generally epithelial cells from the female victim in the case of sexual assault evidence

Normalization: the process of achieving a DNA concentration that fits the optimal window for analysis through either diluting samples that are too concentrated or concentrating samples that are too dilute

NRC I: the first National Research Council report issued in 1992 entitled 'DNA Technology in Forensic Science'

NRC II: the second National Research Council report issued in 1996 entitled 'The Evaluation of Forensic DNA Evidence'

NRY: the nonrecombining region of the Y chromosome

Nuclear DNA: DNA located in the nucleus of a cell

Nucleic acid: a general class of molecules that are polymers of nucleotides; DNA and RNA are the major types

Nucleotide: a unit of nucleic acid composed of phosphate, ribose or deoxyribose, and a purine or pyrimidine base

Nucleus: the cellular organelle in eukaryotes that contains the genetic material

Null allele: an allele that is not detected usually due to a mutation in the template DNA that prevents a PCR primer from binding properly; can result in a true heterozygote being called a homozygote

Obligate allele: required allele(s) at a locus in paternity testing or mixture interpretation after other alleles have been accounted for using available reference samples

Offender hit: a CODIS match between a crime scene sample and an individual found in the offender index

Offender index: the collection of DNA profiles from convicted offender samples that are stored in CODIS

Off-scale data: produced when the emitted fluorescence from the PCR products being measured saturates the detector in an electropherogram; results in flat-topped peaks for STR alleles and pull-up peaks in one or more color channels corresponding to the off-scale peak

Oligonucleotide: a short single-stranded DNA sequence; typically synthesized in a laboratory as in the case of PCR primers

Organic extraction: a method of isolating DNA from cells involving phenol and other organic chemicals

Outsourcing: the utilization of a vendor laboratory to provide DNA analysis services; the originating laboratory typically retains ownership of the DNA data produced

Palindrome: a DNA sequence such as ATCGAT that reads the same when read in the 5′-to-3′ direction on each strand; restriction enzymes often target palindromic sequences

Partial profile: failure to obtain a complete set of results for the DNA loci examined; common causes include degraded or low quantities of template DNA

Paternal inheritance: inheritance from the father

Paternity index (PI): a numerical summary of the strength of the genetic evidence for a match between an alleged father and a child; a likelihood ratio using genetic data that compares how much more likely it would be to have observed the shared alleles between a child and an alleged father if the allele father was the true father of the child versus a random unrelated man of similar ethnic background

PCR: *see* Polymerase chain reaction

PCR product: the DNA amplified as a result of the polymerase chain reaction; also known as an *amplicon*

Peak: the visual image of an allele on an electropherogram; the peak height is correlated to the amount of DNA and the position to its size

Peak height: relative fluorescence intensity of a peak that reflects the quantity of the PCR product being measured

Peak height imbalance: a large difference in peak heights between heterozygous alleles at a locus; usually if peak heights within a single locus are >30% to 40% apart, then a mixture of multiple contributors is considered likely

Peak height ratio: the measurement of one allele's peak height over the other allele's peak height at a single locus in an electropherogram

Pedigree: a chart outlining an ancestral history with squares representing males and circles representing females

Performance check: quality assurance measure to assess the functionality of laboratory equipment, instruments, or procedures that impact the accuracy and/or validity of DNA testing

Personal protective equipment: articles such as disposable (latex) gloves, masks, shoe covers, and eye protection that are utilized by laboratory personnel to provide a barrier to keep biological or chemical hazards from contacting the skin, eyes, and mucous membranes and to avoid contamination of the crime scene or samples being processed in a laboratory environment

Phenotype: the observable characteristics of a cell or organism; the physical appearance or functional expression of a trait

Photobleaching: the photochemical destruction of a fluorophore due to overexposure to light; can complicate the observation of fluorescent molecules

Photostability: the ability of a fluorophore to undergo repeated cycles of excitation and emission without being destroyed in the excited state

Phylogenetics: a method of grouping genetic information together based on similarities in order to infer descent from a common ancestor; this study of genetic diversity enables construction of evolutionary trees and is used to track mtDNA sequence quality

Physical map: a map of the locations of identifiable landmarks on DNA; distance is measured in base pairs.

Picogram (pg): one trillionth of a gram; the DNA from one human cell weighs about 3 pg

Plus A (+A): nontemplate addition by a DNA polymerase at the 3′ end of a PCR product usually in the form of an adenine nucleotide

Point mutation: alteration in the DNA sequence at a single nucleotide in a locus; can be a substitution, insertion, or deletion

Polymarker (PM): a PCR-based DNA test from Roche and Applied Biosystems used in the 1990s involving sequence polymorphisms from six chromosomal locations detected with reverse dot blot assays

Polymerase chain reaction (PCR): an *in vitro* process that yields millions of copies of desired DNA through repeated cycling of a reaction involving the DNA polymerase enzyme

Polymerase, DNA or RNA: enzymes that catalyze the synthesis of nucleic acids on preexisting nucleic acid templates, assembling RNA from ribonucleotides or DNA from deoxyribonucleotides

Polymorphism: difference in DNA sequence among individuals; genetic variations occurring in more than 1% of a population would be considered useful polymorphisms for linkage analysis

Population: a group of individuals residing in a given area at a given time

Population genetics: the study of genetic diversity in populations and how it changes through time

Population substructure: the existence of smaller mating groups within a larger community

Positive control: a known sample taken through an analytical process to verify that the various steps are working properly

Posterior probability: what a judge or jury considers when coming to a verdict after considering all of the evidence in a case; in Bayesian analysis, posterior probability is equal to the prior probability multiplied times the likelihood ratio; sometimes referred to as posterior odds

Power of discrimination: the potential power of a genetic marker or set of markers to differentiate between any two people chosen at random; equal to one minus the sum of the square of the genotype frequencies

Power of exclusion: in the context of parentage testing, the ability of a genetic test to detect an inconsistency between a nonparent and a child

PowerPlex 16: a multiplex STR typing kit from Promega Corporation that coamplifies 15 STRs and the sex-typing marker amelogenin; the STR loci amplified are D3S1358, TH01, D21S11, D18S51, Penta E, D5S818, D13S317, D7S820, D16S539, CSF1PO, Penta D, VWA, D8S1179, TPOX, and FGA

PowerPlex Y: a multiplex STR typing kit from Promega Corporation that coamplifies STRs from 12 regions of the human Y chromosome: the Y-STR loci amplified are DYS19, DYS385a/b, DYS389I/II, DYS390, DYS391, DYS392, DYS393, DYS437, DYS438, and DYS439

Precision: a measure of the closeness of results when experiments are repeated

Preferential amplification: situation in which one allele at a locus is amplified by PCR with greater efficiency than the other allele; this unequal sampling of the two alleles can be due to stochastic fluctuation arising when only a few DNA molecules are used to initiate PCR; can result in a heterozygote allele imbalance or false homozygosity if one of the alleles fails to amplify

Presumptive test: an initial examination of evidence to indicate the possible source of the sample (e.g., blood, saliva, semen, etc.); usually followed up by a confirmatory assay or DNA analysis

Primer: a short preexisting polynucleotide chain, usually 18 to 30 bases long, which targets a specific region of the template DNA and allows a DNA polymerase to initiate synthesis of a complementary strand

Prior probability: in Bayesian statistics, the initially estimated probability of an outcome before all relevant information has been considered; sometimes referred to as prior odds

Probability: the likelihood of the occurrence of any particular form of an event, estimated as the ratio of the number of ways or times that the event may occur in that form to the total number of ways that it could occur in any form

Probability of exclusion (PE): the percentage of the population that can be excluded as potential contributors to a DNA mixture result

Probability of inclusion (PI): the percentage of the population that can be included as potential contributors to a DNA mixture result; calculated by squaring the sum of the frequencies of the alleles present in the mixture at a particular locus

Probative: furnishing evidence or proof that can be used in a court of law

Probe: single-stranded DNA or RNA of a specific base sequence, usually labeled with a fluorescent dye to enable sensitive detection, that are used to detect the presence of the complementary base sequence following hybridization

Procedure: an established practice to be followed in performing a specified task or under specific circumstances

Process control: standardized efforts to manage a set of associated procedures in order to produce a predictable result

Product rule: the combination of genotype frequency estimates from multiple loci achieved by multiplying the individual locus genotype frequencies together; assumes statistical independence between the genetic loci due to recombination

Proficiency test: a quality assurance measure used to monitor performance of an analyst and identify areas in which improvement may be needed; can be internal (produced by the agency undergoing the test) or external (produced by an outside test provider); external proficiency tests can be either open or blind

Profile subtraction: the DNA profile of obligate alleles remaining after removal of alleles accounted for by the known/expected contributor without consideration of associated signal intensities

Profiler Plus: a commercial STR typing kit from Applied Biosystems that utilizes multiplex PCR to amplify and provide genetic information for nine STRs and the sex-typing marker amelogenin; the STR loci examined are D3S1358, VWA, FGA, D8S1179, D21S11, D18S51, D5S818, D13S317, and D7S820

Prokaryote: bacteria with cells lacking a nucleus

Protein: a large molecule composed of one or more chains of amino acids in a specific order; the order is determined by the base sequence of nucleotides in the gene coding for the protein; proteins are required for the structure, function, and regulation of the body cells, tissues, organs, and each protein has unique functions

Protocol: a procedure specified to be used when performing a measurement or related operation as a condition to obtain results that could be acceptable

Pseudoautosomal regions: sections on the tips of the Y chromosome that recombine with the X chromosome

Pull-up: a term used to describe when signal from one dye color channel produces artificial peaks in another, usually adjacent, color (e.g., low-level blue peaks underneath green peaks); off-scale data typically gives rise to pull-up; sometimes referred to as bleed-through or matrix failure

Punnett square: a cross-multiplication square showing possible offspring outcome based on father and mother allele combinations

Purine: a nucleic acid nitrogenous base with a double-ring structure; adenine (A) or guanine (G)

Pyrimidine: a nucleic acid nitrogenous base with a single-ring structure; cytosine (C), thymine (T), or uracil (U)

Q-K comparison: evaluation of question and known samples with one another to reach a decision of inclusion, exclusion, or inconclusive

qPCR: *see* Quantitative PCR

Quality assurance (QA): a system of activities whose purpose is to provide assurance to the producer or user of a product or service that it meets defined standards of quality

Quality control (QC): the overall system of activities whose purpose is to control the quality of a product or service so that it meets the needs of users

Quantitative PCR (qPCR): method used for determining the quantity of DNA template present in a sample through measuring the point at which samples cross a detection threshold relative to a set of standard samples; also known as real-time PCR

Quantum yield: a measure of the efficiency with which an excited fluorophore converts absorbed light into emitted light

Question sample: biological material typically from a crime scene in a forensic case whose source is unknown; compared with known sample(s); abbreviated as 'Q'

Random man not excluded (RMNE): another term for probability of exclusion

Random match: a match in the DNA profiles of two samples, where one is drawn at random from the population

Random match probability (RMP): the chance of a specific profile occurring in a specific population based on observed allele frequencies for that population

RCMP: Royal Canadian Mounted Police; federal police force of Canada

Reagent: a substance used to perform an analytical procedure

Reagent blank control: a negative control that contains no extracted DNA yet is put through the DNA typing process in order to assess possible contaminating DNA present in the reagents or PCR tubes used to amplify the DNA samples

Reannealing: the process of complementary single strands of DNA binding together

Recessive trait: one that is masked by a dominant trait and thus unseen in terms of the phenotype in a heterozygote

Recombination: the process of exchanging DNA between homologous chromosomes that can occur during meiosis; generates new combinations of alleles or genes when passing genetic information between parents and offspring

Reference sample: a sample (typically blood or buccal swab) taken from a known person that is used for comparison purposes to an evidentiary sample; sometimes referred to as the 'K' or known sample

Reference material: *see* Certified reference material

Relative fluorescence unit (RFU): a measure of the signal produced by an ABI 310 Genetic Analyzer or similar capillary electrophoresis system

Renaturation: the reassociation of denatured, complementary strands of DNA or RNA

Repeat unit: a short sequence of DNA that is repeated multiple times at an STR locus

Replication: the formation of an exact copy; with DNA replication each strand acts as a template for a new, complementary strand that is formed according to base-pairing rules (A with T and G with C)

Reproducibility: the ability to obtain the same result when a test or experiment is repeated in another laboratory or segregated by time

Resolution: the ability to separate similar sized DNA molecules

Restriction enzyme: a protein that recognizes specific, short nucleotide sequences and cuts DNA at the those sites

Restriction fragment length polymorphism (RFLP): variation between individuals in DNA fragment sizes cut by specific restriction enzymes; polymorphic sequences that result in RFLPs that are used as markers on both physical maps and genetic linkage maps; RFLPs are usually caused by mutation at a cutting site

Reverse dot blot: a method used to detect DNA that was employed with Polymarker and DQA1 assays; a set of sequence-specific probes is attached to a membrane that is then challenged with PCR products from samples

Review: an evaluation of documentation to check for consistency, accuracy, and completeness of results

RFLP: *See* Restriction fragment length polymorphism; sometimes pronounced 'rif-lip'

Ribonucleic acid (RNA): single-stranded nucleic acid possessing a hydroxyl group at the 2′ position and substituting uracil in place of thymine; comes in several forms including messenger RNA, transfer RNA, and ribosomal RNA—all of which are involved in production of proteins (translation)

RNA: *see* Ribonucleic acid

Run: a batch of samples processed together (e.g., on an ABI 310 Genetic Analyzer)

Scan number: data points collected over time on an ABI 310 or 3100 Genetic Analyzer; form the x axis on an electropherogram and are converted to base pair size by extrapolation to internal size standard peaks

Sequence polymorphism: a locus that exhibits variation in sequence between individuals

Sequence-specific oligonucleotide (SSO) probe: DNA sequences bound to a solid support that are used to capture complementary sequences through hybridization

Sequencing: determination of the order of nucleotides (base sequences) in a DNA or RNA molecule or the order of amino acids in a protein

Serology: discipline concerned with the immunological study of body fluids; laboratory tests that use antigen and serum antibody reactions to characterize biological materials

Sex chromosomes (X and Y chromosomes): chromosomes that are different between the two sexes and are involved in sex determination; in humans, females are XX and males XY

SGM: Second Generation Multiplex; an early STR DNA assay developed by the Forensic Science Service and used in the initial years of the UK's national DNA database; coamplifies the sex-typing marker amelogenin and six STRs: VWA, D8S1179, D21S11, D18S51, TH01, and FGA

SGM Plus: a commercial STR typing kit from Applied Biosystems that utilizes multiplex PCR to amplify and provide genetic information for 10 STRs and the sex-typing marker amelogenin; the STR loci examined are D3S1358, VWA, D16S539, D2S1338, D8S1179, D21S11, D18S51, D19S433, TH01, and FGA

Short tandem repeats (STRs): multiple copies of an identical (or similar) DNA sequence arranged in direct succession where the repeat sequence unit is 2 to 6 bp in length; because STRs generally occur in the 'junk' DNA outside of the constraints of genes, the number of repeat units can vary between individuals in an accordion-like fashion

Silver-stain detection: a method of detecting proteins or DNA molecules in slab gels through chemical development where silver ions are deposited on either the proteins or DNA and then reduced to metallic silver

Single locus probes (SLPs): a form of RFLP testing in which each VNTR probe is specific to a single locus

Single nucleotide polymorphism (SNP): any polymorphic variation at a single nucleotide; most SNPs are biallelic (e.g., either C or T) with the minor allele being observed at least 1% of the time; sometimes pronounced 'snip'

Singleplex: a PCR system that amplifies only one locus

Single-stranded DNA (ssDNA): a form of DNA in which the two strands that normally make up the double helix are separated from one another; ssDNA is more flexible in solution than dsDNA

Sister allele: term given to the second allele present in a heterozygous sample

Slot blot: a commonly used DNA quantitation method prior to the advent of qPCR assays

SLP: *see* Single locus probes (SLPs)

SNP: *see* Single nucleotide polymorphism (SNP)

Somatic cells: any cell in the body except the gametes

Somatic mutation: a mutation after gamete fusion (zygote formation) usually leading to a situation in which the individual has different genotypes in different cells

Source attribution: a statement reflecting that to a high degree of confidence, a tested individual is the source of an evidentiary DNA sample; declared when the random match probability for a particular DNA profile is rarer than a predetermined threshold; an approach first adopted by the FBI Laboratory

Southern blotting: transfer by absorption of DNA fragments separated in electrophoretic gels to membrane filters for detection of specific base sequences by radioactively labeled complementary probes

Spectral calibration: an examination of the contribution of overlap in the emission spectrum of fluorescent dyes used for a specific DNA test on an ABI 31xx Genetic Analyzer; permits the color deconvolution necessary for multicolor STR typing to be performed; the same as a 'matrix' in an ABI 310; a poor spectral calibration leads to pull-up; *see* Matrix calibration

Sperm cell fraction: the portion of a sample produced during differential extraction containing DNA from sperm cells; generally from the male perpetrator in the case of sexual assault evidence

Spike: an anomalous peak that can occur in capillary electropherograms and interfere with data interpretation; this instrumental artifact is typically narrow and produces signal in multiple dye channels

Spurious alleles: alleles assumed to have arrived in a profile via contamination

SSO: *see* Sequence-specific oligonucleotide (SSO) probe

Standard operating procedure (SOP): a detailed listing of all materials required to perform an assay as well as the exact steps required to successfully complete the experiment; SOPs are typically prepared following validation of a new procedure and are expected to be followed exactly when performing forensic casework

Standard Reference Material (SRM): a certified reference material produced by the U.S. National Institute of Standards and Technology

Standards: criteria established for quality assurance purposes that place specific requirements on laboratories and analysts; also refers to well-characterized samples that can aid calibration of measurements

Stochastic: random selection of alleles amplified at a particular locus; more prevalent at low levels of DNA

Stochastic threshold: detection level on an ABI 310 or 31xx Genetic Analyzer where a potential sister allele of a detected peak may fall below the analytical threshold; *see* Interpretation threshold

Stokes shift: difference in wavelength between the maxima of excitation and emission spectra during fluorescence

STR: *see* Short tandem repeats (STRs)

Stringency: specific conditions used in the hybridization of DNA; also refers to a specific parameter used when searching a DNA database

Stutter product ($n-4$): a minor peak appearing one repeat unit smaller than a primary STR allele resulting from strand slippage during the amplification process; usually <15% of the height of the true STR allele; complicates mixture interpretation

Stutter product ($n+4$): a minor peak appearing one repeat unit larger than a primary STR allele resulting from strand slippage during the amplification process; usually <3% of the height of the true STR allele; sometimes referred to as 'forward' or 'positive' stutter

Stutter ratio: calculation of the proportion of a stutter peak height to its parent allelic peak height

SWGDAM: Scientific Working Group on DNA Analysis Methods; formerly known as TWGDAM, Technical Working Group on DNA Analysis Methods; an FBI-sponsored group that develops quality assurance standards and guidelines for laboratories in the United States

SYBR Green: a fluorescent intercalating dye sometimes used for DNA quantitation purposes

Tandem repeat sequences: multiple copies of the same base sequence on a chromosome immediately adjacent to each other (e.g., STR)

Taq **polymerase**: an enzyme derived from the *Thermus aquaticus* bacteria that is capable of withstanding near boiling temperatures; widely used for PCR amplifications because of its thermally stable nature

TE buffer: a commonly used buffer in molecular biology containing Tris and EDTA

Technical leader: typically a laboratory employee who is accountable for the technical operations and is authorized to stop or suspend laboratory operations

Technician: a scientist who performs analytical techniques under the supervision of a qualified analyst; generally does not interpret data or write reports

Technique: a physical or chemical principle utilized to perform analysis of a material

Technology: the practical application of knowledge in a particular field; in the case of forensic DNA analysis, it usually refers to a methodology such as RFLP, STRs, Y-STRs, mtDNA, etc.

Telomere: the terminal regions at the tips of a chromosome

Template DNA: DNA sample added to the PCR reaction and targeted by the PCR primers

Thermal cycler: an instrument used to perform PCR by changing temperatures to heat and cool DNA samples for specified times

Theta (θ) correction: an adjustment made to correct for inbreeding within populations; a value of 0.01 is commonly used for general populations and 0.03 for small, isolated populations where more inbreeding would be expected; often used synonymously with F_{ST}

Thymine: a pyrimidine base; one of the four molecules containing nitrogen present in DNA; designated by the letter T

T_m: *see* Melting temperature

Traceability: establishing a link (through an unbroken chain of comparisons) to an accepted certified reference material—this provides confidence in measurements being made by a particular method; can also refer to the ability to trace the source of uncertainty of a measurement or a measured value

Transcription: DNA to RNA

Transition: a mutation that is purine to purine (e.g., A-to-G) or pyrimidine to pyrimidine (e.g., C-to-T)

Translation: RNA to protein

Translocation: process in which a copy of a gene is inserted somewhere else in the genome

Transversion: a mutation that is purine to pyrimidine or vice versa (e.g., A-to-T)

Triallelic pattern: the detection of three alleles at a particular STR locus

Trisomy: possessing three copies of a particular chromosome (e.g., trisomy 21, which causes Down syndrome)

Uninterpretable: no results can be reported based on available evidence; a DNA profile exhibiting little-to-no results based on lack of amplifiable DNA template

Uniparental inheritance: inheritance from only one parent

Upstream: sequences in the 5′ direction from some reference point on a DNA template

Uracil: a pyrimidine nucleobase that is substituted for thymine when RNA is transcribed; designated by the letter U

UV light: ultraviolet light; portion of the electromagnetic spectrum with shorter wavelengths and higher energy than visible light; nucleic acids absorb light maximally in the ultraviolet range (260 nm), which aids its detection and destruction

Validation: the process by which a sample, measurement method, or a piece of data is deemed useful for a specified purpose; the process of extensive and rigorous evaluation of DNA methods before acceptance for routine use

Variable number of tandem repeats (VNTRs): repeating units of a DNA sequence, the number of which varies between individuals; sometimes referred to as a minisatellite; typically analyzed by restriction fragment length polymorphism (RFLP) methods; can range in size from approximately 500 bp to greater than 20,000 bp

Variance: a measure of the spread of a distribution about its average value

Variant allele: a nonstandard form of an allele due to a mutation or an insertion or deletion relative to other commonly seen alleles

Verification: confirmation by examination that specified requirements have been met

Virtual filters: term given to data collection on the CCD camera of an ABI 310 or 31xx Genetic Analyzer whereby the light intensity in either four or five nonoverlapping regions of the CCD camera is recorded by the software; each region corresponds to a wavelength range that contains or is close to the emission maximum of a fluorescent dye; different virtual filter sets are used to collect light emitted from different fluorescent dye combinations, which are specific to the STR kit used

VNTR: *see* Variable number of tandem repeats (VNTRs)

Whole genome amplification (WGA): a PCR-like method using short, highly degenerate primers to amplify a large number of random sequences spread across the genome; WGA permits sample enrichment with medium quantities of DNA, but is prone to stochastic variation with low amounts of input DNA

X chromosome: one of the sex chromosomes; normal females possess two copies and males one

X-STR: short tandem repeat markers found on the X chromosome that can sometimes be useful in addressing kinship analysis

Y chromosome: one of the sex chromosomes; normal males possess one copy and females none

Yfiler: a multiplex STR typing kit from Applied Biosystems that coamplifies STRs from 17 regions of the human Y chromosome; the Y-STR loci amplified are DYS19, DYS385 a/b, DYS389I/II, DYS390, DYS391, DYS392, DYS393, DYS437, DYS438, DYS439, DYS448, DYS456, DYS458, DYS635, and GATA-H4

Yield gel: diagnostic tool in DNA analysis that aids in determining the quality and quantity of DNA extracted from a sample

Y-STR: short tandem repeat markers found on the Y chromosome that enable male-specific DNA testing and can be useful in cases involving sexual assault; also used in genetic genealogy to trace male lineages

Zygote: cell formed when the nuclear DNA from a father's sperm cell combines with nuclear DNA in a mother's egg, restoring the diploid chromosome count

Abbreviations	
A	adenine
C	cytosine
G	guanine
T	thymine
ABI	Applied Biosystems Incorporated
AmpFLP	amplified fragment length polymorphism
ASCLD	American Society of Crime Laboratory Directors
bp	base pair
CCD	charge-coupled device
CE	capillary electrophoresis
CODIS	Combined DNA Index System

CPE	combined probability of exclusion
CPI	combined probability of inclusion
CRM	certified reference material
DNA	deoxyribonucleic acid
dsDNA	double-stranded DNA
DTT	dithiothreitol
EDNAP	European DNA Profiling Group
EDTA	ethylenediaminetetraacetic acid
ENFSI	European Network of Forensic Science Institutes
FBI	Federal Bureau of Investigation
FSS	Forensic Science Service
HLA	human leukocyte antigen
HRP	horseradish peroxidase
HVI	hypervariable region I
HVII	hypervariable region II
HWE	Hardy–Weinberg equilibrium
IBD	identical by descent
IBS	identical by state
ILS	internal lane standard
ISFG	International Society of Forensic Genetics
kb	kilobase
LE	linkage equilibrium
LOD	limit of detection
LOQ	limit of quantitation
LR	likelihood ratio
Mb	megabase
MLP	multilocus probe
mtDNA	mitochondrial DNA
NCBI	National Center for Biotechnology Information
NDIS	National DNA Index System
ng	nanogram
NIH	National Institutes of Health

NIJ	National Institute of Justice
NIST	National Institute of Standards and Technology
NRC	National Research Council
PCR	polymerase chain reaction
pg	picogram
PI	paternity index
PP16	PowerPlex 16
QA	quality assurance
QC	quality control
qPCR	quantitative PCR
RFLP	restriction fragment length polymorphism
RFU	relative fluorescence unit
RMNE	random man not excluded
RMP	random match probability
RNA	ribonucleic acid
SLP	single-locus probe
SNP	single nucleotide polymorphism
SOP	standard operating procedure
SRM	Standard Reference Material
ssDNA	single-stranded DNA
SSO	sequence-specific oligonucleotide
STR	short tandem repeat
SWGDAM	Scientific Working Group on DNA Analysis Methods
Taq	*Thermus aquaticus*
TE	Tris-EDTA
T_m	melting temperature
U	uracil
VNTR	variable number of tandem repeats
WGA	whole genome amplification
X-STR	X-chromosome short tandem repeat
Y-STR	Y-chromosome short tandem repeat

SI Units of Measurement

Name	Symbol	Value	Scale	Numerical
Yotta-	Y	10^{24}	Septillion	1 000 000 000 000 000 000 000 000
Zetta-	Z	10^{21}	Sextillion	1 000 000 000 000 000 000 000
Exa-	E	10^{18}	Quintillion	1 000 000 000 000 000 000
Peta-	P	10^{15}	Quadrillion	1 000 000 000 000 000
Tera-	T	10^{12}	Trillion	1 000 000 000 000
Giga-	G	10^{9}	Billion	1 000 000 000
Mega-	M	10^{6}	Million	1 000 000
Kilo-	k	10^{3}	Thousand	1000
Hecto-	h	10^{2}	Hundred	100
Deca-	da	10^{1}	Ten	10
		1	One	1
Deci-	d	10^{-1}	Tenth	0.1
Centi-	c	10^{-2}	Hundredth	0.01
Milli-	m	10^{-3}	Thousandth	0.001
Micro-	μ	10^{-6}	Millionth	0.000 001
Nano-	n	10^{-9}	Billionth	0.000 000 001
Pico-	p	10^{-12}	Trillionth	0.000 000 000 001
Femto-	f	10^{-15}	Quadrillionth	0.000 000 000 000 001
Atto-	a	10^{-18}	Quintillionth	0.000 000 000 000 000 001
Zepto-	z	10^{-21}	Sextillionth	0.000 000 000 000 000 000 001
Yocto-	y	10^{-24}	Septillionth	0.000 000 000 000 000 000 000 001

Source: http://physics.nist.gov/cuu/Units/prefixes.html

Appendix 2: Useful Web Sites

Some Internet Web sites will change and many new ones will be added after this book is published. An up-to-date listing of information is maintained at http://www.cstl.nist.gov/biotech/strbase/weblink.htm

General Information

DNA.gov: http://www.dna.gov
DNA Litigation Legal Support Page: http://www.denverda.org/DNA/DNA_INDEX.htm
DNA Policy Community Site: http://www.dnapolicy.net
DNA Resource.com: http://www.dnaresource.com
STRBase: http://www.cstl.nist.gov/biotech/strbase

Organizations

American Academy of Forensic Sciences: http://www.aafs.org

European DNA Profiling Group (EDNAP): http://www.isfg.org/ednap/ednap.htm

European Network of Forensic Science Institutes (ENFSI) DNA Working Group: http://www.enfsi.eu

FBI's Combined DNA Index System (CODIS): http://www.fbi.gov/hq/lab/codis/index1.htm

Forensic Science Society: http://www.forensic-science-society.org.uk

The Innocence Project: http://www.innocenceproject.org

International Society for Forensic Genetics (ISFG): http://www.isfg.org

National Clearinghouse for Science, Technology, and the Law (NCSTL): http://www.ncstl.org/home

National District Attorneys Association (NDAA): http://www.ndaa-apri.org/index.html

National Forensic Science Technology Center (NFSTC): http://www.nfstc.org

National Institute of Justice (NIJ): http://www.ojp.usdoj.gov/nij

National Institute of Standards and Technology (NIST): http://www.nist.gov

National Legal Aid and Defender Association (NLADA): http://www.nlada.org/Defender/forensics/for_lib/Index/DNA

Journals

Electrophoresis: http://www3.interscience.wiley.com/journal/10008330/home

Elsevier forensic products: http://www.forensicsource.org

Forensic Science Communications: http://www.fbi.gov/programs/lab/fsc/current/index.htm

Forensic Science International: http://www.fsijournal.org

Forensic Science International: Genetics: http://www.fsigenetics.com

Forensic Science, Medicine and Pathology: http://www.springerlink.com/content/120561

FSI Genetics Supplement Series: http://www.fsigeneticssup.com

International Journal of Legal Medicine: http://www.springerlink.com/content/1437-1596

Journal of Forensic Sciences: http://www3.interscience.wiley.com/journal/118519059/home

Legal Medicine: http://www.forensicsource.org/periodicals/legmed/home

Proceedings from the International Symposiums on Human Identification: http://www.promega.com/geneticidproc/default.htm

Profiles in DNA (Promega): http://www.promega.com/profiles

Science & Justice: http://www.scienceandjusticejournal.com

Commercial Providers

Applied Biosystems (ABI): http://www.appliedbiosystems.com

Bode Technology Group: http://www.bodetech.com

Forensic Science Service (FSS): http://www.forensic.gov.uk

Forensics Source: http://www.forensicssource.com

Orchid Cellmark: http://www.orchidcellmark.com

Promega Corporation: http://www.promega.com

Qiagen: http://www1.qiagen.com/

Population Databases

EMPOP (European mtDNA Population Database): http://www.empop.org

ENFSI DNA Working Group STR Population Database: http://www.str-base.org

mtDNA Manager: http://mtmanager.yonsei.ac.kr

OmniPop: http://www.cstl.nist.gov/biotech/strbase/populationdata.htm

STR DNA Database: http://www.strdna-db.org

US Y-STR Database: http://www.usystrdatabase.org

Y-STR Haplotype Reference Database (YHRD): http://www.yhrd.org

DNA.gov Training Courses Available as of January 2009

Crime Scene and DNA Basics: http://www.dna.gov/training/evidence

Laboratory Orientation and Testing of Body Fluids and Tissues: http://www.dna.gov/training/forensicbiology

Laboratory Safety Programs: http://www.dna.gov/training/labsafety

DNA Extraction and Quantitation: http://www.dna.gov/training/extraction

DNA Amplification: http://www.dna.gov/training/amplification

Amplified DNA Product Separation: http://www.dna.gov/training/separation

STR Data Analysis and Interpretation: http://www.dna.gov/training/strdata

Population Genetics and Statistics: http://www.dna.gov/training/populations

Communication Skills, Report Writing, and Courtroom Testimony: http://www.dna.gov/training/communicating

Non-STR DNA Markers: SNPs, Y-STRs, LCN and mtDNA: http://www.dna.gov/training/markers

Advanced and Emerging DNA Techniques and Technologies: http://www.dna.gov/training/Technology

DNA: A Prosecutor's Practice Notebook: http://www.dna.gov/training/prosecutors-notebook

Principles of Forensic DNA for Officers of the Court: http://www.dna.gov/training/otc

What Every Law Enforcement Officer Should Know About DNA Evidence: First Responding Officers and *Investigators and Evidence Technicians:* http://www.dna.gov/training/letraining

Appendix 3: Probability and Statistics

The following information is included to provide a background and foundation for the reader on probability and basic statistics. It can be studied in conjunction with Chapter 11 on statistical interpretation of DNA profiles.

Probability

In the case of a rape or murder, there may be no witnesses available to assist in verification of who was the actual perpetrator of the crime. Therefore, DNA evidence developed as part of a criminal investigation of necessity has to be made in the face of uncertainty. While a crime scene sample may match the DNA profile of a suspect, the result is typically cast in the language of probabilities rather than certainty. Probability statements are designed to attach numerical values to issues of uncertainty.

Probability is the number of times an event happens divided by the number of opportunities for it to happen (i.e., the number of trials). The concepts of probabilities can be difficult to grasp because we are often in the mind-set of thinking simply that something either happened or it did not. Probability is usually viewed on a continuum between zero and one. At the lower extreme of zero, it is not possible for the event to occur (or to have occurred). In other words, there is a certainty of nonoccurrence. At the upper end, where the probability is equal to one, the event being measured or calculated did in fact occur. Quite often in scientific determinations, the probability of an event occurring is understood to never be completely zero or completely one. Thus, decisions in science, as in life, often need to be made in the face of uncertainty.

If a weather bureau predicts a 60% chance of rain, then this probability was arrived at because experience has shown that under similar meteorological conditions it has rained 6 out of 10 times. If one of two events is equally possible, such as heads or tails when flipping a coin, then the probability is considered 50% or 0.5 for either one of the events. Probabilities are mathematically described with symbols, such as P or Pr. The probability that an event can occur is given by the notation or formula: $P(H|E)$ or $Pr(H|E) = \ldots$. This notation is shorthand for stating 'the probability of event H occurring given evidence E is equal to ...'. Every probability is conditional on knowing something or on something else occurring.

Laws of probability

The three laws of probability can be summarized as follows. First, as stated earlier, probabilities can take place in the range zero to one. Events that are certain have a probability of one, whereas those that are not possible have a probability of zero. Thus, if a proposition or possibility is false, it has a probability of zero.

Second, events can be *mutually exclusive* meaning that if any one of a particular set of events has occurred then none of the others has occurred. If two events are mutually exclusive and we wish to know the probability that one or other of them is true then we can simply add their probabilities. This concept can be written out in the form:

$$P(G \text{ or } H|E) = P(G|E) + P(H|E)$$

or verbally, the probability of events G or H occurring given evidence E is equal to the probability of event G occurring given evidence E plus the probability of event H occurring given evidence E. In this example, all possibilities are captured by events G or H. Thus, if event G occurred then event H did not and *vice versa*. Another way to write this concept is that $P(G|E) + P(H|E) = 1$ and therefore upon rearranging the equation $P(H|E) = 1 - P(G|E)$. This then means that the probability that H is false is equal to one minus the probability that H is true.

The third law of probability centers on the fact that when two events are independent of one another their probabilities can be multiplied with one another.

$$P(G \text{ and } H|E) = P(G|E) \times P(H|G,E)$$

or verbally, the probability of events G and H occurring given evidence E is equal to the probability of event G given evidence E multiplied by the probability of event H given event G and evidence E.

If the conditioning information (evidence E) is clearly specified and consistent for all possible events, then we can drop the '$|E$' or 'given evidence E' portion of the equation to arrive at:

$$P(G \text{ and } H) = P(G) \times P(H|G)$$

And if G and H are statistically independent or unassociated events then:

$$P(G \text{ and } H) = P(G) \times P(H)$$

To summarize, probabilities fall in the range of 0 to 1. When considering the possibilities of two events occurring, if either one of two mutually exclusive events can occur, their individual probabilities are added (sum rule). Alternatively, if we wish to consider the probability of two independent events occurring simultaneously, then the individual probabilities can be multiplied (product rule).

Likelihood ratios and Bayesian statistics

A *likelihood ratio* (LR) involves a comparison of the probabilities of the evidence under two alternative propositions. In forensic DNA settings, these mutually exclusive hypotheses represent the position of the prosecution— namely, that the DNA from the crime scene originated from the suspect—and the position of the defense—that the DNA just happens to coincidently match the defendant and is instead from an unknown person out in the population at large. In mathematical terms, the likelihood ratio is written as:

$$LR = H_p/H_d$$

where H_p represents the hypothesis of the prosecution and H_d represents the hypothesis of the defense. The likelihood ratio is used in Bayes' theorem to relate the probabilities of the propositions after the evidence to the probabilities prior to the evidence:

$$\frac{Pr(H_p)}{Pr(H_d)} \times \underbrace{\frac{Pr(E|H_p)}{Pr(E|H_d)}}_{\text{Likelihood Ratio}} = \frac{Pr(H_p|E)}{Pr(H_d|E)}$$

(prior odds $\times$ likelihood ratio = posterior odds)

Prior odds relates to the relative guilt or innocence of the suspect. Thus, in order to perform this calculation, one must make assumptions about the prior odds of guilt or innocent. As you might imagine, this approach has not caught on in the United States where the judicial system tries to maintain 'innocent until proven guilty.' However, there is nothing wrong with using the likelihood ratio by itself and have the judge and jury decide on the prior and posterior odds of guilt or innocence.

A good DNA typing system should provide large likelihood ratios when the defendant and the perpetrator of a crime are the same person. Likewise, if they are different people, then the likelihood ratio will be less than 1. Relative levels of likelihood ratios are discussed in the Chapter 11.

Statistics

Statistics is a mathematical science involving the collection, analysis, and interpretation of numerical data. It provides a sense of how reliable a measurement is when the measurement is made multiple times. Statistics involves using samples to make inferences about populations. A *population* is considered in this context to be a set of objects of interest, which may be infinite or otherwise unmeasurable in their entirety.

An observable subset of a population can be referred to as a *sample* with a *statistic* being some observable property of the sample. In the context of DNA testing, the 'population' would be the entire group of individuals who could be considered (e.g., billions of people around the world or those living within a particular country or region). The 'sample' would be a set of individuals from the population at large (e.g., 100 males) who were selected at random and tested at particular genetic markers to try to establish a reliable representation of the entire population. The 'statistic' examined might be the observed allele or genotype frequencies for the tested genetic markers.

Hypothesis testing for statistical significance

One of the most important things to understand about statistics is the concept of hypothesis testing. *Hypothesis testing* is the formal procedure for using statistical concepts and measures in performing decision making. This concept forms the basis for likelihood ratios that were mentioned briefly in the previous section (see also Chapter 11).

Six steps are typically involved in making a statistical analysis of a hypothesis (Figure A3.1): (1) formulate two competing hypotheses; (2) select the appropriate statistical model (theorem) that identifies the test statistic; (3) specify the level of significance, which is a measure of risk; (4) collect a sample of data and compute an estimate of the test statistic; (5) define the region of rejection for the test statistic; and (6) select the appropriate hypothesis.

The first step is to formulate usually two hypotheses for testing. The first hypothesis is called the *null hypothesis*, and is denoted by H_0. The null hypothesis is formulated as an equality and indicates that a difference does not exist. The second hypothesis is usually referred to as the *alternative hypothesis* and is denoted by H_1 or H_A. The null and alternative hypotheses are set up to represent mutually exclusive conditions so that when a statistical analysis of the sampled data suggests that the null hypothesis should be rejected, the alternative hypothesis must be accepted. Thus, the data collected (evidence gathered) should tip the scales toward either the null hypothesis or the alternative hypothesis.

In the context of a forensic DNA evidence examination, the null hypothesis put forward by the prosecution is that the defendant contributed the crime

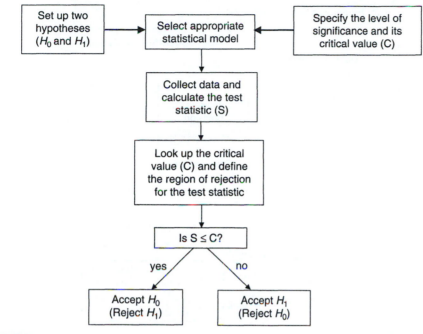

FIGURE A3.1

Flowchart illustrating the steps in hypothesis testing. The null hypothesis (H_0) is mutually exclusive of the alternative hypothesis (H_1). Adapted from Graham (2003).

scene DNA profile while the alternative hypothesis championed by the defense is that someone else other than the defendant contributed the crime scene DNA profile in question. These two hypotheses are then expressed in the form of a likelihood ratio with H_0 or H_p (hypothesis of the prosecution) in the numerator and H_1 or H_d (hypothesis of the defense) in the denominator.

The available situations and potential decisions/outcomes of a hypothesis test are shown in Figure A3.2. There are two types of errors that can be made with hypothesis testing. A type I error involves rejecting the null hypothesis when in fact it is really true. This might be considered a 'false negative.' A type II error on the other hand involves accepting the null hypothesis when in fact it is really false. A type II error is a 'false positive.'

The level of significance, which is a primary element of the decision-making process in hypothesis testing, represents the probability of making a type I error and is denoted by α (D.N.A. Box A3.1). The value chosen for α is typically based on convention and the historical custom, with values for α of 0.05 and 0.01 being selected frequently. The value of 0.05 is equivalent to a 95% 'confidence limit,' while α of 0.01 represents a 99% confidence limit. When we select the significance level (α) of a test, we are setting the probability of a type I error

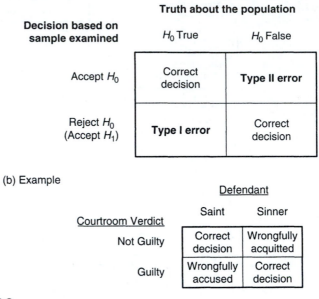

(a) Hypothesis Testing Decisions

Truth about the population

Decision based on sample examined	H_0 True	H_0 False
Accept H_0	Correct decision	**Type II error**
Reject H_0 (Accept H_1)	**Type I error**	Correct decision

(b) Example

Defendant

Courtroom Verdict	Saint	Sinner
Not Guilty	Correct decision	Wrongfully acquitted
Guilty	Wrongfully accused	Correct decision

FIGURE A3.2

(a) Comparison of decisions based on hypothesis testing and the relationship of type I and type II errors. (b) Example demonstrating how type I and type II errors correlate to false positive and false negative results. Adapted from Graham (2003).

('wrongfully accused'). Small *p*-values lead to rejection of the null hypothesis (and acceptance of the alternative hypothesis), while large *p*-values favor the null hypothesis.

The null hypothesis is rejected when the computed *p*-value lies in the region of rejection, which is usually $p < 0.05$. Rejection of the null hypothesis implies acceptance of the alternative hypothesis. When multiple analyses are being performed simultaneously for significance testing, the Bonferroni correction may be applied (D.N.A. Box A3.2).

It is important to recognize that by chance 5% of tests will have *p*-values below $p = 0.05$. Thus, just because a test of significance is below a certain value, the null hypothesis should not necessarily be rejected.

Chi-square test

The chi-square test is a 'goodness-to-fit' test. In other words, how close do observations of an event come to the expected results? The chi square (χ^2)

D.N.A. Box A3.1 What Does It Mean to Be 'Statistically Significant'?

Connected to the process of hypothesis testing is the concept of a statistically significant result, which involves a probability value or 'p-value'. A p-value reflects the probability that a variable being measured would assume a value greater than or equal to the observed value strictly by chance. In mathematical terms this can be described as $P(z \geq z_{observed})$. The threshold whereby a p-value is considered significant is set by an 'alpha value' (α). With the commonly used 95% confidence limit, $\alpha = 0.05$ (since 100–95% is 5% or 0.05).

A variety of alpha values are used in different fields, but probably the most common is 0.05 for a 95% confidence interval around a measurement. Thus, if a p-value is >0.05, then the test statistic and comparison are considered 'not significant.' If the p-value is computed to be between 1% and 5%, then it is generally considered 'significant' in which case the value can be denoted with an asterisk (e.g., 0.0435*). When the computed p-value is less than 1%, it is thought to be 'highly significant' and can be marked with a double asterisk (e.g., 0.00273**).

Thus, in cases where the p-value, which is the probability of obtaining an observed result or a more extreme result, is less than the conventional 0.05, we conclude that there is a 'significant relationship' between the two classification factors. However, it is important to keep in mind that the outcome of the significance testing is very much dependant on how the question is framed as part of the hypothesis testing.

Sources:
Graham, A. (2003). *Teach yourself statistics.* Blacklick, OH: McGraw-Hill.
http://mathworld.wolfram.com/AlphaValue.html
http://mathworld.wolfram.com/P.value.html
http://mathworld.wolfram.com/Significance.html

D.N.A. Box A3.2 The Bonferroni Correction

Carlo Emilio Bonferroni (1892–1960) was an Italian mathematician who developed theories for simultaneous statistical analysis. The Bonferroni correction is a multiple-comparison correction used when several independent statistical tests are being performed simultaneously. While a given alpha value (e.g., 0.05) may be appropriate for each individual comparison, it is probably not sufficient for the set of all comparisons. Thus, the alpha value needs to be lowered to account for the number of comparisons being performed.

The Bonferroni correction lowers the significance level for the entire set of n comparisons by dividing n into the alpha value for each comparison. The adjusted significance level becomes:

$$1 - (1 - \alpha)^{1/n} \approx \alpha/n$$

Thus, a set of 10 comparisons would lower the alpha value from 0.05 to 0.005 (0.05/10) so only p-values below 0.005 would be considered statistically significant rather than the conventional $p < 0.05$.

In the analysis of genetic data for Hardy–Weinberg equilibrium, application of the Bonferroni correction almost always removes the stigma of a locus being below the 5% threshold level. Applying the Bonferroni correction means that the more STR loci being examined, the less sensitive the statistical test since the p-value threshold has been lowered.

Sources:
http://mathworld.wolfram.com/BonferroniCorrection.html
Perneger, T. V. (1998). What's wrong with bonferroni adjustments. *British Medical Journal, 316,* 1236–1238.
Weir, B. S. (1996). *Genetic data analysis II* (Chapter 3, pp. 133–135). Sunderland, MA: Sinauer Associates.

is determined by summing the squared value of the difference between the observed results (obs) and expected results (exp) divided by the expected results:

$$\chi^2 = \sum_{i=1}^{k} \frac{(\text{obs}_i - \text{exp}_i)^2}{\text{exp}_i}$$

The resultant chi-square value is then compared against a table of numbers to see if there is a significant deviation from the 'normal' values expected. High chi-square values indicate discrepancies between observed and expected results. Different 'degrees of freedom' may be applied to data depending on the situation. Paul Lewis at the University of Connecticut has created a nice freeware program that can quickly relate user-input chi-square values and degrees of freedom to their p-value. This program is available at http://lewis.eeb.uconn.edu/lewishome/software.html.

Confidence intervals

Another important statistical concept is that of confidence intervals. Confidence intervals are useful for determining the accuracy of a point estimate. Typically a 95% confidence interval is computed, reflecting the probability that in 95% of the samples tested, the interval should contain the actual value measured.

A 95% confidence interval effectively is the sample average plus or minus two standard deviations. A confidence interval around some value π is a function of the frequency of the observation (p) and the number of individuals or items sampled in a population (n):

$$p - z_{\alpha/2}\sqrt{\frac{p(1-p)}{n}} \leq \pi \leq p + z_{\alpha/2}\sqrt{\frac{p(1-p)}{n}}$$

For 90% confidence intervals, $z_{0.05} = 1.645$ and for 95% confidence intervals, $z_{0.025} = 1.96$:

$$\underbrace{p - 1.96\sqrt{\frac{p(1-p)}{n}}}_{\text{Lower bound}} \leq \pi \leq \underbrace{p + 1.96\sqrt{\frac{p(1-p)}{n}}}_{\text{Upper bound}}$$

Note that the upper bound of the 95% confidence interval is what is used for Y-STR haplotype and mitochondrial DNA frequency estimates with the counting method (see Chapter 16).

Randomization tests

To confirm the validity of data sets, randomization tests are often performed usually with the aid of computer programs. These randomization tests permit an investigator to ask the question 'If the data were collected differently, could the overall results be significantly different?' Permutation tests, such as the 'exact test,' shuffle the original set of genotypes obtained in a population database to examine how unusual the original sampling of genotypes is. This shuffling generates a new genotypic distribution that can be compared to the original one.

Resampling tests, referred to as 'bootstrapping' or 'jack-knifing,' can be performed on data sets as well. Bootstrapping is a computer simulation in which the original n observations are resampled with replacement. Jack-knifing, on the other hand, involves resampling by leaving one observation out of the original n observations to create n samples each of size $n - 1$. Most papers in the literature describing population data sets utilize the exact test with 2000 shuffles although some have reported shuffling as many as 100,000 times.

Since we are only sampling a DNA profile one time in most cases, we perform statistical tests to estimate expected variability if the test were performed again. In the end, a number of statistical tests are performed on genetic data to estimate genotype frequencies since many genotypes are rare and may not be seen in population samples tested.

More than one statistical solution

It is important to recognize that not all approaches are universally accepted and discussion/debate still exists regarding the application of some statistics to forensic DNA typing results (e.g., Bayesian approaches). Models are used in statistics to help interpret data. Yet there are usually assumptions involved so these models are simplified versions of true genetic processes and are attempts to model the real world. The examples provided in this text will be those approaches that are most widely used today largely due to the acceptance of the National Research Council's report on *The Evaluation of Forensic DNA Evidence*, which was published in 1996 and is commonly referred to as 'NRC II.' Both the NRC II report (1996) and the DNA Advisory Board (DAB) recommendations on statistics (DAB, 2000) recognize that rarely is there only one statistical approach to interpret and explain evidence. In fact, the DAB recommendations state, 'The choice of approach is affected by the philosophy and experience of the user, the legal system, the practicality of the approach, the question(s) posed, available data, and/or assumptions'. The DAB further states that simplistic and less rigorous approaches can be employed, as long as false inferences are not conveyed.

REFERENCES FOR FURTHER INFORMATION

Aitken, C. G. G., & Taroni, F. (2004). *Statistics and the evaluation of evidence for forensic scientists* (2nd ed.). Hoboken, NJ: John Wiley & Sons.

Ayyub, B. M., & McCuen, R. H. (2003). *Probability, statistics, and reliability for engineers and scientists* (2nd ed.). Washington, DC: Chapman & Hall/CRC.

DNA Advisory Board. (2000). Statistical and population genetic issues affecting the evaluation of the frequency of occurrence of DNA profiles calculated from pertinent population database(s). *Forensic Science Communications, 2*(3). Available at http://www.fbi.gov/programs/lab/fsc/backissu/july2000/dnastat.htm

Evett, I. W., & Weir, B. S. (1998). *Interpreting DNA evidence: Statistical genetics for forensic scientists*. Sunderland, MA: Sinauer Associates.

Graham, A. (2003). *Teach yourself statistics*. Blacklick, OH: McGraw-Hill.

Lucy, D. (2005). *Introduction to statistics for forensic scientists*. Hoboken, NJ: John Wiley & Sons.

National Research Council Committee on DNA Forensic Science (1996). *The Evaluation of Forensic DNA Evidence*. Washington, DC: National Academy Press.

Planz, J. (2003). Introduction to Forensic Statistics: Probability and Statistics. *Workshop presented at the 14th international symposium on human identification*. Available at http://www.promega.com/geneticidproc/ussymp14proc/stats_workshop.htm

Rumsey, D. (2003). *Statistics for dummies*. Indianapolis, IN: Wiley Publishing, Inc

Index

Note: Page numbers with 'f' refers to figures and with 't' refers to tables.